Mirror of Consciousness

Art, Creativity and Veda

Mirror of Consciousness

Art, Creativity and Veda

ANNA BONSHEK

MOTILAL BANARSIDASS PUBLISHERS
PRIVATE LIMITED • DELHI

First Edition: Delhi, 2001

ISBN: 81-208-1774-5

Also available at:

MOTILAL BANARSIDASS
41 U.A. Bungalow Road, Jawahar Nagar, Delhi 110 007
8 Mahalaxmi Chamber, Warden Road, Mumbai 400 026
120 Royapettah High Road, Mylapore, Chennai 600 004
236, 9th Main III Block, Jayanagar, Bangalore 560 011
Sanas Plaza, 1302 Baji Rao Road, Pune 411 002
8 Camac Street, Kolkata 700 017
Ashok Rajpath, Patna 800 004
Chowk, Varanasi 221 001

Printed in India
BY JAINENDRA PRAKASH JAIN AT SHRI JAINENDRA PRESS,
A-45 NARAINA, PHASE-I, NEW DELHI 110 028 AND
PUBLISHED BY NARENDRA PRAKASH JAIN FOR
MOTILAL BANARSIDASS PUBLISHERS PRIVATE LIMITED,
BUNGALOW ROAD, DELHI 110 007

For
His Holiness Maharishi Mahesh Yogi

PREFACE

In the past 50 years the field of the visual arts has, in some ways, changed dramatically and yet, in other ways, seems relatively unperturbed by our new, global information revolution. With the re-evaluation of art and aesthetics in the digital era, the question of art's universal value seems no longer paramount. Despite this, critics and theorists continue to grapple with the idea of universality. How can the many divergent and contradictory experiences, influences and phenomena that inform cultural discourse, our sense of identity and aesthetics, be comprehended in this light?

Maharishi's Science of Creative Intelligence® curriculum, developed in 1972 by His Holiness Maharishi Mahesh Yogi, articulates the possibility of a universal state of consciousness, the ability to live this permanently in individual and social life, and the potential to express universality in art. It is the Science of Creative Intelligence that connects the main principles of Maharishi Vedic Science® to the main conclusions of modern science and the modern disciplines. The Science of Creative Intelligence presents a unique understanding of creativity—explaining how life unfolds according to the inner dynamics of a universal field of consciousness and thereby establishing a platform for a discussion of universal value in art. Maharishi Vedic Science encompasses a wide range of disciplines and specific technologies of consciousness. (In addition to Maharishi's Science of Creative Intelligence and Maharishi Vedic Science, Maharishi Vedic Science and Technology®, Maharishi's Technologies of Consciousness® (including Maharishi's Transcendental Meditation® program, Maharishi TM-Sidhi® program and Yogic Flying®) are also discussed in this book.)* It should be noted that the diagrams used in this book, as far as is possible, in order to maintain accuracy, follow diagrams used in publications on Maharishi Vedic Science.

Due to the resources and unique educational approach provided by Maharishi University of Management, a detailed and systematic study of the nature and mechanics of creativity from this unique perspective is now possible. Maharishi Vedic Science has the potential to benefit humankind in every generation and all walks of life, being practical and universal in its application. For this reason, the Department of the Science of Creative Intelligence at Maharishi University of

---

*®Maharishi's Science of Creative Intelligence, Maharishi Vedic Science, Maharishi Vedic Science and Technology, Maharishi's Technologies of Consciousness, Maharishi's Transcendental Meditation program, Maharishi TM-Sidhi program, and Yogic Flying are registered or common law trade marks licensed to Maharishi Vedic Education Development Corporation and used with permission. Other aspects of Maharishi Vedic Science referred to in this volume, such as Maharishi Jyotish, Maharishi Vedic Astrology, Maharishi Yagya, Maharishi Sthāpatya Veda, and Maharishi Āyur-Veda, are also service marks, registered or common law trade marks licensed to Maharishi Vedic Education Development Corporation and used with permission.

Management formulated and initiated the Ph.D. program in the Science of Creative Intelligence—facilitating scholarly research and study in this field. This book evolved from research completed while I was a student of this pioneering doctoral program. Although the Ph.D. program in S.C.I. has been taught for over 12 years, relatively little has been written on the visual arts and Maharishi Vedic Science.

Throughout the 1970s and into the 1990s, curriculum development—new core courses, undergraduate and graduate offerings in art history, and studio and design courses—have been developed and continue to evolve under the chairmanship of Michael Cain and the Art Department faculty at Maharishi University of Management. Teaching tools such as the Art Unified Field Chart and an extensive art appreciation video series discussing major works of art in the light of the Science of Creative Intelligence are important historical markers of this consciousness-based approach to art education.

Building upon this, Dr. Lee Fergusson researched archives at the University—documenting lectures on art and creativity given by Maharishi. In collaboration with the art faculty, he structured new foundation courses and curricula; these were evaluated and continue to be updated and taught at Maharishi University of Management, and the substantial volume of research generated by Dr. Fergusson is a resource for some of the material in this book.

Generally speaking, the content of this volume was first explored in the late 1980s; but it was later, as part of doctoral research, that the connections between Maharishi Vedic Science and contemporary art theory were more systematically examined. For this reason, I am particularly grateful to the faculty of the Science of Creative Intelligence Department, the Art Department and Maharishi University of Management as a whole, for making it possible to study and investigate in detail this unique field of knowedge. I would like to thank Dr. Bevan Morris, Dr. Geoffrey Wells, Dr. William Haney III, Dr. Frederick Worth, Dr. John Price, Dr. Thomas Egenes, Dr. Lee Fergusson, Dr. William Sands, Dr. Denise Gerace, Michael Cain, Dr. Jayant Bapat, Peter Freund, Martha Bright, and Mr. N.P. Jain and the editorial staff at Motilal Banarsidass for their advice and comments. It would also have been impossible to complete this work without the support of my parents and family.

I would especially like to express my deepest gratitude to His Holiness Maharishi Mahesh Yogi who has brought to light the profound knowledge of Vedic wisdom in his Vedic Science for the practical benefit of this generation and all generations to come.

CONTENTS

INTRODUCTION

Since the end of the cold war, the demise of modernism and the critical evaluation of totalizing theories, we have seen the development of new hybrid technological cultures and different approaches to understanding art. Many voices can be heard expressing various ideas about identity, meaning, social value, and the definition, function and effects of art. This recognition of cultural relativism is symptomatic of the surge toward ever-increasing hybridity in the cultural and art arenas. "Art" has expanded to "visual culture"—where visual culture includes all the multifarious streams of activities and products which create and define cultural discourse through visual media. Previously held elitist distinctions between fine art and other forms of cultural production (such as folk art, mass media, etc.) have been re-evaluated.

Each decade is associated with a particular trend or development. The 1970s are equated with late-modernism and feminism, the 1980s with postmodernism, and the 1990s with transgender, the body, post-colonialism, digital media and hybridity. Varying theoretical assumptions, political ideologies, and definitions of cultural formation and discourse have contributed to a range of diverse viewpoints. Against this backdrop, *Mirror of Consciousness: Art, Creativity and Veda* looks at visual culture, art, creativity, and the dichotomy of the modern-postmodern axis, in the context of a universal understanding of consciousness. It articulates a new approach to art and theory—one that is appropriate for an increasingly global, technological world—signaling a new direction for the twenty-first century. However, theory alone is limited in its scope and application. Only a comprehensive experience and understanding of universal value in visual culture and life in general can expand any definition and practice of art. This book argues that this experience and understanding can be gained through Maharishi Vedic Science. Brought to light by His Holiness Maharishi Mahesh Yogi, this science provides complete, practical knowledge of consciousness and its expressions[1]—where consciousness is understood to be an unbounded, infinite field of wakefulness that can be experienced by anyone as their own simplest form of awareness. The principles of this science, when applied, present a unique possibility for human life to be lived in a state of infinite creativity, fulfillment and all possibilities.

As with any theory of knowledge, Maharishi Vedic Science has its own terminology and foundational principles. (It should be noted that technical terms like "transcendent" are always connected to their source in consciousness, and therefore, relate to direct experience.) These foundational principles provide the framework for an entirely new approach to art and theory. They offer profound insights into the source of creativity and the definition of culture, art, the artist, the creative process and the purpose and effects of art. For example, an extensive discussion of different kinds of knowledge, including relative and absolute knowledge, can be found in Part II. Later, in Parts IV and V, reference is made to the role of art in unfolding knowledge on the basis of this understanding.

Throughout the ages, artists have sought to express an infinite or universal dimension in art. While this aim is no longer the overarching focus of visual culture, in the 1990s—dissatisfied with art of glamor—artists and theorists began to discuss the need for universal value in art. Some argue that art which does not address the universally human cannot be called art. Partly responding to such developments, this book explains how universal value in art can be viable when viewed from the perspective of Maharishi Vedic Science, because it explains that there is a universal field of life—the source of individual creativity and Nature's creativity—which gives rise to everything in creation[2] and that can be expressed in art. This universal field is a field of awareness or *pure consciousness*. It is infinite and fully awake to itself; pure consciousness is the simplest form of human awareness and can be experienced by anyone through specific technologies. It is also held to be the source of history, tradition and culture; consequently it can be reflected, embodied or represented in visual culture.[3]

As will be seen, Maharishi Vedic Science differs from philosophy and theory in this and other important ways: 1) as noted, it is based on the principle that there is an absolute, infinite, universal field of pure consciousness or *pure intelligence* which, through its *self-referral* nature, creates the manifest universe of forms and phenomena;[4] 2) it presents the details of the structure of pure consciousness in terms of *pure knowledge*, referred to as the *Constitution of the Universe* or the Veda,[5] where consciousness knows itself as both one field and three differentiated values—the knower, the process of knowing and the known; 3) it describes the precise mechanics through which consciousness quantifies itself in terms of this structure of pure knowledge and gives rise to frequencies or impulses which, through a sequential elaboration, develop into the material universe;[6] 4) it provides technologies of consciousness, the Transcendental Meditation (TM) technique and the TM-Sidhi program and Yogic Flying, which allow the individual to experience and operate from this field of pure consciousness;[7] 5) it explains that these frequencies of consciousness are recorded as the Veda and the Vedic Literature, in the language of Vedic Sanskrit;[8] and, 6) it reveals that the human nervous system is the structure of the Veda expressed in terms of the physiology.[9]

A science of *complete knowledge*, Maharishi Vedic Science presents unparalleled insights into the nature of creativity, perception, psychology and the physiology. It not only provides understanding of the universal basis of existence and its expressions, it includes technologies to verify its principles through direct experience—a point that cannot be over-emphasized. Through its exhaustive account of consciousness and numerous studies of the effects of the practice of technologies of consciousness, the principles of this science are supported by rigorous scientific research and theory.[10] Maharishi Vedic Science is referred to as the science of Veda or "knowledge" and presents a unique insight into the nature and value of Vedic texts; the Veda and Vedic Literature are described as impulses of consciousness, rather than religious or philosophical treatises. In this context, the Vāstusūtra Upaniṣad (a Vedic text dealing with art discussed by scholars in connection with Atharvavedic literature and here taken to be associated with Sthāpatya Veda) is examined with respect to consciousness. As considered later, both Maharishi Upaniṣad and Maharishi Sthāpatya Veda are values of the 40 aspects of Natural Law.

In outlining this comprehensive description of consciousness, a new definition of art and its role in individual and collective life can be articulated. For example, Maharishi Vedic Science explains that the universal field of *pure existence* can be experienced as *bliss*; has specific qualities and a precise structure; can be enlivened by the individual to systematically develop full creative potential; and, is expressible in art. Principles such as these are discussed in relation to other theories reviewed in Part I. Part I gives an overview of the notion of universal value and other issues in modern, Indian, and postmodern theory, such as the cultural and historical contextualization of visual culture and theory. Later, as for example in Part IV, the source of language, culture, history and tradition is revealed, according to Maharishi Vedic Science, to be the same universal field of pure consciousness experienced as a state of pure or *absolute knowledge* in individual awareness. By accessing and enlivening this field of pure consciousness, in the state of absolute knowledge, individual life, collective life, and the basis of all cultures can be enriched.

In addition to the identification of consciousness as a universal field, consciousness is also described in Maharishi Vedic Science as *wholeness* or *wholeness on the move*. Wholeness is the "all-comprehensive, eternal reality in its unmanifest, unbounded state of intelligence;"[11] wholeness on the move is the totality of consciousness moving within itself—generating impulses or frequencies within its own unbounded nature. These impulses are impulses of wholeness or the structures of the Veda and Vedic Literature. The Veda and the Vedic Literature comprise 40 aspects or textbooks of *Natural Law*. While the term "Veda" means "pure knowledge', Veda is also referred to as the Constitution of the Universe; "Natural Law" describes the governing intelligence of the universe[12] and wholeness is the nature of self-referral consciousness. Functioning within itself, self-referral consciousness "generates impulses of wholeness (structures of the Veda and the Vedic Literature) which, continuing to evolve, express themselves as structures of Natural Law, evolving into creation."[13] This somewhat abstract theme reveals an unprecedented comprehension of the nature and mechanics of consciousness. Wholeness moves and can be found everywhere in creation—as impulses of the Veda and the Vedic Literature, impulses of self-referral consciousness.

Since the focus of this book involves the application of Maharishi Vedic Science to the domain of art, a generalized review of theory is presented in Part I, *Art as Language Game—Lamenting the Loss of Universal Value*. Part I briefly considers: 1) modernist notions of historical progress in art, the artist as genius, originality, and the art object as a significant or ideal form evoking universal emotion or spiritual experience; 2) Indian theory which holds that art should have a moral purpose and create a peaceful state of mind; 3) the postmodern redefinition of art as a language game—debunking the myth of the avant-garde and a linear or cyclical view of history; and, 4) in response to the shortcomings of postmodernism, a need for universality is articulated, providing a platform for further discussion of universal value in art.

Following this, Part II, *Accessing and Enlivening a Universal Field of Pure Consciousness*, introduces the main principles of Maharishi Vedic Science—including a description of the nature of consciousness, a discussion of the practical technologies of consciousness and their effect on individual and collective life as documented by scientific research. The mechanics of practicing these technologies and the details of higher states of consciousness are considered, revealing that the state of absolute knowledge is the reliable ground of all streams of knowledge and creative experience, and anyone can have access to infinite creativity and become a universal human being.

Entitled *The Veda and the Vedic Literature: The Complete Disclosure of Nature's Creative Mechanics,* Part III investigates more deeply Maharishi's description of the nature of consciousness as expressed in the Veda and Vedic Literature. It considers consciousness in terms of specific Laws of Nature which govern the universe—explaining that the 40 aspects of Natural Law are frequencies or the structuring dynamics of consciousness at the basis of creation. It includes a detailed description of the creative mechanics of Nature's functioning in terms of the Language of Nature, considering the structure of Ṛk Veda or pure knowledge and Maharishi's *Apauruṣeya Bhāṣya. Apauruṣeya Bhāṣya* means "uncreated commentary;" it is the uncreated commentary of the Veda in its progressive, evolutionary, sequential unfoldment into syllables and gaps, ten *Maṇḍalas,* and the entire Vedic Literature. In this sequential progression, through unmanifest frequencies of sound to particles of matter and all forms and phenomena, the precise details of the mechanics of creation are revealed.

On the basis of this understanding of the abstract field of consciousness and its self-referral dynamics, Part IV introduces the reader to Maharishi's insights into history and culture. Entitled *Natural Law: The Universal Foundation of History, Traditions, Culture and Language,* this section explains that the source of the individual and of history, tradition, culture and languages, is the universal field of Natural Law. History is revealed in its infinite context and in terms of the cyclical unfoldment of consciousness. This unique view, in contrast to modern and postmodern perspectives, is important for any understanding of the idea of universal value in art. The issue of cultural context and what are called traditions are addressed in the discussion of the relationship between the individual and society, the basis of culture, how cultural integrity can be strengthened, and the importance of the mother tongue or local language and its relationship to the universal language of the Veda. Part IV, therefore, focuses on how a universal source to both individual and collective life can be located and, when enlivened, can increase individual creativity, strengthen cultural integrity and uphold traditions.

Part V, *The Artist as a Universal Human Being Creating Universal Value in Art and Aesthetics*, then redefines the artist and the creative process by examining several themes: the artist as a universal human being; creating as Nature creates; following specific guidelines in the creation of art which aid in the development of consciousness; the relationship between creativity and suffering; the purpose and effects of art; and, aesthetic value. Having established the details and significance of Maharishi Vedic Science for the expression of universal value in art, Part VI, *Uncovering the Details of the Nature and Structure of Pure Consciousness in the Vāstusūtra Upaniṣad*, analyzes a specific Vedic text on art. It goes into the nature of wholeness and part-to-whole relationships with respect to Maharishi Sthāpatya Veda and considers the distinct perspective of Vedic language theory with its correspondence between sound and meaning. It also examines a reference to "artistic sight" at the beginning of the text, and considers the first and last expressions as complete expressions of the text. Finally, particular sūtras or verses are viewed with respect to the artist, the creative process, form, point, line, grid, geometric forms and number. In this process a parallel emerges between the expressions of the sūtras and the descriptions of consciousness in Maharishi Vedic Science.

While attempting to embrace the comprehensive and extensive range of issues and ramifications surrounding the topic of universal value in art, the main thrust of this book can be simply condensed into two strands of thought: 1) how Maharishi Vedic Science presents the possibility for universal value in life and art; and 2) how some sūtras of the Vāstusūtra Upaniṣad can be viewed in the light of the universal nature and structure of consciousness.

PART I

ART AS A LANGUAGE GAME: LAMENTING THE LOSS OF UNIVERSAL VALUE

Conventionally philosophers have sought to define a universal theory of knowledge and understanding of art. However, cultural production and art have been dominated by the ideas of Western philosophy and science. For this reason, universality in art has often been argued on the grounds of a Eurocentric view, rather than on the grounds of a fundamental universality springing from within different traditions and individual expressions. If one accepts that art practice is driven by theory, in order to comprehend art, it is important to consider the influence of philosophy and different theories of knowledge on artists, art and culture. Furthermore, if theory is the foundation of art, it could be argued that only a universal theory or discourse can be the foundation of universal art. Is such a meta-theory possible? Theory can provide knowledge or the means for the critical evaluation of knowledge claims, but it seems only science can unfold knowledge of natural laws and phenomena; art, on the other hand, is apparently driven by subjectivity and by cultural, social, philosophical and historical forces.

The term "universal" signifies a law, principle or rule. It refers to that which is general rather than particular. In Western philosophy, from Plato through to Kant and Hegel, the notion of an absolute or transcendent—also described as soul or spirit—was linked to universality. Drawing upon these ideas, twentieth-century modernists suggested that universal value can only be expressed as "pure form" in art. As American critic Thomas McEvilley has pointed out, this argument is highly problematic:

> The mainstream tradition in Western philosophy—what Richard Rorty has called the Plato-to-Kant axis—has argued for universal and unchanging criteria of quality that are supposedly valid for all times and places.
>
> There are differences in expression—Plato spoke about objective universals and Kant about subjective universals—but it is a shared idea that correct judgments are based on correct perceptions of universals, and incorrect ones on a misperception of them. Absolute values, in this view, are inborn in all humans identically in all times and all places...This belief implicitly underlay the most influential Modernist criticism...[and] critics...were able to convince others, that they had an especially clear ability to perceive these universals....there is nothing that could be called evidence suggesting that quality is objective and universal, rather than subjective and relative.[1]

Here, McEvilley distinguishes between that which is "objective and universal" as opposed to "subjective and relative." Although McEvilley asserts that no culture's idea of quality can claim a universal validity and even as a law or rule the universal is subject to the conditions of the language game to which it applies, this book will explore the possibility that universal value can be expressed in art and such art appeals to people across cultures, throughout time.

Generally speaking, Western philosophers and aestheticians wanted the artist to embody the spiritual in art by raising art to the level of a realm of pure universality of thought, creating art which evoked universal, detached, aesthetic emotion, and the feeling of pleasure governed by the faculty of taste derived from a "hidden source common to all men."[2] These ideas of taste, formal elements determining universal value in art, and the universal experience of pleasure in response to beauty, were absorbed by modernists as they drew from eighteenth-century and Greek philosophy and adapted ideas from Eastern thought through Theosophy and readings of Buddhism, Tantrism and Zen.

Although the word "modernism" is used to refer to a range of twentieth-century theories and movements which are not homogeneous, a generalized and accepted feature of modern art is the move towards abstraction.[3] Historian David Peters Corbett explains that modernism involves two tendencies: 1) an emphasis on formalism and autonomy of practice; 2) a revolutionary, avant-garde effort to shape new conditions of theory. Whereas "modernism" is associated with style, "modernity"—the hall-mark of a modern society—is characterized by a complex set of social processes such as the emergence of a secularized world-view superseding the religion and tradition, the rise of reason as the legitimized form of intellectual investigation, the dominance of capitalist exchange economies and nation-states, new social and gender roles, class formations and patriarchal relations between the sexes, and the materialist interpretation of value and meaning.[4] In this book the terms modernism and modern theory will be used to refer to art movements as reflected in the stylistic development of art and the theoretical underpinnings of the move toward formalism.

Modernism, as with postmodernism, is often spoken of as a uniquely twentieth-century phenomenon. However, in his essay *Art History or Sacred History* Thomas McEvilley states that the current period is but one in many modern/postmodern cycles, all of which share similar characteristics (one of the earliest documented modernist periods occurred in 600 B.C.E.):

> The apocalyptic mood in which our Modernism and post-Modernism have been viewed has obscured the fact that there have been earlier Modernisms and earlier post-Modernisms. A Modernism is a cultural period characterized by two mutually supportive and mutually validating views about history and selfhood. 1) History seems to have an upward inner directive, a driving force of progress operating within it. In such a situation, innovation and change come to be valued over the stabilizing influence of tradition. There is a sense of confidence in history, which seems to be on one's side. 2) Validated by the inner purpose of

> history, the self inflates. There is an apotheosis of will and personal creativity, as the sources of historical change. Self-expression and originality are revered as the expressions of history's inner directive. There is an heroic view of the self as adventurer, innovator, and guiding force of history. A post-Modernism, on the other hand, is a period when the Modernist faith in history has been lost, usually through political developments. The support of history's inner meaning being withdrawn, the self deflates. History now seems to have no shape and the self no anointed mission. There are attempts to reestablish connections with the traditions destroyed by Modernist innovation.[5]

In addition to the notion of an absolute, modern periods are characterized by a linearly progressive notion of history, a strong sense of self related to the role of the individual in driving history forward, an emphasis on originality and personal creativity, and a tendency to break with tradition. This notion of history is evidenced in twentieth-century modernism, which suggests that abstract art, as pure form, is stylistically superior to, and conceptually more sophisticated than, previous art;[6] such art apparently represents freedom and the originality of the avant-garde.[7]

In contrast, postmodernists view modern theory as a closed system employed by a dominant power group which, in enforcing its own agenda and definition of aesthetic value, restricts artistic freedom, critical judgment, and cultural difference. The critical approach of postmodernism, drawing upon language theory which deconstructs the notion of an absolute signified, undermines the modern notion of universality while making ironic reference to it. The artist, no longer the genius/crusader, is the critic/philosopher evaluating the self in terms of an ever-transformative text. Art is a play of signs in a visual language which is constantly reevaluating itself.

Postmodernists, by undermining the propositions of modern theory, reject so-called totalizing and imperialist modernist claims. They deconstruct the idea of universals, a transcendent or absolute, and the possibility of one-to-one correspondence between an object or idea and that which it signifies. In disallowing the idea of absolute presence, universal value is negated. In this sense, postmodernism appears to be more tolerant of different cultural expressions and philosophies.

Postmodernism is also described as the cultural logic of late-Capitalism, a new approach to knowledge and the new critical phase of art beginning in the sixties.[8] American critic Donald Kuspit observes that postmodernism presents a new anti-transcendental "deconstructive criticality"[9] as opposed to modernism's disguised "transcendental justification" of art. Modern theory is universal and idealist; postmodernism is critical and relativist. Incompatible, a tension or gap is created between the two, yet both are defined in relation to the other.

If "postmodernism" refers to a form of contemporary culture, as English theorist Terry Eagleton suggests, "postmodernity" alludes to a specific epochal change. Postmodernity is:

> A style of thought which is suspicious of classical notions of truth, reason, identity and objectivity, of the idea of universal progress or emancipation, of single frameworks, grand narratives or ultimate grounds of explanation. Against these Enlightenment norms, it sees the world as contingent, ungrounded, diverse, unstable, indeterminate, a set of disunified cultures or interpretations which breed a degree of scepticism about the objectivity of truth, history and norms, the givenness of natures and the coherence of identities. This way of seeing, so some would claim, has real material conditions: it springs from an historic shift in the West to a new form of capitalism—to the ephemeral, decentralized world of technology, consumerism and the culture industry, in which the service, finance and information industries triumph over traditional manufacture, and classical class politics yield ground to a diffuse range of 'identity politics'. Postmodernism is a style of culture which reflects something of this epochal change, in a depthless, decentred, ungrounded, self-reflexive, playful, derivative, eclectic, pluralistic art which blurs the boundaries between 'high' and 'popular' culture, as well as between art and everyday experience. How dominant or pervasive this culture is—whether it goes all the way down, or figures just as one particular region within contemporary life—is a matter of argument.[10]

In his summary of postmodernity, Eagleton displays a certain skepticism; he sees postmodernism as just one aspect of contemporary life. In this book, postmodernism and postmodern theory will refer to the significations of visual culture and the theoretical developments in language theory and philosophy which inform visual discourse and art practice. In this context, art can be defined as signs in a language game pointing to the unnamable. In contrast to both modern and postmodern theory, Indian theory suggests that art is a means to promote individual and social development; it is integral to the development of social cohesion and the continuation of tradition. The artist is not a heroic individual breaking with tradition nor a critical deconstructer of philosophy; rather than developing a personal style, he is expected to work within set guidelines. It is his responsibility to contribute to society by upholding the guidelines which enable his art to achieve its purpose. Art, neither pure form nor the political play of language, is viewed as the product of skill—like other technical activities. It has a moral purpose; it is supposed to aid the viewer in culturing a "good" state of mind.

Indian theory, based on ancient philosophical texts and treatises, is bound, like modernism and postmodernism, to cultural and historical contexts. As with modernism, traditional Indian theories of art and aesthetics posit that art can stimulate universal aesthetic emotion and espouse the idea of an absolute, but, being formless and unmanifest, it is impossible to symbolize. While there are several different approaches to philosophy and art in India which make up what can be referred to as the Tradition, here the works of Pandit and Coomaraswamy are cited. In the unfoldment of creativity, the use of contemplation is mentioned by both Pandit and Coomaraswamy. However, according to Maharishi Vedic

Science, contemplation is not the most effective means for developing the artist's consciousness or expanding creativity. In this and several other important ways, Indian theory and Maharishi Vedic Science differ.

In order to briefly consider these different theories, Part I is comprised of four chapters. Chapter 1, entitled *Modern Art and Theory: Created by a Genius, Art Evokes Universal Aesthetic Emotion,* reviews the main propositions of modern theory: the idea that art expresses the infinite, a transcendent or absolute, and that modern art signifies the goal of history—freedom. Revealing the intimate connection between philosophy, criticism and art practice, modern artists echoed perennial notions—from Plato's ideal forms, Hegel's notion of history and fine art, Kant's description of genius, Clive Bell's idea of formal properties in art eliciting universal aesthetic emotion, to Agnes Martin's description of beaart truth and happiness in relation to art. Outlining another definition of art, Chapter 2—*Indian Theory: Art and Śanta*, considers contemplation and aesthetic emotion, art as skill, inner vision and outer expression, the artist as a maintainer of tradition working within set guidelines, and the purpose of art. Indian theory also speaks of a transcendent and the tasting (*rasa*) of universal aesthetic emotion.

In contrast, Chapter 3, *Postmodern Art as a Pluralist Language Game—Pointing to the Unnamable*, presents a new definition of art. This definition is influenced by contemporary language theory. Art, a language game of arbitrary signs, signifies absence rather than presence in the display of relative knowledge. Postmodern theory and art represent pluralism, the delegitamization of meta-narratives, and the transformation of consciousness. Chapter 4, *Beyond Postmodernism: Universal Art and a New Sense of Self,* examines the criticisms of a postmodern "art of glamor" and the call for universal art. Later sections deal with these themes from the perspective of Maharishi Vedic Science—providing a new understanding of universality and universal principles of art. For example, in Part II, in the description of principles of Maharishi Vedic Science, a universal, subjective field of consciousness, the simplest form of human awareness, will be described and discussed in detail. This absolute, unchanging, subjective realm will be distinguished from the ever-changing world of our common experience and of forms and phenomena—referred to as the objective world. Maharishi Vedic Science, unlike the theories of modernists, postmodernists and Indian aestheticians, includes specific and effective technologies of consciousness as a means to systematically develop creativity.

In addition, Maharishi Vedic Science presents a comprehensive understanding of Vedic knowledge—demonstrating its universal principles and applications. While the term "Vedic" is commonly held to refer to ancient philosophical and religious texts of India, "Veda" means "knowledge" and as will be argued, this knowledge can be understood as universally applicable to anyone in any walk of life.

1

MODERN ART AND THEORY: CREATED BY A GENIUS, ART EVOKES UNIVERSAL AESTHETIC EMOTION

Harking back to Western philosophy, modern critics and artists formulated ideas which, like threads woven together, form the fabric of modern theory. Primary among them is the proposition that pure form can be expressed in art. Pure form, it seemed, embodied universal value or a universal aesthetic. In addition, modern art—the outcome of a linear, historical development of style—was held to be more developed than that of previous eras. Abstraction in art came to signify the superior cognitive development of an evolved, sophisticated culture. According to modernists, the significant form of an authentic fine art expressed universal value through its formal properties and thereby evoked a universal aesthetic emotion, or elation, in the viewer. Similarly, modernists held that in fine art a direct relationship existed between content and form (in Formalist abstraction content is dissolved to become pure form) and the artist's inner insight captured a spiritual emotion or transcendent.

However, in the process of creative practice, despite being a genius, the modern artist did not know the mechanics of his creativity. Art was thus, intuitively inspired and inherently original; it sprang from the uniqueness of individual genius and did not imitate anything outside of itself. Many of these assumptions had their source in the ancient Greek Enlightenment and in nineteenth-century philosophy.[1]

Fine Art Represents Ideal or Pure Form

For modern artists, the concept of pure form in art was paramount. This focus on ideal, significant, pure form has its basis in earlier definitions of art. Throughout the centuries, articulation of the creative process in art involved the notion that something within—an intuitive vision or concept—could be expressed perfectly in art. Arguing that there are universal ideas and particular forms which are copies of ideal forms or ideas, Plato suggested that the idea preceded the particular structure of material form. For example, a carpenter may make a number of beds but there is only one idea "bed." There is the universal bed—the idea; the particular or relative kind of bed, is the actual perceived bed. Furthermore, the artist or painter who makes a two-dimensional image of a bed could only imitate the three-dimensional structure of the bed built by the carpenter; therefore the painter's work, unable to represent all facets of the object simultaneously, [2] was mere imitation—and imitation of the second order. Painting provided only a copy of a copy—whose "original" was the idea. For this reason, according to

Plato, the painter could never actually paint the truth, but only imitate the appearance of things.

In one sense, modern artists attempted to usurp this notion by claiming that abstract Formalism directly represented inner ideas and emotion. It did not imitate anything outside of itself; it was not an imitation of the observable world. By taking this viewpoint art could be elevated to the realm of ideas. To some extent, modernists also re-evaluated Greek philosopher Plotinus' suggestion that high art was artistic representation which imitated not just sensible objects, "but in its highest development, the ideas themselves, of which sensible objects are images."[3] This distinction between imitation and high art evolved further in Hegel's philosophy and in modern theory.

Greek philosophers also felt that an intimate connection existed between art, music, mathematics and nature—certain geometric forms were held to be basic to any understanding of mathematics and the movement of the celestial bodies. Pythagoras maintained that certain numerical values and their relationships in form and sound displayed harmony and, when known and utilized by the artist or musician, reflected fundamental laws of nature.[4] With respect to geometry, Euclid laid out five postulates which defined the point, line and circle from which, he maintained, all geometry could be derived.[5] Pythagoreanism assumed that the natural world had particular formal and aesthetic features and that natural processes possess "harmonies, symmetries, and simplicities;"[6] it also assumed that mathematics is essential to a description and understanding of nature.

Geometry and ideal forms were not merely attractive elements but reflected the unity and design of the cosmos as God intended it. The notion of the artist utilizing mathematical principles to create art guided artists from different cultural traditions throughout the centuries;[7] in the West, when Renaissance artists revived ancient Greek knowledge, artists depicted the human body according to specific mathematical proportions which were felt to express the divine. For this reason, rules of proportion, thought to embody mathematical relationships, were used in both architecture and art.

Transforming these ideas in a modern context, artists such as Marlow Moss, Piet Mondrian and Wassily Kandinsky, attempted to explore fundamental mathematical and harmonic properties in art in a radical new way. Wassily Kandinsky felt that there was a psychological or spiritual foundation to the relationship between color and sound; color directly related to sound—a musical sound provoked an association of a precise color.[8] He also thought that there are universal laws of composition which obliterate difference and are the same for all the arts. By virtue of the relationship between mathematics, art and music, art seemed to share the same aesthetic principles as these other disciplines and apparently reflected the inner workings of nature. These basic ideas surface once again in the work of Steven Holtzman. In his book *Digital Mantras* Holtzman suggests that there is an important connection between sound, color and form. He argues that this relationship has special significance for the investigation of the structure of the cosmos and the creation of digital art and virtual worlds.[9] As is obvious by the title of his book, Hotzman's recent articulation of the connection sound and form draws from Eastern philosophy.

However, the concept of ideal form embodying spirit—culminating in a modernist concept of pure form—drew heavily from Western philosophy and criticism, as did the idea of history as a progressive force. McEvilley emphasizes that the notion of history's progressive move toward an evolved present is a critical, foundational tenet of modern theory.

A Teleological Reading of Art

Transcendental modernism, Thomas McEvilley argues, was formulated in the work of Hegel.[10] His theory of the development of man resulting in Western (specifically Prussian) civilization became the foundation of Clement Greenberg's notion of abstract art's supremacy. In fact, Hegel developed an involved account of history, including three methods of writing history: *original history*, *reflective history*, and *philosophical history*. Reflective history is comprised of four sub-categories, which he described as: *universal history*; *pragmatic history*; *critical history*; and *fragmentary history*. Universal history presents a survey of the entire history of a people, country or the world—where the historian's interpretation predominates over the spirit of the material he is analyzing. Pragmatic history acknowledges the importance of reflecting on events of the past which can be instructional in the present, acknowledging that "examples of good deeds elevate the soul." Critical history involves the evaluation of historical narratives; it is the examination of historiography itself. Fragmentary history, the history of art for example, adopts a universal point of view and can be understood as conceptual history.

While Hegel defined these different approaches to history, his philosophical history asserted that reason was the structuring principle of historical progress. Reason, he defined as substance, infinite power and infinite form or "the infinite material of natural and spiritual life...the infinite content of all essence and truth."[11] Consisting of immutable laws, it was reason as the Divine Idea (wisdom endowed with infinite power which realizes its own aim—the absolute, rational, final purpose of the world),[12] and not chance, that ruled the world. Reason is thought determining itself in absolute freedom; reason leads to Freedom which is the goal of history enjoyed by Spirit. Spirit is Being-within-itself; and, as Hegel suggests in the following argument, it is completely free because it is self-contained:

> When I am dependent, I refer myself to something else which I am not; I cannot exist independently of something external. I am free when I am within myself. This self-contained existence of Spirit is self-conscious, conscious of self.[13]

Spirit is only free in self-containment. Hegel maintained that the whole of history is contained in this self-conscious Spirit and that history is Spirit striving to know its own nature in order to realize Freedom. All this, due to the self-conscious nature of Spirit knowing itself:

> Two things must be distinguished in consciousness, first, *that* I know and secondly, *what* I know. In self-consciousness the two coincide, for Spirit knows itself. It is the judgment of its own nature and, at the same time, the operation of coming to itself, to produce itself, to make itself (actually) into that which is itself (potentially). Following this abstract definition it may be said that world history is the exhibition of Spirit striving to attain knowledge of its own nature. As the germ bears in itself the whole nature of the tree, the taste and shape of its fruit, so also the first traces of Spirit virtually contain the whole of history.[14]

In knowing itself, the self-conscious nature of Spirit generates history and operates in 'time'. In this context, the entire purpose of history is for Spirit to know itself and gain Freedom. For Hegel, the self-knowing character of Spirit is realized in the perfection of man.

This view came under severe scrutiny and criticism because, while he discussed the universal nature of Spirit and its perfectibility in man, Hegel asserted that only the Prussian people could realize that "man is free and that freedom of Spirit is the very essence of man's nature."[15] Therefore "perfection" was not universally applicable. In addition, Hegel's "present" represented the climax of human development; everything previous to it constituted a less evolved state. He dismissed other cultures (and non-Christian religions) as non-progressive. Countries such as India, for example, despite its rich cultural products, "had no history," no final purpose of progress or development.[16] Despite this, Hegel's theory, particularly his notion of the *State* (which represented the perfectibility of man as a collective entity), captivated subsequent philosophers and political ideologues and profoundly influenced modernism as did his definition of art.

Fine Art as the Unity of Form and Content

Echoing the work of earlier Greek philosophers, Hegel stated that the content of a work of art must be the Idea (a genuine, concrete, but spiritual aspect of life), and delineated three criteria for successful art: 1) the content of the Idea should be appropriate for representation (i.e., it should be worthy of expression as art); 2) the content is a particular expression of the universality of the spiritual;[17] 3) the form or shape of the work of art must also be concrete and single, something whole itself. Then art can embody Spirit through a one-to-one correspondence between form and content in a total unified whole.[18] This unity of form and content is found only in Fine Art (as opposed to decorative objects). Fine Art expresses Spirit and is "free," like perfected man. It embodies the status of universal, self-conscious Spirit. Fine Art is, therefore, different from art which: 1) imitates nature, 2) illuminates some experience of the world, and 3) externalizes superficial emotions or feelings.[19] Kant also maintained that Fine Art is produced by the act of freedom, and is distinguished from imitation, handicraft or industrial art.[20]

The aim of Fine Art was, therefore, the revelation of truth in sensuous form. It could not be an object for sensual or cognitive appreciation because it exists alone for the aesthetic perception of the beautiful resulting in imaginative satisfaction. Thus, Hegel asserted that art should express beauty or the "immediate unity of nature and spirit in intuition." In this way, beauty represented the absolute realm of the idea and its truth and goes beyond the relative conditions of a finite reality. In this process, the artist imposes form upon a material substance and provides the potential for the aesthetic experience.

As Hegel stated:

> In art, these sensuous shapes and sounds present themselves, not simply for their own sake,...but with the purpose of affording in that shape satisfaction to higher spiritual interests, seeing that they are powerful to call forth a response and echo in the mind from all the depths of consciousness. It is thus that, in art, the sensuous is spiritualized, the spiritual appears in sensuous shape.[21]

Art was to satisfy "higher spiritual interests." Similarly, modern artist Wassily Kandinsky explained that the artist's task was to create unity between form and content and enhance the "spiritual atmosphere."[22] The unified relationship between form and content and the idea of Spirit in Fine Art persisted through to the twentieth-century, even when the notion of the Spirit was no longer related to Christianity and could, apparently, only be evoked through abstraction.

Ultimately, Formalists would argue that in order to express a universal, spiritual value, art must free itself of particularity and free itself of all content by focusing on pure form; the goal of modern art was still to evoke a universal, spiritual emotion in the viewer but totally unsullied by reference to sensual objects, nature or ideas. Modern art aimed at an absolute aesthetic response.

Significant Form and Universal Emotion

In the 1920s, the critic Clive Bell attempted to redefine art which could evoke universal feeling in his description of significant form. Reminiscent of Plato's ideas and Hegel's particularized Spirit, significant form was modestly defined as a unity of formal properties. Despite the fact that the nature of these formal properties is not clearly demarcated, Engler[23] notes that Bell's concept of significant form implies optimal unity and coherence of compositional patterns of lines and colors, and that this value of unity is an organic unity of wholes rather than parts.

Although many artists were influenced by Eastern philosophy and ideas, McEvilley asserts that Bell's thought, as with other modernist critics and modern artists, was essentially Hegelian in kind:

> By the mid-19th century...artists...could speak of nothing but infinity. Hegel had said that art was an embodiment of the infinite (an obvious contradiction in terms)....The artist James McNeil Whistler, an exponent of the art-for-art's sake attitude that developed from Hegelian artistic millennialism, remarked that 'art is limited to the infinite'...Vincent Van Gogh wrote to his brother Theo, 'I paint infinity.' Countless other examples of this way of speaking could be gleaned from the art discourse of c.1800 to c.1960 AD....Wassily Kandinsky, Piet Mondrian, Yves Klein, Lucio Fontana, Mark Rothko, Barnett Newman.... All these artists spoke of their work in the overwrought religious terms that go back to the age of Hegel—its ability to embody the infinite in finite form—and many of them actually suspected that their works were the last physical artworks, the artworks that immediately preceded the absorption of matter into spirit. Less openly acknowledged by critics and historians than by artists, still this formulation underlies, at the level of presupposition, the essays of Clive Bell, of Roger Fry, of Clement Greenberg, of Sheldon Nodelman, and of many other formalist Modernist writers.[24]

Bell's theory, according to McEvilley, traces its lineage directly to Hegelian millennialism. By focusing on formal elements, over and above the content of art, Bell sought to define a universal property to the aesthetic character of art. Possessing these formal elements, he wrote, art could provoke an aesthetic response.

While Bell acknowledged that each viewer had a different emotional response to a significant work of art, the emotions stimulated by art, he stressed, are the same in principle.

> The starting point for all systems of aesthetics must be the personal experience of a particular emotion. The objects that provoke this emotion we call works of art. All sensitive people agree that there is a peculiar emotion provoked by works of art. I do not mean, of course, that all works of art provoke the same emotion. On the contrary, every work produces a different emotion. But all these emotions are recognizably the same in kind....This emotion is called the aesthetic emotion; and if we can discover some quality common and peculiar to all the objects that provoke it, we shall have solved what I take to be the central problem of aesthetics. We shall have discovered the essential quality in a work of art, the quality that distinguishes works of art from all other classes of objects....What is this quality?...Only one answer seems possible—significant form.[25]

Called significant form, this essential quality defines art which evokes aesthetic emotion. By the same token, significant form is apprehended through aesthetic emotion. This circular argument explains that aesthetic judgment is based on subjective experience. (This perspective also assumes that there are some individuals who are more apt than others to perceive significant form, a position that is criticized by postmodernists.)

Bell continued by stating that "any system of aesthetics which pretends to be based on some objective truth is so palpably ridiculous as not to be worth discussing. We have no other means of recognizing a work of art than our feeling for it."[26] He went on to explain that although all aesthetic theories are based on subjective aesthetic judgment, a theory of aesthetics can have general validity—comparing the state of mind of a mathematician rapt in his studies to that of a person who experiences aesthetic emotion aroused by significant form.[27] He suggested that there is a subjective realm of experience which responds to particular, mentally-conceived or apprehended, formal properties.

As with Kant's criterion of subjective necessity in aesthetic judgment—where subjective necessity is similar to the compulsion involved in making cognitive judgments about an objective empirical fact—subjectivity implies something more than the particular nature of an individual's psychology; it is the subjective basis of the individual. Kant held that judgments made on this basis are universal, since they appear to agree with a universal norm not determined by personal inclinations. In this sense, Kant assumes that there is a universal foundation to the subject which guides judgment concerning art. An aesthetic judgment is one which is made from this platform.

The notion of the subjective faculty of intuition guiding creative expression, aesthetic judgment and insight was supported by both scientists and artists. Einstein, Bohr, and Heisenberg emphasized that intuition and aesthetics guided them in formulating theories. Scientific theories created on what were considered aesthetic grounds were later confirmed experimentally; so much so that the logic governing aesthetic theory in the arts was an essential feature of the modern scientific process.[28] Like modern artists, scientists felt that the mind's perception of beauty finds its realization in nature. The beauty of a scientific theory implies its truth; the intuitive dimension to human inquiry uncovers laws and principles of nature. By identifying an aesthetic inspiration and evaluation guiding scientific insights and thought, modernist's claims seem to be strengthened by science. Extending these ideas, the inner power of the work of art, beauty and the feelings of happiness in response to art, were considered by modern artists Barbara Hepworth and Agnes Martin to be critical to the definition and appreciation of art.

Spiritual Power in Art

Many artists attempted to describe both the subjective realm and the properties of a successful work of art in more specific terms. British sculptor, Barbara Hepworth felt that art's inner, spiritual force and energy created the "power" of the work. Spiritual power, characterized by the qualities of vision, power, vitality, scale, poise, form and beauty, created art's inner force and energy. Like Hegel, Hepworth felt that there should be a unique relationship between form and meaning, form and content; she stated that the material and the meaning of the form must be in perfect equilibrium.[29] She also believed that there are fundamental shapes "which speak at all times and periods in the language of sculpture,"[30] expressing certain eternal principles and relationships.

Great art was defined by Hepworth as affirmative—reflecting the laws of the universe:

> I think that the very nature of art...reflects the laws, and the evolution of the universe—both in the power and rhythm of growth and structure as well as the infinitude of ideas which reveal themselves when one is in accord with the cosmos and the personality is free to develop.[31]

In a description of the creative process, Hepworth stated that:

> Form realization is not just any three-dimensional mass—it is the chosen perfected form, of perfect size and shape, for the sculptural embodiment of the idea. Vision is not sight—it is the perception of the mind. It is the discernment of the reality of life, a piercing of the superficial surfaces of material existence, that gives a work of art its own life and purpose and significant power.[32]

Like Plotinus, Hepworth saw the artist as fathoming the superficial appearance of things, the apparent surfaces of material existence, discerning and exposing reality. Vision was an inner perception of the mind. The perfect form, not just any form or various possibilities of form but one essential form, matched the artist's idea or inner vision. While Hepworth describes a successful work of art in terms of power, certain elemental forms, and the expression of laws of nature, the American painter Agnes Martin feels that only an art of beauty can be called "true art."

Beauty Evokes Elation and Happiness

Stressing the role of the artist's feeling and intuitive perception during the creative process, Agnes Martin, in her description of true art, explains that in art, "our most joyful, subtle, and tender feelings are represented;"[33] for Martin "these feelings are universal and do not change."[34]

Martin locates feeling as the basis of art—suggesting that true art is responded to by people of all cultures in exactly the same way. However, unlike Bell, Martin, using examples such as the Pyramids and Ming pottery, feels that successful art creates the *same* response in each viewer. As with Hepworth, for Martin "positive" art celebrates beauty—the mystery of life apprehended by the mind rather than the eye:

> When I think of art I think of beauty,
> Beauty is the mystery of life.
> It is not in the eye, it is in the mind.
> In our minds there is awareness of perfection...

> All art work is about beauty.
> All positive work represents it and celebrates it.
> All negative art protests the lack of beauty in our experience...
> Beauty is an awareness in the mind.[35]

Martin gives beauty and perfection a privileged status; they are absolute qualities. Beauty, an awareness in the mind, is a mystery, although a universal characteristic of human experience. True art is about beauty; it evokes a specific quality of experience in the artist and viewer. Martin defines what she feels is positive and negative art, claiming that both address the concern for beauty in life.

Criticizing an "art of ideas," Martin suggests that there are two parts of the mind: one that deals with concepts, relationships, categories, classifications and deductions, and another which is an inner level of the mind which says "yes" and "no." The only way for the artist to proceed is through the inner mind which, when it says "yes," brings the feeling of elation called "inspiration."[36] Thus, Martin maintains that true art expresses beauty and illustrates happiness, and is responded to with the same quality of happiness. In contrast, ideational art is only responded to with other ideas and, therefore, is not true art. In her analysis, the difference between universal art and relative art is that the former evokes happiness and the latter stimulates ideas. The implication being that ideas are less universal than the feeling of happiness.

Articulating the process of creative expression, Hepworth and Martin see the artist's and viewer's experience as primary. Through inner vision, the artist creates specific, perfect corresponding forms. In Martin's art, the "figure" she constantly returns to is the grid. For her, the fundamental form of the grid reflects the inner perfection of the mind. These artists, among others, share the view that the artist's goal is to express laws of nature, evolution, or an inner beauty of the mind.

The assumption here is that the mind apprehends beauty through an intuitive process. For modernists, the honing of this somewhat mysterious faculty sets the artist apart as a genius, reflecting earlier ideas articulated by Kant.

The Artist as Genius

The common, Romantic, view presents the artist as a gifted individual with heightened intuition, maintaining spirituality in a society increasingly bereft of it. Often the artist is seen to live and suffer for an art which delivers spiritual meaning for the benefit of humanity. Apparently fitting this description, artists such as Vincent Van Gogh and Jackson Pollock have been canonized. For a time, the life of an artist was assumed to be a tormented one. Madness became associated with creativity and genius.

More recently, critics have examined the life and work of artists like Jackson Pollock in the context of a critical reading of modern theory, providing a less Romanticized view of life.[37] Despite this, it seems that Kant's definition of genius continues to reinforce the Romantic, modern, and often commonly held, concepts of creativity. Kant suggested that the means by which genius takes expression, cannot be known scientifically:

> Genius is a talent for producing that for which no definite rule can be given: and not an aptitude in the way of cleverness for what can be learned according to some rule; and that consequently originality must be its primary property....It cannot indicate scientifically how it brings about its product.[38]

Genius is the talent for producing original art—a talent for which there are no set guidelines. This is why genius is the realm of art and not science.[39] The artist is unable to articulate how the process of creating original art takes place; if he knew the mechanics of his creativity his art would not be original; it would be known beforehand. While knowing the means of creation beforehand would seem to be advantageous, it was seen by many artists as detrimental—inhibiting the immediacy of creative practice.

A genius possesses natural insight and innate ability but, as Kant suggests, genius cannot be taught:

> No *Homer* or *Wieland* can show how his ideas, so rich at once in fancy and in thought, enter and assemble themselves in his brain, for the good reason that he does not himself know, and so cannot teach others....Such skill cannot be communicated, but requires to be bestowed directly from the hand of nature upon each individual, and so with him it dies.[40]

Artistic skill equates with unfathomable insight, lost to humanity when the artist dies. Unlike science, which is able to impart knowledge about its procedures to others in order that they can build upon the work of their forebears, art and genius cannot be learned.

Inherent in Kant's description of genius is the idea that each great artist brings original insight to his work. This concept of originality is central to modernism. Art must be an original expression, in that: 1) it is different from what has gone before, is ever new; 2) the artist does not know how the artwork came about; and, 3) the work somehow embodies original presence, spirit or soul. While originality is a requirement of modern art, postmodern critics and postmodern artists deconstruct this notion (an example of this can be seen in the work of Sherrie Levine, Pat Steir and Lindy Lee).

Indian art theory also finds the notion of originality and genius irrelevant to art but for different reasons, as will be discussed in Chapter 2. For modernists, the artist—as genius and innovator—must always create new insight, new expressions, working in reference to conventions but breaking with them. The avant-garde artist, like a Hegelian hero in the linear move of history, is the progressive radical expressing spirit.

Progress in Art

During the 1940s and 1950s, art critics endorsed the ideas of continual progress in art, the artist as hero/genius, the supremacy of abstract art, art as self-evident revelation, and the claim of painting (as pure, abstracted form) as the ultimate medium to express the absolute.[41] Just as Western philosophers had defined fine art as distinct from decorative or functional art, American critic Clement Greenberg differentiated between high art and kitsch.

High art was abstract, pure form; it did not refer to anything outside of itself; it was for itself, of itself. In support of an absolute art Greenberg stated that:

> The avant-garde poet or artist sought to maintain a high level of art by both narrowing and raising it to the expression of an absolute....'Art for art's sake' and 'pure poetry' appeared, and subject matter or content became something to be avoided like the plague.... Content must become strictly optical and be dissolved completely into form...emptied out into a quality of feeling—which is expressed purely by form.[42]

Modernists conceived of art to be the vehicle for the expression of the absolute—art as pure form expressing feeling. McEvilley claims that this quality of "feeling," unconditioned by content (since modern art had seemingly emptied itself of reference to anything outside itself) was not, in fact, clearly defined by modern critics or artists.[43] But in Greenberg's opinion, painting, by erasing external reference, captured the infinite. Painting was for itself—like Hegel's Being-within-itself. Greenberg also suggested that abstract art more appropriately represented the reality of space as described by modern science:

> What has insinuated itself into Modernist art is the opposed notion of space as a continuum which objects inflect but do not interrupt, and of objects as being constituted in turn by the inflection of space. Space, as an uninterrupted continuum that connects instead of separating things, is something far more intelligible to sight than to touch...but space as that which joins instead of separating also means space as a total object, it is this total object that abstract painting, with its more or less impermeable surface, 'portrays.' The picture plane as a total object represents space as a total object. Art and nature confirm one another as before.[44]

This total, absolute space was represented in painting which no longer focused on isolated or particular forms. Such painting was meant to stimulate in the viewer "absolute emotion." As American painter Barnett Newman stated in 1948: "we are reasserting man's natural desire for the exalted, for a concern with our relationship to the absolute emotions. The image we produce is the self-evident one of revelation."[45]

Greenberg wrote that it was in the search for the absolute that the avant-garde arrived at "abstract" or "non-objective art." Abstract art was for this reason seen as the final moment in art history. The modern artist was the torchbearer of spirit in a mechanistic-industrial age. His avant-garde status guaranteed modernity, the endpoint of history, in the form of absolute art—an art free of content and relative reference. It was also apparently free of political constraints. But, as Kozloff suggests:

> Here [in America], at least, the artist was allowed, if only through indifference, to be at liberty and to pursue the inspired vagaries of his own conscience. Elsewhere in the world, where fascist or communist totalitarianism ruled, or where every energy had been spent in fighting them, the situation was otherwise. Modern American art...now propagandized itself as champion of eternal humanist freedom.[46]

Kozloff asserts that abstract art, despite its claim to be ultimately free, came to represent American humanism. Therefore, in principle, it seemed to stand for democracy and individual freedom—which may be one reason why it became internationally pervasive.

Art historians and critics, in their enthusiasm, even suggested that abstraction represented the mature cognitive development of mankind as opposed to the cognitively undeveloped style of pre-Medieval and Renaissance art.[47] In this way, modernists applied the approach of Hegel's fragmentary history and adopted a universal point of view through conceptual history. By rejecting art which referred to epics, myths, and "primitive" stories as less developed, modern historians reviewed history over a short period of time and in so doing presented its own interests—recounting a series of developments or movements which culminated in abstract art. This art was also defined as "good" in that it apparently "elevated the soul." Here, modern historiography also seemed to conform to the criteria defined in Hegel's fragmentary history.

Reflecting upon modern theory and art, McEvilley states that the non-objective Formalism of modern art:

> Became a 'secular religion'...we all wanted to believe that form in art was a kind of absolute, a Platonic hyper-real beyond conceptual analysis...the worship of form as an absolute is a distant resonance of the Pythagorean/Platonic doctrine of the music of the Spheres—the belief that art vibrations pass constantly through the universe and in fact constitute its inner ordering principles.[48]

In abstract Formalist art, modern theorists and artists attempted to define and create Fine Art that embodied freedom and spirit. Their art did not merely imitate nature, it did not entertain or represent the world of the senses; it aimed to capture absolute emotions. As Zakian wrote of Barnett Newman, his "concept of the sublime is predicated upon the viewer attaining the lofty condition of absolute knowledge, of comprehending the totality of himself and the world in which he exists."[49] Such a goal was far beyond the reach of modernism.

We have seen that modernists saw the historical development of art as resulting in abstraction—an art of pure form—in which the modern artist captured the total space of the infinite, creating work which strove to embody spirit and freedom. Echoing early Greek philosophers and the ideas of Hegel and Kant, modernist critics described Fine Art as that which expresses Spirit or an absolute as opposed to imitative art, functional art or kitsch. Furthermore, the artist/genius, able to intuitively arrive at pure form, could not articulate how his creative process unfolded. This mysterious subjective process of art was echoed in the subjective experience of art.

Despite the acknowledgment of the relativity of emotional response, some modernists argued for a category of aesthetic emotion in which particular emotions (in response to art of significant form) could be classified. Universal feeling or aesthetic response is characterized specifically as happiness, elation, revelation or absolute knowledge. True art, embodying universal value, through unified formal elements or universal forms, is responded to with universal feeling. True art, thus, has universal value; it stimulates this feeling in the viewer, regardless of time, place, and cultural determinants. Due to apparent superior cognitive, cultural and aesthetic development, the modern artist was thought to be conceptually more evolved than his forefathers and modern abstract art, the pinnacle and endpoint of art history.

These ideas were adopted by different cultures throughout the world. McEvilley holds that these propositions, applied through cultural expansionism, have been responsible for the destruction of non-Western cultures:

> The belief that there were universal and unchanging values, and that these values resided in the cultural and social policies of Western Europe and America—essentially, of the colonizing nations—was the characteristic of Modernism. Indeed, it was one of its historical premises. Hegelian Modernism posited history as a force which worked teleologically toward a goal; this force, a subjective universal operating through objective criteria, had to receive definition and leadership from a group of hyper-conscious individuals who would, through superior vision or intuition, see the values toward which history was striving inwardly and help it on its way. The role of the historical avant-garde was assumed by the colonialist nations, much as the Crusaders had once justified conquest as the saving of souls. Modernism, relying on a mysticism of progress and scientific method, saw itself as a global or transcendent viewpoint capable of standing above and judging the countless tribal points of view of other peoples. Lately Modernism has come to seem to be only a tribal view itself, that of Western Christendom since the Renaissance.[50]

Although modernism has been discussed here in terms of an overarching theory, many movements which fall under the rubric of modern art (including the radical, anti-aesthetic of Dada, political art movements such as Constructivism, Futurism, and Social Realism, and later Pop Art) do not necessarily conform to the above criteria. Of these, the more critical movements such as Dada and Pop Art are precursors of postmodernism—critical, relativist, anti-art and anti-absolute. With the advent of a post-colonial world and the development of deconstruction theory, the ideas of "universal value," an "absolute presence," and progress and originality in art, were dismantled. Modern art and theory came to represent one viewpoint among many.

2

INDIAN THEORY: ART AND ŚĀNTA

While there are different schools of philosophy in India, theorists have referred to an overarching traditional approach to art and aesthetics. There are different kinds of art practices in India, but these are often grouped under the term 'Tradition.' As McEvilley notes, "an array of inherited cultural elements—literary, philosophical, religious, artistic, and so on—together make up what in India is called the Tradition in art."[1] However, here, the work of Sneh Pandit and Ananda Coomaraswamy will serve as the main source for the discussion of so-called traditional Indian art theory.[2] Due to the focus on art, the different strands of Indian philosophy will not be examined. However, it is worth mentioning that three different conceptions of philosophy in India have been identified by scholars: 1) the rational, critical, and illuminating review of the contents of theology, economics and political science, called *Ānvikṣiki*, seen as the foundation of action and duty; 2) a system of ideas comprising epistemology, metaphysics, ethics, and soteriology, called *Darśana*; and 3) an intuitive network of views regarding humanity, its nature and destiny, Nature and the Ultimate Reality or God explicit or implicit in the sayings, songs, hymns, talks, and writings of mystics, sages, and saints, called *popular philosophy*.[3]

According to Coward, from the "beginning" (the beginning of Indian philosophical thought—which he locates as sometime before 1000 B.C.E.)[4] Indian philosophy speculated about the "unity and ultimate ground of the world."[5] In this context, "the *Ṛgveda* scripture" is recorded as the earliest philosophical text, with later works being the *Brāhmaṇas* and *Upaniṣads*.[6] As will be discussed in Part III, Maharishi Vedic Science presents a different understanding of the Vedic texts—defining them not as philosophical treatises written by individuals in Indian history but as the record of impulses of self-referral consciousness.

With respect to art, traditional Indian aesthetic theory seems to share some common ground with modern theory, while providing fundamentally opposing definitions of the role and function of art. It holds that art can evoke a universal experience, a tasting of ideal beauty—an intellectual-ecstatic order of being[7]—but, as opposed to modern art, in India, traditionally art is never for itself; its purpose is to fulfill the needs of a patron, viewer or spectator.

> Works of art (*śilpa-karmāṇi*) are means of existence made (*kṛta*, *saṁskṛita*) by man as artist (*śilpn*, *kāraka, kavi*, etc.) in response to the needs of man as patron (*kārayitṛ*) and consumer (*bhogin*) or spectator (*draṣṭṛ*). The production of works of art is never an end in itself; 'the work of the two hands is an otherwise determined element of natural being'; 'all expressions, whether human or revealed, are directed to an end that is over and beyond the fact of expression';

> 'as the purpose, so the work.' Art (*śilpa*, *kāla*, *kāvyai*, etc.) in its becoming (*utpatti*) is the manipulation or arrangement (*saṁskaraṇa*, *vidhāna*, etc.) of materials according to a design or pattern, preconceived (*dhyāta*, *nirmāta*) as the theme (*vastu*) may demand, which design or pattern is the idea or intelligible aspect (*sattva-jñāna-rūpa*) of the work (*karma*) to be done (*kārya*) by the artist.[8]

All expressions of art are created according to a preconceived design or pattern. Only through this is the theme expressed.

Indian art theory and aesthetics also include specific descriptions of: 1) *rasa*—the essence, or the combined aspects of the art object and subjective reactions which those factors evoke; 2) the nature, purpose and meaning of art; 3) aesthetic judgment; and 4) the social role of art.[9]

Tasting Rasa: The Experience of Aesthetic Emotion

As with Western thought, according to Indian theory, aesthetic experience is subjective in nature and gained through intuitive knowledge.[10] Intuitive knowledge is a state of *pure contemplation* without conceptual thought; in this respect, it is similar to Kant's description of aesthetic disinterestedness where the experience of art results in a disinterested "free" pleasure or response—a response not motivated by sensual need but incurred by the beautiful.[11] Intuitive knowledge is not absence of knowledge; it is knowledge through being rather than reasoning. Thus, disinterested contemplation of beauty in nature and art brings about a state of mind which is universal in that it can transcend the individual ego.

Differing from modernist elitism, the aim of Indian art is the cultivation of a dispassionate and disinterested feeling (rather than rational understanding); this feeling is accessible to *everyone*—even though it belongs to the highest order of consciousness.[12] Aesthetic experience, in transcending the ego, intellectual and mental elements of experience, is liberating; it provides illumination, depth and elevation, rather than conceptual knowledge; it seems that Agnes Martin would concur with this account of art and its effect. This elevated experience is a cultivated state rather than a "divine madness" or an unknown creative impulse of innate genius.

The "tasting" or aesthetic experience brought about by the work of art is called *rasa*. Borrowed from Indian medical science, the term *rasa* refers to the soul of art. It is commonly defined as a kind of juice or sap, or the flavor one gets from tasting liquid; in another sense it is taken to be equivalent to *ānanda*, pure bliss or spiritual delight[13] (*rasa* is also discussed in later sections from the perspective of Maharishi Vedic Science). *Rasa* is a special type of feeling which is: 1) free from the adverse effects of actual feeling; 2) achieved when everyday feelings are purified through art and the imaginative faculty of the viewer; 3) possible because the aesthetic situation is unlike everyday life; 4) not a mental construct but feeling proper of a specific kind; and 5) the result of purification which is not religious or moral but aesthetic.[14] It refers to ideal beauty, tasted (*svādyate*) in "pure aesthetic experience."[15]

Accordingly, the:

> Delight or tasting of ideal beauty (*rasāsvādana*), though void of contact with intelligible things (*vedyāntara-sparśaśūnya*), is in the intellectual-ecstatic order of being (*ānanda-cinmaya*), transcendental (*lokottara*), indivisible (*akhaṇḍa*), self-manifested (*svaprakāśa*), like a flash of lightening (*camatkāra*), the very twin of the tasting of Brahman (*Brahmasvāda-sahodara*).[16]

In this sense, the aesthetic experience is considered to be transcendent—here defined as the intellectual-ecstatic order of being which is self-manifested, like a flash of lightening and something akin to the tasting of Brahman.

Apart from the feeling of *rasa*, there are more differentiated human emotions, referred to as *sthayibhava*. Although *rasa* is considered to be more fundamental than *sthayibhava*, these elemental human feelings are the material of aesthetic emotion and have distinct qualities. Since they are basic qualities of human emotion, they are not like passing whim or fancy, but are universal in kind. Thus, all individuals have the capacity for *rasa* and *sthayibhava*. The work of art stimulates these elemental feelings through *udbodhana* or *carvana*, "recollection" or "rumination" respectively.

The viewer in this situation experiences not the ordinary emotion which motivates action, but through a distancing or disinterestedness, a purification of particular emotion and a state of exaltation which results in *śānta* or peace.[17] The emotions experienced by the viewer are "relived" recollected material. This experiencing is not through identification but "the tasting of one's consciousness."[18] In this sense, *Rasa* is more than feeling with the object but becoming the object.

Art as Skill

As opposed to modernists, Indian aestheticians and artists see no distinction between the fine and applied arts. The ancient Greek term *techne*, meaning skillful, which broadly applied to various professions, according to Pandit, is similar to the meaning of the word *śilpa* which includes the arts, crafts and skill. In order to fully develop and refine their skill, until recently in India, both the artist and craftsman, Pandit maintains, were expected to follow a specific routine (similar to that of a saint) the aim of which was to clarify vision, reveal inner laws of outward phenomena, resulting in "right" action, thinking and making.[19]

The idea of skill equating to "right action" pervades Indian art theory. The artist is expected to be an exemplary human being but is not considered set apart from society: He is a skillful individual and knows his craft, working within specific guidelines which serve as grammatical rules in the language of art. He simultaneously develops clarity of mind to hone inner vision.

Inner Vision into Outer Expression

Successful Indian art is the perfect conformity of outward forms to inner vision. *Citra*, which stands for "painting" or "picture," means an object that happens to be an externalization of what was in *chit*, or consciousness; the artist materializes what is in consciousness. If inner vision is confused, unclear, or influenced by considerations that are not pertinent to formal perfection, the artwork will lack artistic quality.

Although Indian art is felt to reflect nature's deeper laws—i.e. the workings of the cosmos, rather than her external appearance—there are different kinds of images serving various purposes. Pandit discriminates, for example, between *murti*, an image of aesthetic value, *pratima*, an icon, or vivid presentation of being, and a *yantra* which, while mathematically symbolic, is not an aesthetic object.

Despite the notion of the perfection of form as paramount in Indian art, unlike modern art, the artist does not strive for "pure form." Art has relative purposes, such as social and functional uses, but if these distort inner vision or impinge upon the formal principles of design and construction then artistic content is diminished.[20] Integrity of form and content must be maintained; in this respect, Indian theory would concur, in principle, with some aspects of Hegel's notion of the relationship of form and content.

However, Coomaraswamy notes that there are two approaches to making art. The first represents the procedure of working from the universal to the particular, the second represents the procedure of working from the particular to the universal. In the first instance the form is already known and is then expressed in art; in the second a thing is perceived sensibly, then the intellect "at work in the heart" discovers the corresponding form. Coomaraswamy indicates that these two approaches can be likened to working from imagination and working from nature or memory.[21] Ultimately, however, art is only properly deduced when it imitates the works of "heaven" or the work of "angelic beings."[22]

Working With Set Guidelines to Create Universal Art

Whereas the modern artist develops his own personal style, the Indian artist works within a set procedural and formal framework. For the traditional Indian artist the idea of individual style and breaking with tradition runs contrary to the definition of what it means to be an artist. The artist follows specific guidelines in order to better express himself and create universal meaning; nothing must be left to chance. The true artist is one who can express himself within the prescribed form.[23]

As with modern theory, Indian theory distinguishes between the knowledge of science and the purpose of art. Pandit states, "if science is the formulation of thought then art is the transformation of feeling."[24] Art is not created to evoke intellectual ideas; it's purpose is to evoke an aesthetic feeling, a tasting of *rasa*, which is impersonal and universal.

The Purpose of Art

Indian theorists suggest that there are three aspects or stages to art: the first is the creative process of the artist; the second is the artwork; and the third is the viewer's response—when the artist's experience is recreated. These three stages occur in one unified process; the absence of any one stage means that the process is incomplete. In fact, there is no room for art which does not communicate to a viewer. The term *pratibha*, meaning creative energy, signifies both the artist's talent and the observer's response. Like Bell's description of aesthetic emotion validating significant form, Pandit remarks that the only proof of the existence of *rasa* in the artwork is the corresponding tasting of *rasa* in the observer, the *sahridaya*.

The artist strives to create a feeling in the observer which is the same as the artist's experience; only a successful artwork will achieve this goal. Since experience is the basic judge of the validity of a work of art, the idea of criticism is redundant; the role of art is to culture aesthetic emotion and not to solicit intellectual inquiry. Pandit states that the work of art is meant to cultivate "good" taste, that is, a *sattvic* state of mind in the viewer—a state of mind free of turmoil. "Good" taste is not a private judgment but a particular state of mind.[25] Therefore, it is impossible to consider the artwork as valid on account of its formal elements or the response of the viewer only; both must be taken into consideration.

Art also aids man to arrive at freedom—*mokṣa* or spiritual liberation;[26] in this sense, art is functional—not in the mundane utilitarian sense of the word, but in helping man to realize a higher value to life. While this view has been construed as religious, Pandit asserts that this is not so. The role of art is to relate human life to cosmic life through fleeting moments of *rasa* by engaging the viewer in life, and not attaining the permanent nature of *mokṣa* through renunciation of life (as does the religious person or *yogi*). In some ways, Hegel's thought might seem in line with this notion; but his ideas were essentially Eurocentric.

By having a moral purpose—culturing the individual to achieve a *sattvic* state of mind, traditional Indian art is seen as integral to a healthy civilization; it has a social value.[27] Furthermore, since all the arts and skills in society are classified as art, there is no "fine art" belonging to an elite group. Pandit suggests that materialism is the cause of such elitist distinctions; life and the arts "cease to be the earnest expression of a whole civilization" but the "symptomatic outburst of a special group."[28] Again, differing from modern theory, artists are felt to be socially responsible beings securing human aims through art that transforms life from drudgery to fulfillment.

Clearly, from this perspective, aesthetic emotion is evoked through art which creates the experience of pure contemplation or an aesthetic disinterestedness. The tasting of one's consciousness, or *rasa*, is the goal of art. The artist does not risk this result by leaving the creative process to chance; he or she works with set guidelines for a prescribed outcome. However, it is the inner vision of the artist that is translated into outer material form. In this, the experience of the artist is recreated in that of the viewer. Thus, the purpose and social role of art is fulfilled; it creates a *sattvic* state of mind, a mind which has achieved *Śānta* or peace. In part V, these themes will re-emerge in the consideration of universal principles of art that expand some of the principles of Indian art in light of Maharishi Vedic Science.

Although this view of art and aesthetics obviously contrasts with Western modern and postmodern theory, both modernism and postmodernism have influenced Indian art and artists. For example, when India adopted a democratic constitution in 1947, a group of artists called the Bombay Progressive Artists Group recommended the adoption of European modern art styles and Formalist tendencies such as abstraction. More recently, artists such as Gulam Mohammed Sheikh use the postmodern device of quotation to explore their Indian identity.[29] While "traditional" Indian art, as defined here, persists, contemporary Indian artists and critics are engaged in developing art theory, redefining visual culture and contributing to the transformation of culture. Some say that the globalization of theory, in fact, reflects a more pervasive colonization of the mind in a so-called "post-colonial" age.

3

POSTMODERN ART AS A PLURALIST LANGUAGE GAME: POINTING TO THE UNNAMABLE

The definition, value and practice of art and aesthetics, have their basis in the philosophy or theory of knowledge that is prevalent at the time for any particular group. As Fehér and Heller note, "the aesthetic value of various arts, although not always explicit in form, will depend on the philosophical system."[1]

> In the first century AD, Strabo recorded...a Scythian initiation rite in which youths would dance in forest clearings clothed in wolf skins. After bonding in this new identity they would regard non-initiates as wolves' prey. It was an effective preparation for power struggles and war, as members of the clan or tribal cult universalized their claim on power by identifying with forces of nature. In the Modernist era, with its claims of universal standards of quality, the elite community of taste might have seemed such a group; certain artworks, especially those of the abstract sublime, were its cultic emblems, like wolf skins. The group for whom the work was made was bonded around its secret meanings; and other groups—*profani*, non-initiates, interlopers—were rendered its social, economic, and cultural prey. While seeming to emphasize universality or sameness, art in the West became a force for divisiveness and exclusion.
>
> With the gradual demise of Modernism during the last three decades, however, there are signs that the art world's cultic ambience is diminishing—or at the very least that its membership base has broadened dramatically. In the 50's and early 60's (the final heyday of Modernism) the range of art that could enter into art history was limited to, basically, abstract paintings out of Paris or New York by white male artists.[2]

Contrasting with the cultic, elitist practices of modernism (which excluded non-Europeans and women), McEvilley states that postmodernism represents a radical paradigm shift. However, although it includes previously marginalized groups, McEvilley and others imply that the postmodern shift could be due to the expansion of modernism. In this scenario, postmodernism is a phase of late modernism[3] or late-Capitalism[4]—continually commodifying art and culture. Even with this reading, postmodernists deconstruct the modernist concepts of universality, originality, the innate genius of the artist, his unique ability to intuitively fathom and express sublime emotion, and the idea of linear historical progress in art. The postmodernist is a philosopher, linguist, performer, story-teller, critic, shaman or appropriator; she examines the production of meaning in art, analyzing and criticizing modernist propositions rather than assuming they are true. Drawing upon contemporary philosophy, Postmodernists define art as visual language that, rather than signifying presence, points to its absence. As conceptual artist Joseph Kosuth explains, the role of the artist is not to represent universal value or significant form but to generate new rules in a language game revealing that the unsaid is unsayable.[5]

In presenting a critique of modernism, then, postmodern theory posits an infinite variety of discourse as opposed to one unifying theory. In addition, whereas modernists favored a linear model of History, the postmodernist model can be described as "an array of dissimilar line fragments flung randomly down on the page, some intersecting others, some paralleling others, some more or less isolated."[6] This heterogeneous, counter-meta-narrative model seems more appropriate because, "every ethnic group or bonding group or community of taste or belief will write and rewrite its own fragment of history, and probably in many conflicting versions."[7] Despite this overall shift in theory, it seems that there are different postmodernisms. At least two can be identified: deconstructive postmodernism and revisionary postmodernism. The first undermines the notion of progress, revealing a non-linear play of difference; the second adopts a neo-humanist approach.[8] Deconstructive postmodernism has had a significant impact upon art and theory, through the influence of semiology and philosophy—especially the work of Ferdinand de Saussure, Jacques Derrida and François Lyotard.

Language as Arbitrary Signs

In many cultures, and prior to the twentieth century in the West, language had a unique relationship to that which it signified (the word for apple, for example, was thought to correspond intimately to the thing "apple"). This idea extended to art in as much as the form of the art object was felt to directly embody content or spirit—the essence of art. Postmodernists maintain that such a claim for language and for art is baseless. As visual language, art is a play of arbitrary signs that cannot embody a self-evident presence or transcendent. While in modern theory, the self or the centered subject is the foundation of art and language, for postmodernists, there is no unified self unconditioned by social, cultural and historical factors from which artistic expression originates. There is no modern artist who is a hero and genius expressing the presence of spirit through revelatory insight; the "word," or *logos* does not represent the original language of God. Incorporating the work of Saussure and Derrida, postmodernists view the self or self-consciousness as mediated by language—by the social language of the world and not the divine.

In the early part of this century, Saussure developed his semiology—a science which studies the life of signs within a society—proposing that an arbitrary relationship exists between the linguistic sign (the word) and that which it signified. The sound-image (the material element such as the mark on paper or sound) he called the *signifier.* The concept (an immaterial idea to which the signifier refers) he termed the *signified.* The combined *concept* and *sound-image* associated with a word is known as the *sign.* Saussure stated that only a conventional rather than an intrinsic bond exists between the sign's material element and its content or meaning—the signifier and the signified. Every language has its own terminology for a single object or concept which has come about through the historical and cultural development of any nation, culture, or group of people. Meaning, therefore, is generated in language not through terms which are naturally imbued with absolute meaning, but through difference.

However, Green notes that Saussure's approach does assume that the observer could in principle have the entire structure of another's language as an object of thought. This Structuralist perspective privileged the system of language (*langue*) over speech (*parole*) such that the social structure of language became more significant than individual speech acts. For this reason, the primary role of individual consciousness (as presence articulated through speech) was less significant than the system of language as a whole and its influence in shaping individual consciousness.

Applied to art, this approach shifts the emphasis away from the idea of art that embodies a transcendental realm through individual insight, and shifts it toward the role of social conditions in shaping visual culture. Despite this, the structure and formal aspect of the work of art still holds prominence.

Absence of Presence

Extending these ideas, Derrida developed his theory of deconstruction. Deconstruction usurps the notion of absolute presence and questions the notion of a universal transcendental signified, denying the possibility of absolute value. Derrida creates new meaning in language. For example, he coined a neologism, *différance*, which, in contrast to traditional philosophy, defines not a transcendental unity but an "a chain of differing and deferring substitutions" unceasingly dislocating itself.[9] *Différance*—a constant difference and deference of meaning—signifies the play of signs within language. It is, among other things, the active, moving discord of different forces that question the primacy of presence as consciousness. It also negates logocentrism—which privileges the spoken word over the written word:

> As Aristotle saw it, voice and breath have an immediate relationship with the mind that naturally reflects the divine *logos*. Between *logos* and mind is a relationship of natural signification—the mind mirrors things by natural resemblance. Between mind and speech there is a relationship of conventional symbolization. Spoken language is a first conventional symbolization of the inner reflection of the *logos*. Written language is a second, further removed convention.[10]

Western philosophy had posited that naturally speech, before writing, represented the divine or the origin of language. This proposition informed modern theory. However, for Derrida, there is no divine *logos* fundamental to language; the "immediate presence" of the subject or speaker is not directly related to the word or object;[11] meaning is always located within a "gap" between signifier and signified, self and other. Rather than a name or physical expression of ineffable Being, there is only a play of names which reveal the impossibility of expressing Being or ultimate presence.

As discussed earlier, in Hegel's content and form and Greenberg's formalism, meaning was felt to be completely correspondent with form or structure; there was a special, unique relationship between artistic insight and divine insight, Being or absolute presence. Postmodern art, on the other hand, applying Derrida's deconstruction theory, questions the notion of absolute presence existing prior to a work of art.

With respect to *différance*, Green argues that it has its roots in Hegel's notion of contradiction, where everything comes into existence out of opposition to what it is not. However, while Hegel's binary opposition is transcended through synthesis in a greater whole there is no such possibility with *différance*. For Derrida there is only a structure of differences; there is no possibility of pure self consciousness.[12] Deconstruction theory also assumes that the text or writing (indeed, the whole structure of language within which meaning is defined and redefined) is primary; it is "writing," the play or active moment of differentiation, which creates the force of all language. This definition of writing expands the conventional notion of the simple script of texts; for Derrida, "writing" also includes the neuronal traces in the brain—which Freud identified as memory. In the same way, Derrida alludes to DNA as a "writing" or the trace present in all living substances. In his materialist approach "writing," and not the divine word, forms consciousness.

Since Derrida privileges writing over speech, he rejects the idea that mental concepts are transparently meaningful. Therefore, there is no self-conscious realm of knowing or absolute knowledge which precedes difference. He states that there is no "master-name" of Being because the sign (writing) presents the thing in its absence; the sign is always *deferred presence* and can never represent *original presence*. As visual language or a play of signs, art similarly cannot embody consciousness as self-presence or Being, but only indicate absence.

In deconstruction theory, no ideas or sounds exist prior to a linguistic system; there are only conceptual and phonic differences without positive terms. There is no pure speech, pure thought, pre-actualized meaning, and no transcendental system with a reservoir of perfect expressions or meaning. Applying this argument to art, there can be no pure form embodying an absolute. Indeed, pre-actualized meaning can only be understood as a "blind origin" or pure absence. In this sense, there is always an unrealizable external outside to any discourse; any unifying system of philosophy becomes impossible. In art, here is no unified expression of perfect form but many signs and relationships between signs. It is worth mentioning that the architectural style of deconstructivism combines reference to both the style of Constructivism and the theory of deconstruction; it works against the notion of wholes, symmetry and any spatial definition based on traditional or modern aesthetic theory.

As one critic puts it, deconstruction allows movement from the particular to the particular without a transition through the general or universal; there is movement from *chora* (sacred, local, particular space) to *chora* without *topos* (universal, abstract space). This post-structuralist perspective parallels the process of electronic art in this technological age. Involving equipment that can make jumps, rather than step-by-step logic, aesthetic practices like collage can represent deconstructive thinking in a computer environment. Electronic media seem to lend themselves to non-hierarchical processes and deconstructive thought.

As mentioned earlier, in Saussure's analysis the observer could in principle have the entire structure of a language as an object of thought. In contrast, Derrida's *différance*, cannot be the object of thought. Despite this, it can be seen as a transcendental, albeit ungraspable, precondition for the possibility of thought, because, rather than a horizontal, non-hierarchical plurality of meaning, *différance* represents the foundation for the play of meaning and its production (as in the analogy of textual movement as rhizome). [13] Derrida deliberately employs terms such as *différance* and *pharmakon* (the latter signifying both remedy and poison) to illustrate the elusiveness of determinate meaning and present a semantic paradox. Through this approach, he aims to undermine totalizing theories, and apparently bring ethical and critical judgment to philosophy and its applications. Although he does not replace the universalizing assumptions of traditional philosophy and modern theory with a simple relativism, his application of materialist theories of meaning to phenomenology creates something problematic and mysterious in itself. [14] Curiously, Derrida's language theory imposes its own totalizing view in the negation of presence through infinite difference and absence.

Just as traditional philosophy influenced modernists, language theory and deconstruction informs postmodernists. Postmodernism embraces political, cultural, historical, social and psychoanalytic parameters rather than simply focusing on the assumed universal, transcendental, and formal developments.[15] It denies the artist the role of inspired, spiritually insightful genius creating original art works which embody presence. Art, a play of *différance*, is a text which can never disclose universal value. Artists who espouse deconstruction theory find the notion of art embodying a significant presence redundant and misleading.

In a sense, Derrida's theory may not aim to be relativist but when applied to art it often becomes just that, and it is this relativist notion of art which critics of deconstructive postmodernism resist.

> What Derrida and other post-structuralists try to deconstruct is the absolute truth value of any relative manifestation of an absolute center, of which we generally have no direct, shareable experience and therefore cannot legitimate. Textualists

argue that there is no absolute in the relative, and from this they infer that there is no absolute, that everything is language or difference.[16]

Language Games and Knowledge

Some say that postmodern art is a language game, affecting the formation of culture through the transformation of consciousness. Coined by Wittgenstein, the term "language game" refers to various types of utterances in different modes of discourse. Wittgenstein's view both gave language a scientific basis (to articulate what can be spoken) and revealed how language can indicate what cannot be spoken. He indicated that different language games are used as part of an activity or form of life, e.g., giving orders, forming and testing a hypothesis, guessing riddles, etc.[17] Each game includes rules defined by the group which employs it but those rules change according to the needs of the group. Due to the differences between individual experience, perception and derivation of meaning, in any language game, there can be no universal definition of meaning. Involving an interactive play of forces—artist, viewer, social and historical context—similarly, there are many possible responses to, and readings of, art. Just as words have no *a priori* or intrinsic meaning and are used according to definitions laid down by the people who generate rules of a language game, art has no *a priori* significance.

In his book *The Postmodern Condition: A Report on Knowledge*, Lyotard defines two distinct language games which provide two kinds of knowledge—*narrative knowledge* and *scientific knowledge*. The former is related to day-to-day living and making judgments while the latter is employed by science. Art and cultural discourse are a part of narrative knowledge because it includes social or *customary knowledge* (of which art is a part). As discussed earlier, modernists legitimized theory by claiming, like science, in art there are objective universals. Lyotard, however, sees a clear demarcation between narrative and scientific knowledge stating that it is narrative knowledge which is important for art because through it culture is formed.

Scientific Versus Narrative Knowledge: The Formation of Culture

Lyotard clarifies the difference between narrative and scientific knowledge by explaining that narrative knowledge is related to concepts of internal equilibrium and conviviality, and includes notions of "know-how," "knowing how to live," "how to listen," etc. while scientific knowledge is a set of denotative statements. Narrative knowledge, going beyond determination and application of truth, encompasses ethical wisdom, technical qualification, and visual sensibility. It includes aesthetic judgment: aesthetic value is determined by the relative criteria of beauty, truth and efficiency articulated by the social group of the "knower." Such criteria are established through consensus and conformity. For this reason, there is a relationship between this kind of knowledge and social custom.

This way of legitimizing statements has often been called "opinion," but Lyotard holds that it is consensus within a group that allows knowledge to be legitimate for that particular group; each group has its own value system agreed upon by the group. In this way, culture is shaped by consensus. This kind of knowledge, often takes a narrative form and is called customary knowledge. Culture, in this scheme, can be said to be determined by the kind of narrative knowledge generated and upheld by it. Narrative knowledge determines criteria of competence and application—as narratives circumscribe what should be said and done in a culture. Since narrative knowledge also requires a participatory, interactive role of the speaker and the listener, it is instrumental in the formation of social bonds. In terms of popular stories narrative knowledge: 1) defines positive or negative models (e.g., the successful or unsuccessful hero in myth); 2) lends itself to various language games; and 3) often requires particular rules in the transmission of narratives. It takes place "in time," has a value in terms of rhythm (e.g., in sacred chants) and includes ritual and art.

Scientific knowledge, on the other hand, "requires that one language game, denotation, be retained and all others excluded;" it requires the production of verifiable or falsifiable statements about referents accessible to the scientific experts.[18] While modernists wanted to validate art using criteria appropriate to the language game of science, postmodernists accept that science and art, or scientific and narrative knowledge, are separate models or language games with their own criteria and rules.

Scientific knowledge aims to be "true;" for example it seeks to discover fundamental laws that function in nature and to show how these laws operate and can be used through specific technologies. Scientific knowledge, does not, according to Lyotard, use language games that combine to form a social bond; only narrative knowledge is central to the identity and formation of culture and society. The sociological character of narrative knowledge, with custom and art included in its range, determines its relative nature. Postmodernism, as part of contemporary narrative knowledge, similarly, affects social life but does not disclose truth or absolute presence. By creating social consciousness, language games determine a culture or period's world-view.

Since narrative and scientific knowledge have a different criteria for legitimizing statements, judging the validity of one on the basis of the other is impossible. As Thomas Kuhn notes, even within science the criteria that govern one paradigm are not necessarily compatible with those of another. In science, a researcher engaged in *normal science* does not test the paradigm itself, but takes the rules which govern the paradigm for granted.[19] One could say that a paradigm is a kind of language game which, at a critical juncture (when individuals question or create new rules) alters, and a new language game is formed. Modernists, like the researcher engaged in normal science, do not put the rules or assumptions to test. Postmodernists, on the other hand, attempt to constantly question rules and assumptions. It is accepted that new paradigms emerge and develop over time;

like maps, they provide information about the terrain while being constantly redrawn.

Drawing upon these ideas, postmodernists define art as a set of codes or conventions which convey meaning to a particular people at a given time. To understand art of another culture one must try to enter into a cultural discourse governed by different assumptions than those of one's own. The criteria that inform visual culture for a particular group, will differ from group to group. Different language games operate in different circumstances, cultures, or disciplines. Not only is language instrumental in forming consciousness but social custom and cultural practice define knowledge and individual thought and action. However, while the postmodern definition of knowledge aims to eradicate imperialist or totalizing theories, many people suggest that postmodernism is also totalizing in its claims.

Master Narratives and Aesthetics

Richard Rorty suggests the distinction between scientific and narrative knowledge resembles the positivist demarcation between scientific method and unscientific, political, religious, or common sense discourse. Narrative knowledge is held on an equal footing with science,[20] but some critics feel that postmodern theory remains just theory; it provides no practical social implementation of its propositions. Even Lyotard's rejection of totalizing theories has been criticized as simplistic, reductionist and "terroristic"[21] because postmodernity, like modernity, is a master narrative itself. The term *post* in relation to modernism accepts the modernist historical, totalizing perspective. By rejecting all totalizing systems one falls prey to the same problem of totalization. Many critics argue for theory which conceptualizes macrostructures *and* differences, observing that although some narratives of legitimation may seem dubious, *all* grand narratives should not be rejected.[22] This kind of approach is in keeping somewhat with revisionary postmodernism.

With respect to aesthetics, sociological aesthetician, Janet Wolff states that even though art needs a new theory of the aesthetic, postmodernists, by "textualizing" the social, collude with modern theory. She favors a new formalism in the study of the visual arts, "which without abandoning ideological critique or social history, enables the art critic to pay attention to the structural features and content of works."[23] In understanding that meaning is derived, not through the perception of universal phenomena which predate language[24] but through socially-acquired language, in art, appreciation and assessment vary within a society or period. Therefore, Wolff states that if one wanted to argue for universal aesthetics, any criteria of judgment and taste would have to overcome the relativism of time, place, social and economic status. Is this possible? Wolff says no.[25]

Its seems there is no universal criteria of value, taste, judgment, or coherence, which can be applied through aesthetics, art or science; each area of knowledge has its own rules—like a game. In the same way, each culture has its own customary knowledge. For example, Maruyama notes that Japanese and European concepts of architectural space differ significantly due to the cultural determinism defined by their linguistic origins.[26] While European spaces conform to an Aristotlian identity principle serving one specialized function, Japanese spaces reflect a more flexible condition where a room can serve various functions at different times of the day.[27] In addition, researchers note that not all societies or periods see the same colors, despite the fact that, from the physiological point of view, the experience of color should be the same for all races (Homer's translators are unable to find precise equivalents of Greek terms for specific colors).[28] Some argue that this kind of linguistic and perceptual difference is due to fundamentally different conceptions of the world, while others suggest that the difference in a conception of the world springs from the linguistic differences between groups or races.

From this discussion, it can be seen that critics and theorists find aesthetic judgment is defined by the relative criteria of beauty and taste determined by language. Even elemental factors such as architectural space and color are conceived of and perceived differently by different groups and cultures. Thus, art and aesthetics can only reflect relative judgment and value or the world-view of one group among many. Critics now apply a multivalent reading of art and aesthetics, spanning psychological, social, ecological, historical readings of art and art's formal and spiritual meaning. In this milieu, artists such as Joseph Kosuth suggest they can create art that forms consciousness.

Art as a Language Game Forms Consciousness

Preserving the notion of art's ability to convey significant meaning, Kosuth believes that art's role is, in a Wittgensteinian sense, to preserve "silently what was of value in art," to point to that which is inexpressible.[29] Kosuth suggests that Wittgenstein's insight was based on his admission of the inability of traditional philosophy to speak of the "unsaid"—unlike modernists who felt that art could express the unsayable (the transcendent) through significant, pure form. For Kosuth, art can only point to the unsayable. Art cannot represent absolute presence—or the totality of meanings. Indeed, for the postmodernist, a work of art can only indicate absence.

> The work of art 'presents' in the perceptible space-time-matter, something—a gesture—that cannot be presented there. This 'presence' cannot be a presentation. It remains silent. And this is its sign. The work is mute not because it is made of colors and forms but because it is inhabited by this 'presence.' Thought is also an art, because we think in sentences, and the sentences themselves also 'present' gestures of the space-time-matter of language. Sentences, supposedly speaking of something to someone, remain tacit on the subject of their referent and their destination.[30]

Art can, however, affect consciousness by creating new rules in its language game. Kosuth maintains that when new rules or shifts are accommodated by art they become part of the game. Once this happens the new rule forms part of culture. For example, the idea of a radical avant-garde is now institutionalized. It is an intrinsic part of Western culture and shapes our consciousness. In this sense, in its ability to modify culture, art alters consciousness.

> Wittgenstein's '*unsayable*' constituted the significant value, because for him it underscored exactly those elements that cannot be verified by language. We can note, however, a process of cultural verification which occurs in art when *language game(s)* of art accommodate an additional shift, and adjust to a new *rule*. The change (rupture, inclusion) becomes institutionalized and is incorporated into the *reality* of the game, thereby forming part of the horizon of culture which produces consciousness.[31]

Art for Kosuth is not about presenting self-contained pictures of the world. It is not about reflecting a "*presumed view* of a unified society...and a world-view that is no longer credible."[32]

Without meaning inherently embodied in the art object, traditional pictorial statements cease to communicate with society. For Kosuth, only critical, examined meaning in art can be "true" because aesthetic considerations of taste, beauty, etc., relate purely to decorative value. Any aesthetic consideration is extraneous to an object's function or "reason to be."[33] In contrast to Agnes Martin's view, the artist is by definition a critic; art which produces uncritical or unexamined meaning it is mere decoration.

> It is necessary to separate aesthetics from art because aesthetics deals with opinions on the perception of the world in general. In the past one of the two prongs of art's function was its value as decoration. So any branch of philosophy which dealt with 'beauty' and thus, taste, was inevitably duty bound to discuss art as well.[34]

Although Kosuth wants art to remain out of the realm of taste and judgments of beauty, in a sense, his ideas follow on from Hegel's delineation between fine art and decorative art, and Greenberg's formalist art versus kitsch. Indeed, art is still meant to carry profound meaning and affect consciousness. In fact as Kosuth states, in the contemporary era, "after philosophy and religion" art is probably the one "endeavor that fulfills what another age might have called 'man's spiritual needs."[35]

Contemporary art, by breaking with the modernism, presents a proposition within the context of art as a comment on art. Wolff suggests that it is our aesthetic intention or attitude which defines what is circumscribed as art (something becomes art—from ethnic objects plundered and displayed in a gallery to Duchamp's ready-mades—to the extent that it is *considered* to be art). Kosuth sees art as philosophy. Either way, art is a linguistic statement and not embodied presence.

Since art can point to the unsayable, it has an ability beyond science which, by definition, only deals with the sayable (using only verifiable or non-verifiable propositions). While modernists saw a unifying link between art and science (both aim to uncover the "music of the spheres"); postmodernists hold that art and science are different language games. Only one of them generates culturally-specific meaning. The postmodern language game of art, dispensing with the idea of an origin or cause (among other things) no longer supports the notion of originality and the avant-garde. In this sense, the progressive development of history (with the present representing the culmination of civilization revealed in the original art work expressing pure form) is dismissed.

Art, Originality and Repetition

As discussed earlier, one of the key features of modern art is its apparent originality. This characteristic is dependent upon the artist's ability to express his own individuality and fathom absolute emotion. Art is an original expression by the avant-garde artist. Postmodernists negate the notion of original form or presence through reproduction and repetition. Similarly, art critics deconstruct the notions of originality and the avant-garde in their criticism of modern art and museum practice. Modern art was expccted to have the look "of having risen out of nothing, out of the exhaustion of a past sequence that then leads to a creative break through the intervention of a world historical great individual."[36] This look granted the art object the status of a miracle; it became an "original" art work.

Despite this observation, post-structuralist critic Rosalind Krauss argues that modern avant-garde creative practice was, on the contrary, founded upon "repetition and recurrence" rather than originality. She uses the example of the grid to illustrate this principle, and claims that the grid as a figure is, "impervious both to time and to incident, [it] will not permit the projection of language into the domain of the visual, and the result is silence."[37] In this sense, Krauss asserts that the grid for modernists became a referent for the origin of art itself. For those whom "the origins of art are found in an empirically grounded unity, the grid-scored surface is the image of an absolute beginning;" it is "a stereotype which is constantly and paradoxically rediscovered."[38] From another perspective, McEvilley suggests that Agnes Martin, who employs the grid in her work, sees it as a kind of transformative realm somewhere between the universal and the particular.[39] In fact, the silence indicated by the grid, Krauss maintains, for modernists represented an audible perception of the origins of art—even though, logically, it is impossible to "hear" silence. Indeed, like Greenberg's pure form, the grid denies the perceived spatial quality of nature; it can be thought of as a purely cultural object.

The modernist notion of originality, ironically, reinforces itself through contradictory multiple references to itself. Many artists may "discover" and rediscover the grid—repeating "original discoveries" of this figure. Likewise, as Krauss puts it, the entire modernist discursive practice of the museum, historian and artist, is geared toward perpetuating the myth of originality regardless of the ever-present reality of the copy as the underlying condition of the original. She states that when museums routinely posthumously reproduces an artist's work (as in the case of Rodin's *Gates of Hell*), the "aura" of the original is recreated repeatedly throughout time.[40] Postmodern art demonstrates this—repeating, copying or quoting images that have become part of the lexicon of art. The language of art is the purveyor of meaning rather than an art object. Art seems to become a copy for which there is no original. It indicates lack of presence through absence; the copy indicates lack by means of the trace.

Art History: A Non-Linear Array of Possible Styles

Postmodern theory, in dispensing with the Hegelian concept of Being and the idea of presence, also rejects Hegel's view of history and time—generated from within an originating self-conscious Spirit leading to perfected civilization. The idea of abstraction as the pinnacle of art's development was compelling for modernists, as evidenced in Gablik's *Progress in Art*—which applied Piagetian theory to the "evolution" of art from imitative and naturalistic to conceptual, comparing historical art styles to stages of childhood cognitive development. In this scenario, twentieth-century European art represented a more highly-developed cognitive state than that of the Medieval and Renaissance period (and by implication a more evolved status than art of other cultures). Historian Hans Belting commented that according to Gablik, "art has evolved to its highest and most authentic form only in our own century [and] mankind has supposed to have undergone a mental development from figurative thought toward abstract and operational thought, just as it occurs in childhood."[41] Later, Gablik redirected her inquiry in *Has Modernism Failed?* observing that the "art-for-art's sake" movement of modernism severed its relation with other cultural attitudes and in doing so failed to realize its aim: to awaken the spiritual in humankind.

Clearly, different cultures have their own models of history; the cyclical (circular or spiraling) model and eternal present model are employed by what McEvilley describes as "pre-Modern" societies and Avatamsaka Buddhism.[42] Ironically, by classifying models as "pre-modern," by inference McEvilley cites these approaches in reference to modernism and precludes them from the contemporary debate. While the cyclical and eternal present models were apparently subscribed to by 1960s and 1970s artists, the Western modernist model continues to dominate; as McEvilley states, the "residual Modernist model might be visualized as a straight line that continues past the so-called end of Modernism, but fades as it goes, becoming a kind of ghost of itself."[43]

With respect to the adoption of the Hegelian model by non-European cultures, McEvilley suggests that some writers have revised the Hegelian structure and applied it to support what he refers to as a "pan-African" or "pan-Indian" view. Cheikh Anta Diop, a Senegalese writer, and Indian author Paramesh Choudhary trace the historical roots of civilization back to Africa and India Diop, arguing that ancient Egypt was a black African society, reverses the modernist hierarchy. Choudhary suggests that all of North Africa as far as Mauritania, and most of the Near East, showed no trace of civilization until they were colonized from the Indus Valley. Both identify their own cultures as central to the beginning of "civilization". But, as McEvilley has noted, there are other models of history; history can be viewed as 1) a continuum or 2) as many histories—like line fragments. On a continuum, he states, all possible art styles exist; the "dissimilar line fragment" model is incompatible with the upward linear progression model,[44] and in art many possible styles are valid; no one style (such as abstraction) represents the pinnacle of human development. Unlike the modern view, postmodern art histories deny the teleological march of European civilization, challenging the idea that pure form or abstract art represent the ultimate expression of fully-cognitively developed, free individuals. Each work and style is, rather, one among many possibilities.

Colonialism is seen to be the force behind the modernist teleological analysis of art. In our so-called post-colonial era, with different concepts of history, terms like quality, moral judgment, high art, low art, and history signify categories defined by the rules of the language game of a particular culture. Cultural production and visual culture represent the plurality of voices in the world. Art has its value as a proposition within a language game which seeks to define or uncover meaning pertinent to the participants of the language game (it is interesting to note that this view of history superficially seems to echo Hegel's category of critical history which examines its own claims). As McEvilley notes:

> We are entering a period when every ethnic group or bonding group or community of taste or belief will write its own fragment of history, and probably in many conflicting versions. A more or less unconnected array of micronarratives will replace, for a time, the single meta-narrative.... A more copious, ample meta-narrative may begin to articulate itself, made up of the interactions of many fragments rather than imposing itself upon them.[45]

With many voices writing their own histories in different ways, it may be, as McEvilley states, that "a new meta-narrative cannot be conceived to encompass them all without becoming indiscriminately accommodating to contradiction" and, in this sense, perhaps "History" is over while "histories" endure.[46] Despite this argument, the idea of a meta-narrative which accommodates contradiction is not an impossible concept—as revealed in Part IV. In the binary opposition of modernism and postmodernism, both are understood in relation to one another. The problem with postmodernism is that while it aims to be "ethical," as "part of the global project of cultural decolonization," it is primarily the West that, in continuing to apply its own models (colonialist or de-colonialist), defines and transforms cultures. In fact, Kumkum Sangari refers to postmodernism as "an institutionalized 'third-worldism'...[that makes] an attempt to re-annex the colonial subject...through the application of recent de-essentializing critical theories pitted against bourgeois, colonial, Enlightenment value systems."[47] As noted earlier, postmodern theory can also be criticized as invasive and totalizing in its deconstructive approach.

To summarize, if art has become philosophy undergirded by language theory, then its agenda is no longer to capture a universal, spiritual value to life but to invent new rules in a language game. Art deconstructs itself to transform language and culture and form consciousness. Art and culture are not driven by a desire to reveal or mimic an absolute, but to constantly critique these assumptions. In this sense, postmodern theory assumes that socially-constructed language governs and forms consciousness. Art, a language game which can redefine culture, is no longer an object of beauty but a critical statement about modern culture itself. Art shows that the unsayable is beyond expression. This critique has arisen in response to the failure of theories of knowledge to provide a systematic means of experiencing and comprehending an absolute value of life. Language itself seems unequipped for such an enterprise. Given this understanding, many theorists and feel that postmodernism is bereft of universal value; it allows for a variety of style but does not speak to the universally human in mankind.

Some critics even find deconstructive postmodernism mysterious, colonizing and totalizing, and Lyotard's relativism impractical and dissuasive of useful meta-narratives. If modernism was the style of a colonizing force, postmodernism extends this principle by "re-annexing the colonial subject." Furthermore, in art, textual analyses are deemed restrictive, missing a sociological interpretation of aesthetics. As Ihab Hassan writes, the argument between the *One* of Modernism and the *Many* of postmodernism is now being eclipsed:

> Let Postmodernism now work itself out as it might. Perhaps all we have learned from it is what the gods have taught us in both myth and history: that even in their own omnivorous eyes, the universe is not single, but still One and Many as it shows itself to our sight.[48]

The co-existence of one and many presents a paradox but paradox does not have to be problematic; it serves as the basis of the dynamic nature of our own consciousness and the perpetual creation and recreation of the material universe. As discussed in Parts II and III, the co-existence of opposites exists at the basis of life. Creating art with this experience and understanding, as is considered in Part V, the universal can be expressed and found in the particular.

4

BEYOND POSTMODERNISM: UNIVERSAL VALUE IN ART AND A NEW SENSE OF SELF

Despite the postmodern move toward relativism, critics lament the lack of universal significance in art. They argue for an art which speaks of universal value created by an artist who is an exemplary human being and suggest that art has to reflect a holistic view of man's relationship to nature and culture. Art practice can no longer simply focus on "art for art's sake" but must have some social, moral, ecological or spiritual purpose to be meaningful and to influence collective awareness such that the global, ecological and social destiny of humankind can be preserved. Some critics refer to postmodern art as art of glamor—arising because art is bereft of universal meaning and social respect. In this scenario, the artist has become a "postmodern ape," denying art its ability to speak from innermost being. Clearly, critics have articulated a need for universal value in art and for the artist to be an exemplary human being.[1]

Lack of Universal Value in Contemporary Art

In his essay *The Problem of Art in the Age of Glamor*, Donald Kuspit states that we live in a capitalist "age of glamor" where the value of art is determined by monetary worth, and where "the history of art has become the history of art auction prices, confirmed by textbooks that are auction catalogues in all but name."[2] Art is currency, with all its allure. The more art is worth the more glamorous it becomes. Whereas spiritual or aesthetic value were the determining factors in the judgment of a work of art in the past, today its value is based on art's ability to afford glamor.

Kuspit defines glamor as the effect art has in making us feel good about ourselves. Art is not an object from which we derive aesthetic enjoyment through contemplation but rather a narcissistic object of consumption; "we consume the glamorous looking art object to satisfy a deep psychic need, an especially pressing one in our barren world, which offers few narcissistic consolations, certainly no transcendental ones."[3] The world we live in is a kind of postmodern wasteland, where consumerism dictates culture. As Jameson points out, postmodernism is a reaction to the commodification of the modernist aesthetic but which itself is immediately commodified. Aesthetic production has become completely integrated into commodity production; postmodernism is simply an expression of late-Capitalism.[4]

In this age of consumerism, the love of art is self-love in disguise. Art offers solace by presenting the illusion of integrity, a cohesive self; today's artist can no longer be taken as an exemplary human being since his art, which is more an expression of his own personal concerns than of his experience of examples of human universals, is essentially narcissistic. Such art, "has little human interest apart from what it tells us about the artist;" the artist no longer has a universal voice.[5] Similarly, others criticize the narrowness of art which isolates itself from humanity and sociological and ecological issues.[6]

Kuspit even criticizes postmodern artists who supposedly create art which addresses social, political or historical concerns. Speaking of the American artists Jenny Holzer and Leon Golub, and the German painter Anslem Kiefer, Kuspit claims that Holzer flaunts her superior insight while Golub exploits the popular awareness of violence. The nationalistic "brooding" in Kiefer's work is elevated not because of its universal voice but because "humanness is chic." In addition, he describes Peter Halley's abstract works that refer to modernism as completely betraying "the human universality of absolute art from Piet Mondrian to Barnett Newman."[7] He goes on to further criticize appropriation art by stating that:

> The implicit purpose of the work of appropriation artists is to strip the human voice from the art they appropriate. Or else, as in appropriation art which pretends to give pride of place to that voice, such as that of Julian Schnabel—who is always painting the wounded heart—it is aped. The dregs of the human voice are visible, not its substance.[8]

What wc are witnessing, says Kuspit, is the de-evolution of the human in art; the artist has become a postmodern ape. Postmodern appropriation art does not attempt to speak with a universal voice because to do so is unsophisticated and provincial. The ultimate outcome of this "narcissistic aestheticism" is the denial of the existence of human universals altogether. Despite this human universals remain.

In his lament of the loss of universal value in art Kuspit sums up the short-comings of postmodern commodified art:

> Once upon a time to say art was important meant it seemed inevitable, which also meant that it seemed to speak with a universal human voice. It did not just exist for itself. The experience of the art's inevitability involved the feeling that it articulated what seemed impossible yet necessary to articulate. It also meant that what the art made articulate was something that we felt we were just about to make articulate ourselves—that the art was on the tip of our own tongue, as it were. It gave us the sense of spontaneously articulating what was inarticulate yet that we felt we knew 'naturally.' It articulated what we could not quite articulate but were perpetually on the verge of articulating. The sense that art did not simply address people from the outside but spoke to them from their innermost being, which it seemed to grasp better they themselves could, articulated their desire and sense of reality better than they knew them, was once basic to high art, giving it its special human value and social respect. The attempt to create the

> sense of speaking from inside of the universally human has been abandoned by high art. Art that even pretends to do so loses face....Indeed, today, as Gedo says, 'the mandarinate is embarrassed about professing any value system at all,' that is, about making any art that has inner relevance to human universals.[9]

This statement articulates the problem of art which does not speak to people from their innermost being. It does not carry human value, nor does it warrant social respect or have any lasting relevance. When art has no lasting meaning or relevance, attention is refocused on the creativity of the artist—who must produce new styles, be witty, ironic and innovative at all costs. When this occurs universal value is set aside. Such rampant innovation is the institutionalized form of the avant-garde. Some critics feel that this situation arises because artists no longer give expression to what is common knowledge in society; in fact, there are no common beliefs held by people today:

> Previous to the concept of the artist as estranged from society was the fact of the artist giving concrete expression to the beliefs that were central to it. The artist was seen not as an alienated visionary or formalist researcher into visual knowledge but primarily as someone who gave expression to what was common knowledge.[10]

Critics suggest that while modernists, by breaking with the past, created art which became incomprehensible to the common viewer, postmodernists, by making appropriation, conceptual, and psychoanalytic art, continue to divorce art from everyday language and recognizable art media. This can result in alienation of the viewer. Furthermore, as Banks suggests, the avant-garde, being institutionalized by capitalist society, is no longer pertinent to radical art. Avant-gardism supported dissenting individualism and created a polarity between the individual and society; the modern artist became an art terrorist. The postmodern artist is equally estranged from society because he merely creates objects of glamor, commodities, rather than universally-significant art.

Returning to the discussion of Indian art, as mentioned in Chapter 2, theorists like Pandit would no doubt ascribe this problem to the materialist nature of contemporary society—where artists are more concerned with fashion than significance in art. In either case, the sense is that the artist somehow is unable to communicate anything of real profundity to his audience. Art can no longer contribute to society, it can only become another object for consumption. It is worth noting that Banks also criticizes conceptual artist Joseph Kosuth, whose ideas were articulated in Chapter 3; Banks argues that Kosuth is an elitist because Kosuth refers to individuals who can only appreciate traditional painting as art as illiterate, uncultured dingbats. Apart from the fact that Kosuth dismisses people who are unfamiliar with conceptual art, Banks notes that traditional media should not be overlooked since they have an important role in communication. Despite these arguments, the problem goes deeper than the question of the medium or materials of art. Taking a more comprehensive view, Jameson claims that the subject (including the artist) in today's postmodern world is unable to conceptualize her relationship to the global, multinational communicational network in which everyone is caught up; thus the individual needs to develop what he calls *cognitive mapping*—a way of articulating her place in the global system. The aesthetic of the future would be an aesthetic of cognitive mapping, defining the sense of the individual's relationship to place and any "national" and "global" identity. Many theorists and artists dealing with internet art and electronic media recognize the importance of the impact of information technology on visual culture, cultural production, aesthetics and theory. With the development of the internet and electronic media, theory, science, technology and art have converged. Looking to the descriptions of physics, those engaged in articulating and developing our understanding of this convergence, find that consciousness and reality are interrelated and constructed.

> Physicists have found compelling evidence that the only time electrons and other quanta manifest as particles is when we are looking at them. What implications might this have for the complex images we observe everyday? In virtual reality we know that the human brain actually participates in its own deception to create a continuous simulated reality? How does our attention affect what we observe in the ultra mediated world?[11]

Reality—virtual or otherwise—seems to be created through the attention of the mind. However, for the creation and experience of virtual reality the functioning of a kind of bio-apparatus (the combined functioning of computer, mind and body) is necessary; mind, body and computer technology together facilitate experience. On a social or collective level, the internet has also been identified as a cultural space; it is a "space" or field in which social and cultural interaction and the creation of new hybrid cultures occurs. By facilitating social and economic changes it is seen to highlight the complex interactions of a global consciousness.

> It may be argued that socially, a substantial part of human attention is focused on the global exchanges of our...economy, now boundlessly enveloping the world.... World financial indices generate real time, numerically encoded information regarding our most elaborate global exchanges. When looking at streams of this data graphically, one might suggest they represent a kind of electrocardiogram of a portion of the earth's brain activity.[12]

Clearly, digital media and new technologies have an important impact on all areas of life, including our sense of identity, the construction of reality, and the formation of culture. There is a growing awareness of the interconnectedness between everything. With electronic media, intelligence is seen to be liberated from constraints of body and place. Science tells us that the distinction between so-called inner and outer realities or worlds is no longer clearly demarcated.

> A close scrutiny of life reveal that living creatures are not material entities separated from their surroundings but rather regulatory interfaces of interactions occurring between "their" [so-called] internal and external environments. Life is an emergent condition whenever and wherever certain complex internal and external tensions meet one another and find some dynamic balance. Life is a "boundary conditions" phenomenon. To maintain continuity under constantly changing circumstances, life must endlessly (1) monitor the boundary conditions and (2) act towards responding at once to internal and external demands."[13]

There is a constant exchange or dynamic between internal and external phenomena. Ultimately, any sense of reality is affected by our subjective interaction with the world. As quantum physics suggests, what we see and know of the world is not the real physical world but an "inferred surface produced by our interaction with the world contained in our observing instrument, the mind."[14] Some argue that the internet is breaking down centralized forces of change and that the importance of the individual mind in constructing the "inferred surface" of our reality is leveling hierarchies. Postmodernism, important in the 1980s, has been eclipsed by post-colonialism and theory arising from the convergence of investigations into consciousness, science, art, and new technologies.

In summarizing, it seems that the pluralist approach of postmodernism is limited, perhaps due to the fact that society no longer shares common beliefs and values in our increasingly hybridized global culture. On one level, the individual appears insignificant against the backdrop of global development—with the accelerated growth of technology, and economic exchange. On another level, we recognize our complicity in constructing our reality and influencing social and economic forces. In embracing pluralism, variety and freedom of expression are enhanced. Postmodernism supports pluralism but resists provision of a meta-narrative; many narratives can operate and define cultural identity in the context of the global community. It seems there is need for a universalizing, global awareness within which the individual can locate herself, her own geographical, cultural and national concerns, identity and voice, and from which she can speak of her ethnicity and universality simultaneously. These issues are reviewed in Parts IV and V in the discussion of how artists can create a universal art and be exemplary human beings—"articulating what we were just about to articulate ourselves", creating art of universal and social significance, and redefining cultural identity. But where does aesthetic experience fit into this picture?

Aesthetic Disinterestedness and a New Sense of Self

In an effort to redefine aesthetic value, Kuspit applies a psychoanalytic reading of aesthetics and the purpose of art, stating that any theory of aesthetics is based upon the notion of *disinterested attention* and *disinterested pleasure.* The disinterested aesthetic attitude is one of *contemplation*, where the object of attention provides no utilitarian function. Thus, aesthetic disinterestedness is associated with form and it occurs when something is held outside the normal arena of conventional need.

As Kant defined it, the disinterested attitude is a mode of direct awareness rather than conceptual thinking, moral or utilitarian judgment. In this sense (as modernists also claimed) it is inherently subjective. Although subjective, the disinterested aesthetic attitude is completely disconnected from desire for the object or concern for its existence. Thus, subjectivity is equated with a special direct awareness which is not linked to sensual pleasure or intellectual concerns. It is, as Kuspit calls it, an "aesthetic transcendence" which implies having an emotional distance from the object.[15] This state resembles a "quasi-Buddhist" sense of desirelessness or detachment. Here, Kuspit notes the similarity of this state with that described by Eastern religion as "non-attachment." However, Kuspit implies that it was more accurately described by Malevich as a non-objective sensation and feeling which is beyond human organizations. Such aesthetic emotion, while associated with spirit or transcendence, it is not the exclusive preserve of art, state or religion.

Kuspit emphasizes that what designates art as art is the experience of aesthetic disinterestedness itself. Despite this, as discussed in the previous Chapter, Wolff proposes that the aesthetic attitude can be experienced in response to anything. She claims that by placing something in the art context it can solicit an aesthetic response. In this sense, her definition of art is broader than Kuspit's. For Kuspit, it is the art created form, in contrast to any other kind of form, which is a deliberately designed means of creating aesthetic transcendence.[16] Like Bell, he asks the question: What is it about the form of art which creates this effect? He observes that most aestheticians define the work of art as that form which must display a constructed *unity* which resonates with the coherence and form given to the self. Art must have a formal unity—a reconciliation of conflicting formal elements, a balance of formal forces which are analogous to the balancing of psychic forces.

This view of art and aesthetic disinterestedness is derived from philosophy and modern aesthetic theory, but Kuspit adds a psychological factor to the analysis. He mentions that aesthetic experience is a kind of hypersensitivity of, or hyperalertness to, the formal elements of the work. This hyperalertness is indifferent to the narrative or iconographic identity of the work. The aim of art, Kuspit suggests, is to create a feeling of something beyond reach. As with the play of *différance* in language, for Kuspit aesthetic disinterestedness permits a free intellectual-emotional play as a way of articulating possibility. For this reason, he feels it has purpose within its apparent purposelessness and paradox. Aesthetic disinterestedness can conceive its own unity while acknowledging its lack:

> It is a free play that exists to give form to the self...aesthetic disinterestedness can speculatively imagine and conceive its own unity. At the same time, in this state of self-creation as it were, it implicitly acknowledges its lack of unity....Beyond both sensing and reasoning, such psychic activity reminds us that the self has no

> final, perfect form, while at the same time speculatively positing one, that is, a transcendental illusion of selfhood. (The great variety of styles of art—modes of formal unity—testifies to the 'impossibility' of final form)....Art is not reparative regression to an old mode of being-self, but a means of progressing to a new sense of self—a means of speculatively working through to and articulating the real possibility of achieving a new sense of self.[17]

Art serves to promote the sense of a formal unity which corresponds to a unified self—not a reality of being, or a return to some innocent unmediated self, but a possible new sense of self. As revealed by the failure of modern and postmodern art, one ultimate formal unity is impossible in art. The formalist dream of an absolute form is replaced by the possibility of many formal unities, varied but equivalent, positing the illusion of a transcendental, but unrealizable, potential unified self. As Sherrie Turkle[18] suggests, with the internet and electronic media the play of multiple selves or identities is made possible.

This issue of our sense of self, the positing of a unified self and its significance for art, is considered in greater detail in Parts II and V, which outline the development of the self according to Maharishi Vedic Science. In this science, the normal changing waking state of consciousness is held to be only one state in several stages of human development.

As we have seen, critics of postmodernism like Kuspit lament the loss of universal value, suggesting that postmodern art is socially bankrupt and that the artist is a postmodern ape. Postmodern art no longer speaks to the innermost self of the viewer but becomes another commodity in our age of glamor. In this milieu, there seems to be a need for a universal art which can evoke aesthetic disinterestedness, creating the feeling of the possibility of a new sense of self or an integrated unity. With a new approach, art could have profound transformative meaning and aesthetic value and could support human development. By suggesting that art should have both a constructive role in shaping society and culture and the ability to provide a new sense of self, critics express concern not only for the state of art and aesthetics but also for the theory of knowledge that informs culture.

Obviously no one theory has been able to: 1) provide artists with a means to experience a universal field of consciousness, 2) fully develop the artist and society, 3) help the artist to express universal value, and 4) culture aesthetic sensibility. The various debates concerning the relative nature of knowledge and the arts confirm the difficulty of trying to define, let alone create, universal value in art. Therefore, any discussion of art and universal value can only proceed within a broader context of an understanding of the relationship between the individual, language, culture, tradition, the historical development of humankind, and knowledge. By exploring these themes and the nature of consciousness, as defined in Maharishi Vedic Science, the following sections provide a platform for the consideration of how universal value can be expressed in art and aesthetics.

PART II

ACCESSING AND ENLIVENING A UNIVERSAL FIELD OF PURE CONSCIOUSNESS

While the Vedic texts and their knowledge are considered part of Indian history, philosophy and culture, Vedic knowledge as comprehensively unfolded in Maharishi Vedic Science, reveals that the Veda and the Vedic Literature are eternal impulses of pure, self-referral consciousness that can be directly perceived and known on the simplest level of human awareness. Comprised of three words—Maharishi (meaning great, *Mahā*, seer or knower, *Ṛishi*), Vedic (signifying pertaining to Veda—where Veda denotes knowledge, pure knowledge, or complete knowledge), and science (referring to the practical, systematic, verifiable, and reliable nature of this knowledge)[1]— Maharishi Vedic Science provides total knowledge of all phases of existence, from the absolute, unmanifest basis of life in consciousness to its expression in terms of manifest forms and phenomena. Maharishi Vedic Science is a science of consciousness and its expressions. It is a science of complete knowledge structured within the self-referral consciousness of the seer or knower. In perceiving the fabrics of his own self-referral consciousness, the structure of pure knowledge or the Veda, Maharishi has brought to light the details of this universal field.

As Maharishi explains, as the total science of all aspects of life, Vedic Science intellectually analyzes "all values in the field of relative life and the absolute state of self-referral consciousness;"[2] it includes knowledge of universal principles, including the first principle of nature's functioning which illustrates the self-referral, self-interacting dynamics of pure consciousness—consciousness in knowing itself differentiates the values of knower, process of knowing and known within its undivided nature.[3] Through the interaction of these values, consciousness generates frequencies and Laws of Nature which govern and structure matter and create the entire universe.

Vedic Science not only divulges how consciousness is the unmanifest basis of creation, but it also provides technologies of consciousness for accessing this knowledge on the level of experience:

> How creation comes out—how consciousness becomes matter and how matter in nature behaves with utmost orderliness, absolutely following the laws of nature—this is Vedic Science. Vedic Science is this state of knowledge, and it includes the procedures for gaining this knowledge of the ultimate self-referral unity which underlies the whole creation and expresses itself in innumerable, divergent ways.[4]

Here Maharishi explains that Vedic Science is the state of knowledge itself—the self-referral unity of knower, process of knowing and known experienced through the Transcendental Meditation technique as absolute Transcendental Consciousness—the simplest form of human awareness.

In the last 20 years, various scholars have explored the principles of Vedic Science as applied to education, art practice, art education, acting, architecture, deconstruction theory, literature, psychology, physics, sociology, and ideal political administration (as illustrated in the Rāmāyana), but the significance of this science has not yet been explored in the context of art theory.[5] This book aims to address this issue. Furthermore, intellectual arguments in favor of a universal absolute, as criticized by contemporary theory, are not supported by evidence of or a means to experience such a realm. Consequently, postmodernists suggest that absolutes relate to philosophical ideas rather than any absolute level of reality which can be experienced and applied for practical outcomes in life and art. It could be said that the human mind or consciousness, considered by contemporary theorists to be formed by language, cannot express in linguistic or visual terms the range of its conceptual ability. However, Maharishi Vedic Science reveals that a universal field of pure consciousness is the source of the individual mind and also the source of language, culture and art. This universal field of pure consciousness, the spiritual value of life and the simplest form of human awareness, is the source of all streams of creativity and the foundation of material creation.[6]

While spirituality has been associated with art, philosophy and religion it could more precisely be said to correspond to the inner, universal value of life beyond religious, philosophical or relative difference. According to Maharishi Vedic Science, the inner spiritual realm is pure consciousness, the Self or pure awareness of everyone. This Self or *Ātmā* is the infinite, unbounded, universal nature of the Self as opposed to the individualized, localized sense of self.[7]

Discussing human development in terms of spirituality (or lack of it), Maharishi indicates that intellectualism (which is commonly associated with the domain of philosophy) has failed to improve the mental chaos of modern life. While it is commonly thought that modern man is too engrossed with glamor and materialism, he emphasizes that the "achievements of material science, the glamour of increased material comfort, and the joys of the material world" are not responsible for the degeneration of life or the "decadence of even the human qualities" in man.[8] In any situation where the outer material value of life dominates, the inner, universal source is hidden. Art seems to mirror this phenomenon. For example, as Krauss suggests, in contemporary life we are separated from nature by a wall or billboard of signs generated by postmodern, technological culture. Postmodern art of glamor, a diverse array of signs, is like this billboard.[9]

When materialism dominates, Maharishi points out, effective technologies are needed for re-enlivening the universal field of pure consciousness. In this context, he notes that neither detachment and renunciation nor gross forms of ritualism have brought peace or happiness for humankind, but the non-sectarian technologies of the Transcendental Meditation technique and the TM-Sidhi program can harmonize the material or outer world and spiritual or inner value of life, by re-enlivening universal, pure consciousness.[10] It should be noted that Maharishi does not dismiss the value of ritual but defines it in terms of action from the level of pure consciousness. In this context, the Vedic technology called *Yagya* is discussed in more detail in Part III.[11] With effective technologies of consciousness the underlying inner aspect is revealed, known, and lived in daily life, benefiting the individual and society.

Reconciling or holding together opposite values is a fundamental property of consciousness. Inherent within pure consciousness is the phenomenon of *absolute administration* or the ability to hold together opposites through the value of Natural Law, the *infinite organizing power of Nature*.[12] This theme of opposites co-existing surfaces again in Maharishi's description of the self-referral nature of consciousness in terms of unity (self-referral) and diversity (object-referral) and silence and dynamism. The idea of sequence and quantification of the singular, unbounded, infinite field of consciousness is also related to the nature of consciousness to be one and many at the same time.

As considered in Chapter 5, *Pure Consciousness: The Universal Self-Referral Source of Creation,* due to the simultaneous silent and dynamic values of consciousness, consciousness can be understood as a straight line. In discussing the level of consciousness where there are impulses but no differences, Maharishi also relates how basic geometric forms—the circle, triangle and square—emerge from within consciousness. While these descriptions of pure, self-referral consciousness may seem highly abstract, the practical technologies for research of this abstract realm allow their verification on the level of experience. The individual can subjectively experience the universal, absolute field of pure consciousness and effectively enrich life on the levels of mind, body, behavior, and the environment and through art and culture.

Chapter 6, *Developing Higher States of Consciousness through the Practice of the Transcendental Meditation Technique, the TM-Sidhi Program and Yogic Flying*, discusses the role of technologies of consciousness in the growth to higher states of consciousness and their effect in individual and collective life. These advanced states of consciousness are normal stages in the development of human potential. Each state of consciousness has its corresponding knowledge or world. Knowledge is different in different states of consciousness. Despite this, there can be a reliable, absolute, universal knowledge that is of immense practical value to life. The means to unfold this absolute knowledge is furnished by the technologies of consciousness. The TM-Sidhi program cultures self-referral performance referred to as *Saṁyama*. This self-referral performance promotes growth to higher states of consciousness and the ability to function from the field of infinite creativity. The *Yogic Flying* technique also promotes skill in action and generates an influence of harmony in the environment. The results of the practice of these technologies are documented by scientific research, as revealed in

Chapter 7. Entitled *Scientific Research on Maharishi's Technologies of Consciousness,* Chapter 7 reviews the beneficial effects of the practice of these mental techniques on the development of human potential, improvement of mind-body co-ordination, skill in action, increased creativity, and enhancement of individual and collective life. All these factors are important to art practice and theory.

5

PURE CONSCIOUSNESS: THE UNIVERSAL SELF-REFERRAL SOURCE OF CREATION

Presenting a profound understanding of the nature of consciousness that has applications in all areas of knowledge, art and theory, Maharishi Vedic Science identifies an unmanifest, absolute source of creation—pure consciousness—which, through a self-referral dynamic, gives rise to the subtle aspects of the ever-changing, manifest creation of forms and phenomena. As Maharishi explains, "consciousness is that one element in nature on the ground of which the infinite variety of creation is continuously emerging, growing, and dissolving. The whole field of change emerges from this field of non-change."[1] This description is corroborated by modern physicists who identify a unified field as the source of all the fundamental laws (such as gravity, weak, strong and electromagnetic fields).[2] The unified field, through a process of spontaneous symmetry breaking, gives to the basic constituents of matter. In this sense, modern science lends support to this fundamental principle: a non-changing, unmanifest field is the source of the ever-changing, relative field.

In Maharishi Vedic Science, the unmanifest field is the universal field of absolute, pure consciousness subjectively experienced through technologies of consciousness. The manifest creation is the objective world of forms and phenomenon. In its progression from the absolute to the relative, from abstract to concrete, life is found to have subtle and more gross levels of expression. This principle is illustrated in the human physiology: DNA represents the underlying intelligence of the body. DNA structures RNA and proteins. These, in turn, give rise to the cells, tissues, and organs of the physiology. According to Maharishi Vedic Science, DNA is an expression of the field of self-referral consciousness or pure intelligence. Thus, the self-referral functioning at the basis of the physiology is the reality of every cell of the body.

While the body is can be understood as made up of levels of expression from the more subtle molecular and cellular levels to the gross level of organs, from another perspective every aspect of the body is the self-referral functioning of the intelligence of the DNA. This self-referral functioning is the demonstration of Nature's administration or the self-referral value of pure, unmanifest consciousness on the level of the DNA. As Maharishi notes: "The administration in Nature is demonstrated in the functioning of DNA, which promotes RNA (various types);" RNA, in turn, transforms itself into material particles and the different aspects of the physiology.[3]

Therefore, while everything in creation is made up of levels or layers, creation is also the continuous play of self-referral consciousness. As Maharishi explains, "The infinite diversity and dynamism of creation is just the expression of the eternally silent, self-referral, self-sufficient, unbounded field of consciousness—pure wakefulness, unbounded alertness, pure intelligence, pure existence, all knowingness."[4] The nature of this field of consciousness is such that it contains within it opposite values; the opposites co-exist at that abstract level. Since this is the basis of all life, this principle can be located within everything.

From microcosm to the macrocosm, every cell in the body and each planet in the universe is the expression of self-referral consciousness; self-referral consciousness is nothing other than the simplest form of awareness of the individual. This means that the phenomenal world is the expression of individual awareness in its most expanded state.

The Self-Referral Nature of Pure Consciousness

As noted above, pure consciousness is an infinite, unmanifest field of pure awareness or wakefulness—also described as pure intelligence in Maharishi Vedic Science.[5] Pure wakefulness is awake to itself. In being awake to itself, it discriminates various values of its own nature. Thus, the intelligence of consciousness differentiates values within itself. Consciousness is both single and divided. It is a single field of consciousness, but being awake it knows itself in terms of different values. Opposites do not cancel each other out but co-exist on this level.

In being aware of itself, consciousness is self-referral; it intellectually conceives of differentiated values within its own infinite singularity.[6] As Maharishi points out:

> Consciousness is that which is conscious of itself. Being conscious of itself, consciousness is the knower of itself. Being the knower of itself, consciousness is both the knower and the known. Being both the knower and the known, consciousness is also the process of knowing. Thus consciousness has three qualities within its self-referral singularity—the qualities of knower, knowing, and known—the three qualities of 'subject' (knower), 'object' (known), and the relationship between the subject and object (process of knowing). Wherever there is subject-object relatedness; wherever subject is related to object; wherever subject is experiencing object; wherever subject (knower) is knowing object, these three together are indications of the existence of consciousness.[7]

In this explanation, consciousness is characterized as singularity; but it has three qualities distinguished within its self-referral nature. The existence of consciousness is revealed by a subject-object relationship. Such a relationship occurs wherever the three values of the knower, the process of knowing and the known can be identified.

This description bears some resemblance to Hegel's notion of Spirit or Being-within-itself within which "the whole of history" is contained. However, unlike Hegel's philosophy, Maharishi Vedic Science provides a completely detailed account of the dynamics of self-referral consciousness—corroborated by: 1) subjective experience in the form of the individual testimony of practitioners of the Transcendental Meditation, TM-Sidhi program and Yogic Flying, as discussed in the next chapter; 2) objective verification through extensive scientific research on the effects of the practice of these technologies of consciousness, considered in Chapter 7; 3) as mentioned previously, theoretical understanding and the discovery of the unified field by modern science; 4) the Vedic texts which, as will be discussed in Part III, are the actual record of impulses of self-referral consciousness knowing itself; and 5) the discovery of Veda in the physiology—where these impulses of consciousness recorded in the Veda and the Vedic Literature are shown to correspond to the functions and structure of the physiology, also discussed in Part III.[8] Demonstrating its universal application, any individual can learn Maharishi's technologies of consciousness and begin to experience this level of existence. Pure consciousness is not a philosophical notion; it is the reality of everyone's own simplest form of awareness—a universal reality. As considered in Chapter 6, with access to this level of awareness, the individual can be a universal human being.

In his description of the nature of this universal field of self-referral consciousness, Maharishi points out that the universe, with the observer, contains the three values of the subject or knower, the process of knowing, and the object, and, in this way, indicates the nature of consciousness:

> The universe with its observer expresses the three values of observer, process of observation, and object of observation; therefore it is the indicator of the existence of consciousness.[9]

With its observer observing creation, the universe itself demonstrates the existence of consciousness. He also adds that: "The universe, with its observer, is the expression of consciousness in its self-referral state."[10] The universe as the known or observed value, and the observer as the knower involved in the process of knowing or observing, represents the self-referral phenomenon of consciousness.

Since the universe is nothing other than the expression of self-referral consciousness, when the observer is conscious of the universe, he is ultimately conscious of his own self-referral state: "The observer, being conscious of the universe, is conscious of his own self-referral state."[11] This reality represents the total realization of consciousness. As Maharishi explains, "The reality that the universe is the observer himself is the reality of the total disclosure of consciousness. It is the total potential of consciousness; it is the total reality of consciousness."[12] This phenomenon, where the universe is known to be the self-referral consciousness of the observer, is discussed in Chapter 6 which considers the development of higher states of consciousness.

Describing the nature of consciousness, Maharishi adds that in its self-referral state, consciousness knows itself and nothing else; it is *pure* consciousness: "When we say total reality of consciousness, we mean consciousness in its self-referral state, when consciousness knows itself and nothing else. This state of consciousness is pure consciousness."[13] In contrast, when consciousness knows other things it is called object-referral.

The object-referral value of consciousness arises because consciousness has intelligence. Maharishi notes that objects can only be perceived by virtue of intelligence, and that intelligence differentiates or divides the singularity of pure consciousness:

> Another state of consciousness is when it knows other things; then it is known to be object-referral consciousness, because all objects can only be perceived by virtue of the intelligence quality of consciousness, which creates the observer and process of observation within the singularity of the self-referral state of consciousness.[14]

By virtue of the intelligence value of consciousness the object-referral state (where the observer and process of observation are identified) is created within the singularity of pure, self-referral consciousness. Object-referral is created by the intelligence quality of self-referral consciousness; it is located within self-referral consciousness. Consciousness is two things at the same time; it is self-referral and object-referral. This principle is expressed in the following Vedic expressions, translated by Maharishi as:

वृत्तिसारूप्यमितरत्र ।

Vṛtti sārūpyam itaḥ atra

(*Yog-Darśana*, *1.4*)

"Tendencies (of the observer) emerge from here,"

स्वरूपेऽवस्थानम् ।

Svarūpe avasthānam

(*Yog-Darśana, 1.3*)

"Self-referral state—and remain here (within the self-referral state)."[15]

Maharishi also translates "*Vṛtti sārūpyam itaḥ atra*" as "Frequency of self-interacting dynamics of consciousness in one unbounded, silent ocean of consciousness—pure wakefulness"[16] and "The frequencies of self-referral consciousness emerge <u>from</u> self-referral consciousness and remain <u>within</u> self-referral consciousness."[17] There is self-referral and object-referral but both are, ultimately, within consciousness. Both are intelligence functioning within itself, in one unbounded field.

While the self-referral value of consciousness is unified or singular, the object-referral value is diversified. As Maharishi states: "This reality of consciousness, that by nature consciousness is self-referral and object-referral at the same time, makes it obvious that the nature of consciousness is both singularity (self-referral), and diversity (object-referral)."[18] With this understanding, knowledge of consciousness encompasses knowledge of the unmanifest field of self-referral consciousness at the basis of creation—referred to as "the Ultimate Reality"—and the mechanics or transformation of singularity into diversity.[19]

The state of pure, self-referral consciousness is also identified as Transcendental Consciousness—where "consciousness is open to itself and is no longer open to others. It is completely self-referral."[20] "Transcendental" means "to go beyond." Transcendental Consciousness refers to that level of consciousness which is beyond the relative states of consciousness. During the practice of the Transcendental Meditation technique (which will be discussed later in the context of the development of higher states of consciousness) the state of Transcendental Consciousness can be subjectively experienced and verified. Maharishi describes Transcendental Consciousness as a fourth state of consciousness, where the mind transcends the commonly experienced waking, dreaming and sleeping states of consciousness. It is an absolute, non-changing, unbounded state of pure wakefulness or singularity called *Kaivalya*.[21] As noted above, from one perspective life is comprised of an absolute, infinite, unbounded field of pure consciousness and an ever-changing, relative field of diverse existence, forms and phenomena. While the absolute is eternal, universal, infinite, pure consciousness, it is also lively wakefulness. It is a field of all possibilities, of pure potentiality. This value of intelligence, as Maharishi points out, is inherent within, and can be seen displayed in, relative creation:

> We see things around us exist. We also see that things around us change and evolve. We also see that there is order in evolution—an apple seed will only grow into an apple tree, etc. Thus it is obvious that existence is endowed with the qualities of intelligence—existence breathes life by virtue of intelligence. By virtue of intelligence everything in creation is aware of itself, is aware of its own existence—is conscious of itself, and at the same time it is aware of its environment. It is self-referral (it knows itself), and it is object-referral (it knows itself as the object of knowing). Thus existence is intelligence, it is consciousness. Consciousness is the existence of everything, and consciousness is the intelligence of everything.[22]

Existence is intelligent. Everything "breathes life" by virtue of intelligence. Existence evolves and develops by virtue of intelligence. Everything in creation (existence) is aware of itself because of this value of intelligence; it is aware of itself and of its environment and is therefore both self-referral and object-referral.

In this way, Maharishi explains that existence is intelligence or consciousness. Self-referral consciousness is existence or the foundation of everything:

> The self-referral state of consciousness is that one element in nature on the ground of which the infinite variety of creation is continuously emerging, growing, and dissolving. The whole field of change emerges from this field of non-change, from this self-referral, immortal state of consciousness. This interaction of the different intellectually conceived components of this unified, self-referral state of consciousness is that all-powerful activity at the most elementary level of nature. That activity is responsible for the innumerable varieties of life in the world, the innumerable streams of intelligence in creation.[23]

These intellectually-conceived or discriminated qualities of self-referral consciousness—the knower, process of knowing and known—interact with one another and this activity is responsible for the different expressions of intelligence in creation. The singularity of consciousness, through its self-referral dynamics, creates all the Laws of Nature which govern the diversified modes of existence.

The fountainhead of all the Laws of Nature, pure, self-referral consciousness is the total potential of Natural Law. Natural Law is the force of evolution guiding life. This single self-referral field creates and governs life including "all field of existence, all kinds of intelligence" which emerge from this "unbounded, eternal field of intelligence."[24] Consciousness is the self-sufficient source of creation; creation evolves by virtue of, and finds its fulfillment within, self-referral consciousness.

> Consciousness is the existence of everything, and consciousness is the intelligence of everything. Consciousness is wakefulness, unbounded alertness, pure intelligence, pure existence, self-referral fullness, all knowingness—the self-sufficient and unmanifest source, course, and goal of all creation. Those who practice Maharishi's Transcendental Meditation [technique] experience these qualities of consciousness in their own Transcendental Consciousness.[25]

In addition, Maharishi has identified specific qualities of pure consciousness[26] which, through the practice of his technologies of consciousness, can be enlivened in human life and in the art of the artist.[27] Of these values, self-referral and pure knowledge (with its infinite organizing power) reveal the dynamic nature of consciousness and, while pertinent to the understanding of any field of knowledge, are particularly significant for art.

The Three-In-One Structure of Pure Knowledge

The self-referral state of pure consciousness, is also described as the three-in-one structure of pure knowledge.[28] In Maharishi Vedic Science, the three values of self-referral, pure consciousness—observer, process of observation and observed, or knower, process of knowing and the known—are referred to as Ṛishi, Devatā and Chhandas respectively. These three aspects of consciousness in their unified status are called Saṁhitā. The word Saṁhitā means "to put together." It is one word with two roots—"hi" meaning "to put" and "san" which indicates "together." In this sense, Saṁhitā means the togetherness of Ṛishi, Devatā, and Chhandas or the unified state of the three. Maharishi points out that, "togetherness is called Saṁhitā:"[29]

> The knower, the known, and the process of knowing which connects the knower and the known—when these three aspects of knowledge are seated one within the other, that is called Samhitā. Samhitā is the collectedness of knower, known, and knowledge.[30]

In "Vedic language this 'three-in-one' structure of consciousness is called Saṁhitā of Ṛishi, Devatā, Chhandas—Saṁhitā (unity) of Ṛishi (knower), Devatā (dynamism of the process of knowing), and Chhandas (the known)." [31] The term Veda means "pure knowledge"— the "solid mass of knowledge" where the knower, process of knowing and known are the same structure of knowledge.[32] Thus, Veda is the three-in-one structure of pure knowledge. Due to consciousness knowing itself in terms of three and one simultaneously, Maharishi points out that there is an infinite frequency or vibration within consciousness:

> In that pure consciousness we have three values—observed, observer and observation—and we have one unified state of the three. Here we have one and three at the same time. When we have one and three together in that self-referral state of pure consciousness, there is that infinite contraction for remaining one and there is that quick expansion to become three. When they are simultaneously three and one there is infinite dynamism.[33]

"In this togetherness of one and three, we find infinity pulsating."[34] Infinity pulsates and creates frequencies. These frequencies give rise to the entire manifest creation. Since this dynamic structure is that governing intelligence at the basis of creation, the "three-in-one structure of pure knowledge," Maharishi explains, "is the absolute structure of perfect administration."[35] Why is it perfect? Because it administers the activity of the entire universe with complete orderliness. It administers the universe through the simultaneous phenomenon of analysis and synthesis (where analysis denotes the discrimination of elements or the principle of diversification in terms of the three differentiated values of Ṛishi, Devatā and Chhandas, and synthesis signifies the unification of diversified elements or the unified value of Saṁhitā). Therefore, the three-in-one structure of pure knowledge holds together the spontaneous theme of diversification in a unified, integrated state and in so doing, administers from that level all the activity of the universe.

This three-in-one structure is found to be Ṛk Veda (the first aspect of the Veda and the Vedic Literature), identified by Maharishi as the Constitution of the Universe since it comprises the fundamental principles that uphold, structure, and govern all life. As noted in Part III , Ṛk Veda, the self-referral unity at the basis of creation, governs the laws which uphold the manifest universe just as the constitution of a nation sustains the laws which maintain order in the nation.[36] As Maharishi states, "Ṛk Ved is the functioning Constitution of Creation, which is ceaselessly governing the entire creation."[37] In contemporary theory much is made of the impossibility of any experience of an infinite, absolute realm and the theme of paradox. In Maharishi Vedic Science, the absolute reality of pure consciousness can not only be experienced but contains within it opposing qualities; it is the opposing values of intelligence within the structure of consciousness which renders consciousness wakeful and alert.

Saṁhitā: Coexistence Of Contradictory Values

The three-in-one structure of consciousness or pure knowledge, Saṁhitā of Ṛishi, Devatā, and Chhandas, as noted above, involves opposite values:

> Consciousness is the unity or coexistence of two qualities of intelligence that are contradictory to each other: 1) Singularity of self-referral Saṁhitā, and 2) Diversity of Ṛishi, Devatā, and Chhandas. It is interesting to note that the quality of alertness in the nature of consciousness is due to the coexistence of these two opposite values within its structure. Togetherness of these contradictory qualities within the structure of consciousness renders consciousness wakeful, alert, and lively. Consciousness is the lively field of all possibilities.[38]

The quality of alertness is due to the contradictory values of singularity and diversity within the structure of consciousness. The word "wakefulness" describes the character of pure consciousness and conveys the Saṁhitā value which is unbounded wholeness fully awake within itself. With respect to the aspects of Ṛishi, Devatā and Chhandas and their values, Maharishi explains how the different qualities of Saṁhitā and Ṛishi, Devatā and Chhandas create and generate the transformations within consciousness at the self-referral level. The Ṛishi value is one of witnessing, while Devatā is dynamism and Chhandas is the hiding quality of consciousness:

> The word 'witnessing' conveys the quality of Ṛishi, the seer, within the wakeful quality of Saṁhitā. The sense of action, or activity, or dynamism in the witnessing value of Ṛishi (which is essentially the wakeful quality of Saṁhitā), actually creates the relationship between Saṁhitā and Ṛishi and generates the transformations of one into the other.[39]

Maharishi further explains that "This dynamism within the nature of Saṁhitā, connecting Ṛishi and Saṁhitā, creating the relationship of Saṁhitā and Ṛishi, is the eternal dynamism of Devatā within the nature of Ṛishi"[40] and that the quality of hiding or obscuring, also inherent within the nature of self-referral consciousness, is called Chhandas:

> Ever present within the qualities of Ṛishi and Devatā is the quality of hiding; the Ṛishi value hides the value of Saṁhitā, and Devatā value hides the value of Ṛishi. Saṁhitā, fully awake within itself, being self-referral, is with reference only to itself. In this sense the self-referral value has a quality of hiding, in that when it opens to itself it is not open to anything else. Saṁhitā, open to itself, is not open to Ṛishi, Devatā, or Chhandas; similarly, Ṛishi, open to itself, is not open to anything else; similarly, Devatā, open to itself, is not open to anything else. Thus it is clear that the self-referral quality has within its own nature the covering quality called Chhandas.[41]

When each value of consciousness is open to itself and nothing else it covers other values of its own nature; this covering quality is Chhandas. The self-referral nature of consciousness, being wakefulness, thus possesses the qualities of witnessing, dynamism and hiding. Unlike contemporary theory, not only does Maharishi Vedic Science identify a universal, abstract self-referral field of pure consciousness, but it also provides an incredibly detailed account of its structure. As discussed, Saṁhitā, pure wakefulness, has these three values of Rishi, Devatā, and Chhandas awake within its own singularity. As Maharishi points out:

> Saṁhitā, in its own self-referral nature, fully awake within itself, has Ṛishi, Devatā, and Chhandas qualities also fully awake within it. That is why it is Saṁhitā of Ṛishi, Devatā, and Chhandas—the three-in-one structure of self-referral consciousness—Transcendental Consciousness.[42]

This three-in-one structure of self-referral consciousness can be subjectively experienced and verified as one's own simplest form of awareness—Transcendental Consciousness. Maharishi Vedic Science does not end with a simple description of self-referral consciousness; it contains the entire disclosure of the mechanics of creation.

One and Many: Unity and Diversity

As mentioned above, the three diversified values of Rishi, Devatā, and Chhandas represent the diversifying aspect of consciousness within the unity of Saṁhitā. The one unified value and the three diversified values of consciousness are two contrary aspects of consciousness but nevertheless co-existing.

Despite their opposing values, instead of completely neutralizing themselves, unity and diversity support each other in the direction of *evolution*, where evolution refers to the unfoldment of self-referral consciousness in terms of creation and its progressive development. Maharishi explains:

> The quality of self-referral Creative Intelligence, maintaining balance between Unity and Diversity, inspires them to support each other into steps of creation—steps of evolution, promoting infinite creative momentum which is displayed in the eternal process of evolution.[43]

Creative Intelligence is pure consciousness in its creative, self-referral mode. The steps of creation and creative momentum governing the evolutionary unfoldment of life in a harmonious and balanced and sequential development occur by virtue of the balance of unity and diversity, self-referral and object-referral consciousness, the three-in-one structure of consciousness. This progressive unfoldment or evolution of consciousness occurs through the quantification of consciousness.

Located within the process of diversification or quantification is sequence and the theme of counting—the expansion from one to many, and ultimately, to infinity. Inherent within the unified value of Saṁhitā are discrete values or seeds of diversity. In this sense, consciousness diversifies itself and in so doing creates specific quantified values which can be counted from one to two to three to many. Maharishi teaches that these quantified values are being derived by the intelligence of pure consciousness itself:

> Where do you have one and two initially? The seer, the intelligence, in its self-referral state, it becomes the observer, and the observer becomes the observed; then there are two. Then we have all the logic to know that one is Ṛishi, Devatā and Chhandas; one is observer, observed, observation. These innumerable values are all the values of intelligence because it is the intelligence which argues within itself—I am one, I am two, I am three, I am the observer, observed, observation, and this and this and this.[44]

The intelligence of the seer divides itself. In this sense, the entire creation can be known and understood to be the quantification of one's own self-referral consciousness. Indeed, this experience is fully realized in Unity or Brahman Consciousness, a level of human development which is described in the following chapter.

In order to experience diversity as one's own self-referral consciousness the individual has to be living pure wakefulness; consciousness must be permanently lively, alert and infinitely expanded. It is worth noting that, as Maharishi explains, it is this experience of consciousness multiplying itself which is the basis of mathematics. As Maharishi explains:

> It is an *experience* of consciousness multiplying itself that has set mathematics to life. The phenomenon of the expansion of consciousness—one fullness going,

and going, and going—this experience is the basis of mathematics. Mathematics is not the imagination of some wise dreamers. Had it been so, it would have been gone long before now. Mathematics comes from this experience, this phenomenon in nature. It's a solid, concrete phenomenon on the level of consciousness. That is the reason why mathematics has continued.[45]

In this context, the foundation of mathematics *is* the *experience* of self-referral consciousness and its sequential unfoldment. As Maharishi explains, "Basically the mechanics of transformation of self-referral intelligence into the ever-expanding universe is available to us in countable stages in the structure of Ṛk Veda."[46] Part III goes into this structure and dynamic in more detail.

Continuing with the theme of consciousness in terms of one and many at the same time, Maharishi points out this principle is expressed in the Vedic Literature as, "एकोऽहम् *Ekoham*—'I am one'; बहु स्याम् *Bahu syām*—'May I be many."[47] In addition to this, creation can be discussed in terms of innumerable particles, each of which is essentially Saṁhitā, within the unbounded field of pure consciousness.

Every Point is Saṁhitā and Infinitely Correlated with Every Other Point in Creation

In the infinite, singular, silent field of self-referral consciousness, Maharishi explains, consciousness finds itself to be made of "points."[48] With respect to the three-in-one structure of consciousness, Saṁhitā is found at every point in creation. Every grain of creation is Saṁhitā of Ṛishi, Devatā, and Chhandas or the structure of self-referral consciousness:

> Each point is Saṁhitā, and each point is Saṁhitā of Ṛishi, Devatā, and Chhandas. Each point has pure wakefulness in three values of knower, knowing, and known because it is pure wakefulness. So there is knower, knowing, and known, and there is one flat, uniform, eternally the same, basis of three in eternal unity.[49]

In order to help us comprehend this phenomenon, Maharishi adds that Saṁhitā, pure wakefulness or pure self-referral consciousness, is that wakeful quality which, being awake to itself, creates a move within its own infinite, unbounded nature. He describes it as "one unbounded ocean of consciousness in motion within itself"[50] and compares this move to the stirring of water in a dish. The stir, or move, creates a ripple, a wave, throughout the whole body of water:

> When totality moves it moves to bring together infinity, the two ends of infinity. For example, if you take water in a deep dish, fill it and stir it at one end, the moment you start to stir one holistic wave goes through the whole dish. The entire water begins to move.

> Such is the move of that pure wakefulness which is eternally awake within itself. It moves, and where does it move? It moves connecting its own point after point, and point after point, and point after point. On that level, the point and point are not separated; points are not separate because pure wakefulness is unified and that unified wholeness we call the infinite correlation level of pure intelligence, where one point is infinitely correlated with every other point.[51]

Since each point, like a wave in the dish, is intimately connected to the other, each point, while discrete, is part of the greater body of water. In this sense, every point is infinitely correlated. As Maharishi indicates, "every point of consciousness is infinitely correlated with every other point."[52]

Thus, in one unbounded ocean or field of consciousness, when the total field moves,[53] due to its infinite nature, the entire field "brings together the two ends of infinity."[54] The whole field stirs. In this description Maharishi gives us a picture of how there can be one infinite, unbounded, holistic value of consciousness, and an infinite number of points within that unboundedness which are all fundamentally interconnected.

Incidentally, as will be discussed in Chapter 6, Maharishi also points out that it is due to these internal dynamics of self-referral consciousness that a field effect occurs as a result of the Transcendental Meditation technique and the TM-Sidhi program; through the stirring of self-referral consciousness, the practice of this technology generates coherence in the physiology, coherence throughout the environment, and coherence throughout the universe.[55]

Maharishi also uses an analogy of waves of water stirred in a dish to describe the move within self-referral consciousness and emergence of diversified values:

> Take a dish full of water. Create a gentle stir in the water by tilting it and leaving it. First you will see one holistic stir, one holistic wave generated throughout. If the process of stirring continues, specific waves develop in different structures within that one holistic wave—the initial holistic wave sequentially develops into waves of specific categories. This is how one holistic wave naturally gets broken into many waves.[56]

The frequencies of self-referral consciousness are like "waves" in a ocean, or water in a dish.[57] Each wave, or each point in creation, is one of an infinite number which together make up the infinite diversity of the universe. According to the same principle, every individual is an expression of consciousness, making up the diversity of cultures in the world.

This understanding may provide an additional perspective on the argument brought forward by theorists exploring the connections between quantum physics, technology, art, science and aesthetics—as mentioned in Chapter 4.

Puruṣa and Prakṛti in Every Grain of Creation

Continuing with the idea of points within consciousness or the characteristics of each grain in creation, in the terminology of Maharishi Vedic Science, there are two values called *Puruṣa* and *Prakṛti* within every aspect of creation. These two values represent silence and dynamism. From modern physics, on one level material creation can also be understood, to be made up of particles. As we have seen, in Maharishi Vedic Science, the manifest universe is described in terms of points or grains of creation which relate to consciousness; each grain in creation has the values of *Puruṣa* and *Prakṛti*. *Puruṣa* is the silent, uninvolved, witnessing value of intelligence which is fully alert within every grain of creation, and *Prakṛti* is the dynamic or Creative Intelligence aspect inherent within the silent value of intelligence. As Maharishi teaches, "The intelligence within every grain of creation has the silent quality of intelligence (*Purush*), and the creative quality of intelligence (*Prakṛiti*), with reference to that particular grain of creation."[58] Along with *Puruṣa,* there is *Prakṛti*, the creative quality of intelligence with reference to that particular grain of creation.[59]

Maharishi goes on to describes the holistic value of all the innumerable values of *Puruṣa* in the universe as *Puruṣottama*. *Ottama* or *Uttama* means "superlative" or of "supreme quality"; thus, *Puruṣottama* means "holistic rulership" in Vedic terminology.[60] Rulership refers to that governing property of absolute administration at the basis of creation introduced earlier in the discussion of the three-in-one structure of pure knowledge or Saṁhitā. As Maharishi explains:

> Considering the congregate of all the innumerable *Purush* in the universe, and considering that whole is more than the collection of parts, we find the innumerable *Purusha* in the universe with reference to innumerable diversified values in the universe. The quality of these innumerable *Purush* must be different to the *Purush* with reference to the whole of the universe. This absolute, holistic quality of *Purush* is *Purushottam* (holistic value of the innumerable values of *Purush* in the universe) and within the nature of this *Purushottam* is the holistic nature of *Prakṛiti* of all the innumerable *Prakṛiti* with reference to all the innumerable *Purush* in the Universe. This is holistic *Prakṛiti* of holistic *Purush.*[61]

The field of *Puruṣottama* is the totality of consciousness within which the innumerable points (values of Saṁhitā) are all infinitely correlated. The level of *Puruṣottama* is the total intelligence of Natural Law which administers the whole universe from the self-referral, holistic value of intelligence. Maharishi equates *Puruṣottama* with the totality of Saṁhitā or *Brahma.* He describes *Brahma* as the total value of Natural Law which governs the universe in an orderly, evolutionary way—that intelligence which rules its own expressions and expands itself, spontaneously maintaining its own expressions in absolute order.[62]

Thus, in the lively dynamic of self-referral consciousness at the basis of creation and our own consciousness, silence and dynamism—*Puruṣa* and *Prakṛti*.—are located.

Silence and Dynamism: Co-Existing Values of Pure Wakefulness

On the level of human awareness characterized by pure wakefulness, silence and dynamism coexist; pure wakefulness is that comprehension of the simultaneity of silence and dynamism. Maharishi points out that in silence becoming dynamism (and vice versa), the creativity inherent within singularity resides.[63] In this context, as he elaborates, all the creative and evolutionary processes which structure the universe can be said to emerge from pure wakefulness:

> In its pure wakefulness, human awareness comprehends the details of its own structure and finds that the silent value of its own nature is co-existing with the dynamic value of its own nature. This co-existence of silence and dynamism presents a picture of silence partaking of dynamism and dynamism partaking of silence. This phenomenon of silence ceaselessly partaking of dynamism and dynamism ceaselessly partaking of silence within the structure of pure wakefulness displays creativity within the singularity, which forms the basis of all creative and evolutionary processes of the diverse universe.[64]

Singularity evolves or progresses into its divided nature without actually losing its status as one. Retaining its holistic character, pure wakefulness is one unified wholeness of silence and dynamism at the same time. Within the structure of wakefulness, singularity is seen as duality. This dynamic describes the mechanics of creation and reveals that the mechanics of creation are lively within the structure of singularity. Maharishi describes it in the following way:

> Here, within the structure of wakefulness, we see singularity in terms of duality; here, within the structure of pure wakefulness, we see the mechanics of creation—we see duality within the structure of singularity. This gives us the understanding of the mechanics of creation being lively within the structure of singularity.[65]

Maharishi further teaches that pure wakefulness is the alertness of silence and dynamism. In entertaining one another, each must be supremely alert lest one is neutralized or annihilated by the other:

> Pure wakefulness, being awake in the two values within its structure, exhibits the quality of lively intelligence, the quality of consciousness. By virtue of its wakeful nature it knows itself completely. The interchange of silence and dynamism within the nature of pure wakefulness demonstrates the mechanics of creation; it explains how unity is duality and how the process of evolution is

> sustained within it. Pure wakefulness locates the dynamics of creation within itself and locates the structures of creation within its own unmanifest self-referral state—dynamic silence. It comprehends the COLLAPSE of dynamism into silence and silence into dynamism.[66]

Maharishi reveals that the phenomenon of the interchange of silence and dynamism demonstrates how the mechanics of creation occurs and how the process of evolution is sustained. Being awake to the two values of silence and dynamism within its own structure, pure wakefulness displays the value of intelligence.

How does this intelligence express itself? Maharishi points out that dynamism "collapses" into silence, and silence "collapses" into dynamism in an infinite dynamic and that this phenomenon of "collapse" presents the simultaneous reality of both silence and dynamism. Pure wakefulness locates this eternal interaction of the two basic values of its own nature. In this sense, as Maharishi explains, pure wakefulness locates the mechanics of creation unfolding, and the deeper structures of creation, within self-referral consciousness.

This eternal interaction of silence and dynamism can be heard on the level of consciousness; the sound of creation unfolding is the sound of the eternal interaction of silence and dynamism—the collapse of dynamism into silence and silence into dynamism. These values of silence and dynamism are also discussed in terms of consciousness as a straight line.

Consciousness as a Straight Line

The straight line represents two values of silence and dynamism. As Maharishi reveals, silence represents the non-wave like character of the straight line and the progression of the straight line represents dynamism—a straight dynamism.

In the context of the experience of pure wakefulness and the functioning of mind, Maharishi also describes the activity of enlightened awareness in terms of a straight line. He explains that when the dynamism of thinking is supported by the state of silence, there is no wastage of energy. In this sense, the straight line is silent—it is not a wave with peaks and troughs; it is dynamic because it is progressive. A progressive move is characterized by a straight line; it is a "straight dynamism" functioning according to the principle of least action. As Maharishi notes, "when motion is in waves its speed is less because the direction is up and down, and sideways. In a straight line the motion is direct and therefore faster. A straight line represents infinite frequency, the field of silence, where energy is not dissipated in up and down directions."[67]

In another context, Maharishi goes on to discuss consciousness as the straight line of life which knows only infinity, bliss, the value of pure knowledge and its infinite organizing power:

> On that level where line is a plane, a field, without boundaries, an endless unbounded straight line—a straight plane of no boundaries, on that level of life, all possibilities are always lively and form the basis of all creation.[68]

The straight line is unbounded, endless, a plane of no boundaries at the Transcendental basis of creation—the level of all possibilities. This is the field of self-referral consciousness.[69]

Being self-referral, the process by which this field evolves, is referred to by Maharishi as a self-referral loop, "the entire field of consciousness is structured in self-referral loops of infinite frequency."[70] Maharishi describes this process of the self-referral evolution of consciousness in terms of "flow and stop;" it can be said to go backward and forward but entirely within its own unboundedness. Thus, progress occurs on the ground of non-change and "distance" is only a move forward or backward.

This principle of evolution, Maharishi explains in terms of steps or stages—using the analogy of walking. One foot and then another goes ahead but whatever distance one covers the feet are simply going backward and forward.[71] "Forward" or "backward" movement here describes the move *within* consciousness—that Ultimate Reality described as a straight line. In effect, there is no in or out; or rather it's all in and all out simultaneously. This principle is further described by Maharishi as the "lamp-at-the-door"—inside and outside are illuminated simultaneously. One is in and out at the same time.[72] This situation characterizes the state of pure consciousness.

Consciousness is wholeness, the totality, all-pervasive, infinite, all-encompassing, moving within itself. Ultimately there is no "in" and "out" of consciousness, but within this field there is a move. In this sense, the state of pure consciousness is bi-directional; it is self-referral and object referral. As Maharishi explains:

> Now that state of Being [pure consciousness] is both ways at the same time. Outside lighted, inside lighted, but what do we mean by in and out in that state? In and out is the reality of dynamism and silence. On that level both are the same. Dynamism and silence, dynamism and silence. But if we take it to be in and out then it is with infinite speed in and out. It's a straight line representing silence and dynamism only when the dynamism is of infinite frequency—when at no time is it out or in; it is in and out at the same time.[73]

The straight line represents silence and dynamism when the dynamism inherent within consciousness is of an infinite frequency. Pure awareness, thus, has the characteristic of a "lamp-at-the-door;" it is in and out with infinite speed and is therefore neither in or out, or rather it is simultaneously "in and out."

Recalling Derrida's concept of *différance*, and the move or force of language through a continual deferring and differing of meaning within language, there seems to be a parallel idea at work; it could be said that there is no "in" or "out" of language. However, Derrida denies any possibility of a Transcendental realm. In Maharishi Vedic Science, the description of the mechanics of self-referral consciousness apply to the most abstract realm of life. Language is this play of self-referral consciousness within consciousness. Indeed, Part III describes how all of creation is the play of self-referral consciousness or the language of the Veda.

With respect to the understanding of consciousness as a line, it is also interesting to note that the Greeks described line in relation to point. Plato called the point the beginning of a line; the difference between the point and line, according to Aristotle, is that the former is indivisible and the latter is divisible. Returning to this theme, Part VI reviews specific sūtras of the Vāstusūtra Upaniṣad in terms of consciousness as a straight line. Other ancient definitions of the point and line describe the point as: the indivisible beginning of all magnitudes; an extremity which has no dimension; an extremity of a line. An-Nairīzī also stated that if one wants to know the essence of a point (a thing more simple than a line) one should, in the sensible world, think of the center of the universe and the *poles.* As discussed in Chapter 1, in ancient Greek thought, philosophy, science and in traditions throughout the world, mathematical principles were held to reveal the workings of nature or the divine.

In Maharishi Vedic Science the basic structure and nature of consciousness, itself, is found to correspond to fundamental mathematical principles.

Consciousness as the Source of Geometric Forms and Alphabets

As discussed earlier, life can be understood to be made up of layers: abstract or subtle levels to gross or more concrete levels of creation—for example, in the physiology this is demonstrated as levels progressing from the intelligence of the DNA, to RNA, proteins, cells, tissues, organs etc. In the unfoldment of pure consciousness (the most abstract level of life) to more expressed levels of matter, Maharishi explains that at the level where pure consciousness begins to develop into the grosser expressions of material creation, the finest impulses of consciousness are lively.

While the whole creation is made up of layers, the subtlest level of these layers is the self-referral basis of creation: "Physical sciences inform us that the whole creation is built up of layers of energy, one inside the other. The subtlest constitutes the innermost stratum of creation."[74] In Maharishi Vedic Science the physical or material world is referred to as the relative:

> In the physical world, which we shall call the relative or the relative field of existence, several forms of energy are known. These forms are eternally changing into one another according to the laws of physics.[75]

While specific laws govern the manifestation of phenomena at each layer or level, according to Maharishi, there is a subtle level of impulses of almost no differences from where all the different values and layers of creation arise; "From the most quiet transcendental level, nature performs, and it performs within itself. It is the self-referral activity of natural law that is responsible for absolute order in creation."[76] That self-referral activity, Maharishi adds,

> Is the most basic performance in nature. It transcends all activity of natural law in the relative field, but yet is always lively as the basis of the classical, physical world. It is the most refined level of quantum-mechanical activity of nature, from where absolute orderliness controls, commands and governs all affairs of the universe.[77]

Knowledge of this range of life is important for the artist, who, Maharishi points out, should have open to his awareness "all aspects of life" from "the grossest relative aspect to the sublest relative aspect to that eternity which lies beyond the sublest relative, the Absolute."[78] The different levels of creation all have as their source a field of impulses; from this level of innumerable impulses arise forms, colors, time and space, all the elements and the finer particles in creation, all the numbers, alphabets, and the fundamental geometric forms—triangle, circle and square:

> The source of all differences in creation is at a level which, in itself, is free from all differences. When there are impulses in this field, these impulses can be of an innumerable nature. From there arises the green color, orange color, yellow color, this and that form; from there arises time and space, all the elements, and all the finer particles. Therefore, on that level where there are no differences, the possibility of all differences starting from there is very clear. That is the level from where all the triangles come out, all the circles come out, all the squares come out, all the numbers—one, two, three—come out, alphabets come out, and creation expresses itself.[79]

The building blocks of creation emerge from a field of impulses. From the level of no differences arises the possibility of all differences and all forms.

This level is not the absolute, despite the fact that the absolute is the ultimate source of the variety in creation.[80] It can be understood as waves or vibrations on an infinite ocean. The forms and phenomena of creation are the different values or impulses; in this sense, the whole of creation can be understood as comprised of waves or frequencies of consciousness.

This seems to run counter to McEvilley's comment about the Platonic/Pythagorean doctrine of the music of the spheres and the belief that art vibrations pass constantly through the universe and constitute its ordering principles. Clearly, "art vibrations" of modern formalism do not constitute the ordering principles of the universe. However, frequencies of a unified field—a universal, self-referral consciousness that structures the universe and all of life—can be understood to permeate and give rise to all forms and phenomena. Granted, if the artist could function from this level, then presumably, his or her art could embody or represent that universal level of consciousness. Part V discusses how, when the artist starts to function from the level of self-referral consciousness, this can become a possibility.

When the individual begins to function from this level of Nature's functioning, he or she performs action from the "main switchboard" governing creation; for instance, as Maharishi indicates in the performance of the TM-Sidhi program (specifically the Yogic Flying technique which is discussed in detail in Chapter 6) the individual is in control of:

> Nature's central switchboard, from where Natural Law governs the universe. From here the individual can command all channels of Nature's creativity and the invincible organizing power of Natural Law. An order from the Prime Minister commands the total authority and resources of the nation for its implementation. Similarly, any intention projected from the Unified Field of Natural Law commands the infinite organizing power of Natural Law for its immediate fulfillment.[81].

The individual who perceives and comprehends the mechanics of nature's functioning at this level—the level of impulses—realizes, along with the details of consciousness, the source of color, time and space, forms, all the elements and finer particles, triangles, circles, squares, numbers and alphabets. In this sense, Maharishi Vedic Science brings fulfillment to the aspirations of traditional philosophy and modern theory. It locates the deepest level of life and reveals that this can be our daily reality. Access to this level would be of great value to any artist who wished to create an art embodying the deepest structure and mechanics of the universal field of consciousness.

As mentioned in Chapter 1, number and simple geometry as expressed in ideal form and proportion are of prime importance in traditional art and architecture seeking to represent or embody the eternal. These principles were derived mathematically. In Maharishi Vedic Science, number, fundamental forms, and basic "geometry," are understood to be ultimately generated from the universal field of self-referral consciousness, the Creative Intelligence of the individual. Mathematics is defined as something more expansive and all-inclusive than computations, formulas and proofs; "Vedic Mathematics" involves the self-referral consciousness of the individual, the source and common basis of all the activity in the universe, and unfolds the mathematics of consciousness itself in the individual's own awareness.

These mathematics are the mathematics functioning at the basis of all life; as Maharishi points out, the technology to achieve this is the Transcendental Meditation technique which:

> Is the programme of Vedic Mathematics [the technology of Natural Law] because it enlivens and utilizes the holistic value of Natural Law to materialize an

> all-directional effects in all fields of space and time. It is this theme of Vedic Mathematics available through Transcendental Meditation that promotes absolute order from the common basis of all activity in the universe—the self-referral, unified field of consciousness.[82]

Vedic Mathematics is the experience, enlivenment and utilization of the holistic value of Natural Law, self-referral consciousness. To develop expertise in this field of Vedic Mathematics, Maharishi adds, one should gain Transcendental Consciousness through the practice of the Transcendental Meditation technique and act from the most settled level of mind and optimize brain functioning through the TM-Sidhi program. Then one can gain the support of Natural Law and enjoy all thought, speech, and action free from stress, strain, problems or failures.[83]

As noted above, the infinite, unbounded field of pure consciousness generates impulses through its self-referral mechanics and administers the universe by virtue of holding together contradictory values—unity (Saṁhitā or self-referral) and diversity (Ṛishi, Devatā and Chhandas or object-referral). In the process of the quantification of consciousness, sequence, number, and fundamental forms unfold. It is clear that consciousness can be described from different perspectives; it has both the values of silence and dynamism. It is a field of all possibilities. All of creation is comprised of subtle to gross levels or layers as well as being frequencies of self-referral consciousness.

The theme of paradox or coexistence of opposites defines the basic functioning of self-referral consciousness—how diversity emerges from singularity, or rather how diversity is just the move of consciousness within itself. In Maharishi Vedic Science, every grain of creation is seen to contain values of silence and dynamism, *Puruṣa* and ***Prakṛti.*** The two values of silence and dynamism coexisting are referred to as the straight line of consciousness. Although these descriptions of consciousness seem abstract, in providing technologies of consciousness (the Transcendental Meditation technique, TM-Sidhi program and Yogic Flying), Maharishi Vedic Science allows the individual to access pure, self-referral consciousness and operate from this level. Then one has access to all the Laws of Nature, the switchboard of the entire creation. This ability is highly advantageous for any individual, and any artist.

6

DEVELOPING HIGHER STATES OF CONSCIOUSNESS THROUGH THE PRACTICE OF THE TRANSCENDENTAL MEDITATION TECHNIQUE THE TM-SIDHI PROGRAM AND YOGIC FLYING

Without a technique to develop consciousness, according to Maharishi, knowledge remains incomplete and the individual thinks, acts and speaks from a limited experience and understanding of life.[1] With specific technologies of consciousness one can rise to enlightenment. The most effective techniques for developing consciousness are the Transcendental Meditation technique, the TM-Sidhi program and Yogic Flying. The Transcendental Meditation technique is known world-wide as an easy, effortless mental procedure which allows individual awareness to experience Transcendental Consciousness and harness the infinite organizing power of Natural Law. The TM-Sidhi program and Yogic Flying further promote activity from the level of Natural Law, increase mind-body co-ordination and the ability to achieve outcomes by mere intention, and also accelerate growth to higher states of consciousness.

While the term "enlightenment" in Western art history is associated with eighteenth-century Rationalism, here it denotes a state of human existence characterized by perfection. In Maharishi Vedic Science perfection is characterized by a problem-free life, perfect health, and the ability to spontaneously fulfill one's desires—desires which are life-supporting for the individual, society and the environment. An enlightened individual is a 'perfect' human being because he or she functions "spontaneously according to Natural Law, does not make mistakes and does not create problems for himself or for others."[2]

The common experiences of suffering and struggle throughout the record of human existence have made us skeptical about the possibility of perfection and permanent happiness. At face value, history does not seem to support this possibility but there are records of highly developed and harmonious periods of life documented in texts and oral traditions of different religions and cultures. Despite the fact that these accounts are often not recognized by modern historians as "history"—as will be discussed in Part IV—they present instances when administration was perfect and life on an individual and social level was lived in fulfillment.

According to Maharishi Vedic Science, perfection is the birth-right of everyone; it is the direction in which life evolves. Perfection does not mean a dull, eventless existence. Perfection in life is lived in bliss and fulfillment, where the a field of all possibilities is open to one; this is the life of a universal human being. Technologies of consciousness furnish the means to realize this goal.

Perfection and enlightenment, on a collective level, are characterized by a society where universal value is naturally expressed, all the diverse tendencies of individual life are netted in harmony; the world family is a "beautiful mosaic of different cultures."[3] A harmonious society is made up of individuals whose behavior, thinking and action is naturally life-supporting. For the artist, enlightenment encompasses the ability to make the piece of art speak the "fullness of life" so that "it tells the story of life and keeps on telling the story of life to generations in the eternity of time."[4] For this reason, Maharishi explains that because art has its source in the transcendent, "the skill of the artist lies in knowing what consciousness is and what it is made of."[5] This is possible in higher stages of human development where the individual displays skill in action, possesses highly developed mind-body co-ordination and the ability to simultaneously focus sharply and maintain broad comprehension.[6] Skill in action is enhanced through the development of higher states of consciousness through the regular practice of the Transcendental Meditation technique and the TM-Sidhi program.

The practice of the Transcendental Meditation technique can be thought of as a professional tool for the artist because, as Maharishi states: "It is vital for the study of art, much more than for the study of any other field, that the artist spontaneously live the completeness of life. Only then will his strokes spontaneously be the impulse of life."[7] The word "life" here denotes the field of pure consciousness—that which gives rise to creation and which is the source of existence itself. From the perspective of Maharishi Vedic Science, the artist has to have "the capacity to live the unbounded along with the boundaries."[8] For this the artist must be living Cosmic Consciousness or higher states of consciousness—where absolute knowledge is gained.

As discussed earlier, modern artists sought to create work which would give the experience of absolute knowledge—a goal which is absurd to postmodernists. However, according Maharishi Vedic Science, considering the normal development of higher states of consciousness and the unfoldment of absolute knowledge at the basis of all relative knowledge, it is possible to envisage how absolute knowledge might be experienced and embodied in art.

The Universal Human and Higher States of Consciousness

Psychologists and sociologists have recognized that people can experience altered states of consciousness and there are different states of the consciousness. On the individual level one can speak of the conscious and subconscious mind; on the social level there are values of collective consciousness which define social awareness. According to Maharishi Vedic Science, with respect to individual awareness, there are seven states of consciousness. The three commonly experienced states of waking, sleeping, and dreaming are called *Jāgrat Avasthā* or *Jāgrat Chetanā*, *Swapn Avasthā* or *Swapn Chetanā*, and *Sushupti Avasthā* or

Sushupti Chetanā, respectively. The four further states of consciousness are Transcendental Consciousness (*Turīya Avasthā* or *Turīya Chetanā*), Cosmic Consciousness (*Turīyātīt Avasthā or Turīyātīt Chetanā*), God Consciousness (*Bhagavad Chetanā*), and Unity or Brahman Consciousness (*Brāhmi Sthiti* or *Brāhmi Chetanā*)—the mature state of enlightenment. Maharishi teaches that any individual can develop higher states of consciousness and gain enlightenment—where the individual can breathe "life in Cosmic Reality"—through the practice of the Transcendental Meditation technique and the TM-Sidhi program.[9]

The Transcendental Meditation technique allows the conscious mind to settle down to its least excited state of Transcendental Consciousness, thereby transcending or going beyond the three relative states; as Maharishi explains: "this is a state of inner wakefulness with no object of thought or perception, just pure consciousness."[10] This process is described as follows:

> Maharishi's Transcendental Meditation Technique is a simple, natural, effortless procedure practiced for 15 to 20 minutes in the morning and evening while sitting comfortably with the eyes closed. During this technique the individual's awareness settles down and experiences a unique state of restful alertness—as the body becomes deeply relaxed, the mind transcends all mental activity to experience the simplest form of human awareness—Transcendental Consciousness—where consciousness is open to itself. This is the self-referral state of consciousness.[11]

As discussed in the previous chapter, in Transcendental Consciousness the mind no longer has as its object thoughts or perceptions and the individual experiences inner wakefulness—where consciousness is open to itself and is self-referral.

Transcendental Consciousness is described as a field of *bliss-consciousness*; therefore, the "flow of the mind toward this state is natural"[12]—for the mind spontaneously moves toward this field of bliss. In effect, through the practice of Transcendental Meditation, the mind moves in the direction of subtler levels of experience until it reaches this field of bliss, Transcendental Consciousness:

> Through Transcendental Meditation, the attention is brought from gross experience to subtler fields of experience until the subtlest experience is transcended and the state of transcendental consciousness is gained. The march of the mind in this direction is so simple as to be automatic; as it enters into experience of a subtler nature, the mind feels increased charm because it is proceeding towards absolute bliss. Once the mind reaches transcendental consciousness it no longer remains a conscious mind; it gains the status of absolute Being. This state of transcendental pure consciousness, also known as Self-consciousness, Self-awareness, *Samadhi*, represents the complete infusion of cosmic Being into the individual mind.[13]

Paralleling the earlier description of layers of creation, in this passage Maharishi introduces the notion that there are layers of experience from gross to subtle, from subtle to more subtle, and ultimately to the most subtle experience of bliss. The experience of pure bliss-consciousness, which is also referred to as absolute Being, self-consciousness, self-awareness or *Samādhi*, represents the "complete infusion of cosmic Being" or cosmic existence (pure consciousness) into the individual mind.

Levels of the Mind and the Process of Transcending

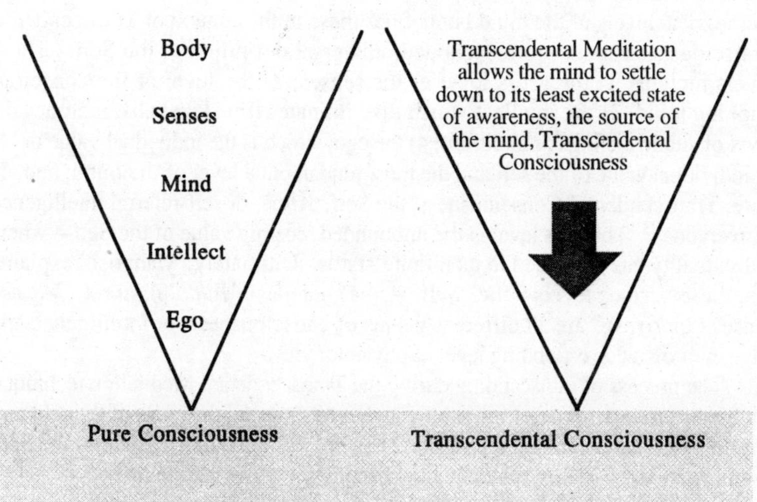

According to Maharishi Vedic Science, there are various levels of the mind, from the Transcendental level of Pure Consciousness, to the subtle levels of the ego (the sense of "I" or individuality) and intellect (the discriminating and synthesizing aspect of the mind), to the thinking mind and the more expressed or gross levels of the senses and the body.

Furthermore, as the following statement explains, the practice of the Transcendental Meditation technique allows the individual to develop her creative potential and eradicate the stress and strain in the nervous system that inhibits the flow of creativity.

> The experience of Transcendental Consciousness develops the individual's latent creative potential, while dissolving accumulated stress and fatigue through the deep rest gained through the practice of Transcendental Meditation. This experience enlivens within one's awareness creativity, dynamism, orderliness,

> and organizing power, which results in increasing effectiveness and success in daily life. Transcendental Meditation can be easily learned by anyone. People of all cultures, religions and educational backgrounds practice this technique.[14]

As noted above, Maharishi describes pure consciousness as a field of infinite creativity, and locates it beyond the relative field of differences. The Transcendental Meditation technique, by enlivening this field, can increase creativity and promote effective and successful behavior in the life of the individual regardless of cultural background. Therefore, this technique does not require a particular educational, philosophical or religious orientation. Utilized by the artist, it can allow access to infinite creativity and organizing power.

As with modern psychology, Maharishi Vedic Science identifies several hierarchical levels of the mind but defines these in the context of Transcendental Consciousness and a more expanded, universal definition of the Self. These levels include: 1) the gross level of the senses; 2) the level of the conscious thinking mind; 3) the intellect which discriminates (this level also includes the level of subtle feelings or intuition); 4) the ego, which is the individual value of "I" or individual value of the self and the most fundamental level of the mind; and, 5) pure, Transcendental Consciousness, the Self, *Ātmā*, or self-referral intelligence of everyone.[15] This last level is the unbounded, cosmic value of the Self—where individuality has expanded to its infinite status. Ultimately, Maharishi explains that these various levels—the "Self (*Ātmā*), intellect (*Buddhi*), mind (*Manas*), senses (*Indriyas*)," are all different values of consciousness, or intelligence and have their own corresponding level of physiology.[16]

The process of transcending during the Transcendental Meditation technique facilitates the experience of the subtler and even more subtle levels of thought and physiological functioning until the mind reaches this unbounded status of the Self. Established in this status, the individual becomes a universal human being.

The Physiology of Higher States of Consciousness

On the physiological level, Maharishi explains that Transcendental Consciousness corresponds to a certain state of the nervous system which "transcends any activity and is therefore completely different from that state of the nervous system which corresponds to the waking state of consciousness"[17]:

> When the mind transcends during Transcendental Meditation, the metabolism reaches its lowest point; so does the process of breathing, the nervous system gains a state of restful alertness which, on the physical level, corresponds to the state of bliss-consciousness, or transcendental being. In order that the consciousness of the waking state may be maintained along with transcendental bliss-consciousness, it is essential for the nervous system not to lose this state of restful alertness corresponding to bliss-consciousness. At the same time the

> nervous system should maintain a metabolic rate corresponding to the activity taking place in the waking state.[18]

The metabolic rate and breath rate in the physiology decreases during the transcending process and the physiology reaches a state of restful alertness corresponding to Transcendental Consciousness but, as Maharishi continues to state, in order to maintain higher states of consciousness the metabolic rate of the waking state of consciousness should also be maintained. Even when the individual is no longer practicing Transcendental Meditation and is engaged in activity, the physiology is increasingly able to maintain that state of restful alertness (and maintain bliss consciousness) along with the waking state. This happens through repeated experience of transcending and then performing daily activity. The human physiology becomes more and more accustomed to a cycle of deep rest and activity and is more and more able to sustain pure, bliss consciousness:

> For transcendental consciousness to become permanent and co-exist with the waking state of consciousness, it is necessary that the two states of the nervous system corresponding to these two states of consciousness should co-exist. This is brought about by the mind gaining alternatively transcendental consciousness and the waking state of consciousness, passing from one to the other. This gradual and systematic culture of the physical nervous system creates a physiological situation in which the two states of consciousness exist together simultaneously.[19]

Maharishi uses a analogy to illustrate this phenomenon. The process of alternating Transcendental Consciousness and waking consciousness is like dipping a cloth in dye and then drying it in the sun. The sun bleaches the dye from the cloth but at the same time some of the dye remains and becomes fast. Over time, through the repeated dipping and leaving the cloth to dry in the sun, the cloth becomes permanently colored. The process of transcending familiarizes the nervous system with transcendental, pure consciousness and eventually the physiology begins to support two styles of functioning simultaneously.[20]

Through the Transcendental Meditation technique the awareness is repeatedly taken to the field of unboundedness, pure wakefulness. Pure wakefulness, as discussed in the previous chapter, contains within it its own point value.

> Maharishi's Vedic Science, practically creating the repeated experience of transcending, spontaneously takes the awareness to the finest point of wakefulness, and there is the experience of unboundedness [the Unified Field of Natural Law]—unbounded pure wakefulness along with the point value of wakefulness.[21]

The awareness is taken from the level of common waking state consciousness to infinite unboundedness. Unboundedness contains within it its own point value. Here the co-existence of opposites is experienced within the individual's awareness:

> This experience, repeated through regular practice, gives rise to the natural ability of comprehending infinity within a point. This gives rise to the ability to enjoy every isolated experience remaining submerged within the unbounded ocean of bliss—self-referral dynamic nature of pure wakefulness. This is the basis of life in freedom, life in bliss, life in its full potential of eternal silence and eternal dynamism—life in full enlightenment.[22]

The Process of Transcending

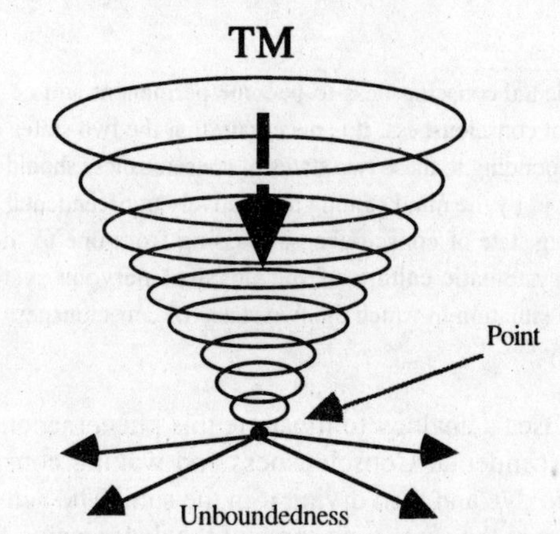

Through the Transcendental Meditation technique, the repeated experience of transcending is practically created, taking the awareness to the finest point of wakefulness —the experience of unbounded pure wakefulness along with the point value of wakefulness.

The repeated experience of transcending allows the individual to gain the experience of pure wakefulness and the point value of wakefulness—to grow in the ability to appreciate infinity within each isolated experience while "submerged" within unboundedness, bliss consciousness. By means of the alternation between the experience of Transcendental Consciousness during the Transcendental Meditation technique and the dynamic activity of daily life, Transcendental Consciousness gradually becomes infused into the mind and is maintained permanently, even in the midst of waking, dreaming, and sleeping.[23] This stage of development of consciousness is called Cosmic Consciousness, *Turīyātīt Avasthā* or *Turīyātīt Chetanā*.

Related to the previous chapter's account of the nature of consciousness, it is clear that Maharishi Vedic Science emphasizes the significance of experiencing pure consciousness versus mere intellectual speculation about it.

Cosmic Consciousness: The Fifth State Of Consciousness And Its Corresponding Physiology

Despite the fact that there are further stages in the development of consciousness, the fifth state of consciousness is referred to as "enlightenment" because at this point of development the individual is permanently established in pure consciousness. In the early stages of the practice of Transcendental Meditation the two levels of function (bliss consciousness and the relative states) are unable to occur at the same time, but by gradually alternating from one to another this "physiological inhibition" is overcome when the individual attains Cosmic Consciousness. As Maharishi explains:

> The two levels begin to function perfectly at the same time, without inhibiting each other and still maintaining their separate identities. The function of each is independent of the other, and that is why this state of the nervous system corresponds to cosmic consciousness, in which Self-awareness exists as separate from activity. Silence is experienced with activity and yet as separate from it.[24]

As with other states of consciousness, this fifth state of consciousness, *Turīyātīt Chetanā*, is also characterized by its own physiological parameters—a restful alertness maintained in the midst of dynamic activity. As noted in Chapter 7, scientific research supports this description[25] of the absolute phase of life (the silent, universal field of pure consciousness) and the relative phase (the ever-changing world of activity) being appreciated simultaneously:

> It is well known that there exist in the nervous system many autonomous levels of function between which a system of coordination also exists. In the state of cosmic consciousness, two different levels of organization in the nervous system function simultaneously while maintaining their separate identities. By virtue of this anatomical separation of function, it becomes possible for transcendental consciousness to co-exist with the waking state of consciousness and with the dreaming and sleeping states of consciousness.[26]

With the awareness permanently established in pure consciousness, the individual is identified with that level of life which Maharishi describes as the "Government of Nature"—that level which governs the activity of the entire creation.[27] Any action is performed from this level of the Cosmic Self is life-supporting for the actor and his or her environment. Despite this, on the level of experience there is still a separation between the absolute and relative values of life. This apparent separation diminishes in the development of God Consciousness and Unity Consciousness.

God Consciousness and Unity Consciousness: The Sixth and Seventh States of Consciousness

Maharishi describes two further stages of human development, a sixth and seventh state of consciousness, which he terms God Consciousness or *Bhagavad Chetanā* and Unity Consciousness or *Brāhmi Sthiti* or *Brāhmi Chetanā*.[28] While in *Turiyatīt Chetanā* the unbounded nature of self-referral consciousness is experienced as separate from the relative boundaries of daily life, in *Bhagavad Chetanā* this distinction is increasingly diminished through refinement of perception. Maharishi explains that in order to develop God Consciousness the nervous system needs to be cultured further so that it comes to function in an integrated manner, and that this integration on the level of the nervous system results from refinement of the mind's functioning.[29]

The integration of the two styles of functioning of the nervous system occurs through extremely refined mental activity.

> In order to define activity of this quality [mental activity of ultimate refinement], we must analyse the whole range of activity. The activity of the organs of action is the most gross, the activity of the senses of perception is more refined, the mental activity of thought is finer still, and the activity of feeling and emotion is the finest of all. One could further classify different levels of quality in emotional activity, such as anger, fear, despair, happiness, reverence, service and love. The activity of devotion comprises the feelings of service, reverence and love, which are the most refined qualities of feeling. It is through the activity of devotion that cosmic consciousness develops into God-consciousness.[30]

As discussed previously, not only are there various levels of existence, but there are also specific levels or values of human activity and emotion.

Within the hierarchical range of human activity, the subtlest level of emotion—specifically feelings of service, reverence and love which make up the activity of devotion—plays the most significant role in the development to *Bhagavad Chetanā*. When constantly open to this activity, the required physiological integration occurs. In *Bhagavad Chetanā* perception moves, from the surface level of particular objects, in the direction of comprehending deeper and more subtle levels of matter;[31] the individual begins to appreciate the finer values of creation. The experience attained in *Turīyātīt Chetanā* is heightened or glorified through the ability to perceive the most refined or subtle value of objects of experience.

In a further stage of development, in the seventh state of consciousness called Unity Consciousness or *Brāhmi Sthiti*, the universal, transcendental value of the object of perception is appreciated and the object is found to be nothing other than self-referral consciousness. The experiencer and the object of experience, both brought to the infinite value of consciousness, are perceived as unified on the level of consciousness.

In this unified state of consciousness, Maharishi explains that "the experiencer and the object of experience have been brought to the same level of infinite value, and this encompasses the entire phenomenon of perception and action as well. The gulf between the knower and object of his knowing has been bridged."[32] The experience in unity consciousness or *Brahmī Chetanā* is encapsulated in an expression from Ṛk Veda which Maharishi translates as:

> दुरे दृशं गृहपतिं अथर्युम्
> *Dūre dṛśaṁ gṛhapatiṃ atharyum.*
> (*Ṛk Veda, 8.1.1*)

> The light of God, which was experienced within one's own Transcendental Consciousness, is found shining throughout the whole creation to the very farthest point.[33]

In this state the individual is able to cognize the infinite value of the object. The individual knows, directly on the level of his or her consciousness, the complete structure of reality and therefore has complete knowledge—the totality or Brahman;[34] and as Maharishi adds: "In this state, the full value of knowledge has been gained, and we can finally speak of complete knowledge."[35]

In Brahman Consciousness or Unity Consciousness everything is known to be the impulses of one's own consciousness; one has total knowledge. Total knowledge spans

> Knowledge of the universe to knowledge of totality, *Brahm* (the Self), which is the unified state (togetherness) of the knowledge of the universe, the knowledge of the Veda, and the knowledge of the Self—the blossoming of total knowledge in the Self.[36]

The expression *Ahaṃ Brahmāsmi,*[37] which Maharishi translates as "I am totality—I am singularity—I am self-referral consciousness,"[38] describes the identity of one who has risen to this state. Brahman means "the totality" or total knowledge of the full range of life.[39] Just as Brahman Consciousness is the

> Awakening of the pure nature of consciousness to its own self-referral reality—the unified reality of the diversified universe—which renders individual life to be a field of all possibilities—infinite organizing power of the Unified Field of Natural Law spontaneously upholding individual life.[40]

One who is living Brahman Consciousness can know anything, do anything and accomplish anything[41], and is living in accord with Natural Law. As a universal human being, he or she is able to express universal value in every thought, every word, and every action because Brahman—the Creative Intelligence of Nature—governs every aspect of their life. This phenomenon is described in Ṛk Veda as:

यातीनाम् ब्रह्मा भवति सारथिः ।

Yatīnāṁ Brahmā Bhavati Sārathiḥ.

(*Ṛk Veda, 1.158.6*)

"Those established in self-referral consciousness—Cosmic Intelligence—for them, Cosmic Intelligence, the Creator, *Brahmā*, is the charioteer, the administrator of all their actions."[42] The infinite organizing power of one's own Transcendental Consciousness "becomes the guiding light of every thought and action, promoting success in every undertaking and actualizing and spontaneously engaging the infinite organizing power of the Unified Field of Natural Law."[43]

This level of intelligence is referred to by Maharishi as the Light of *Brahm*, the basic light of life, the total light of Natural Law, the Light of the Self, Cosmic Creative Intelligence, *Mother Divine* or *Brāhmī Śakti*. Maharishi indicates that the term "Mother Divine" refers to the supreme Cosmic Creative Intelligence which, at this level, is the basis of all performance.[44] For those who are established on this level of awareness, the self-referral structuring dynamics of pure knowledge with its infinite organizing power, performs anything.

> This is the merger of diversity into unity: the whole reality, being self-referral, is visualized in terms of unity, pure wakefulness, where every aspect of diversity has been dissolved, and having dissolved all the variations of unity, the spirit of unity rejoices in its ultimate sovereignty. For eternity, there is nothing other than that one exalted, supreme sovereign Mother Divine, the source of creation—supreme Creative Intelligence in her magnanimity, supreme invincibility, totality, pure potentiality—the source of everything.[45]

Maharishi continues to point out that:

> This is the supreme intelligence that pervades all the specific areas of governing—all the governing dynamics of all the specific structuring dynamics contained within this generality of pure singularity. It is alliance with this level of intelligence that awakens the all-knowing, all-possible, infinite organizing power.[46]

According to Maharishi, this state of Brahman Consciousness can only be gained through Vedic Science:

> It is only through Vedic Science that one individual person can become a lively embodiment of Natural Law. That is what is known as the totality, Brahman. Unity consciousness in the midst of all the diversified structures of knowledge and all activities, performances, behavior, interchanges, and exchanges—all lively in one unity consciousness and unity consciousness lively in one human personality—that is the representative of Natural Law, Brahman Consciousness, the totality.[47]

The goal of enlightenment cannot be gained through affectation. It is developed from within, from the level of the individual's own consciousness. As Maharishi explains, devotion on the level of thinking and assuming "an attitude of feeling (mood-making)"[48] cannot create unity. Characterized by behavior spontaneously performed from the level of pure wakefulness and a physiology fully established in the value of the Veda, enlightenment naturally dawns through the practice of technologies of consciousness.

Knowledge is Different in Different States of Consciousness

In higher states of consciousness the individual is united with the source of creation—pure consciousness[49] but, as Maharishi teaches, "to rise from the waking state of consciousness to God-consciousness, one has to pass through the states of transcendental consciousness and cosmic consciousness."[50] One state leads to another—from waking state, to Transcendental Consciousness, Cosmic Consciousness, God Consciousness, and, ultimately, Unity Consciousness.

Maharishi explains that these states of consciousness are very different from one another; just as they have their own particular style of neurophysiological functioning they also have their own characteristic knowledge:

> They are as different from one another as spectacles of different colors through which the same view looks different. When the same object is cognized in different states of consciousness, its values are differently appreciated. Life is appreciated differently at each different level of consciousness.[51]

Here the term "cognition" refers to the direct perception and knowledge of an object. The object perceived in Cosmic Consciousness appears different to the same object cognized in Brahman Consciousness. In the latter case, the object is seen and known to be self-referral consciousness. In this sense, knowledge can be said to be different according to different states of consciousness.

Whereas "the superficial aspect of knowledge is knowing and understanding," Maharishi explains that "the real nature of knowledge is the state of knowingness, the state of pure consciousness"[52]—gained in Transcendental Consciousness. Transcendental Consciousness represents the real nature of knowledge—the absolute state of knowledge where the knower, known and process of knowing are all consciousness, all are "one solid mass of knowledge."[53] When absolute knowledge dawns in Transcendental Consciousness, the basis for reliable knowledge is gained. Maharishi emphasizes that in the relative states of waking, dreaming and sleeping consciousness, knowledge is unreliable; it constantly changes. Even, in the waking state of consciousness, knowledge is subject to change. However, Maharishi Vedic Science holds that there is an absolute, reliable basis to all streams of knowledge; this is the universal knowledge of the knower himself which dawns in Transcendental Consciousness. This understanding contrasts with the postmodern theory of knowledge which is based only on a waking state view of knowledge and language.

For the artist, without universal knowledge—without a technology to unfold universal knowledge—there is no guarantee one can become a universal human being and create art that reflects universal value. There has to be a situation where reliable, universal knowledge—knowledge that is not dependent upon relative concerns or varying values of consciousness—can be gained. As Maharishi elucidates:

> When we consider consciousness, there are different states of consciousness. We are aware that consciousness changes from night to morning to noon to evening. Sometimes we're dull, sometimes asleep, sometimes very wide awake in the morning. Consciousness is a changing value. And knowledge changes with the changing value of consciousness.[54]

He goes on to explains that:

> Different states of consciousness have different values of knowledge. There has to be a way to have reliable knowledge. Otherwise, as the values of consciousness change, knowledge is apt to change. And in the changing spheres of knowledge one finds inconsistency, chaos, confusion. A stable level of consciousness is required, one that will not change, so that knowledge of an object could be reliable. A non-variable level of consciousness has to be structured in the level of one's awareness. There is a level of consciousness that can be made to be non-variable. That is Transcendental Consciousness, unbounded awareness.[55]

Only in Transcendental Consciousness is universal, non-changing, absolute knowledge available.

This universal status of knowledge remains established in higher states of consciousness but these other states have their own unique sphere of knowledge. As Maharishi points out, "Cosmic Consciousness is another state of knowledge where the transcendental, absolute field of pure consciousness—knowingness—is appreciated along with the relative, ever-changing world."[56] Knowledge in Cosmic Consciousness develops into God Consciousness. In God Consciousness there is knowledge of the finer values of creation along with the experience of knowingness. Finally in Unity Consciousness the separateness of the Self and activity dissolve into the state of Unity. The individual gains *complete knowledge* of the reality of life and perceives the object as impulses of his or her own self-referral consciousness.

While in Transcendental Consciousness (the state of pure, absolute knowledge) no *external* object of perception is involved (the knower, the known, and the process of knowing are the same infinite value of pure consciousness), in Unity Consciousness even the external object of perception is perceived as impulses of self-referral consciousness. This is the final step of knowledge in Brahman Consciousness, when complete knowledge dawns.

Vedic Science provides knowledge of, and the means to experience, all seven states of consciousness: "It is obvious that each state of consciousness has its own world. Maharishi Vedic Science is the complete science of all the seven states of consciousness and of all their corresponding worlds."[57] As we have seen, unlike other theories, this complete science identifies a state of *pure knowledge* or *absolute knowledge*—where the knower knows himself as pure, Transcendental Consciousness, a state of unchanging, reliable knowledge. This state of absolute knowledge is the foundation of the fifth, sixth and seventh states of consciousness. Only in Unity or Brahman Consciousness is the external object perceived as one's own self-referral consciousness; then one enjoys complete knowledge—where everything is seen in terms of the Self.

On the level of behavior, when one's awareness is established in absolute knowledge, the individual spontaneously acts according to Natural Law. With the support of the infinite organizing power of Natural Law knowledge is universal by nature and in application. This understanding of knowledge and its relationship to consciousness differs from relativist theories which propose that consciousness is formed through man-made language and cultural determinants. Only with this universal knowledge of the absolute, can the artist be a universal human being and create universal art. Maharishi explains that complete knowledge "is available in the field of pure intelligence, pure consciousness, pure wakefulness—Transcendental Consciousness, and that "Transcendental Meditation is the technology to develop pure consciousness, pure intelligence—the basis of **complete knowledge**."[58]

Perfection and the TM-Sidhi Program

While the Transcendental Meditation technique cultures the direct experience of pure consciousness, the TM-Sidhi program allows the individual to operate from this level and more rapidly develop higher states of consciousness and complete knowledge. As Maharishi elaborates, "the most simple human awareness is Transcendental Consciousness, gained through Transcendental Meditation, and the ability to function in that Transcendental Consciousness comes through the TM-Sidhi Program."[59] As with the Transcendental Meditation technique, the aim of the TM-Sidhi program is to attain higher states of consciousness:

> The TM-Sidhi Programme is an advanced aspect of the technology of Maharishi Vedic Science. It trains the individual to think and act from the level of Transcendental Consciousness, greatly enhancing the co-ordination between mind and body. The individual gains the ability to enliven Natural Law to support all avenues of life to fulfill his desires.[60]

The TM-Sidhi program not only promotes growth to higher states of consciousness but also generates a life-supporting or coherent influence in society and the environment. When practiced by the square root of one percent of a population, the TM-Sidhi program generates coherence for that population. Maharishi explains that, "coherence means togetherness—that is a situation in which differences cease to dominate and friendliness begins to reign."[61]

As described earlier, Maharishi teaches that in Unity Consciousness the individual can know anything, do anything right and accomplish anything because the impulses of one's consciousness are the impulses of Natural Law. Any desire and action emerges from the level of Natural Law and is therefore inherently supportive of the individual, society, and the environment. That desire is generated and fulfilled from the level of Nature's functioning. Maharishi refers to this phenomenon as "perfection in life"—balance in daily life through spontaneous right action which enjoys the full support of Natural Law. Right action is discussed further in Chapter 16. The term "*Sidhi*" means "perfection."[62] The quality of action, or perfection in life, is based on the alignment of individual intelligence with supreme Cosmic Intelligence."[63] While the practice of the TM-Sidhi program develops mind-body co-ordination and a refined nervous system free from stress and strain, any completely successful performance of this program requires perfect mind-body co-ordination. Through specific mental formulas or *Sūtras*, this program enables an individual to begin to operate from the field of pure consciousness, the level of nature's functioning and create a desired result:[64]

> The original Sanskrit meaning of 'sidhi' is 'perfection', and each of the TM-Sidhi procedures is a technique for producing perfection in one specific channel of the functioning of the mind and/or mind-body co-ordination. Thus, there are sidhi procedures to enhance the abilities of all the senses and of the organs of action, sidhis that develop internal abilities and emotional virtues, as well as sidhis pertaining to higher creative abilities such as being able to fly, or know the past and future. Maharishi has emphasized in his interpretation of the sidhis that their primary value is to develop enlightenment—self-realization or perfection. Patanjali describes the inner transformation of awareness as a means of establishing permanent wholeness of awareness—*kaivalya*—singularity.[65]

The TM-Sidhi program, "evolved by Maharishi from the *Rig Veda* and *Yoga Sutras* of Patanjali," is designed "to strengthen the ability of the nervous system to experience pure consciousness, while simultaneously developing one particular channel of mind-body co-ordination."[66] Thus, through the TM-Sidhi program experience and knowledge of Nature's creative mechanics can develop. Is there an simple analogy to indicate how this program works?

Psychophysiological Pathways—Expressions of Natural Law

As mentioned previously, Maharishi explains that developing mind-body co-ordination is like gaining access to the switchboard of nature. A switchboard is a central organizational site for channels of communication and activity. Similarly, while all the laws or "streams of organizing power in nature"[67] governing the universe reside within pure consciousness, they each govern different fields of excitation in nature. Gaining access to pure consciousness gives one access to the source of all the Laws of Nature. While these laws have their expression in the relative, changing aspects of life, Maharishi explains that "the absolute non-changing phase of life is inherent deep within them."[68] Each law embodies the status of the non-changing value of pure consciousness. Pure consciousness is not only the basis of creation but also the most fundamental level of human awareness; therefore, each law is an impulse of the individual's own consciousness. Thus, in the practice of the TM-Sidhi program, the individual gains access to the switchboard of Nature's functioning. Anything can be accomplished from there.

Furthermore, the individual's specific psychophysiological pathways are actually expressions of specific laws of nature emerging from pure consciousness.[69] This principle is corroborated by Nader's discovery (discussed in Part III)—where the Veda is shown to correspond to the human physiology. Due to this relationship between the individual's psychophysiological pathways and corresponding Laws of Nature, the TM-Sidhi program directly unfolds the ability to create specific phenomena or qualities from the level of pure consciousness by utilizing those Laws of Nature. Maharishi therefore states:

> The mechanics of the TM-Sidhi techniques can be understood in terms of enlivening different values of the laws of nature within consciousness. The total value of natural law is contained in unbounded awareness, and each TM-Sidhi technique exercises the mind to act in accordance with, or be in tune with, a specific aspect of natural law. The effect of the specific technique is simply the result of this attunement.[70]

It is only by functioning from the level of self-referral consciousness (the home of all the Laws of Nature) that it is possible to create a desired effect.[71] In fact, perfect mind-body co-ordination permits successful performance of the technique. But the successful performance of the TM-Sidhi program is, indeed, dependent upon the degree to which the individual is able to operate from this universal field. Put another way, the degree to which the *Sidhis* (the specific techniques of the

TM-Sidhi program) can be successfully performed, depends upon the degree to which pure, self-referral consciousness is established in individual awareness

Self-Referral Performance—Saṁyama

In Maharishi Vedic Science, the mechanics of the TM-Sidhi program are referred to as *Saṁyama*. *Saṁyama* involves the simultaneous application of three modes of awareness: *Dhāraṇa* or steadiness of mind, *Dhyāna* or transcending, and *Samādhi* or Transcendental Consciousness.[72] All three occur during the practice of the TM-Sidhi program, allowing the individual to actualize the Sidhi phenomenon. Maharishi discusses the performance of *Saṁyama* as "the process by which the junction point between the absolute, silent level of awareness and the relative, active states of awareness is enlivened within consciousness."[73] It takes place at the point where the active mind has become so subtle as to merge with the unboundedness of pure consciousness.

From this level, each TM-Sidhi technique enables the mind to function in accordance with a specific aspect of Natural Law[74] and the lively field of all possibilities is utilized in terms of specific impulses of consciousness. Maharishi further elaborates upon this phenomenon by quoting from the *Prajāpati Smṛti*:

> अहरहः सन्ध्यामुपसित
> वेदो नित्यमधीयताम् ।
> *Aharahaḥ sandhyām upasita*
> *Vedo nityam adhīyatām.*

This formula states, "devote yourself to the connecting point, to the junction point:" As Maharishi points out

> The junction point in its ultimate sense is the point of connection between the unmanifest and the manifesting process, the point where the value of consciousness gets transformed into matter and energy; where the immovable, non-changing starts to move and becomes converted into change.[75]

The TM-Sidhi program helps train the individual to operate from that level where "consciousness gets transformed into matter and energy," or the junction point—from where the "non-changing starts to move and becomes converted into change."[76]

As the self-referral process of consciousness is the basis of all action and all forms and phenomenon in creation, when generated from this level, Maharishi explains that a particular effect can be achieved by mere intention.

Skill in Action: Utilizing Nature's Principles

The TM-Sidhi program develops mind-body co-ordination. It can be appreciated as a breakthrough in the development of human potential. This kind of mind-body co-ordination demonstrates skill in action. Skill in action seems like a common phrase. Typically we think of athletes, dancers or artists as having this ability. But "skill in action" has a deeper significance in Maharishi Vedic Science. It refers to the principle of least action identified by physics—the ability to perform action with the least effort and maximum effectiveness.[77] Skillful action is evolutionary action or action in accord with Natural Law; it supports the individual, her family, society, the environment, and the entire universe. This kind of action occurs only when the individual operates from the silence of Transcendental Consciousness because, then, it is spontaneously computed from the level of the total organizing power of Natural Law.

Action in silence is action from the level of infinite correlation:

> The Principle of Least Action (Physics) is only realized on this level of action in SILENCE, where action yields maximum results with minimum effort. Minimum effort is available in silent wakefulness where consciousness is self-referral—where consciousness is the fully awake, fully alert field of the infinite organizing power of Natural Law. The full potential of intelligence is available in this quality of action in silence.[78]

This action in silence, Maharishi continues to explain:

> Is action from the level of infinite correlation—from the level of the 'field', where the total energy of Natural Law is utilized to fulfil the intention. Action propelled from this level of silence consumes least energy and utilizes the total organizing power of Natural Law (Principle of Least Action) to hit the target with maximum speed and least resistance.[79]

Indeed, when an individual engages in activity from the level of Transcendental Consciousness he or she utilizes the full potential of their brain physiology.[80]

Holistic Brain Functioning

Holistic brain functioning is referred to as use of the "brain reserve" which co-ordinates the senses and the self-referral functioning of the brain. Maharishi indicates that without the experience of Transcendental Consciousness this area of brain physiology is not accessed:

> Experience in the waking state of consciousness has its basis in the functioning of the five channels of physiological structure of the brain with reference to the

> sense of hearing, sense of sight, sense of taste, sense of touch, and sense of smell. At the same time it requires the functioning of the total brain physiology that co-ordinates all these five channels. This co-ordinating theme of the physiological network displays the supreme level of co-ordination from the physiology of the cortex, the seat of the self-referral state of consciousness. Those who do not experience Transcendental Consciousness through the Transcendental Meditation and TM-Sidhi Programme do not put this level of the physiology to function, they do not have access to the fourth state of consciousness—Transcendental Consciousness—which gives entry into higher states of consciousness leading to Brahman Consciousness, or Unity Consciousness, where the total creative potential of life is not ignored during the activity of intelligence in any specific area.[81]

Research indicates that those individuals who practice the Transcendental Meditation technique, and more specifically, those who practice the TM-Sidhi program, have access to the brain reserve—access to the holistic functioning of the brain whilst engaged in activity involving the five senses.[82] Over time, with the practice of the Transcendental Meditation technique and the TM-Sidhi program the individual begins to operate from the level of pure, self-referral consciousness, allowing the individual to rapidly develop toward higher states of consciousness. The increased holistic functioning of the brain and enhanced mind-body co-ordination achieved during the practice of the TM-Sidhi program is demonstrated in Maharishi's Yogic Flying technique.

Operation from the Unified Field of Natural Law—Yogic Flying

Yogic Flying one of the TM-Sidhi techniques described by the *Yogatattvo Upaniṣad* as developing in three stages: hopping; floating; and flying. The term Yogic Flying as Maharishi uses it, refers to all three stages. The increased mind-body co-ordination evidenced in Yogic Flying is enjoyed by virtue of the principle of *Saṁyama. Saṁyama* is evidenced in Yogic Flying when, through the application of a specific mental formula, the body lifts up from the ground:

> The demonstration of 'yogic flying' illustrates that the individual human nervous system has sufficient, integrated complexity to function at that level of the unified field. It proves the nervous system's capability to function at the level which all the laws of nature are unified. From this perspective, the brain wave coherence which is maximum during 'yogic flying' represents an upsurge of coherence from the level of the unified field itself.[83]

Self-referral performance, as noted above, is the basis of the practice of the TM-Sidhi program, where, as Maharishi explains, the transformation of self-referral consciousness from one phase to another occurs.[84] Maharishi emphasizes that the "proof of thought emerging from self-referral consciousness is that while practicing the *Flying Sūtra* during the TM-Sidhi Programme, the body lifts up and moves forward in the air."[85] How can we further comprehend this phenomenon?

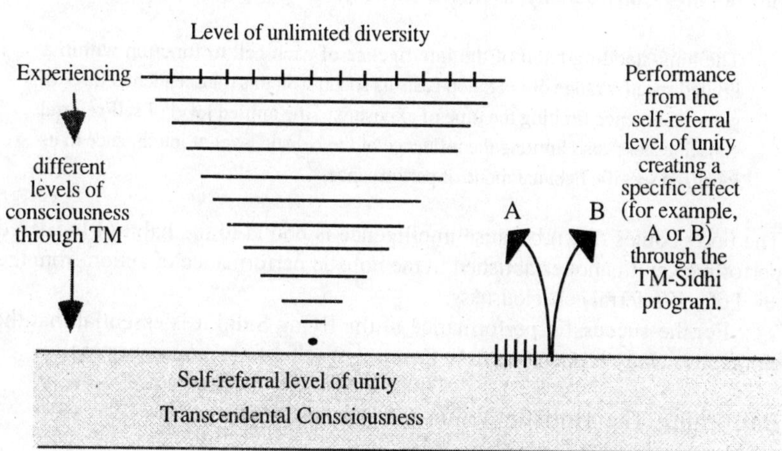

The Transcendental Meditation technique trains the mind settle down to the level of self-referral unity, the simplest form of awareness. The TM-Sidhi program trains the individual to operate from that level to create specific outcomes.

Maharishi explains that:

> When the all-pervading, unqualified level of intelligence, which is the common basis of all the different levels of intelligence of the different cells and parts of the body, is fully lively, then it enlivens the holistic intelligence of all the specific levels of intelligence in the whole physiology and puts them all to function under the irresistible supreme influence (command) of this all-pervading pure intelligence in the body; and because the conscious mind has accessed this level of intelligence with the intention to fly, every level of intelligence in the body under the indomitable influence of the command of pure intelligence to fly, every level of intelligence functioning in different parts of the body is spontaneously taken over by the overall intention to fly, and inevitably the body as a whole spontaneously and most naturally comes under the full influence of the intention

> of the *Sūtr* (*Flying Sūtr*)—the body lifts up. The phenomenon of the intention holds the body in the air.[86]

In the first phase of Yogic Flying (called hopping) the intelligence of the cells of the body still have the habit of functioning within a limited range—overshadowing the transcendental level of pure intelligence. This inhibits the time of exposure to that self-referral value of consciousness and the intelligence of the cells in the body—being in the habit of limited function—cannot sustain self-referral functioning. Consequently, as Maharishi states, the body does not remain afloat:

> The long-standing habit of the intelligence of each cell to function within a limited specific range of operation casts its shadow on this transcendental level of pure intelligence limiting the time of exposure to the unified level of self-referral consciousness, also limiting the influence of the holistic level of intelligence to its localized specific habitual mode of performance.[87]

The body comes down because intelligence is bound to the habit of localized performance; it is not established in the holistic performance of action from the level of self-referral consciousness.

For the successful performance of the flying Sidhi it is essential that the entire physiology is operating from the level of self-referral consciousness.

Enlivening The Holistic Value Of Puruṣottama

The holistic value of *Puruṣottama*, discussed in Chapter 5, is enlivened in the human physiology through the practice of the TM-Sidhi program. *Puruṣottama* is holistic rulership—the totality of consciousness within which the innumerable values of Saṁhitā are all infinitely correlated. It is the value of holistic *Prakṛti* of holistic *Puruṣa*—all values of silence and dynamism. As Maharishi outlines:

> When a Yogic Flyer, performing from the level of Transcendental Consciousness, experiences the lifting up of the body, he experiences two qualities of his own consciousness: dynamic (which lifts the body), and silent (which quietly witnesses the dynamism within its own nature). The phenomenon of Yogic Flying brings to experience three qualities of consciousness: dynamic (*Prakṛiti*), silent (*Purush*), and the witness of both (*Purushottam*).[88]

Not only does the individual experience these three values of consciousness, every cell in one's physiology is the site of the lively integration of the two values of *Puruṣa* and *Prakṛti* and every fiber of every cell is awake to the holistic value of the cell. In this sense, the whole body is enlivened, or awake to, the quality of the holistic intelligence of *Puruṣottama*—that quality of intelligence enlivened in the physiology of the Yogic Flyer. As Maharishi goes on to explain:

> Enlivenment of all *Prakṛiti* and *Purush* qualities of intelligence of the innumerable cells of the physiology is the basis of the lively integration of the two qualities of intelligence present within each cell; each cell becomes fully enlivened—the total intelligence of the physiology of each cell is fully integrated with the intelligence of each grain of the cell physiology (cell membrane)—every fiber of the cell wakes up in the total intelligence of the holistic value of the cell. This being the situation regarding every cell in the body, the whole body wakes up in the quality of holistic intelligence—the *Purush* and *Prakṛiti* value of each cell become the parts of the grand *Purush* and *Prakṛiti* value—the whole body is awake in the quality of supreme *Purush* and supreme *Prakṛiti—Purushottam*. This is the grand awakening of the *Purushottam* quality of intelligence in the physiology of everyone.[89]

The evidence of this enlivenment of *Puruṣottama* in the individual physiology is that complete mind-body co-ordination which results in the Yogic Flying practice itself. It is the integration of consciousness and the physiology which generates "supreme mind-body co-ordination—that level of consciousness which witnesses both *Prakṛiti* and *Purush,*" the total infinite organizing power of Natural Law.[90]

This total infinite organizing power of Natural Law is infinite dynamism and infinite silence at the same time. *Puruṣottama* involves bi-directional intelligence, referred to by Maharishi as "lamp-at-the-door"[91]—the value of intelligence which illuminates "inside" and "outside." *Puruṣottama* is that quality of intelligence witnessing both silent *Puruṣa* and dynamic *Prakṛti* at the same time. *Puruṣottama* is total intelligence or *Brahma.* Maharishi points out that the quality of intelligence called *Puruṣottama* is available not only on the level of the individual—when the human mind is in its settled state (the self-referral state of Transcendental Consciousness)—but also available on the level of the universe. This is why a group of Yogic Flyers functioning from the level of Transcendental Consciousness, identifying with the level of *Puruṣottama* intelligence on the individual level and creating the phenomenon of group flying, generate the value of *Puruṣottama* in the intelligence of the whole group of Yogic Flyers:

> The phenomenon of Yogic Flying enlivens *Purushottam*, the Unified Field of all the Laws of Nature (*Parā Prakṛiti of Param Purush*); it enlivens the administration of the Unified Field of Natural Law; it enlivens the administration of *Purushottam*; it enlivens the administration of the Government of Nature; it enlivens Veda; it enlivens order in the universe—it transforms entropy into order.[92]

Maharishi elsewhere translates *Para* as the "transcendent";[93] hence, *Parā Prakṛti* is the Transcendental *Prakṛti* of *Param Puruṣa* or Transcendental *Puruṣa.* When a group practices the TM-Sidhi program of Yogic Flying together they collectively create an influence of *Puruṣottama* in the atmosphere and coherence is generated in society because *Puruṣottama* is that level of intelligence which contains all levels of intelligence—indeed the whole universe—within it. This effect of creating orderliness in the environment is documented by the scientific research on the collective effect of the practice of the TM-Sidhi program discussed further in the following chapter. Having discussed the technique and its effects, what is the subjective experience of this phenomenon?

Accounts of the Experience of Yogic Flying

Throughout history, there have been accounts of more than 200 individuals from various cultures—including the people of Europe, Asia, and the first nation peoples of North America and Australia—who could fly or levitate. Many of these individuals recorded having pleasant experiences during this phenomenon. Practitioners of the TM-Sidhi program and Yogic Flying technique report feelings of bliss, joy, and vitality, and of being "strong and invincible" and "integrated."[94] While the major of people would think of this phenomenon as unnatural, Maharishi emphasizes, the phenomena of the Sidhis, including the Yogic Flying technique, are completely normal and are simply the outcome of the mind-body co-ordination of the stress-free nervous system:

> The performance of the Sidhis, which in the days of ignorance were termed superhuman powers, is not superhuman. Everything is within the normal range of man's ability—to handle the whole of cosmic life is within the range of everyone's own nature, because it is the same nature. The gardener who handles the sap handles not only the pink of the flower, but the green of the leaf, the stem and all parts of the flower. So it is by handling our own nature that we handle the nature of anything, of everything.[95]

The performance of the Sidhis is not just a normal phenomenon, it is also beneficial to the practitioner and his our her environment. This holistic effect of the practice is well documented. As Maharishi indicates, the *Yoga Sūtras* state that negative trends in society can be neutralized through the coherence generated by the group practice of this technology, as the following expression states:

> तत् सन्निधौ वैरत्यागः ।
>
> *Tat sannidhau vairatyāgaḥ.*
>
> (*Yoga Sūtra*, 2.35)

This is severally translated by Maharishi as: 1) Conflicts get dissolved in the environment of Yogic Performance—integrated, balanced mind, 2) In the vicinity of the phenomenon of Yog, Yogic Flying, conflicting tendencies disappear. The unifying influence neutralizes the diversifying qualities in the area,[96] and, 3) In the vicinity of coherence (Yoga), hostile tendencies are eliminated.[97]

Research on the effect of the group practice of this technology shows reduced negative tendencies and increased positive trends in society. These techniques also facilitate research in consciousness[98]; the individual researches (experiences, cognizes, witnesses, operates from, develops and gains knowledge of) his or her own self-referral consciousness at the basis of creation.

> Research in consciousness requires experience of the whole field of consciousness, the whole range of activity of the mind, intellect, and ego—the Self—which are different levels of the ocean of consciousness.[99]

The practice of these technologies of consciousness also promotes success in action and spontaneous engagement of the infinite organizing power of Natural Law. As Maharishi points out, researching in the field of consciousness through Transcendental Meditation

> Enlivens the total potential of intelligence in human physiology, and trains the physiology to function in the most natural way, in the most orderly manner, according to Natural Law—daily experiencing self-referral consciousness in order that the infinite organizing power of one's own Transcendental Consciousness (one's own nature, one's own simplest form of awareness, the nature of one's Self) becomes the guiding light of every thought and action, promoting success in every undertaking and actualizing and spontaneously engaging the infinite organizing power of the Unified Field of Natural Law.[100]

In this way, Maharishi's Vedic technologies of consciousness provide the means for the development of perfection in the individual and society—where spontaneous administration becomes a natural part of life. Natural Law, governing from within individual and collective consciousness, promotes harmonious and life-enhancing trends.

The individual, a universal human being, can perform action from the level of Saṁhitā, total intelligence, the total potential of Natural Law called *Brahma.* As Maharishi points out, "activity promoted by pure consciousness is the activity upheld by the infinite organizing power of the Unified Field (Saṁhitā) of Natural Law."[101] Such activity, Maharishi explains:

> Is commonly known as 'support of Nature,' because not knowing the principle of success through one's action, one thinks that one is supported by powers outside oneself, but in fact the phenomenon of support of Nature is the phenomenon of one's own pure consciousness—self-referral consciousness.[102]

On one level, one could think of 'good luck' as Support of Nature; but this is not the entire picture. Support of Nature is the functioning of one's own self-referral consciousness—enhanced through the collective practice of the Transcendental Meditation and TM-Sidhi program.

These technologies allow the individual to experience and unfold higher states of consciousness enabling normal human abilities and action from the level of infinite creativity. This level of intelligence, a universal field of human awareness commonly missing from contemporary life, is described in Maharishi Vedic Science as beyond cultural difference—the source of creation, the source of diversity. This is why Maharishi Vedic technologies can help enable anyone to live life as a universal human being.

While the theory and practice of Maharishi's technologies of consciousness have been considered here, the following chapter introduces some of the scientific research on the effects of the individual and group practice of these techniques.

7

SCIENTIFIC RESEARCH ON MAHARISHI'S TECHNOLOGIES OF CONSCIOUSNESS

The practical value of Maharishi Vedic Science has been demonstrated by extensive empirical research on the benefits of the Transcendental Meditation technique, the TM-Sidhi program and Yogic Flying. More than 500 scientific research studies, conducted at over 214 different institutions in at least 27 countries over the past 40 years, show that these technologies of consciousness enhance and increase creativity.[1] Collectively, this research supports the principle that a unified field of pure consciousness exists and that regular experience of it promotes growth and development in many areas of life. Increased creativity and intelligence, improved health and quality of life, decreased negativity and increased positive tendencies in society have been shown to result from the practice of these technologies of consciousness.

The first empirical research on the Transcendental Meditation technique supported Maharishi's explanation in 1966 that the Transcendental Meditation technique produces a fourth style of psychophysiological functioning known as "restful alertness" or Transcendental Consciousness.[2] Following this initial research, many studies confirmed that the experience of Transcendental Consciousness is distinguishable from the commonly experienced states of waking, dreaming and sleeping. This fourth state of consciousness experienced by practitioners of the Transcendental Meditation technique has corresponding physiological changes: including respiration rate, enhanced alpha and theta EEG (electroencephalographic) power, coherence in frontal and central regions of the brain, and faster H-reflex recovery. Studies such as these have established clear evidence of a unique style of physiological functioning developed through the practice of the Transcendental Meditation technique. On the subjective, experiential level, research also reveals that this technique increases happiness and harmony in daily life[3]—providing evidence of the growth of specific qualities of pure consciousness and corroborating testimonies of "boundless infinitude, beautiful bliss, total silence."[4] When lived in daily life, these qualities can be expressed in art and have a profound, nourishing and uplifting effect on the viewer. Growth of pure consciousness, it seems, is indicated by increased cognitive development, increased perceptual ability and improved health.

Cognitive Development, Perceptual Ability and Health

As commonly accepted, creativity and intelligence are areas of concern for the arts. In the areas of cognitive development, studies suggests that technologies of consciousness can play a significant role in the development of human potential. For example, researchers found that subjects who practiced the Transcendental Meditation technique display: 1) increased creativity on measures of flexibility, originality and fluency in creative thought;[5] 2) superior synthetic and holistic thinking demonstrated by better spatial localization;[6] 3) enhanced tonal memory; increased intelligence and decreased neuroticism;[7] and 4) enhanced organizational ability of the mind—a quality important to memory and abstract thinking.[8]

In addition, research on field independence demonstrated that the practice of the Transcendental Meditation technique produces a shift in the quality of attention and perceptual style in the direction of increased perceptual acuity, increased field independence and ego-distance.[9]

Field independence is held to be a measure of an individual's part-to-whole awareness and is thought to refer to an analytic style of perception or an ability to perceive items as distinct from their background; field independence is displayed as the ability to simultaneously experience the discrete parts of a stimulus field and the overall context in which they appear and is valuable for the creative individual who is dealing constantly with part-to-whole relationships.[10] Pelletier suggests that increased field independence is indicative of improved pattern recognition and increased accuracy of perceptual judgment. It indicates the ability to focus on a specific area without losing broad comprehension.[11]

This ability in meditators, according to Maharishi, actually demonstrates developed consciousness:

> Scientific research has shown that through regular practice of the Transcendental Meditation and TM-Sidhi programme individuals grow in field independence. This means that when they are focusing sharply on any one area they do not naturally lose the broad comprehension of the total field of their concern.[12]

He continues to state that, "This means that while they are attending to any one part no other parts are left out of their consideration." With this understanding, one would expect that the artist, who is dealing with many levels of concern or many parts within the context of the creation of a "whole" work or performance, would benefit from increased field independence. Examining this principle, Lee Fergusson conducted studies analyzing the relationship between field independence, grade point average (GPA), and art achievement, in college fine art students who practiced the Transcendental Meditation technique and a non-meditating comparison group.[13] The meditating group showed significantly higher levels of field independence, apparently reflecting a greater ability to maintain broad comprehension while focusing on parts. Expanding the idea of field independence, Maharishi points out that in Vedic terminology field independence "conveys the characteristic quality of intelligence, which blossoms through the practice of Transcendental Meditation, and has its relevance in the word *Moksha*—freedom from boundaries."[14] *Mokṣa* here does not simply mean the freedom to choose or freedom in a general sense, but freedom as a state where the relative boundaries of life do not impinge upon or govern activity and experience. This definition extends Pandit's description of the Indian concept of *Mokṣa* discussed in Chapter 2. *Mokṣa*, life free of relative boundaries, is gained through Yog. Yog is not just the practice of specific postures, it is the state of Transcendental Consciousness experienced through the regular practice of the Transcendental Meditation technique. *Mokṣa*, a characteristic of enlightenment, is described as "liberation from all pain and sorrow through Yoga, or Union with the Supreme."[15] As will be discussed in Part V, art can have a value in helping to promote experience in the direction of transcendent.

According to Maharishi Vedic Science, not only can the artist enhance his part-to-whole awareness, but he can also gain freedom or *Mokṣa* through the practice of technologies of consciousness. Then the possibility of creating art which embodies the universal value of freedom can be realized. Visual culture may speak beyond cultural and historical contexts. Any artistic work requires skill and mental acumen to actualize conceptual initiatives in material form; skill implies mind-body coordination. The practice of the Transcendental Meditation technique has been found to produce both short- and long-term improvements in complex sensory-motor performance[16] and can be considered as a practical technique to enhance and develop perceptual ability applicable to the field of art. As noted earlier, in Maharishi Vedic Science, skill in action is defined as "performance conducted under the unifying influence of self-referral intelligence" or natural performance—performance "without stress or strain," "according to the evolutionary direction of Natural Law."[17] Gaining this type of skill should be advantageous to any individual.

Performance "without stress or strain" is evidenced in some of the research conducted on health and personality. For example, secondary symptoms of post-traumatic stress disorder were shown to decrease as a result of the practice of these technologies—measured by personality and health variables in Cambodian undergraduates.[18] In addition, college art students who practiced the Transcendental Meditation technique were generally healthier than non-meditating students.[19] Improved health, intelligence and creativity are all factors which are commonly appreciated to be valuable in the development of creative potential. For this reason alone, the practice of these technologies of consciousness can be valuable for artists. However, there is a broader application that is especially relevant to those who are concerned with art and social responsibility, collective consciousness and the environment.

Coherence in Mind-Body Co-Ordination through the Practice of the TM-Sidhi Program and Yogic Flying

A powerful method for developing consciousness, the TM-Sidhi program positively impacts individual and collective life. For example, with respect to individual mind-body co-ordination, studies show that during Yogic Flying individuals experience enhanced neurophysiological integration as measured by the degree of EEG coherence at the time when the body lifts up in the air.[20] The high degree of neurophysiological integration suggested by this study supports the explanation of improved mind-body coordination as the basis of the performance of Yogic Flying. Using a measure called "coherence" determined through a sophisticated computer analysis of brain wave data identifying episodes of highly synchronized brain wave activity from different parts of the brain, studies show a high level of synchrony across all areas of the brain during meditation in practitioners of the Transcendental Meditation technique. Furthermore, long-term meditators show higher levels of coherence; however, it is during the practice of the TM-Sidhi Yogic Flying technique that maximum coherence is seen. In addition, when comparing the effects of the same individuals voluntarily jumping or practicing Yogic Flying, researchers found that coherence occurred only during Yogic Flying. This result can be understood in the light of Maharishi's description of the performance of the flying *Sūtra* from the level of self-referral consciousness:

> From this measurement of total brain functioning we infer that during 'flying' the corresponding level of consciousness is in the self-referral, dynamic state, where consciousness is open to itself; and this state of fully awake, pure consciousness is stimulated by the intention of the *Sūtr*.[21]

Maharishi points out that it is "as if the unqualified, self-referral state of fully awake consciousness is qualified or coloured by the intention of the *Sūtr*."[22] EEG coherence can be said to correspond to the self-referral level of functioning of the brain during flying. The intention of the flying *Sūtra* appears to qualify the unqualified value of self-referral consciousness. While studies show increased mind-body co-ordination and EEG coherence as a result of the Transcendental Meditation technique and TM-Sidhi program, further research has documented the effect of these technologies on collective life.

Increasing Harmony in Society

Many artists and theorists suggest that art can: transform individual and collective consciousness, be socially responsible, and create balance in the environment. While these goals are worth pursuing, it can be argued that the practice of the TM-Sidhi program and Yogic Flying are the most powerful artistic tools for the realization of these goals.

As Maharishi explains, when a small fraction of a population practices the Transcendental Meditation technique the population displays more orderliness and increased quality of life; he comments that "the contentment and serenity gained through this action of meditation produce harmonious and life-supporting influences for the whole world."[23] When a group practice the TM-Sidhi program, an even smaller number is required to increase positivity and decrease negative trends.

As discussed earlier, Maharishi indicates that the principle of generating coherence in society is expressed in the *Yoga Sūtras* in the following phrase: In the vicinity of coherence or *Yoga* hostile tendencies are eliminated. As early as 1960, Maharishi explained that with the practice of the Transcendental Meditation technique by just 1% of a population positive trends would increase in that population. Since then, research has supported this prediction. When more than 1% of a city's population practice this technique, negative tendencies in that city, such as crime, sickness and conflicts decline, and positive tendencies are strengthened.[24] In keeping with scientific protocol, this phenomenon has been named the *Maharishi Effect.*

Maharishi discusses the basis of this phenomenon in terms of the *collective consciousness* of society, which he describes as the fundamental force governing the quality of social life. Although the term collective awareness is used in common parlance and by art critics,[25] here collective consciousness refers the wholeness of consciousness of a population. The quality of any collective consciousness relates to the degree of pure consciousness lively in the life of the people (as id discussed later on Part IV). Furthermore, each level of society,[26] Maharishi explains, has its own characteristic collective consciousness (such as family consciousness, community consciousness, city consciousness, state or provincial consciousness, national consciousness and world consciousness) and, just as the consciousness of an individual determines the quality of his thought, the collective consciousness of a social group has its own reality reflecting the level of consciousness of its individual members. In this context, Maharishi points out:

> As individual consciousness grows, collective consciousness rises; and as collective consciousness rises, individual consciousness grows. Individual consciousness is the basic unit of all levels of collective consciousness—family consciousness, community consciousness, national consciousness, and world consciousness—influencing them all and being in turn influenced by them.[27]

Coherence and order in collective consciousness indicate that the individuals are living more in accord with Natural Law or pure consciousness; the qualities of the Unified Field—including perfect balance and perfect order—are more lively within the group. The practical result of this is displayed in improved quality of life in society—measured by less traffic fatalities, less incidents of disease, a rise in stock market indices, more harmonious social behavior and peace among nations.[28]

This phenomenon is analogous to a law of physics. The Third Law of Thermodynamics demonstrates the creation of orderliness through reduction of activity or excitation in a system. The coherence exhibited by certain systems, such as superconductors, lasers and superfluids, can be understood as simply a manifestation of the quantum level of infinite correlation where everything is connected to everything else.[29] Even if a small fraction of the units of a system are acting in an orderly or coherent fashion a transition to orderly behavior in the system as a whole will spontaneously occur.[30] Similarly, during the practice of the Transcendental Meditation and TM-Sidhi program the mind settles down to its least excited state of awareness, the source of thought, and experiences an increased coherence in mind and body. When a critical number of individuals practice this technique simultaneously and within close proximity, that infinite correlation value of the unified field of Natural Law is stimulated. Orderliness increases in the environment and society. Like a wave coming in from the ocean on which everything bobs up and down together, the coherence generated by just a few people from their own self-referral consciousness,—the Unified Field of Natural Law—brings support of Natural Law to collective life.[31]

As Maharishi points out: "A universal principle in nature is that internally coherent systems possess the ability to repel external influences, while incoherent systems are easily penetrated by disorder from outside."[32] In keeping with this principle, Maharishi introduced the TM-Sidhi program in 1976, explaining that the effect of the group practice of this technology (where the group numbered only the square root of 1% of a population) would more effectively raise the level of positivity and coherence within the collective consciousness of that population. Called the *Extended Maharishi Effect*, this phenomenon has also been well documented in research studies performed around the world[33] and may be largely responsible for the positive trends in recent world events.[34] In fact, research showing a highly significant relationship between increases in the size of a coherence creating group at Maharishi University of Management and improvements in U.S.-Soviet relations[35] support this hypothesis for the United States.

Maharishi explains that with the group practice the TM-Sidhi program by the square root of one percent of a nation's population, national consciousness becomes integrated, cultural integrity is strengthened, and life is lived more in accord with Natural Law. The result is the development of self-sufficiency and an "invincible armor" for the nation—repelling any external negative influences.[36] In practicing this technology in sufficiently large groups the nation is able to maintain its traditions and culture while adapting to productive change. On the global level, Maharishi has pointed out that to ensure permanent world peace a "coherence creating group" equaling the square root of 1% of the world's population is required.[37] In this way, both the Transcendental Meditation technique and the TM-Sidhi program not only improve individual life but contribute significantly to global quality of life.

One important demonstration of the effectiveness of this technology occurred in 1993 when 4,000 coherence creating experts gathered together to collectively practice TM-Sidhi program in Washington D.C. (which then had the highest crime-rate of any capital city in the world). Preliminary research indicates that violent crime dropped in the city by at least 18% below the predicted levels for that time of the year.[38] In this way, research provides support for the existence and accessibility of a universal field of self-referral, pure consciousness and the positive benefits to individual and social life resulting from the individual and group practice of the Transcendental Meditation technique and the TM-Sidhi program. Through the practice of these technologies Maharishi explains that life on earth can be transformed from suffering and international conflict to mistake-free life, prosperity, harmony for all nations, and peace on earth.

With an understanding of the fundamental, universal nature of human consciousness, its self-referral dynamics, qualities and properties, and the availability of technologies to unfold experience and knowledge of this realm, a new paradigm is emerging for the development of art theory and practice.

PART III

THE VEDA AND THE VEDIC LITERATURE: THE COMPLETE DISCLOSURE OF NATURE'S CREATIVE MECHANICS

Creativity and its development can be said to be the foundation of artistic and cultural expression. If creativity has its basis in the universal functioning of Nature or Natural Law, complete knowledge of Nature's creative mechanics would be extremely valuable to the artist. With this knowledge infinite creativity could be accessed. From the perspective of Maharishi Vedic Science, creativity can be comprehended in terms of: the sequential unfoldment of the Veda and Vedic Literature, the dynamics of our own self-referral consciousness, and the intelligence which structures our own physiology. The evolution of the Veda and Vedic Literature is the unfoldment of Nature's creative mechanics—which, as introduced in Part II, can be cognized on the level of one's self-referral awareness.

Unlike contemporary theory, Maharishi Vedic Science holds that the Veda and the Vedic Literature are not just individually inspired texts but the expression of pure consciousness elaborating upon its own self-referral structure through sound or frequencies. The sounds of the Veda and the Vedic Literature *are* the expressions of our own Transcendental, self-referral consciousness. Consciousness, in knowing itself, is self-referral and generates the three-in-one structure of pure knowledge—creating an infinite frequency and the innumerable frequencies or sounds at the basis of creation.

These frequencies the sounds of the Veda and the Vedic Literature, Laws of Nature, identified in Maharishi Vedic Science as: *Ṛk Veda, Sāma Veda, Yajur-Veda, Atharva-Veda, Śikṣā, Kalp, Vyākaraṇ, Nirukt, Chhand, Jyotish, Nyāya, Vaiśeṣik, Sāṃkhya, Yoga, Karma Mīmāṁsā, Vedānt, Gandharva Veda, Dhanur-Veda, Sthāpatya Veda, Hārīta Saṁhitā, Bhel Saṁhitā, Kāśyap Saṁhitā, Charak Saṁhitā, Suśrut Saṁhitā, Vāgbhatt Saṁhitā, Mādhav Nidān Saṁhitā, Śārngadhar Saṁhitā, Bhāva Prakāś Saṁhitā, Upaniṣad, Āraṇyak, Brāhmaṇa, Itihās, Purāṇ, Smṛti, Ṛk Veda Prātiśākhya, Śukl-Yajur-Veda Prātiśākhya, Atharva Veda Prātiśākhya, Atharva Veda Prātiśākhya (Chaturadhyāyī), Kṛṣṇ-Yajur-Veda Prātiśākhya (Taittirīya), Sāma Veda Prātiśākhya (Puśpa Sūtram)*—and referred to as the 40 aspects of the Veda and the Vedic Literature.[1] These sounds are the perfect rhythm of the Veda which, containing those impulses of consciousness, have been orally preserved by Vedic pundits over time.[2]

As Maharishi points out, "Veda is not written by anyone; it is not a composition. It is the self-interacting rhythm of the Veda that is responsible for the perfect orderliness that we see in the activity of nature."[3]

The language of the Veda, Vedic Sanskrit—as recorded in the "books" of the Veda and the Vedic Literature—is the direct expression or embodiment of the self-referral mechanics of consciousness. Therefore, the relationship between the concept or sound-image and the sound is not arbitrary; in fact, each sound or expression (the syllables, words, lines (*Pādas*) and verses (*Ṛichās*) of the Veda) directly corresponds to its form. The specific frequency or impulse of consciousness is the basic reality of its form. Frequencies structure matter. Furthermore, the sounds of the Veda are the forms of sound that correspond to the physiology; as Maharishi indicates: "Sound has a form, form has a sound; form is physiology, sound is the frequency that structures physiology."[4] This principle has been vividly illustrated in the work of Dr. Tony Nader who has located the Veda and the Vedic Literature in the human physiology. In addition, while each expression can have various levels of meaning, the ultimate value of meaning—intimately related to its sound—is found on the level of self-referral, Transcendental Consciousness or *Ātmā.*

In his description of the Veda and the Vedic Literature, Maharishi identifies Ṛk Veda, the structure of pure knowledge, as the first, holistic aspect of all the 40 values listed above. He describes the other aspects of the Vedic Literature as containing all the Laws of Nature which govern the structuring dynamics of Natural Law.

Ṛk Veda is the first, holistic aspect; it is the three-in-one structure of pure knowledge which contains the infinite organizing power that governs the universe. It is the structure of self-referral consciousness and can be understood in terms of: 1) Saṁhitā of Ṛishi, Devatā and Chhandas; 2) the dynamic of infinity collapsing to its point value; 3) the interchange of silence and dynamism; 4) the flow and obstruction to flow of pure intelligence in terms of the "whirlpool" or spiraling dynamic within the infinite ocean of consciousness; 5) the relationship between its syllables (or expressions) and gaps, and the mechanics of the gap; 6) a self-referral *Maṇdala* or circular form; 7) its sequential elaboration into the Vedic Literature; 8) the 40 qualities of intelligence brought out by the Veda and Vedic Literature; 9) the self-referral loops which the Vedic Literature highlights in the structuring mechanics of Ṛk Veda, and, 10) the practical disciplines or knowledge that different aspects of the Vedic Literature unfold.

These details are contained within Maharishi's "uncreated commentary" or *Apaureṣeya Bhāṣya* —the unmanifest commentary of the Veda. As Maharishi explains, the Veda presents its own commentary on its own self-interacting dynamics; this commentary is heard on the level of self-referral consciousness. This is why the impulses or sounds of the Veda and the Vedic Literature are not considered as relative, linguistic utterances or inscriptions, but the actual frequencies of Natural Law governing creation—heard by anyone on the level of their own simplest form of awareness or Transcendental Consciousness.

This field of self-referral consciousness—the field of Natural Law—is the "sequentially progressive Vedic sequence"[5] or the sequence of sounds or frequencies in terms of the syllables and gaps of the Ṛk Veda and the Vedic Literature. While Ṛk Veda embodies the holistic value of Natural Law, Maharishi points out that through its self-referral performance it develops into the other aspects of the Vedic Literature—aspects of Natural Law or Laws of Nature involved in the structuring dynamics of Ṛk Veda. Ṛk Veda evolves into:

> Clusters of Natural Law, clusters of the holistic value of Natural Law—different specific systems, which basically inspire the activity of the self-referral holistic performance of Natural Law.[6]

In this sense, there is one holistic value of Natural Law which could be described as an aggregate of clusters or specific systems that promote the self-referral performance of Natural Law.

The entire play of Natural Law, the self-referral dynamics of consciousness, takes place on the ground of *Ātmā,* the Self. However, the source of the different areas of Natural Law taken together is the meeting point of unity and diversity which is simultaneously self-referral (with reference to Saṁhitā) and object-referral (with reference to Ṛishi, Devatā, and Chhandas).[7] As Maharishi explains, the different aspects of the Vedic Literature categorically express different modes of consciousness, "which constitute the structuring dynamics of Ṛk Veda"[8]. Ṛk Veda involves the entire Vedic Literature in the materialization of its structure.[9] Thus, Ṛk Veda is the compact form of the unmanifest frequencies of the Vedic Literature.

Dealing with Ṛk Veda as this self-referral structure, Chapter 8 is entitled: *Self-Referral Consciousness as the Structure of Ṛk Veda: The Holistic Value of Natural Law at the Basis of Creation*. This chapter describes how Ṛk Veda provides its own uncreated commentary or *Apauruṣeya Bhāṣya* in terms of the expressions of Ṛk Veda (the syllables, words, etc.) and the gaps between them. It also considers how Ṛk Veda unfolds progressively in packages of knowledge or Natural Law and how the Vedic Literature provides a further elaboration on the structure of pure knowledge—detailing the various relationships and interactions between Saṁhitā and Ṛishi, Devatā, and Chhandas.

Chapter 9, *The Maṇḍala Structure of Ṛk Veda,* goes deeper into the form and structure of the Veda—considering the relationship of the ten *Maṇḍalas* of Ṛk Veda in terms of consciousness. Due to the self-referral nature of consciousness, the evolution of the Vedic Literature unfolds in feedback loops of Ṛishi, Devatā, Chhandas and Chhandas, Devatā, Ṛishi. Each aspect of the Vedic Literature is a quality of intelligence; each highlights specific sets of Laws of Nature engaged in promoting values of Ṛishi, Devatā and Chhandas within Saṁhitā. These qualities of intelligence and values of Ṛishi, Devatā, Chhandas and Chhandas, Devatā, Ṛishi, are the structuring dynamics of self-referral consciousness.

Chapter 10, *The Forty Aspects of the Veda and the Vedic Literature and their Qualities of Intelligence: Impulses of Consciousness as the Structuring Mechanics of Ṛk Veda*, introduces the forty aspects, their specific qualities of intelligence, how they highlight the structuring mechanics of Ṛk Veda and their self-referral unfoldment in clusters or feedback loops in terms of Ṛishi, Devatā and Chhandas values. It also introduces the correspondence of these forty aspects to specific structures and functions in the physiology.

In order to examine the Veda and Vedic Literature in more detail, the subsequent chapters deal with the four Vedas and the different clusters of the Vedic Literature, including: Chapter 11, *The Absolute Values of Each of the Four Vedas: Ṛk, Sāma, Yajur, and Atharva Veda*, Chapter 12, *The Vedānga and the Darśana: The Expansion and Submergence of Self-Referral Consciousness and the Phenomenon of Cognition*, Chapter 13, *Upa-Veda: The 'Subordinate Veda' or Third Cluster of the Vedic Literature*, Chapter 14, *Āyur-Veda, Brāhmaṇa, and Prātiśākhya: The Final Three Clusters of Natural Law*. Maharishi's account of specific values of the Veda and the Vedic Literature and their role in the structuring dynamics of self-referral consciousness or Ṛk Veda reveals their universal significance, demonstrating that they can be appreciated as going beyond philosophical treatises or documents relating epics and legends.

This consideration of the Veda and Vedic Literature will be relevant to the discussion of history, tradition, and culture later in Part IV, the consideration of art and aesthetics in Part V, and the analysis of the Vāstusūtra Upaniṣad from the perspective of consciousness in Part VI.

8

SELF-REFERRAL CONSCIOUSNESS AS THE STRUCTURE OF ṚK VEDA: THE HOLISTIC VALUE OF NATURAL LAW AT THE BASIS OF CREATION

According to Maharishi Vedic Science, Ṛk Veda is the seed of the whole universe. The structure of Ṛk Veda has within it, in seed form, the complete knowledge of all the Laws of Nature which govern the activities of the different solar systems, galaxies, and all the evolutionary processes, forms and phenomena in the universe. Ṛk Veda can be understood as the encyclopedia of complete knowledge whose meaning is ultimately contained in its structure. It is the first unmanifest expression of consciousness—the fundamental structure which gives rise to the vast universe and all of life. It is the unified state—Saṁhitā—of all the Laws of Nature that structure creation. All the Laws of Nature relate to the three fundamental values of intelligence, fundamental values of the universe, as introduced in Chapter 5, called Ṛishi, Devatā, and Chhandas.

Discussed earlier, self-referral consciousness includes both the unifying and diversifying aspect of consciousness; it comprises all the Laws of Nature considered together and separately. Ṛk Veda is that value of self-referral consciousness that contains all of the Laws of Nature together while the rest of the Vedic Literature considers specific sets of Laws. As Maharishi explains: "Ṛk Ved is the consideration of all the Laws of Nature together in their unified state, whereas every other aspect of the Vedic Literature considers every set of laws with reference to Ṛishi, Devatā, Chhandas, separately."[1] Ṛk Veda is the total potential of Natural Law with reference to the unified qualities of Ṛishi, Devatā and Chhandas within the nature of Saṁhitā—that level of consciousness constituting the structuring dynamics of the Constitution of the Universe with reference to the holistic quality of consciousness.[2]

It is the first aspect of the Vedic Literature and embodies the totality of Natural Law and all other aspects of the Vedic Literature. In order to comprehend this abstract reality this chapter presents Maharishi's account of the nature of Ṛk Veda—which is essentially the structure of our own self-referral consciousness. In so doing, it provides a description of the mechanics, structure and sequential unfoldment of this abstract, field of consciousness—underlying our experience, notions, and experience of individual and social consciousness.

Ṛk Veda: Absolute Administration

As Maharishi indicates, the process of the evolution of consciousness, as discussed in Chapter 5, occurs by virtue of the self-referral nature of consciousness which, through the phenomenon of absolute administration, harmonizes the principle of difference or duality:

> Absolute consciousness is the phenomenon of holding together the two opposite values—singularity (togetherness) of diversity (observer, process of observation, and observed)—holding together singularity and diversity. Administration is the phenomenon of integrating opposite values. The reality of absolute administration is stability in its silent, dynamic structure. It is silent, it is dynamic; it is unity, it is diversity; it is connectedness and at the same time it is disconnectedness. In the process of expansion of the ever-expanding universe, it is unifying at the same time it is diversifying—it is obviously diversifying but basically unifying—maintaining diversity in a unified state.
>
> Holding together opposite values is the nature of absolute administration; holding together opposite values is the nature of perfect administration, ideal administration. This is the ideal administration at the basis of all creation. In this we have the display of infinite organizing power—opposite values held together. This value of the infinite organizing power of Natural Law is completely available in the first book of creation, Ṛk Ved, and its allied Vedic Literature; and in this scientific age it has been glimpsed by modern science in the Unified Field Theories of Quantum Physics.[3]

Self-referral consciousness is the only level from which ideal or absolute administration can be achieved, because it is the only level capable of sustaining these opposite values. This is the dominion of absolute administration.

In the field of contemporary theory, the term "absolute administration" would be deemed an impossibility but in Maharishi Vedic Science absolute administration reveals and defines the reality of consciousness. It denotes the fundamental reality of every individual's self-referral awareness, the capacity to simultaneously entertain opposites—infinity and point, absolute silence and infinite dynamism, Saṁhitā and Ṛishi, Devatā and Chhandas, singularity and diversity, self-referral and object referral—the capacity to entertain difference on the ground of unity. The term absolute administration, therefore, includes all values of unity and difference.

In addition, while it is within the nature of pure consciousness, the source of manifest creation, to hold together opposites, it does not necessarily follow that everything should be categorized according to antithetical pairs (a grouping which postmodern theory usurps and evades). While Maharishi Vedic Science everything in creation can be categorized in terms of the three values of Ṛishi,

Devatā and Chhandas (and other values of consciousness), the diversity of creation is expressed in infinite variety and difference.

The Constitution of the Universe

The principle of holding together opposites demonstrates that absolute administration is the infinite organizing power of Natural Law (available in Ṛk Veda) where opposites are maintained in unity. As the Constitution of the Universe, Ṛk Veda is the structure of pure knowledge and infinite organizing power which governs the emergence of the different Laws of Nature; it is the kernel of the Vedic Literature and "the unity of diversified values."[4] This Saṁhitā quality of consciousness "holds the reins of all activity in the universe."[5]

> Ṛk Ved is the functioning Constitution of Creation, which is ceaselessly governing the entire creation. It illustrates how the self-referral state of pure intelligence evolves creation from within its unmanifest singularity; and how systematically it is organized from within itself, so that the infinite diversity of the universe is sustained in a unified state of absolute order and harmony. The structure of Ved in pure knowledge, pure intelligence, pure consciousness—total potential of Natural Law—is the all-time, eternal Constitution of Creation. Ṛk Ved is the total potential of the structure of pure knowledge and its infinite organizing power. From its eternal, self-referral, unified state of pure intelligence, the total potential of Natural Law organizes the system of emergence of different Laws of Nature.[6]

Ṛk Veda sustains the universe in a state of absolute order; for example, the movement of the planets creates the daily and seasonal cycles through which life evolves and flourishes. These cycles are governed by Natural Law. Maharishi goes on to point out that for the individual who is established in the singularity of fully awake, self-referral consciousness, the infinite organizing power of Natural Law governing existence, guides their action; this action is appropriate for the time, place, the individual, his or her culture, the environment and the universe. Nothing is outside of one's domain. Action from this level is completely life-supporting, infinitely creative, and guided by universal principles and governed by "perfect administration"—called the eternal Cosmic Administration.[7]

Perfect administration, Maharishi continues to explain, is administration or activity generated from the level of this Unified Field of Natural Law;[8] it is the phenomenon of knowledge or knowingness, the phenomenon of least action, the phenomenon of the self-interacting dynamics of the self-referral state of consciousness.

At this level unity is ruling itself. As expressed in the Upaniṣads, this principle states:

तत् ष्ट्वा तदेवानुप्राविशत् ।

Tat sṛṣṭvā tad evānuprāviśat.

(*Taittiīya Upaniṣad, 2.6.2*)

"The administrator is present in everything that he administers; the creator is present in every grain of creation."[9] As Maharishi teaches

> Being Saṁhitā of Ṛishi, Devatā and Chhandas, Ved, pure knowledge, is that self-sufficient level of intelligence, that is the creator, the process of creation, and creation at the same time. It is the material from which the creator creates and it is also at the same time the object of creation.[10]

This level of self-referral consciousness governs itself in all its various manifestations whether the individual is awake to this reality or not—just as the sun rises each morning whether we are awake to see it or not.

Governing Through the Principle of Least Action

From the perspective of Maharishi Vedic Science, Ṛk Veda presents, through the principle of least action, the governance of the Constitution of the Universe in the eternal language of Natural Law. Any individual can begin to perform action from this level of Nature's functioning. Any activity generated from this level occurs with the minimum expenditure of energy and greatest efficiency; it requires least effort because:

> The energy consumed in activity is simultaneously replenished from its source in eternal silence, which is pure wakefulness, absolute alertness, pure subjectivity, pure spirituality, self-referral state of consciousness—Transcendental Consciousness on the human level of existence—easily gained through my Transcendental Meditation. This level of intelligence is the Unified Field of Natural Law.[11]

Expended energy is automatically replenished from the level of pure consciousness, the self-referral state of one's own Transcendental Consciousness, which is an inexhaustible reservoir of creativity and intelligence or energy. There is no depletion of energy. Maharishi points out that Natural Law functions in this manner because the orderly dynamics of Nature are founded on the ground of eternal silence. Therefore, Natural action—action in accord with Natural Law or *Dharma*,—does not create any strain,[12] stress, or negative influence in the individual or the environment.

Natural Law or *Dharma* is the "invincible power of nature which upholds existence"; it "maintains evolution and forms the basis of cosmic life" by supporting all that is helpful, and discouraging all that is opposed, to evolution.[13] It is that absolute order which is eternally nourishing to all, governing the perfect administration of life.[14] *Dharmas*—the plural of *Dharma*—represent the different powers or Laws of Nature "upholding different avenues of the way of evolution."[15]

Dharmas take expression as different modes of activity which keep the whole stream of life in harmony so that life is lived in accord with *Dharma* and every aspect of life is properly balanced with every other aspect of life.[16] These Laws of Nature are different aspects or values of intelligence. Modes of Creative Intelligence or values of Ṛishi, Devatā, and Chhandas, they form the building blocks of creation at the unmanifest basis of creation; they are the various aspects of Vedic Literature or different values of consciousness in terms of Ṛishi, Devatā, Chhandas values, which uphold life everywhere.

The Blueprint of Creation

Ṛk Veda is the total potential of Natural Law or *Dharma*. It is the blueprint of creation, containing all the various Laws of Nature. It contains in one package the structure of the universe. Unlike a set of propositions about the nature of reality, Ṛk Veda actually presents the fundamentals which form the building blocks of creation, including the human physiology.[17] Ṛk Veda is eternal. It is the intelligence which structures every grain of creation.

All the streams of order in the universe, all the Laws of Nature, have their basis in the structure of Ṛk Veda. Ṛk Veda is universal, absolute. Neither foreign to anyone nor culturally specific, it is that level which gives rise to all times and places, to all of diversity. It is the universal reality of everyone's own self-referral consciousness and can be experienced by anyone through the Transcendental Meditation technique. Therefore, it is possible to maintain connectedness to this source of life at all times.

On the level of Ṛk Veda, all the diversified projections of self-referral consciousness maintain the connection to their source in consciousness. The diverse values of consciousness expressed in all the diverse aspects of creation (which are all a projection of self-referral consciousness) are unified in Saṁhitā, pure wakefulness:

> All fields of creation are the diverse projections of self-referral consciousness, and as they always maintain connectedness with their source, the entire field of diversity is the field of consciousness. That is why self-referral consciousness administering itself means the entire material universe is administered by consciousness.[18]

Maharishi Vedic Science also identifies how this field of self-referral consciousness gives rise to frequencies and material particles.

Audible Frequencies of Sound Give Rise to Matter

The process of evolution of consciousness, from unmanifest sound into audible frequencies of sound, gives rise to material particles. How can these frequencies be audible at this abstract level? These frequencies of sound can be heard by the individual on the level of self-referral awareness when consciousness is fully developed. While the self-referral value of awareness is the structure of Ṛk Veda, within this structure emerge specific quantified qualities of intelligence, inclusive of the *Tanmātrās*. Maharishi points out that the "five qualities of intelligence"[19] referred to as the *Tanmātrās*[20] come to the level of mind that experiences them as five *Vṛttis* or fluctuations of intelligence.[21]

The term *Vṛtti* means frequency—"frequency of self-referral consciousness,"[22] "frequency of self-interacting dynamics of consciousness,"[23] or "tendency."[24] Maharishi adds that the cognition of this self-referral process belongs to the intellect:

> This cognition belongs to the intellect and various *Vṛttis* of it, various fluctuations of it, come to the level of mind and the mind experiencing the five values. What are these five values? From where do they come? The five values we call *Tanmātra*: " *Tan*" and " *Mātra*," or "*Tat*" and " *Mātra*," means "the measure of That." " *Tat* " means Brahman. *Tat tvam asi*; Thou art Brahman. *Tanmātra*, is the measure of That. What measures it? The *Vṛttis*, the *Vṛttis* of wakefulness.
>
> But what are the *Vṛttis* of wakefulness and where are these *Vṛttis*? All the five *Vṛttis* are expressed in the names of the five *Mahābhūtās*, the five elements: *Ākāsha, Vāyu, Agni, Jal, Pṛthivi.* These five, the self-referral wakefulness, self-referral dynamics of consciousness, are the self-referral dynamics of intelligence, the intelligence which cognizes Saṁhitā and Ṛishi, Devatā and Chhandas.[25]

Whereas Maharishi explains that the *Tanmātrās* are the five qualities of intelligence or material particles, he indicates that the *Mahābhūtās* are the five elements out of which creation is constituted.[26]

> All areas of individual life—ego, intellect, mind; the five senses of perception and five of action; the five fundamental elements (*Mahābhūtās*), which constitute the individual physiology; and the five qualities of intelligence (*Tanmātrās*, fundamental to the five elements)—constitute the entire universe.[27]

With respect to the human physiology, the five *Tanmātrās* and five *Mahābhūtās* are referred to respectively as: i) the five principles underlying all material expressions—space (emptiness), gaseous state, heat (and light), fluidity, and solidity, and, ii) space, air, fire, water, and earth.

These ten aspects are described by Nader as referring to the various metabolic, lymphatic, endocrine processes and all that maintains the constancy of the internal milieu of the physiology.[28] Everything in the universe, including the human physiology, can be understood as made up of these qualities—the "measure" of Brahman or Totality.

Śruti is Heard on the Level of Consciousness

When the individual hears the frequencies of self-referral consciousness, that which is heard is called *Śruti*. As discussed earlier, due to the co-existence of one and three a move is created within consciousness. This move is the fluctuation of consciousness heard as sound or *Śruti*.[29] As Maharishi explains, in the cognition of Saṁhitā or self-referral consciousness, specificity emerges and sound is generated:

> In this cognition of Saṁhitā and, at the same time, Ṛishi, Devatā and Chhandas, there is the emergence of specificity [within] generality. So there is a move, and in that move, wherever there is a move, there is sound, there is *Śruti*.[30]

According to Maharishi *Śruti* is "that which is heard"[31] on the level of self-referral consciousness. The mechanics of transformation of "unity into diversity form the fundamental processes of creation, and these fundamental processes are displayed as *Shruti*, the sounds of the Veda and the Vedic Literature" which are heard on the level of consciousness.[32] Departing from the understanding provided by Coward,[33] this description of *Śruti* involves the experience and knowledge of consciousness:

> Since time immemorial, Veda has been known as *Shruti*, but no one has defined *Shruti* as श्रुत् (*Shrut*) इ (I)—श्रुत् (*Shrut*) means 'heard' and इ (I) means 'Devatā'. *Shruti* is the Devatā in the form of sound, the administrator of the universe in the form of sound—that which is totally heard—that which is heard for its specific tone without sacrificing its general, non-specific, holistic, absolute basis. It is specific and non-specific at the same time—it is specific, fully awake in its holistic quality, which is non-specific. It is the sound that is heard by itself; it is energy and intelligence at the same time, because its existence is on the level of self-referral consciousness.[34]

Here, Maharishi emphasizes that *Śruti* is the value of energy and intelligence, the Devatā, or administrator of the universe, in terms of sound which is heard by itself on the level of self-referral consciousness. The move of self-referral consciousness creates sound heard as *Śruti* and *Śruti* gives rise to *Viśwa*, the universe. In this move of consciousness the fundamental constituents of material creation are generated.

Fundamental Constituents of Creation—the Move of Consciousness

With this understanding, the cognition and emergence of the *Mahābhūtās* is further elucidated by Maharishi in terms of Saṁhitā observing itself as the knower, process of knowing, and known values of consciousness:

> In the nature of Saṁhitā, when Saṁhitā looks upon itself as the knower, knowing and known, there is a shift. There is some *Vāyu* there, some shift, some impulse, some frequency, some sound in the self-referral state. The self-referral state examining its own nature finds within itself these *Vṛttis,* the *Vṛttis* of *Vāyu,* and then the sound is carried through. It is not only an isolated sound because it is not an isolated move; it's the move of the Totality.[35]

Maharishi continues to explain that this move is

> A move of the total infinite field of the ocean of pure intelligence. It is the infinite field of the unbounded wakefulness, pure wakefulness, knowing itself, functioning within itself, reverberating within itself, in its singularity of Saṁhitā.[36]

In the shift or move of the total field of consciousness there is the frequency which has the characteristic of *Vāyu* or air. Similarly, within the self-referral functioning of consciousness, of Saṁhitā with its values of Ṛishi, Devatā, and Chhandas and their interaction, there is the value of unmanifest, eternal space.

Maharishi points out that it is this differentiation between and interaction among the values of Saṁhitā of Ṛishi, Devatā, and Chhandas that creates the elements:

> In the popping up of Ṛishi there is dynamism and that is the Devatā. In the dynamism there is overshadowing of silence, an overshadowing of Saṁhitā and popping up of Ṛishi, so altogether there is Ṛishi, Devatā and Chhandas, three values; Ṛishi, Devatā and Chhandas, three values functioning within themselves by virtue of some space. There is space; unboundedness, pure wakefulness, that is that eternal space, unbounded in its magnitude. This fully awake ocean of consciousness, fully awake ocean of intelligence, knowing itself as pure singularity of Saṁhitā has the diversified values of Ṛishi, Devatā and Chhandas but this diversification is in the unmanifest state because Saṁhitā is unmanifest. It is unmanifest because it is ever the same, but nevertheless it has space in itself.[37]

The diversification taking place within the unmanifest, is by virtue of eternal, unbounded space. In this, there is the quality of flow. Due to this quality of flow, or the fluctuation of *Vāyu*, there is friction, which, Maharishi goes on to state, causes warmth or heat. The value of warmth or heat is the value of *Agni*. *Agni*, in turn, has the property of melting; in melting it flows in the value of *Apa*, or water. *Apa* solidifies or crystallizes and forms the quality of *Pṛthivi*, or earth. As Maharishi teaches:

> Wherever there is flow there is friction. Along with sound there is some heat, some warmth, some *Agni.* Wherever there is *Agni* in the state of flow, the *Agni* melts whatever is there, so it gets melted, and that is intelligence. Intelligence melts to flow, and that flow is the value of *Apa*, the value of water, and once it begins to crystallize in crystals, it is *Pṛthivi.* Thus, *Ākāsha, Vāyu*, *Agni, Jal, Pṛthivi,* they are all the specific values in the non-specific eternally the same, pure awakening, pure wakefulness of self-referral consciousness. There are so many qualities and all these qualities are the qualities of pure wakefulness. It is in these five qualities, that the totality of pure intelligence is measured. These five qualities become the measure; they are the measure, the quantitative values of the pure, eternally the same, wakefulness. Quantitative we can say, qualitative we can say, but these five values they are known as *Tanmātrās* on the level of Ṛishi, Devatā and Chhandas.[38]

The five fundamental qualities of intelligence known as the *Tanmātrās,* are the measure or instrument of quantification of the total field of pure consciousness and come about due to the dynamic of Ṛishi, Devatā, and Chhandas. This dynamic is a fundamental property of self-referral consciousness, contained in the structure of Ṛk Veda.

In this context, Maharishi points out, the further values of *Sattva, Rajas*, and *Tamas* and *Vāta, Pitta*, and *Kapha* emerge from the three values of Ṛishi, Devatā, and Chhandas:

> From Ṛishi, Devatā and Chhandas, *Sattva, Rajas,* and *Tamas* qualities spring and from these five values on the same level, values of intelligence, values of consciousness, from these five come the five elements having the qualities of *Sattva*, *Rajas* and *Tamas* and these three values Ṛishi, Devatā and Chhandas in terms of *Vāta*, *Pitta*, and *Kapha,* and from here begins the whole creation.[39]

Sattva, Rajas, and *Tamas* are described elsewhere by Maharishi as the three *guṇas* which constitute three forces or tendencies which interact with each other; "The entire creation consists of the interplay of the three gunas—sattva, rajas and tamas—born of prakriti, or Nature."[40] *Prakṛti* is Creative Intelligence governing the process of evolution which involves *Rajo-guna*, required to create a spur, and *Sato-guna* and *Tamo-guna* to uphold the direction of movement.[41]

Vāta, Pitta, and *Kapha*, referred to in Maharishi Vedic Science as three *Prakṛtis* or *Doṣas* are principles or precipitated values of consciousness; these "principles of *Vāta, Pitta,* and *Kapha* correspond to Rishi, Devatā and Chhandas, respectively."[42] Furthermore, *Vāta Prakṛti* has the qualities of *Ākāsha* and *Vāyu*,

Pitta has the properties of *Agni* and *Apa* (also called *Jala*), and *Kapha* has the qualities of *Apa* and *Pṛthivi*; the whole of creation can also be categorized according to these three.[43] The principles of *Vāta, Pitta*, and *Kapha* are important to Āyur-Veda which is an aspect of the Vedic Literature and a branch of Maharishi Vedic Medicine. Through the detection of imbalance in *Doṣas* in the physiology health can be restored by creating balance at that level.

The five *Tanmātrās* or material particles, give rise to the sensory systems of the human physiology (i.e., hearing, sight, etc.) and the five elements. These inherent qualities of intelligence are the cause of the emergence of the quantified values of intelligence which form the elementary particles, sensory systems, and different aspects of the human physiology.[44] In presenting the *Tanmātrās* in the context of the modes of consciousness which arise in the TM-Sidhi program, physicist, John Hagelin, extends this discussion to the direct, subjective experience of the mechanics of self-referral consciousness.

Modes of Consciousness Identified as Subtle Elements

In his account of the parallel between fundamental quantum fields, the *Tanmātrās* and subjective experience during the TM-Sidhi program, Hagelin outlines the above dynamic progression in terms of the physics of five fundamental spin types at the level of quantum fields. In his analysis he locates a correspondence between objective structures and subjective experience:

> Of the numerous 'modes' of consciousness which arise in the context of the TM-Sidhi program, five correspond to 'objective' modes said to be responsible for material existence. These are the so-called 'subtle elements' or *tanmatras*.... (These tanmatras must be distinguished from the five 'gross elements' or *mahabhutas*, also called akasha, vayu, agni, etc., which have previously been identified with classical space-time and the four states of bulk matter, i.e. gaseous, plasma, liquid, and solid, respectively...). A very similar structure is observed within the framework of quantum field theory, where there are also five fundamental categories of quantum field or "spin types' consistent with relativistic causality and renormalizability, which are responsible for the entire material universe. These are the spin-2 graviton (responsible for space-time curvature and the force of gravity), the spin-3/2 gravitino (appearing only in the context of a supersymmetric field theory), spin-1 force fields, spin-1/2 matter fields, and the spin-0 Higgs fields responsible for symmetry breaking. There appears to be a striking correspondence between the five tanmatras and these quantum-mechanical spin types.[45]

Here, Hagelin identifies a correspondence between the categories of the quantum field and the *Tanmātrās* (subjective modes of consciousness arising in the TM-Sidhi program). He states that the pairings of: *Ākāsha* and *Vāyu* in *Vata Prakṛti* correspond to the unification of the spin-2 graviton and the spin-3/2 gravitino in the context of the *gravity superfield*. *Agni* and *Jala* in *Pitta Prakṛti* parallel the combination of spin-1 force fields and spin-1/2 "gauginos" in *gauge superfields*; and, *Apa* (or *Jala*) and *Pṛthivi* in *Kapha Prakṛti* correspond to the spin-1/2 matter fields and their spin-0 supersymmetric partners which give rise to *matter superfields.*[46]

From the side of physics, direct experience, and Maharishi Vedic Science, the fundamental constituents of creation can be known and understood. Essential constituents or qualities of consciousness correlate to particular quantum fields. It is the process of intelligence quantifying itself which gives rise to the fundamental material properties of creation. Matter is constituted of frequencies of consciousness which can be cognized by the fully awake awareness. As noted in Chapter 4, the understanding of the interconnectedness between so-called subjective and objective or inner and outer realms has been established by physics; for example, the only time electrons and other quanta manifest as particles is when they are "observed". However, it is Maharishi Vedic Science that presents the details of the frequencies at the basis of creation—expressed in Ṛk Veda and the Vedic Literature as the dynamics of transformation of self-referral consciousness.

As Maharishi states, "the material and non-material expressions of creation have specific frequencies (sounds). These fundamental frequencies, non-material values, are the sounds of the Vedic Literature."[47] The mechanics of transformation of self-referral consciousness evolving into the ever-expanding universe are "available to us in countable stages" in the structure of Ṛk Veda, brought out in Maharishi's *Apauruṣeya Bhāṣya*[48]—the uncreated commentary of this universal structure of consciousness at the basis of creation. While the general principles of how consciousness becomes matter have been touched upon, the precise mechanics of this process of unfoldment is elaborated in Maharishi's *Apauruṣeya Bhāṣya.*

The Uncreated Commentary of the Veda—Apauruṣeya Bhāṣya

According to Maharishi Vedic Science, the commentary of the Veda is not "authored" by anyone; Veda provides its own uncreated commentary through the syllables and the transformations within the gaps between each syllable or expression of the Vedic hymns. This is why Ṛk Veda is referred to as "uncreated commentary":

> "*Bhāshya*" means commentary, "*Apaurusheya*" means uncreated—self-generated—eternal; no space-time value can be allotted to it; no creator can be assigned to it. *Apaurusheya Bhāshya* means a commentary that is not written by anyone; *Apaurusheya Bhāshya* of Ṛk Ved means that Ṛk Ved has been cognized as the most complete, absolute expression of pure knowledge and its infinite organizing power.[49]

This timeless, eternal commentary of Ṛk Veda[50] presents the structure of Veda as the structure of absolute order. There are two aspects of Veda, the words and the gaps between them—referred to as the *Mantra* (words) and *Brāhmaṇa* (gaps) of the Veda.[51] The gaps are the structuring dynamics of the words; together they constitute Veda. The Veda actually provides its own commentary on its structure—the syllables, words, expressions of Ṛk Veda—and the transformations of the gaps between them.

While this phenomenon of self-commentary by the Veda is referred to as Maharishi's *Apauruṣeya Bhāṣya,* Maharishi emphasizes:

> I have not written any commentary on Ved, but I have found that everything is the expression of Ved and as such everything is the commentary of Ved; I wish to repeat, everything is the expression of Ved, starting from the structuring dynamics of Ved itself, as expressed in the Vedic Literature, which naturally proceeds in its spontaneous course of evolution expressing itself in the different values of material creation and in the whole ever-expanding universe.[52]

This reality of the structure and evolution of consciousness as the Veda, and everything in creation, is simply an expression of the unfoldment of consciousness. Here the term "evolution" refers to the progressive development of self-referral consciousness which unfolds by virtue of infinite frequency through various frequencies of sound and specific Laws of Nature, into matter. Maharishi's cognition reveals that the Veda is its own commentary—but that anyone can find the commentary of the Veda within the text of the Veda. The text is the sounds or *Śruti* of everyone's own self-referral consciousness.[53] The cognition of the uncreated commentary of the Veda is within the range of the everyone's own awareness.

Furthermore, Ṛk Veda unfolds discrete "packages" of knowledge—each containing totality. Each expression of Ṛk Veda, from the first letter, the first syllable, the first word, the first line, to the entire ten *Maṇdalas* or chapters, presents a complete package of knowledge of the total value of consciousness in ever more elaborated versions of itself. For example, Maharishi points out that the first letter of Ṛk Veda "A" contains the totality of consciousness—total knowledge. "A" represents the Self or *Ātmā*: "the first expression of Ṛk Veda अ (A), the totality of Ṛk Veda, indicates the self-referral state of consciousness, or intelligence, or the self-referral state of the Self—*Ātmā*—of everyone."[54] The first syllable "Ak" also contains the total expression of knowledge. In the same way, the first word of Ṛk Veda, "*Aknim*," brings out a more elaborated expression of total knowledge and the first *Pāda* or line of Ṛk Veda; "*Aknim ile purohitam*," encompasses a yet more elaborate expression of the totality of consciousness, and so on. The whole of Ṛk Veda itself is the compact expression of total knowledge. The Vedic Literature further unfolds the details of the structuring mechanics of Ṛk Veda; as Maharishi states, the entire Vedic Literature is a "commentary in its own right" which is the "total engineering of creation."[55]

Like a seed, a young plant and, then, the mature tree, at each stage of progression in its growth, the entire tree is contained. The whole of the Veda and the Vedic Literature is an elaboration of the dynamics contained within "A," the first letter, and "Ak," the first syllable, of Ṛk Veda—the expression of the infinite value of consciousness collapsing to its point value.

Ṛk Veda Emerging from Infinity and its Point

As introduced in Chapter 5, consciousness can be understood in terms of infinity and its own point or as an infinite field with innumerable point values. This dynamic can be described with respect to the first letter of Ṛk Veda, "A," which contains total knowledge of the range of consciousness from infinity to point. The sound of "A" is the holistic sound at the unmanifest basis of creation. It contains complete knowledge. This sound emerges from the relationship of infinity with its point within singularity. It is the flow of Ṛishi, Devatā, and Chhandas within Saṁhitā. As Maharishi explains, it is "the intellectually conceivable sound of the silent holistic dynamism of self-referral consciousness"[56]:

> The eternal basis of creation on this level of the holistic sound, अ (A), has been described as the tumultuous uproar (*Nāsadīya Sūkta—Ṛk Veda, 10. 129*) of the move of eternal void—the unmanifest holistic value of self-referral consciousness, and the consequent emergence of the holistic sound, अ (A); and in this process of evolution of consciousness, the breaking of the holistic sound, अ (A), into different frequencies, which constitute the structuring dynamics of the Veda.[57]

When it moves, the eternal void creates a tumultuous uproar—the emergence of the sound "A" and all the following diversified sounds. The holistic sound breaks, or diversifies, into different frequencies, different sounds (alphabets, vowels and consonants) which are the structuring dynamics of the Veda available in the different areas of the Vedic Literature.

The details of these structuring dynamics of Ṛk Veda are elaborated in Maharishi's *Apauruṣeya Bhāṣya*—disclosing how the sounds of the Veda reveal the form of the Veda, and how the transformation of one sound to another takes place in the gaps.

The Significance of Speech: "Ak" as the Total Potential of Natural Law

As introduced above, each aspect of the Veda, from the first letter, the first syllable, the first word, the first *Pāda* or line, the first *Ṛichā* or verse, to the first *Sūkta,* the *Maṇḍala*, and so forth, is the totality of consciousness in multiple elaborated versions. The first syllable of Ṛk Veda, अक् (Ak), contains the total expression of knowledge in seed form. Subsequent expressions contain more elaborated versions of complete knowledge.

Phonetically, these expressions of knowledge are highly significant. As Maharishi points out, अ (A) is pronounced with the full opening of the mouth and expresses the fullness of consciousness; क् (K) is the stop value of अ (A), which when pronounced requires the closing of the throat and expresses the cessation of sound. Maharishi explains that the syllable अक् (Ak) contains the expression of the total range of Natural Law from fullness to emptiness: अ (A) represents infinity and क् (K) its own point value. अक् (Ak) is the value of consciousness as infinity collapsing onto its own point:

> The pronunciation of अ (A) requires full opening of the mouth, indicating that अ (A) is the expression of the total value of speech. अ (A) presents unbounded totality, अ (A) is the total potential of speech. Pronunciation of क् (K) requires complete closing of the channels of speech (the throat). अ (A) fully opens the channels of speech; क् (K) closes the channels of speech. Full opening followed by full closing displays the phenomenon of collapse of the unbounded field (of speech) to the point value (of speech). The whole range of speech is in this collapse; all sounds are contained in this collapse, and all the mechanics of transformation of one sound into the other are also contained in this collapse.[58]

The entire range of speech is found to exist in the phenomenon of the collapse of consciousness from its infinite value into its point value. It can be said that the study of the phonetics of Veda essentially is the study of one's own consciousness.

In his description of the collapse of "Ak," Maharishi explains that the term "*Kṣara*" embodies the collapse taking place by virtue of "A," which is the totality of consciousness—the total field of Natural Law collapsing to its point value of "K," the quantified value of infinity. The total mechanics of transformation of consciousness, all the sounds and the transformations of one sound into another, are found in the collapse of अक् (Ak), the *Kṣara* of अक् (Ak), which occurs in the transcendental field of self-referral consciousness, the simplest form of human awareness.

Obviously speech is central to this understanding of consciousness and its expression in terms of sound. The actual formation of the sounds by the human nervous system involve the various transformations of consciousness—the Laws of Nature that structure sound and form. For this reason, the recitation of the sounds of the Veda and the Vedic Literature, according to Maharishi Vedic Science, has the effect of aligning individual consciousness with Natural Law (the universal field of self-referral consciousness) and the sequence through which consciousness manifests as form. In pronouncing these sounds the brain physiology is enlivened:

> The flow of the Vedic Text starts with अ (A). The pronunciation of अ (A), the holistic sound, first enlivens the whole brain physiology; every fibre of the brain wakes up; the intelligence in every fibre of the brain wakes up and moves in perfect synchrony with the intelligence of every other fibre. At this stage all the brain matter, the intelligence present within every fibre of the brain, is alert an two levels: (1) holistic (total) awareness of the total intelligence of the total brain physiology, and (2) within this holistic awakening of the intelligence of the brain is the most delicate activity of each fibre of the brain matter.[59]

In pronouncing and listening to the sounds of the Veda and the Vedic Literature the universal holistic value of consciousness is enlivened in the total brain physiology *and* in each fiber of the brain. This demonstrates the profound value of speech (with respect to the Veda and the Vedic Literature) and its importance for the brain physiology. Preliminary scientific research on the effects of reading the Vedic Literature has already been conducted at Maharishi University of Management, U.S.A., showing changes in the brain's functioning.

This perspective is the antithesis of contemporary theory (discussed in Chapter 3) where there is no transcendental value or physiological correlate to language and where writing or language is held to be more fundamental that speech. Although in deconstruction theory writing is thought of as any separation of the unitary cry into different parts or the neural traces in the brain (the "unitary cry" signifies Rousseau's concept of the origin and nature of primal verbal expression), deconstruction does not include a transcendental level of speech or meaning. There is no one-to-one relationship between signifier and signified (the concept and the sound-image).

It is interesting to further note that, according to Maharishi Vedic Science, when the Veda is cognized on the level of self-referral awareness, the actual form of the script can appear within consciousness. The frequencies appear as the words of the Veda and Vedic Literature. As Maharishi points out

> The structure of Veda, the sequential unfoldment of sound, which at the same time is the sequential unfoldment of the form (of the sound), is the sequential unfoldment of *Shruti*, that which is heard by self-referral consciousness, and *Darshana*, that which is seen by self-referral consciousness.[60]

The sounds of the Veda, the impulses of consciousness in the form of the script of the Veda, are "seen" (*Darśana*) on the level of self-referral consciousness by self-referral consciousness. These sounds structure the forms in creation. "All the material and non-material expressions of creation have specific frequencies (sounds). These fundamental frequencies, non-material values, are the sounds of the Vedic Literature."[61] Since these sounds are also the frequencies which structure the physiology and the universe, for the Veda and the Vedic Literature there is a correspondence between consciousness, speech, text, the physiology, and the entire creation.

Here अक् "Ak" has been discussed as the compact expression and form of Veda; the mechanics of Veda are contained in अक् "Ak." The entire structure of creation is contained in अक् "Ak;" अक् "Ak" is the form of the Veda. Maharishi explains that Veda also has a name which contains the dynamics of consciousness in its sound—this name is ऋक् Ṛk.

The Sound of "Ṛk": The Collapse of Dynamism from Infinity to Point

In his description of the nature of Ṛk Veda, Maharishi points out that while अक् (Ak)—the form of the Veda—is the collapse of silence, ऋक् (Ṛk)—the name of the Veda—is the collapse of dynamism.

Ṛk: Infinity Collapsing to its Point Value and the Collapse of Dynamism and Silence

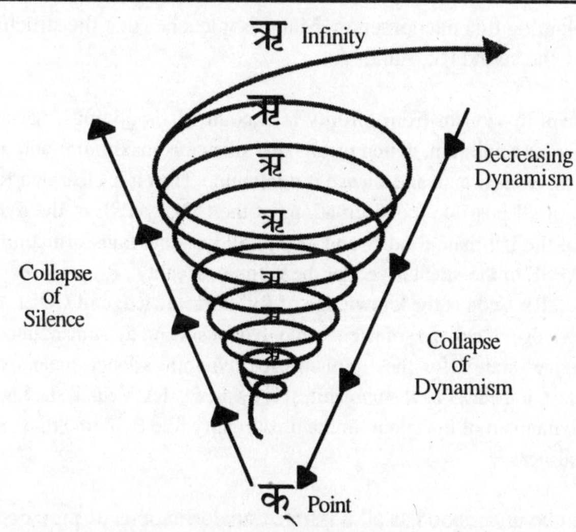

The sound of Ṛk is shown as the collapse of infinity, in a decrease of dynamism, spiraling to its point value. Ṛk represents all possible transformations from infinity to a point and from point to infinity, from dynamism to silence and silence to dynamism.

The actual sound of the name of Ṛk Veda (ऋक्, Ṛk) contains the entire dynamics of consciousness in terms of its transformation from infinity to a point.[62] Again, unlike the understanding of linguistic utterances in contemporary theory, Ṛk, here, literally embodies the dynamics of self-referral consciousness—in terms of dynamism collapsing to its point value. Illustrating this principle, Maharishi points out that the word Ṛk, when pronounced, displays dynamism from infinity to a point; the sound "ऋऋऋऋ" (ṚṚṚ) displays dynamism, whereas the sound क् (K) displays stop of dynamism. Infinity is expressed in the former. Its point value is expressed by the latter. In this way, "Ṛk Veda" means knowledge of Ṛk—knowledge of this dynamic relationship between consciousness as infinity and as a point. Whereas the form of the dynamics of this transformation is contained in the first syllable of Ṛk Veda—अक् (Ak), the relationship between "ऋऋऋऋ" (ṚṚṚ) and क् (K), as discussed above, displays the collapse of dynamism to its point through decreasing dynamism. As dynamism decreases, silence increases. Silence increases until dynamism reaches its minimum value of क (K) which displays maximum silence. Therefore, the structure of Ṛk displays the maximum value of dynamism in ऋ (Ṛ) and the maximum value of silence by क (K). At this level, Maharishi emphasizes, silence and dynamism are both unmanifest. The dynamic between silence and dynamism is an unmanifest activity displayed by Ṛk Veda.

In explaining this phenomenon, Maharishi teaches that the structure of Ṛk, as displayed by the sound Ṛk, stands for:

> Collapse of dynamism from infinity to a point. It is obvious that at क (K) dynamism is minimum, which means that silence is maximum; and at ऋ (Ṛ) dynamism is maximum and silence is minimum. Thus it is clear that Ṛk Veda is Veda of all possible transformations of the COLLAPSE of the dynamism aspect of the Ultimate Reality and also of all possible transformations of the COLLAPSE of the silent aspect of the Ultimate Reality. Ṛk presents dynamic silence. Ṛk Veda is the knowledge of Ṛk, the knowledge of COLLAPSE—the knowledge of collapse of silence into dynamism and dynamism into silence. As 'silence' stands for the 'unmanifest', dynamic silence means dynamic unmanifest, it means that the unmanifest is dynamic. Ṛk Veda is the knowledge of the dynamism of the silent, unmanifest reality, the field of Transcendental Consciousness.[63]

Ṛk Veda can be understood as all possible transformations of pure consciousness, the Ultimate Reality, in terms of dynamism and silence. There is both silence and dynamism together. Ṛk Veda is the knowledge of the dynamism of the silent, unmanifest reality of the field of pure Transcendental Consciousness. "Ṛk demonstrates potential of dynamism and potential of silence co-existing in the reality of the unmanifest transcendental reality at the source of creation."[64] The silence of the unmanifest is completely lively. Silence and dynamism co-exist and can be understood in terms of infinity and its point. It is important to highlight this phenomenon of consciousness. As philosophical interpretations have revealed, speculative propositions about an unmanifest realm do not include a means to experience and know this reality. Maharishi Vedic Science presents a vivid description of the unmanifest source of creation and a means to experience this reality in individual awareness. In fact, the syllable Ṛk, Maharishi points out, contains the field of pure knowledge associated with both theory and its applied aspect—pure knowledge and its infinite organizing power; it expresses the science and technology of pure consciousness.

In his description of Ṛk, Nader affirms that the whole range of possible human experience is expressed by the name "Ṛk;" 'Ṛ' represents reverberating dynamism or the range of all possible experience, and 'K' represents the point value of isolated moments of experience. Our perception involves the focus of attention of the subject onto an object (i.e., a sound or smell).[65] In this process the unbounded consciousness or *Ātmā* of the subject converges onto a point value (the object) revealing that the dynamics of Ṛk operate on the level of human experience.

Ultimately, knowledge of Ṛk is knowledge of the total range of human experience. It is knowledge of totality, knowledge of the Self (*Ātmā*) in terms of *Brahma*, the Totality—where everything in creation is known to be an expression of one's own self-referral consciousness. This state is the state of Brahman Consciousness discussed in Chapter 6. As Maharishi points out:

> Ṛk demonstrates the Ultimate reality in its self-referral state—total reality in its self-referral state. This reality of the Self is *Brahm*—अयं आत्मा ब्रह्म *Ayam Ātmā Brahma (Māndukya Upanishad, 2)*. Thus, Ṛk Veda is pure wakefulness—fully awake self-referral level of reality—singularity, totality, one unbounded ocean of consciousness in motion—and this is the reality of myself, yourself, and all this.[66]

Ṛk is the move of one's own self-referral consciousness and embodies the dynamic of silence and dynamism as infinity collapses to its point value. In sum, contrasting with contemporary language theory, Vedic language displays the reality of one's own self-referral awareness and demonstrates the significance of the Vedic terms.

In a further consideration of Maharishi's teaching about the nature of Ṛk, the collapse of infinity to its point value can also be understood in terms of Saṁhitā and Ṛishi, Devatā, and Chhandas values which create "Ṛks," "whirlpools" or spirals within consciousness.

Whirlpools Within the Infinite Field of Consciousness

As discussed in Chapter 5, consciousness can be described as an ocean with innumerable points. All these points are connected, like waves on the ocean. When the ocean stirs, it moves connecting its own point after point. Maharishi elaborates further on this aspect of consciousness by explaining that it is an infinite field of intelligence which, through its creative process, flows like a river. As mentioned previously, the flow is due to the wakeful quality of Ṛishi within pure consciousness and the obstruction to this flow is due the emergence of Ṛishi within Saṁhitā. This obstruction is referred to as Chhandas, the quality that hides. In this obstruction, just like the flow of a river when restricted, a "whirlpool" is created.

Due to the Ṛishi quality of consciousness within the nature of Saṁhitā, Saṁhitā cognizes or knows itself; the dynamism inherent within this phenomenon of cognition is the value of Devatā and Chhandas, in turn, is the hiding quality. This whole process, the flow of intelligence and the subsequent obstruction of that flow, is described by Maharishi as follows:

> It is the Chhandas value (within the self-interacting dynamics of Ṛishi, Devatā, and Chhandas, within the absolute singularity of Saṁhitā quality of consciousness) that obstructs the flow of the creative process as the Ṛishi quality emerges within the Saṁhitā quality of consciousness. What happens is that the process of emergence of Ṛishi, initiated by the Devatā (dynamism) quality of consciousness gets obstructed by Chhandas. It is like the flow of a river, when obstructed, creating a whirlpool. Thus it is clear that the intelligence quality of consciousness, at the Saṁhitā level of consciousness, has a built-in value of flow. The quality of flow is available within the nature of Saṁhitā, and within this structure of flow there is that quality that obstructs the flow, Chhandas. The flow is due to the wakeful quality of Ṛishi (that sees) by virtue of the dynamism of Devatā. Obstruction to flow, obstruction to the eternal continuum of the singularity of Saṁhitā, is due to the emergence of Ṛishi within the structure of Saṁhitā. The obstruction to flow is called Chhandas, the quality that hides.[67]

In this description of the flow of intelligence, the quality of flow inherent within Saṁhitā, the wakeful quality of Ṛishi (which sees or cognizes itself by virtue of the dynamism of Devatā) is responsible for the value of flow, but the emergence of Ṛishi within the eternal continuum (the singularity of Saṁhitā) causes obstruction. This obstruction is called Chhandas.

It is this obstruction of the flow of the eternal continuum of Saṁhitā, which creates "whirlpools" within the nature of Saṁhitā. While "flow" is due to "Ṛishi emerging within the Saṁhitā" and Devatā is involved "in this process of emergence of Ṛishi," the obstruction of flow is "provided by Chhandas inherent in the nature of Saṁhitā."[68] This, Maharishi continues to explain:

> Gives us a picture of the flow and obstruction to flow creating whirlpools within the nature of Saṁhitā level of consciousness. The sound of the whirlpool within the self-interacting dynamics of Ṛishi, Devatā, Chhandas is expressed by the syllable Ṛk.[69]

The sound of this self-interacting dynamics of self-referral consciousness, Ṛishi, Devatā, and Chhandas within Saṁhitā creating the "whirlpool," is expressed by the name of the Veda, Ṛk. This self-referral dynamic of Ṛishi, Devatā, and Chhandas within Saṁhitā creates the form of the Veda; "the name is Ṛk and the form (structure), present within the name, is the Saṁhitā of Ṛishi, Devatā, and Chhandas. Saṁhitā of Ṛishi, Devatā, and Chhandas is the form (or structure) of the Veda, whose name is Ṛk."[70]

Maharishi Vedic Science not only describes the details of "Ak" and Ṛk, in its whirlpool dynamic, but also outlines how the mechanics of transformation of consciousness into sound is available in the gaps between the syllables and words of the Vedic hymns.[71]

The Transformation and Structure of Organizing Power in the Gap

The gaps between each expression of Ṛk Veda are the transformation points for the dissolution of one sound and the emergence of the following sound. Therefore, the structuring dynamics of the sequential flow of the *Ṛichās* or verses can be located in the gap. The creative process whereby one syllable is transformed into another occurs in the silence of the gap.

Contemporary language theory also identifies a gap between the signifier and signified but this gap denies a direct correspondence between sound and meaning. It does not refer to a unmanifest realm of transformation. Maharishi Vedic Science reveals that sound and meaning are completely correspondent; the gap is the unmanifest realm of transformation between one sound and another, as each develops into the other in the evolution of sound. Maharishi explains that every syllable coming into being takes shape by virtue of the organizing power of pure knowledge functioning in the gap which precedes it.[72] The area of the gap is the unmanifest, silent value of speech; it is pure, self-referral consciousness. One sound dissolves into the pure state of self-referral consciousness. From there a new sound emerges. While the organizing power inherent in the first syllable dissolves into self-referral consciousness, the organizing power lively in the self-referral state of consciousness in the gap organizes the creation of the next syllable.

Maharishi explains that not only is this how the Veda and the Vedic Literature evolve but, because the Veda and the Vedic Literature are the structure and mechanics of self-referral consciousness at the basis of creation, it is how the entire manifest universe evolves. The universe is the expression of the organizing power inherent within this self-referral structure (the gaps between the syllables of the Veda):

> The structure of organizing power located in the gap between two syllables presents the unmanifest structure of the organizing power in the gap, and the syllables (Primordial Sounds) are the expressions of the manifest structure of the organizing power. The organizing power thus is seen moving in waves constituting the manifest and unmanifest, evolution and dissolution. The organizing power proceeds giving rise to the process of evolution and dissolution.[73]

The Vedic expressions represent the evolution and dissolution of various values of consciousness expressed in terms of frequencies or syllables of the Veda; these impulses structure the phenomenal world. The precise dynamics of the transformation in the gap between each syllable can be described in terms of: 1) silence and dynamism; 2) the values of Ṛishi, Devatā, and Chhandas; and 3) four stages of transformation in the gap.

The Four Stages of the Gap

According to Maharishi Vedic Science there are four values of transformation within the gap between one syllable and another—called *Pradhwaṁsābhāva*, *Atyantābhāva*, *Anyonyābhāva*, and *Prāgabhāva*. *Pradhwaṁsābhāva* is the value by which a sound dissolves into silence; this stage of silence is called *Atyantābhāva*. The next stage, *Anyonyābhāva*, is the value of dynamism. The emergence of the new sound is *Prāgabhāva*. While the value of silence within the gap, *Atyantābhāva*, is a silent point of all possibilities, the structuring dynamics of what happens in the gap, *Anyonyābhāva*, represents dynamism.

The Four Stages of the Gap

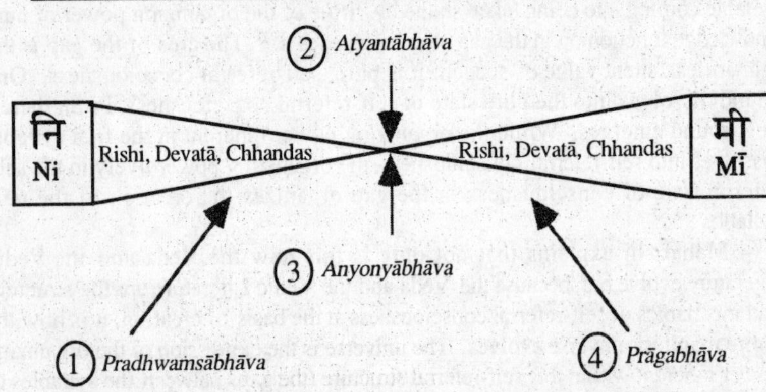

In this diagram the syllables "Ni" and Mī" are shown with the four transformations of the gap. Pradwaṁsābhavā denotes the dissolution of 'Ni,' Atyantābhāva is the value of silence, Anyonyābhāva is the dynamic value of consciousness, and Prāgabhāva is the emergence of the next sound or syllable which in this case is 'Mi.' The values of Ṛishi, Devatā and Chhandas are involved in this transformation from one sound to the next.

Maharishi indicates that because the dynamic between silence and dynamism is a self-referral loop, *Atyantābhāva* is *Anyonyābhāva*. *Atyantābhāva* illustrates "a self-referral loop of silence, and in this looping back of silence, silence is naturally expressed as dynamism. So the loop of silence is the loop of dynamism. This is how *Atyant-abhāv* is *Anyonya-abhāv*."[74] As in his description of the simultaneous co-existence of opposites of silence and dynamism on the level of self-referral consciousness, Maharishi maintains that this level of intelligence "which holds together *Atyant-abhāv* and *Anyonya-abhāv* is the totality—*Brahm*."[75] In this context, *Brahm* is located between silence and dynamism, the two aspect of *Ātmā*. As Maharishi states, "It [*Brahm*] can be seen as sandwiched between the two aspects of *Ātmā*—silence (*Atyant-abhāv*) and dynamism (*Anyonya-abhāv*)."[76]

He goes on to state that the value of *Atyantābhāva* (illustrating the silence of *Puruṣa*) is *Anyonyābhāva* (which demonstrates dynamism or *Prakṛti*.). At this level *Puruṣa* is correspondent with the quality of *Prakṛti*. These two qualities of intelligence or consciousness are eternally in the state of union at this level of the gap.[77] In the process of one sound dissolving and another emerging all four stages of the gap are involved. The sound or syllable collapses into the gap and dissolves into silence (*Pradhvaṁsābhāva*). A new sound is structured and emerges from the gap (*Prāgābhāva*).

Since the values of Ṛishi, Devatā, and Chhandas, are involved in this process, the gap can also be understood in terms of the self-referral dynamic of intelligence. "Another interesting feature of this analysis of the gap," Maharishi points out, "is the technology of consciousness—the display of the self-referral level of intelligence as the quality of Creative Intelligence."[78] As he continues to explain, this display of the self-referral level of intelligence is

> The display of the performance of silence (silent performance of Ṛishi) demonstrating Devatā within Ṛishi and displaying Chhandas (hiding quality of consciousness). When we focus on Ṛishi, Devatā becomes unavailable; when we focus on Devatā, Ṛishi becomes unavailable. This unavailability of Ṛishi of Devatā gives rise to the quality of Chhandas.[79]

Ṛishi, Devatā and Chhandas are all part of the transformation of one sound into another in the unmanifest mechanics of the gap. Along with this description of transformations within the gap between one syllable and the next, Maharishi unfolds details of specific divisions of Ṛk Veda in terms of his *Apauruṣeya Bhāṣya*.

Maharishi Vedic Science presents the Vedic language as the sequential unfoldment of consciousness—revealing that subsequent sounds elaborate on previous ones and that sounds comment on transformations within the gaps.

Divisions of Ṛk Veda—Sequentially Elaborated Values of Natural Law

As mentioned earlier, each sound, from the first sound of the first syllable of Ṛk Veda (अक् Ak) to the more elaborated syllables, words (अग्निम्, *Aknim*), *Pādas* or phrases (अक्निम् इले पुरोहितं, *Aknim ile purohitam*), *Ṛichās* (verses), the 192 *Sūktas* (hymns) and the ten *Maṇḍalas* (chapters) of Ṛk Veda, are an expression of the totality of Natural Law. They are complete and holistic structure of the Constitution of the Universe. Each expression of Ṛk Veda contains the totality of Natural Law.[80] Each complete expression is contained in the previous and provides a package of knowledge. As Maharishi points out:

> The ten *Mandals* of Ṛk Ved are available in the first *Mandal*; the first *Mandal* is available in the first *Sūkt*; the nine *Ṛichās* of the first *Sūkt* are contained in the first *Richā*; the three *Pad* of the first *Richā* are contained in the first *Pad*; the eight syllables of the first *Pad* are contained in the first syllable, अक् (Ak); अक् (Ak) is available in अ (A); अ (A) is the expression of the holistic value of speech, which is available in the *Ātmā*, the Self of everyone.[81]

The entire structure of Ṛk Veda (the syllables, verses, chapters and the gaps between each syllable, verse, etc.) is the embodiment of the eternal dynamism and silence at the basis of the infinite organizing power of Natural Law. The structure of Ṛk Veda unfolds according to a specific number and sequence—not only in terms of sound and Ṛishi, Devatā, and Chhandas values, but also the eight *Prakṛtis*.[82]

The Eight-Fold Collapse of Fullness Contained in 'Ak'

The structure of Ṛk Veda can be further understood in terms of multiples of Ṛishi, Devatā, and Chhandas and the eight *Prakṛtis* (*Ahaṃkāra* or ego, *Buddhi* or intellect, *Manas* or mind, *Ākāsha* or space, *Vāyu* or air, *Agni* or fire, *Jala* or water, and *Pṛthivi* or earth). These eight *Prakṛtis* arise as a result of the eight stages of collapse of fullness (the fullness of "A" to the emptiness or point value of fullness "K"). As mentioned above, "fullness" refers to the infinite value of consciousness and "emptiness" to the point value of consciousness.

The first syllable अक् (Ak), Maharishi teaches, contains the *Kṣare*, or collapse, of A—the collapse of fullness to emptiness. The nature of this collapse is elaborated by the first *Pada* of the second *Ṛichā* of the first *Maṇḍala* of Ṛk Veda. अक् (Ak) describes the collapse of fullness of consciousness, represented by अ (A), within itself to its own point value, represented by क् (K). This collapse—the eternal dynamics of consciousness knowing itself, occurs in eight stages. Through an eight-fold collapse the sound or syllable collapses into the gap (*Pradhvaṃsābhāva*) and becomes silence—the silent point value of all possibilities (*Ātyantābhāva*). The structuring dynamics of what happens in the gap (*Ānyonyābhāva*) takes place and the mechanics by which sound emerges (*Prāgabhāva*) unfolds in an eight-fold sequence.

Maharishi explains that the eight stages of collapse are separately elaborated in the eight syllables of the first *Pāda* of Ṛk Veda (as is illustrated by Nader[83]). In this way, the first eight syllables of the first *Pāda* of Ṛk Veda comment on the first syllable अक् (Ak). These eight syllables correspond to the eight *Prakṛtis* (*Ahaṁkāra*, *Buddhi*, *Manas*, *Ākāsha*, *Vāyu*, *Agni*, *Jala*, *Pṛthivi*)—the fundamental qualities of intelligence which constitute the divided nature of consciousness. Thus, the dynamics of अक् (Ak) are seen sequentially progressing into a "single straight line of pure knowledge, the first *Richā* or hymn of Ṛk Veda."[84]

The eight syllables of the first line of the first verse of Ṛk Veda unfold the eight values of *Ahaṁkāra*, *Buddhi*, *Manas*, *Ākāsha*, *Vāyu*, *Agni*, *Jala*, *Pṛthivi* with respect to the Ṛishi value of consciousness. The next eight syllables (syllables nine to 16) of Ṛk Veda unfold the *Ahaṁkāra*, *Buddhi*, *Manas*, *Ākāsha*, *Vāyu*, *Agni*, *Jala*, *Pṛthivi* values in terms of the Devatā quality of consciousness. The following eight syllables (syllables 17 to 24) unfold *Ahaṁkāra*, *Buddhi*, *Manas*, *Ākāsha*, *Vāyu*, *Agni*, *Jala*, *Pṛthivi* with reference to the Chhandas quality of consciousness—making a total of 24 different values.

The Dynamics of the Gap Elaborated in Subsequent Expressions

Emerging from the 24 unmanifest gaps or *Sandhi* between the 24 syllables of the first verse (first *Richā*) of Ṛk Veda, the corresponding 24 *Pādas* or lines of the next eight *Richās* (*Richās* two through nine) provide the next level of self-elaboration of Ṛk Veda. A another level of complexity can be seen in the relationship of the 192 gaps between the 192 syllables of *Richās* two through nine. These give rise to the corresponding 192 *Sūktas* (hymns) of the entire first *Maṇḍala* of Ṛk Veda.[85] There are striking parallels between this picture of the unfoldment of consciousness and the understanding of structures at the basis of matter and of the physiology discovered by modern science.

Ṛk Veda, Quantum Physics and DNA

According to Hagelin, there are eight fundamental degrees of freedom or modes of the string, in Superstring theory, which admit three interpretations. These three, defined as Hilbert Space, Operators and States,[86] have been correlated with the three values of Ṛishi, Devatā and Chhandas:

> With these interpretations afforded by the Quantum Principle, one obtains the identical 3 x 8 = 24-fold structure corresponding to the first *Richā* (verse) of Ṛk Veda. The next stage in the sequential elaboration of the self-interacting dynamics of the Unified Field is found in the free-fermionic formulation of the string in four dimensions, as quantified by a corresponding four-dimensional Lagrangian.... In this more expressed formalism, all bosonic degrees of freedom associated with the original, abstract space-time arena are fermionized, except for two right-moving and two left-moving coordinates needed to account for the four-dimensional structure of classical space-time geometry.

> This yields precisely 64 fermionic degrees of freedom intrinsic to the string itself.... When these 64 string fields are interpreted with respect to Hilbert Space, Operators, and States, this gives 3 x 64 = 192 fundamental expressions of Natural Law...in precise correspondence with the first *Sūkta* of Ṛk Veda.[87]

The same mathematical correspondence can be identified in the structure of the DNA in the physiology. DNA is expressed through 64 different varieties of codons in the genetic language with reference to three categories which have been identified as corresponding respectively to the values of Ṛishi, Devatā and Chhandas: 1) specific pieces of information, 2) the arrangement of information in a code, and 3) that which manifests in material structure. The 64 varieties of codons with reference to these three categories gives 192 units of DNA:

> The triplet code of the DNA is made up of these three bases—Ṛishi, Devatā, Chhandas—three modes or characteristic qualities intrinsic to their nature, making 64 x 3 = 192 units of DNA found throughout the length of the DNA. All the cells of the body are continually talking to each other through messengers (neuropeptides, transmitters, hormones,...), the communication network (these 192 units) of the DNA,...correspond to the fundamental expressions of Natural Law available in the 192 *Sūkta* of Ṛk Veda—self-referral fluctuations of consciousness in the self-interacting dynamics of the Unified Field of Natural Law.[88]

The "mathematical" principles of the structuring dynamics of the self-referral field of intelligence, therefore, seem to be expressed in quantum physics (identified by Unified Field theory), the intelligence of DNA itself, and in the structure of Ṛk Veda. This suggests that the same intelligence is involved in structuring individual consciousness, the universe and the physiology.

As seen above, Maharishi Vedic Science presents a holistic insight into the relationship of consciousness and matter. However, the ten *Maṇḍalas* of which Ṛk Veda is comprised can also be described in a further mathematical and sequential unfoldment of self-referral consciousness.

Maṇḍala Ten's 192 Sūktas Comment on the Gaps Between the 192 Sūktas of Maṇḍala One

Ṛk Veda is made up of ten *Maṇḍalas* that are not simply "chapters" of a text. The entire first *Maṇḍala* of Ṛk Veda comments on the mechanics of transformation inherent in the 192 gaps between the syllables of *Ṛichās* two through nine. These mechanics of transformation are the transformations of self-referral consciousness giving rise to syllables of sound—or expressions of self-referral consciousness. The 192 gaps between the 192 *Sūktas* of the first *Maṇḍala* give rise to the corresponding 192 *Sūktas* of the tenth *Mandala* of Ṛk Veda.

The first *Maṇḍala* consists of 191 *Sūktas* and one unmanifest or *Avyakta Sūkta*, discovered by Maharishi, which makes a total of 192 *Sūktas*. In this way, the circular, cyclical, eternal structure of the first *Maṇḍala* with its 192 *Sūktas* is complemented by the 192 syllables of the tenth *Maṇḍala*. The tenth *Mandala* fills, or comments on, the gaps of the first *Maṇḍala* such that the two comprise a complete embodiment of the transformations of consciousness in terms of sound and silence.[89] Since अक् (Ak) is the first expression of pure knowledge, each successive expression and gap in its specific orderly unfoldment provides more elaborated expressions or commentaries on that first syllable. As Maharishi points out:

> In my *Apaurusheya Bhāshya* I have mentioned that the ten *Mandals* of Ṛk Ved are available in the first *Mandal*; the first *Mandal* is available in the first *Sūkt*; the nine *Ṛichās* of the first *Sūkt* are contained in the first *Ṛichā*; the three *Pād* of the first *Ṛichā* are contained in the first *Pād*; the eight syllables of the first *Pād* are contained in the first syllable, अक् (Ak); अक् (Ak) is available in अ (A); अ (A), the continuous sound, stands for *Ātmā*—infinity; and क् (K), whose pronunciation stops the flow of speech, establishes the relationship between infinity and its point. अ (A) indicates *Ātmā* and क् (K) indicates the point of *Ātmā*.
>
> अक् (Ak) establishes the relationship between infinity and its point; अक् (Ak) is *Ak-kshar*, the *kshar* of अ (A), the collapse of अ (A) onto its own point, क् (K); अक् (Ak) expresses the collapse of infinity onto its own point; अक् (Ak) stands for the total dynamic potential of the Self of everyone, the *Ātmā* of everyone; अक् (Ak) expresses the relationship of अ (A) with its point क् (K), and in this dynamism of अक् (Ak) the total structure of Ved is lively.[90]

In this analysis, Maharishi not only discusses the deeper significance of the syllables and words of Ṛk Veda, but considers the dynamics within the gaps between each expression and how subsequent expressions comment on the previous gaps. The letter अ (A) "the first letter of Ṛk Ved, is the expression of the holistic value of Ṛk Ved, and also stands to express the *Ātmā*, the Self of everyone."[91] अ (A) contains all the transformations and expressions of sound. अ (A) is the value of infinity, one's own pure consciousness or *Ātmā*, and क् (K) is the point of *Ātmā*—revealing the dynamic and reality of one's own consciousness. The entire unfoldment of Veda in terms of syllables and gaps, *Mantra* and *Brāhmaṇa*, is contained in अक् (Ak)—the first syllable of Ṛk Veda.

While other commentaries miss the value of consciousness, the dynamics of the gaps, syllables, words and phrases of the Vedic hymns, Maharishi presents his profound cognition of the mechanics of self-referral consciousness. Other commentaries focus on words and phrases from a relative, waking state perspective—which is necessarily limited, unable to uncover the universal nature of these expressions. The description of the precise mechanics and structure of

Ṛk Veda, demonstrates the depth and scope of Maharishi Vedic Science and its importance for any artist wishing to unfold universal value in life and in art.

Pure knowledge, the self-referral structure of pure consciousness, is the fundamental structure of the artist's own awareness—that field of infinite creativity, the basis of all forms and phenomena, of all languages, cultures and artistic expression. But the description of the structure of Ṛk Veda does not end here. Fundamental to any understanding of the nature of Ṛk Veda as the self-referral dynamics of consciousness or pure knowledge, is its circular or *Maṇḍala* form.

9

THE MAṆDALA STRUCTURE OF ṚK VEDA

The ten *Maṇdalas* of Ṛk Veda are discrete aspects of self-referral consciousness. Therefore, they function in a self-referral loop. Due to this self-referral nature of consciousness, the Veda has a *Maṇdala* form. As Maharishi emphasizes, it is by virtue of the fact that it has the function of a self-referral loop, that the Veda has a circular form:

> All aspects of the Vedic Literature, in the process of structuring Veda, function together simultaneously; so the structure of Veda is structured by those mechanics whose dynamism is always self-referral. That is the reason why the structure of Veda is self-referral, and as such the structure is in a circular form, a *MAṆDALA* form. The obvious conclusion is that the structure of Veda is in the *Maṇdala* form, and each structure of the Vedic literature (being the structuring dynamics of Veda) is in a *Maṇdala* form—we call it a self-referral loop. Being in a circular form, a *Maṇdala* form, each aspect of the Vedic Literature breathes immortality, eternity.[1]

Both Ṛk Veda and the entire Vedic Literature have the same eternal, circular structure. As Maharishi points out, the circular form of the Veda also applies to the different aspects of the Vedic Literature:

> The theme of composition in the Vedic Literature is so orderly and profound that it can be best understood by a circle, which denotes the passage of never-ending eternity. Every aspect of the Vedic Literature (from the beginning to end of Nyāya, from the beginning to end of Vaisheshik, from the beginning to the end of Yoga, and likewise in every aspect of the Vedic Literature) has the same marvellous theme of orderly progression of knowledge as is present in the sequentially evolving Ṛk Veda.[2]

The *Maṇdala* form embodies the eternal, self-referral nature of consciousness. In addition to this, Maharishi indicates that from one perspective all of the ten *Maṇdalas* of Ṛk Veda arise from and are connected to one "point" which contains the total potential of Natural Law, as Lester notes:

> Each of the ten mandalas arises from and is connected to one central "point," which contains the total potential of natural law. Maharishi...explains that this total structure of the ten mandalas of *Rig Veda* is contained at each point of the universe. Thus, the total potential of natural law is available at every point of the universe.[3]

The first *Maṇḍala* contains the fullness of knowledge of Natural Law; it is the total potential of Natural Law, the seed of the entire Ṛk Veda.

As mentioned above, it has 192 *Sūktas* or parts, and represents Brahman or totality. (Each *Maṇḍala* ranges in its number of *Sūktas*—the average being approximately 100 *Sūktas* per *Maṇḍala*—and each *Sūkta* consists of between five and 50 verses; the entire Ṛk Veda consists of approximately 10,000 verses).

The Ten Maṇḍalas and Eight Prakṛtis

According to Maharishi Vedic Science, the second through to the ninth *Maṇḍalas* present the eight *Prakṛtis* or the eight fundamental qualities of intelligence which constitute the divided nature of pure consciousness.[4] As Lester states:

> In his description of the eternal structure of the Veda, Maharishi...has shown that each of the ten mandalas is primarily responsible for the manifestation of some specific aspect of natural law. The first mandala contains the fullness of knowledge of natural law and is considered as the seed of the entire *Rig Veda* and the entire functioning of natural law in the universe. The second through sixth mandalas contain the laws responsible for governing the five subtle elements, or *tanmatras*, forming the basis for all the physical aspects of the universe: *prithivi* (earth) tanmatra, *jala* (water) tanmatra, *agni* (fire) tanmatra, *vayu* (air) tanmatra, and *akasha* (space) tanmatra....The ten mandalas of *Rig Veda* exist eternally within the structure of the unified field and contain in seed form all the laws of nature responsible for governing all the processes in the universe....The seventh through tenth mandalas are concerned with the subjective aspects of life: mind, intellect, ego, and Self, respectively.[5]

Maṇḍalas two through to six contain the laws governing the five *Tanmātrās*, including: *Pṛthivi* (earth), *Jala* (water), *Agni* (fire), *Vāyu* (air), and, *Ākāsha* (space), respectively. The remaining three *Prakṛtis* (*Manas* or mind, *Buddhi* or intellect, and *Ahaṁkāra* or ego) are governed by the qualities of intelligence contained in *Maṇḍala* seven, eight, and nine, with *Maṇḍala* ten representing *Ātmā* or the Self. The ten *Maṇḍalas* thus contain the entire mechanics of self-referral consciousness in terms of the collapse of totality through eight stages of transformation.

As Maharishi has pointed out, the ten *Maṇḍalas* form the actual structure of the Ṛk Veda existing eternally within the unified field of self-referral consciousness. As discussed earlier, the "Ṛk," or "whirlpool" displays infinity collapsing to a point value. The *Maṇḍala* structure of Ṛk Veda can be seen to also embody the collapse of wholeness. Again, as noted earlier, the form of the Veda embodies the structure of the dynamics of self-referral consciousness; the first syllable of Ṛk Veda, अक्, "Ak", displays the form of self-referral consciousness—from totality expressed by अ, "A" to its point value of क्, "K" in a whirlpool of collapse.

The Maṇḍalas of Ṛk Veda as a Design Principle

The structure of Ṛk Veda in terms of its ten *Maṇḍalas* is used as the basic design of the ground plan of the Maharishi Center for Perfect Health and World Peace, in the city of Fairfield, U.S.A.[6] In reference to this design, Maharishi describes further the different *Maṇḍalas*; "the First and Tenth Mandalas display the self-interacting dynamics of *para,* and Mandala Two to Nine, these eight mandalas—Second, Third, Fourth, Fifth, Sixth, Seventh, Eighth, and Ninth—display the knowledge and organizing power of the eight *prakritis.*"[7] Maharishi continues to point out that:

> These eight prakritis we already know—*bhumir, apo, 'nalo, vayuh, kham, mano, buddhir eva cha, ahankara itiyam me bhinna prakritir ashtadha*. This is the eight-divided prakriti. The emergence of the eight *aparaprakritis* from the ground of *paraprakriti*, that is really the ground of real Fairfield.[8]

As noted earlier, *Para* means "transcendent" and *Prakṛti* means "nature."[9] *Paraprakṛti* is the ground of pure knowledge. Pure knowledge is always lively in its self-referral dynamics—the dynamics of *Paraprakṛti.* As Maharishi explains, "in the nature of paraprakriti is the dynamics of the eight-divided nature" of the eight *prakṛtis*."[10] As a site, Fairfield can be understood as the field of pure knowledge with its infinite organizing power which is fair, or impartially nourishing, to all.

In addition to this discussion and understanding of the ten *Maṇḍalas* of Ṛk Veda, the relationship between the first and tenth *Mandalas* is described in terms of different values of fullness and emptiness. Fullness refers to the total expression of consciousness or Natural Law and emptiness is its opposite.

The 192 Sūktas and Gaps of the First and Tenth Maṇḍalas and their Expression as Values of Fullness

The 192 *Sūktas* of the first *Maṇḍala* of Ṛk Veda progress from wholeness of consciousness as expressed in the first *Sūkta*, the value of fullness, to the value of emptiness in the opposite *Sūkta* on the *Maṇḍala* (*Sūkta* number 97). Accordingly, each *Sūkta* has its complementary value directly opposite to it on the circle (see the diagram below).

Then, from *Sūkta* 97, the *Sūktas* progress again to fullness, with the last *Sūkta* (number 192) expressing 100 percent fullness of Natural Law. Each *Maṇḍala* starts and ends with fullness—completing the circle. The first and last expression of any aspect of the Vedic Literature is a total expression of that value of consciousness it reveals and represents. As Maharishi points out, the first letter of Ṛk Veda अ (A) and the last letter इ (I) both represent wholeness; the first letter is the wholeness of silence, the last is the wholeness of dynamism.[11] In sum, the

192 *Sūktas* of the first *Maṇḍala* express the changing qualities of pure consciousness from fullness to emptiness back to fullness. To reiterate, *Maṇḍala* one, taking the *Sūktas* as progressing round a circle, starts from *Sūkta* one and finishing at the same point on the circle with *Sūkta* 192. In addition, each *Sūkta* has a counterpart opposite to it on the circle. *Sūkta* one represents fullness; its opposite (*Sūkta* 97) is the *Avyakta Sūkta* representing emptiness. This means that the combined sum of the first *Sūkta* (representing complete fullness) and the 97th *Sūkta* (representing emptiness) is the total value of fullness of pure consciousness or 100 percent Natural Law. The same total value is found when the value of any two *Sūktas* opposite each other on the circle are added.

Every *Sūkta* and its opposite on the *Maṇḍala* (for example, the 49th *Sūkta* and the 145th *Sūkta* and so on) combine to contain the entire range of Natural Law from fullness to emptiness:

> Maharishi's Apauruṣeya Bhāṣya explains the geometric arrangement of the suktas in Rik Veda. Maharishi points out that the 192 suktas of Rik Veda naturally exist in the form of a mandala....Each sukta is a mathematical quantity of fullness. The suktas express a mathematically calculable value of the full range of natural law, from fullness to emptiness. The first sukta is 100% fullness. Progressing clockwise around the mandala from the 1st to 97th sukta, this 100% value decreases incrementally. As the value of fullness of a sukta decreases by an increment, the value of emptiness of the sukta increases by that same increment....In the 97th sukta (Maharishi's *Avyakta* or unmanifest sukta), which is diametrically opposite the first sukta, the value of fullness is nil and the value of emptiness is 100%. Then, as this progression continues around the mandala from the 97th sukta to the 192nd sukta, fullness increases incrementally until the 100% value of the first sukta is once again reached.
>
> Maharishi...explains that the Avyakta sukta completes the perfect complementarity of Rik Veda's first mandala. With the Avyakta sukta the circular arrangement of suktas in the first mandala maintains the perfect balance and wholeness of pure consciousness. This is because each sukta has its complimentary sukta directly facing it on the other side of the circle.
>
> When two complementary suktas are added, they always create wholeness....Due to the perfect balance of opposite yet complimentary values among the suktas, Maharishi...points out that the mandala is an eternal circular cyclical structure of natural law and forms the fundamental origin of complementary relationships in nature and mathematics.[12]

The eternal, circular form of the *Maṇḍala* is not arbitrary; it is highly significant not merely because of its "geometry," but because this is, according to Maharishi Vedic Science, the nature and structure of self-referral consciousness—the basis of creation.

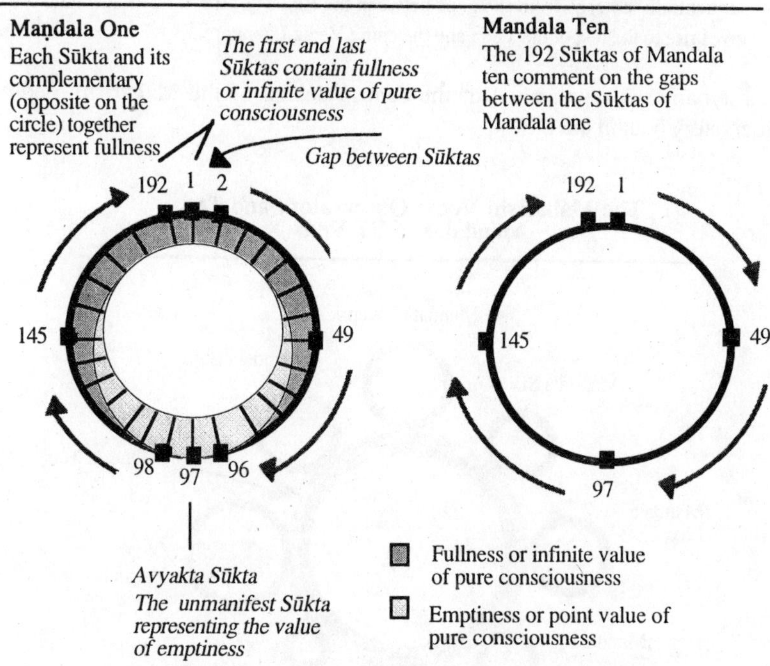

The 192 Sūktas of the first Maṇdala of Ṛk Veda express the progression from fullness of pure consciousness, or the total percent of Natural Law, as expressed in the first Sūkta (Sūkta 1), to emptiness of pure consciousness expressed in the Avyakta or unmanifest Sūkta (Sūkta 97) and back to fullness again in the last Sūkta (Sūkta 192). Due to this progression on the circular structure of the Maṇdala, each Sūkta sits opposite to its counterpart. Each pair of Sūktas directly opposite each other on the Maṇdala together represent fullness. The transformations within the gaps between the 192 Sūktas of the first Maṇdalas are commented on by the 192 Sūktas of the tenth Maṇdala. In this sense, the first and tenth Maṇdala are intimately related.

As mentioned previously, in his *Apauruṣeya Bhāṣya,* Maharishi reveals that the transformations in the gaps between the 192 *Sūktas* of the first *Maṇdala* are commented upon by the 192 *Sūktas* of the tenth *Maṇdala.* Then, *Maṇdalas* two through nine emerge from the gaps between the *Ṛichās* of the first *Sūkta* of the first *Maṇdala*:

> Ultimately, in subsequent stages of unfoldment, [the] 192 syllables of the 1st Sūkta (stanza) [of the first Mandala] get elaborated in the 192 Sūktas that

> comprise the 1st Mandala (circular cyclical eternal structure) of Ṛk Veda, and from the gaps between these 192 Sūktas emerge the 192 Sūktas of the 10th Mandala; the remaining Mandalas 2-9 (corresponding to the eight Prakṛitis) sequentially emerge from the gaps between the Ṛichās of the 1st Sūkta. This gives rise to the rest of the Veda and the entire Vedic Literature.[13]

This dynamic is represented in the central design of the Maharishi Vedic Observatory built in the U.S.

The Maharishi Vedic Observatory and Ten Maṇḍalas of Ṛk Veda

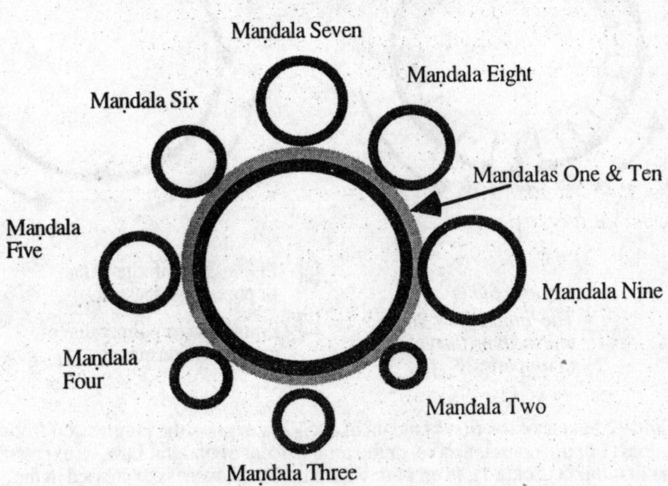

The ten Maṇḍalas as a central design of the Maharishi Vedic Observatory. (After: Maharishi Vedic Observatories Corporation, Maharishi Vedic Observatory, Fairfield, IA, 1996, p. 20-21 & 24).

The precise relationship of the ten *Maṇḍalas* of Ṛk Veda has been employed in the design and architectural form of the Maharishi Vedic Observatory which contains specific *Yantras* or Vedic instruments and comprises a central design of the ten *Maṇḍalas* of Ṛk Veda. It is suggested that when viewing the structure (this diagram can be found illustrated more fully in *Maharishi Vedic Observatory*[14]) a spectator will enjoy a balancing influence. As a technology for aligning individual life with cosmic life, the observatory is designed to allow the individual to gain the benefit of the orderly functioning of Nature's cosmic performance from his or her perspective on earth. Hagelin notes, "The Maharishi

Vedic Observatory... expands the awareness and re-establishes the relationship between human intelligence and cosmic intelligence—spontaneously and automatically."[15] It connects the inner intelligence of the structure of Ṛk Veda to the cosmic intelligence which governs the movement of the planets and the human physiology. The structure is, in a sense, a product of both art and science. It is a site which connects human life with cosmic life, providing a map of inner and outer worlds. One could even describe it as a site-specific work which integrates the total range of Vedic knowledge and acts as a technology for enhancing creativity in the viewer.

In this consideration of the nature and structure of Ṛk Veda according to Maharishi Vedic Science, it is clear that pure consciousness, due to its self-referral nature, has a dynamic structure despite the fact that it is "singularity", infinite and unbounded. This structure of Ṛk Veda holds together opposite values, unity and diversity and contains complete knowledge in seed form—all the evolutionary processes and all forms and phenomena in the universe. According to Maharishi's *Apauruṣeya Bhāṣya*, the sequential unfoldment of the structure of consciousness is systematic and orderly, proceeding according to the dynamic nature of self-referral consciousness, generating the syllables or sounds of the Veda. Described in Ṛk Veda itself as the "eternal void" of absolute self-referral consciousness, this "tumultuous uproar" is heard on the level of fully awake awareness.[16] By virtue of the move of the eternal void the holistic sound of "A" emerges and breaks into the various sounds of the Vedic Literature. In this way, the universal field of pure consciousness, through its own dynamic, generates impulses—the unmanifest sounds which structure creation.

While it is within the capability of human consciousness to perceive, hear, and know the details of Ṛk Veda, one requires a clear, fully awake consciousness to perceive this reality. This ability is especially important for any artist who wishes to imbue his or her work with universal value. As Maharishi explains, "the artist should know what consciousness is and what it is made of."[17] This may imply that in order for the artist to really create universal art he or she should know the structure and sequence of the Veda and the Vedic Literature—the dynamics through which nature creates the entire universe.

10

THE FORTY ASPECTS OF THE VEDA AND THE VEDIC LITERATURE AND THEIR QUALITIES OF INTELLIGENCE: IMPULSES OF CONSCIOUSNESS AS THE STRUCTURING MECHANICS OF ṚK VEDA

As emphasized previously, unlike other descriptions of the Vedic or Sanskrit texts, Maharishi Vedic Science reveals that the Veda and the Vedic Literature are modes of self-referral consciousness—frequencies or impulses of Natural Law involved in the structuring mechanics of Ṛk Veda. In Maharishi Vedic Science "Veda" refers to Ṛk Veda, the structure of pure knowledge, Saṁhitā of Ṛishi, Devatā, and Chhandas, and the four Vedas—Ṛk, *Sāma, Yajur* and *Atharva Veda*. "Vedic" is that which "pertains to" Veda, or pure knowledge. The phrase "Veda and Vedic Literature" refers to Ṛk Veda and the 39 aspects of the structuring dynamics of Veda—totaling 40 aspects of the Veda and Vedic Literature.

In his description and identification of the Veda and the Vedic Literature, Maharishi explains that Ṛk Veda is "the self-generated sound of the self-interacting dynamics of the self-referral state of consciousness,"[1] where Ṛk Veda is the unmanifest sound at the "basis of all categories of sounds displayed in the Vedic Literature." These different aspects of the Vedic Literature express different:

> Modes of consciousness, which constitute the structuring mechanics of Ṛk Ved. That is why there is an inseparable connection between the structure of Ṛk Ved and the different structures of the Vedic Literature.[2]

All the different aspects of the Vedic Literature are the structuring mechanics of consciousness involved in forming the structure of Ṛk Veda or pure knowledge. As mentioned previously, Ṛk Veda comprises all the Laws of Nature; it is Saṁhitā of Ṛishi, Devatā, and Chhandas, the Constitution of the Universe—that body of fundamental principles which govern the activity of the universe. Ṛk Veda is the holistic expression of dynamic silence in self-referral consciousness. Maharishi indicates that while the structuring dynamics of Ṛk Veda involve 40 qualities of Natural Law brought out by the Veda and Vedic Literature,[3] this holistic value of Natural Law has its seat in the Self of everyone, called *Ātmā*. *Ātmā* is the seat of the holistic value of Natural Law.

Maharishi goes on to point out that the Vedic Literature expresses the different modes of consciousness in terms of Saṁhitā, Ṛishi, Devatā, and Chhandas values and is involved in the structuring mechanics of everything in the universe. With access to and proper knowledge of these structuring dynamics the individual can achieve anything. As Maharishi explains, those sounds which construct self-referral consciousness that have been heard by the ancient Seers in their own self-referral consciousness—are available to anyone in one's own self-referral consciousness. They are:

> The sounds that are available to us in the Ved and the Vedic Literature. Through proper use of these sounds, the entire Vedic Technology, the whole engineering of creation, all the secrets of Nature's silent functioning, is available to us.[4]

Nature's infinite creativity and organizing power are available through proper use of the sounds of the Veda and Vedic Literature.

As a complete science of consciousness, Maharishi Vedic Science thus reveals the practical value of the Veda and Vedic Literature—how all the Laws of Nature can support individual and collective life. This knowledge is vital for any discipline—including art and theory. With respect to recent developments in Maharishi Vedic Science, Nader has uncovered the one-to-one correspondence between the Veda and the Vedic Literature and the structures and functions of the human physiology. In this discovery, the role of intelligence (expressing itself as the sounds of the Veda and Vedic Literature) is shown in the structure, function, maintenance, evolution and development of the physiology. Self-referral intelligence or consciousness, unfolding in self-referral loops, is the intelligence of the physiology and all of creation.

The mechanics of creativity which structure the universe are the same mechanics of creativity which govern perception, cognition and the domain of mind-body coordination and development. In knowing these mechanics, the artist knows the precise and intimate details of his or her own creative process.

The Self-Referral Loops of the Vedic Literature

Although there are "hundreds of textbooks"[5] which unfold the divisions and subdivisions of different areas of Natural Law,[6] in identifying 40 aspects of the Veda and the Vedic Literature which bring out a particular value of Saṁhitā, Ṛishi, Devatā or Chhandas in the elaboration of the self-referral dynamics of consciousness, Maharishi Vedic Science presents a completely new and precise understanding of the nature of Veda. In fact, the unfoldment of the 40 aspects of the Veda and Vedic Literature can be understood as a further elaboration of Maharishi's *Apauruṣeya Bhāṣya*. Each aspect brings out a more elaborate package of knowledge. These 40 aspects have been identified by Maharishi in groups, branches or clusters, forming self-referral loops, bringing out values of Saṁhitā of Ṛishi, Devatā and Chhandas.

The structure of the 40 aspects of the Veda and the Vedic Literature is elaborated upon below and illustrated in the diagram on subsequent pages.

1) Ṛk Veda is the structure of pure knowledge, self-referral consciousness, Saṁhitā of Ṛishi, Devatā and Chhandas in its compactified state.

2) Sāma Veda, 3) Yajur-Veda, and 4) Atharva-Veda are the following three Vedas that bring out Ṛishi, Devatā and Chhandas values respectively. Maharishi explains that all the four Veda, Ṛk, Sāma, Yajur and Atharva, are independent qualities of wholeness but contain the other within each. This is because they are all four Absolutes within one Absolute, *Ātmā.*[7] The next six aspects of the Vedic Literature bring out the first self-referral loop of Rishi, Devatā and Chhandas and Chhandas, Devatā and Ṛishi, respectively; they are 5) Śikṣā, 6) Kalp, 7) Vyākaraṇ, 8) Nirukt, 9) Chhand, and 10) Jyotish. Starting and ending with a Ṛishi value, or with wholeness, they are known collectively as the *Vedānga* or "limbs" of the Veda. After the Vedānga, the subsequent self-referral loop is the *Upānga* and comprises: 11) Nyāya, 12) Vaiśeṣik, 13) Sāṃkhya, 14) Yoga, 15) Karma Mīmāṁsā, and 16) Vedānt. Referred to as the Upānga, or "subordinate limbs" of the Veda, they are also called the six systems of Indian philosophy, or the *Darśana*. These six aspects bring out Ṛishi, Devatā and Chhandas, Chhandas, Devatā and Ṛishi qualities in another loop.

Categorized as the *Upa-Veda*, the next self-referral loop includes 17) Gandharva Veda, 18) Dhanur-Veda, 19) Sthāpatya Veda, 20) Hārīta Saṁhitā, 21) Bhel Saṁhitā, 22) and Kāśyap Saṁhitā. The Upa-Veda thus continue to elaborate Rishi, Devatā and Chhandas and Chhandas, Devatā and Ṛishi values, respectively. Also grouped under the heading Upa-Veda[8] or *Āyur-Veda*[9] and including 23) Charak Saṁhitā, 24) Suśrut Saṁhitā, 25) Vāgbhatt Saṁhitā, 26) Mādhav Nidān Saṁhitā, 27) Śārngadhar Saṁhitā, and 28) Bhāva Prakāś Saṁhitā, the next self-referral loop of Rishi, Devatā and Chhandas and Chhandas, Devatā and Ṛishi also highlights specific qualities in the structuring dynamics of Ṛk Veda.

Collectively called the *Brāhmaṇa* and forming another self-referral loop, the following branch of the Vedic Literature comprises 29) Upaniṣad, 30) Āraṇyak, 31) Brāhmaṇa, 32) Itihās, 33) Purāṇ, and 34) Smṛti which again bring out specific Ṛishi, Devatā and Chhandas and Chhandas, Devatā and Ṛishi values.[10] Finally, the sixth branch, the *Prātiśākhya*, highlights the wholeness value of consciousness, rather than specific parts. The Prātiśākhya include: 35) Ṛk Veda Prātiśākhya, 36) Śukl-Yajur-Veda Prātiśākhya, 37) Atharva Veda Prātiśākhya, 38) Atharva Veda Prātiśākhya (Chaturadhyāyī), 39) Kṛṣṇ-Yajur-Veda Prātiśākhya (Taittirīya), and 40) Sāma Veda Prātiśākhya (Puśpa Sūtram). They connect the parts with the whole, revealing the value of *Brahm* or Totality—the complete value of consciousness lived in the state of Brahman Consciousness where everything is seen in terms of the Self, *Ātmā.*[11] The theme of evolution is complete; *Ātmā* is *Brahm*. Including Ṛk Veda, each aspect of the Vedic Literature is predominantly associated with a specific aspect of self-referral consciousness in constructing the seed of diversified creation—Ṛk Veda itself. The self-referral loops demonstrate the nature of consciousness to elaborate itself in diversified values while remaining connected to the source—self-referral consciousness.

The Forty Aspects of the Veda and the Vedic Literature

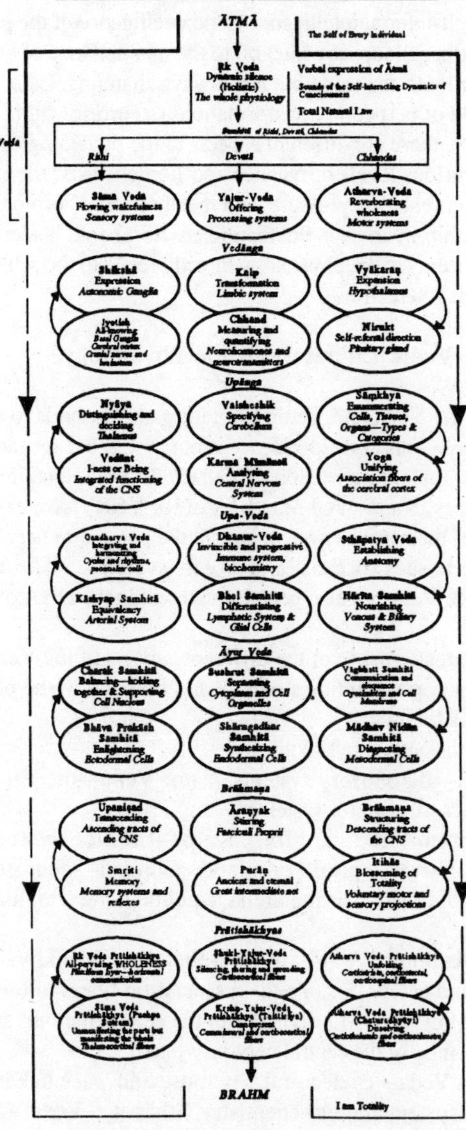

In Maharishi's Vedic Science, the forty aspects of the Veda and the Vedic Literature highlight the qualities and values of self-referral consciousness; they unfold in a specific sequence and self-referral loops. Each aspect also has its correspondence in the physiology.

They unfold the simultaneous move toward diversification and toward unity, maintaining balance and the flow of evolution from wholeness to wholeness.

Since this self-referral intelligence is the intelligence of the physiology, Nader explains that feedback loops are integral to the maintenance of balance within the body. The body looks the same but it is always changing. Like a flowing river, it is a dynamic field of perpetual transformations occurring within sets of feedback loops. Ultimately, there are different aspects to the physiological feedback loops accounting for various levels of balance and homeostasis; for example: specific levels of temperature, blood pressure, and metabolic and hormonal activities must be maintained within in an ever-fluctuating environment. Nader emphasizes that the cybernetic systems in the physiology directly relate to the self-referral feedback loops of the Vedic Literature.

The Veda and Vedic Literature in the Physiology

Every aspect of the Veda and Vedic Literature corresponds to some part of the human physiology. This correspondence is not trivial, but reveals that the human physiology is a complete expression of Veda and Vedic Literature. For example, the syllables, verses, *Sūktas*, and *Maṇdalas* of Ṛk Veda "have been mapped in the entire structure of the nervous system and all the peripheral nerves controlling the activities of the tissues, organs, and organ systems. The basic theme of organization of Ṛk Veda has also been located within the DNA of every cell of the body." [12]

The unique relationship of the different aspects of the Veda and the Vedic Literature to their corresponding structure and function in the physiology, [13] has been articulated as follows:

Rk Veda—the entire physiology;

Sāma Veda—the sensory systems, Yajur-Veda—the processing systems, and Atharva-Veda—the motor systems;

Śikṣā—autonomic ganglia, Kalp—limbic system, Vyākaraṇ—hypothalamus, Nirukt—-pituitary gland, Chhand—neurotransmitters and neurohormones, Jyotish—basal ganglia, cerebral cortex, cranial nerves and the brain stem;

Nyāya—thalamus, Vaiśeṣik—cerebellum, Sāṃkhya—cells, tissues, organs—types and categories, Yoga—association fibers of the central nervous system, Karma Mīmāṁsā—12 divisions of the central nervous system, Vedānt—integrated functioning of the central nervous system;

Gandharva Veda—cycles and rhythms, and pacemaker cells, Dhanur-Veda—immune system and bio-chemistry, Sthāpatya Veda—anatomy, Hārīta Saṁhitā—venous and biliary system, Bhel Saṁhitā—lymphatic system and glial cells, Kāśyap Saṁhitā—arterial system;

Charak Saṁhitā—cell nucleus, Suśrut Saṁhitā—cytoplasm and cell organelles, Vāgbhatt Saṁhitā—cytoskeleton and cell membrane, Mādhav Nidān

Saṁhitā—mesodermal cells, Śārngadhar Saṁhitā—endodermal cells, Bhāva Prakāś Saṁhitā—ectodermal cells;

Upaniṣad—ascending tracts of the central nervous system, Āraṇyak—fasciculi proprii, Brāhmaṇa—descending tracts of the central nervous system, Itihās—voluntary motor and sensory projections, Purāṇ—great intermediate net, Smṛti—memory systems and reflexes;

Ṛk Veda Prātiśākhya—plexiform layer—horizontal communication, Śukl-Yajur-Veda Prātiśākhya—corticocortical fibers, Atharva Veda Prātiśākhya—corticostriate, corticotectal, and corticospinal, fibers, Atharva Veda Prātiśākhya (Chaturadhyāyī)—corticothalamic and corticoclaustral fibers, Kṛṣṇ-Yajur-Veda Prātiśākhya (Taittirīya)—commissural and corticocortical fibers, Sāma Veda Prātiśākhya (Puśpa Sūtram)—thalamocortical fibers.[14]

This and other correspondences of Veda and the Vedic Literature with the physiology only further emphasize the universal significance of the Vedic texts as impulses of Natural Law structuring the body and its neurophysiological functioning and provide important new applications for the field of medicine and the creation of a disease-free society.

Forty Qualities of Intelligence

In the discussion of the nature of the Veda and Vedic Literature with respect to consciousness, Maharishi explains that each of the 40 aspects highlights a specific quality of consciousness. Ṛk Veda is the expression of *dynamic silence (holistic)* in self-referral consciousness while Sāma Veda highlights the quality of *flowing wakefulness* involved in structuring Ṛk Veda. The other aspects (listed as follows) highlight further qualities involved in the structuring of Ṛk Veda:

Yajur-Veda—*offering,*
Atharva-Veda—*reverberating WHOLENESS,*
Śikṣā—*expression,*
Kalp—*transformation,*
Vyākaraṇ—*expansion*,
Nirukt—*self-referral direction,*
Chhand *measuring* and *quantifying*,
Jyotish—*all-knowing*,
Nyāya—*distinguishing* and *deciding,*
Vaiśeṣik—*specifying*,
Sāṃkhya—*enumerating*,
Yoga—*unifying,*
Karma Mīmāṁsā—*analyzing,*
Vedānt—*I-ness* or *Being*,
Gandharva Veda—*integrating* and *harmonizing*,
Dhanur-Veda—*invincible* and *progressive*,
Sthāpatya Veda—*establishing,*
Hārīta Saṁhitā—*nourishing,*

Bhel Saṁhitā—*differentiating*,
Kāśyap Saṁhitā—*equivalency*,
Charak Saṁhitā—*balancing—holding together*,
Suśrut Saṁhitā—*separating*,
Vāgbhatt Saṁhitā—*communication* and *eloquence*,
Mādhav Nidān Saṁhitā—*diagnosing*,
Śārngadhar Saṁhitā—*synthesizing*,
Bhāva Prakāś Saṁhitā—*enlightening*,
Upaniṣad—*transcending*,
Āraṇyak—*stirring*,
Brāhmaṇa—*structuring*,
Itihās—*blossoming of Totality*,
Purāṇ—*ancient* and *eternal*,
Smṛti—*memory*,
Ṛk Veda Prātiśākhya—*all-pervading WHOLENESS*,
Śukl-Yajur-Veda Prātiśākhya—*silencing*, *sharing*, and *spreading*,
Atharva Veda Prātiśākhya—*unfolding*,
Atharva Veda Prātiśākhya (Chaturadhyāyī)—*dissolving*,
Kṛṣṇ-Yajur-Veda Prātiśākhya (Taittirīya)—*omnipresent*,
Sāma Veda Prātiśākhya (Puśpa Sūtram)—*Unmanifesting the parts but manifesting the whole*.[15]

As noted, each of these 40 aspects brings out some value of Natural Law, where Natural Law contains all the Laws of Nature which structure the universe—each one deals with either a Ṛishi, Devatā or Chhandas quality of consciousness in the self-referral unfoldment of consciousness, the structuring dynamics of Ṛk Veda.

If Ṛk Veda is the seed, then the different values of the Vedic Literature represent the evolution and full blossoming of the seed into the flower, fruit and tree.[16] For this reason, Veda is understood as the "reality of the structure of the unstructured field of consciousness" while the Vedic Literature unfolds the mechanics of that structuring process[17] and is, therefore, the literature of consciousness.[18]

The various parts of the Veda and the Vedic Literature in different contexts, also reveal multiple values of knowledge. For example, with respect to the levels of the mind identified in his Vedic Science (i.e. *Ātmā* or the Self, *Buddhi* or intellect, *Manas* or mind, and the *Indriyas* or senses), Maharishi points out that while the holistic value of Natural Law [Ṛk Veda] has its seat in the Self (*Ātmā*) of everyone, the specific parts of Natural Law [the Vedic Literature] have their seat in the intellect (*Buddhi*), the divisions of these have their seat in the mind (*Manas*) and their subdivisions have their seat in the senses (*Indriyas*) and each of these hierarchical levels has its own corresponding level of physiology.[19]

While this is one level of analysis, the following chapters deal primarily self-referral consciousness, its dynamics and sequential elaboration in terms of Veda and the Vedic Literature, mentioning briefly connections between consciousness and the physiology. In each instance, Maharishi Vedic Science provides an unparalleled perspective on the ultimate nature of the Vedic texts.

11

THE ABSOLUTE VALUES OF EACH OF THE FOUR VEDAS: ṚK, SĀMA, YAJUR AND ATHARVA VEDA

In Maharishi Vedic Science, the four Vedas are described as values or impulses of intelligence or consciousness moving or flowing within itself. They are understood to contain the other within each; they are four Absolutes within one Absolute or *Ātmā*.[1] *Atmā* is that unbounded field of pure, self-referral consciousness fully awake within itself, and within which the impulses (*Vṛttis*) of the four Vedas arise. As Maharishi explains

> ***Ātmā*** fully awake within itself has four qualities—self-referral *Vṛittis* (impulses) within its self-referral, unmanifest reality—the ocean of WHOLENESS, infinity, in the state of pure wakefulness. These *Vṛittis*—Ṛk, Sāma, Yajur, and Atharva qualities of intelligence—are the self-expressed *Shruti*—that which is heard by *Ātmā* itself in its eternal state of Unity, *Brāhmī Chetanā* —fully awake *Ātmā*—the state of *Brahm*—*Ayam Atmā Brahm.*[2]

These four qualities are all independent qualities of wholeness—bringing out the value of *Brahm*, or Totality. As Maharishi points out, *Ātmā*, in being awake to itself, generates these *Vṛttis*, Ṛk, Sāma, Yajur, and Atharva qualities of intelligence, which are the *Śruti*, that which is heard on that self-referral level by *Ātmā*.

Mentioned earlier, in this sequential progression or evolution of consciousness, *Ātmā* gives rise to Veda, *Śruti* or sound, which is the basis of the manifest universe or *Viśwa*. When *Viśwa* is seen as the self-referral dynamics of *Ātmā*, then *Ātmā* is *Brahm*, the Totality. This whole range of evolution, from *Ātmā* to Veda, to *Viśwa* to *Brahm*, is the range of the Veda and the Vedic Literature. As considered in the previous chapter, Ṛk, as indicated by its name, on the unmanifest level, contains the whirlpool dynamic or collapse of dynamism to silence. As Maharishi indicates, it contains both infinite dynamism and infinite silence.

> Ṛk Veda is the knowledge of ऋक् (Ṛk), the expression of ऋ (Ṛ) and क् (K). ऋ (Ṛ) represents dynamism and क् (K) represents point of dynamism or silence. Thus the expression ऋक् (Ṛk)—dynamism and silence together—is easily pictured in the formation of a whirlpool, which has dynamism ऋ (Ṛ) at the surface and concentrated dynamism at its point क् (K). It is the expression of infinite dynamism and its direction—move towards its point. This means that the dynamism of ऋक् (Ṛk) is self-referral; it is moving from infinity to its point.

> Thus it is obvious that ऋक् (Ṛk) is the expression of WHOLENESS—self-referral WHOLENESS. Both values—all silence and all dynamism—are contained in the syllable ऋक् (Ṛk). ऋक् (Ṛk) is the expression of Totality.[3]

In this description Ṛk Veda is defined as the quality of dynamic silence which is completely holistic. It contains all possibilities within its fold. This quality of dynamic silence is not a incidental attribution; it is the fundamental nature of Ṛk. Ṛk is dynamic silence—the dynamic silence of self-referral consciousness which is completely holistic. The same principle applies to all the qualities of the Vedic Literature involved in the structuring dynamics of Ṛk.

Earlier, Ṛk Veda was described as made up of a specific number of *Sūktas.* Similarly, in the physiology, the *Sūktas* of Ṛk Veda correlate to the nervous system and the entire physiology. For example: of the 192 *Sūktas* of the first *Maṇḍala* of Ṛk Veda which contains total knowledge, *Sūkta* 1 corresponds to layer 1 of the cerebral cortex. The cerebral cortex is the surface of the cerebral hemisphere and is approximately 2-4 millimeters thick. The complimentary *Avyakta* or "unmanifest" *Sūkta, Sūkta* 97, corresponds to the silent filum terminale, a silent fiber at the tip of the spinal cord, at the bottom level of the nervous system, which has no activity or expression.

Sūktas 2-4 and *Sūktas* 98-100 relate respectively to the excitatory and inhibitory stimuli of corpus callosum and corona radiata (the corpus callosum and corona radiata refer to parts of the brain; the corona radiata are the pair of radiations of nerve fibers extending to and from the cortex); *Sūktas* 5-28 and 101-124 correspond to the excitatory and inhibitory stimuli of the 24 cranial nerves and *Sūktas* 29-96 and 125-192 relate to the excitatory and inhibitory stimuli of the spinal nerves.[4] These complimentary stimuli—excitatory or inhibitory—are necessary for experience. For example, to get visual information certain neurons are inhibited while others are excited; likewise, in moving an arm, particular muscles are activated (agonists) while others are inhibited (antagonists)—allowing for differentiation and balance in each sensory and motor experience. Thus, the complimentary excitatory and inhibitory stimuli reflect the opposing values of dynamism and silence within Ṛk.

The mechanics and correspondence of the physiology with Ṛk Veda, in terms of Maharishi's *Apauruṣeya Bhāṣya* (including the sequential unfoldment of Ṛishi, Devatā and Chhandas values, the four stages of the gap, the eight *Prakṛtis,* and all the *Sūktas* and *Maṇḍalas* of Ṛk Veda with respect to perception, motor functions and experience via the body[5]) are identified in detail by Nader—showing that the body is the precise expression of Veda and Vedic Literature.

The same analysis can be applied to the following three of the four Veda—Sāma, Yajur and Atharva Veda. Sāma Veda is the flow of self-referral consciousness or wholeness within Ṛk; it is the flow of intelligence within itself. Following on from this, Yajur-Veda is the dynamics of that flow and Atharva Veda is the value of vibrating intelligence. Sāma is the flow of the Ṛishi quality within Ṛk, Yajur is the dynamism of Devatā quality within Ṛk and Sāma, and

Atharva is the finest measure of infinity in terms of Chhandas which represents the hidden dynamics of the relationship between Ṛk, Sāma and Yajur. As Maharishi points out:

> Sāma is the flow of WHOLENESS—the flow of the Ṛishi quality within Ṛk; Yajur is dynamics of flow—the dynamism of Devatā quality within Ṛk and Sāma; and Atharva is vibrating intelligence—the qualityless reverberation of WHOLENESS—the qualityless eternal silence indicated by अ (A). It is the vibrating, unmanifest relationship between Ṛk, Sāma and Yajur; it is Chhandas, the finest measure of infinity—the hidden dynamics of relationship between Ṛk, Sāma, and Yajur—between Saṁhitā, Ṛishi, and Devatā. Sāma, Yajur, and Atharva all have their own unmanifest status, their own quality within the Saṁhitā of Ṛk Veda.[6]

Maharishi also describes Atharva as the pure power of intelligence and the finest wave of Creative Intelligence which is "the self-sufficient unit of intelligence, the self-referral tool of consciousness reverberating in itself."[7] This level of Atharva is the "basis of the technology of consciousness"[8] and is therefore related to the means by which consciousness is developed.

As mentioned above, despite the fact that each of the four Veda bring out some specific aspect of self-referral intelligence; each contains the other. Maharishi teaches that Sāma contains Yajur, Yajur contains Atharva and Atharva "can be seen as containing Sāma, Yajur, and Ṛk within it."[9] He explains this in terms of the absolute status of the all the four Vedas, where each is an absolute reality.

> All these four independent qualities of WHOLENESS—Ṛk, Sāma, Yajur, and Atharva—should be understood as absolute values of WHOLENESS. Each being independent of each other contains the others within it. This question on the reality of the four Veda in one wholeness of *Ātmā* is resolved when we understand them all as absolute realities. Each being Absolute (non-relative) can be easily seen to be one within the other—four Absolutes in one absolute value of *Ātmā*—Totality—*Brahm*.[10]

Again, Maharishi Vedic Science provides deep insights into the nature of the four Veda. They are *Vṛttis* or impulses of intelligence—the different qualities of intelligence, as intelligence moves within itself, within its own unbounded wholeness.

These qualities are self-sufficient but, because they are absolutes, contain the other within each. In this description one can locate the notion of discriminated values of wholeness within wholeness. There are multiple absolutes but these are contained within one absolute value of *Atmā* which is *Brahm*—the Totality—that which contains all values.

Sāma Veda—Flowing Wakefulness

As discussed above, Sāma is the flow of intelligence or pure wakefulness. Maharishi indicates that wakefulness is pure alertness. "This alertness is due to the coexistence of two opposite values—silence and dynamism;"[11] these two opposite values are contained in the structure of Ṛk—dynamic silence. With respect to the quality of wakefulness, "for silence and dynamism to entertain each other, each must be supremely alert lest one be neutralized by the other."[12] Due to being awake in these two values of silence and dynamism, pure wakefulness "exhibits the quality of lively intelligence, the quality of consciousness."[13]

Maharishi points out that pure wakefulness locates the dynamics of creation within itself and in its self-referral state, pure wakefulness is the seer of Ṛk, it is Ṛk.[14] Therefore, Ṛk can be understood further in terms of Sāma Veda, that flowing aspect of intelligence. Silence, or self-referral consciousness, flows. Since it is eternal, it is a continuous flow; Sāma is this flow of consciousness.

> This flow is the reality of the process of self-referral expressing the dynamism inherent in silence—dynamism, the quality at the basis of silence that maintains it as an eternal continuum and gives it the characteristic quality of flowing wakefulness.[15]

The structure of Sāma is located within Ṛk; it is the flow within the structure of pure wakefulness. In the physiology, Sāma Veda corresponds to the sensory systems. They include all peripheral and central sensory receptors and nerves, ascending spinal cord sensory columns and their relays and connections, the basal ganglia, thalamus and the sensory neocortex. Nader indicates that through these channels the wakeful physiology receives the flow of experience and in so doing sustains flowing wakefulness. Both on the level of consciousness and physiology, Sāma brings out the value of flowing wakefulness. Sāma Veda also highlights the sets of Laws of Nature which promote the quality of Ṛishi within Saṁhitā, self-referral consciousness.[16]

Yajur-Veda—Offering

If Sāma is flowing wakefulness, then, as Maharishi points out, Yajur is that value of offering—where silence offers itself to dynamism and dynamism offers itself to silence or, similarly, where the three values of knower, process of knowing, and known, offer themselves to each other in the creation of a fourth value of knowledge.

According to Maharishi Vedic Science, Yajur-Veda relates to *Yajan*, defined as "offering" or "sacrificing" and also referred to as *Yagya*. However, here, *Yagya* refers not to sacrifice as in relinquishment or loss on a relative level or to an arcane ritual but to the process of offering that takes place on the level of consciousness. This understanding extends other translations of the term. The activity of *Yagya* is the process through which knowledge can be fully expressed. This is a deeper sense of the meaning of offering; it elaborates the unmanifest phenomenon of the dynamic interaction between the three values of Ṛishi, Devatā and Chhandas—or knower, process of knowing and known—and their unified status within self-referral consciousness, the structure of Ṛk. As Maharishi points out

> Knowledge is *Yagya.* Knowledge (*Gyān*) emerges with the coming together of knower, process of knowing, and known—the unity of the three—knower, process of knowing, and known creating the fourth element—knowledge. All three offer to each other their separate identities, and the whole process of each merging with the others blossoms into the fourth value—knowledge. This process of offering (or sacrificing) is the activity that is called *Yagya,* which is the activity, or process, for knowledge to blossom.
>
> The process of *Yagya*—dynamism offering itself to silence and silence offering itself to dynamism ऋक् (Ṛk) is the process of *Yajan*—*Yagya*—the knower is offering himself to the known, and the known is offering itself to the knower through the process of *Yagya,* which puts them together in one structure of knowledge; and because the whole process of offering (sacrificing) is the process of flow, it is clear that the structure of *Yajan* (*Yagya*) is the structure of Ṛk as it is also the structure of Sāma; it is the blossoming of the full awakening of consciousness—all the three Veda, Ṛk, Sāma, and Yajur, in one's own self-referral consciousness.[17]

Gyan means knowledge. The phenomenon of offering, referred to as *Yajan* or *Yagya* and brought out by Yajur, is in the structure of knowledge. It is the structure of Ṛk and of Sāma because this dynamic of the offering of the knower, process of knowing and known to knowledge, is in the process of flow. Offering, along with flowing wakefulness, describes the dynamics of self-referral consciousness which can be experienced in one's own simplest form of awareness, Transcendental Consciousness or *Ātmā.*

In the physiology, Yajur-Veda is identified as the processing systems which has two main divisions—the somatic system and the autonomic nervous system. It is worth noting that Yajur-Veda is divided into two sections: 1) *Śukla* Yajur-Veda and 2) *Kṛṣṇ* Yajur-Veda. *Śukla* means white and *Kṛṣṇ*, black, so they signify opposites. *Śukla* corresponds to the somatic system which is open to awareness and *Kṛṣṇ* refers to the autonomic nervous system which is not generally speaking under conscious control. The autonomic nervous system is that part of the nervous system concerned with control of involuntary bodily functions—regulating the functions of the glands (in particular, the salivary, gastric and sweat glands, the adrenal medulla, smooth muscle tissue, and the heart) and may act on these tissues to reduce or slow activity or to initiate their function. Furthermore, Śukla Yajur-Veda has 15 *Śākhās* or branches which correspond to the 15 modalities of the processing of the somatic sensory systems. Nader observes that the 15 *Śākhās* and 15 modalities are also both grouped according to two categories. Kṛṣṇ Yajur-Veda has 86 *Śākhās* or divisions. In the physiology there are 86 'head ganglia' which deal with the processing of the autonomic modalities. The autonomic ganglia are clusters of sympathetic or parasympathetic cell bodies located outside the central nervous system (the hypothalamus is the part of the brain which releases factors that activate the pituitary gland and autonomic nervous system). Channeled through the autonomic ganglia and cranial nerve autonomic nuclei under the control of the hypothalamus, the 86 'head ganglia' correspond to the divisions of Kṛṣṇ Yajur-Veda.

As is evident, this vision of Yajur-Veda brought out by Maharishi Vedic Science reveals the involvement of Yajur-Veda in the structure of Ṛk and Sāma. Fundamentally, with reference to consciousness, Yajur-Veda contains the particular sets of Laws of Nature which promote the quality of Devatā, the process of observation or the "dynamism of observing within the witnessing quality of Ṛishi"[18] within Saṁhitā.

Atharva Veda—Reverberating Wholeness

In this discussion of the four Vedas, Atharva Veda can be understood as that quality which elaborates the bi-directional flow of intelligence within *Ātmā*, the reverberating wholeness value of consciousness. With flow in two directions, the neutralization of flow occurs maintaining non-flow or silence within flow. As mentioned above, silence can be described as flowing toward dynamism and dynamism towards silence. This phenomenon is located within Ṛk. As Maharishi explains:

> The phenomenon of flow in two opposite directions in the structure of Ṛk can be seen in terms of neutralizing the flow in each direction and maintaining perpetual silence in the flow. The picture is of a series of points of silence constituting the flow. This continuous structure of points of silence within the flowing structures of Ṛk Veda, Sāma Veda, and Yajur-Veda produces such points in the field of self-referral motion in Transcendental Consciousness—points of silence fully awake—points of silence without motion throughout the passage of evolution, which is the reality of creation.[19]

Due to the phenomenon of flow or motion in opposite directions—the flow of silence towards dynamism and the flow of dynamism towards silence—points of non-motion are generated. This is the structure of the self-referral phenomenon in the process or passage of evolution of consciousness. These points can also be described as a juncture where the flow of silence and the flow of dynamism cross.

Maharishi explains that this crossing point is a structure which is lively within itself but is without direction, or, rather, is all-directional.[20] This point is:

> A 'pulsating quality.' This is the vision of ATHARVA—the *Tharva* of अ (A)—reverberating WHOLENESS within क् (K), the point of speech—*Vṛittis* of *Atmā*, unmanifest sound, emerging from the self-interacting dynamics of WHOLENESS—Transcendental Consciousness—the vibrating potential, the self-referral dynamics at the basis of everything.[21]

Although the description of consciousness as a straight line and as a series of points was introduced in Part II, the discussion of consciousness in terms of its points is here elaborated upon by Maharishi with respect to the four Veda and specifically Atharva Veda. These points, having a pulsating quality, are the vibrating potential, reverberating wholeness of अ (A) within क् (K), the *Vṛittis* of *Ātmā*, unmanifest sound, emerging from within our own Transcendental Consciousness.

The value of the point can also be discussed in terms of the letter क् (K). As noted in the previous section, according to Maharishi's *Apauruṣeya Bhāṣya* the sounds of the Veda (the letters, syllables etc.) elaborate the dynamics of consciousness and evolve discrete, holistic expressions or packages of knowledge. The letter क् (K), in this understanding, represents the stop value of the collapse of अ (A) to क् (K). क् (K), however, also contains within its pronunciation the letter अ (A); while क् (K) is the point, अ (A) is unboundedness. As Maharishi explains

> The letter क् (K) has two aspects to its pronunciation. First is stop, point, and second is अ (A)—unbounded. क् (K) represents point and unboundedness—क् (K) represents point shifting to unboundedness. In the first stage of this shifting the point becomes the point of the point. The point of the point gaining the reality of unboundedness is the faintest fibre of unbounded silence—अ (A). This point of the point is Atharva—the finest fibre of unbounded silence, fully awake in itself at the basis of all the Veda and the Vedic Literature—the structure of Law and its evolution in the universe.[22]

The finest fiber of unbounded silence, is Atharva, the point of the point. It is the first stage of the shifting of point to unboundedness. This finest fiber of unbounded silence is fully awake within itself, the basis of the Veda and the Vedic Literature and the basis of all creation. Like the other three Veda, Atharva can be seen to be the absolute structure at the basis of creation.[23]

In Atharva, then, as Maharishi points out, one direction of flow can be said to offer itself to another, generating a state of non-flow—the "self-reverberating fibre of eternal silence—Atharva."[24] In this sense, Yajur is found within Atharva. When point offers itself to its own point, this is referred to as *Yajan*, the point gains unboundedness through offering. This is called *Yagya* or "the Atharva—eternally going on at the basis of creation."[25] With reference to consciousness,

Atharva Veda comprises those sets of Laws of Nature which promote Chhandas—the object of observation, hiding the dynamism of Devatā in the witnessing quality of Ṛishi within Saṁhitā.[26]

Atharva Veda also has 9 *Śākhās* or branches. In the physiology, it is expressed as the motor systems and correlates to the muscle groups found in the musculoskeletal system which are also comprised of 9 divisions: head, neck, upper limbs, thorax, back, abdomen, pelvis, perineum, and lower limbs. These muscle groups have the value of Chhandas in that they involve covering, hiding, expanding and moving all over the body.

According to the above discussion, Ṛk, Sāma, Yajur, and Atharva can be seen to be aspects of consciousness or pure wakefulness. They are the structures of knowledge having their own identity but which can be found within each other. The four Vedas represent the values of pure knowledge, Saṁhitā of Ṛishi, Devatā and Chhandas, the three-in-one structure of pure knowledge, identifying diversified values within *Ātmā*—unbounded, Transcendental Consciousness. While the structuring dynamics of these four Vedas are available in the Vedic Literature, taken together as a whole, the Veda and Vedic Literature is the field of Natural Law which evolves from sound to matter to the universe. As Maharishi points out

> The structuring dynamics of the four structures of knowledge with their divisions and subdivisions are available in the Vedic Literature, which constitutes the quality of pure wakefulness—the *Ātmā* of everyone. This whole field of the Veda and the Vedic Literature is the field of Natural Law, which evolves from the frequency of sound to matter and to the whole orderly universe.[27]

These fundamental categories of Saṁhitā, Ṛishi, Devatā and Chhandas, as discussed in previous chapters, can be seen to be the basic values of everything in creation. They are the basic modes of intelligence which structure creation. Everything can be categorized according to these. In terms of the Laws of Nature, their holistic value is expressed in terms of Saṁhitā and their specific values in terms of Ṛishi, Devatā and Chhandas. In the language of Āyur-Veda (the fourth cluster or self-referral loop of the Vedic Literature and the branch that deals with health or life-span) everything can be categorized in terms of the precipitated values of Ṛishi, Devatā and Chhandas— *Vāta, Pitta,* and *Kapha.* Maharishi describes this relationship of Ṛishi, Devatā and Chhandas and *Vāta, Pitta,* and *Kapha* with respect to Saṁhitā and balance in the physiology.

> Looking to the total picture it is obvious that the holistic value of the Laws of Nature is expressed in terms of the Unity (Saṁhitā) of the three categories (Ṛishi, Devatā, Chhandas) in which the intelligence of all the Laws of Nature are classified. These four modes of intelligence—Saṁhitā, Ṛishi, Devatā, Chhandas—are physiologically expressed in terms of balance of *Vāta, Pitta,* and *Kapha* (terminology of Āyur-Veda). The unified values of these, the holistic

> value of the physiology—the balanced state of *Vāta, Pitta,* and *Kapha*—is the total holistic value of intelligence—the total organizing power of Natural Law that sustains the infinite diversity of the universe. This becomes clear from the knowledge that *Ātmā*, the Self—WHOLENESS—the total potential of Natural Law—expresses itself through the four fundamental values of the Vedic Literature (Ṛk, Sāma, Yajur, and Atharva Veda), and these frequencies of the unmanifest reverberate as the material structure of the DNA in terms of its four fundamental codes—A,G,C,T (Adenine, Guanine, Cytosine, Thymine). Thus it appears that the four kinds of frequencies—Saṁhitā, Ṛishi, Devatā, Chhandas—have been discovered on the level of the physiological expressions of Natural Law—the building blocks of the DNA; we see DNA as the total physiological expression of Natural Law.[28]

Here, Maharishi Vedic Science locates a correspondence between the intelligence of Natural Law or pure consciousness in terms of its holistic, flowing wakefulness, offering and reverberating wholeness qualities brought out by Ṛk, Sāma, Yajur and Atharva Veda (the four frequencies of Saṁhitā, Ṛishi, Devatā, Chhandas) and the building blocks of the DNA—Adenine, Guanine, Cytosine, Thymine (A,G,C,T).

While the values of Saṁhitā, Ṛishi, Devatā, Chhandas are elaborated by the four Vedas, the diversified aspects of Ṛishi, Devatā, Chhandas—in terms of a six-fold self-referral loop which emerges when the values of Ṛishi, Devatā, Chhandas begin to interact with each other—are brought out in the rest of the Vedic Literature in a precise mathematical sequence. The first self-referral loop in this sequence is called the Vedānga.

12

THE VEDĀNGA AND THE DARŚANA: THE EXPANSION AND SUBMERGENCE OF SELF-REFERRAL CONSCIOUSNESS AND THE PHENOMENON OF COGNITION

The Vedic Literature, Maharishi explains, unfolds in self-referral loops—revealing the expansion and return to the source in the self-referral move of consciousness. As mentioned earlier, the Vedic Literature is comprised of six clusters of Natural Law. These clusters are made up of self-referral loops which highlight the dynamics of Ṛishi, Devatā, and Chhandas, and Chhandas, Devatā and Ṛishi. The first self-referral loop or cluster of Natural Law is the Vedānga. The word "*Anga*" means limb; the "Veda-Anga" are referred to as the limbs of the Veda.[1] These "limbs" include Śikṣā, Kalp, Vyākaraṇ, Nirukt, Chhand, and Jyotish and embody specific qualities of consciousness related to the expanding and contracting elements fundamental to the creative process. In this way, these six aspects of the Vedic Literature form the first self-referral loop of the Vedic Literature which follows on from the four Veda.

Maharishi explains that Śikṣā is one of the "structuring dynamics of Ṛk Veda"[2] which highlights the quality of expressing involved in structuring Ṛk Veda; it also brings out the Ṛishi value in the structuring dynamics of Saṁhitā. It is the expressing quality of intelligence available in self-referral consciousness or *Ātmā.* Kalpa, highlighting the sets of Laws of Nature promoting the quality of Devatā within Saṁhitā, brings out the transforming quality of intelligence. Following this, Vyākaraṇ and Nirukt highlight the expanding and self-referral qualities of intelligence respectively. Vyākaraṇ promotes the sets of Laws of Nature which highlight the Chhandas quality within Saṁhitā in the move of consciousness towards expansion; Nirukt promotes the sets of Laws of Nature the support Chhandas within Saṁhitā but in the self-referral direction toward the source in this loop. As Maharishi explains, opposite to the direction of expansion displayed by Vyākaraṇ, Nirukt constitutes the structuring dynamics of Ṛk Veda with reference to the self-referral quality of consciousness, which is inherently directed toward the source in pure consciousness.[3]

On another level, Vyākaraṇ is known to deal with grammar and Nirukt with meaning of the Veda and Vedic Literature. Chhand displays the measuring and quantifying quality of intelligence. Also translated as "metre" or rhythm, it highlights the sets of Laws of Nature which support the value of Devatā within Saṁhitā and is responsible for the precise structure of the Veda and the Vedic Literature in terms of meter. Finally, Jyotish, constituting the "all-knowing" quality of intelligence, is the value of *Jyotish-mati-pragyā*, "all-knowing intelligence" or fully awake consciousness[4]—and the last in the unfoldment of this self-referral loop. It highlights the sets of Laws of Nature engaged in the promotion of the quality of Ṛishi within Saṁhitā and brings out the wholeness of all-knowing intelligence. On the level of experience, *Jyotish-mati-pragyā* is gained in higher states of consciousness when awareness includes everything in its range—all action is computed from the level of absolute administration, the field of Natural Law which governs the universe. This all-knowing quality of intelligence includes the prediction of all dynamic processes; on the level of awareness this is available as *Ṛtam-bharā pragyā* in the self-referral consciousness or *Ātmā* of everyone.[5] Jyotish is also referred to as Vedic Astrology since, on an applied level, it is the science of transformation and prediction which can free life from unhelpful influences and circumstances. Maharishi has developed his Vedic Astrology and Maharishi Yagya programs to help create enlightenment in individual and collective life:

> The Maharishi Vedic Astrology and Maharishi Yagya programs are for the development of enlightenment—life free from dependence on surroundings and circumstances, and mastery over one's own destiny. The Maharishi Vedic Astrology program—Maharishi Jyotish program—comes from that level of all-knowing intelligence, 'Jyotishmati Pragya', that can fathom the influence of the threads of karma in all directions. The Maharishi Yagya program is a means to accomplish perfection in life. Everything is possible through Maharishi Yagya performances.[6]

Yagya was discussed earlier with respect to the offering quality of consciousness highlighted by Yajur-Veda—the offering of the knower, process of knowing, and known, to knowledge. Yagya refers to performance on the level of Natural Law, the level of self-referral consciousness. Operating from this fundamental level, through Yagya anything can be transformed. Yagya, here, is that Vedic technology, or Vedic engineering, which promotes enlightenment. As a science, Maharishi Vedic Astrology uses a precise mathematical approach involving knowledge of the cycles of time that bring about all transformations; it explains how the Laws of Nature are responsible for change and how life unfolds sequentially in steps of evolution and provides means for averting the danger that has not yet come.

Furthermore, in disclosing the intricate connections between the universe and the human body, Maharishi Jyotish reveals that the solar system and the universe influence the human brain, the cell, and the DNA. For example, there is a one-to-one relationship between the *Grahas* (planets) and the DNA: the hydrogen bonds which make up the central axis of the DNA correspond to the sun (*Sūrya*); the heaviest constituent of DNA, guanine, corresponds to Jupiter (*Guru*), the heaviest planet; similarly, adenine corresponds to Saturn (*Śani*), cytosine to Mars (*Mangal*), and thymine to Venus (*Śukra*); the sugar corresponds to Mercury (*Budh*); the phosphate corresponds to the moon (*Chandra*); and the enzymes which act within the DNA (but are not a real part of the DNA) correspond to the ascending and descending lunar nodes called the shadowy planets or *Rāhu* and *Ketu* in Jyotish. In the brain the correspondence is shown as: the sun (*Sūrya*)—the thalamus, the moon (*Chandra*)—hypothalamus, Mars (*Mangal*)—amygdala, Mercury (*Budh*)—subthalamus, Jupiter (*Guru*)—globus pallidus, Venus (*Śukra*)—substancia nigra, Saturn (*Śani*)—putamen, *Rāhu*—nucleus caudatus (head), and *Ketu*—nucleus caudatus (tail). In the cell the correspondence can be seen as: the sun (*Sūrya*)—the nucleus, the moon (*Chandra*)—cytosol, Mars (*Mangal*)—mitochondria, Mercury (*Budh*)—membranes, Jupiter (*Guru*)—golgi apparatus, Venus (*Śukra*)—endoplastic reticulum, Saturn (*Śani*)—lysosomi, *Rāhu*—endosome, and *Ketu*—pores. The influence from the universe on the brain is identified in the correspondence of the twelve zodiac signs, or *Rāśis* and twelve cranial nerves.[7] While all the details of these components of the physiology and the influences of the different planets cannot be covered here, the identification of such a relationship reveals that the microcosm and the macrocosm are intimately related—a feature that is highly significant for Jyotish and Maharishi Vedic Science.

In the physiology, Nader states that Jyotish corresponds to the basal ganglia, cerebral cortex, cranial nerves and brain stem. The brain stem includes groups of neurons which participate in the regulation of sleep-waking cycles and other biological rhythms. Nader goes on to discuss how the 9 *Grahas* (planets), the 12 *Bhāvas* or houses, the 12 *Rāśis* (zodiac signs), and the 27 *Nakśatras* or constellations also correspond to specific aspects of the physiology. The *Grahas* relate to the basal ganglia, the thalamus and the hypothalamus; the 12 *Bhāvas* correspond to 12 cortical areas, the 12 *Rāśis* correspond to the 12 cranial nerves; the 27 *Nakśatras* correspond to the 27 mono-aminergic groups of the brainstem. Looking in more detail at the thalamus, as noted above, Nader finds it corresponds to the Sun or *Sūrya.* Since the thalamus occupies a central place in the brain—all the basal ganglia and sensory and motor inputs connect to it—it has an important role in the physiology. It also is related to the body's orientation in space. The firing patterns of the neurons in the thalamus are altered by the direction one faces—influencing the brain functioning and the physiology. In this sense, the body is programmed to respond to direction and orientation with respect to the sun. (This point is significant to another area of the Vedic Literature, Sthāpatya Veda, which will be considered later).

With regard to the evolution of time, in Jyotish time is categorized according to specific divisions; for example:

100 *Truti*	=	1 *Tatpara*,
30 *Tatpara*	=	1 *Nimeṣa*,
18 *Nimeṣa*	=	1 *Kāṣṭhā*,
30 *Kāṣṭhā*	=	1 *Kalā*,
30 *Kalā*	=	1 *Ghatikā*,
2 *Ghatikā*	=	1 *Kṣaṇa* (*Muhūrta*),
30 *Kṣaṇa*	=	1 day.[8]

Further divisions of time identified in Maharishi Vedic Science are in terms of specific cycles in the rise and fall of Natural Law throughout eternity; these are discussed in Part IV. In general, Jyotish can be understood as that all-knowing quality of intelligence lively within *Ātmā*, the science of transformations on the level of consciousness, and the specific cycles which influence individual life. Jyotish also brings out the last quality in the first self-referral loop of the Vedic Literature—highlighting the sets of Laws of Nature that promote Ṛishi within Saṁhitā—elaborating a new value of wholeness in reference to the source.

With respect to this move of self-referral consciousness as a whole, the Vedānga bring out the principles governing expansion and contraction of infinity and its point value on the level of consciousness:

> Shiksha, Kalpa, and Vyakaran unfold the principles governing the process of expansion from a point towards infinity, the sequential elaboration of the Veda into its expressed values. Nirukta, Chhandas, and Jyotish, reveal the principles that govern the contraction of infinity to a point, the process through which the more elaborated structure of the Veda is referred back to its source.[9]

As aspects of the Vedic Literature, the Vedānga are seen to represent the dynamics of a self-referral loop of consciousness elaborating values of Ṛishi, Devatā or Chhandas and Chhandas, Devatā and Ṛishi, specific qualities of intelligence within *Ātmā*. Looking at the Vedānga in the physiology, it has been shown that the 36 books of Śikṣā correspond to the 36 autonomic ganglia and some of the tissues and organs to which they connect;[10] Kalp corresponds to the limbic system (both Kalp and the limbic system have four main divisions of 19, 8, 1 and 12, respectively); Vyākaraṇ corresponds to the hypothalamus; Nirukt to the pituitary gland, Chhand to the neurohormones, neurotransmitters, and their receptors acting on the end-organs classified into eight organ systems; and, as noted above, Jyotish corresponds to the basal ganglia, cerebral cortex, cranial nerves and brain stem.[11] Maharishi also teaches that these six aspects of the Vedic Literature collectively explain how to preserve, know, and use the Veda on the level of self-referral consciousness.[12] Therefore, they can be seen to unfold the dynamics of self-referral consciousness and also involve a practical application in the preservation, use and attainment of knowledge.

The next self-referral loop illuminated by the Vedic Literature is often referred to a the six *Darśana*, and is described in Maharishi Vedic Science as representing the practical means of gaining knowledge or the phenomenon of cognition.

Darśana: The Phenomenon of Cognition

As a self-referral loop following the Vedānga, the *Darśana*—Nyāya, Vaiśeṣik, Sāṁkhya, Yoga, Karma Mīmāṁsā, and Vedānt—elaborate further Ṛishi, Devatā and Chhandas, and Chhandas, Devatā and Ṛishi values, respectively.

Commonly referred to as the six systems of Indian philosophy or the six *Darśanas*, Nyāya, Vaiśeṣik, Sāṁkhya, Yoga, Karma Mīmāṁsā, and Vedānt have been described as the six systems of gaining knowledge. They represent the practical means of gaining knowledge of the Veda and provide complete knowledge of Natural Law.[13] In contrast to the definition provided by scholars such as Coward[14] who equate *Darśana* with a system of ideas comprising epistemology, metaphysics, ethics and soteriology, Maharishi translates *Darśana* as "form"[15] or "cognition"[16]—again, bringing the understanding of the Vedic Literature back to experience. Ultimately, *Darśana* is the phenomenon of cognition. The six *Darśanas* "unfold the reality of cognition:"

> Cognition is fundamentally the phenomenon of intelligence. Cognition is the path to awaken intelligence to the reality of what one cognizes. Levels of cognition take the intellect from the surface levels of sensory perception to deeper levels of intellectual cognition, until the intellect, transcending the boundaries of the senses, ultimately transcends its own intellectual limitations. What is left is the field of pure existence, pure intelligence—unbounded, limitless, infinite, eternal, immortal totality, the ultimate wholeness, *Brahm*—pure knowledge, the Veda, lively in human awareness—Veda realized on the level of its own intelligence, Saṁhitā of Ṛishi, Devatā, Chhandas, the Ultimate reality of human consciousness. This is *Brahma Vidyā*, the knowledge of totality, the knowledge of Natural Law.[17]

Darśana refers to more than systems of philosophy. It represents the phenomenon of cognition where "cognition" is a technical term revealing the process of transcending and gaining complete knowledge of self-referral consciousness. *Darśana* is the process of gaining finer or deeper levels of cognition until one ultimate transcends intellectual limitations and gains totality. It involves intellectual understanding, the process of gaining enlightenment, and the experience of enlightenment. This understanding of *Darśana* is considered further in terms of "artistic sight" (in Part V and VI) when Maharishi explains "there is an art of seeing in which you see behind the surface expressions."[18]

Maharishi has also discussed *Darśana* with respect to Vedic Mathematics. Vedic Mathematics is defined as the system of simultaneously sustaining all values of relationship.[19] It is the mathematics of self-referral consciousness and all the relationships generated on this level of awareness.

> Vedic Mathematics is self-referral; its source is self-referral; its course is self-referral; its goal is self-referral. Being self-referral, Vedic Mathematics is a quality of pure wakefulness—all-knowingness.

> Vedic Mathematics is that level of Creative Intelligence from where all the number systems and all the mathematical structures systematically and sequentially emerge in the most orderly way, and while maintaining the perfect

> structure of Unity (Saṁhitā), cause the appearance of diversity (Ṛishi, Devatā, Chhandas).[20]

Vedic Mathematics is the quality of pure wakefulness and all-knowingness. All-knowingness was mentioned earlier with respect to Jyotish and *Ṛtam-Bhāra Pragyā.*. In Part II, the level of *Ṛtam-Bhāra Pragyā* was described as the source of all numbers, alphabets, colors and of all squares, circles and triangles. This level of Vedic Mathematics maintains unity and diversity, Saṁhitā and Rishi, Devatā, and Chhandas simultaneously; from here all number systems and mathematical structures are generated. Since Vedic Mathematics is the mathematics of consciousness, it can be cognized by the fully awake level of individual awareness. As Maharishi points out

> The cognition of Vedic Mathematics is most delightful. It is available to fully alert consciousness—*Ṛitam-bhāra-pragyā*; it is available within the *Ātmā* of everyone, in the self-referral consciousness of everyone; it is available as the structuring dynamics of each *Sūtra* of the Veda and Vedic Literature, particularly in the Darshan Sūtra of the Veda, and most vividly in the structuring dynamics of the Vedānt Sūtra.[21]

(Here, "Darshan *Sūtra*" collectively refers to the six *Darśana*: "Nyāya Darshan Sūtra, Vaisheshik Darshan Sūtra, Sāṁkhya Darshan Sūtra, Yoga Darshan Sūtra, Karma Mīmāṁsā Darshan Sūtra, Vedānt Darshan Sūtra."[22]) This cognition, available in the sūtras of the six *Darśana*, is the quality of consciousness maintaining the simultaneous individuality and unity of Saṁhitā and Ṛishi, Devatā, Chhandas. In this theme of Vedic Mathematics creativity is characterized by opposing qualities. As Maharishi explains

> It is the quality of Creative Intelligence of consciousness which designs or structures the relationship between Saṁhitā and Ṛishi, Devatā, Chhandas; it unites Saṁhitā with Ṛishi, Devatā, Chhandas and at the same time separates Saṃhitā from Ṛishi, Devatā, Chhandas—it maintains their individual identity in their togetherness. Here at this level, the intelligence quality of consciousness is Creative Intelligence on the ground of Vedic Mathematics, and this creativity is characterized by opposing qualities—the unifying and diversifying.qualities of consciousness. This illustrates the nature of Vedic Mathematics, organizing activity within the silent nature of self-referral consciousness. This system of simultaneously sustaining all values of relationship is Vedic Mathematics, which we call mathematics of relationship; it handles all diversifying and unifying values of evolution simultaneously.[23]

For this reason, Vedic Mathematics is the "balancing power between two opposing qualities";[24] it is a field of all possibilities demonstrated by Nyāya, the first of the *Darśana.*

Nyāya—Distinguishing And Deciding: The Lamp-At-The-Door

Nyāya upholds contradictory values simultaneously[25] and has been described by Maharishi as "the-lamp-at-the-door"—that aspect of awareness which illuminates inside and outside. In this sense, it's bi-directional; characteristically, it is seen to present equally valid but contradictory lines of argument. Nyāya also highlights distinguishing and deciding qualities involved in structuring Ṛk Veda. These distinguishing and deciding qualities simultaneously comprehend opposites—holistic and the specific values at the same time. With respect to the physiology Nyāya corresponds to the thalamus which, similarly, has a discriminative and integrating role. Nader explains that almost all thalamic nuclei project to, and receive input from, the cerebral cortex—allowing the cortex to modulate input according to ongoing activity. Elsewhere, Maharishi refers to Nyāya as the science of reasoning cognized and expounded by Gautama which presents 16 points for testing the procedure of gaining knowledge.

Vaiśeṣik—Specifying

Also in this context, Vaiśeṣik, as cognized and expounded by Kanada, analyses the special qualities (or *Viśeṣa*) which distinguish one object from other objects. Following Nyāya in the self-referral loop, Vaiśeṣik brings out the quality of specifying with respect to consciousness and, in the physiology, corresponds to the cerebellum—that aspect of the physiology which is able to see facts and specific values within the spectrum of possibilities and that compares specific performance with intention. Through internal and external feedback signals, the cerebellum compares central information corresponding to an intended goal or a desired trajectory with actual motor response.[26] There are 10 lobules of the cerebellum which are divided into two sections (right and left); the cerebellum has approximately 370 small gyri (or folds). These lobules, sections and gyri correspond to the 10 chapters of Vaiśeṣik which have two divisions each and 370 *Sūtra* in total.

Sāṁkhya—Enumerating

Following Vaiśeṣik is Sāṁkhya. Sāṁkhya highlights the enumerating value involved in the structuring of Ṛk Veda, comprising the sets of Laws of Nature which are engaged in promoting the quality of Chhandas—which hides the dynamism of Devatā within the witnessing quality of Ṛishi—within Saṁhitā. Cognized by Kapila, Sāṁkhya means "pertaining to number;" it holds that knowledge of an object will not be complete without the knowledge of its components.[27] In the physiology, Sāṁkhya corresponds to the cells, tissues, organs—their types and categories.

In reference to growth to enlightenment, Maharishi points out that the first three Darśana—Nyāya, Vaiśeṣik and Sāṁkhya[28]—can be thought of as presenting the intellectual path to enlightenment, and the second three—Yoga, Karma Mīmāṁsā, and Vedānt—as presenting the experiential nature of the path to enlightenment. The first three deal with objective means of gaining knowledge while the second three unfold the subjective means of gaining knowledge. As Maharishi explains:

> Nyaya analyses the correctness of the procedure for gaining objective knowledge. Vaisheshika sets forth the criteria for analyzing the special qualities that differentiate one object from another. Sankhya enumerates the twenty-five essential categories of existence pertaining to the object. While these first three systems are primarily concerned with the objective means of gaining knowledge, the second three systems are primarily concerned with the subjective means. Yoga establishes the knower in the state of non-variability of subjective knowledge. Karma Mimamsa brings to light the knowledge of the finest impulses of the laws of nature within the field of consciousness of the knower. Vedanta then unifies the subjective and objective values in the realization of the simultaneous coexistence of silence and dynamism in the nature of the Self.[29]

Here Yoga is defined as the means of establishing the knower in the non-variability of subjective knowledge. This level of subjective knowledge is absolute knowledge, knowledge of the Self, *Kaivalya*.

Yoga—Unifying

Dealing with the subjective means of gaining knowledge, the last three *Darśana* reveal the unifying, analyzing, and I-ness or Being qualities of consciousness. Yoga, cognized by Patanjali, represents the unifying quality of consciousness within Saṁhitā which, as Maharishi points out, is expressed by the last Yoga Sūtra: चितिशक्तिरिति ॥ *Chiti Śaktiriti* (*Yoga Darśana,* 4.34), "The power of consciousness is infinite; its content is Veda—Saṁhitā of Ṛishi, Devatā, Chhandas."[30] The word "Yoga" means "union" and can refer to the path to, and experience of, union in Transcendental Consciousness: "Yoga, the path of Union, is a direct way to experience the essential nature of Reality."[31] The purpose of Yoga is to gain knowledge by direct perception.[32] It is a practical science of life which lays open to direct experience the field of absolute, pure consciousness, making available to direct experience the different levels of relative creation; its technologies are the Transcendental Meditation technique and TM-Sidhi program which develop Yogic consciousness.

In another context, in his *Commentary on the Bhagavad-Gita: Chapters 1-6,* Maharishi points out that there are eight "limbs," or eight spheres, of Yoga referred to as *Aṣthanga Yoga*. For many years, he explains, these eight limbs were regarded as different steps in the development of the state of Yoga,[33] but, in actuality, each limb is designed to create the state of Yoga in the sphere of life to which it relates.[34] The eight spheres of Yoga are:

1) *Yama*, the five qualities of observance;
2) *Niyama*, the five rules of life;
3) *Āsana*, the sphere of posture;
4) *Prāṇāyama*, the sphere of individual breath;
5) *Pratyāhāra*, the sphere of life lying between the senses and their objects;
6) *Dharaṇa*, the sphere of life that lies between the senses and the mind;
7) *Dhyāna*, the sphere of life that lies between the mind and pure consciousness; and
8) *Samādhi*, the state of Transcendental Consciousness.

The last three limbs were considered in Part II in the discussion of the self-referral mechanics of the TM-Sidhi program referred to as *Saṁyama*. The mechanics of *Saṁyama*. occur through the simultaneous application of these three modes of awareness: *Dharaṇa*, or steadiness of mind, *Dhyāna* or transcending, and *Samādhi* or Transcendental Consciousness. The term, Yoga, often associated with sets of postures (the field of *Āsana* which is one sphere of Yoga), actually deals with direct experience and the gaining of *Samādhi*. One can gain Yogic consciousness through the practice of the Transcendental Meditation technique and the TM-Sidhi program. As Maharishi teaches, with continuous practice of all eight limbs of Yoga, the state of Yoga grows simultaneously in all eight spheres of life.[35]

Nader has identified Yoga in the physiology as the association fibers of the cerebral cortex. The Yoga sūtras—the characteristic sounds or frequencies of Yoga—are seen to correspond to the actual structure of the brain physiology:

> The cortex is highly convoluted with folds called gyri and grooves called sulci. The set of association fibres connecting adjacent gyri are called U-fibres. They are anatomically identified on the basis of the folds of cortical gyri to which they connect. The longer association fibres are fasciculi and the fibres connecting the right brain with the left brain are the corpus callosum and anterior commissure. It was possible to divide the total number of association fibres into 195 sets. They correspond to the 195 sūtras of Maharishi Yoga. The cerebral cortex is divided into four lobes named for the overlying bones of the skull: Occipital, frontal, parietal and temporal lobes.
>
> The cortical areas in each lobe are historically distinctive. These lobes correspond to chapter 1-4 of Yog Sūtras, respectively. One more thing to observe is that the dimensions of the brain and the length of the sūtras also correspond to each other. The overall understanding is that the sequence of syllables of the sūtras and the physical structures of the brain meaningfully and purposefully correspond to each other....From the correspondence of the structure and function of the Yoga sūtras and the association fibres of the cortex—both display the mechanisms of unification, integration, and

> coordination—we infer that the sounds generated by the sequential activity of the association fibres are the sequentially organized sounds which make a sūtra—the sound of a sūtra. Therefore, the unifying function of brain physiology is demonstrated in the frequencies of the sequentially placed syllables of each sūtra. Maharishi Yoga brings out the quality of unity and diversity and hides, or covers, diversity. As such, it has predominantly a Chhandas value.[36]

Nader goes on to discuss this correspondence in more detail, showing the actual sūtras of Yoga and their counterparts in the brain physiology. In this way, Yoga can be understood: 1) on the unmanifest level in terms of its the self-referral mechanics of consciousness, the structuring dynamics of Ṛk Veda, 2) the level of the eight limbs of Yoga and the path to and state or experience of *Samādhi,* 3) the actual brain physiology itself. Maharishi also discusses Yoga with respect to the stages of the gap, the relationship of Yoga to Karma Mīmāṁsā and to Vedānt in terms of the dynamics of consciousness and the experience of higher states of consciousness. In two of the four stages of the gap—on the level of self-referral consciousness—the process of Yoga corresponds to *Pradhwamsābhāva* (the first stage of the gap discussed earlier in terms of the dissolution of sound) and the state of Yoga is *Atyantabhāva, Kaivalya* (the value of silence).[37]

Karma Mīmāṁsā—Analyzing

Whereas on the level of consciousness Yoga is the unifying quality of intelligence, Karma Mīmāṁsā is the analyzing value of intelligence. Cognized and expounded by Jaimini, Karma Mīmāṁsā, deals with the analysis of *Karma* or action—action at the level of self-referral consciousness.[38] It is the Mīmāṃsā (analysis) of *Karma* of the self-interacting dynamics of Saṁhitā of Ṛishi, Devatā, and Chhandas. In this sense, it is the analysis of the structuring dynamics of consciousness within *Kaivalya*, the singularity of consciousness or Yoga.

Action was mentioned in Part II, in terms of individual action or *Karma*—only action from the level of self-referral consciousness can take into account any influence and create a life-supporting effect; such action is in accord with *Dharma* or Natural Law. This relationship of individual action and *Dharma* is considered in more depth in Part IV; individual action performed from the self-referral level of Nature Law is defined as action which has the power and support of Saṁhitā of Ṛishi, Devatā and Chhandas.

On the unmanifest level, Maharishi explains, Karma Mīmāṃsā "is the analysis of the performance of Saṁhitā within itself that locates the dynamics within the silent structure of Saṁhitā;"[39] it analyzes all the differentiated values of consciousness expressed in the different aspects of the Vedic Literature, and deals with the analysis of infinity and its point—the eternal dynamic of consciousness at the self-referral level of action:

> The analysis of Ved comes from looking into the structure of Ved, and the structure of Ved emerging from the structuring dynamics of the Ved, the Vedic Literature. The structuring dynamics of Ved emerges from *Ak-kshar*, and *Ak-kshar*, the collapse of infinity onto its own point, is the *Karma* of infinity and its point, and the *Karma* of infinity and the *Karma* of the point of infinity is the eternal relationship of infinity and its point. Infinity is made of its points; infinity exists because of its points, and therefore the relationship of infinity and its points is the relationship on the self-referral level. Thus *Karma* of infinity and its point is self-referral *Karma*. Self-referral *Karma* is the eternal state of *Karma*; *Karma* is eternal within that level of intelligence which is self-referral. Thus the element of *Karma* is where the doer, the doing, and the done are in their togetherness—Saṁhitā of Ṛishi, Devatā, Chhandas—the Ved. Analysis of this structure of Ved (analysis of the Saṁhitā of Ṛishi, Devatā, Chhandas) finally comes to an end in self-referral performance—self-interacting dynamics. In this state of self-referral dynamism, the analysis of *Karma* comes to an end at its source and the analyst finds himself fully awake within himself without anything else.[40]

The *Karma* of infinity and its point is identified as the eternal relationship of infinity and point within the self-referral dynamics of consciousness, which gives rise to the structuring mechanics of the Veda and the Vedic Literature. This *Karma* of infinity and its point is the *Karma* of self-referral consciousness.

As noted above, Yoga is silence or *Kaivalya*. When one dives into this silence of *Kaivalya* one finds infinite silence and point of silence. Infinity is found to be made up of points (as described in the earlier discussion of Atharva Veda, the point can be located at the crossing of silence and dynamism). As Maharishi points out, the relationship of infinity and its points is the relationship on the self-referral level.

> So Karma Mīmāṁsā, or as it is called, Pūrva Mīmāṁsā (initial analysis), is the *Mīmāṁsā* (analysis) of the dynamic nature of silence (the state of Yoga)—the dynamic nature of Saṁhitā in terms of Ṛishi, Devatā, Chhandas—three in Unity—three within one unified WHOLENESS—analysis of Saṁhitā in terms of Ṛishi, Devatā, Chhandas.[41]

Karma Mīmāṁsā is the analysis of the dynamism within silence or the dynamic value of Saṁhitā in terms of Ṛishi, Devatā, Chhandas. Maharishi goes on to add that this analysis extends to the analysis of Ṛishi, Devatā, Chhandas in terms of the clusters of Natural Law as available in the Veda and Vedic Literature and the analysis of these in terms of their divisions and subdivisions.[42]

Vedānt—I-ness or Being

When the analysis of *Karma* comes to an end, in the state of self-referral dynamism, the analyst is awake to himself. This is described as the state of Unity

Consciousness or Vedānt. Then the finest value of creation is seen to be nothing other than one's own self-referral awareness. This is Vedānt. Vedānt, Maharishi teaches, means "the end of the Veda" and is concerned with knowledge.[43] In its role in the structuring dynamics of the Constitution of the Universe or self-referral consciousness, Vedānt represents "I-ness" or Being. This "I-ness" is *Ātmā*—that which remains when the analysis of *Karma* comes to an end, when the analyst is left to himself.[44] It is that self-referral intelligence within Veda—the "final analysis" of the Veda, the final analysis of Saṁhitā of Ṛishi, Devatā, Chhandas.[45] This is why, Maharishi explains, Vedānt is the end of the Veda.

> The last stage of analysis of Veda (Vedānt) is that level of intelligence which has completed the analysis of Veda and is left to itself. The analyst remains awake in his own Self and finds that I an all that there is without a second. This is the merger of diversity into unity; the whole reality, being self-referral, is visualized in terms of Unity, pure wakefulness, where every aspect of diversity has been dissolved, and having dissolved all variations of Unity, the spirit of Unity rejoices in its ultimate sovereignty.[46]

In Vedānt, unity is known to be the ultimate reality. In terms of the transformations or stages of the gap, this unified state is that level of intelligence which is where "the analyst himself and which remains all by itself—*Atyantābhāva* and *Anyonyābhāva*—the state of intelligence which is in the state of the gap."[47] The state of the gap is both silence, *Atyantābhāva*, and dynamism, *Anyonyābhāva*, together.

Looking at the role of the last three *Darśana* in this six-fold, self-referral loop and its return to the source, Yoga highlights the unifying quality in the structuring mechanics of Ṛk. It comprises the sets of Laws of Nature which promote Chhandas within Saṁhitā. Karma Mīmāṁsā, highlighting the analyzing quality involved in structuring Ṛk Veda, comprises the sets of Laws engaged in promoting the value of Devatā—the dynamism of observing within the witnessing quality of Ṛishi—within Saṁhitā. Karma Mīmāṁsā, has one book with 12 chapters and 60 *Pāda* or divisions. These have been correlated with 12 divisions of the central nervous system which cover the complete sensory-perceptual and motor experience and which is the organizer or switchboard by which the activities of the body are orchestrated and integrated.

For the *Darśana*, the self-referral loop is complete in Vedānt; Vedānt highlights the value of I-ness or Being with respect to consciousness. It comprises specific sets of Laws of Nature which promote the Ṛishi quality of self-referral consciousness in the structuring of Ṛk Veda. Appropriately, Vedānt corresponds to the integrated functioning of the central nervous system. It includes the 4 lobes of the cortex and the 16 nuclei of the thalamus. Nader states that the four chapters of Vedānt correspond not only to the four lobes of the cortex but also to the four categories of fasciculi described in Yoga; the 16 divisions that correspond to the 16 values or nuclei of the thalamus relate to the 16 aspects found in Nyāya. Finally, the 192 subdivisions or *Adhikaraṇa* of Vedānt correspond to the 192 *Sūktas* of the first and tenth *Maṇḍalas* of Ṛk Veda. Thus, Vedānt gives holistic experience. In this sense, and in highlighting Ṛishi, it brings another level of wholeness and unity.

In this penetrating insight into the nature of Yoga, Karma Mīmāṃsā and Vedānt, with respect to the structuring dynamics of self-referral consciousness, the value of the development of the experience of self-referral consciousness is evident. The knowledge of these *Darśana* is not just for intellectual contemplation; they unfold the experience of higher states of consciousness.

In sum, the *Darśana* can be generally understood to unfold the value of cognition—cognition of the self-referral dynamics of consciousness, the knowledge of *Brahm—Brahma Vidyā.* Clearly the different aspects of the Vedic Literature not only bring out different values of knowledge but represent the details of self-referral consciousness and the different states of consciousness themselves. In this way, Maharishi unfolds the most universal understanding of these "texts," revealing that they are impulses of our own self-referral consciousness that structure our physiology and the whole manifest universe.

The following self-referral loop called the Upa-Veda elaborates further the nature of self-referral consciousness and its dynamics.

13

UPA-VEDA: THE SUBORDINATE VEDA OR THIRD CLUSTER OF THE VEDIC LITERATURE

Following the *Darśana*, the next self-referral loop in the unfoldment of the Vedic Literature is referred to as the Upa-Veda. Upa-Veda means "subordinate Veda" and comprises Gandharva Veda, Dhanur-Veda, Sthāpatya Veda, Hārīta Saṁhitā, Bhel Saṁhitā, and Kaśyap Saṁhitā—bringing out the values of Ṛishi, Devatā, Chhandas, Chhandas, Devatā and Ṛishi, respectively. The first three clusters of the Vedic Literature—Vedānga, Upānga or *Darśana*, and Upa-Veda—are dedicated to *Śruti* in the total expression of Natural Law. The last three clusters, Āyur-Veda, Brāhmaṇa, and Prātiśākhya, are dedicated to *Smṛti*. *Smṛti* is the quality of memory—where memory refers to value of awareness which does not forget its unmanifest value even when it is in terms of fluctuations. *Smṛti* is discussed in more detail in Chapter 14, as part of the Brāhmaṇa loop. However, as Maharishi explains, in the evolution of Law (i.e., the sequential development of Veda from "Ak") one can understand this evolution in terms of qualities which initiate the process and qualities in the opposite direction:

> It is interesting to find that in the total expression of Law, half of the structure is dedicated to *Shruti* and half is dedicated to *Smṛiti*.. The values which initiate the process of evolution are categorized as *Shruti*, and those in the opposite direction are categorized as *Smṛiti*. This is the reason why traditionally *Shruti* and *Smṛiti* are taken to be two aspects of the same structure of knowledge, the Veda, and their extension is available in the thirty-six values of the Vedic Literature. Three clusters of the Vedic Literature belong to *Shruti*—Upa-Veda, Vedānga, and Upānga, and three belong to *Smṛiti*—Brāhmaṇa, Āyur-Veda, and the Prātishākhyas. It is necessary to know that understanding *Shruti* and *Smṛiti* as separate is just for the purpose of understanding their unique quality in order to understand them on their own basis; it is for the sake of understanding, otherwise in reality they are an inseparable continuum. For example, the path from home to school is always the same one path; one finds it different only on the return journey when one comes from school to home. At every point of the path, both directions are available.[1]

Here Maharishi identifies the six clusters of Natural Law—from the Vedānga, Upānga, Upa-Veda, Āyur-Veda, Brāhmaṇa to the Prātiśākhya—and their divisions as 36 aspects of the Vedic Literature. The first three clusters belong to *Śruti*, the second three to *Smṛti*; but this separation is merely for the purpose of understanding since both values are really one continuum. This evolution of *Śruti* and *Smṛti* in both directions is also seen elaborated in the ten *Maṇḍalas* of Ṛk Veda, the structure of pure knowledge.

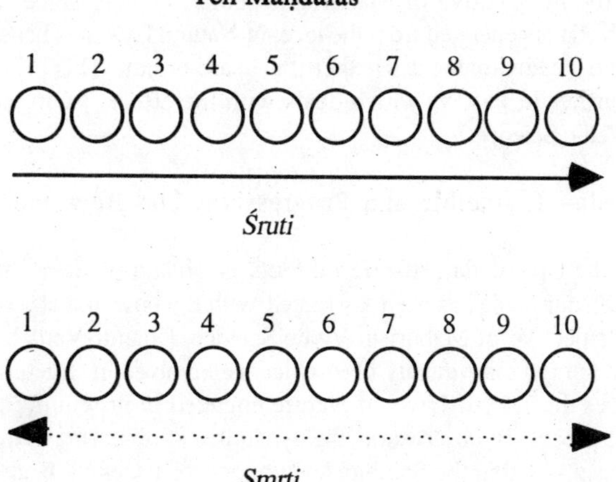

Maharishi illustrates this diagramatically by representing ten circles (the ten *Maṇḍalas*) in a row with an arrow initiated from the first *Mandala*, pointing from left to right, in the direction of the tenth *Maṇḍala.* This indicates the evolution of *Śruti.* The evolution of *Smṛti* is shown by what at first appears to be the same picture; a row of ten circles—the ten *Maṇḍalas*—with a line underneath. But this line is bi-directional; it has an arrow at both ends. It is also less distinct, as if dynamically indicating the possibility of movement in both directions.[2]

The third self-referral loop or cluster of Natural Law of the Vedic Literature which is dedicated to *Śruti* includes Gandharva Veda, the music of Nature.

Gandharva Veda—Integrating and Harmonizing

Gandharva Veda brings out the integrating and harmonizing quality of intelligence or consciousness involved in structuring Ṛk Veda and highlights the sets of Laws of Nature which promote the value of Ṛishi within Saṁhitā. Commonly known as the discipline of Indian classical music, Maharishi Gandharva Veda specifically enlivens Natural Law by matching with the swings of Nature. It mirrors the rhythms of Nature. Enlivening values of Natural Law lively at specific times of the day and by eliminating stress in the atmosphere, Gandharva Veda upholds evolution in waves of bliss and produces a healthy environment for the individual and society. This is how it has a harmonizing and integrating effect on the whole of society. In the physiology, Gandharva Veda is found as the seven sympathetic ganglia on each side of the spinal cord which participate in the modulations of the rhythms of the heart. These correspond to the seven *Swaras* or musical notes of

Gandharva Veda—SĀ, RE, GA, MA, PA, DHA, and NI. These seven impulses are connected to four thoracic segments which correspond to the flat notes RE, GA, DHA, and NI (Nader also notes that the parasympathetic or vagal innervation also connected to the heart corresponds to the sharp note MÁ).[3]

From the perspective of Maharishi Vedic Science, since the effect of Gandharva Veda is generated from the level of Natural Law, it is beneficial for the individual and the environment whether it is heard or not. This principle will be discussed further in Part V, which deals with the effects of art as defined by Maharishi Vedic Science.

Dhanur-Veda—Invincible and Progressive: The Bow and Arrow

The next in the Upa-Veda self-referral loop, is Dhanur-Veda. 'Dhanu' means 'bow' and Dhanur-Veda has been associated with the bow and arrow or defense. From the perspective of Maharishi Vedic Science, Dhanur-Veda highlights the invincible and progressive quality of intelligence involved in structuring Ṛk Veda and comprises the sets of Laws of Nature engaged in promoting the value of Devatā—the process of observation, the dynamism of observing in the witnessing quality of Ṛishi—within the Saṁhitā level of consciousness.[4] It also represents the individual and cosmic bio-chemistry. It is that invincible and progressive quality of intelligence that structures the immune system and the bio-chemistry.[5] In fact, with respect to the physiology, Dhanur-Veda can seen on three levels: 1) the DNA, 2) the bio-chemical reactions or transformations, 3) the vertebrae of the spine. Firstly, the DNA, in its self-referral silence and dynamism, is projected onto the entire human physiology; this phenomenon is correspondent to the 'Self' or *Ātmā* (DNA) projected onto *Brahm* (body). Secondly, also demonstrative of the theme of bow and arrow associated with Dhanur-Veda, the bio-chemical reactions project one state into another in their transformations. Thirdly, each vertebra is divided into four parts which correspond to the four chapters of Dhanur-Veda. There are 33 vertebrae in total and each chapter of Dhanur-Veda contains a number of *Sūtras* equaling a multiple of 33.[6]

In general, the theme of Vedic defense has been well articulated in Maharishi Vedic Science. Maharishi explains that Vedic Defense has four strategies with reference to the four values of intelligence: Saṁhitā, Ṛishi, Devatā and Chhandas (Ṛk Veda, Sāma Veda, Yajur-Veda and Atharva Veda). The field of Saṁhitā is transcendental, beyond reproach, eternally invincible and is, therefore, absolute defense. This level of consciousness, Maharishi indicates, was bestowed on the battlefield to Arjuna—the principal hero of the Bhagavad-Gītā.[7] The remaining strategies of defense—with reference to Ṛishi, Devatā and Chhandas—are called *Adhyātmik*, *Adhidaivik*, and *Adhibhūtik*. The *Adhyātmik* or *Yogic* aspect of defense is the practice of Yogic Flying by a small percentage (3%-5%) of the military personnel—creating an abstract, indomitable, invincible armor for the nation. Yogic Flying was discussed in Part II in the context of the TM-Sidhi program. Research studies on the effect of the group practice of this program show that when only the square root of 1% of a population practice this technology, war deaths and crime rate decrease. Therefore, this *Yogic* aspect of defense is extremely effective. Maharishi adds that the *Yogic* strategy of defense is with reference to Ṛishi and is dedicated to the silent quality of Saṁhitā, the silent transcendental field of consciousness beyond space and time, the level of invincibility.[8] *Yogic* defense, the *Adhyātmik* aspect of Vedic Defense, is the "total value of defence" because through it the integration of collective consciousness is always maintained. When collective consciousness is coherent an invincible armor is created, disallowing the birth of an enemy or disruption from outside influences. This concept is also discussed in Part IV, in connection with cultural integrity.

The second, *Adhidaivik* aspect of Vedic Defense is related to the influence of the *Grahas, Rāśis*, and *Nakṣatras.* This *Daivik* aspect involves the Devatā aspect of Saṁhitā—the dynamic aspect of Saṁhitā or the unified dynamism of all the Laws of Nature and the influence of the *Grahas* or planets, the *Rāśis* or zodiac signs, and the *Nakṣatras* or constellations. The *Grahas, Rāśis*, and *Nakṣatras*

> Are aspects of the physiology of the individual, and have their counterparts in Cosmic Life. The *Grahas, Rāshis*, and *Nakshatras* project their positive and negative influences on the individual and on national life. It requires an all-time vigilance to ensure their influence is always nourishing and supporting to life, so that individual and national consciousness is saved from any negative influence. This is called *Graha Shānti* in India.[9]

As mentioned in Chapter 12, the relationship of the individual to, and influence of, the *Grahas, Rāśis*, and *Nakṣatras* is dealt with in Maharishi Jyotish and Yagya. This is just one way in which the various areas of Vedic knowledge are interconnected. The last quality of Vedic Defense is the material or physical means of preventing the enemy involving the use of weaponry. Maharishi explains that the subject matter of this *Adhibhūtik* means of defense is available in Dhanur-Veda and Sthāpatya Veda.[10] While the use of the *Adhibhūtik* means of defense is brought out in these two aspects of the Vedic Literature, Sthāpatya Veda provides details of how the built environment can be constructed so that life can be aligned to Natural Law.

Sthāpatya Veda and Vāstu Vidyā: Establishing Life in Accord With Natural Law

Referred to as ancient Indian architecture and design, Sthāpatya Veda involves much more than design, planning and building. Maharishi Sthāpatya Veda is devoted to the establishment of life in accordance with Natural Law. It highlights the establishing quality of intelligence or consciousness in the structuring mechanics of Ṛk Veda,[11] unfolding the sets of Laws of Nature engaged in promoting the Chhandas value within Saṁhitā. As Maharishi points out,

"Sthāpatya Ved is the total potential of Natural Law with reference to the quality of CHHANDAS, the object of observation, within the nature of Saṁhitā level of consciousness;" it constitutes the structuring dynamics of Ṛk Veda, "with reference to the quality of consciousness, which ESTABLISHES everything in the light of Natural Law." [12] In terms of our physiology, Sthāpatya Veda is the establishing quality of intelligence which structures the anatomy; it deals with structure and the relationships of structure—the integration of the parts to the whole. [13] For example, the structure of the nerves of the spinal cord "is especially established by the principles of Sthāpatya Veda" since the spinal cord (and the nerves that issue from it) represent a major part of the Veda. [14] The spinal cord, with its 35 segments or nerves on either side (the eight cervical nerves; the twelve thoracic nerves; the five lumbar nerves; the five sacral nerves; the five coccygeal nerves) present two symmetrical parts which total 70 divisions. These 70 divisions correspond to the 70 chapters of Sthāpatya Veda.[15]

The brain and the spinal cord are also discussed by Maharishi in terms of an "inverted tree" [16]—where the brain is the seed with its roots, the spinal cord and its nerves is the trunk with its branches, and the branches have leaves which correspond to specific *Sūktas* of Ṛk Veda. Reference is made to an inverted tree, an Aśvattha tree (also called the holy fig tree in Indian scholarship) and a World tree, in the Vedic hymns and the Bhagavad-Gītā:

उर्ध्वमूलमधः शाखमश्वत्थमं प्राहुरव्ययम् ।
छन्दांसि यस्य पर्णानि यस्तं वेद स वेदवित् ।।

Ūrdhvamūlamadhaḥ shākham aśvattham Prāhuravyayam,
Chhandāṁsi Yasya Parṇāni Yastaṁ Veda Sa Vedavit.

(*Bhagavad-Gītā, 15. 1*)

Maharishi translates this expression as, "Ṛk Veda speaks of the eternal Ashvattha, the World Tree, whose roots are on top and branches with leaves below. They are the Vedic hymns. He who knows it knows the Veda." [17] The Vedic hymns, Ṛk Veda and Sthāpatya Veda, are equivalent to the "inverted tree"—the World Tree, the eternal *Aśvattha* (with roots on top and branches and leaves below)—this is expressed as the structure of the human nervous system. [18]

Scholars such as Coomaraswamy have noted this reference to the inverted tree in the Vedic texts, suggesting it can be equated with Brahman while also mentioning that this concept arises in other traditions. Here, Maharishi Vedic Science furnishes a profound understanding of the inverted tree with respect to consciousness, the Vedic hymns and the physiology—providing not only a penetrating insight into this concept but also one which has enormous practical value. The World Tree is the structure of the Veda in the human physiology. Specific *Sūktas* of Ṛk Veda and chapters of Sthāpatya Veda not only relate to one another but also correspond to the nervous system. The implications of this knowledge are far reaching.

On another level, Sthāpatya Veda is described as "Vedic Architecture" or architecture based on complete knowledge. Vedic Architecture is architecture which: 1) is supported by the theories of modern science (physics, chemistry, mathematics etc.) and completely scientific; 2) takes into account the consciousness of the builder and architect—both must be developed in order to realize architecture in accord with Natural Law; and, 3) must conform to the measurements and formulas of Sthāpatya Veda that provide procedures and programs for constructing architecture in accord with Natural Law and according to which the eternal structure of the universe itself has been laid out.[19] It encompasses architecture, town and city planning, and the arts, each of which plays the role of establishing the human physiology with respect to the cosmic physiology—the anatomy of the universe. Maharishi Sthāpatya Veda is also referred to as *Vāstu Vidya*—knowledge of *Vāstu.* It is the mathematical formulas of *Vāstu Vidya* that are used in Maharishi Sthāpatya Veda.[20] As discussed further in Part VI, *Vāstu* refers to place or site, the site within which consciousness resides.

This science of Maharishi Sthāpatya Veda considers the harmonious interrelationship of all the different structures of man-made design, and how these structures can be aligned with the cycles of Nature. Any artistic, architectural, or environmental form which aims to be in accord with cosmic life, and to create harmony and a life-supporting influence, must embody the structure and orderly properties of self-referral consciousness. In this context, Maharishi Sthāpatya Veda is the most supreme "system of country, town, village, and home planning in accord with natural law" which takes into account the solar and lunar influences on the earth "connecting individual life with cosmic life, individual intelligence with cosmic intelligence."[21]

Highlighting the precision of *Vāstu Vidya*, Maharishi Vedic Science reveals that the field of Vedic Architecture is the field of Vedic Mathematics. Vedic Mathematics was discussed earlier with respect to the unfoldment of the *Apauruṣeya Bhāṣya* of Ṛk Veda and with respect to cognition or *Darśana*. Maharishi points out that Vedic Mathematics has one basic principle, expressed in the *Bṛhad-Āraṇyak Upaniṣad* as: *Pūrṇat pūrṇam udachyate*—"from fullness emerges fullness—from fullness is structured fullness—from total Natural Law emerges total Natural Law."[22]

> In the process of transformation, or evolution, it is the Totality that is reborn again and again—नवो नवो भवति जायमानः *Navo-Navo bhavati jāyamānaḥ* (*Ṛk Veda, 10.85.19*). This means that in the sequential flow of evolution of Natural Law, all its expressions, at every step of evolution, are sustained in the quality of WHOLENESS. This makes it clear that total Natural Law expressing itself in terms of Ṛk Veda, Sāma Veda, Yajur-Veda, and Atharva Veda, and all the other thirty-six values of the Vedic Literature—the forty (4 + 36) fundamentals of creation—give the destiny of every progressive step of the process of evolution, which is the nature of creation. This is because the whole process of creation has

> its basis in the self-interacting dynamics of Saṁhitā—the self-interacting dynamics of Ṛk Veda—and the emergence of new values, and the continuum of the emergence of new values—Sāma, Yajur, and Atharva—evolve through the principle of पूर्णात् पूर्णमुदच्यते *Pūrṇāt pūrṇam udachyate*—fullness of unmanifest Veda (Saṁhitā) giving rise to the fullness of unmanifest Veda (Ṛishi, Devatā, Chhandas).[23]

Fullness is the total value of self-referral consciousness or Veda. Through the evolution of consciousness fullness (Saṁhitā) gives rise to fullness (Ṛishi, Devatā and Chhandas)—diversified values of fullness, but fullness nevertheless. In this way, any new values of Natural Law are sustained in wholeness and remain connected to the source—Saṁhitā. This means that the evolutionary process is always supported by Natural Law, always balanced, always holistic, always nourished by that eternal, infinite value of pure consciousness. Nothing is lost to fullness.

This process of creation is on the ground of *Atyanta-Abhāva*. *Atyanta-Abhāva* is the field of silence or Absolute Abstraction. Maharishi goes on to point out that on this level is the reality of Absolute Wakefulness, *Ṛtam bharā pragyā*.[24] As mentioned before, in Part II *Ṛtam bharā pragyā* was described as that level of almost no differences from where all differences arise—that level from where all triangles, circles, squares, alphabets, and colors, spring. It was also referred to in Chapter 12 with respect to Vedic Mathematics and cognition (*Darśana*) as that level of fully alert consciousness—available within the *Ātmā* of everyone, the self-referral consciousness of everyone, available as the structuring dynamics of each *Sūtra* of the Veda and the Vedic Literature, particularly the *Darśana Sūtras* but especially the *Vedānt Sūtras*. Maharishi adds that on this level of Absolute Wakefulness or *Ṛtam bharā pragyā*:

> On this level of awakening is the unity of Saṁhitā of Ṛishi, Devatā, and Chhandas. From here, every step of evolution is the togetherness of three —Saṁhitā of Ṛishi, Devatā, and Chhandas—it is the mathematics of the Absolute value that prevails. This is the reality of पूर्णात् पूर्णमुदच्यते *Pūrṇāt pūrṇam udachyate*—from Saṁhitā, Ṛishi, Devatā, and Chhandas emerge the structures of fullness—Sāma Veda, Yajur-Veda, and Atharva Veda—each is specific without losing its generality; its specificity is embedded in its generality. When specificity is in terms of generality—Totality—the non-specific level of WHOLENESS—then the specific structure is Vedic.[25]

The process of creation or evolution takes place on the ground of Absolute Abstraction. The reality of wakefulness or awakening is on this level—where every step of evolution involves the three values of Ṛishi, Devatā, and Chhandas within Saṁhitā. The values of Sāma, Yajur and Atharva Veda, structures of fullness, emerge from these values of Saṁhitā, Ṛishi, Devatā and Chhandas. In this way, specificity is always in terms of generality, the holistic value of Natural

Law. This is the definition and actuality of a Vedic structure—it embodies Totality, the parts are always in reference to the whole, self-referral consciousness (Part VI returns to this principle of wholeness in its introduction to the Vāstusūtra Upaniṣad). Every structure has the total value of intelligence, holistic and specific, within its inner intelligence. In this sense, the purpose of Sthāpatya Veda is to establish any building, village, city or country, in full alignment with the structuring dynamics of the whole universe, which maintains the connectedness of everything with everything else.

This is why Vedic Architecture is that architecture which is not only upheld by modern science and its disciplines, but takes into account the development of consciousness of the builder and architect, who ideally are living higher states of consciousness, functioning at that level of awakening—*Ṛtam bharā pragyā*, and why the measurements and guidelines according to Sthāpatya Veda must be taken into account for any structure to display Vedic Mathematics, the mathematics of the evolution of Natural Law.

The formulas of Sthāpatya Veda create the effect of harmony and stability in life because the individual is essentially Cosmic in nature; the structures and functions of the of the physiology are an exact replica of the Cosmic Physiology—the physiology of the universe. Natural Law is common to both. As mentioned in Part II and earlier in this section, every grain of creation is governed by that intelligence which structures the universe. The intelligence of every grain of creation is in tune with the whole cosmos. Structurally, the infinite diversity of the ever-expanding universe is upheld by one unified wholeness of intelligence.

The first step of design and construction representing the principle of fullness emerging from fullness is the establishment of the central point of the structure, the *Brahma-Sthān*. The *Brahma-Sthān* is the seat of wholeness. From this point wholeness expands. When the construction of houses, villages and towns is not based on this system of Vedic Architecture problems in life arise. There is lack of balance between individual and cosmic counterparts (i.e. the influence from the sun, moon, directions etc.)—due to the intimate relationship between the microcosm and the macrocosm. The intelligence which structures the cell, is the same intelligence that structures the universe. Nader indicates that all the forty qualities of intelligence, available in the Vedic Literature as the form of sound, can be located in the nucleus of the cell, the cell, and the whole physiology—which has its counterparts in the whole universe. That intelligence governs every grain in creation and all the galaxies and planets, including our own planet—keeping everything in harmony.

The movement of the planets affects our life, creating cycles which promote our continued existence. Recent research has also confirmed that the brain is sensitive to orientation, position and direction in space.[26] The thalamus is one aspect of the brain that is involved with this sensitivity to orientation. The firing patterns of the neurons in the brain differ according to direction and orientation. This value of direction and its influence is taken into account in Sthāpatya Veda in several ways but primarily with respect to the orientation of a building. Indeed, auspicious and inauspicious influences due to directions are clearly outlined.

Taking into account this influence, when the house and entrance faces East, enlightenment, affluence and fulfillment for the inhabitants are predicted. North is the only other direction for enhancement of what can be termed auspicious results. A North orientation is said to bring prosperity and happiness. According to Maharishi Sthāpatya Veda, all remaining orientations have the propensity to promote inauspicious influences, for example: constant fear (entrance and house facing Southeast); all negative influences, problems and suffering (South); influence of quarreling (Southwest); poverty and lack of creativity and vitality (West); mental inconsistency and instability (Northwest); and less outer success (Northeast).[27]

An ideal city which is built according to *Vāstu* (the science of Sthāpatya Veda) with all the roads running North to South and East to West—operates like a superconductor. Unlike an ordinary electrical conductor which can be penetrated by an external magnetic field, a superconductor (as illustrated by the Meissner Effect in quantum physics) disallows the penetration of an external magnetic field. This is due to the orderly, coherent collective functioning of its electrons. The impenetrable status of the superconductor is, thus, maintained in the face of the outside influence.

This principle is analogous to the *Maharishi Vāstu Effect* in Maharishi Sthāpatya Veda. A city that is not designed according to Natural Law with roads running in all directions, leads to problems in life. The ideal city has appropriate *Vāstu*—employing ideal orientation (roads running North/South and East/West) and appropriate cross ventilation—enriches city life with the evolutionary power of Natural Law, generating coherence, order and harmony in society. Effectively, the negative influences remain at the border or boundaries of the *Vāstu* site.[28]

Practically speaking, by applying this knowledge to city and town-planning and architecture, financial resources can be saved, and the individual and society can enjoy greater success, health and fulfillment. Exploratory research has already been conducted at Maharishi University of Management examining principles of Maharishi Sthāpatya Veda such as orientation. This discussion provides an insight into the practical nature of the discipline of Sthāpatya Veda and the fundamental value of intelligence which Sthāpatya Veda highlights in the structuring mechanics of Ṛk Veda.

As mentioned above, Sthāpatya Veda brings out the Chhandas value in the self-referral loop of the Upa-Veda. Both the anatomy and the physical structures of the architectural environment are Chhandas values, in the sense that they deal with material structure. Since Sthāpatya Veda involves the establishment of wholeness in every part, and is that Vedic discipline that encompasses the arts, it is considered further in Part VI.

Hārīta, Bhel, and Kaśyap Saṁhitā: The Self-Referral Move in the Loop of Upa-Veda

Following Sthāpatya Veda in the self-referral loop of Upa-Veda, as Maharishi points out, Hārīta Saṁhitā highlights the nourishing quality of self-referral consciousness or *Ātmā*. With reference to consciousness, Hārīta Saṁhitā comprises the specific sets of Laws of Nature that are engaged in promoting the quality of Chhandas within the Saṁhitā level of consciousness and in the physiology, it corresponds to the venous and biliary systems. Next in the self-referral loop is Bhel Saṁhitā which highlights the differentiating quality of intelligence and comprises the Laws of Nature which promote Devatā—the process of observation, the dynamism of observing in the witnessing quality of Ṛishi—within the Saṁhitā level of consciousness.

Bhel Saṁhitā corresponds to the lymphatic system and the glial cells in the body. The lymphatic system pertains to the lymph vessel which collects lymph from the lymph capillaries and converges with other lymphatics to form the thoracic and right lymphatic ducts. The glial cells concern glia—the non-nervous or supporting tissue of the brain and spinal cord. Nader explains that the glial cells originate from the spongioblasts of the neural tube and include the astrocytes and oligodendrocytes. He states that the term Bhel indicates the values of evolution which maintains balance between the destructive and creative forces—unifying and differentiating at the same time. This role is served by the glial cells which maintain the nervous system by holding it together but by also allowing the neurons and their processes to be differentiated. Each neuron is well-defined in its activity and well-differentiated when acting in harmony and coordination with other neurons. Furthermore, there are 120 chapters in Bhel Saṁhitā. As for the nervous system, it is divided into two parts as described under Karma Mīmāṁsā—60 for astrocytes and 60 for oligodendrocytes; this makes 120 which correspond to the 120 chapters of Bhel Saṁhitā.

In the self-referral sequence, the move from Gandharva Veda (integrating and harmonizing), Dhanur Veda (invincible and progressive) to Sthāpatya Veda (establishing) and then to Hārīta Saṁhitā, (nourishing), Bhel Saṁhitā (differentiating) and Kaśyap Saṁhitā, brings us to the quality of equivalency within self-referral consciousness. This quality of equivalency highlighted by Kaśyap Saṁhitā is that value of intelligence that structures the arterial system in the body. This system—carrying the blood to the heart—is a key part of our physiological functioning. On the level of consciousness, Maharishi explains that the quality of equivalency is available everywhere. The manifest is, ultimately, unmanifest; Saṁhitā is equivalent to Ṛishi, Devatā and Chhandas. Everything in the universe is the play of self-referral consciousness.

In effect, as Maharishi indicates, another example of this quality on the level of consciousness, is the "dynamic silence of the syllable क् (K), which puts Ṛishi, Devatā, and Chhandas in one category—Saṁhitā."[29] Kaśyap Saṁhitā, as the final aspect of this self-referral loop highlighting the value of equivalency, brings out the wholeness value, revealing that the manifest is unmanifest and that Ṛishi, Devatā and Chhandas are equivalent to Saṁhitā.

The next self-referral loop in the unfoldment of the Veda Literature is collectively referred to as Āyur-Veda and is the first in the last three clusters of six values of the Vedic Literature (Āyur-Veda, Brāhmaṇa, and Prātiśākhya) which, as mentioned at the outset, are dedicated to *Smṛti.*

14

ĀYUR-VEDA, BRĀHMAṆA AND PRĀTIŚĀKHYA: THE FINAL THREE CLUSTERS OF NATURAL LAW

The remaining three clusters of Natural Law, as mentioned earlier, are dedicated to *Smṛti* and comprise Āyur-Veda, Brāhmaṇa and Prātiśākhya. Āyur-Veda means knowledge or science of life-span and deals with creating balance in all areas of life: mind, body and environment. It is the fourth self-referral loop or cluster of the Vedic Literature—comprising Charak Saṁhitā, Suśrut Saṁhitā, Vāgbhatt Saṁhitā, Mādhav Nidān Saṁhitā, Shārngadhar Saṁhitā and Bhāva Prakāsh Saṁhitā.

The next in the sequence, is the Brāhmaṇa—the fifth cluster of Natural Law. The term Brāhmaṇa, used to refer collectively to the self-referral loop of Upaniṣad, Āraṇyak, Brāhmaṇa, Itihās, Purāṇ and Smṛti, also refers to one of its aspects. Similarly, Smṛti, the value of memory described with respect to the self-referral direction or opposite to *Śruti* in the evolution of Natural Law, is also an aspect of the self-referral loop of Brāhmaṇa. The value of Smṛti brings out the mechanics of "memory" with respect to self-referral occur at every level in the evolution of Natural Law.

Finally, Prātiśākhya is that cluster of Natural Law which brings out the wholeness value—connecting all the parts to the whole—elaborating Brahman as identified by the specific qualities of intelligence they represent: all-pervading WHOLENESS; silencing, sharing and spreading; unfolding; dissolving; omnipresent; unmanifesting the parts but manifesting the whole. These six qualities of intelligence correspond to Ṛk Veda Prātiśākhya, Śukl-Yajur-Veda Prātiśākhya, Atharva Veda Prātiśākhya, Atharva Veda Prātiśākhya (*Chaturadhyāyi*), Kṛṣṇ-Yajur-Veda Prātiśākhya (*Taittirīya*), and Sāma Veda Prātiśākhya (*Puśpa Sūtram*), respectively.

In one instance, Maharishi explains that the Prātiśākhya are different in their role to the other aspects of the Vedic Literature in that they put all the values of the structuring dynamics of Ṛk Veda detailed in the other aspects in the context of their source. Thus, they reveal that all the different aspects of the Veda and Vedic Literature are united at one point, the non-differentiated field or unmanifest singularity of Natural Law.[1]

Like those before them, all of these three clusters of Natural Law unfold specific values in the structuring mechanics of Ṛk Veda, self-referral consciousness. In the Āyur-Veda loop, Charak Saṁhitā is seen as the wholeness value of the total grouping—it contains the others within it.

Āyur-Veda: The Fourth Self-Referral Loop of the Vedic Literature

In his description of the Āyur-Veda self-referral loop, Maharishi explains that the word Charak, the name of the first aspect, contains in its sound and meaning total knowledge—*Brahma Vidyā,* the total knowledge of Natural Law. "Cha" meaning "and" represents togetherness, or Saṁhitā—the togetherness of the two values of silence and dynamism or the togetherness of the separate values of *Ātmā* and its expressions—intellect, mind, body, and behavior. Charak highlights the balancing—holding together and supporting qualities of intelligence. These values account for the relationship of unity with diversity which is contained in the word "Charak".[2] As Maharishi explains

> In the word 'Charak', 'Cha' means 'and', which means togetherness—Saṁhitā—the togetherness of the two values of silence and dynamism (bosonic and fermionic tendencies)—togetherness of the separate values (qualities) of *Ātmā* and its expressions—intellect, mind, body, behaviour, etc. 'Cha' puts together the unmanifest self-referral dynamism of *Ātmā* and its expressions, the Laws of Nature, and their evolutionary nature. This means that 'Cha' expresses Totality—*Brahm*—which is expressive of the unmanifest and all its manifestations as the ever-expanding universe.[3]

Here the silence and dynamism of self-referral consciousness is identified also as the bosonic and fermionic tendencies, fundamental fields in the terminology of physics. In further analyzing the word Charak, Maharishi points out that after "Cha", the syllable "Ra" can also be described in terms of its significance on the level of consciousness. "Ra", Maharishi indicates, is comprised of two sounds र् (R) and अ (A)—र् (R) "reverberation, indicative of the finest impulse of holistic silence expressed by अ (A)—*Atharva'*[4]:

> It represents the reverberating intelligence of the finest particle of the wave function of the universe reverberating in itself—present here, there, and everywhere as the unmanifest intelligence at the unmanifest basis of every particle in creation.[5]

The expression from Ṛk Veda which illustrates this principle states:

दूरे दृशं गृहपतिम् अथर्युम्

Dūre dṛśaṁ gṛhapatim atharyum

(*Ṛk Veda*, *7.1.1.*)

Far, far away the indweller of the house, the Self, is seen reverberating.

This means that even the most distant point is seen in terms of the Self, self-referral consciousness. This is the reality of Brahman Consciousness, *Brahm.* The reverberating intelligence of finest particle of the wave function of the universe (in the language of physics) is found reverberating within itself, everywhere.

Maharishi continues to explain that in the word Charak, the अ (A) of र् (R) with the following letter क् (K) expresses अक् (Ak)—the first syllable of Ṛk Veda (discussed in the beginning of this section as the compact expression of total knowledge). Thus, as Maharishi indicates, 'Charak' comprises complete knowledge of all the Laws of Nature. As he points out

> Then in the word 'Charak', the अ (A) of र् (R), together with the following क् (K), express अक् (Ak), the first syllable of Ṛk Veda—the collapse of reverberating WHOLENESS onto its own point, generating all the Laws of Nature responsible for the expression of Totality in specific values. Thus the name 'Charak' contains the complete knowledge of all the Laws of Nature, which on one side have the ocean of intelligence—Veda—Mantra and Brāhmaṇa (knowledge and organizing power)—and on the other side their expressions in the ever-evolving material creation. In this way, Charak is the light of life eternally maintaining *balance—holding together* and *supporting* WHOLENESS of life on the level of *Ātmā* and all its expressions on the levels of intellect, mind, body. senses, and behaviour. Charak is total knowledge—*Brahma Vidyā*; it presents the total knowledge of Natural Law.[6]

Charak contains the knowledge of the Laws of Nature which have on one side Veda (made up of the *Mantra* and *Brāhmaṇa*, here described respectively as knowledge and organizing power, also known as the words and gaps of the Vedic hymns), and on the other side the expressions of the Laws of Nature in material creation. This is why Charak is the quality of maintaining balance, holding together and supporting wholeness—the Totality of consciousness—on all levels of life. Charak Saṁhitā is the expression of this level of *Brahma Vidyā* which is available in self-referral consciousness—*Ātmā.* With this understanding, it is possible to locate in Charak the value of Smṛti—the role of maintaining the "opposite direction" to the direction of evolution brought out in the first three clusters of the Vedic Literature dedicated to *Śruti.*

Maharishi goes on to explain that the break down of balance between Ṛishi, Devatā and Chhandas results in the preponderance of Ṛishi, Devatā or Chhandas values which create the divisions of the body. However, the harmony of the Ṛishi-predominating, Devatā-predominating, and Chhandas-predominating structures of Natural Law which are the parts of the body, is within the range of Charak. Ultimately, Charak highlights Ṛishi, as Maharishi points out:

> Breaking down the balance between Ṛishi, Devatā and Chhandas expresses Natural Law in terms of the predominance of Ṛishi, Devatā, or Chhandas values,

> which produces the *Angas*, or divisions and subdivisions of the body. The total body belongs to Charak, and the harmony of differences is also within the range of Charak; that means Ṛishi-dominating, Devatā-dominating, and Chhandas-dominating structures of Natural Law are also kept in harmony, but they are parts of the body, divisions of the body. This is Charak, Suśrut, and Vāgbhatt Saṁhitā in *Ātmā*—the unified value of Ṛishi, Devatā, and Chhandas. Ṛishi———> Charak Saṁhitā; Devatā ———> Sushrut Saṁhitā; Chhandas ———> Vāgbhatt Saṁhitā. Each have their divisions and subdivisions, which are available subjectwise in the names of their chapters, and in the detailed material within each chapter.[7]

Charak, Suśrut, and Vāgbhatt Saṁhitā in *Ātmā* represent the unified value of Ṛishi, Devatā, and Chhandas. Charak is that aspect which contains within its range the total body, the harmony of differences (Ṛishi-dominating, Devatā-dominating, and Chhandas-dominating structures of Natural Law which are divisions or parts of the body) but which also highlights Ṛishi in this fourth cluster of Natural Law.

Suśrut Saṁhitā brings out the separating quality of intelligence. In terms of physics, this separating quality of Suśrut is described as the process of sequential symmetry breaking which separates the different quantum fields at the basis of creation in the progression toward larger distance scales; the fields become different and their mutual interaction becomes restricted.[8] This phenomenon demonstrates this separating quality. Suśrut Saṁhitā is that aspect of the Vedic Literature which is the expression of this level of reality in self-referral consciousness—*Ātmā*. Maharishi explains that this area

> Of consideration of 'progression towards larger distance scales' is covered by all values of the Vedic Literature, elaborated with reference to Ṛishi-predominant Charak Saṁhitā, Devatā-predominant Sushrut Saṁhitā, and Chhandas-predominant Vāgbhatt Saṁhitā. The far-distant evolution of the universe is maintained in an orderly way, and in this is the dignity of the Saṁhitā element of intelligence in which the place of Sushrut Saṁhitā is very important; it separates in a way that the separation, or differentiation, in the passage of evolution, however far it may go, will always remain within the range of Yoga—the field of unifying power. The value of larger distance scales is relevant when we consider the observer at a point in the infinity of space and time. The reality is that the unified WHOLENESS is omnipresent and there is no place far or near to it; it is an area of infinite correlation, so from whatever distance one is already always associated with it. This is why it is equally available in all places.[9]

Suśrut Saṁhitā is that aspect which separates in such a way that separation or differentiation always remains within the range of that unifying value of Yoga. As mentioned previously, Yoga means union and is that aspect of the Vedic Literature that brings out the unifying value of self-referral consciousness. So separation can occur while always remaining unified; differentiation takes place but without disconnection from self-referral consciousness.

As stated above, there is no far or near point on the level of wholeness—which is one's own self-referral consciousness—because this is an area of *infinite correlation.* It is by virtue of this aspect of infinite correlation, as discussed in Part II, that the effects documented in research on the group practice of the Transcendental Meditation and TM-Sidhi Program can be achieved. Through the practice of these technologies of consciousness the individual is increasingly able to function from that level of self-referral consciousness—beyond space and time. The reality of wholeness is that it is omnipresent; it is present everywhere. This principle, Maharishi explains, is described in the Upaniṣad in the expression:

> अणोरणीयान् महतो महीयान्
>
> *Aṇoraṇīyān Mahato-mahīyān*
>
> (*Katha Upaniṣad*, *1.2.20*)
>
> (The Self is) smaller than the smallest, bigger than the biggest.

The Self, or the Totality of Brahm, is present everywhere—in every grain of creation in the ever-expanding universe. Total Natural Law "is available in the finest particle of creation where Totality is available in terms of the finest value on the level of infinite correlation."[10] For this reason, through the practice of the Transcendental Meditation and TM-Sidhi Program, the mind can re-establish its integrated state—allowing the individual to access and function from this level. As Maharishi points out

> निवर्तध्वम् *Nivartadhwam (Ṛk Veda, 10.19.1)* awakens the memory of the mind to realize the silence within itself, and re-establishes its natural integrated state wherever it is, regardless of its present placement in space and time. In this regard all the dynamics of Natural Law available in the Vedic Literature are involved. Special reference can be made to the organizing power of Brāhmaṇa, the invincible and progressive quality of Dhanur-Veda, the establishing quality of Sthāpatya Veda, and the separating quality of Sushrut Saṁhitā.[11]

Nivartadhvam means to retire; it can be understood as relating to the process of transcending in the practice of Transcendental Meditation technique. It is the awakening of the memory of the mind to silence—the silence of its own Nature. It is the re-establishment of the mind's natural integrated state which can occur anywhere, regardless of one's location in space and time. In this context, while all the dynamics of Natural Law—all the aspects of the Vedic Literature—are involved in this process, Maharishi specifically emphasizes the role of the organizing power of Brāhmaṇa, the invincible and progressive quality of Dhanur-Veda, the establishing quality of Sthāpatya Veda, and the separating quality of

Suśrut Saṁhitā. He identifies the interconnectedness of these different aspects of the Vedic Literature.

As with other clusters of the Vedic Literature, Āyur-Veda can be understood to relate to, or contain, the total value of Natural Law. However, Āyur-Veda, as mentioned earlier, means the knowledge or science of life-span; in this sense, its domain encompasses the creation of balance in all areas of life: mind, body and environment. With respect to the role of Āyur-Veda and the relationship between consciousness and matter, immortality and mortality, Maharishi explains that Āyur-Veda:

> Maintains balance between consciousness and matter, between change and non-change, and between mortality and immortality. If we interpret Āyur-Veda in terms of balance, then Āyur-Veda will mean that quality of intelligence which will balance the relationship of infinity and its point, immortality and its constituent segments of mortality. In this sense Āyur-Veda is the science and technology of raising mortality to immortality; it is the science and technology of the analysis of immortality—immortality in its constituent parts of mortality—the finite constituent parts of infinity.

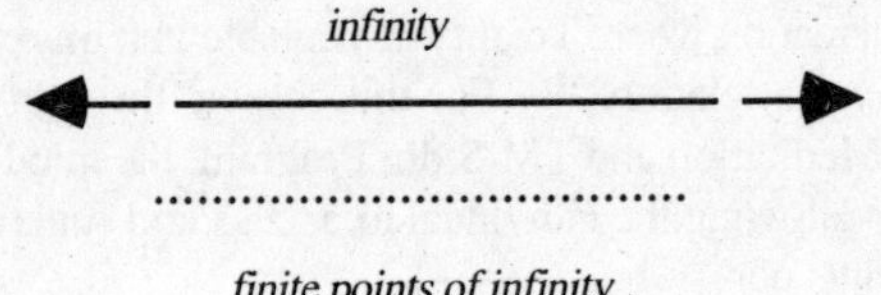

Āyur-Veda is defined as:

आयुर्वेदोऽमृतानाम्

Āyur-Veda Amṛtānām

(*Charak Saṁhitā, Sūtra Sthānam, 25.40*)[12]

Āyur-Veda is the science and technology which raises finite values (mortality) to infinity, pure consciousness (immortality). As stated before, in the self-referral feedback loop, this fourth cluster of the Vedic Literature involves Charak Saṁhitā, Suśrut Saṁhitā, Vāgbhatt Saṁhitā, Mādhav Nidān Saṁhitā, Shārngadhar Saṁhitā and Bhāva Prakāsh Saṁhitā which bring out Ṛishi, Devatā, Chhandas and Chhandas, Devatā and Ṛishi, respectively.

Comprising the holistic value of Āyur-Veda, described above in the analysis of its name, Charak Saṁhitā highlights the balancing, holding together and supporting quality of intelligence. In the physiology it structures the cell nucleus. The cell is the basic structural and functional unit of all organisms; it is the smallest structure capable of performing all the activities vital to life. The cell nucleus is an organelle (a component or structure within the cell that is specialized to serve a specific function in cellular activities) containing the genes. The genes, in turn, carry the hereditary factors of the cell. The cell nucleus, as part of the basic unit of the physiology, corresponds to the quality of intelligence of Charak Saṁhitā.

In the cluster of Āyur-Veda, after Charak Saṁhitā, Suśrut Saṁhitā is the separating quality of intelligence, bringing out a Devatā value. In the physiology it structures the cytoplasm and cell organelles. The cytoplasm, also called protoplasm, is the substance within the cell's plasma membrane external to the nucleus. It comprises the internal environment of the cell (outside of the nucleus). In this respect, Charak and Suśrut Saṁhitā are intrinsically interrelated. Following Suśrut Saṁhitā, Vāgbhatt Saṁhitā—the communication and eloquence quality of intelligence—brings out a Chhandas value. Maharishi explains that the activity of Vāgbhatt on the Saṁhitā level—the level of infinite correlation—is the reality of communication. It is the phenomenon of *Ayonya-Abhāva* (infinite dynamism) in *Atyanta-Abhāva* (infinite silence). "It is the phenomenon of *Ayonya-Abhāva* in *Atyanta-Abhāva.*—Absolute Abstraction."[13]

The quality of intelligence brought out by Vāgbhatt Saṁhitā structures the cytoskeleton and the cell membrane. The cytoskeleton is the complex internal structure of the cytoplasm consisting of microfilaments and microtubules—the microtubule, for example, provides functions of support, structure and transportation in the cell. Thus, with respect to the physiology, Charak, Suśrut, and Vāgbhatt Saṁhitā structure integral components of the cell.

In the further unfoldment of the self-referral loop, the last three values—Mādhav Nidān Saṁhitā, Shārngadhar Saṁhitā and Bhāva Prakāsh Saṁhitā—highlight the specific qualities of diagnosing, synthesizing, and enlightening which can be seen to promote Chhandas, Devatā and Ṛishi values, respectively. The phenomenon of diagnosis upheld in Mādhav Nidān—conducted by the Āyur-Vedic physician, is a quality lively in Saṁhitā which gives rise to the differentiated values of Ṛishi, Devatā and Chhandas.

Maharishi points out that "the most basic value of this is in attention when attention is self-referral."[14] Diagnosis involves the perception or differentiation of distinct values. On the level of Saṁhitā, as explained in previous chapters, when attention is self-referral it distinguishes differentiated values within its own unbounded nature. With this analysis, in the value of diagnosing, Mādhav Nidān Saṁhitā unfolds a fundamental principle of consciousness.

The next in the Āyur-Veda self-referral loop, Shārngadhar Saṁhitā, brings out the synthesizing value of intelligence. As Maharishi points out, in "Saṁhitā, all possible configurations of Ṛishi, Devatā, Chhandas are synthesized. Therefore, Shārngadhar Saṁhitā is the technique for *synthesizing* all aspects of life."[15] In putting together differentiated elements, Shārngadhar Saṁhitā plays a unifying role, revealing the tendency of curving back in this feed-back loop.

Next, Bhāva Prakāsh Saṁhitā, as Maharishi explains, is the "emergence of *Bhāva* in the *Abhāva*; that means the blossoming of the concrete from the abstract unmanifest."[16] The *Abhāva* is that unmanifest level from where the concrete, *Bhāva*, arises or emerges. Maharishi elaborates upon this phenomenon with respect to the dawning of enlightenment and the unfoldment of the syllables of the Vedic texts in terms of his *Apauruṣeya Bhāsya.*

> Enlightenment is the quality that causes the blossoming of WHOLENESS. (This is *Bhāva* from within the field of *Abhāva*.) The first inception of this phenomenon is the blossoming of *Anyonya-Abhāva* from *Atyanta-Abhāva*, and the evolution of *Anyonya-Abhāva* to *Prāg-Abhāva*, and further to the concrete expressions of *Bhāva* in the letters, syllables, and words of the Vedic Text—the essentially progressive expression of the Vedic Language, the Language of Nature.[17]

Anyonya-Abhāva, the value of infinite dynamism, blossoms from *Atyanta-Abhāva*, infinite silence, and then evolves to *Prāg-Abhāva* (the emergence of sound) and the expression of *Bhāva* as the letters, syllables and words of the Vedic Text. The unmanifest creates concrete values or expressions of sound which structure form.

In the physiology, Mādhav Nidān Saṁhitā structures the mesodermal cells, Shārngadhar Saṁhitā structures the endodermal cells and Bhāva Prakāsh Saṁhitā structures the ectodermal cells. The mesoderm is the middle of the three primary germ layers in the embryo which give rise to connective tissues, blood, blood vessels and muscles. The endoderm is the inner layer of cells of an embryo and the ectoderm is the outermost of the three primary germ layers, giving rise to the nervous system and the epidermis of the skin. From this outer layer of cells of the developing embryo are developed the skin structures, the nervous system, organs of special sense, the pineal and part of the pituitary and suprarenal glands. Thus, all these aspects of the Vedic Literature promote the development and structure and function of the physiology.

Elaborating further on the nature and significance of the Vedic Literature as a whole, Maharishi explains that the process of metabolizing knowledge is the domain of Āyur-Veda:

> The truth us that today we stand in possession of total knowledge and the means to realize it: listen to Veda; read Vedanga; apply Upānga; transform through Brāhmaṇa; harmonize through Upa-Veda; metabolize through Āyur-Veda; and live wholeness of life—*Brahm*—Totality—through the Prātishākhyas.[18]

Continuing with the last two clusters of the Vedic Literature in the unfoldment of Natural Law, the next in sequence is the Brāhmaṇa—that which transforms.

The Brāhmaṇa: The Fifth Cluster of Natural Law

Dealing with transformation, Brāhmaṇa is the infinite organizing power of Natural Law. The term Brāhmaṇa is used to refer to the six-fold cluster of this aspect of the Vedic Literature and also to one of the six values within the self-referral loop. The Brāhmaṇa includes Upaniṣad, Āraṇyak, Brāhmaṇa, Itihās, Purāṇ, and Smṛti.

Upaniṣad is the transcending quality of intelligence and, with reference to consciousness, comprises the specific sets of Laws of Nature that promote Ṛishi within Saṁhitā. The unexpressed Transcendental level is the fundamental level of consciousness itself. With respect to Upaniṣad, Maharishi explains that the characteristic qualities of "Ṛk Veda, Sāma Veda, Yajur-Veda, and Atharva Veda in the field of Transcendental Consciousness convey the characteristic features of this level of reality"—the reality of the transcendental level.[19] The self-referral motion in the self-referral transcendental field of consciousness is the basis of diversity.

After Upaniṣad, Āraṇyak is the stirring quality of intelligence involved in structuring Ṛk Veda. It comprises the Laws of Nature which promote the quality of Devatā within Saṁhitā. Following this, Brāhmaṇa is the structuring quality of intelligence and contains the sets of Laws of Nature engaged in promoting Chhandas—the object of observation which hides the dynamism of Devatā in the witnessing quality of Ṛishi—within the Saṁhitā level of consciousness. Also promoting Chhandas, Itihās is the next of the six aspects in this self-referral loop and is the blossoming of Totality quality of intelligence. Then, Purāṇ, the ancient and eternal quality of intelligence, comprises the specific Laws of Nature which promote Devatā within Saṁhitā; finally Smṛti, the quality of memory, is the last aspect of the self-referral loop of Brāhmaṇa.

With reference to consciousness, Smṛti, comprises the sets of Laws of Nature which promote Ṛishi within Saṁhitā. This value of memory can be understood with respect to the self-referral direction or opposite to *Śruti* in the evolution of Natural Law and denotes the mechanics of "memory" inherent within the self-referral dynamics that occur at every level in the evolution of Natural Law. Smṛti brings the move within this self-referral loop full circle.

Upaniṣad—Unfolding the Self

Maharishi explains that the Upaniṣads involve knowledge of the path of unfolding the Self—the path of Self-realization. "Upaniṣad" has often been translated as meaning "sit nearby the teacher" but, as Maharishi explains, it can be translated as "sit near to the Self" or "sit near to the Veda",[20] gaining the knowledge of the Self or *Ātmā Vidya*.

While there are hundreds of Upaniṣads, there are 10 to 15 main books; in terms of the physiology, these correspond to the ascending tracts or pathways in the nervous system—which are 10 to 15 in number. Despite this, as Nader points out

> There are hundreds of ascending pathways comparable in number to approximately 300 Upanishads. They carry a large number of modalities of transmission of sensory information, position sense, temperature, touch, muscle tension, etc. They are anatomically positioned in the area surrounding the grey matter.[21]

He also states that the position of these within the central nervous system, the main seat of the Veda, is analogous to the idea of Upaniṣad—sitting near Veda. As discussed previously, Veda is identified in the physiology in the nerves of the spinal cord. Structurally speaking, then, Upaniṣad literally sits near Veda. Nader further notes that, in higher states of consciousness, the sensory pathways corresponding to Upaniṣad become the channels through which everything starts to be perceived in terms of *Ātmā*, the Self.[22] Therefore, the sensory pathways of Upaniṣad in the physiology are integral to the actual experience of the Self—pure consciousness or *Ātmā*—in higher states of consciousness.

The Upaniṣad comprise the specific sets of Laws of Nature that are engaged in promoting the quality of Ṛishi, or silent witnessing value, within Saṁhitā. Clearly, from this perspective, Upaniṣad can be understood as that aspect of consciousness which reveals the transcending value of consciousness; it is knowledge of the process of transcending through which one arrives at the Transcendent, the Self. The Upaniṣad also describe the reality of higher states of consciousness—namely when the seemingly distinct realms of absolute and relative are found to both be fullness, wholeness or self-referral consciousness—as illustrated by the verse mentioned earlier:

> पूर्णमदः पूर्णमिदं पूर्णात्पूर्णमुदच्यते ।
> पूर्णस्य पूर्णमादाय पूर्णमेवावशिष्यते ॥
>
> *Pūrṇamadaḥ pūrṇamidaṁ pūrṇāt pūrṇam udacyate*
> *Pūrṇasya pūrṇam ādāya pūrṇam evāvaśiṣyate*
>
> (*Isa Upaniṣad*) Introductory verse.
>
> That is full; this is full. From fullness fullness comes out. Taking fullness from fullness, what remains is fullness.

These "two fullnesses" together (which can be described as the fullness of the absolute and the fullness of the relative) represent the state or knowledge of Brahman or *Brahma Vidyā.* The knowledge of the Self or *Ātmā* (knowledge of the Absolute—pure consciousness) has become the complete knowledge of Brahman where both "this" and "That" are full—both are self-referral consciousness. *Ātmā Vidya* becomes *Brahma Vidyā.*

As Maharishi explains, "The philosophy of two fullnesses [is] found in the Upaniṣads: this is full and That is full, "*pūrṇamadaḥ pūrṇamidaṁ*"—That Transcendental unmanifested absolute eternal being is full, and this manifested relative ever-changing world of phenomenal existence is full. The Absolute is eternal in its never-changing nature, and the relative is eternal in its ever-changing nature."[23]

This theme is also expressed elsewhere in the Upaniṣad as the *Mahāvakyas* or "great sayings:"

> अहं ब्रह्मास्मि ।
>
> *Ahaṃ Brahmāsmi.*
>
> (*Bṛihadāraṇyaka Upaniṣad, 1.4.10*)
>
> I am That, or "'I am totality'—the state of full enlightenment," or "I am totality—I am singularity—I am self-referral consciousness."[24]
>
> तत् त्वमसि ।
>
> *Tat tvam asi.*
>
> (*Chāndogya Upaniṣad, 6.11*)
>
> Thou art That.
>
> सर्वं खल्विदं ब्रह्म ।
>
> *Sarvaṁ khalvidaṁ Brahma.*
>
> (*Chāndogya Upaniṣad, 3.14.1*)
>
> All this is That, or "All this is totality"[25]
>
> प्रज्ञानं ब्रह्म ।
>
> *Prajñānaṃ Brahma.*
>
> (*Aitareya Upaniṣad, 3.5.3*)
>
> And That is consciousness.

This last expression is translated by Maharishi as follows:

> Fully awake, self-referral dynamism (of the universe) born of the infinite organizing power of pure knowledge, the Veda—fully awake totality of individual consciousness is *Brahm*, which comprehends the infinite dynamism of the universe in the infinite silence of the Self.[26]

These expressions describe the state of Brahman consciousness when everything is seen in terms of self-referral consciousness. Upaniṣad, a popular aspect of the Vedic Literature, in this sense, goes beyond philosophy. It encompasses the experience of transcending and the physiological structures which act as channels for that experience. Next in the self-referral loop of Brāhmaṇa is Āraṇyak—of which Maharishi Vedic Science has provided an in depth description.

Āraṇyak: Stirring the Ocean of Consciousness

Maharishi's description of consciousness as an ocean made up of points (Part II) and the discussion of the first syllable of Ṛk Veda, "Ak," as the collapse of infinity to its point, can be understood with respect to Āraṇyak. Through the stirring value of consciousness which is Āraṇyak, "A" spirals into "K" and "K" spirals into "A". The total field of consciousness, aware of its points, creates the whirlpool dynamic. Āraṇyak is that mode of consciousness which develops the Veda from its first syllable, its first sound, stirring the total field of consciousness to create specificity or points.

In discussing this aspect of the Vedic Literature further, Maharishi considers the word Āraṇyak:

> The word Āraṇyak = Āraṇi + Ak. Āraṇi is the instrument which stirs; Āraṇi is अक् (Ak). That means अक् (Ak) is Āraṇi, अक् (Ak) is the instrument that stirs; अक् (Ak) is Āraṇi—Āraṇyak. अक् (Ak) is अ (A), wholeness, infinity, and क् (K) point of wholeness, stop. अ (A), being aware of its point, is the first stir of wholeness within itself; it is the display of self-referral consciousness. This stir is अक् (Ak), which is the first syllable of Ṛk Ved, the source of Ṛk Ved. Wholeness, awake within itself, is aware of its points. That awareness is wakefulness, wholeness, aware of its entirety—totality—and also aware of its points. The picture is that of wholeness in the shape of a stir within itself—a whirlpool within itself. Stirring is the quality of अक् (Ak). अ (A) spirals into क् (K) and क् (K) spirals out into अ (A). Āraṇyak is the means of developing the Ved from the first syllable, अक् (Ak). Stirring अ (A) to create क् (K), stirring totality to create specificity, stirring wholeness to generate points.[27]

Āraṇyak facilitates the development of the Veda from "A" to "K", stirring "A" or wholeness so that it creates points within itself.

In this context, Maharishi adds that, अक् (Ak) is the means to create Veda, or the knowledge to create Veda in one's awareness, or the means to gain total knowledge—knowledge of infinity and knowledge of the point—to develop *Ātmā* from *Jīva* and *Brahma* from *Ātmā*.[28] *Jīva* is the individual or point value of consciousness; *Ātmā* is singularity or potential unity of pure consciousness; *Brahma* is totality, the cosmic value of *Jīva*, or the wholeness of consciousness moving within itself creating its own points within itself.[29] This process, where consciousness is stirring back and forth, *is* Āraṇyak.[30] It is represented as the churning of the ocean (which is ultimately consciousness) in various aspects of the Vedic Literature.

Considered legend by post-Vedic Sanskrit scholars, the story of the churning of the ocean has been found in the *Mahābhārata, Rāmāyaṇa, Matsya Purāṇa, Viṣnu Purāṇa, Brahmāṇḍa Purāṇa, Padma Purāṇa*, the *Śrīmad-Bhāgavatam, Āgneya Mahāpurāṇa*, and the *Skanda Mahāpurāṇa*.[31] In Maharishi Vedic Science this "legend" actually describes how consciousness moves within itself and creates differentiated values within its own nature. The universal significance of the story of the churning of the ocean is revealed; the churning, is, in effect, the self-referral dynamics of consciousness—experienced and cognized by the individual as the fundamental activity at the basis of creation. Maharishi points out that the principle of self-referral consciousness stirring back and forth within the ocean of consciousness is illustrated in the Bhagavad-Gītā:

प्रकृतिं स्वामवष्टभ्य विसृजामि पुनः पुनः ।

Prakṛtiṁ svām avaṣtabhya visṛjāmi punaḥ punaḥ
(*Bhagavad-Gītā, 9.8*)

"Taking recourse to my own self-referral nature, I create again and again."[32] This expression describes the stirring of self-referral consciousness, the creative mechanics of Natural Law, which is eternally occurring and generating all the diverse forms and phenomena in creation.

The churning of the ocean of consciousness involves the silent and dynamic values of the gap (*Anyonya-Abhāva* within *Atyanta-Abhāva*). In the self-referral loop or "churning" of consciousness, silence and dynamism become each other in an infinite dynamic. This fundamental process upholds the process of evolution. This phenomenon determines the development or emergence of the first word of Ṛk Veda, अग्निम् *Aknim*:

> क् (K) spiralling out into अ (A) creates nothingness, न (NA), and creates dynamism in nothingness, इ (I), and generates Hum, म् (M). This is how the first word of Ṛk Veda is formed. This is how Āraṇyak brings to light the dynamism (*Anyonya-abhāv*) within the unmanifest न (NA—*Atyant-abhāv*), through the churning process lively within अक (Ak). So the subject matter of Āraṇyak is अक् (Ak), the first syllable of Ṛk Ved from where the structure of Ṛk Ved emerges.[33]

Here Maharishi points out that the first syllable of Ṛk Veda contains the stirring quality of अक (Ak) spiraling into क (K). Out of अ (K) develops the emergent word, *Aknim.* The first syllable serves as an eternal momentum which propels or causes the evolution of the structure of Veda. The structure of this eternal momentum is *Āraṇi*—the forward and backward sense of motion.[34]

While the structure of अक (Ak) is exemplified as *Araṇi*, the instrument which stirs is described by Āraṇyak. Through the stirring of wholeness or अ (A), Ṛk, the point value of wholeness, is created:

> अक (Ak) is considered as the instrument to stir totality and locate a point in it. Ṛk gets created; point gets created—from that stirring, the function of अक (Ak), the ocean of silence, in being aware of its point, generates dynamism. Wholeness looking to point and point looking to wholeness, this is the picture of the stir back and forth within the nature of wholeness.[35]

Āraṇyak is the phenomenon of stirring—the stir of silence to dynamism, dynamism to silence—the churning of the ocean of consciousness within itself creating its own point and unfolding the ever-evolving values of Ṛk Veda. This analysis demonstrates how Maharishi Vedic Science expands the understanding of the Vedic texts given by post-Vedic scholars. Maharishi Vedic Science provides unparalleled insights into the universal reality and meaning of the Vedic Literature.

Āraṇyak is also identified as the stirring quality of intelligence in the physiology that structures the fasciculi proprii. As Nader points out, the spino-spinal fasciculi or fasciculi proprii are short, crossed and uncrossed, ascending and descending fiber systems which begin and end within the spinal cord. He goes on to explain that all groups at various levels (and within the same level of the spinal cord) are interconnected with this intrinsic spinal pathway. The spinal cord, as discussed earlier, represents most of the expressions of Ṛk Veda; Ṛk Veda is, in turn, the elaboration of "Ak". Therefore, the fasciculi proprii "effectively constitute a whirlpool of activity interconnecting and stirring the structures which represent "Ak" in its material expression" in the physiology.[36]

Nader goes on to state that the fasciculi are arranged like a forest around the central gray matter of the spinal cord. "Āraṇyak" can also be translated as "forest." There are six main divisions of Āraṇyak. With respect to the fasciculi proprii, there are six groups of fibers corresponding to the (right and left) ventral, lateral and dorsal sections.

In this way, Maharishi Vedic Science locates the value of Āraṇyak on the level of consciousness and the physiology—giving an unprecedented account of this aspect of Natural Law.

Following Āraṇyak is the Brāhmaṇa in this self-referral loop.

The Structuring Quality of Brāhmaṇa

As Maharishi points out, Brāhmaṇa, as one of the structuring dynamics of Ṛk Veda, highlights the structuring quality of intelligence involved in structuring Ṛk Veda. With reference to consciousness, Brāhmaṇa comprises the specific sets of Laws of Nature that are engaged in promoting Chhandas—the object of observation—within the Saṁhitā level of consciousness. There are 15 principal

Brāhmaṇa which correspond to the 15 main descending tracts in the spinal cord (there are three remaining Brāhmaṇa which, Nader states, correspond to the corticotectal, corticopontine and corticobulbar tracts). Brāhmaṇa is that value of infinite organizing power inherent within the gaps of the Vedic syllables and expressions.

In the dissolution and emergence of sound there are four stages of the gap (as discussed in Chapter 8) and there is the dynamic or resonance of infinite dynamism within infinite silence (*Ānyonya-Abhāva* in the nature of *Atyanta-Abhāva*) within the gap.[37] Brāhmaṇa, representing the organizing power available on the level of the gap, unfolds the structuring quality of self-referral intelligence.

After Brāhmaṇa, the next aspect in this self-referral loop, Itihās, highlights the blossoming of Totality quality within self-referral consciousness.

The Full Blossoming of Natural Law through Itihās

Itihās highlights the blossoming of Totality quality "involved in the structuring of Ṛk Veda."[38] Totality is Brahman; the complete value of Natural Law. In analyzing the name Itihās further, Maharishi explains that "*Iti* is the end; *hāsa* is the laughter: the end of the laughter of Nature. That means the total expansion of the expression of bliss."[39] Itihās comprises the *Mahābhārat* and the *Rāmāyaṇ* is the history of consciousness as living examples of the full range of possibilities inherent within self-referral consciousness[40]—the field of bliss. Self-referral consciousness is bliss; the story of Rāma is the story of bliss. "In the language of the Rāmāyana, this is *Rāma rāsa,* the essence of Rāma."[41] Both aspects of the Itihās—the *Mahābhārat* and the *Rāmāyaṇ*—describe the interactions of the field of bliss and its unfoldment as the expression of bliss.[42] In this context, Itihās represents the full blossoming of *Ātmā*, including: 1) *Ānanda Khan*, the concentrated expression of total happiness or bliss; 2) *Chit Khan*, the concentrated expression of total consciousness; and 3) *Gyān Khan*, concentrated total knowledge.[43]

The various tellings of the *Rāmāyaṇ* throughout South Asia, reveal that it is a vital component of numerous traditions and cultures.[44] In Maharishi Vedic Science the *Mahābhārat* and *Rāmāyaṇ* are held to present knowledge of the Veda in behavioral form through the actions of heroes and heroines (the *Mahābhārat* has many heroes and the *Rāmāyaṇ* has one main hero). It is through the Itihās that "Veda is seen to be practical, is put on the comprehensive level, on the field of behavior—behavioral comprehension of the entire infinite dynamism of the structure of pure knowledge, the Veda."[45] William Sands examines this perspective and investigates how the *Rāmāyaṇ* can be analyzed for its principles of ideal political administration as defined by Maharishi Vedic Science.[46] Indeed, Maharishi explains that, "Rām, in [the] Rāmāyaṇ, is portrayed as the embodiment of *Dharm*—Natural Law—*Purushottam*—the abstract, unmanifest, absolute ruler of the ever-expanding universe."[47] Rāma is the embodiment of the "supreme quality of order, freedom, bliss, and the ability to nourish all."[48] He is the

Totality—pure spirituality, self-referral intelligence, the total potential of Natural Law. Thus, Rāma could be defined as a universal human being. Rāma, a role model for humanity, demonstrates behavior from the field of Absolute Administration—the level of Natural Law. As Maharishi points out:

> [The] Rāmāyaṇ presents the eternal record of perfection is every field of life. Every single person, at every level of his evolution, finds a living example of perfection in Rāmāyaṇ. Here, in the context of government, the Absolute Theory of Government locates perfect administration in Rāmāyaṇ.[49]

In this context, the *Rāmāyaṇ* presents an example of life lived from the level of Absolute Administration, the level of Nature's government. Ultimately, in revealing the "blossoming of totality" quality of self-referral consciousness, Itihās deals with "history" in the broadest sense of the term.

With reference to consciousness, Itihās comprises the sets of Laws of Nature that promote the quality of Chhandas within Saṁhitā. In the physiology there are 7 spinal processes (two superior, two inferior, two lateral, and one posterior) and there are 7 cervical vertebrae which hold and support the neck and head. These groups of 7, Nader states, correspond to the 7 chapters of the *Rāmāyaṇ*. In addition, the laminae of Rexed, parts of the spinal column, correspond to the books of the *Mahābhārat*. This discussion again reveals how there are various levels of understanding of the Vedic texts. According to Maharishi Vedic Science, underlying them all one principle remains—the Veda and the Vedic Literature are expressions of self-referral consciousness, the structuring dynamics of Veda, the evolution of Natural Law.

Following Itihās in the self-referral loop of the Brāhmaṇa is the ancient and eternal quality of intelligence—Purāṇ.

Purāṇ: Elaborating the Dynamics of Self-Referral

In his description of the ancient and eternal quality of consciousness in the display of the performance of silence in the gap, Maharishi explains that the Puraṇ bring out the values of Ṛishi, Devatā, and Chhandas in terms of the transformation within the gap in the evolution of consciousness. He points out that there are different kinds of gaps in the structure of Ṛk Veda. For example, there are six values of Saṁhitā within the gap—these are the values of Saṁhitā in terms of the evolving values of Ṛishi, Devatā, and Chhandas, and the values of Chhandas, Devatā, and Ṛishi merging back into Saṁhitā in a self-referral feedback loop.

This emergence and submergence (brought out by Vyākaraṇ and Nirukt) proceeds with infinite frequency; the 18 Purāṇ unfold this transformation of silence into dynamism and dynamism into silence—the dynamic of the eternal continuum. In this context, the different kinds of gaps are expressed in the ancient quality of consciousness (Purāṇ) in terms of Cosmic Creative Intelligence, called *Devī*; as Maharishi explains:

If we count the different kinds of gaps in the whole structure of Ṛk Ved we will be delighted to sequentially unfold the qualities of the gaps in sequence expressed sequentially in the whole range of Devī Purāṇ (the ancient quality of consciousness in terms of *Devī*), Cosmic Creative Intelligence, the fundamental element of the structuring dynamics of Ved.

The whole dynamics of the structuring mechanics that structure the Ved (being in the gap) is complete in terms of six values of Saṁhitā; that means Saṁhitā evolving into Ṛishi, Devatā, Chhandas, and Chhandas, Devatā, Ṛishi in sequence merging back into the state of Saṁhitā.

In this eternal theme of emergence and submergence—emergence of Ṛishi, Devatā, Chhandas from Saṁhitā, and submergence of Ṛishi, Devatā, Chhandas back into Saṁhitā—the qualities of emergence and submergence (Vyākaraṇ and Nirukt) take place with infinite frequency, because of the self-referral state of intelligence in which the structuring dynamics of consciousness structure the Ved in its potentially evolving structure. All the eighteen Purāṇ bring out the reality of the eternal continuum of transformation of silence into dynamism and dynamism into silence.[50]

The Self-Referral Feedback Loop of Ṛishi, Devatā, Chhandas and Chhandas, Devatā, and Ṛishi

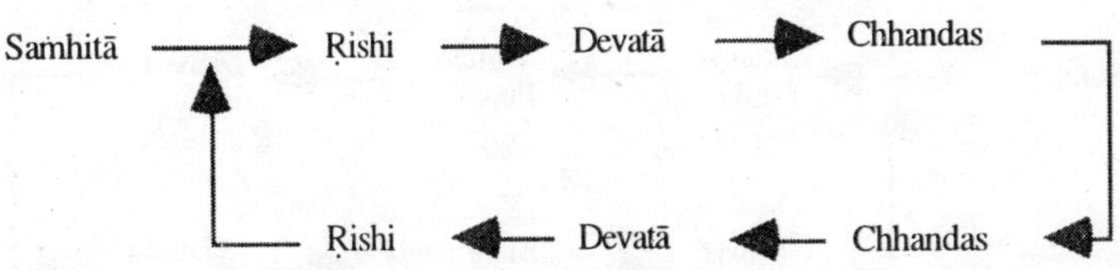

In the eternal theme of emergence and submergence—the emergence of Ṛishi, Devatā, Chhandas from Saṁhitā, and the submergence of Ṛishi, Devatā, and Chhandas back into Saṁhitā—the qualities of emergence and submergence take place with infinite frequency. The Purāṇa bring out the details of this six-fold self-referral feedback loop which takes place within the gap.

Maharishi goes on to explain that there are 18 ancient, eternal qualities of consciousness (18 Purāṅ) because there are three kinds of self-referral feedback loops determined by Ṛishi, Devatā, and Chhandas:

The 18 Purāṇ in terms of Self-Referral Loops of Ṛishi, Devatā and Chhandas

Ṛishi in its own feedback loop:

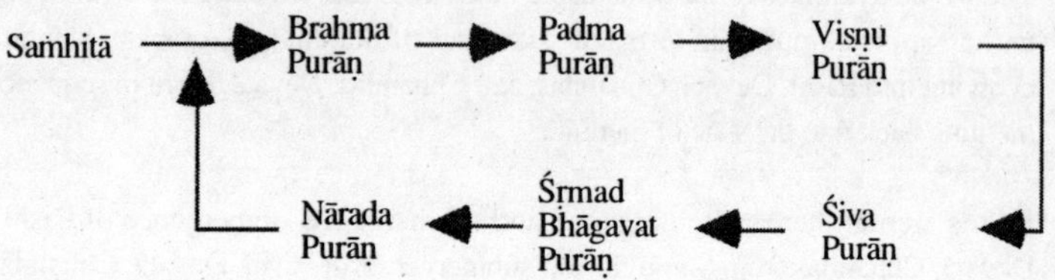

Devatā in its own feedback loop:

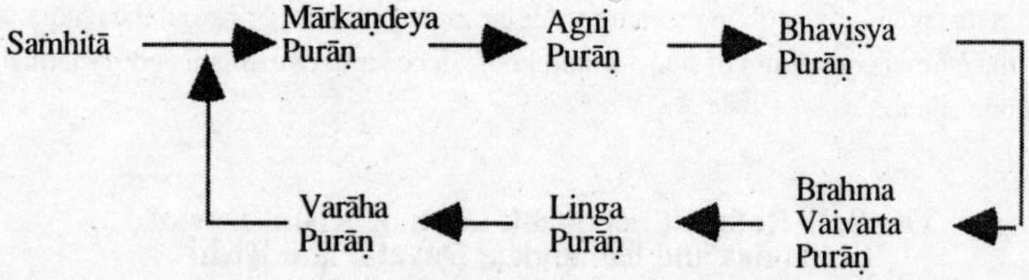

Chhandas in its own feedback loop:

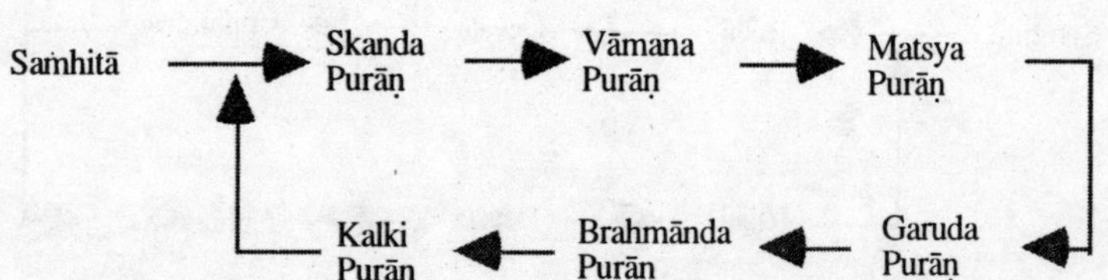

The Purāṇ bring out the details of this six-fold self-referral feedback loop which takes place within the gap in terms of Ṛishi, Devatā, and Chhandas.

The relationship between the point of Ṛishi and infinity of Ṛishi: between the point of Devatā and infinity of Devatā; and between the point of Chhandas and infinity of Chhandas is available in the eighteen Purāṅ—eighteen ancient, eternal qualities: Ṛishi in its own feedback loop: Devatā in its own feedback loop: and Chhandas in its own feedback loop: these three in the theme of emerging, and then Chhandas in its own self-referral loop, Devatā in its own self-referral loop, and Ṛishi in its own self-referral loop, sequentially forming a loop of six values,

> sequentially giving rise to a mutual loop within the Saṁhitā constructing the unity of three in terms of six values, and in turn these six values are displayed in terms of Ṛishi, Devatā, Chhandas, and these are the eighteen Puraṇ.[51]

Through six-fold self-referral feedback loops—one Ṛishi self-referral loop, one Devatā self-referral loop and one Chhandas self-referral loop (18 values of transformation of self-referral consciousness)—the 18 Purāṇ reveal the various values of the transformation of self-referral consciousness. Maharishi explains that the entire Ṛk Veda is encompassed in the range of each Purāṅ. With reference to Devatā, the spread of every Purāṅ from beginning to end is available in sequence in the gaps from the beginning of Ṛk Veda (the first syllable—अ, "A") to the end of Ṛk Veda (the last syllable, इ, "I"). Maharishi adds that the same is true for the 18 Smṛti—with reference to Chhandas, and for the 18 Itihās—with reference to Ṛishi, and for every aspect of the Vedic Literature. As he points out:

> It is interesting to see that the structuring dynamics of Ved, as available in each of the Vedic Literature in terms of their Sūtras, follow the same sequential order of Ṛk Ved from the beginning to the end of its spread. It is the same sequence of evolution of the structure of Ṛk Ved.[52]

It is worth noting that while the Purāṅ can be understood to embody transformations within the gaps in the sequential order of the unfoldment of Ṛk Veda, on the expressed level they also contain models of teaching (with reference to the codes of conduct and behavior contained in the Smṛti). As outlined in Maharishi Vedic Science, the Purāṅ and the Itihās present "living examples of the full range of possibilities inherent within the unified field of natural law."[53]

The Value of Memory or Smṛti in Maintaining Unity

As noted above, according to Maharishi Vedic Science, the word Smṛti means "memory," and refers to the memory of the ultimate unity of Saṁhitā. In terms of individual experience, when Smṛti is lively in awareness action is performed from the level of Saṁhitā—the total potential of Natural Law. The field of universal, pure consciousness is ever maintained along with the fluctuations of consciousness, which appear as the diversified values of relative creation. As Maharishi explains

> Awareness is just memory. If I remember something, that thing is open to the awareness. Smṛiti means 'memory.' So the aspect of Vedic literature that is called Smṛiti deals with the character of awareness. It is concerned with how the awareness could be such that when it is in terms of fluctuations or excitations it does not forget its unmanifest value. In other words, when the awareness is acting in terms of specific values of Natural Law, the non-specific, general character of Natural Law is not out of awareness. When the totality of Natural

> Law is out of awareness then we say that a man is ignorant of his own nature. When the totality of Natural Law does not disappear from memory then the individual is established in enlightenment. He is living the totality of life through all his individual expressions. The individuality is in tune with universality through memory of the totality of Natural Law being maintained.[54]

In this context, Smṛti deals with the basic value of awareness or intelligence, and reveals "the nature of the connection between the unmanifest and the manifesting process of nature."[55] Smṛti, the awareness of Saṁhitā in the midst of diversity, is not simply the emergence of thoughts in the mind associated with past experience.

Recalling the postmodern notion of the play of language, discussed in Part I, writing or language is equated with "brain writing"[56] or the neuronal traces in the brain. This understanding of language connected to neuronal traces in the brain, Freud defined as "memory." Applying this to his deconstruction theory, Derrida alludes to DNA as a kind of "writing" or trace present within living substances. One could say that Maharishi Vedic Science goes much further by identifying the script of the Veda, the impulses of self-referral consciousness, as the basis of DNA and demonstrating that the language of the Veda and the Vedic Literature corresponds directly to the human physiology. Memory, as a intrinsic aspect of consciousness, in this sense, is more than a trace in a linguistic chain of arbitrary signs. Smṛti or memory is an intrinsic aspect of self-referral awareness—it is the nature of fully awake consciousness; it is that fully awake, self-referral consciousness which structures the entire physiology and generates perception and the functioning of the mind. In Part V, we will again return to this discussion of memory in the consideration of the creative process in artistic expression.

Continuing with the analysis of Smṛti in the Brāhmaṇa self-referral loop, Maharishi also discusses the 18 divisions or books of Smṛti in terms of ideal modes of conduct through which the individual can evaluate his or her level of attunement with Natural Law;[57] but he emphasizes that, when used in this sense, the Smṛti are only a guide for the individual who is growing in higher states of consciousness. They are not to be taken as prescriptive. Trying to follow these codes of conduct without being established on the level of Natural Law would cause strain and confusion because: firstly, the individual can only act from his or her level of consciousness; and, secondly, the Smṛtis apparently present conflicting instructions when viewed without the experience of enlightenment.

In terms of experience and in another context, Maharishi discusses the lack of memory explaining that when the track of memory is lost one is disconnected from the rhythm of life.[58] Due to the excitement of the mind, balance is lost and delusion results. This state of delusion obscures the track of memory and the intellect ceases to function properly.[59] In contrast, the enlightened individual, does not forget the value of his own self-referral consciousness; both the unmanifest unified field of pure consciousness and the manifesting process as fluctuations of that field remain in his awareness:

> The Smṛitis emphasize that the unmanifest state and the manifesting process both have to remain in one's awareness. This is healthy awareness, enlightened consciousness of the individual in which one does not forget the total potential of Natural Law when one is expressing oneself in limitations and boundaries.[60]

From this perspective, it could be argued that for the artist who wishes to create universal art, it is essential that the unmanifest and the manifesting process remain in awareness at all times. Smṛti should be lively at all times. If not, it has to be re-enlivened.

Maharishi adds that "when the Smṛiti is lost, that is, when memory of the unbounded is no more, then the 'correctional institution' of pure knowledge is introduced."[61] Pure knowledge is that integrated state of awareness, where knower, process of knowing and the known are unified within Saṁhitā. Pure knowledge is regained through the practice of the Transcendental Meditation technique and the TM-Sidhi program. The primary mistake the intellect made in favoring diversity at the expense of unity is thus corrected through experience of pure knowledge. Maharishi states that as long as mind is one-sided and

> Subjected only to activity without the direct influence of Being, it fails to become a successful mediator. It fails to safeguard the freedom of the self from the influence of action, and at the same time fails to safeguard action from the limitations of individuality, so that activity remains without the direct support of the almighty power of Nature.[62]

Any action performed without Smṛti lively in awareness is confined to the limitations of individuality. It is not universal and does not have the support of Natural Law (the almighty power of Nature). During the process of transcending the mind is reconnected with Natural Law through the intellect.

Maharishi states that "the intellect is the finest aspect of one's subjective nature. As long as the intellect is intact there's every hope of advancement and fulfillment in life."[63] The intellect, as such, plays a part in "remembering" its unmanifest nature—self-referral consciousness. Through this process, the value of memory or Smṛti can be understood as correcting the "mistake of the intellect" (where the intellect favors diversity at the expense of unity)—called *Pragya-Aparadha* in Maharishi Vedic Science.[64]

Ultimately, the value of Smṛti presents the universal definition of memory, and the role of this aspect of consciousness in revealing the fundamental reality of our own self-referral awareness.

Prātiśākhya: Unfolding *Brahma Vidyā*—Knowledge of *Brahma*

In Maharishi Vedic Science, the last cluster of the Vedic Literature or Natural Law—the Prātiśākhya—are seen to bring out the value of Brahma, Totality or wholeness. Comprising Ṛk Veda Prātiśākhya, Śukl-Yajur-Veda Prātiśākhya,

Atharva Veda Prātiśākhya, Atharva Veda Prātiśākhya (*Chaturadhyāyi*), Kṛṣṇ-Yajur-Veda Prātiśākhya (*Taittirīya*), and Sāma Veda Prātiśākhya (*Puśpa Sūtram*), these six, respectively, are the qualities of: 1) all-pervading WHOLENESS; 2) silencing, sharing and spreading; 3) unfolding; 4) dissolving, 5) omnipresent; and 6) unmanifesting the parts but manifesting the whole. In the physiology, these six qualities structure different layers of the cerebral cortex. The all-pervading WHOLENESS value of intelligence of Ṛk Veda Prātiśākhya structures the plexiform layer—horizontal communication (cerebral cortex layer 1), the silencing, sharing and spreading quality of Shukl-Yajur-Veda Prātiśākhya structures the corticocortical fibers (cerebral cortex layer 2), the unfolding quality of intelligence of Atharva Veda Prātiśākhya structures the corticostriate, corticotectal, and corticospinal fibers (cerebral cortex layer 5), the dissolving quality of Atharva Veda Prātiśākhya (*Chaturadhyāyi*) structures the corticothalamic and corticoclaustral fibers (cerebral cortex layer 6), the omnipresent quality of intelligence of Kṛṣṇ-Yajur-Veda Prātiśākhya (*Taittirīya*) structures the commisural and corticortical fibers (cerebral cortex layer 3), and the unmanifesting the parts but manifesting the whole quality of Sāma Veda Prātiśākhya (*Puśpa Sūtram*) structures the thalmocortical fibers (cerebral cortex layer 4). As Nader notes, in the physiology the Prātiśākhya are represented by the gray matter of the cerebral cortex where all the diverse expressions, all parts of knowledge, are integrated to form a wholeness which is more than the sum of the parts. He adds that this aspect of the physiology, realizes its full potential when its holistic functioning sustains the experience of pure consciousness in perception, thought and action. When this is achieved totality and point are seen together—in one unbounded ocean of consciousness in motion.

As discussed in Part II, recent research by Lyubimov conducted on individuals who practice the Transcendental Meditation technique and the TM-Sidhi program indicates the occurrence of more holistic brain functioning. Nader notes that in several experiments, using computerized electroencephalography, control subjects responded to sensory stimuli by activating (as expected) small localized areas of the brain that correspond to the particular stimulus. Lyubimov found that subjects practicing the Transcendental Meditation technique and the TM-Sidhi program tested under similar conditions responded by enlivening the whole brain. This finding, Nader suggests, can be seen to be indication of the enlivenment of the full value of the Prātiśākhya.[65]

In discussing six qualities of intelligence brought out by the six Prātiśākhya, Maharishi points out that they reveal the non-material material field of intelligence which is motivated both by the direction of expansion and the direction toward the source at the same time. This is by virtue of bi-directional awareness—where the two directions of emergence and submergence (given by Vyākaraṇ and Nirukt respectively) are simultaneously revealed. The Prātiśākhya highlight the value of bi-directional intelligence.

> Like the cotton that gets woven into the thread, or the earth that gets moulded by the potter, consciousness is given one direction by Vyākaraṇ and an opposite direction by Nirukt, but that reality (intelligence) which is itself motivated in two opposite directions is brought to light by the Prātishākhyas.[66]

That self-referral consciousness is the absolute administration of Natural Law where the holding together of opposites is maintained in the broadest sense—extending from the state of unity or Ṛk Veda to the field of diversity which includes the whole range of multiplicity, reaching the farthest end of infinity.

Maintaining Unity in Diversity

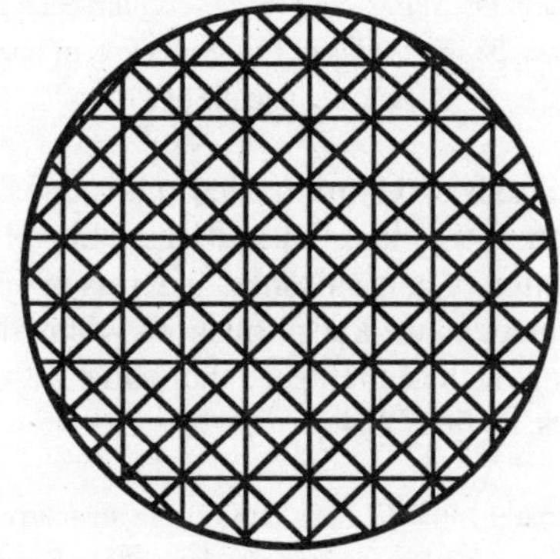

The Prātiśākhya connect the farthest ends of infinity and maintain one homogeneous wholeness of intelligence.

As considered earlier, this phenomenon of absolute administration is a phenomenon of self-referral consciousness. It is everyone's own simplest form of awareness. Administration through Natural Law takes the individual or *Jīva* from his status as *Ātmā* to the Cosmic value of *Brahma*—the total functioning of Natural Law at every point in creation. Thus, the theme of administration is understood and experienced as the self-referral dynamics of one's own awareness where *Jīva* becomes *Brahma.*[67] In this state of Brahman Consciousness, Maharishi teaches, the government of Nature, governing through the Natural Law, administers life and promotes evolution at every phase of existence.[68] Individual activity, performed from this level of Saṁhitā or Cosmic Creative Intelligence is completely nourishing to all life; it is completely universal. With this understanding, the purpose of study of the Vedic Literature is extended. It enlivens within the student's awareness that value of self-referral consciousness displayed by each aspect of the Vedic Literature.[69] Furthermore, when the individual is fully awake in her own self-referral awareness the Veda and the Vedic Literature are appreciated for their universal, Transcendental value; the individual perceives the most fundamental value of the expressions of the Vedic Literature and the mechanics of transformation in the gaps between each expression. This, especially, is the domain of the Prātiśākhya, as Maharishi explains:

> The student of the Prātishākhyas appreciates the transcendental element beyond the expressed words (*Mantr*) and, visualizing the mechanics of transformation or the structuring dynamics of the words of the Vedic Literature, spontaneously familiarizes his awareness with the organizing power of Creative Intelligence inherent within the word. He also appreciates the reality of the sequence of gaps (between the *Mantras* and the *Sūtras*) and locates, within each gap, the Creative Intelligence that presents the mechanics of transformation of one syllable into the other, one *Mantr* into the other, one *Sūtr* into the other.[70]

As discussed earlier, the details of the mechanics of this transformation from one word or expression to another is laid out in Maharishi's *Apauruṣeya Bhāṣya.* This picture of the evolution of consciousness in terms of syllables and gaps—where the syllables comment on the transformations within the gaps in a precise sequential manner—dawns in the enlightened individual's awareness. Whatever field the individual studies, he finds that:

> Everything is so transparent that he sees behind the structure and behind the meaning of the sound the all-meaningful wholeness, Saṁhitā, the Veda, percolated with Vedānta; and finally the reality of himself.[71]

The Prātiśākhya, Maharishi adds, "awaken that intelligence which makes every aspect of the Vedic Literature a mirror on which the student of Vedic Science sees himself."[72] The Vedic Literature is a mirror of one's own consciousness; one sees one's Self.

In this sense, the Prātiśākhya bring to light the wholeness within every aspect of Ṛk Veda, as Maharishi explains: re-establishing "the significance of the whole within every part, the quality of Saṁhitā, wholeness, everywhere."[73] When one is awake in the totality of the Self, including all the structuring dynamics of the Veda and the Vedic Literature, one finds oneself in all fields of knowledge and all types of experiences—past, present and future. The individual gains mastery over Natural Law, the field of infinite creativity, and becomes a lively expression of the total engineering of creation and evolution.

In his description of the value of this last cluster of Natural Law, Maharishi presents an extensive account of the role of the Prātiśākhya; he explains that they:

—bring to light wholeness within the Constitution of the Universe, Ṛk Veda;

—re-establish the significance of the whole within every part by establishing Saṁhitā or wholeness everywhere;

—explore the Ultimate Reality, the essential content of the Veda and hold together diversifying and diversified Laws which constitute the specific structuring dynamics of the Veda;

—present the Veda and Vedic Literature in terms of the infinitely correlated, holistic structure of intelligence where separate values are seen in terms of togetherness, oneness, connectedness or wholeness and connect the farthest ends of infinity and maintain one homogenous wholeness of intelligence;

—present the individual structuring dynamics of Veda in terms of the wholeness of the Constitution of the Universe, bringing out the hidden underlying common basis of the structuring dynamics of Veda;

—bring to light non-material material field of intelligence or consciousness motivated by the structuring dynamics of Vyākaraṇ (in the direction of expansion) and simultaneously by the structuring dynamics of Nirukt (in the direction of the source);

—explore the junction point between any and every two expressions of the Vedic structure

—are at the basis of all values of the Vedic structure and, as such, unfold one Ultimate Reality—the Unified Field of Natural Law;

—locate the essential field of Intelligence, Saṁhita, expressed by Śikṣa, transformed by Kalp, given direction by Vyākaraṇ and Nirukt, hidden by Chhand and fully awake in terms of Jyotish on the level of *Jyotish Mati Pragya*—where everything can be known;

—explore the nature of basic reality which blossoms into different values of Upānga and Upa-Veda and all other aspects of the Vedic Literature and make every value transparent so that *Atyanta-Abhāva*, infinite silence, shines through everything, Vedānt shines through the structuring dynamics of Veda so that connectedness characterizes Veda and Vedic Literature in the reality of *Brahm*, wholeness shines through all the parts;

—locate Veda and Vedic Literature in Self-referral *Ātmā*;

—scan every structure of Veda and Vedic Literature and examine the relationship of one with another by examining the gaps between them;

—locate different kinds of *Atyanta-Abhāva* and the corresponding quality of *Anyonya-Abhāva* in the gaps;

—visualize the existence of Veda and Vedic Literature within the Ultimate Reality, the absolute silence of *Atyanta-Abhāva*, Absolute Abstraction, pure intelligence;

—unfold the whole field of total science and the technologies of consciousness;

—establish the wholeness of the Constitution of the Universe in every part of it (i.e., in every grain of creation);

—substantiate Vasiśtha's cognition which unfolds the whole range of the Prātiśhākhya:

दूरे दृशं गृहपतिम् अथर्युम्

Dūre dṛśaṁ gṛhapatim atharyum

(*Ṛk Veda, 7.1.1.*)

Far in the distance is seen the owner of the house reverberating;

—present a storehouse of knowledge which is a must for every government;

—awaken that intelligence which makes every aspect of Vedic Literature a mirror on which the student of Vedic Science sees himself;

—promote the study of any *Mantra* (word) or *Sūtra* (phrase) in a way that one sees the form of the written text but simultaneously appreciates the Transcendental value of each *Sūtra* and the wholeness of Saṁhitā, the common basis to all *Sūtra*;

—nourish and enrich the student of Vedic Science and allow the student to appreciate the Transcendental element beyond expressed words (*Mantra*) and visualize the mechanics of transformation of the words of the Vedic Literature;

—spontaneously familiarize the student's awareness with the organizing power of Creative Intelligence inherent within the word. The student appreciates the gaps and the mechanics of transformation in gaps, finding that Vedānt unfolds in Veda, Veda unfolds in Vedānga, Vedānga unfolds in Upānga, and so forth, until every aspect blossoms into Veda and Vedānt, every aspect unfolds the Transcendent, *Brahm*;

—allow the student to find everything so transparent that, whatever aspect of the Vedic Literature is studied, behind the structure and behind the meaning of sound, all meaningful wholeness is seen, percolated with Vedānt the student sees the reality of himself; and

—facilitate all types of experiences—past, present and future are found in the Transcendental nature of the student's own Self, his or her own awareness. The awareness of student is the lively expression of total engineering of creation.[74] The technology to realize this goal, Maharishi emphasizes is the Transcendental Meditation technique.

In discussing this and the other values of the Vedic Literature, it is clear that from the perspective of Maharishi Vedic Science these "texts" are not considered to be the writings of individual authors but the structuring dynamics of everyone's own self-referral consciousness. Consciousness in its most expanded sense, is wholeness.

As described in this section, the move of wholeness within itself generates the Veda and the Vedic Literature. As Maharishi points out:

> Fully awake, fully alert consciousness—singularity, wholeness, aware of itself—spontaneously displays self-referral dynamism in terms of the sound of the Veda. This is how wholeness, functioning within itself, generates impulses of

> wholeness (structures of the Veda and Vedic Literature, which, continuing to evolve, express themselves as structures of Natural Law, evolving into material creation. Wholeness appears as the Veda, Veda appears as the Laws of Nature, and this is the management of WHOLENESS—wholeness managing itself through its own managing intelligence, the Laws of Nature that create, maintain, and evolve the entire ever-expanding universe within the structure of wholeness.[75]

All 40 aspects of the Veda and Vedic Literature are involved in and highlight the structuring dynamics of the structure of Ṛk, and bring out the values of Ṛishi, Devatā, or Chhandas within the Saṁhitā value of self-referral consciousness. The move of wholeness as the creative process of Natural Law, Maharishi explains, progresses in a systematic manner illustrated by the sequential unfoldment of Ṛk Veda and the Vedic Literature. Each aspect of the Vedic Literature unfolds a specific quality of consciousness in the sequence of unfoldment of self-referral dynamics consciousness; consequently, the Vedic Literature presents itself in clusters of Natural Law, or self-referral feedback loops. In revealing this aspect of consciousness, the transcendental value of the sounds of Ṛk Veda and the Vedic Literature and their expression in terms of Natural Law, Maharishi uncovers the deeper significance of these texts; the language of the Veda can be understood as universal; a direct relationship exists between sound and form. This intimate correspondence between name and form, and sound and meaning, in the Vedic language is revisited in the discussion of the Vāstusūtra Upaniṣad in Part VI. From the perspective of Maharishi Vedic Science, relative utterances and inscriptions of speech and writing (and all artistic expressions) have their source in self-referral consciousness.

Maharishi emphasizes that while it can be said the Veda and Vedic Literature can be appreciated on various levels (for example, the epics of the *Mahābhārat* and the *Rāmāyaṇ* have their value as stories about heroic individuals who represent the embodiment of Natural Law) on the level of *sound alone* the verses of these epics reverberate those qualities of consciousness which, when heard or recited by the individual, enliven that corresponding value of consciousness in the awareness and the physiology of the listener and speaker. Therefore, in listening to or reading the Veda and Vedic Literature one is involved in developing consciousness.[76] Given this understanding of consciousness, how can art aesthetic value be redefined? While Part V will go on to answer this question, the following section returns to concepts of history introduced in Part I, and discusses how history and culture, tradition and language are understood in Maharishi Vedic Science. In this way, a platform for the comprehension of a universal basis to visual culture will be established, encompassing re-definitions of historiography, cultural integrity, tradition, and the importance of using one's mother tongue.

PART IV

NATURAL LAW: THE UNIVERSAL FOUNDATION OF HISTORY, TRADITIONS, CULTURE AND LANGUAGE

According to Maharishi Vedic Science, the history of humankind can be understood in terms of the unfoldment of time and events in discrete stages within the infinite continuum of self-referral consciousness or Natural Law. From this broad perspective, a universal basis to history, tradition, culture, language and collective consciousness can be identified. The range of history is infinite but it unfolds in cycles of Natural Law.

While Maharishi's perspective of history contrasts with the modern and postmodern models, it sheds light on the Indian view of cyclical development. As mentioned before, Maharishi explains that his Vedic Science is an eternal and universal science of consciousness, despite the fact that the Vedic tradition has been preserved in India. In this chapter then when Maharishi is quoted as speaking of the Indian approach to history he is referring to the Vedic approach, as presented in his Vedic Science, as opposed to the modern Western model. In his commentary on the Bhagavad-Gītā, (a text which, Maharishi holds, is both a universal expression of the Veda and a historical document in its own right) Maharishi discusses the Indian/Vedic conception of history. Within the cyclical unfoldment of Natural Law there are four main divisions or *Yugas* in which people engage in different ways of living. These different ways of living reflect the degree to which the people are able to live Natural Law in daily life. Each *Yuga* represents a different percent of Natural Law being lived by the people. At any time, the purpose of history is to inspire the individual and society to evolve in the present, preparing the ground for a better future.[1] In Chapter 15, *The Purpose and Dynamic of History: The Rise and Fall of Natural Law in the Cyclical Unfoldment of Consciousness*, this view of history is described, expanded and applied to an analysis of different theories of art over time.

History is not the only factor of collective life which is governed by Natural Law and specific Laws of Nature. The traditions which maintain the integrated functioning of society are also governed by Laws of Nature. Chapter 16: *Traditions: Different Modes of Activity Governed by Dharmas* considers how, just as there are Laws of Nature which sustain and co-ordinate the body, there are those which govern and co-ordinate the relationships between individuals within a family and families within society.[2] This chapter looks at the dynamic interplay between individual, family and social consciousness and the relationship of these to pure consciousness. Even a profession of an individual or family can be understood in terms of Laws of Nature or *Dharmas*; all the various professions in society, when they uphold life in accord with Natural Law, play a role in the progress and evolution of individual and collective consciousness.[3] This contrasts somewhat with modernist notion of the privileged artist's originality and uniqueness of expression.

Along with tradition, Maharishi maintains that one's culture plays a significant role in promoting evolution. Chapter 17: *Culture as the Expression of Specific Laws of Nature—Governing Geography Climate, Mannerisms, Language and Accents of Different Peoples*, considers how there is a universal and particular value to culture; "the holistic value of Natural Law handles the holistic value of culture—universal culture"[4] while specific values of different Laws of Nature give rise to particular cultures and the geographic and climatic conditions which shape them. These Laws of Nature are specific values of Natural Law that structure the physiology of the individual and shape the characteristic aspects of a culture or nation—including the mannerisms, artistic expressions, and local language of the people. While there is a universal value to culture, each individual culture is governed by its own inner ordering principles or Laws of Nature which support the development of that group by maintaining cultural integrity. A nation that enjoys cultural integrity is invincible; it cannot be disturbed by outside influences. It is firmly established in the universal basis of culture—the field of Natural Law.[5]

As discussed in Part II, Natural Law can be enlivened through the practice of Maharishi's Technologies of Consciousness. The effect of these technologies is evidenced by research showing that, when practiced by a sufficiently large group, collective stress in a population is dissolved and quality of life increases. In any culture or nation there are different tendencies. When society operates with the support of Natural Law, every person can be fulfilled in his own activity while contributing to the whole. The key is the development and expansion of individual and collective consciousness through the practice of the technologies of Maharishi Vedic Science. Through the enlivenment of the universal basis of all cultures—pure consciousness or *Ātmā*—these technologies strengthen cultural integrity and those traditions which are useful to life[6]. Similarly, different cultural expressions, different values of visual culture, can generate contextualized meaning while also embodying universal significance.

One aspect of culture is the local language or "mother tongue" of the people. Maharishi explains that it is important for people of a specific culture to use their mother tongue to strengthen and maintain cultural integrity. He points out that the mother tongue is the closest language to the universal language of the Veda. It therefore supports the physiology of the individual.[7] Clearly, history, tradition and culture are, here, not defined as socially constructed, dead or outmoded; each play a vital role in promoting evolution and helping unfold universal value in life.

15

THE PURPOSE AND DYNAMIC OF HISTORY: THE RISE AND FALL OF NATURAL LAW IN THE CYCLICAL UNFOLDMENT OF CONSCIOUSNESS

The purpose oi nistory, according to Maharishi Vedic Science, is to promote the development of consciousness by inspiring today's generation with past events. Maharishi indicates that "the study of history has a definite purpose and place in the life of an individual. Its aim is to educate the mind of the present with information from the past in order to ensure a better present and a better future."[1] At face value, this view of history seems to resemble Hegel's idea of pragmatic history—where events of the past are instructional in the present. However, Hegel's ideas are not commensurate with the principles of evolution and progress in Maharishi Vedic Science. Hegel's category of original history completely rejected "myth" as non-historical. Subsequently, Western historians have overlooked historical details recorded in oral traditions of other cultures. As Maharishi explains, "modern historians tend to reject as non-history any series of events for which they fail to find a proper chronological order."[2]

Modern historians assume that descriptions of higher states of human development, documented for example in the Vedic Literature, are imaginative literature or mythology rather than actual accounts of reality.[3] Maharishi adds that, "it is deplorable that such precious accounts of life on the highest human level as are to be found in the historical material of ancient India should have been regarded as myth."[4] By rejecting such accounts, so-called "objective" methods of writing history dismiss important records and oral traditions. Speaking of the Bhagavad-Gītā, Maharishi explains that although it deals with fundamentals of life it is also a historical record relating events that took place 5,000 years ago.[5] As such, it provides an account of how life can be lived according to *Dharma* and forms the core of an authentic record of Indian history. Maharishi indicates that the Bhagavad-Gītā has been dismissed as mythology "because the narrow vision of modern historians, tied to rigid chronology," fails "to understand it as a historical record."[6] Furthermore, on another level, as part of the *Mahābhārata* (one of the Itihās discussed in Part III), the Bhagavad-Gītā is not only a historical document but also an expression of the self-interacting dynamics of consciousness.

The Western approach to history has, to some degree, misinterpreted and misrepresented the traditions of various cultures and is not without its problems (as stated in Part I). In the 1980s scholars felt it was impossible to locate any consensus in historical studies. Some noted that the study of history seemed to be governed by factional polarization or fragmented chaos. History as a discipline ceased to exist.[7] According to Maharishi Vedic Science, the main problem with the study of history has been the lack of understanding of its governing principle—the mechanics by which consciousness unfolds in terms of time and events. Modern historiography considers events in terms of a limited framework, without comprehending the relationship between human life and the universal field of consciousness governing the entire field of existence. Going beyond the limited vision of modern historians and even Hegel's notion of universal history, in Maharishi Vedic Science history can be seen as the story of the eternal continuum of pure consciousness or Natural Law quantifying itself in various expressions of knowledge.

Maharishi Vedic Science also holds that an enlightened historian is able to maintain a vision of the whole span of time beginning from the day of creation. This infinite conception of time is based upon the experience of pure consciousness. As outlined in his discussion of a verse from the Bhagavad-Gītā, against the backdrop of the infinite, Maharishi points out, time unfolds in specific eras:

> Time is a conception to measure eternity. Indian historians base their conception of time on eternal Being; for them eternity is the basic field of time. To arrive at some conception of the eternal, the best measure will be the life-span of something that has the greatest longevity in the relative field of creation. This, according to the enlightened vision of Vyasa, is the Divine Mother, the Universal Mother, who is ultimately responsible for all that is, was and will be in the entire cosmos.
>
> The eternity of the eternal life of absolute Being is conceived in terms of innumerable lives of the Divine Mother, a single one of whose lives encompasses a thousand life-spans of Lord Shiva. One life of Lord Shiva covers the time of a thousand life-spans of Lord Vishnu. One life of Lord Vishnu equals the duration of a thousand life-spans of Brahma, the Creator.
>
> A single life-span of Brahma is conceived in terms of one hundred years of Brahma; each year of Brahma comprises 12 months of Brahma, and each month comprises thirty days of Brahma. One day of Brahma is called a Kalpa. One Kalpa is equal to the time of fourteen Manus. The time of one Manu is called a Manvantara. One Manvantara equals seventy-one Chaturyugis. One Chaturyugi comprises the total span of four Yugas i.e. Sat-yuga, Treta-yuga, Dvapara-yuga and Kali-yuga. The span of the Yugas is conceived in terms of the duration of Sat-yuga. Thus the span of Treta-yuga is equal to three quarters of that Sat-yuga; the span of Dvapara-yuga is half that of Sat-yuga, and the span of Kali-yuga one quarter that of Sat-yuga. The span of Kali-yuga equals 432,000 years of man's life.[8]

To try to cover all the events of the history of the infinite, as Maharishi indicates, would be somewhat futile. As can be calculated, if a *Kali-Yuga* is 432,000 human years, *Dwāpara-Yuga*, *Tretā-Yuga*, and *Sat-Yuga* are, respectively: 864,000, 1,296,000, and 1,728,000 years in length. In turn, a *Chaturyugi* consists of 4,320,000 years; a *Manvantara* equals 306,720,000 years; one *Kalpa* (14 *Manus* or 14 times one *Manvantara*) is 4,294,080,000 years. A *Kalpa* is one day of *Brahmā*. and one single life-span of *Brahmā* is 154,586,880 million years. A life-span of *Viṣṇu*—being one thousand times the life-span of *Brahmā*—is 154,586,880 billion years. The life-span of *Śiva* is one thousand life-spans of *Viṣṇu* or 154,586,880,000 billion years, and the life-span of Mother Divine (of which, Maharishi notes, there are an innumerable number) is one thousand life-spans of *Viṣṇu* or 154,586,880,000 trillion years.

Mother Divine, was discussed in earlier chapters as the "supreme Cosmic Intelligence" which Maharishi equates with the experience of "I am"—where there is nothing else but pure existence and one is fully awake to one's own self-referral consciousness, where diversity is merged into unity.[9] It is the infinite value of Creative Intelligence, "the source of creation—supreme Creative Intelligence in her magnanimity, supreme invincibility, totality, pure potentiality—the source of everything."[10] An enlightened historian, Maharishi emphasizes, bases his or her conception of time on that which has the greatest longevity in the relative field—this value of Mother Divine. Therefore, the vast range of history, Maharishi points out, cannot be listed item-by-item. As he asserts, by applying a chronological order to history, historians actually mar the purpose of history.

> Now consider the time of creation: for how many billion trillion years the world has been! Even if the account of one year were to occupy a page or a single line, how could anyone possibly read such a history and apply its lesson to his life? This is why chronological order was not maintained by Indian historians. Apart from being impractical, it was considered to be unnecessary, useless and damaging to the very purpose of history. All this should be borne in mind by those modern historians who tend to reject as non-history any series of events for which they fail to find a proper chronological order.[11]

Since the purpose of history is to spur the individual on to a better future, Maharishi emphasizes that it is the *value* of events which bear significance. He suggests that only certain events are worth studying—those events which throughout the vast span of time integrate men and women's lives in the present and help the individual to spontaneously behave more in accord with Natural Law or *Dharma*.[12] In this context, history should help further human development. As Maharishi teaches, the eternal basis to history is the evolution of consciousness. It is the quantification of pure consciousness as discrete values of time—unfolding series of cycles which correspond to specific eras in which people live varying percentages of Natural Law. This cyclical progression takes the form of different *Yugas* which can be understood in terms of the rise and fall of Natural Law as reflected in the change of religious codes or precepts.

This cycle can also be considered in the light of politics, social change and other areas—such as the idea of universal value in art and culture.

Sat-Yuga: Living 100 Percent of Natural Law

Sat-Yuga is defined as that period when 100 percent of Natural Law is lived; life is characterized by perfection. Perfection refers to perfect health in mind and body, life-supporting behavior, and spontaneous fulfillment of desires on the individual and collective level. *Sat-Yuga* is an era when life is lived in an integrated and harmonious manner; where all individual trends are netted in harmony. Maharishi describes such an era by stating:

> As long as one hundred per cent value of Natural Law is lived in daily life, people spontaneously act in accordance with Natural Law; or, in the language of religion, act in accordance with the 'Will of God'; and, in the language of science, live life according to Natural Law—a state of perfect physiological, psychological, sociological, and ecological integration—ideal mental and physical health. When one hundred per cent value of Natural Law is lived in daily life every code of conduct of every religion will finally be fulfilled, because the fulfillment of all religions is daily life lived according to all the Laws of Nature; pure knowledge, the Veda, and its infinite organizing power enjoyed by all is the most natural state of life. Such a period in Vedic history is called *Sat-Yuga*. This is a period when mastery over Natural Law belongs to almost everyone. The infinite potential of life, the field of all possibilities, is ever awake, eternally lively in everyone's self-referral, Transcendental Consciousness.
>
> This heritage is spontaneously passed on from generation to generation, and the age has a name: the Age of Enlightenment. In *Sat-Yuga*, consciousness on both levels, individual and collective, is in perfect accordance with Natural Law, and therefore every aspect of life is evolutionary. Society is ideal, and nations invincible. The family of nations enjoys perfect health in every way. The administration of society is as perfect and automatic as administration of the universe: no one sees who administers; administration is so quiet, and yet every impulse is evolutionary.[13]

In *Sat-Yuga*, an age which may sound unachievable to the contemporary man, people enjoy perfect physiological, psychological, sociological and ecological integration. Action is performed from the level of the cosmic administration of the Constitution of the Universe, which spontaneously computes the right (most life-supporting) action for any given moment in a given context—cultural or otherwise. Many great minds have tried to articulate a vision of such an age, calling it Utopia or Heaven or simply a society which can live in peace and harmony.

However, Maharishi stipulates that *Sat-Yuga* is an age when people spontaneously enjoy mastery over Natural Law. As discussed in Part II, with the development of consciousness through the Transcendental Meditation technique and the TM-Sidhi program, one can gain mastery over Natural Law—the ability to operate from the level of the Constitution of the Universe, the total potential of Creative Intelligence.[14] The phrase "mastery over Natural Law" refers to the ability to live from the holistic basis of life; it does not refer to a manipulation of partial values of life without knowledge of the whole (as with the approach of modern technologies which have damaging side effects). Individual action, promoted from the level of Natural Law, spontaneously and automatically takes into account the appropriate life-supporting influence for the rest of society and the environment. Ethical, moral and social concerns are automatically computed. Nothing is "inappropriate." Furthermore, life in enlightenment, life lived according to Natural Law, does not imply a static existence (which critics of the ideal or Utopian model fear). The field of pure consciousness itself, as discussed previously, generates an infinite, self-referral dynamic: silence and dynamism together—giving rise to the play of difference on the ground of unity. Life is an ever-evolving field of change but pure consciousness is the basis of this change and variety. The immense array of diversity can be enjoyed on the basis of unity because life can be lived anchored to the unifying foundation of pure, self-referral consciousness.

Enlightenment, on the collective level, is characterized by ideal life and invincibility for every nation. As emphasized above, in *Sat-Yuga*, both individual and collective consciousness is in accordance with Natural Law. Life is evolutionary. On a global level, the family of nations enjoy perfect health and the administration of society is automatic—like the administration of the universe.[15] In this "ideal" world, everyone is fulfilled; nations live in harmony. Individuals and society are governed by the same laws which effortlessly govern the activity of the entire universe through the silent administration of Natural Law. Maharishi elaborates by stating that no one sees the "administrator" but every aspect of administration of Natural Law is completely evolutionary. All the different tendencies in life are able to function together without discord. The key to ideal living and perfect administration is spontaneous behavior in accord with Natural Law—from the level of self-referral consciousness. When life is lived collectively in accord with Natural Law, society, ecology and the environment enjoy balance—the seasonal cycles come on time and all of life is totally life-supporting.[16]

Different Values of Natural Law: Tretā, Dwāpara and Kali-Yuga

While *Sat-Yuga* is that period when the complete value of Natural Law is lived in daily life, Maharishi explains that the other *Yugas*—*Tretā-Yuga*, *Dwāpara-Yuga* and *Kali-Yuga*—denote those periods when a lesser degree of Natural Law is lived by the people. For example, 75 percent of Natural Law is lived in *Tretā-Yuga*, 50 percent in *Dwāpara-Yuga*, and 25 percent in *Kali-Yuga*.[17] Thus, the infinite continuum of time is measured in terms of these discrete stages—evolving cyclically from one to the other.

As the degree of Natural Law lived in daily life decreases, the period of *Sat-Yuga* gives way to *Tretā-Yuga*, then *Dwāpara-Yuga*, and finally, *Kali-Yuga*. In *Kali-Yuga*., over time, almost zero percent of Natural Law is reached. At this point life swings back to 100 percent of Natural Law again.[18] The phenomenon of the decline of Natural Law occurs due to the gradual loss of pure consciousness in human awareness—a loss of the full value of Natural Law lived in daily life. When almost zero percent of Natural law is reached, the pendulum swings back—to 100 percent again. The progressive lack of wakefulness, the lack of 100 percent of pure consciousness, causes a lack in man's ability to maintain and live the full degree of Natural Law. At the point of almost zero percent, Natural Law is latent in its pure potentiality and is awakened again in human life. The cycle swings once again to *Sat-Yuga* The phenomenon of this swing back to 100 percent from zero percent of Natural Law is referred to as the "Great Leap" by Maharishi[19] and is brought about by the discovery of the lively field of pure potentiality of Natural Law in human awareness through the practice of technologies of consciousness. This cycle demonstrates the different percentages of Natural Law lived by people during the different eras or *Yugas*.

Religious Codes and The Unfoldment of Pure Consciousness in Daily Life

The various teachings of moral, religious, and political codes can also be considered in the context of the cycle of the *Yugas*. These different teachings of moral, religious, and even political codes which spring up throughout time are the expression of the principle of orderliness at the basis of creation governed by the Constitution of the Universe—Ṛk Veda.[20] Ṛk Veda is that holistic value of Natural Law which governs life with complete efficiency and order. This absolute, orderly structure of self-referral consciousness is infinitely flexible; it is a field of all possibilities. Maharishi points out that this universal structure of the Veda has been cognized and explicated by enlightened individuals throughout the ages, in many different languages in the scriptures of different religions. It is the same universal structure of pure knowledge which is cognized in terms of the light of God or as Natural Law by different individuals. As he explains, this field of all possibilities:

> Is cognized in so many different ways by so many enlightened sages, saints, and seers—messengers of God—in so many different languages, in so many different lands, throughout the ages in the long infinity of time. We have

inspiring records of these beautiful cognitions as the holy scriptures of different religions.[21]

However, when the message gets diluted and looses its relevance, new religions emerge. As Maharishi explains:

> We have inspiring records of these beautiful cognitions as the holy scriptures of different religions; but when the original message gets distorted in time, it ceases to be useful; people naturally lose interest in something that is not useful. This is how religions fall, giving rise to new ones with a fresh message of the same old, eternal light of God. Veda, the structure of pure knowledge, because of its absolute perfection, continues to be appreciated by the enlightened in their own pure consciousness—spontaneous revelations, generation after generation.[22]

In this sense, the scriptures of various religions essentially convey the message of the "light of God." Terms such as the "light of God," "stillness," "peace," can all be understood to describe pure consciousness. In the terminology of religion "heavenly life" is "life in the light of God"; using the terminology of science "ideal life" is "life in accord with Natural Law"—lived from the level of pure consciousness and characterized by orderliness, harmony and peace.

When understood from the perspective of higher states of consciousness, descriptions such as those recorded by seers throughout time represent the documentation of self-referral consciousness experienced by individuals of diverse traditions. Veda continues to be appreciated and the religious codes that spring up define parameters for individual and social behavior. Religious codes provide guidelines for behavior when man is unable to spontaneously live the full value of Natural Law. Ultimately, as Maharishi notes, "every religion is the highest possible expression of Natural Law at its time and place of origin."[23] However, the different religious codes which spring up correlate to the degree of Natural Law being lived by the people. This explains why different expressions of religious codes in the form of different religious sects emerge:

> As Natural Law declines in human awareness, religious codes arise to help man and guide him to maintain the ability to live Natural Law as much as he can. The decline of Natural Law in the life of the people should be understood in terms of the decline of man's ability to spontaneously live Natural Law in daily life. As Natural Law continues to decline through the passage of time, man's ability further deteriorates, and he ceases to be capable of living up to the full value of the religious codes. Diluted or simplified expressions of the religious codes, in form of the codes of different sects of the same religion, arise in response to the need of the time. By the time Natural Law is expressed in its zero value in daily life, it has reached the lowest limit of its extreme range. The acceptance of suffering by religion is the indication of the complete decline of Natural Law in daily life. Thence comes the point of return. The beauty is that at this point in

> time the total value of Natural Law is in its pure potentiality; it is fully awake within itself. This fully awake potential of Natural Law naturally begins to express itself in daily life. This is the **great leap** of the nature of Natural Law within itself from its zero level of expression to its one hundred per cent level of expression in practical life.[24]

As man's ability to live according to the effortless, holistic functioning of Natural Law decreases over time, he loses the ability to function in accord with Natural Law and is unable to live by the religious codes. Due to the need of the time, new codes—which are more simplified—spring up and are expressed as guidelines of religious sects in that religion. Then, when suffering becomes a tenet of religion, zero percent of Natural Law has been reached.

The Cyclical Unfoldment of Time in Terms of the Four Yugas and Their Respective Degrees of Natural Law

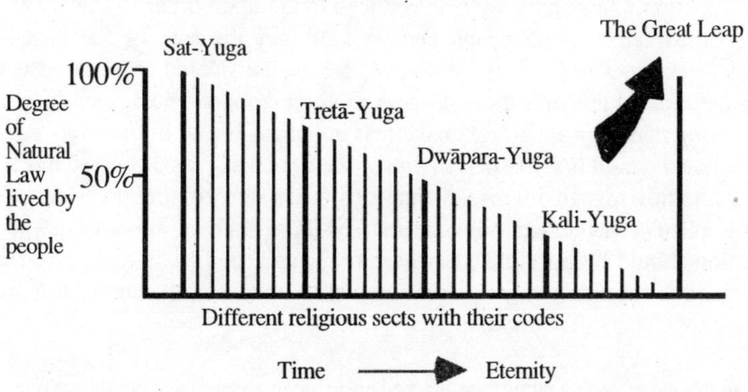

The cycle of Natural Law swings from 100 percent value, through all its gradations in terms of religious codes, back to its 100 percent value. Here the rise and fall of religions in the corridor of time eternal is indicated in terms of the Yugas, the idea of different religious sects springing up, and the degree of Natural Law spontaneously lived in life.

Maharishi Vedic Astrology states that we are now living in the 5101st Vedic year of *Kaliyuga*:

> According to the *Surya Siddhanta*, the major text on Vedic Astronomy, fifty years of the life of Brahma are over. Currently we are living in the first Kalpa (day of Brahma) of the 51st year. In this Kalpa, 6 Manvantaras of 71 Chaturyugas have passed, and in this 28th Caturyuga, the Kritayuga, Tretayuga, and Dwaparayuga are also passed.[25]

Generally speaking, in *Kali-Yuga*, there is a disconnection from the universal source of life; there is a rise of struggle and suffering. When zero percent of Natural Law is reached *Kali-Yuga* comes to an end. Technologies of consciousness are introduced so that human life can return to an age of 100 percent Natural Law. Nader comments that Maharishi Vedic Science is now providing the knowledge of how to live life in accord with Natural Law, after:

> Thousands of years of struggling history of life on earth, Maharishi has joyfully shown the script of Veda and Vedic Literature lively within the fibres of the human physiology and has provided simple programmes to enliven the full Vedic potential—full potential of Natural Law—within the physiology of everyone.[26]

The Relationship between National Law and Natural Law

When a nation is no longer able to act in accord with Nature's infinite organizing power, national laws have to be introduced to maintain order in society and to protect the interests of the people and the land they inhabit. In *Sat-Yuga* such codes of conduct or laws, in one sense, can be considered to be unnecessary because individuals and the nation as a whole spontaneously act in a life-supporting manner—incurring no distress in human life or in the environment. While many would find this description of life unrealistic, as discussed in Part II, research showing an increased quality of life due to the practice of the Transcendental Meditation technique and TM-Sidhi program indicates that such a situation should be possible. Furthermore, many traditions and sacred texts describe this condition of life. For example, from the fourth century B.C.E. the writings of Chuang-Tze exclaim:

> In the age of perfect virtue they attached no value to wisdom nor employed men of ability. Superiors were [but] as the higher branches of a tree; and the people were like the deer of the wild. They were upright and correct, without knowing that to be so was Righteousness; they loved one another, without knowing that to do so was Benevolence; they were honest and leal-hearted, without knowing that it was Loyalty; they fulfilled their engagements, without knowing that to do so was Good Faith; in their simple movements they employed the services of one another, without thinking that they were conferring or receiving any gift. Therefore their actions left no trace, and there was no record of their affairs.[27]

Descriptions such as these, contrary to the opinion of modern historians, can be viewed as records of life lived in accord with Natural Law and not mere conceptions or mythology.

With respect to history, Maharishi emphasizes that it is the "display of the impact of the evolutionary impulse of Natural Law on the collective consciousness of every nation"[28]—the demonstration of the degree to which

Natural Law is lived by the nation or group. History includes in its range the documentation of the decrease, and violation, of Natural Law. When people violate Natural Law stress increases and coherence is lost in collective and national consciousness.[29] Maharishi points out that when this occurs, Natural Law affects changes in society.[30] Any changes in the life of nation (i.e., changes in social, cultural, political, economic, legal and constitutional structures) result from a evolutionary response and demonstrates the degree to which national life is in tune with the natural law of the land. From one perspective, even revolutionary change can be said to aim at neutralizing stress in collective consciousness in order to create the opportunity for problem-free existence and progress. However, it is more advantageous to create change through peaceful evolution. According to Maharishi Vedic Science, it is only the practice of technologies of consciousness that can provide the means for peaceful evolution to occur.[31]

> Any change in the life of the nation occurs as a natural evolutionary response demonstrating the extent to which national life is in congruence with the natural law of the land; concomitant with changes in the level of coherence in collective consciousness in any nation, natural law creates unique changes in its social and cultural, political and economic, legal and constitutional structures. Revolution aims at neutralizing stress in collective consciousness and providing a new fresh ground for problem-free existence and progress.[32]

It is important to emphasize that it is not necessary for a nation to go through the stress of revolutionary change. According to Maharishi Vedic Science, through the practice of the Transcendental Meditation technique and TM-Sidhi program evolutionary change can take place, neutralizing collective stress "day-by-day so that the life of the nation is progressively more in accord with natural law."[33] When society lives more in accord with Natural Law, national laws reflect this change. There is less need for the reinforcement of national laws because life is spontaneously more life-supporting. Thus, the percentage of Natural Law being lived by a nation at any time will not only determine the quality of life the nation enjoys, but also the degree of political and economic change and effectiveness.

Spontaneous Action in Accord with Natural Law

As noted previously, Maharishi emphasizes that life can only be lived in accord with Natural Law in a *spontaneous* manner because it is impossible to know all the elements that constitute Natural Law.[34] It is not possible to intellectually calculate the ramifications of every thought and action. Therefore, it is not enough to analyze a thought or action after the fact. As Maharishi indicates, regarding the outcome of thought and action, it is impossible to reverse the damage of a negative thought once it has emerged. Only through complete harmony with Natural Law—thinking and acting from the level of Natural Law—can the individual (and collective) spontaneously prevent negativity from arising. The Transcendental Meditation technique and TM-Sidhi program help facilitate development toward spontaneously life-supporting thought and action. On this basis, the accomplishments of the individual can really make a significant contribution to the life of his or her people.

Natural Law's Hierarchical Levels of Administration

In its move to express the totality of its own Nature through the cycle of 100 percent to zero percent of Natural Law being lived in daily life, Natural Law expresses itself in different degrees that define the cycle of time:

> A cycle of time is created on the basis of the rising and falling values of Natural Law in the practical fields of life. This cycle of time exists in the timeless, infinite continuum of the fullness of Natural Law.[35]

Swinging from 100 percent through to zero percent and back to 100 percent of Natural Law, cycles of time are generated. With 100 percent of Natural Law in daily life, life is lived spontaneously in accord with Nature's functioning. Perfect administration of Natural Law is lived and enjoyed.

With respect to this perfect administration of Natural Law and the specific Laws of Nature, Maharishi indicates that in life there are several hierarchical levels of administration: 1) the holistic administration of the ever-expanding universe, the level of pure knowledge, Saṁhitā—the structure of total knowledge, total intelligence or *Puruṣottama*; 2) the administration of the parts of the universe governed by specific Laws of Nature (for example, the laws governing a galaxy or solar system); 3) administration of life on earth; 4) administration of the holistic value of human life on earth, including the Laws of Nature that administer life in each part of the globe—"the Natural Laws of the land that give rise to specific cultures of the land;"[36] 5) the Laws of Nature that administer specific values of individual life; 6) "administration of the whole nation through man-made law based on the man-made constitution of every country" and "administration of the states or provinces of the nation"[37] based on their constitutions; 7) administration of cities and towns based on their constitutions. Each subsequent level is administered by the previous levels. For any administration to be perfect it must maintain connectedness with the source of all the Laws of Nature—the first level of administration.

Clearly, the different phases of Natural Law are contained within the holistic value of Natural Law. For this reason, while in *Sat-Yuga* life is ideal, the history of the other periods is not forgotten. As Maharishi points out, "the grand cycle of the expressions of Natural Law can never be forgotten."[38] The history of the different degrees of Natural Law as lived through the different epochs of human life on earth is remembered because, "it is all this taken together that expresses the full value of Natural Law in the eternal continuum of life."[39] So the purpose of history remains the same: to promote evolution and reveal the eternal continuum of life.

The changes in the *Yugas* have been considered here in terms of religious codes and national laws, however, this analysis can be applied to other areas of life as well.

Different Degrees of Natural Law and Universal Value In Art

Applying the above principles to art and aesthetics, it could argued that when 100 percent of Natural Law is lived by the people and the artist is living in accord with Natural Law, art automatically displays the full potential of Natural Law. Visual culture displays the universal value of pure consciousness and its qualities. Such art is life-supporting, culturally appropriate, environmentally beneficial and promotes an evolutionary response in the viewer. In this context, "beauty" may be defined as the full expression of universal, pure consciousness in the work of art. The value of *Sattva* (the creative impulse of pure consciousness) would be intimately related to beauty. Displaying *Sattva*, art or visual culture uplifts and inspires the viewer and the nourishes the environment.

This definition of art—where universal aesthetic value is commensurate with evolutionary significance—follows directly from the principle that there is an underlying field of pure consciousness which has specific qualities, creates from within itself the entire phenomenal world, and promotes the evolutionary development of life in all its phases. In addition, since pure consciousness is a field of all possibilities one could assume that there are an infinite variety of art forms which may embody universal value. Just as every person is different and yet everyone is the expression of Creative Intelligence—every unique physiology is a lively expression of the Veda. As Maharishi points out, "the Creator has tremendous Creative Intelligence in him. How many faces has he designed but he wants to see no two faces alike."[40] Similarly, different expressions of art (appropriate for different cultures at different times) could embody universal value. Different kinds of art can express the qualities and sequentially unfolding structure of consciousness. This theme is examined in the context of the rise and fall of Natural Law and is referred to again in Part V.

As Maharishi notes, "in the course of history cultures display varying amounts of creativity."[41] In considering universal value in art with respect to the unfoldment of Natural Law, it could be argued that the definitions of the value and purpose of art throughout history reflect the level of collective consciousness at that time. The different art theories of specific eras reflect the degree of Natural Law being lived by the people and by the artist at that time. One could reexamine the term *Zeitgeist* in this context. In this analysis, there are two factors: 1) the degree of Natural Law being lived collectively in a given era, and 2) the degree of Natural Law being lived by the artist. While the former influences art and theory, the latter may influence theory but may also go "beyond" the prevailing *Zeitgeist*. In this sense, it would be possible for an artist to have unique insight and the ability to express universal value even though it may not be appreciated in his or her time. While an artist's work may not be appreciated in by his or her own generation, it could, however, speak to the collective consciousness of another generation.

With respect to pure knowledge, Maharishi teaches that in the long corridor of time, enlightened individuals have cognized the Veda and expressed its reality as they realized it.[42] Therefore, it is possible for seers to cognize the reality of the universal field of pure knowledge in any era. Similarly, it is possible that an artist could live a greater degree of Natural Law than commonly experienced in his or her time. If so, it seems likely that the degree of Natural Law he or she lives would be embodied in his or her work. According to this argument, one would expect that some works of art could transcend the limitations of their time. Art could embody universal value in any era. Despite the relationship between the individual and the epoch within which they live and work, an individual could be a universal human being in an age when the population is not living 100 percent of Natural Law. This point of view presents the idea of exceptions to the norm.

From another angle, it could be said that specific trends or ideas in art and theory represent the apparent relevance or irrelevance of universal value at any given period. For example, at a time when universal value is no longer considered valid or significant, the idea of universal value in art and history is negated. In the 1980s, the end of art and art history was declared by both historians and artists;[43] art had apparently reached its apotheosis. Historians such as Niall Ferguson, and art historians, Norma Broude and Mary Garrard, have re-examined and re-written history, and, in so doing, have redefined historiography itself. In the last 20 years universal value (particularly as the embodiment of the spiritual) seemed have little value. But, when theorists like Gablik and Kuspit argue for a re-visionary or universal art, a new approach again emerges; one that addresses the need for universality. This development seems to reveal a shift in collective consciousness.

Applying the principles of Maharishi Vedic Science to art, it would appear that art's relative meaning and expression can simultaneously be enlivened by universal content, universal value, and universal meaning, if the artist is performing from the level of Natural Law. When the artist and society live 100 percent Natural Law, the artist and the viewer enjoy the maximum effect of the universal value of art, but when 100 percent of Natural Law is no longer lived, the concern for universal relevance in art declines. Art history can be seen to involve a cyclical fluctuation in the definitions of art and theory. When art is declared to be "dead" or when "only the dregs of the human voice are visible and not its substance" the sense for a need for universal value and relevance rises again.

Looking at history from the perspectives of modernism, Indian theory, postmodernism and Vedic Science, we see that they vary substantially. The modern approach is linear and "progressive", the Indian approach is cyclical, and the postmodern view presents an array of line fragments with no unifying theme or direction.

Modernist Model of the Historical Development of Art

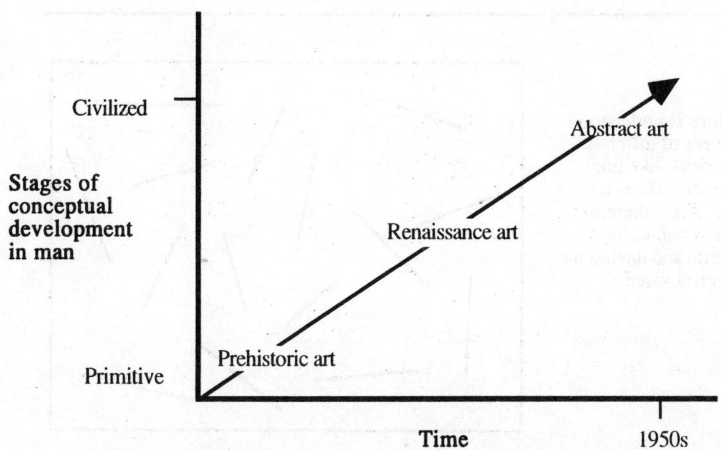

The modernist view presents art history as the successive, linear development of art styles toward more advanced, conceptual expressions of an absolute. The artist/genius, a historical figure/ hero, propels art forward. The culmination is abstract art—art of a more conceptually developed, civilized, free human being.

Maharishi Vedic Science explains that history is not only cyclical, but that this cyclical unfoldment occurs on the ground of the infinite continuum of pure consciousness. In this eternal cyclical phenomenon, different values of Natural Law are lived and expressed in an never-ending progression. Encompassing the notions of progression, cyclical development, and diverse readings of history according to differing degrees of Natural Law as embodied in collective consciousness, Maharishi Vedic Science extends other theories. More importantly, it includes the ultimate range of time, infinity, and identifies human evolution within this context. The different views of history are founded upon different fundamental assumptions about knowledge, evolution, human consciousness, the individual and culture. Without the understanding and experience of pure consciousness, meaning in art and the development of art history is comprehended from relative perspectives in the context of language games. Any absolute value or meaning which may lie beyond these issues is not only invalid but considered mystifying. According to Maharishi Vedic Science, history reveals the myriad changes of collective consciousness over time through a cyclical progression. In this progression, life has its source in the absolute, universal foundation of pure consciousness even when that source is apparently no longer visible or available.

The Postmodern View: No "History" But Only "histories"

History is understood in terms of different histories—like line fragments thrown on a page. Art is therefore seen as culturally-specific and having no universal value

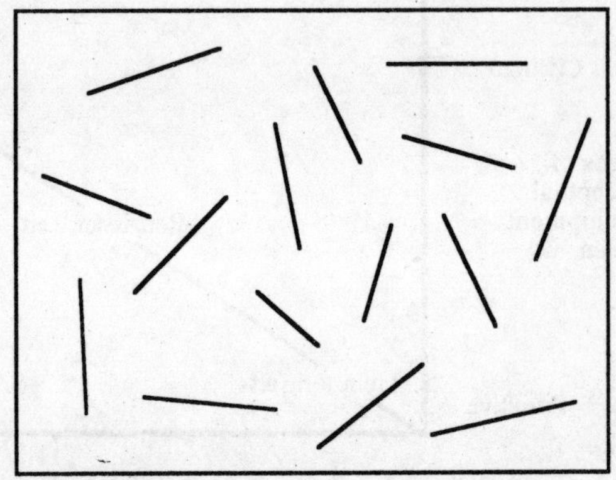

The postmodern view of history analyzes art from many different perspectives, for example: socio-political, cultural, and psychoanalytic readings. The concept of progression is deconstructed through the rejection of the notion of an absolute presence which can be embodied in art. All art styles are valid since all convey meaning within a particular language game or discourse.

When individuals begin to live more in accord with Natural Law the universal value of life is reintroduced into the lexicon of art. Perhaps, today, this phenomenon is evidenced in a growing concern for universal value in art. When universal value is expressed in art, artists can fully enhance life. Art history, from this perspective, recognizes that artistic achievements of the past can inspire people in the present to evolve and live more of Natural Law in daily life. Universal value in art does not eradicate difference or relative meaning. On the contrary, when unity is the dominating factor in art, difference is appreciated more fully.

As we have seen, the history of universal value in art can be viewed from a cyclical perspective where time stretches out to infinity and where art and theory reveal their ability to describe and embody universal value. This cyclical view of art history differs from the modern and postmodern views but extends both. The postmodern approach, which asserts that there are only "histories" like line fragments on a page with no universal underpinning, supports and give equal emphasis to the various histories of different cultural groups. In the cycle of Natural Law described by Maharishi Vedic Science, the histories of every cultural group are understood with respect to their universal basis and as part of the unfoldment of time and events throughout eternity. This approach to history also illuminates the Indian cyclical model. The cyclical unfoldment of Natural Law (or the history of the unfoldment of consciousness in collective life) demonstrates the manner in which the experience and principles of consciousness are found to be expressed in daily life over the long span of time.

16

TRADITIONS: DIFFERENT MODES OF ACTIVITY GOVERNED BY DHARMAS

With respect to family and community, according to Maharishi Vedic Science, there are Laws of Nature called *Dharmas* which support the individual, family and society. As discussed in earlier chapters, the holistic and specific values of Natural Law (the Veda and the Vedic Literature) structure the human physiology [1] and all of creation. In this context, there exist different hierarchical levels of administration of life which govern different levels of collective life. Maharishi explains that there are also Laws of Nature governing and maintaining the well-being of the family and society. The family structure (and tradition itself) is governed by specific Laws of Nature which promote evolution and keep the whole stream of life in harmony.[2] He goes on to explain:

> The laws of nature maintaining the well-being of the whole body consist of a collection of the laws maintaining its different parts, together with others added to coordinate different limbs. The laws of the evolution of the body likewise are the sum total of those governing the evolution of different limbs, along with those coordinating them. In a similar way, there are dharmas which govern individual evolution and there are dharmas which connect and coordinate different individuals. These latter are said primarily to govern the evolution of society.[3]

Just as there are specific laws which uphold the body and coordinate different limbs of the body, there are laws which govern and co-ordinate different individuals in society and ensure the evolution of society as a whole. In a further description of *Dharmas* Maharishi points out that:

> 'Dharmas', the plural of dharma, signifies the different powers of nature upholding different avenues of the way of evolution. They take expression as specific modes of activity or different ways of righteousness, which keep the whole stream of life in harmony—every aspect of life being properly balanced with every other aspect—and moving in the direction of evolution. As these specific modes of activity are passed on from generation to generation, they form what we call traditions. It is these traditions which are referred to as family dharmas.[4]

Different Laws of Nature uphold particular avenues in the way of evolution; these avenues are expressed as activities referred to as "ways of righteousness." Thus, modes of activity performed by individuals of each generation form traditions or family *Dharmas*. Such activities are defined as righteous action or action which is in accord with Natural Law. In this context, family traditions help to structure life in the direction of evolution. Family *Dharmas* are the powers of different principles "which uphold the coordination between different members of a family, at the same time enabling every member, consciously or unconsciously, to help every other member on his path of evolution."[5]

Tradition in general has an important role in the evolution of society, and allows for the smooth progression of life. For this reason, tradition is very useful. Just as grammar, by virtue of its restrictions, allows one to communicate and generate enriched values of meaning, tradition can provide a stable framework for the expression of progressive creativity. If a new grammar or alphabet were constantly being created, this would be counter-productive to communication. Breaking with tradition to create ever new modes of activity can restrict creativity. Using this analogy, creativity and freedom can be seen to be enhanced by tradition. Without tradition, Maharishi points out, society has no stable basis:

> A society without tradition has no basic stability or strength of its own; it is like a leaf left to the mercy of the wind, drifting in any direction without any stability and basis of its own. In the name of modern education, the societies of many countries are drifting away from old tradition. The result is a wild growth of faithless people, without tradition, whose society exists only on the superficial gross level of life.[6]

While this point can be appreciated, it should be noted that, according to Maharishi Vedic Science, only traditions which are governed by Natural Law can really allow the individual to be most creative and support the progressive evolution of collective life.[7] The tradition which has survived the longest seems more likely to represent the genuine path of evolution. The oldest traditions are more likely to be those which are most useful, since they have persisted over time. However, it is those traditions which are based on the universal value of truth, or pure intelligence, which are eternal and remain useful generation after generation.

Therefore, while family *Dharmas* and the traditions they support maintain the development of human life, it is possible that some activities defined as traditions or rituals may not useful in promoting evolution. These so-called non-useful activities will be cast off by a culture over time. With respect to activities which are not life-supporting, Maharishi points out that *Adharma* (meaning absence of *Dharma*) thwarts the evolutionary process and when "*Adharma* prevails, the great power of nature, which maintains the equilibrium between positive and negative forces, is lost, and the process of evolution is thereby obstructed."[8] When evolution is obstructed, suffering increases. Suffering is detrimental to life. This is why it is important that the family *Dharmas* and traditions are maintained. Clearly, the process of development and evolution in society and culture is a complex dynamic. This evolving dynamic is related to changes in collective consciousness and the unfoldment of time in specific eras or *Yugas* as discussed in Chapter 15.

Since there is a relationship between each individual and the family, and between each family and the community, it is obvious that there are influences generated from, and between, the various components that make up society—individual, family and society.

The Interconnectedness of Individual and Community Consciousness

Any group has its own collective consciousness. It has a collective consciousness which is more powerful than either the intelligence of the isolated individuals who form the group or the mere sum of their intelligence.[9] The group consciousness of a community or nation has an intelligence of its own which is more than the constituent parts taken together. Despite this, a community, nation or group of people can be considered in terms of specific components—for example, 1) individual, 2) family, 3) the community as a whole. With this example, for any group there is an influence from the individual on the family (and vice versa) and from the family on the community (and vice versa). When individuals within a family or community are living more in accord with Natural Law then the Laws of Nature which support the smooth functioning of intra-family and community relations are enlivened, traditions are strengthened and the evolution of individual and society is promoted.

According to Maharishi Vedic Science, the collective consciousness of a group includes all aspects of the group: physical, climactic, sociological, cultural and ecological. It outlasts individuals who contribute to it at any one time. This group consciousness is sensitive to the various fluctuations of experience in all its constitutive elements. Maharishi teaches that the integrity of the group can only be strengthened from the level which transcends the various elements of that group—namely, the universal level of pure, self-referral consciousness. By enlivening Natural Law in individual and collective consciousness, this level of life (governing the orderly functioning of the constituents of society and its internal relationships) can promote the harmonious, coherent functioning of a society or nation—thereby strengthening the traditions which allow society to progress in the fastest possible manner.

The dynamic interaction between the various elements of society make up the sociological structure of a culture—the relationship between Natural Law, the individual, the family, society, and its traditions. With this understanding, Maharishi emphasizes that the destruction of social order with its family *Dharmas* "is the greatest loss to any nation."[10] Since family *Dharmas* govern relationships between individuals within a family, when they are broken "people living together do not know how to live in such a manner that their way of life naturally helps each of them to evolve. The result is the loss of the path of evolution and the increase of disorder and chaos in the family."[11] Maharishi maintains that life in such a family is so unhappy it could be described as "hell." Consequently, the maintenance of family *Dharmas* is held to be very important to the happiness and fulfillment of individual life. While family *Dharmas* have been discussed here in terms of Laws of Nature and the maintenance of evolution in life, they can also be considered with respect to work activity, profession or vocation.

Dharma and Profession

Family *Dharma* can also refer to an established tradition where people born of a particular family engage in the profession of that family.[12] By working in the profession of one's parental heritage one can work more efficiently and productively, benefiting oneself and society. If the activity of a profession is familiar and comfortable, Maharishi notes, it is more likely that the individual will not become overly tired.[13] Being more efficient in one's work means that there is more time to allow for development of consciousness, and, by developing higher states of consciousness, one can succeed and be more effective in one's work. A society which lives according to Natural Law lives comfortably with the support of family *Dharmas* and traditions.[14]

While *all* the qualities of Creative Intelligence are in every aspect of life differences in profession occur by virtue of the preponderance of some qualities over others.[15] This principle has been considered in previous sections. For example, the three values of Ṛishi, Devatā and Chhandas in their precipitated form become the three *Doṣas* of *Vāta, Pitta* and *Kapha*. These in turn correspond to the five elements: *Vāta* has the characteristics of *Ākāsha* or space and *Vāyu* or air; *Pitta* has the value of *Agni* or fire and *Apa* or water; and Kapha includes the elements of *Apa* and *Pṛthivī* or earth. According to Maharishi Āyur-Veda, these *Doṣas* are like basic building blocks of creation.

In various combinations, balance or imbalance, they influence the emotional and physical attributes of each human psychophysiology—governing the body-type and disposition of an individual. The predominantly *Vāta* constitution tends to display characteristics associated with that quality. Everything in creation (the seasons and times of the day, etc.) is governed by these values or *Doṣas*—with a greater preponderance of some values in one aspect of creation than in others.

This gives some understanding of how, when all the qualities of pure consciousness are present in everything, there can be innumerable variety and difference. As Maharishi points out, when "all the qualities of Creative Intelligence are present in everything in creation then what makes the difference is the expression of some qualities more than others in different things."[16] This accounts for the differences in creation and in society:

> When we consider our society, the same formula applies. People are different, tastes are different, likings are different, and professions are different, but every profession, every impulse of liking, every undertaking is nothing other than the

> expression of Creative Intelligence. This being the case, when the conscious mind reaches the pure field of Creative Intelligence it becomes saturated with all the qualities of Creative Intelligence, and then wherever and in whatever area of living those qualities that are needed express themselves more. This is why, when a man meditates he becomes more capable in any undertaking. He becomes more efficient in any field of thinking; he becomes efficient in every field of decision-making. He begins to display more expressed values of Creative Intelligence in whatever phase his awareness progresses.[17]

By contacting and enlivening the field of Creative Intelligence—the field of Natural Law—through the practice of the Transcendental Meditation technique, Maharishi reveals that the mind becomes saturated with all the qualities of this infinite field. Then, when the individual engages in activity, the appropriate qualities express themselves. In this way, whatever activity she is engaged in, the individual is more effective. The values of Creative Intelligence, or Natural Law, are expressed spontaneously and appropriately for any given undertaking. With respect to any specific profession, Maharishi indicates that the different values of each profession represent personal expressions of Creative Intelligence. The different professions in life represent the myriad aspects of the progressive value of Creative Intelligence or Natural Law:

> The artist, the scientist, the astronomer, the historian, the economist, and the politician, all these different phases of social activities and personal expressions of Creative Intelligence belong to the progressive nature of Creative Intelligence.[18]

He continues to point out that Creative Intelligence extends to all areas of knowledge: psychology, environmental values or ecology, physics, chemistry, and astronomy. All these areas are involved in every progressive impulse of Creative Intelligence.[19] Only, it is the discriminative value of Creative Intelligence which is wide awake, distinguishing what value should be used here and there, what value should be used later, and what value should be completely left out.[20]

Ultimately, all the qualities which are expressed in activity are "present in the unmanifest value of Creative Intelligence," and that "the unmanifest value of Creative Intelligence is a universal existence" which is present everywhere—"deep within everything and on the surface of everything."[21]

The whole value of Creative Intelligence—the holistic value of Creative Intelligence—is everywhere. In this sense, Creative Intelligence is omnipresent; it's omnipresent because it has to take care of every expression and every step of progress of everything in creation. This wholeness of Creative Intelligence is holistic.[22] So there is the holistic value of Creative Intelligence and there are the different expressions that manifest in the diversity of life. In human life, in different professions, Maharishi points out that

> Whether one is an economist, an astronomer, a politician, a scientist or an artist, all the values of Creative Intelligence are there; it is [simply] a matter of who is making use of what. The whole thing is there. For example, in a big home the library is there, the kitchen is there, the drawing room is there, the bedroom is there; it is just a matter of who uses what most.[23]

While all possible values are available in the multiple variety of creation, regarding different activities and professions, it is simply a matter of preference. In this description of the holistic nature of Creative Intelligence and the role of its discriminating value, every aspect of life, every expression of Creative Intelligence, every individual has inherent within him or her all the qualities of Creative Intelligence. However, Creative Intelligence, or Natural Law, computes that value which is necessary (i.e., most appropriate) for the successful evolution of life. In the case of a flower, specific values govern the formation the petal, the leaf, the stem, etc.—distinct components of the plant which contribute to the holistic growth of the plant. In the same manner, people are predisposed to different professions and activities—they engage in different relative *Dharmas* which uphold society.

Development of Heart and Mind

In discussing different activities and professions further, Maharishi refers to professions as falling into two main categories: 1) "heart" governed activities; and 2) "mind" governed activities. He gives the example of the former being related to activities such as motherhood and art and the latter to scientific endeavor. However, despite this general categorization of the professions, Maharishi does emphasize that these two tendencies are present in everyone. He explains that the hero of the Bhagavad-Gītā, Arjuna, is developed in both "heart" and "mind". Both aspects are fully developed in any enlightened individual.[24] From a modernist perspective, the artist is generally held to be more intuitive than the scientist but Maharishi suggests that both the heart (defined as the harmonizing value) and the mind (referred to as the discriminating value) must be developed to the maximum for each individual to be effective in any profession and in personal life:

> When we were considering the development of Creative Intelligence in society, the point was made very clearly that with the growth of Creative Intelligence the individual members of the society become enriched, fully developed. This means that the differences in society will grow—economists will become very successful economists and politicians will become very successful politicians.[25]

Maharishi goes on to explain that:

> The growth of difference along with the growth of unity is what Creative Intelligence produces. The heart will be more emotional, more fluid; love will be universal love. The whole field of life will be so smooth that we are found slipping everywhere, and at the same time, the intellect will be so precise that we will slip nowhere! This ability to slip in stability is the expression of full life. This is that enormous flexibility that increases with the growth of Creative Intelligence until a time comes when every little individuality may breathe infinite unboundedness of life. This is the growth of flexibility through the development of Creative Intelligence.[26]

When Creative Intelligence is fully lively, differences grow but are seen on the ground of unity; the heart is more fluid and flows in universal love—creating harmony among individuals; and the discriminating value of the intellect, with finely-tuned precision, ensures that life remains firmly established in the orderly, life-supporting, efficient functioning of Natural Law. These values grow, regardless of one's profession. Life can be stable and flexible, discriminating and harmonious.

One's Own Dharma is the Dharma of the Self

With respect to different professions or activities, the area of expertise of each individual is important for that particular person and for the development of society. In this context, Maharishi points out that it is better, even when it appears less meritorious, to perform one's own *Dharma* (the activity that is most-evolutionary for oneself) as opposed to performing someone else's *Dharma*. The reason for this assertion is that different people are at different levels in the process of evolution, and "each level has its own guiding principle, a standard of its own," i.e., its own *Dharma*.[27] A person who goes by their own level of consciousness will evolve more quickly.

In an "age of glamor," where one is subjected to numerous and conflicting signs, this is a useful principle. As Maharishi points out:

> So far as the process of evolution is concerned, one's own dharma is the most suitable even though it may appear 'lesser in merit' when compared with the dharma of another. The true merit of dharma is in its usefulness in promoting evolution in the most effective manner. Life at one stage, when promoted by the dharma of that stage to a higher stage, begins to be governed by the dharma of that higher stage. This is how, stage by stage, life evolves through the dharma of different stages of evolution. The comparative merit of the dharma of one's present state may be less than the dharma of a higher state, but its merit in its own place is greater by far.[28]

This is so, because, as Maharishi continues to explain:

> If a man were to try to follow a dharma suitable for one of higher development, he would not be able to put it into practice successfully and thus would waste his time and energy. This may go so far as to entail loss of the path of his evolution.[29]

In this description of *Dharma*, Maharishi places emphasis on following the guiding principle: The standard for activity and progress should be appropriate for the person's level of development. Action is more effective which most suits the individual at a specific time in his or her development. All activities and professions that are in accord with Natural Law help the individual to evolve and progress in life. Different professions have their merit since each has its purpose in promoting life and aiding evolution for a specific individual. This perspective seems to differ from the modernist, elitist view of the artist's profession. According to modernists, as discussed in Part I, the artist's activity is unique in relation to other professions. It is the artist, not the scientist, who expresses genius.

From the perspective of Maharishi Vedic Science, various activities or professions serve their purpose in helping people to evolve; any profession—ceramicist, studio potter, painter, sculptor, film-maker, webmaster, or scientist, musician, etc.—has its value; "genius" can be expressed in all of them. As discussed in detail in Part V, anyone can unfold inner genius. Unlike modern theory (which elevates the fine artist and sets him apart from society) infinity creativity is the birthright of everyone. In further considering this theme of one's *Dharma*, Maharishi explains that each person has the ability to do as he or she wishes and can therefore chose any activity in life, but as he states:

> Because a man has freedom of action, he is certainly capable of trying to assume the role of action belonging to different levels of evolution. This means that he is capable of attempting to perform actions suitable to the dharma of another. But if he performs such actions, he loses the continuity of progress on the level from which he could evolve. This is the greatest danger to life: that one lives life, time goes by, without any progress on the path of evolution.[30]

It seems important that the individual does not try to perform actions which are not suitable for them. It is better for each individual to continue to perform activity within the guidelines or principles of action for his or her area of expertise and his level of development in terms of consciousness. Despite this, in today's fast-paced world, where standards of behavior and action may not be clearly defined, knowing one's *Dharma* can be problematic.

Since the workings of Natural Law are incomprehensible, how can we know what our *Dharma* is and what action to perform at any given time? Maharishi points out that one cannot intellectually comprehend all the implications of action—the outcomes of action, the effects of action, or understand those occasions when one is unable to perform certain actions. To understand action and the implications of action, one has to understand the "laws of nature and the cosmic law which underlies all of them."[31] Maharishi teaches that one can begin in this direction by practicing of his technologies of consciousness. The practice of these technologies eradicates stress from the nervous system and thereby lessens the chances of non-life-supporting activity; it also allows for an increasing appreciation of Natural Law. As discussed in Parts II and III, "right" action is performed spontaneously from the level of pure consciousness—the total potential of Natural Law—through the enlivenment of *Smṛti*, the quality of "memory," fully awake consciousness or Saṁhitā.

Providing further insight into the effect of so-called "wrong" and "right" action, Maharishi emphasizes that everything in the universe is interconnected. Like waves on the surface of the ocean each person has their own individuality but no-one is isolated from the influence of other individuals. "Every wave has its own course to follow, but this course is dependent on that of every other wave. The life of any individual is a wave in the ocean of cosmic life, where every wave constantly influences the course of every other."[32] As Maharishi indicates:

> Everything is so intimately connected with every other thing in creation that it is not possible to distinguish completely the existence of one from the other. And the influence of one thing on every other thing is so universal that nothing could be considered in isolation. We have already mentioned that the universe reacts to an individual action. Therefore the question of right and wrong is a highly complicated problem. A person who knew all about everything in creation and could determine the influence of any action of any individual on any stratum of existence—he alone would be able to say for certain whether that action was right or wrong. Right is that which produces good influence everywhere. Certainly right and wrong are relative terms, and nothing in the field of relative existence could be said to be absolute right or absolute wrong, but, even so, the right and wrong could only be judged by the influence of good or bad. If something produces relatively good influence everywhere it would be said to be right.[33]

Here, right and wrong are acknowledged to be relative terms or values but, despite this, Maharishi does go on to say that right action would be that action that produces relatively good influence everywhere. "Right" action is action in accord with Natural Law. It is action performed in higher states of consciousness (i.e., Cosmic Consciousness, God Consciousness, and Unity Consciousness) from the level of *Ātmā*, pure, self-referral consciousness. With respect to the ramifications of action, in principle, the idea of interconnectedness is accepted and understood in the field of physics—and also in other areas of life (e.g., business, international politics, sociology, and ecology). However, as mentioned in Part II, in Maharishi Vedic Science everything is understood to be infinitely correlated at the universal level of Natural Law. Therefore, while the individual has free will and freedom of action, any action he performs incurs a corresponding reaction.[34] On a collective level, as Maharishi states, "when people behave rightly, a corresponding atmosphere is naturally produced, and when such an influence is dominant, the individual's tendencies are affected by it."[35] Collective "right" action, therefore, generates an influence of coherence in the society and environment. The individual is protected by that influence. This means that even if he is prone to follow a course of non life-supporting action, he will be protected by the coherent influence around him.[36]

Conversely, Maharishi points out that when an atmosphere is saturated with non life-supporting influences, it is not possible for virtue "to survive for long."[37] For this reason, it is essential that coherence is generated in collective consciousness to furnish a supportive atmosphere for individuals in all walks of life. This can be achieved through the practice of the Transcendental Meditation technique and TM-Sidhi program. The unseen governing force of life, enlivened through the practice of these technologies, increasingly guides individual action. Here we can see that there are two aspects to gaining the support of Natural Law: 1) through one's own development of consciousness and subsequent actions; and 2) through the influence of a coherent or *Sattvic* environment. Maharishi emphasizes that Natural Law as the supreme organizer is "always right"; therefore, by aligning oneself with Natural Law one can also be "always right."[38]

A country aligned with Natural Law creates a nation where all wrongs cease, where those actions which jeopardize evolution and the growth of life to bliss-consciousness cease. With respect to performing one's own *Dharma*, rather than abruptly abandoning their current level and loosing continuity of evolution, Maharishi explains that each individual can raise their present level of evolution. This is achievable through the practice of his Transcendental Meditation technique and the TM-Sidhi program. In practicing these technologies progress on the path of evolution is ensured.

Extending this discussion further, Maharishi points out that, ultimately, "one's own *dharma*" literally means the "*dharma* of the Self," or Absolute *Dharma*, and "another's *dharma*" refers to the relative *Dharma* of the three *guṇas*—the play of the relative experienced as separate from the Self.[39]

Absolute Dharma—Dharma of the Self—is Everyone's Dharma

Through practice of the Transcendental Meditation technique one takes recourse to the *Dharma* of the Self—absolute bliss-consciousness or Absolute *Dharma*. By living the *Dharma* of the Self (which is everyone's *Dharma*) one takes recourse to Natural Law. Activity is supported by the "influence of almighty Nature" as opposed to the "*Dharma* of another"—the field of the three *guṇas* or the play of the relative. In enlivening all the Laws of Nature the individual is more likely to meet with success in every undertaking. As Maharishi indicates:

> When a man is established in his own dharma, the dharma of the Self, his activity is carried on under the direct influence of almighty Nature and enjoys Its full support; whereas if he partakes of the dharma of another, the dharma of the

> three gunas, he loses the support and patronage of almighty Nature in cosmic life, and his activity becomes limited by the limitations of individual life.[40]

In order to maintain optimum progress and evolution, one should station oneself at that point where the absolute, universal field of the Self, the field of Natural Law, guides action and brings fulfillment to activity—at each stage of development. When individuals collectively begin to function from the *Dharma* of the Self, the rich traditions of each culture (including different kinds of visual art and culture) naturally flourish. Referring to India, Maharishi explains that those traditions still maintained, day by day, uphold the different qualities of Nature's intelligence.

Traditions in India—Upholding Different Qualities of Nature's Intelligence

As discussed in Maharishi Vedic Science, in the earth's orbit around the sun (a total of 360 days of our calendar year), the quality of time and of life changes from day to day. These changing values of Natural Law are commonly celebrated in India.[41] These celebrations are designed to serve the purpose of unifying, harmonizing and integrating national consciousness.

> This national tradition of recognizing, upholding, cherishing, and celebrating different qualities of Nature's Intelligence day by day and night after night naturally unifies, integrates, and harmonizes the collective consciousness of the whole population of India every day, day after day throughout the year. This tradition has always been, and will always be, a great nourishing, unifying, integrating, and harmonizing power for national consciousness. The dawn of every new day in India awakens one specific quality of Nature's Intelligence, and this quality of the day is traditionally enlivened in the awareness of the individual...as the Sun moves from morning to noon to evening.[42]

These traditional celebrations are mindful of the unfoldment of time; they are a means to enliven the specific Laws of Nature or qualities of Nature's Intelligence that distinguish each day from another—governing life or the quality of life at that time. Each day of the calendar year brings a new quality of Nature's Intelligence—celebrated and enlivened in awareness. This is why the festivals are maintained and cherished. Festivals are means of enlivening the structures and functions of specific Laws of Nature. As Maharishi indicates:

> India has a tradition of celebrating festivals with reference to the structures and functions of the Laws of Nature as they have been portrayed in the Vedic Literature in terms of *Ganpati*, *Shiva*, *Vishṇu*, *Sūrya*, *Devī*, etc. Every year, as a routine of the Indian calendar, all the qualities of Creative Intelligence that administer life are celebrated: *Vasant Panchami*, *Maha Shivarātri*, *Rām Navmi*,

> *Krishṇ Janmāshtami*, *Ganesh Chaturthi*, *Navarātri* (celebrating *Maha Durgā*), and *Dīpāvalī* (celebrating *Maha Lahshmī*), etc.[43]

In the Vedic Literature, these Laws of Nature have been portrayed as *Gaṇpati*, *Śiva, Viṣṇu*, *Sūrya, Devī*, etc. Maharishi clearly indicates that they portray the structures and functions of specific Laws of Nature.

Nader states that these Laws of Nature have their correspondence in the physiology. In this unique analysis, he shows that *Gaṇpati* can be found in the human brain—indicating diagramatically how the components of *Gaṇpati* (or *Ganesh*) directly represent aspects of the brain itself.[44] He points out that the pons, the name of a major part of the brainstem responsible for controlling awareness, behavioral performance and the inputs and outputs of the brain, represents the head of *Gaṇpati*.. Emanating from the pons are the cranial nerves which facilitate motor and sensory innervation to the skin, muscles and joints. Other functions mediated through the pons are vision, hearing, olfaction, taste and the control of viscera, breathing, heart rate, blood pressure, coughing and swallowing. The ears of *Gaṇpati* represent the cerebellum which governs balance, eye movement, bodily equilibrium, limb movement, the balancing of action with intention and the planning and initiation of movement. The medulla represents the trunk of *Gaṇpati* and serves as a pathway for the functions of the pons (the head of *Gaṇpati*). Then, the trigeminal nerve roots represent the eyes of *Gaṇpati* which mediate sensations from the skin, muscles and joints in the face, mouth and teeth. Finally, Nader notes that a group of nerves at the base of the pons together represent the tusks of *Gaṇpati*. These are responsible for balance, eye movement, postural reflexes, and orientation of the head in space.[45] In this way, Nader identifies the specific quality of Nature's Intelligence or Law of Nature portrayed in the Vedic Literature as *Gaṇpati* as corresponding to particular aspects of the brain physiology and functioning. *Gaṇpati* represents both Laws of Nature that govern the brain physiology and qualities of Nature's Intelligence at times in the calendar year.

Maharishi Vedic Science brings to light these intricate relationships between qualities of Nature's Intelligence and the course of time, the structure and function of the physiology and the value of collective consciousness and national life. With respect to the enlivenment of these Laws of Nature in national consciousness and the smooth administration of national life through India's government, Maharishi points out that:

> It is very important that those who hold the reins of national administration understand how the daily routine of celebrating the different values of the administering intelligence of Nature help to create and maintain a perfect government. First it should be understood by every Member of the Indian Parliament that it is the collective consciousness that is the real administrator of the nation. Government is the mirror of the nation—whatever is the quality of

> collective consciousness, that is the quality of government: On the day of *Maha Shivarātri*, the whole national consciousness wakes up in the quality of *Shiva*.[46]

As noted earlier, in the discussion of the *Yugas* and collective consciousness, a nation's collective consciousness has its own value. In terms of government, in Maharishi Vedic Science, the actions and effectiveness of the government of a nation is held to reflect the level of collective consciousness of the nation. The government is an "innocent mirror" of national consciousness. For this reason, it is important that collective consciousness is lively in the value of Nature's Creative Intelligence, the value of Nature's spontaneous administration. Only then will government be effective in meeting the needs of society and every individual.

The festivals mentioned above are seen, in Maharishi Vedic Science, not as archaic rituals, but as a means to enliven the Laws of Nature that govern the smooth functioning of society, the unfoldment of the different qualities of each day, the physiology and national consciousness. They are a means to awaken those qualities of intelligence in the individual and society as a whole. In this sense, traditions play a vital, living role on all levels of national life. The tradition of worship in the different temples is also understood in this light. For example, it is seen to serve the purpose of:

> Maintaining integrated national consciousness hour by hour and day by day, and this quality of integration in national consciousness naturally upholds an integrated national government in the same way as a fully alert mind maintains full alertness of the body.[47]

Although revisionary postmodernism seems to support the revival of traditions, without a deep understanding of the basis of tradition and culture, the danger is that visual culture becomes a smorgasbord of style or that a culture's intellectual property is misappropriated or misused.

While tradition has a value in promoting evolution, as is discussed in the following chapter, culture also accelerates progress toward higher stages of human development.

17

CULTURE AS THE EXPRESSION OF SPECIFIC LAWS OF NATURE: GOVERNING GEOGRAPHY, CLIMATE, MANNERISMS, LANGUAGE AND ACCENTS OF DIFFERENT PEOPLES

Culture, according to Maharishi Vedic Science, is governed by specific Laws of Nature which structure and govern a people or a nation. However, as Maharishi points out, culture can be considered from both a universal and a specific perspective:

> The holistic value of Natural Law handles the holistic value of culture—universal culture—whereas specific values of different Laws of Nature are concerned with the specific culture of an individual country or the specific area of a country; these are the Laws of Nature that give rise to the specific geographic and climatic conditions, accents of speech, languages, and trends of society on all levels of life—spiritual, social, and material. [1]

In locating both universal culture and individual values of culture, Maharishi identifies, at the basis of culture, the same foundational principle spoken of in previous sections; unity gives rise to diversity. One and many co-exist. One holistic value of Natural Law handles the holistic value of culture. Different Laws of Nature are concerned with the specific culture of a country or particular area of a country. The specific values of Laws of Nature concerned with culture give rise to particular geographic and climatic conditions, accents and language of a population. The religious, social and economic trends can also be thought of as values of Laws of Nature and as expressions of the degree of Natural Law that is being lived by the people. Culture, from this perspective, is not governed by the members of a social group or nation but is ruled by Natural Law and has a very specific role in the development of life. As Maharishi explains:

> The word 'culture' has a very, very great and profound meaning. It includes everything concerning life. Life is made up of so many elements, and the behavior of all these elements put together constitutes the process of evolution of life. All these elements and their inter-relationships are ruled by Natural Law. Everything negative belongs to violation of Natural Law. Everything positive is a fruit of life lived in accordance with Natural Law. [2]

Culture refers to "everything concerning life." This includes the various components and behaviors of individual and collective life which together constitute the process of evolution—the progression of life toward enlightenment. The different elements and their relationships which constitute culture are governed by Natural Law or *Dharma.* When life is lived in accord with Natural Law it is fulfilling, harmonious, and progressive. Life which is not in accord with Natural Law promotes tendencies which are life-damaging. Ultimately, Maharishi points out that "only that which is in accordance with the laws of evolution can last. Anything that does not conform to these laws is thrown off by nature."[3] Therefore, in the process of evolution, only life-supporting influences will prevail.

Culture, thus, is a part of the process of evolution itself. Culture, including all the elements of life together, promotes evolution—the progressive development of life toward higher states of consciousness.[4] In fact, the word "culture," meaning "to refine," in Maharishi Vedic Science refers to the process of evolution, itself—this progressive refinement of life as it develops towards fulfillment. As Maharishi teaches:

> Culturing life, that is refining the crude values, is like refining gold ore, where fine, pure gold particles are mixed up with mud. Through the refining process the ore is cultured from a crude muddy form to a refined gold. In the same way, the culture of a country puts the crude human element, starting from birth, through the evolutionary process of refinement to produce very cultured, refined, and enlightened persons. An enlightened person is one who does not violate any laws of nature. It is the laws of nature which are responsible for the creation and evolution of life. When a person acts in harmony with the laws of nature, he steps on the effortless and royal road of evolution. In evolution, life grows in steps of fulfillment and the person continually goes from more to even more and still more fulfillment. In the higher stages of fulfillment is the joy of life and strength. We call this inner fulfillment the integration of life, because mind and body act in full co-operation and co-ordination. Such culturing of life is culture according to natural law. The nation's cultural integrity is built up on this basis of integration within the individual.[5]

Refinement of the human element takes place from birth to maturity through the agency of the culture of a country. Why is this significant for society? The goal of the process of refinement is to produce enlightened individuals who do not violate any Laws of Nature—laws responsible for the creation and evolution of life. The individual, through this process, becomes more fulfilled, joyful, and integrated. The cultural integrity of any nation is built upon this integration in individual life. Culture influences individual life; individual life influences cultural integrity. For this reason, Maharishi explains that evolution is really the goal of all cultures and that culture is the basis for progress in any land.

While cultural values help the individual evolve, the omnipresent, universal value of culture—pure self-referral consciousness—is not influenced by the specific characteristics of any particular culture. The universal basis of culture is not affected by difference; it is beyond social determinism. It is the source of the individual mind—the simplest form of human awareness. On the individual level, a fully-cultured state of mind is one which is established in this self-referral state of consciousness, "where the unbounded range of pure intelligence is available in the form of infinite Creative Intelligence endowed with the total potential of infinite organizing power."[6]

Natural Law and Levels of Administration

As stated in Chapter 15, there are seven different hierarchical levels of administration. The first is the holistic administration of the ever-expanding universe, the level of Saṁhitā or total knowledge. The second is the administration of the parts of the universe governed by particular Laws of Nature (such as the laws governing a galaxy or solar system). The third is the administration of life on earth; the fourth level includes the administration of the holistic value of life on earth and includes the Laws of Nature that administer life in each part of the globe—the Natural Laws that give rise to the specific cultures of the land. This level must remain connected to the first and subsequent levels of administration to be holistic. Then, all the different aspects of culture are supported by the holistic values of Natural Law, the field of total knowledge.

LEVELS OF ADMINISTRATION

1. *Holistic administration of the ever-expanding universe—Saṁhitā, total knowledge—source of all levels of administration*

2. *Administration of parts of the universe governed by particular Laws of Nature (i.e. governing a galaxy or solar system)*

3. *Administration of life on earth*

4. *Administration of holistic value of life on earth and laws which administer life in different parts if the globe*

5. *Laws of Nature that administer individual life*

6. *Man-made laws of the country, states and provinces, based on their constitutions*

7. *Administration of cities and towns based on their constitutions*

The fifth level involves the Laws of Nature that administer values of individual life while the sixth level is the administration of the nation through the man-made constitution of the country and the administration of the states and provinces of the nation based on their constitutions. The seventh level of administration is the administration of cities and towns based on their constitutions. Each level is administered by the previous; for any one to remain perfect it must maintain connectedness with the source of all the Laws of Nature which is the first level of administration—total knowledge, Saṁhitā. In this analysis, the man-made constitution and laws of any land are related to the Laws of Nature which govern life in that place.

Different Cultures, Climate and Geography

As mentioned above, the Laws of Nature which govern climate and geography are more fundamental than man-made laws. Maharishi explains that certain factors structure cultural values. These factors arise by virtue of Natural Law and the Laws of Nature governing the geographic and climatic conditions of a place, society, family and individual. The different properties of the natural environment (such as the desert in one locale, fertile soil in another, heat, mountains, lowlands etc.) influence the culture of the people living in that area—creating the difference in accents, mannerisms, traditions, and different forms of behavior described by the people as their ancestral tradition. Thus, with their varying traditions and languages and accents, different cultures arise due to the variation in climatic and geographic conditions. As Maharishi explains

> That is why even within small countries, habits and mannerisms change, and even accents of the same language are different from area to area. Just one mile this way and one mile that way, habits, traditions, and accents change. The people justify the differences by saying: 'This is our ancestral tradition.'[7]

Cultural differences, including habits imbibed in the children from the parents, values of right and wrong for that society, accent, and parental heritage, can be understood as relating to the differences in climate and geography. As Maharishi points out, man everywhere is the same universal man, but the different climatic and geographical conditions create different procedures which culture the physiology and the psychology of the individual in that locality. Culture is governed by Laws of Nature and the conditions of the environment and, like a fertilizer, stimulates personal evolution.

This definition of culture is somewhat more expansive than the definition provided by Lyotard discussed in Part I. While Lyotard locates culture as part of customary knowledge, constituting criteria of valid narrative knowledge in a particular social group that influences culture, his understanding of culture is based on the idea of language games and disallows any notion of a universal level of culture or laws that govern geography and climate. In Maharishi Vedic Science not only do the climatic and geographic conditions—considered as natural factors—play an integral part in shaping culture, but so also does the unmanifest field of pure consciousness, the home of Natural Law. Could the recent move toward the revival of culture and traditions indicate an upsurge in the degree of Natural Law being lived by the people of the world?

It is worth noting that there is, in today's "post-colonial" era, increased concern for First Nation peoples and the revival of cultural traditions. This new trend is evidenced in art practice which aims to recontextualize traditional culture and redefine national identity and material and visual culture. Such changes could also be part of a larger shift toward ever more complex cultural hybridity, where the concept of a integrated culture is unimaginable. Despite this, events throughout the world reveal a desire for the (re)establishment of cultural or national identity—often related to issues of the land. This phenomenon is worthy of more lengthy consideration, particularly in the light of specific values of Natural Law and the cycle of the *Yugas* mentioned earlier. However, regarding the role of culture as defined by Maharishi Vedic Science, the key point here is that the specific values of culture actually sustain life for a particular group. For the full development of the individual, traditions and cultural values have to be preserved or life will not be sustained. Therefore, cultural values are essential to the preservation of life.

As Maharishi Vedic Science reveals, while all the specific values of life which enrich human existence in a particular locale constitute culture, it is the Absolute—with its impulse to know itself from the field of infinite creativity on the level of Natural Law—that gives rise to all cultures. The inherent, self-referral value of Absolute, pure consciousness gives rise to cultures.

> All the values that enrich life in a particular geographical area constitute its culture. Creativity is the source of all culture. The infinite potential of creativity lies in the state of pure intelligence—unmanifest, unbounded, absolute. The unmanifest Absolute is self-sufficient. It cultures itself from within its own nature. All cultures are the expression of the eternal impulse of the Absolute to know itself.[8]

For this reason, this field of the Absolute, the field of self-referral pure consciousness, has to be enlivened in the life of the people. Then the source of all cultures will promote the expression of cultural difference; lost traditions and ways of living which were and are evolutionary and life-supporting will be revived.

Five Fundamentals of Progress and Cultural Integrity

As discussed previously, Maharishi teaches that culture and tradition are strengthened through the enlivenment of Natural Law. He goes on to describe the mechanics of this phenomenon in terms of five fundamentals of progress: Stability; Adaptability; Integration; Purification; and Growth:[9]

> The fundamentals of Progress are the same as the fundamentals of Culture. They are stability, adaptability, integration, purification, and growth. By virtue of the element of stability being lived in national life, any influence coming from

> outside (cultural, economic, political, religious, or intellectual) will not be able to overthrow cultural integrity. By virtue of the liveliness of the element of purification in national life, any influence coming from outside will spontaneously be purified. Whatever aspect of it is life-supporting will be naturally integrated due to the elements of adaptability and integration. By virtue of the element of growth, outside influences will promote progress without damaging cultural integrity. Enlivening the qualities of stability, adaptability, integration, purification, and growth in the life of the individual, family, community, and country, the Transcendental Meditation programme presents the practical possibility of harmonizing the ever-changing nature of progress with the non-changing nature of culture.[10]

To maintain individual and cultural integrity the five factors mentioned above must be lively in individual and collective life. For example, in order for a culture to be strong and self-sufficient it must be stable. Here stability refers to the degree to which life is anchored in pure consciousness or Natural Law. Stability is gained through enlivenment of the immovable basis of life—the field of Natural Law.

While stability is crucial to the maintenance of cultural integrity, adaptability is also vital to any culture. When an influence comes from another country, the people need to be stable in their own mannerisms but if the mannerisms of the other country are more inspiring they can be adopted. In an ideal situation, the assimilation of a new influence involves purification and then integration—so that assimilation does not disturb cultural integrity. Purification and integration simply mean that whatever is not life-supporting in a culture is left out; it is not taken on by the host culture. Whatever is life-supporting and progressive is adopted. In this way, culture may take on a new influence without loosing its particular evolutionary values. What is adopted (or left out) occurs on the basis of the administration of Natural Law—that field which can spontaneously compute the most appropriate action for any situation. Dynamic and progressive development can occur but the universal and life-supporting values of culture are maintained.

When the five fundamentals are enlivened within the culture, the new influences that are adopted strengthen the culture. In contrast, a culture that does not possess and display these values will have the propensity to adopt life-damaging influences. Unsuitable for the geographic and climatic conditions, these influences will lead to that culture's degradation. Despite the identification of an ever-increasing cultural hybridity in contemporary life, in today's global economy with its advanced information technologies, the maintenance of cultural integrity is vitally important for many individuals and groups.

The term "cultural hybridity" at face value may not seem congruent with the evolution of culture operating according to the five fundamentals of progress. To be life-supporting, any transformations in culture would involve the enlivenment of Natural Law. As Maharishi explains, "in every nation it is very important that the people of every generation remain connected to their cultural values. Life according to one's culture means life spontaneously in the evolutionary direction of Natural Law."[11] Indeed, he points out that if even the value of one culture is threatened, the dignity of the whole world is at stake. Because every culture contributes to the whole, the value of each one must be maintained. As Maharishi teaches:

> Nature loves variety. World harmony is not based on the fusion of different cultures. It depends on the ability of each culture to maintain its own integrity on the basis of the infinite adaptability that characterizes life lived in accord with the laws of nature. Like the many-coloured pieces of a mosaic or the varied tunes of an orchestra, each fully integrated culture contributes to form a harmonious world.[12]

It is only through the maintenance of cultural integrity in each culture that a bond can be formed between all cultures which will form the basis of world harmony.[13] For this reason, from the perspective of Maharishi Vedic Science, maintenance of cultural integrity is not a naive desire to hold onto unrealizable and unrealistic visions of a cultural unity or unique identity. Nor is it simply an outmoded concept. Cultural integrity is a necessary part of the development of human life toward peace and harmony in higher states of consciousness. Cultural integrity can be strengthened through the practice of technologies of consciousness.

The Transcendental Meditation Technique and TM-Sidhi Program: Promoting Cultural Integrity

The most powerful tools for the development of cultural integrity are Maharishi's technologies of consciousness because, as discussed in Part II, these technologies enliven in individual and collective consciousness the holistic and specific values of Natural Law simultaneously. Furthermore, enlivening all the five fundamental values in the individual and in culture, the practice of the Transcendental Meditation technique and the TM-Sidhi program provide a universal means to strengthen culture. They nourish all cultures at their foundation. These technologies allow one to live more and more the value of Natural Law or pure consciousness. As Maharishi indicates

> To live one's culture, one must live life according to Natural Law. All activity in nature begins from the common ground of silence which is found in the mind's settled state of awareness. Through the [Transcendental Meditation] technique, whenever we reach the settled state of mind we get some blessing from the home of all the laws of nature, and our actions become more evolutionary. The basis of growth is culture, and the basis of culture is life according to Natural Law.[14]

Since experience during meditation allows the individual to contact and, over time, become established in this home of all the Laws of Nature, the Transcendental Meditation technique and TM-Sidhi program help each individual to spontaneously live their own culture. When the individual becomes established in higher states of consciousness his or her action is more evolutionary. Evolutionary action strengthens culture. In addition, individual growth is promoted by a stable and adaptable culture. There is a reciprocal relationship between individual and culture. In this sense, living life in accord with Natural Law strengthens both cultural integrity and individual life.

Cultural integrity represents all the values that are necessary to promote and culture life, and to live life spontaneously in an evolutionary direction. Just as the word "culture" implies the actual culturing of life toward greater fulfillment, all the values in a society—community, state, or nation—that go to culture life enhance cultural integrity. Maharishi defines the result of cultural integrity as "happiness, affluence, and harmony within the nation and complete impenetrability from any disturbing influences outside."[15] In this sense, cultural integrity is the foundation for national invincibility. "Invincibility" is characterized by: 1) "freedom from fear of invasion and disturbances from beyond the nation's frontiers;" 2) "coherence and togetherness among the various elements which make up the nation's internal structure;" and 3) "complete lack of fear from natural calamities."[16] Invincibility, as discussed in the consideration of Vedic Defense in Part III, encompasses the nation's ability to be free from outside attack, to demonstrate internal coherence through harmonious existence of diversified elements, and balance in nature. But can harmony be realistically achieved between all the different tendencies in society?

Individuals of any nation are involved in different activities and have different tendencies, desires, likes and dislikes but it is possible for differences to co-exist and for individual aspirations to be fulfilled without detriment to others. Every individual can perform life-supporting action, thereby nourishing and fulfilling personal interests along with family, social, and national interests. For a nation living in accord with Natural Law, seasons come on time, crops are plentiful, and there are no natural disasters such as droughts, famine, earthquakes, or floods. Scientific research, as discussed in Part II, indicate a move in the direction of "invincibility" as a result of the group practice of this technology. War deaths, conflict, crime and disease are shown to subside in a population when a sufficient number of individuals of that population practice these technologies.

Maintaining Unity and Nourishing Difference in World Cultures

As with his description of the significance of family life and the maintenance of family *Dharmas*, in his discussion of cultural integrity Maharishi refers to the importance of sustaining cultures:

> People from one land, when they live in another's always miss their old habits and surroundings. This is not just a psychological weakness. The fact is that each land has a different culture according to its geographic and climatic conditions. So in each land the human nervous system is cultured differently, starting from birth. When a person moves to another land, his nervous system tries to adapt and often does succeed to a large extent. But even if the person fails to adapt to just one small factor, that will become a drag for him and the host culture, because he will not be able to cohere fully with his environment.[17]

Maharishi points out that the only effective way of dealing with this issue is to enliven the universal, unifying value of culture and the five fundamentals of progress through the practice of the Transcendental Meditation technique and TM-Sidhi program. By enlivening this unifying value of consciousness and allowing Natural Law to structure and compute the most evolutionary steps of progress, one's culture is strengthened and all cultures are supported. The most life-supporting action and outcome will be computed by Natural Law.

In a specific example where Maharishi discusses management training and cultural values, he emphasizes it is essential that, "foreign ideologies do not dominate the life of the manager and the system of management that connects him with his field of responsibility,"[18]—"management in every country should fundamentally be based on the cultural values of the country."[19] This kind of management training is achieved when the holistic value of Natural Law is enlivened in the life of the manager and the people, and the spontaneous ability to maintain cultural values is promoted.

As noted above, every culture is essential to the development of world consciousness. The process of strengthening each culture so that each one supports the other but remains invincible within itself can occur in a peaceful, harmonious manner.[20] On the collective level, as Maharishi points out, all nations can radiate the unique values of their separate cultures, as well as "the universal value of togetherness." Each culture can support and enjoy the other, while remaining "serene within itself."[21] With the growth of greater friendship and harmony, cultures can be revitalized.

Clearly, the so-called post-colonial period of the 1990s signaled collective change—even if only in the call for the end of foreign domination. Despite this, neither contemporary theory and nor present government can countenance the idea of invincibility. Maharishi Vedic Science reveals that individuals and organizations, by expanding their limited thinking, can promote "universal coherence" in world consciousness.[22] Universal coherence is achieved through the establishment of sufficiently large groups of practitioners of the Transcendental Meditation technique and TM-Sidhi program. As discussed in Part II, these groups can create coherence for the nation, eliminating fear and disharmony. In this sense, it is through the accomplishments of man, as Maharishi points out, that the level and quality of life in his nation are determined:

> When a lot of individuals begin to unfold their hidden genius, national and world consciousness become coherent, and perception of similarities begins to dominate in the atmosphere, instead of perception of differences. People begin to live in accord with Natural Law, that is, in accordance with the culture of the land. It is Natural Law that maintains life everywhere and gives every nation its cultural traditions.[23]

When many individuals enliven the value of Natural Law, and unfold their hidden "genius," people become more creative. World consciousness becomes more coherent, more unified and increasingly driven by life-supporting tendencies. With coherent collective consciousness cultural traditions are supported and flourish, the perception of similarities comes to the foreground rather than the focus on differences. Differences thrive but the underlying unity of life—Saṁhitā, the holistic value of Natural Law—provides the ground for harmony and progress rather than discord. People live in accordance with Natural Law enjoying the culture and the land which supports them. As is clear, this discussion hinges on Maharishi's principle that there is a basic element in life—"the Light of *Brahm*" the field of Transcendental Consciousness—favoring all life and promoting evolution.[24] This basic element, as discussed in Part II and III, is the total potential of life which gives rise to the entire manifest universe and is realized as the simplest form of human awareness through research in consciousness.

Research in consciousness (achieved through the practice of the Transcendental Meditation technique and the TM-Sidhi program) can therefore be understood as the cornerstone of Vedic Science and, time after time, has been the focal point of knowledge throughout the ages—forming the core of various systems of knowledge, cultures, and artistic expressions:

> Philosophies developed around this central point of knowledge; systems of administration developed from this central point of knowledge which governs the universe. Systems of social order and culture sprang from this central point of knowledge. All streams of knowing and knowledge emerge from this and converge onto this central point of knowledge. All streams of organizing power emerge from and converge onto this central point of knowledge. All poets and writers rejoice in formulating their thought, speech, and action in the light of this central point of knowledge. All aspirations and all success is derived from this central point of knowledge.[25]

As Maharishi goes on to point out:

> Throughout the history of time, research in consciousness has led everyone to the same ultimate discovery—the discovery of the supreme light of pure intelligence, which expresses itself in its own language, the Language of Nature,

> the language of the Veda, the mother of all languages. The same Ultimate Reality finds expression through all languages throughout time.[26]

This underlying principle that the field of pure consciousness can be experienced and known through research in consciousness, that life can be lived according to Natural Law, has been cognized by enlightened individuals throughout the ages.

As Maharishi emphasizes, certain individuals who wanted to teach and give advice to others throughout history have taken recourse to this theme of research in consciousness; religions, philosophies, systems of administration, social order and culture—all streams of knowledge—ultimately find their source in this fundamental principle of knowledge.[27] With this in mind, Maharishi maintains that when any artist (regardless of their cultural background) successfully captures this universal value of life, his or her art withstands the test of time and continues to inspire the people generation after generation.[28] Since all streams of knowledge and organizing power "emerge and converge onto this central point of knowledge," and since culture (including artistic expressions) takes recourse to the infinite creativity and organizing power of pure knowledge, any culture living the full value of Natural Law can be said to emerge and converge onto this central point of knowledge. In this way, culture and art which mirror Natural Law emerge from the self-interacting dynamics of consciousness, the three-in-one structure of pure knowledge, and converge to the same point.

This dynamic and the sequential unfoldment of knowledge, as discussed in Part III, is recorded in the universal language of the Veda, the language of consciousness, which Maharishi points out underlies all languages.

The Relationship Between Vedic Language and One's Mother Tongue

The mother tongue of every group of people—whether a tribe or a nation— is structured and upheld by the local Laws of Nature which govern the life of the individuals who make up that group. The mother tongue is therefore very important. Like tradition and culture, Maharishi explains that language is upheld by the Laws of Nature that structure the physiology; the mother tongue "is structured and upheld by local Laws of Nature which structure the physiology of the individual."[29] Since Vedic language is the "Language of Nature which is upheld by universal Laws of Nature, which are the common basis of all the physiological structures in the universe,"[30] an intimate relationship exists between Vedic language, the mother tongue, and one's physiology. Maharishi emphasizes that the mother tongue is the closest to the Vedic language than any language for any group of people; it is vital that individuals, a nation or group uses the mother tongue. In teaching the youth, or in any educational setting, Maharishi recommends that the local language be used so that there is no gap in communication.[31] The use of the one's own language preserves the cultural integrity of the people by enlivening the Laws of Nature which structure the physiology of the individual and the character, traditions, and social fabric of the culture.

As a result of the value of the sounds of the Veda and the Vedic Literature and their relationship to the native language and the physiology, in translating Sanskrit texts into the mother tongue, people can preserve their basic culture. In today's global environment, one's own culture "requires support for survival due to the influence of all kinds of foreign cultures."[32] The language of the Veda and the Vedic Literature (impulses of pure, self-referral consciousness which structure life) strengthens the local Laws of Nature which uphold the mother tongue and the cultural integrity of the people, because culture, art, and the local languages of every culture, are expressions of Veda—pure knowledge and its organizing power. For this reason, the mother tongue, can be said to directly express or embody Natural Law in the most appropriate way.

Ultimately, there is a direct correspondence between language and meaning or sound and form for every language, even though different words are used in different languages. Therefore, while pure intelligence expresses *itself* in its own language (the language of the Veda—which is why Maharishi refers to the Vedic language as the mother of all languages), pure intelligence is also expressed in the different languages of different peoples throughout history. The validity and importance of each local language and culture in promoting evolution is clearly brought out in Maharishi Vedic Science, which reveals the relationship between pure consciousness, its expression as its own universal language, the individual physiology, the culture and traditions upheld by specific Laws of Nature, and the different local languages. Every aspect of human life (individual, social, cultural, traditional, artistic—the geographic and climatic conditions in which a group of people live, and the mother tongue) has its basis in the universal field of pure consciousness which can be enlivened in individual and collective consciousness.

As outlined in this section, this discussion of history, tradition and culture, expands upon the perspectives of modern, postmodern and Indian theory. In Maharishi Vedic Science, history can be seen in the larger context of the cyclical rise and fall of Natural Law in the infinite span of eternity. This infinite cycle perspective extends other views by defining history with respect to consciousness. History's purpose is seen to promote evolution and inspire people in the present with events from the past to create a better future. Similarly, tradition is understood in relation to the universal field of Natural Law. Traditions or ways of living are sustained by family and social *Dharmas* or Laws of Nature which, having their basis in Natural Law, govern and support the relationships between individuals in social life. Traditions based on Natural Law are not empty, reified forms of behavior but maintain life in the evolutionary direction. Along with traditions, culture plays a critical role in the development of individual life but when the inner value of pure consciousness is hidden, culture and traditions are not upheld.

With this understanding, it could be argued that to identify universal principles in art (as expressed in the various artistic traditions of the world) the artist, the art historian, and the art critic need to develop the ability to experience the field of pure consciousness (i.e., know what consciousness is and what it is made of). Then, in expressing universal value, the artist does not have to sacrifice tradition or individuality. He or she can reflect in art the various qualities and characteristics of the universal field of pure consciousness while capturing the spirit of his or her time. The historian can bring to light those evolutionary events to inspire people to evolve in the present. Critics can locate the universal in art.

Returning to a theme raised in Part I, according to Lyotard, the subjective and objective tendencies of life were represented by narrative and scientific knowledge—the former being instrumental in the formation of social bonds and culture, the latter dealing with verifiable propositions or objective knowledge. Maharishi Vedic Science gives a deeper insight into knowledge by revealing that the basis of all streams of knowledge is the field of pure consciousness with its three-in-one structure of pure knowledge, where Ṛishi (the knower or subject), Devatā (the process of knowing or relationship between subject and object) and Chhandas (the known or object) are unified one within the other. This structure of knowledge gives rise to all streams of knowledge, all kinds of intelligence, and all the professions. This fundamental structure, identified as the Constitution of the Universe, generates all the Laws of Nature which give rise to societies and different cultures. It is the governing constitution which governs traditions, cultures and language. If art is created from the level of pure knowledge, it embodies, or speaks for, this source of all cultures even when it is formed in the visual language of one culture. Aesthetic judgment and ethical wisdom (discussed by Lyotard as the realm of customary knowledge) are also, ultimately, expressions of Natural Law operating through specific Laws of Nature and cultural codes. In this context, Vedic language (the language of Nature which unfolds the totality of complete knowledge) is not socially determined but is the very structure of individual consciousness and the individual physiology. Vedic language unfolds absolute knowledge which gives rise to all theories of knowledge and takes into account all perspectives. With complete or absolute knowledge every action supports ecological, social, national, global and individual balance and growth. All levels of life ("subjective" and "objective") are simultaneously nourished. Life in lived in unity consciousness.

Furthermore, viewed from the level of Unity Consciousness or fully awake value of Saṁhitā, different world-views can be appreciated as different concepts of Natural Law—reflecting the degree of Natural Law being lived at the time and the governance of Laws of Nature upholding life in a particular region or culture. In contrast, if one is living partial values of Natural Law then the understanding of life and Nature held by the people will be explained only to that degree. Just as knowledge is different in different states of consciousness, the world-view of a group or people depends on the degree of Natural Law enlivened and displayed in collective consciousness. Similarly, paradigms can be understood to be models that reflect the ability of human intelligence to fathom the precise workings of nature at any one time. Different paradigms spring up over time and like the

Yugas, in the cycle of the fall and rise of Natural Law, reflect the degree of Natural Law lived at any particular time period. This cycle of Natural Law represents the mechanics of Nature's functioning operating on the collective level.

As we have seen, cultures differ; but if people of different cultures are living 100 percent of Natural Law, the universal reality of pure consciousness will be seen as the basis of all cultures. Complete knowledge will be accessible. Only when people are not living 100 percent of Natural Law do they fail to share the comprehensive and complete knowledge of the workings of Nature. When experience and understanding is grounded in the transcendental level of pure consciousness, a common reality is known to all and difference can be fully appreciated.

Clearly, traditions, culture, language, art and visual culture in a society which is living Natural Law are specific to the land and the people but are also firmly established in the universal field of life. In such a setting, there is no dichotomy between "nature" and "culture": Culture is the expression of the Laws of Nature that govern a particular people, their land, the climate in that region, the language, the traditions, and their art. The mechanics through which Natural Law constructs and orchestrates the natural world are the same mechanics which underlie human life on the individual, social, cultural, national, and international levels. Any enlightened individual, living in accord with Natural Law, gains the support of Nature. His or her behavior reflects the balance, orderliness, and precision of Nature's functioning, and in every regard upholds tradition and culture. With respect to world peace, harmony among cultures depends on the ability of each one to maintain its own integrity on the basis of "the infinite adaptability that characterizes life lived in accord with the laws of nature"[33] and not on the fusion of cultures. "Like the many-coloured pieces of a mosaic or the varied tunes of an orchestra, each fully integrated culture contributes to form a harmonious world."[34]

It seems, therefore, that the attempt to impose concepts of universality and social order which are not based on the experience of pure consciousness but on individual or governmental conceptions of social policy, can never cater to all the different tendencies and interests of various cultures. Only the universal field of Natural Law can compute and guide the activity of life such that all cultures with their different artistic expressions can flourish. With the knowledge of Maharishi Vedic Science, as Maharishi points out, every country can now "enjoy the infinite creativity of the organizing power of Natural Law"[35] and grow in cultural integrity. This has profound implications for art and visual culture.

PART V

THE ARTIST AS A UNIVERSAL HUMAN BEING CREATING UNIVERSAL VALUE IN ART AND AESTHETICS

Pure self-referral consciousness, in its dynamic unfoldment into Laws of Nature and the entire manifest universe, has been described as the basis of history, tradition and culture. With this understanding, topics such as the artist, creative process, art object, aesthetics, and visual culture, as defined by modernists, postmodernists, Indian theory, and art critics, can be reconsidered. Since Maharishi Vedic Science provides not only knowledge about Nature's creative mechanics but also technologies to access the infinite creativity of Natural Law, it enables artists of all cultures to cognize and represent universal mechanics of creation. According to Maharishi Vedic Science, art is the direct expression of the level of consciousness of the artist. If the artist is living the full value of Natural Law, the artwork will express that universal, unbounded value of consciousness. The tools to achieve this are the Transcendental Meditation technique and TM-Sidhi program. These technologies facilitate: 1) experience of pure consciousness and access to infinite creativity; 2) knowledge of the creative mechanics of Nature or one's own consciousness; 3) the ability to become a universal and exemplary human being; and 4) the creation of universal art which creates and evolutionary effect on the viewer and the environment.[1]

With access to infinite creativity—and knowledge of the creative mechanics of Nature—the artist can accomplish anything. Through the development of consciousness, the artist can become a universal human being and to begin to express universal value in art. Such an artist, enlightened and knowing what consciousness is and what it is made of, creates as Nature creates—from the field of infinite creativity. All performance is life-supporting, artistic and exemplary. Once thought to be a rarity, artistic genius can now be developed in a scientific, systematic way; genius is systematically enlivened in anyone through Maharishi's technologies of consciousness. A genius, according to Maharishi Vedic Science, is someone who can overcome obstacles, achieve his goal with maximum success and minimum expenditure of energy. He or she is a supremely creative person whose every achievement is beneficial to the environment. A less creative person meets with seemingly insurmountable difficulties in life. But the artist/genius lives higher states of consciousness and is able to maintain broad awareness while focusing sharply. Fulfilled, such a person: gains support of Nature; enjoys bliss; is naturally and spontaneously happy, loving and harmonious; always thinks in terms of life-supporting values instead of opposition, disharmony and criticism; and lives the full value of life. As a universal human being, the artist is a role model for society—performing life-supporting activity and living life in freedom.

This individual brings a life-supporting influence to the world. This can be said to be the most significant role the artist can play. The artist can be a role model in any transition period.

A transition period, or phase transition, is defined as the phase between a period when a only limited degree of Natural Law is lived by the people and a period when people enjoy a fuller expression of Natural Law in daily life. This idea was discussed in the previous section which considered the development of history in terms of *Yugas*. In the transition from an unenlightened age (a period when people live almost zero percent of Natural Law) to an age of enlightenment (an era when 100 percent of Natural Law is lived in daily life) the artist can be role model for society. Through exemplary and transformational performance the artist can change the trends of time. Chapter 18, *The Role of the Artist: Spontaneously Functioning from the Level of Natural Law*, specifically addresses this discussion of the artist's role.

With respect to the creative process, for the universal or enlightened artist, the process of creating follows the same creative mechanics of Nature. The artist stands as a Cosmic Creator and expresses the full value of consciousness in art. Individual creativity springs from the infinite reservoir of Creative Intelligence and not from a limited sense of self. Individual creativity can demonstrate the creative mechanics of Nature, and, in so doing, reflect the dynamics and structure of Veda. The work of art mirrors the structure of self-referral consciousness—which is the fundamental structure and dynamic of the human physiology, every grain of creation, every form and phenomenon. In terms of the artist's creative process, the artist's own unbounded consciousness collapses onto a point value—an idea, inspiration or inner vision—and in a sequential unfoldment, this thought or picture is transferred into form. In order to transport this inner value of consciousness onto the outer material object or performance requires great flexibility and creativity on the part of the artist. The art object mirrors the creative mechanics of Nature. It is lively in the self-referral dynamics of consciousness.

For the artist to best develop infinite flexibility and creativity, Maharishi explains that the creative process itself should be systematic and specific, and not governed by chance. By "holding" or envisaging the entire work of art within his or her unbounded consciousness and then, over time, transferring it into material form, the work of art spontaneously exhibits the qualities of unboundedness, immortality and bliss. These three qualities are qualities of the unified field of pure consciousness and are embodied in artistic expression. Infused with these qualities, art is held to create a life-supporting response in the viewer.[2] This outcome occurs when the artist is enlightened.

Since the thoughts of an enlightened artist spring from the field of pure creativity or pure consciousness, they are not motivated by individual consequences or past experiences embossed on the mind as impressions—a process described in Maharishi Vedic Science, as part of the cycle of experience, impression and desire. Creative Intelligence or self-referral consciousness is understood to be the origin of thoughts and ideas and of the material object. The flow of energy and intelligence on the deepest level of the mind gives rise to thought which is the structure of the object on the level of the thinking mind. With this understanding, the thought and the object are woven of threads of energy and intelligence, the fabrics of self-referral consciousness.

In the creation of art, Maharishi also explains that the nervous system can be refined or cultured. This is one of the benefits of creative practice. But the creative process of art is no substitution for the technologies of consciousness which effectively promote evolution to higher states of consciousness. The idea of refinement of life through art runs contrary to contemporary ideas about the role of art and art practice which often prescribe shock and chance. It is commonly thought that creativity and suffering go hand in hand. From the perspective of Maharishi Vedic Science, creativity and suffering are completely opposed to one another. In Chapter 19, entitled *The Creative Process: Operating from, the Level of Nature's Creative Mechanics*, individual or artistic creativity is viewed in reference to these topics, while Chapter 20, *Universal Art and Its Effects,* deals with the art object and the effects of art. The aesthetic value and purpose of the work of art can be understood in terms of its ability to evoke the experience of unboundedness in the viewer. This means that the viewer's consciousness is drawn in the direction of the Transcendent. From this perspective, art promotes evolution by inspiring the viewer to experience bliss. Bliss is universal. It is the essential nature of life. The different cultural meanings and styles of a work of art can have their basis in a universal value which provokes in the viewer a feeling of inspiration and upliftment—aiding progression towards enlightenment. The purpose of art, in this sense, is to inspire the viewer to evolve toward higher states of consciousness and experience the unified Self or Saṁhitā.

Universal art is markedly different from other art; it has an evolutionary effect whether the viewer sees it or not. In fact, this is one criterion that successful art should meet. Successful art fulfills a social and environmental role by creating harmony and unity in "culture" and in "nature" by radiating qualities of consciousness and contributing to coherence in collective consciousness. Chapter 21, *Aesthetic Value and Aesthetic Response: Leading the Viewer Toward Bliss and a Unified Self*, explores the idea of aesthetic experience in response to art and its contribution to a new sense of self. Themes introduced in Chapter 4 articulated by Kuspit, are again revisited and expanded. By noting comparisons with precepts of modern, Indian, and postmodern theories, this section finalizes the discussion of art. It contributes, with the earlier chapters, to an overall picture of Maharishi Vedic Science, acting as a platform for Part VI which examines the Vāstusūtra Upaniṣad.

18

THE ROLE OF THE ARTIST: SPONTANEOUSLY FUNCTIONING FROM THE LEVEL OF NATURAL LAW

According to Maharishi Vedic Science, an artist is a person who is living higher states of consciousness, who has mastered the art of living in accord with Natural Law. He or she is not simply an artisan or generator of language games. This definition of the artist differs from the modern, postmodern and Indian perspectives. Both modern and postmodern theories distinguish between art and science (or narrative knowledge and scientific knowledge); for modernists, artistic insight or genius, unlike science, cannot be taught. The modern artist/genius has innate abilities, is an avant-garde hero who breaks with tradition, and creates original art. Postmodernists suggest this concept propagates elitism. In contrast to both, Indian theory sees the artist as a facilitator or artisan who follows an established tradition. In this sense, originality and avant-gardism are opposed to the purpose of art. Maharishi Vedic Science presents an entirely new understanding of the function of science in the development of art and the artist, the nature of genius, and the role of the artist, redefining each of these areas with respect to consciousness.

Firstly, Maharishi suggests that the artist's creative ability and inner genius can be scientifically and systematically developed through practice of his technologies of consciousness. Secondly, genius is the spontaneous expression of Creative Intelligence or pure consciousness in individual life. Because Creative Intelligence is the essential nature of everyone's consciousness, it is possible for anyone to be a genius. Thirdly, while Maharishi identifies a difference between art and science, the scientific approach of Vedic Science and the Science of Creative Intelligence [1] are crucial to the development of art and the artist. In today's hi-tech world artists employ the tools of technology—creating electronic art that extends new frontiers of visual culture. However, it is only through systematic development of consciousness can the artist become a universal human being and a role model for society—whatever art he or she creates. [2]

Developing the Artist Through Science

Maharishi generally distinguishes between the disciplines of art and science by explaining that science is the systematic knowledge of thing and art is the systematic expression of a thing. [3] While the scientist investigates different levels of life (for example, the molecular, atomic and the sub-atomic levels) in order to gain knowledge of the laws which govern the finer levels of creation, the artist applies knowledge to create an expression of life. The scientist investigates the subtle phases of creation. The artist, knowing something on the causal level, creates and applies that value to the surface or expressed level of life.[4] In this sense, art is an applied science. Despite this distinction, in both instances the artist and the scientist attempt to fathom the deeper values of creation, but it is the artist who, in living life established Transcendental Consciousness, spontaneously expresses the universal source of existence in a work of art. According to Maharishi Vedic Science, the subjective approach of art can be strengthened through the application of science. Vedic Science brings system to art.

Modernists assumed that in employing an "objective" approach science could not fathom the spiritual or subjective realm of experience—the domain of art. Art was superior to science; it uncovered the subjective, mysterious realm of inner experience. In a similar pairing of opposites, postmodernists argue that, unlike science, art is a part of narrative knowledge and customary knowledge (which involve the formation of social bonds and questions of value, taste and ethical judgment); scientific knowledge alone employs denotative statements about knowledge claims. On the other hand, Maharishi Vedic Science provides complete knowledge of the subject, (the knower), object (the known), and the process that links the two (the process of knowing), by unfolding the three-in-one structure of pure knowledge in human awareness. This structure is the dynamic basis of all subjective and objective values and their relationships, the basis of all streams of knowledge (objective and subjective), the basis of tradition, culture, and of all aspects of life. This structure can be enlivened in one's awareness and is the basis of all streams of science and art.

Furthermore, it is through the knowledge and technologies of Maharishi Vedic Science and Maharishi's Science of Creative Intelligence, that the subjective discipline of art can be developed in a scientific, systematic and reliable way. Art no longer has to be an expression of chance.[5] As noted at the beginning of this book, Maharishi's Science of Creative Intelligence is the theory and practice of the development of higher states of consciousness. It unfolds the infinite creativity of individual consciousness. As Maharishi explains, it brings spontaneous discipline to art:

> This is the first generation in the long history of art for whom the objectivity of science is enlivened by the subjectivity of art. In fact, the objectivity of science is utilized by the Science of Creative Intelligence to develop the subjectivity of the artist. This generation is thereby profoundly capable of displaying the whole range of art and its role to express the fullness of life in the boundaries of living—the totality of life expressed in small, small expressions. This is the first generation that sees art and science not only coming together but one becoming the breath of the other. The Science of Creative Intelligence is born to bring in system, born to bring spontaneous discipline to art, born to bring harmony into that which is spontaneously comprehensive and specific at the same time.[6]

Art involves the knowledge of how Creative Intelligence unfolds in a sequential, step-by-step fashion to create the manifest universe. Artistic expression is a systematic procedure, akin to science, but in an application of the knowledge of the Laws of Nature as opposed to an investigation of them. It is a systematic procedure because the artistic or creative individual, in expanding consciousness, begins to know the full details of consciousness. He or she knows the details of the unfoldment of the mechanics of self-referral consciousness, the Veda—the field of infinite creativity—and creates in the same way that Nature creates.

Indeed, Maharishi points out that systematic thinking is required in the life of both the artist and the scientist: "One step after the other, each very well systematized, is the natural thinking of the artist. Systematic, uncluttered, uninvolved, faultless thinking is the natural style of thinking in the life of the scientist, too."[7] Just as in nature, everything is "very dignified" because "everything in creation follows certain laws and everything is systematically set;"[8] the artist's creative practice and life, following Nature's creative dynamics, naturally exhibit the orderly, systematic progression of Natural Law.

As described in Part II, through the technologies of Maharishi's Science of Creative Intelligence and Maharishi Vedic Science the subjectivity of the artist is effectively developed so that he or she can systematically and spontaneously know and express the full range of Creative Intelligence in art. With this scientific approach, system, spontaneous discipline, and harmony can be brought to the field of art. This means that art can more effectively express the universal, infinite value of life within the confines of an object, performance, film, etc..[9]

The Development of Genius

The skill of a successful artist was at one time (as in Kant's day) thought to belong to only a few, but now it can be systematically developed in anyone. Maharishi maintains that genius does not have to be restricted to a few artists because, in this scientific age, the great skill of expression can be developed in a natural way. A genius is defined as a person who *knows* the mechanics of the creative process (as discussed in Parts II and III); a genius is able to create, think and behave from the level of pure, self-referral consciousness. By systematically developing consciousness genius can be expressed:

> Although art has always been taught, it had been thought that it was some inborn faculty that structures the artist, his vision and skill. But those days have gone when the genius of man was thought to belong to a few people born with a high level of consciousness. Now is the time when physics has declared the existence of a field of all possibilities located in the state of least excitation of consciousness. With this understanding about the different levels of creation, the unfoldment of the innermost level of life and its display on the surface values of living has become simple and easy. This scientific development of the full potential of life is such a common phenomenon today through the Science of

> Creative Intelligence that the development of the full potential of art in everyone's life is and must continue to be a very natural phenomenon. In this scientific age, art is no longer an expression of chance. [10]

Through development of consciousness, every individual can unfold inner genius and be an "artist". Creativity, here, is no longer a rare skill reserved for an elite few. It is also no longer a question of chance.

Having stated that anyone can be a genius, Maharishi distinguishes between genius and "non-genius". A genius is a naturally creative person with very clear consciousness who can create without struggling, clearly visualize the goal and achieve it; this person's life is characterized by success, progress and achievement—not only for himself but for his family, community, nation and the environment. Therefore, genius is defined by the degree of creativity that is displayed in a person's actions. Creativity is the ability to do less and accomplish more, to sustain an obstacle-free process of re-creation. A less creative person is unable to overcome obstacles, and cannot see a means to achieve a desired goal. As Maharishi emphasizes:

> There is a difference between the creativity of a genius and the creativity of a non-genius. A genius is a naturally creative person. A creative person is someone who is able to do less and yet accomplish more, someone who doesn't have to struggle in order to create: this is creativity. A non-creative person, however, because he can't surmount the obstacles on the way to creation, will struggle. Thus, creative means that the individual can create and sustain the process of re-creation without encountering obstacles; obstacles on the way don't come up because the creative person is powerful enough to overcome them.[11]

Maharishi continues to point out that

> Because a genius is a person with very clear consciousness, he sees things so clearly that he doesn't even experience obstacles or resistance to creativity; he just keeps on progressing on the steps of greater achievement. While some less creative individuals cannot see a way, a genius not only sees the way but achieves the goal: this is a genius, a creative person. With greater application of creativity comes more comfort for the doer. Greater comfort for the doer means greater achievement for both the whole atmosphere and the doer himself.
>
> This is the value of applying Creative Intelligence, and this is the value that a genius has; he just sees things clearly, and this is because the basis of the life of the genius is more natural. His awareness is broader, widened awareness is the basis of a genius. [12]

In this sense, as Maharishi indicates, "facility and ease in the field of achievements is what marks the steps of a genius, the steps of a creative man." [13]

Things go easily for a genius. There are no obstacles. The genius, having broad or wide awareness, sees things clearly and is able to apply the infinite value of Creative Intelligence, which creates the entire creation, to any undertaking. He or she sees the goal and achieves it with minimum expenditure of energy and maximum success. Individual creativity unfolds in the same orderly fashion as Nature's creativity, and the outcome of this creative process is beneficial to everyone.

According to Maharishi Vedic Science, then, genius can be understood as innate; it is the outer expression of everyone's inner, Transcendental, pure consciousness. Anyone can access this unseen reservoir of infinite creativity through Maharishi's technologies of consciousness. While Maharishi contrasts the genius and the non-genius, everyone can unfold their inner genius. This view contrasts with modern, postmodern and Indian theories. Modernists see genius as unfathomable—only a few individuals are born with it. Postmodernists suggest "genius" is a arbitrary value— a modernist concept obscuring the role of cultural parameters in forming individual and social consciousness. Indian theorists, such as Pandit, explain that genius and individuality—tied up with originality—are opposed to the purpose of art. The artist is expected to work within clear guidelines of tradition to create a prescribed outcome.

The Artist: A New Definition

In Maharishi Vedic Science, an artist is a person who is living higher states of consciousness. If art is to embody the universal, absolute within the boundaries of the object or performance, then the artist must be established in the universal, unbounded value of pure consciousness. He or she must be at least living Cosmic Consciousness[14]—the fifth state of consciousness discussed at length in Part II. Cosmic Consciousness is that level of awareness in which the individual can maintain unboundedness along with the ability to focus sharply. As Maharishi explains:

> In cosmic consciousness, the artist not only gains the ability of simultaneously maintaining broad comprehension along with sharp focus but also the ability to express, through his imagination and feeling, the unexpressed level of Being in such a way as to make it concrete.[15]

He further indicates that

> Cosmic consciousness is the ideal awareness of the artist, because in this state of consciousness the artist can spontaneously maintain unbounded awareness while maintaining boundaries and can depict the unbounded value onto the bound; unbounded awareness gets transported onto the finite values of his strokes on paper. He is able to sustain that unboundedness, and he is able to move that unboundedness through his brushes.[16]

This idea of maintaining broad comprehension and sharp focus refers to the ability to sustain unbounded, pure awareness, while engaging in activity and express that unbounded awareness in creative practice. The capability of the mind to operate according to this principle has been demonstrated by measures of field independence, as discussed in Part II. As Fergusson found, meditating college art students showed increased field independence in comparison to non-meditating students. Maharishi explains that field independence is an indication of broad awareness and ability to focus. Both broad awareness (encompassing the whole) and cognizance of detail (the parts) are simultaneously the domain of consciousness. With respect to higher states of consciousness, the successful field of the artist is Cosmic Consciousness because in this state "his awareness plays and displays the full reality of life"[17]—it encompasses broad, unbounded awareness and ability to focus on the parts.

Although the full reality of life is gained in Cosmic Consciousness, the *full liveliness* of life is experienced only in Unity Consciousness, or Brahman Consciousness—the most developed state of consciousness. As Maharishi points out, "the totality, the unboundedness, the infinity—is expressed in every boundary of living only in Unity Consciousness."[18] For this reason, it is necessary for the artist to be in Cosmic Consciousness for his or her art to reflect the deeper values of consciousness—despite the fact that, in actuality, one is a fully developed artist in Unity or Brahman Consciousness. Unity Consciousness is the more developed state, but the full value of life starts "to be enjoyed, viewed and lived even from the level of Cosmic Consciousness."[19] Therefore, an artist who wants to express the universal value of the infinite must be enjoying Cosmic Consciousness—permanently living the full value of awareness. Then, the artist's life reflects the absolute, infinite, eternal field of Creative Intelligence. Then art, in expressing that eternal Cosmic value, has a life-supporting impact on the viewer and the environment.

Part II discussed how the artist can begin to live this state of consciousness. The practice of the Transcendental Meditation technique and TM-Sidhi program provide the means. These technologies of consciousness are essential for any artist, indeed any person, who wants to develop higher states of consciousness. As Maharishi points out, "It is very, very necessary that the students of art have the regular practice of Transcendental Meditation because it's the only way whereby all stresses and strains can be removed and that most desired level of consciousness can be generated."[20] Through these technologies the human nervous system can be cultured so that the individual gains the ability to maintain the vision of infinity while acting in infinite values and can develop the ability to enliven and operate from the field of infinite Creative Intelligence:

> From unmanifest to unmanifest, from infinity to infinity is the range of Creative Intelligence, and this is within the comprehension of the vision of the human mind. Human vision, human awareness, has that ability not to lose the value of infinity when it is indulging in the fields of finite values; infinite and finite both.

> To this extent, the body has to be cultured, the physiology has to be modified, and regular practice of leading our awareness to the unmanifest, bringing the awareness to the field of action—meditation and action, meditation and action—keeps on modifying the physiology day after day. The hope is that one day the physiology will rise to a level of effectiveness or efficiency such that the functioning of the nervous system will be able to have that unbounded awareness established while our mind is engaging within boundaries, perception, action, and all work. In this state fullness is never lost.[21]

This mental technique has a corresponding effect on the physiology. By taking the awareness to the field of the infinite and then coming out into activity, the physiology is modified day by day. The body is cultured such that the nervous system is able to maintain unboundedness permanently. Taking recourse to practice of the Transcendental Meditation technique and then engaging in daily activities afterwards, the artist can begin to maintain the unbounded awareness of Transcendental Consciousness and can express the universal value of pure consciousness in the limitations of the art object/process. As Maharishi points out:

> The purpose and function of the artist is to manifest the unmanifest. This is so profoundly and completely accomplished through Transcendental Meditation. Every stroke of an artist should spontaneously fall in the right place with the right shades, colors, intensity, and so on. This will occur only when his awareness operating on the brushtip does not lose contact with that area where the brush is going to fall. There has to be harmony between inner consciousness and outer performance. The artist has to have a synchronous mind. Only in the synchrony of the mind will this compactness and concentratedness, this synchrony of the heart, be found operating. The feelings of the artist should be so precise, so full, that they overflow, and this synchrony in the awareness of the artist is what makes an artist a creator. This synchrony increases with Transcendental Meditation, and therefore Transcendental Meditation is the art of art.[22]

The Transcendental Meditation technique can be thought of as a professional tool for the artist.[23] It is the "art of art."

The Art of Living Bliss Consciousness

Living bliss consciousness, the enlightened artist is fulfilled—established in pure consciousness. He or she displays artistic behavior in every aspect of life. Such a life is one of fulfillment, a "life lived in the wholeness of one's own consciousness which is bliss consciousness."[24] A fulfilled person achieves success in every undertaking. 'Success' means "support of Nature or the expression of Nature in increasing degrees of fullness."[25]

At the opposite end of the spectrum, as Maharishi points out, an individual who does not know the mechanics of the creative process cannot be defined as an artist:

> One is not an artist, one is not the expresser of life that an artist should be, if one is weeping, if the heart is cramped while the brush is going forward and the drops of color are spread unknowingly, by accident here and there. This is not the expression of an artist.[26]

This unequivocal definition, discussed further in Chapter 19, is at variance with the popular idea that meaningful "great" art is associated with angst or suffering. Clearly, from the perspective of Maharishi Vedic Science, an artist or creative person is not simply one who paints or sculpts; an artist is someone who can perform action from the level of Natural Law and express Creative Intelligence or pure consciousness in every action. As Maharishi points out, a creative person is one who has mastered the "art of living":

> In order to express creative intelligence, we do not have to take a brush to a piece of paper or a hammer to a stone. Creative intelligence sings the glory of life in every phase of perception and action. There is a wave of creative intelligence and life expresses itself through that wave. In order to be creative, we do not have to start writing. Living life is the expression of the full value of creative intelligence. Not allowing ourselves to be dumped into the inertia of stresses and strains and suffering—this is the art of living, and this belongs to the developed value of creative intelligence.[27]

Maharishi goes on to explain that "living life, living the fuller values of life, is the expression of the art of living, and this develops spontaneously when the inner latent value of creative intelligence is enlivened on the level of our awareness."[28] Aspects of the qualities and behavior that are displayed in individual life as one grows in the art of living are outlined as follows:

> What we are—how radiant, how happy, how loving, how harmonious; how much we think in terms of life-supporting values instead of dwelling in oppositions, disharmony, criticisms and speaking ill of others; how much we express the value of life—in simple terms, how good we are to ourselves and to others. This is the display of life, this is the art of living.[29]

The degree to which we are happy, loving, harmonious, thinking in terms of life-supporting values instead of being caught up in oppositions, criticisms and speaking ill of others, reveals the degree to which we are displaying the art of living. The art of living, Maharishi points out, is structured in the individual when awareness is established in the field of Creative Intelligence:

> This is the art of living which is spontaneously structured when our awareness is established in the pure field of Creative Intelligence. It is in that area that the unbounded range of Creative Intelligence is comprehended spontaneously, and in the unbounded comprehension of the whole value of Creative Intelligence lies the key to the development of artistic life, the development of scientific life, the development of the ability to live the full value of life.[30]

Having mastered the art of living, the full value of Creative Intelligence is displayed in one's life. This means that one is not "dumped into the inertia of stress" and does not struggle; there are no obstructions to creativity. Skill in the science or art of living means the full value of Creative Intelligence or self-referral consciousness is lively in thought, speech and action. As considered above, there are indicators of more creative behavior: the creative individual: 1) is naturally and spontaneously happy, loving and harmonious; 2) thinks in terms of life-supporting values instead of opposition and disharmony; 3) does not speak ill of others; 4) is good to himself or herself and to others; 5) is spontaneously aware of the unbounded range of Creative Intelligence; and 6) lives the full value of life—lives higher states of consciousness. In this context, demonstrating enlightened behavior, the artist is a role model for the rest of society.

The Artist as a Role Model

In Maharishi Vedic Science, the transition from life lived in a non-life-supporting manner (where a small degree of Natural Law is lived) to an era of life-supporting action (where action is in accord with Natural Law) is referred to as a phase transition. Maharishi explains that in a phase transition the artist is an example to society:

> During the phase transition, the role of an artist in society is to create a model human—an individual who is growing in the ability to express the full value of life. The life of an artist should always be a model to all other people in society. We have the tradition of the artist gaining respect in society, gaining honor in society. This tradition occurs because artists are breathing life to expose something that lies behind the scene. An artist takes a flat piece of paper and produces a face, a lively face. With just one dimension, he is able to produce two, three, or four dimensions.[31]

Having eradicated stresses from the nervous system through the practice of technologies of consciousness, the artist can be an inspiration to other individuals. Living higher states of consciousness and displaying the qualities of a universal human being in every action, the artist becomes an example for society. This is because the life of an enlightened artist is saturated with the experience of bliss. This quality of bliss is spontaneously embodied in all activity, including art.

This understanding of the artist and his or her role is quite different from modern and postmodern definitions—the former seeing the artist as an individual hero/genius who does not know the source of his creativity, whose work is created by chance, and the latter defining the artist as a player of language games. Maharishi Vedic Science extends the concept of genius to include the inner creativity of the individual which is latent within everyone, not just an elite few. It also expands ideas outlined in Indian theory by defining the artist as one who is living higher states of consciousness and who can express the infinite within the finite. More importantly, this complete science of consciousness provides technologies whereby this can be achieved and explains how the creative process in art unfolds in a sequential and precise manner—as in Nature's creative mechanics.

19

THE CREATIVE PROCESS: OPERATING FROM THE LEVEL OF NATURE'S CREATIVE MECHANICS

There are three important principles in Maharishi Vedic Science which inform the artist's the creative process: 1) the need for the development of the inner value of consciousness by tapping infinite, unbounded field of creativity; 2) comprehension of Nature's creative mechanics of Nature; 3) the forming of a picture within the imagination which is subsequently expressed in outer material form. The artist must first have unbounded consciousness, access to pure creativity and knowledge of the creative mechanics of Nature. Only then can he or she imagine any form on the level of consciousness and, keeping that inner picture lively day-after-day in all its precise detail, transform or transport that inner picture into art. In addition, Maharishi Vedic Science presents a unique understanding of ideas of authorship and action, originality, creativity and suffering, which contrast with modern and postmodern theories.

Artist as Creator: Displaying the Creative Mechanics of Nature's Functioning

As intimated in the earlier chapters, from the perspective of Maharishi Vedic Science, the artist can be understood as an individual creator who, in expanding his or her awareness to the level of the Cosmic Creator, is able to create as Nature creates. The "Creator" is the initiator and originator of the cosmic creation who has unparalleled Creative Intelligence, as Maharishi points out:

> That great artist, the Creator, has tremendous creative intelligence. How many faces he has designed, no two faces he wants to see alike—what a great artist! He has used all the knowledge of all the laws of nature functioning together. Therefore, the whole creation is the systematic knowledge through which the Almighty has displayed his artistic ability.[1]

It is this Creative Intelligence of the "Cosmic Creator" which creates every person and every creature in existence through application of the all the Laws of Nature. Creative Intelligence involves the systematic application of absolute knowledge in artistic expression. In this sense, Creative Intelligence could be described as the primal cause since this infinite value of pure consciousness is the originator of life.

From this perspective, each expressed value of creation (including, for example, each individual person) is a work of art created through the systematic unfoldment of self-referral consciousness in a sequential manner. As noted earlier, every physiology is structured in an orderly way and upheld by the Laws of Nature that govern the functioning of the mind and body. But many different expressions of consciousness are found in manifest form. No two faces "are alike." Each individual has a unique character, physical appearance and nature governed by many factors (influences at the time and place of birth, one's family tradition, the geography and climate, the *Doṣas* that are predominant in the physiology, the experiences and conditions of life, etc.—all of which are governed by Laws of Nature administered by Creative Intelligence).

Despite the differences in expression, the same orderly unfoldment of Natural Law is responsible for the emergence of everything in creation. Each creative expression is original and unique but, in the process of its creation, follows a specific sequence of expression through the sequential unfoldment of Veda—as discussed in Part III. As described in the Upaniṣads, in the process of creation, the Creator creates and then enters into his creation: तत्सृत्वा तदेवानुप्राविशत् । *Tat sṛṣtwā tad evānuprāviśat* (*Taittirīya Upaniṣad, 2.6*).[2] Maharishi translates this verse as "Having created the creation, the Creator entered into it"[3] or "the Creative Intelligence of the Veda, having created its home, the physiology, dwells within it."[4] This expression explains that the Creator—pure Creative Intelligence or the Veda—not only creates creation (including the physiology) but can be found, or resides, within it. This is the reality of self-referral intelligence, which, as discussed in Parts II and III, is both responsible for and dwells in every point or grain of creation. This is why, Maharishi adds, self-referral consciousness is referred to as the "field" (*Kṣetr*) and the "in-dweller of the field" (*Kṣetragya*) at the same time:

> For scholars of Vedic knowledge, this level of reality—self-referral intelligence, whose self-referral dynamism constitutes the sound of the Veda and the script (form) of the Veda at the unmanifest basis of creation—is *Kshetragya* and *Kshetr* at the same time. It is the Creator and the creation at the same time. It is the Creator that creates creation from within itself.[5]

Self-referral intelligence is the Creator that creates creation from within itself and dwells within that creation. It is both the Creator and the creation, simultaneously. This level of self-referral intelligence, Maharishi reveals, is the Creator, the process of creation and the creation altogether in itself—the Saṁhitā of Ṛishi, Devatā and Chhandas. The same dynamics of self-referral consciousness operate at every point in creation; from this perspective there is no "inside" and "outside" to creation.

The so-called original cause is pure, self-referral consciousness but it is everywhere present in creation at every moment. There is no outside "origin" external to life or individual consciousness, as expressed in a verse from the Bhagavad-Gītā:

प्रकृतिं स्वामवष्टभ्य विसृजामि पुनः पुनः ।
भूतग्राममिमं कृत्स्नमवशमं प्रकृतेर्वशात् ॥

Prakṛtiṁ svām avaṣṭabhya
visṛjāmi punaḥ punaḥ,
bhūtagrāmamimaṁ kṛtsnam
avaśaṁ prakṛtervaśāt.
(Bhagavad-Gītā, 9.8)

Translated by Maharishi as: "Taking recourse to my own self-referral nature, I create again and again. Creation and administration of creation, both are a natural phenomenon on the basis of my self-referral consciousness,"[6] this verse describes the creative, self-referral nature of consciousness. Self-referral consciousness, which is the simplest form of everyone's own awareness, is the creator and administrator of creation. It is both "originator" and the creative mechanics through which creation emerges. In terms of the artist, Maharishi points out that, in creating the work of art, he too expands his status to the Cosmic Creator by virtue of the same principle.

> The artist, while creating, stands as a creator, and that status of the creator, howsoever small, takes the vision to a very big Creator of the entire cosmic life. So an artist as a Creator, as one who expresses himself, tells the story of creation: when an artist expresses himself, he tells the whole story of creation. The Upanishads describe this aspect of the Creator in a very beautiful expression. They say, "Having created, he enters into creation." The expression of a piece of art is the expression of the life of the artist. Just this phenomenon is described in terms of the Creator entering his creation, and when the Creator enters his creation, the creation becomes lively. When the artist expresses himself in a piece of art, which is an automatic phenomenon, spontaneously the creation contains its creator. This phenomenon of the piece of art containing the expression of the heart and mind of the artist is itself the promotion of life. The artist promotes life on a lifeless piece of paper or stone.[7]

Maharishi continues to explain that

> The artist is instrumental in the greatest display of life: the display of life through the lifeless. This is the territory of an artist. By incorporating the lifeless into the value of his own life, he promotes life into that area. That is why an artist is held high above his fellowmen.[8]

Whatever the status of the artist, from whatever level of consciousness he or she creates, the piece of art speaks of his or her level of consciousness. When the artist is enlightened, the full value of the universal, unmanifest will be infused or expressed in the relative manifestation of art. The artist's life, which has its basis in pure consciousness, is transferred into the work of art. Life is thereby instilled into the lifeless object.

In this sense, the "originator" of life is naturally expressed in the work. Both the universal value of pure consciousness and the specific qualities, which the artist expresses by virtue of his or her unique physiology and culture (as influenced by the climatic and geographic conditions of the land) are expressed in the work of art. While the artist is described as the creator of the work of art, it is really Creative Intelligence that, operating through the artist, creates art. Without expansion of awareness, the artist erroneously assumes authorship of action.

Creativity and Authorship of Action: The Cycle of Impression, Desire and Action

The artist who is not cognizant of his own infinite creativity (his own unbounded state of awareness) assumes authorship of creative action. He sees himself as an originator of action but does not fully comprehend the mechanics of creation or his role as a creator. In his commentary on the Bhagavad-Gītā, Maharishi points out that it is folly for the individual to assume authorship of action because action, in the relative sphere of life, is carried out by the three *guṇas* born of *Prakṛti* or Creative Intelligence. It is only when the individual does not comprehend the workings of the three *guṇas*, the play of the relative and its relationship to the absolute status of his own awareness, that he presumes he is the author of action. In addition, the motivation of desire and action can be understood differently in different states of consciousness. Acting upon a thought, in waking state consciousness, one is bound to a cycle of experience, impression, desire, action, and further experience, in a continuous cycle of cause and effect. As Maharishi points out:

> Experience results when the senses come into contact with their objects and an impression is left on the mind. The impulse of this new impression resonates with an impression of a similar past experience already present in the mind and associates itself with that impression. The coming together of the two gives rise to an impulse at the deepest level of consciousness, where the impressions of all experiences are stored. This impulse develops and, rising to the conscious level of the mind, becomes appreciated as a thought. This thought gaining the sympathy of the senses, creates a desire and stimulates the senses to action.[9]

Experience occurs when the senses engage objects of perception. An impression is then left on the mind. This new impression associates itself with some similar past experience already located in the storehouse of the mind. The collision of the two impressions, creates an impulse which, as it rises to the thinking level of the mind, is acknowledged as a thought; then, in concert with the senses, a new desire emerges and spurs one to action. In contrast, as Maharishi goes on to point out, when the mind is in unison with Being or pure consciousness, it becomes as if one with the Laws of Nature and desire arises as a result of the need of Nature rather than in response to "individual" thoughts:

> When the mind comes into full unison with Being, it gains the very status of Being and thus itself becomes the basis of all activity in nature. Natural laws begin to support the impulses of such a mind: it becomes as if one with all the laws of nature. The desire of such a mind is then the need of nature, or, to put it another way, the needs of nature are the motive of such activity. [10]

Desire, in this case, is really an expression of the needs of Nature; or, as Maharishi puts it, the needs of Nature are the motive of activity. According to Maharishi Vedic Science, when individual awareness is not based in the awareness of pure consciousness (unity or Saṁhitā), activity is governed by the cycle of desire, action, impression and further desire. [11] Stimulated through the collision of present experience and past impression, a thought arises, gains the sympathy of the senses and a desire is born—spurring one on to activity and experience which promotes the cycle, of desire, action and impression, once again.

Although this word "impression" seems analogous to Derrida's idea of trace or memory, in Maharishi Vedic Science it refers to the phenomenon where a particular experience registers in the subject's consciousness. Maharishi gives a detailed explanation of the mechanics by which an experience is registered in the mind and later recalled. He points out that when something is perceived through the senses, such as a beautiful rose, the impression of it is stored in the brain. This process is analogous to the mark made when a line is drawn on a stone; the line endures by virtue of the material nature of the stone; "when Being is not established in the mind, the impression made by the object is like the impression of a line cut into stone, difficult to erase."[12] This describes the situation when self-referral consciousness or Being is not established in the mind.

Likewise, when another experience creates a new impression it is stored along with other similar previous impressions—just as letters are sorted and stored in a post office. When this new impression collides with a past impression a thought emerges. [13] In this context, a memory in waking state consciousness can be understood as the emergence of a thought due to a collision of impressions within the mind's storehouse of impressions, triggered by experience.

As noted above, for the individual who is operating from the level of waking state consciousness only, activity is motivated by this cycle of impression, desire and action. In the case of the artist, it could be said that some past experience is governing the thought that arises in the mind spurring the desire to create. Stimulated in this way, art expresses some value of the artist's experience and level of consciousness but may not embody the full value of Natural Law, and therefore would not necessarily be universally purposeful or evolutionary in the absolute sense. From one perspective, the artist who is bound by the cycle of impression, desire and action, will naturally assume authorship of any action, even though it is, in effect, the three *guṇas* governed by *Prakṛti* that are responsible for the action. Conversely, the individual or artist who is living higher states of consciousness performs action due to the need of nature and the environment. This artist realizes that the universal, Cosmic value of Natural Law governs both action and the outcome of action. He or she is not bound by a localized, individual sense of self and does not assume authorship of action.

Maharishi further explains that the individual mind is the expression of pure consciousness as 'molded' by all the impressions of past experience. For this reason, it is important for the cycle of desire and action to be broken for the individual to be free of the binding influence of past impressions. Otherwise individual life, in the relative states of consciousness, is determined by past experience and impressions stored in the mind.[14] Just as the seed shapes the pattern of the tree, the impression of past experience shapes Being, or pure consciousness, into a specific pattern of the individual life-force. From the perspective of higher states of consciousness as described in Maharishi Vedic Science, an artist who is living Cosmic Consciousness is free from the binding influence of this cycle. The artist appreciates her own unbounded consciousness, the Self, as separate from activity.

Similarly, in God Consciousness, while the finer values of creation are appreciated, a separation is still perceived between the Self and the object or activity. Only in Brahman Consciousness does the artist perceive and know that the object and activity in the relative field are the play of his own self-referral consciousness. Despite the difference in the three states of Cosmic Consciousness, God Consciousness, and Unity or Brahman Consciousness, common to all three states is the realization that self-referral consciousness or Creative Intelligence (and not the localized, individual notion of ego or self) is the governor of activity. In the waking state of consciousness the individual identifies with the object of experience and the different values of experience in the relative field. Therefore, one's conception of the self is governed by relative factors. In higher states of consciousness the self is known and experienced as the Self—the unchanging, infinite field of pure consciousness, where the knower, known and process of knowing are unified. In Brahman Consciousness, the state of the unity is known to be the basis or ultimate reality of all differentiated values. The Self is unified with everything in creation. One experiences wholeness, or a supreme state of unity. This is not an intellectual notion but the ultimate reality on the level of experience.

Maharishi goes on to discuss why, in higher states of consciousness, impressions do not leave an indelible trace on the mind. He notes that when the individual is living Cosmic Consciousness, the impression of the object does not overshadow the mind. As he points out, when "Being is maintained, the impression of an object on the mind is just enough to give an experience. It is like the impression of a line drawn on water which is simultaneously erased."[15] In waking state consciousness impressions dominate; in Cosmic Consciousness the unbounded field of pure consciousness is dominant. In Cosmic Consciousness perception occurs but there is no permanent register of the effect of experience. Like a line drawn on water or air, there are no impressions deep within the mind to promote or bind the individual to the cycle of impression, desire and action.

Put another way, if bliss-consciousness is not permanently in the awareness, experiences gained through the senses leave deep impressions stored in the brain. When the experience is one of unbounded bliss, like the concentrated taste of honey on the tongue no other sweet taste can overshadow or compete with that concentrated flavor or bliss.[16] The value of bliss disallows "tastes" or experiences to overshadow the mind; "because the mind is full of the value of Being, and Being is in Its nature bliss-consciousness, impressions of a transitory experience naturally fail to make a deep impression on the mind."[17] Memory, in this context, can be understood as the trace of some deep impression on the mind.

Memory, Psychology and Art

Many contemporary artists deal with memory in their work. This activity can be seen as means of retrieving forgotten histories which contribute to individual and collective identity and a sense of self. This is particularly the case with art that deals with Diaspora, displacement and hybridity; King writes that, through the:

> The re-enactment of history is a significant gesture of retrieval; an opportunity to grapple with an unspeakable past. Memories, our own or others, can be hoarded and stashed in an effort to chronicle personal and compelling moments. Since memories are never anonymous, they contribute to the unfolding of personal and collective stories and narratives.
>
> Papers, photographs, fragments and images are keys to reclaiming distant memories. Many visual artists use records and material objects as documentation with which to resurrect their past experiences and those of their families. Often using literary means, visual artists who archive their past employ text as well as images in poetic and haunting ways. Quotation and citation form the kernel of this psychology of retrieval and act of preservation.[18]

As discussed in Part IV, histories can be understood in the context of the larger unfoldment of eternity in terms of *Yugas* and time. Eternity or infinity is the underlying nature of everyone's own consciousness.

Therefore, in complete enlightenment, where the individual enjoys *Jyotish Mati Pragya*, it is possible for all of the past, present and future to be known. Everything can be available to awareness. This is the most expanded understanding of the role of memory. In order to entertain eternity, this infinite value of memory, *Smṛti*, must be lively in one's awareness. As discussed in Part III, *Smṛti* means memory or awareness and is one aspect of the Veda and Vedic Literature. *Smṛti* is that value of pure wakefulness which does not forget its own unbounded, unified, holistic nature while engaged in activity (the "parts" of life). If the artist is living the full value of memory or *Smṛti,* the infinite, eternal value of awareness will dominate. The details of individual and collective history can be seen against the backdrop of his or her own infinite awareness. Nothing is lost or irretrievable. Furthermore, those values which are most life-supporting will be highlighted. In this situation, the Laws of Nature which structure family, a culture, history, tradition, language and sense of identity are spontaneously enlivened. Anything that was life-supporting, anything that was previously lost, can re-emerge.

As mentioned in Part IV, those traditions which are most life-supporting can be re-awakened and cultural integrity strengthened through the practice of the Transcendental Meditation and TM-Sidhi program. The practice of these technologies supports cultural difference and the heritage of different peoples while nourishing the underlying unity of them all. Thus, by enlivening pure consciousness—the source of the mind and culture—artists can effectively re-enliven their cultural heritage and tradition; they can "retrieve" or reawaken those foundation principles which structure culture, memory and heritage.

It is worth noting that the disciplines of modern psychology and psychoanalysis (that inform contemporary theory) do not necessarily acknowledge pure consciousness as the source of the mind. They do not take into account the potential for the individual to evolve to higher states of consciousness—despite mention of a possible unified self. Contemporary theory defines the self in terms of past events, linguistic and social determinants, and an unobtainable unified self.[19] Fitting the description of waking-state consciousness (with its the cycle of impression, thought , thought as memory, desire and action), the individual experiences changing notions of selfhood. On the other hand, Maharishi Vedic Science (encompassing Maharishi Vedic Psychology[20]) provides a new definition and understanding of past experience, our sense of self, identity and the development of consciousness.[21] The actual, unchanging nature of the self, in Maharishi's Vedic Psychology, is the infinite, unbounded field of pure consciousness—a field of infinite creativity, the Cosmic Self. On the ground of this Cosmic Self, the play of relative life—including the individual sense of ego, the functioning of the mind and subsequent action—can be appreciated.

With this understanding, any lack of knowledge of the mind's source, results in a restricted concept of memory. Indeed, memory, as understood by modern psychology, Maharishi points out, can actually be instrumental in weakening the mind.[22] For example, when psychology brings to the conscious mind the trauma of a person's past, "even for the purpose of enabling him to see the cause of his stress and suffering [it] is deplorable, for it directly helps to strengthen the impressions of a miserable past."[23] It can depress the person's consciousness in the present by overshadowing it with the memory of past events. Maharishi notes that it is actually a blessing that we normally forget the past, even though the present is a result of past experience, because, "the fact remains that the past represents less developed states of consciousness, and the present belongs to a more developed state. Therefore it is only a loss to overshadow the more evolved present with memories of the less developed past."[24] The past can be seen as instructive in the present when it inspires evolution; this is the purpose of history as discussed in Part IV. Ultimately, the nature of the self is not just the accretion of memories of events and emotions, but an infinite reservoir of intelligence and creativity.

In this context, Maharishi indicates fairly unequivocally that the "subjects of psycho-analysis [could] be saved from the unfortunate results of digging into the mud of a miserable past"[25] by practicing the Transcendental Meditation technique. Then consciousness can be developed and the individual mind strengthened by gaining experience of Transcendental bliss-consciousness, the home of all the Laws of Nature. Then the infinite value of memory—*Smṛti* or total wakefulness (memory of the self-referral unity at the basis of creation) is enlivened in individual awareness. From this level, the individual can create and do anything. The Self is infinite and all possibilities are lively.

Given this discussion, it is clear that authorship of action, creativity and memory can be understood differently in different states of consciousness. In terms of individual experience, the person who has expanded awareness, who knows the mechanics of how the manifest universe unfolds, realizes that his own self-referral, pure consciousness is the cause of activity but is a silent witness to it. He remains uninvolved, as it were. As Maharishi points out, even though the entire activity of life is generated from the silent level of pure consciousness, pure consciousness remains uninvolved with the creative process. When the individual is established in pure consciousness, he is established in the silent witnessing value. However, activity—the play of the relative—continues to unfold. The foundation of this experience can be located in the nature of consciousness itself; there are two values to consciousness—*Puruṣa* and *Prakṛti*, silence and dynamism. Both co-exist.

This provides a new perspective on the idea of individual authorship and individual expression. In the waking of state of consciousness, without the experience of pure consciousness or the Self, the individual relies on localized values of memory and external circumstances to define himself. The artist has access to limited creativity and can only express relative value in art. Maharishi Vedic Science presents a more detailed and profound understanding of individual authorship and action with respect to creativity. To some extent, it illuminates the critical postmodern argument that individual "originality" and "authorship" are concepts used to determine and inflate arbitrary "value" or "worth" in art.

However, according to postmodernists there can be no individual creative act which expresses Being. Following the proposition that writing (which does not include ideas or sounds that exist before the linguistic system) is more important than speech acts or individual expression, there is no original idea or thought which exists prior to writing or the system of language. With no ultimate origin or source, there is no pure originality. Everything already exists in a state of potentiality. Thus, language (i.e., cultural language or visual language as text) is more important than individual authorship.

Going back to the discussion of language in Parts III and VI, from the perspective of Maharishi Vedic Science, Vedic language—Veda and the Vedic Literature—is the unmanifest sound of self-referral consciousness knowing itself. Therefore, it is the basic sound and form of creation; sound corresponds to form and form has a sound. If the artist creates from this unmanifest level, the frequencies that structure creation are enlivened in the work of art. In this context, it would make sense to say that nothing exists outside of the system of language, since the language of the Veda is the structure, and structuring dynamics, of creation. According to Maharishi Vedic Science, Vedic language, the language of Nature, gives rise to all languages. It is the source or origin of all linguistic expression. With this understanding, the idea of something being "original" is valid. However, it can also be said to be a copy of what was in consciousness. This theme will be considered further in Chapter 20.

Pure Consciousness as the Origin of Thought

From the perspective of Maharishi Vedic Science, speech, linguistic utterances, writing, all artistic expressions, visual and material culture, have their source in the self-referral functioning of pure consciousness. This self-referral functioning of consciousness is the simplest form of human awareness, a universal field at the basis of the individual mind. Thoughts are expressed through the apparatus of the individual mind and arise as speech. Action is the outcome of the expression of consciousness from the universal source of the mind.

If the artist is to create universal art, it is crucial that the artist's awareness is established at that level of infinite, universal, pure consciousness—the silent source of all thoughts and action. All the manifest expressions of life spring from this field of *pure creativity* through the agency of Creative Intelligence. Therefore, pure intelligence can be thought of as the unmanifest origin of all manifestations and the artist's creative intelligence has its source in that universal field of existence. As Maharishi points out:

> Creative intelligence springs, like a banyan tree, from the center of its seed, in which seemingly there is only a hollowness. In that unmanifest center, that abstract area of the seed, lies the potentiality of the whole tree, the unexpressed source of all its expressions. The nature of that unmanifest potency is to create, and it remains the unmanifest centre of every creation. In it, creativity is inherent, latent, as yet unexpressed, and so we call it *pure* creativity. Pure creativity, pure intelligence is the *absolute* field of creative intelligence, the unmanifest origin of all its manifestations, in the same way that the apparently empty center in the banyan seed is the unmanifest origin of the leaves, flowers, fruit, and so on of the fully-grown banyan tree.[26]

Pure creativity, Maharishi explains, is that inherent, latent, unexpressed creativity at the unmanifest center of all manifestations. He goes on to point out that:

> A man's creative intelligence has its origin in that one absolute existence, and so everything may be cognized in its maximum creative potentiality because absolute existence is absolutely creative. We can say, too, that all relative expressions of creativity have their source in pure intelligence, since creative *intelligence* is both absolute and relative. The whole of individual and cosmic life is fundamentally creative because it goes on and on; it is progressive, evolutionary; and the whole of life is fundamentally intelligent because it proceeds systematically, containing its own order and unfolding in an overall orderly way, unifying individual purposes in a multi-purpose flow.[27]

Life is creative because it is progressive and evolutionary. Furthermore, the artist's creativity has its source in "absolute existence" which is "absolutely creative." Therefore, human intelligence has the ability to cognize that origin of life and of its own creativity which is infinitely progressive and evolutionary. As indicated in earlier chapters, it is through the alternation of rest and activity, meditation and action, that the source of creativity becomes established in awareness. One way in which Maharishi explains this is by pointing out that awareness is open to both ends of thought: i) the source of thought in absolute, pure consciousness (or silence), and ii) the outcome of thought in action. When one is fully awake, knowledge is always lively; ideas gain the support of comprehensive vision because there is increasing awareness of both ends of thought:

> He who is ever awake keeps knowledge alive however far he proceeds. By developing this alternation of rest and activity, awareness opens to a more comprehensive vision. By thus increasing awareness of both ends of thought we open a highway from silence to greater activity, and thereby greater access for the flow of Creative Intelligence. Like an army's lines of communication, it must be cleared for speedier interchange between base and battlefield, until every aspect of the battle gains the immediate benefit of the base—overall insight, abundant provisioning, and harmonious co-ordination for the more powerful activity.[28]

In this analogy, the lines of communication on the battlefield represent the flow of Creative Intelligence, without resistance, between the source of thought and its goal. In this sense, ideas or thoughts can be comprehended as the flow of Creative Intelligence—expressions of pure consciousness or pure creativity—where the individual, established in pure consciousness, has no stresses embedded within his physiology. These ideas, originating from the field of Natural Law, are cosmic in scope and arise as a direct response to the need of the time. As discussed earlier, such ideas are not just individual thoughts governed by past impressions. They serve the purpose of enhancing and enriching individual, social and cosmic life. These ideas and expressions are, therefore, simultaneously Cosmic and individual because the individual has risen to his Cosmic status. This does not mean that a social, cultural or historical value will not be present in the work of art, but that the absolute, unbounded, universal status of the work of art will allow it to transcend the boundaries of time and place, and be appreciated by anyone.

Returning to the idea of originality and authorship, from the perspective of Maharishi Vedic Science, in one sense, one could say that individuality is an expression of Veda. The individual physiology is structured out of Veda. Veda is the sound of impulses of consciousness giving rise to creation. Veda presents its own commentary on its own dynamics.

Veda is the language of Nature, the play of self-referral consciousness, the source of individual thought. The whole range of existence, thought and action, is contained in one syllable "A"—the totality of consciousness, the seed of all possible expressions of language and consciousness. Any idea is always already present in seed form as one of the infinite number of possibilities that exist within the continuum of pure consciousness. Fundamentally, any apparent "original idea," with attached authorship, if it is fully expressed from the level of self-referral consciousness, is the total expression of originality, all possibilities of the infinite, within finite boundaries.

When the author has attained the status of Cosmic Creator, "authorship" is no longer determined by localized individuality. Any uniqueness and originality is due to the need of the time and to the specific Laws of Nature which govern, and are expressed in, any action, phenomenon or form arising in a given situation and place. Uniqueness and originality is not an end in itself; it relates to the evolutionary unfoldment of Natural Law. Again, authorship and originality can be understood to be different in different states of consciousness.

In addition to this, Maharishi Vedic Science gives a detailed insight into the mechanics of thought, intuition, and the actual structure of a thought in its relationship to the object.

The Flow of Energy and Intelligence: The Mechanics of Thought and the Structure of the Object

The thinking mind, in Maharishi Vedic Science, is but one aspect of several hierarchical levels of the mind: 1) pure consciousness or the Self; 2) ego or individual self; 3) the intellect; 4) the thinking mind; 5) the senses; 6) the body and organs of action; and 7) the environment. Within this hierarchical structure, intuition is a subtle value of the intellect and is more fundamental than the active thinking level of the mind. Recalling the earlier discussion, postmodernists favor critical thought since intuition seems potentially mystifying. Modernists feel that intuition is a mental ability which is of particular significance in artistic expression. From the perspective of Maharishi Vedic Science, all levels of the mind are involved in creative expression. In experiencing and cognizing the creative mechanics of Nature (one's own self-referral consciousness) the creative process is systematic, orderly, and evolutionary. It involves the intellect, thought and action. Maharishi Vedic Science demystifies the creative process—revealing the connection between thought and its form.

While pure consciousness is beyond thought and expression (and is therefore ultimately "indescribable"), consciousness generates it own unmanifest commentary in the form of the language of the Veda. In this sense, pure consciousness is beyond language, but produces language. It is beyond thought but produces thought. It is beyond the object but creates the object. Maharishi points out that "thought is the first physical expression of the material structure of its object;"[29] this means that thought is the first subtle expression of the object on the level of the thinking mind. Thoughts can be understood as the expression of unmanifest sound that structures the psychophysiology. Thought, generated by Creative Intelligence registers on the level of the thinking mind. Creative Intelligence is that field of pure creativity, pure intelligence, which gives rise to all manifestations and which channels itself through all the senses, all the bodily movements and all thoughts and decisions.[30]

Maharishi goes on to explain that we can understand thought as lying in between two phases of Creative Intelligence, referred to earlier as absolute and relative:

> Every activity has its basis in thinking. The Empire State Building or the post office tower has its basis in the thought of its architect. One impulse of his thought started the whole train of building activity. Between the absolute and relative phase of creative intelligence there is thought. For a thought to arise and continue there must be energy present, and that energy must be directed in a systematic way for it to reach its aim.
>
> Creative Intelligence is one, but its creativity arises from its energy and its intelligence is directed by its thought which partakes of that energy. Creative intelligence is an impelling force of life by reason of its energy and intelligence. Although thought is an impulse of creative intelligence, in totality it is built of creative intelligence. Thought is the first *physical* expression of the material structure of its object—the concrete building is present in the architect's thought. Thought is an expression of Creative Intelligence woven with the threads of energy and intelligence.[31]

Here, Maharishi points out that a thought is built of Creative Intelligence; it is the subtle physical expression of the material structure of its object woven with the threads of energy and intelligence. Indeed, it is energy and intelligence, or the fluctuations of intelligence, which heard on the level of self-referral awareness as *Sūtras*—the Veda and the Vedic Literature. "Sutra" means "thread". In this sense, the object is made up of threads of intelligence. In Part III, in the discussion of the sounds of the Veda, Maharishi defined *Śruti* as the sounds of the Veda and the Vedic Literature; these threads of intelligence are the Devatā—the administrator of the universe—heard as sound on the level of self-referral consciousness. *Śruti* is Devatā in terms of "energy and intelligence at the same time, because its existence is on the level of self-referral consciousness."[32] Maharishi teaches that *Śruti* is the specific representative of total creativity, total intelligence, which is:

> One with the absolute status of total organizing power, which is unshakeable, immutable, unimpeachable. It is the sound of the self-referral level of intelligence—self-referral level of consciousness—the scintillating light of Creative Intelligence heard as sound—*Shruti.*[33]

The light of Creative Intelligence, on the self-referral level, is heard as sound or *Śruti.* As mentioned in Part III, *Śruti*, audible frequencies of sound, form the basis of material particles or *Tanmātrās*. These are measured by the five *Vṛttis* in terms of the five *Mahābhūtās* or elements—*Ākāsha*, *Vāyu*, *Agni*, *Jal*, and *Pṛthivi*. The value of intelligence, through the qualities of flow, friction, heat and crystallization, form the five elements and all of material existence.

In terms of our experience, it is worth noting that Maharishi also explains that, governed by Creative Intelligence, the flow of thoughts have direction and energy, direction and purpose:

> We know thoughts flow out because they have a purpose. Creative intelligence cannot be purposeless; it has a direction until its fulfillment is reached. Their flow derives from the energy, and the direction from the intelligence of creative intelligence. This impelling force of life is organized spontaneously, and its expressed value is joy in creation. The more a man's intelligence is displayed, the more joy comes, not only to him but also to the surroundings. In creation is the joyous display of life. And as we have experienced, it comes about increasingly by the alternation of silence and activity: rest and work, night and day. Absolute and relative. Creative intelligence, this impelling life force, is structured in this repeated cycle of stop and start.[34]

Thoughts are described here as directed by the impelling life force, Creative Intelligence—the evolutionary force of Natural Law. In the case of the artist or architect, for example, he may have a vision of a work of art or an entire building in his mind. Maharishi explains that "one impulse of thought" starts the whole train of building activity: design, planning, and construction.[35] This activity has its basis in thought. However, for that one thought to continue to be developed it must have energy and direction.

The creative impulse is generated from the infinite energy value of Creative Intelligence, while the intelligence value of Creative Intelligence gives direction to the thought. In this sense, Maharishi points out, the thought partakes of the energy of Creative Intelligence. The thought, he adds, is an impulse of Creative

Intelligence but it is, in actuality, "in totality," made up, or built, of Creative Intelligence. Thought is therefore both the expression of Creative Intelligence and the fabric of Creative Intelligence simultaneously.[36]

The Flow and Obstruction to Flow in the Cycle of Stop and Start

In the above description, the impelling life force is said to be structured in the repeated cycle of stop and start. This stop and start can be located in the dynamic of self-referral consciousness, in terms of the flow and obstruction of flow of intelligence. As discussed in Part III, the flow of intelligence is due to the wakeful quality of Ṛishi which "sees" by virtue of the dynamism of Devatā. The eternal continuum of *Kaivalya* or Saṁhitā is obstructed by Ṛishi; this obstruction to the flow of intelligence is called Chhandas.[37] The Chhandas value of consciousness, within the absolute singularity of Saṁhitā, obstructs the flow of the creative process; because the Ṛishi quality gets obstructed by Chhandas, there is flow and obstruction to flow. This "stop and start" is the self-referral feedback loop of consciousness where intelligence flows "forward" and "backward." This whole dynamic occurs within consciousness. The values of Ṛishi, Devatā and Chhandas and their elaboration into further differentiated values of Ṛishi, Devatā and Chhandas, as mentioned in previous chapters, can be understood to form the basic building blocks of creation. They constitute the different Laws of Nature, which take expression as different modes of activity, different modes of intelligence which structure creation.

The artist's thoughts and ideas, generated from the level of the Creative Intelligence, the universal language of the Veda, are expressions of Natural Law. Ultimately, the whole range of possible human thought and experience, as noted by Nader earlier, is expressed in the syllable "Ṛk", where "Ṛ" represents reverberating dynamism and "K" represents the point value of isolated moments of experience.[38] Perception involves the subject's focus of attention onto the object. In this process the unbounded consciousness or *Ātmā* of the subject converges onto its point value (an object) and identifies with it. Similarly when the mind entertains a thought, attention focuses on the thought and the unbounded awareness collapses to a point value. This dynamic of Ṛk operates at every point in creation.

In this context, it could be said that the fully developed artist can know, on the level of his own awareness, how his or her thoughts and ideas come about because the generation of thought is simply the unfoldment of self-referral consciousness—the collapse of unboundedness to its point value within wholeness, the infinite field of pure Creative Intelligence. The thought of the object and the object itself are woven with the threads of Creative Intelligence. They are created from, and made of, Creative Intelligence.

Without the experience of self-referral consciousness thoughts are as if disconnected from that field of energy and intelligence. Individual ideas do not fathom the structure of consciousness, and the individual does not know the source of his ideational process or the mechanics of perception in terms of the collapse of infinity to a point. Furthermore, obstacles can thwart the progress of idea realization.

In this respect, Maharishi Vedic Science provides a detailed account of the mechanics whereby the universal field of pure consciousness is found to be both the source of thought and the object. Here, thought and the levels of the mind have been discussed with respect to the creative process of Nature's functioning.

The process of creating art can be considered further in terms of the transference of an inner image or concept onto outer form or matter.

Forming a Picture Within Consciousness —Transporting it into Matter

According to Maharishi Vedic Science, there is one important prerequisite to successful creative expression: the artist must have clear, unimpeded consciousness in order to conceptualize or envision the work of art and then create it according to that inner vision. This principle implies that the artist knows, prior to creating her creation, the details of the work of art—the entire work of art is formed in consciousness and then translated into material form. In this respect, the creative process mirrors the creative mechanics of Nature. Again, there is an intimate relationship between consciousness, thought and the object.

As Maharishi explains, "the basic requirement of an artist is the skill of transporting consciousness onto matter, but the basis on which he could successfully create in this way is his own consciousness."[39]

In order to transport consciousness into matter the artist should have: firstly, a stress-free nervous system; secondly, that awareness which corresponds to the finest value of almost non-fluctuating Transcendental Consciousness; and thirdly, a complete vision of the work of art in her own consciousness, which is then transferred to paper, stone, wood (and digital media, film, etc.)— whatever material is appropriate.

The first point has already been discussed; in reference to the second Maharishi explains:

> The awareness of the artist has to correlate the finest area of almost non-fluctuating transcendental consciousness with the grosser areas of action. The inner has to be expressed into the outer.
>
> If there is co-ordination established between the inner and the outer, between the inner unmanifest finest feeling with the outermost gross expression, if there is a habit, a facility, of expressing the finest emotions to the gross without losing the grip of the finest, then the flow of the inner emotions into the outer expressions of art will be very perfect.[40]

The inner absolute value of consciousness is expressed through the artist's fine feelings or emotions. Maharishi points out that:

> The artist must be able to balance the finest inner emotions with the gross outer expressions; only then will they flow fruitfully from within and without. These expressions go out when they do not lose contact with the inner value of consciousness, and they go in when they do not lose the ability of performance in the gross. Only then is the definition of the artist satisfied.[41]

Maharishi, here, clarifies his definition of "artist". The definition of the artist is valid if the individual is able to balance finer inner emotions and outer gross expressions. The artist is that person who has the ability to harmonize the inner and outer values—to express the inner value of consciousness in material form. In order to achieve this goal the artist has to have a balanced, stress free heart and mind—working in synchrony, not in conflict. The most delicate values of heart and the most discriminating, systematic values of the mind work in tandem to express the deepest, universal value of pure consciousness in the work of art.

For this, Maharishi emphasizes the need for the artist to practice technologies of consciousness. The Transcendental Meditation technique is seen to be a requirement for any artist wishing to express universal value. However, the TM-Sidhi program is also an important technology of consciousness because it increases creativity by enlivening and activating Transcendental Consciousness through the performance of *Saṁyama*.

Saṁyama as discussed in Chapter 6, involves the three modes of awareness, *Dharaṇa* (steadiness of mind), *Dhyāna* (transcending), and *Samādhi* (pure, Transcendental Consciousness). Operating from this level of self-referral consciousness, the field of infinite correlation, the artist can achieve his or her goal in a spontaneous, effortless manner.

The Development of Artistic Sight

Ultimately, the artist can, through the development of higher states of consciousness gain "artistic sight." Maharishi defines artistic sight as the ability to perceive the inner divine or celestial value of life rather than just its surface expressions:

> Artistic sight is that sight which sees inside the surface expressions of life. So there is the art of seeing in which you see behind the surface expressions, the art of hearing in which you hear behind the words being spoken, and the art of touching in which you feel behind the touch, you feel behind the sight, you sense something there. No matter what you are hearing, you have your target on the divine level in every hearing. This is Vedic hearing. The formula that is sung about it is, *Bhadram karnebhih shrinuyama deva* [Rig Veda, 1.89.8; Nrisimhapurvatapaniya Upanishad, 1.1.]. Bhadram is divine, the finest value of

> hearing. However, the verse specifies that you hear through the ears, not that you just hear, but that you have divine hearing through the ears. This means that the gross is to be experienced in a lively state in terms of the subtle or the subtlest.
>
> When the ears have been trained to capture the divine value, when the divine value is there at the subtle level of every word, then you will be hearing the transcendental value of sound and the gross will not be the field of hearing. In such a state of consciousness, the subtle will always be enjoyed, and that will be the art of hearing. No matter what you hear, you will only hear that which nourishes the ears and the mind and the intellect and the ego. This means that you will only hear what is nourishing to life and you will unhear that which should not be heard.[42]

The TM-Sidhi program helps facilitate the development of this "artistic" perception because it promotes growth to higher states of consciousness. In higher states of consciousness the transcendental value of thought opens to view. In time, the transcendental value of the object is perceived. If having artistic sight means perceiving the deepest structure and reality of the object of perception, this faculty would seem important to any artist who seeks to embody the subtle value of creation in his or her work.

As noted in previous chapters, Maharishi describes the mechanics of creation as unfolding in terms of frequencies—the creation and dissolution of one sound into the next as recorded in the Veda and the Vedic Literature. In promoting higher states of consciousness, the TM-Sidhi program can enliven these mechanics in individual consciousness. The entire mechanics of the structuring of the Veda are enlivened in the human brain physiology through the TM-Sidhi program; in this way, the individual can begin to know what consciousness is and what it is made of.

In effect, the source of design is the artist's own consciousness. That is why, when the artist has balanced the extremes of inner silence and outer activity, the inner insight of the artist springing from the lively impulses of Creative Intelligence is translated into outer activity. The art work can be created in the same sequential manner as Nature creates, embodying the structure of self-referral consciousness. As Maharishi explains:

> Here is the source of design where insight can be easily depicted in outer activity. Without these extremes being balanced (innermost with outermost), creative intelligence suffers because it cannot create with the speed it should. This is what the Science of Creative Intelligence can give a man, by opening his awareness to these two extremes of deep silence and tremendous activity intelligently directed. We open our awareness to that most potent origin of thought in order to extend to the full its field of action.[43]

Without balance between inner and outer aspects of life, between silence and activity, absolute and relative, Creative Intelligence cannot flow unobstructed. Balance is created in the human physiology through the practice of the Transcendental Meditation technique and the TM-Sidhi program.

The Magnitude of the Artist's Skill: Fixing or Holding the Image Within Consciousness Over Time and Transferring it into Form

Successful art is the expression of bliss and always embodies the fullness of life in a spontaneous manner; the extent of the artist's skill (the degree to which he can achieve this result) depends upon the level of comprehension of the artist's consciousness. Using the example of Renaissance artist Michelangelo, Maharishi describes the artist's vision and skill:

> The magnitude of this skill depends upon the comprehension of the artist's consciousness; how much an artist can comprehend, on that will depend the skill of expression. You remember that the very great and beautiful artist Michelangelo said that he was merely scraping out or exposing the figure that already existed in the piece of marble. He saw the figure in the marble and what he did was scrape out the figure; he scratched out the undesirable deposits of the marble surrounding the figure. Where was that figure structured? Certainly it existed in the marble, but it was a copy of the structure on the consciousness of the artist. The artist comprehends or conceives of a figure—maybe a long face with a short nose—in his consciousness, and then he wants to depict it on marble, on paper, on clay, or on wood; he carves the wood, but he carves the wood to match the picture he contains in his awareness.
>
> To first comprehend in great detail, with great accuracy, and then keep that comprehension alive day after day, week after week, month after month, year after year, until the image has been completely portrayed on the wood or on the marble or on the paper or on the canvas—that is art. The artist enjoys having that figure in his awareness. And he has it permanently fixed in his awareness because, if he goes to the market and sees so many things in nature, so many faces and so many articles in creation on his way to the store and coming back, none of these impressions erase the beautiful model that he wants to create. This is 'knowledge is structured in consciousness' and 'knowledge is the basis of action'. All these strokes of the artist—all his movements, all his activity—move in accordance with what he holds on the level of his awareness. The ability to portray exactly that image is the skill of art, so the basis of the artist is wide and clearly detailed comprehension. This ability to comprehend precisely and retain that comprehension during the act of expressing it is the joy of the artist. What is happening when the artist has a figure in his consciousness and he tries to create it? He is expanding his consciousness, and expansion of awareness, being the

> nature of life, is a joy; it is a wave of life. The artist lives in the waves of expansion, in the waves of evolution, all the time in the waves of growth.[44]

Here Maharishi clearly delineates how the artist has a definite picture in his awareness and, holding onto that picture, maintains that figure on the level of his awareness over time until it has been successfully transported onto the stone or requisite medium. The picture is so lively on the level of the artist's awareness that he enjoys the expansion of the picture from the level of consciousness to the outer object. This process, in itself, is evolutionary for it involves setting up the goal in awareness and maintaining that vision amidst the daily, weekly, monthly, and yearly activities that can distract the mind. A true artist is not distracted by outside intrusions; the permanent feature of his inner vision is a delight to him. It certifies his ability to maintain broad comprehension, the unboundedness of awareness, along with boundaries and, furthermore, to channel his creativity in a specific direction without deviating from the goal.

With fully awake consciousness, Maharishi points out, the artist has absolute knowledge at his or her disposal. Nothing can swerve the artist off the path which leads to the achievement of the goal. With the structure of pure knowledge in awareness, action is supported by the infinite organizing power of Nature. There is no obstacle to creation. The source (the initial picture) and the goal (the art work) are the two ends of thought on the highway from silence to activity. This process occurs spontaneously. This is why Maharishi explains that great artists do not need to follow the rules that students are required to study:

> The whole thing is a very spontaneous activity. All those great artists of the past and the present, don't go by the laws that the students study, the laws of how to produce a piece of art. Spontaneously they express themselves, and their expressions constitute the laws or the principles of producing art. The most successful artists have displayed the most nourishing pieces of art, whether in literature of in any other field of art, in a very spontaneous manner. The more their performance is spontaneous, the more it brings the full value of life.[45]

Skillful activity for the great artist is spontaneous. The great artist knows the mechanics of her creative expression, but because she is established in pure consciousness, her art naturally constitutes the laws or principles of creating art. The artwork embodies the universal principles of creativity and art without effort or excogitation. Such a condition becomes possible when the artist is living higher states of consciousness.

As is described in Part I, Indian theorists state that traditional artists are expected to start with a preconceived design or pattern.[46] The work of art is defined as the perfect outer expression of an inner vision. *Citra*, which Indian theorists refer to the painting, picture or image, is an object which externalizes what was in *Chit*, referred to as consciousness. While the principle of expression is touched upon in Indian theory, the mechanics by which this phenomenon is achieved and developed systematically is made fully comprehensible through the principles of Maharishi Vedic Science. From the perspective of his Vedic Science, Maharishi explains that the ability to externalize what is on the level of *Chit* or consciousness can be developed—by growing toward higher states of consciousness through the practice of the Transcendental Meditation technique and TM-Sidhi program. Through this practice, the artist's consciousness is expanded. He develops the ability to maintain the image within consciousness over time and transport the image onto a specific medium. Connecting the inner universal value of consciousness to the outer expression, the expression of pure consciousness is facilitated.

In order for the artist to "mold consciousness in any shape" through the universal principles of creativity, his nervous system must be pure, that means, it must be free of stress. This is why the practice of the Transcendental Meditation technique is crucial:

> Here is the need for Transcendental Meditation in the life of an artist. In order to mold in his consciousness any shape, any detailed form including the fine fabrics of what he wants to create, he must be able to hold it in his awareness, not only with eyes closed but he is able to have that picture in his awareness even with his eyes open, with his hands moving, and with his sense of discrimination active.
>
> He will take red or yellow or this proportion, so many items pulsating in his consciousness, but he is able to hold onto the beautiful shape he wants to create on paper. For this it is necessary that his consciousness is pure and should not have any foreign material in it. For consciousness to be pure, one has to have stress-free nervous system.[47]

The prerequisite for the production of successful art, then, is the artist's stress-free nervous system. Only then, the artist can balance two levels—inner and outer. In the coming together of the two, the absolute within the relative, comes bliss or *Ānanda*.

The Expression of Bliss

Vibrating impulses, Maharishi explains, result from the union of the unchanging unmanifest and intelligence (*Sat* and *Chit*); these impulses are bliss—*Ānanda*. Through the creative process, Creative Intelligence fluctuates within itself and creates bliss. In fact, the three values of *Sat*, *Chit*, and *Ānanda* form the absolute character of Creative Intelligence. From this level of Creative Intelligence consciousness moves and when it moves it flows in the waves of bliss. When the artist is living in higher states of consciousness and her creative process follows Nature's mechanics, creation is the flow of bliss. Her art spontaneously embodies bliss. Bliss is the self-referral dynamic of consciousness unfolding, experienced by the individual living higher states of consciousness. As Maharishi explains

> There is a word in Sanskrit, *Sat Chit Ānanda*. *Sat* is that which never changes, *Chit* is intelligence, and *Ānanda* is bliss. This unmanifest, non-functioning value of Creative Intelligence is an eternal reality of life, and that is why it is called *Sat*—that which never changes. It is on this never-changing value of pure intelligence and pure existence that the whole universe and its phenomenal phases are structured. *Chit* is intelligence or consciousness. *Ānanda* is the result, bliss is what vibrates as a result of the union of *Sat* and *Chit*. When that unmanifest, never-changing value comes along with consciousness, that pure, unbounded, unmanifest existence and intelligence together bring about the third impulse of life, *Ānanda*, bliss. These three in their unmanifest value formulate the absolute nature of what we call Creative Intelligence. From the unmanifest value consciousness starts to move, and as it moves on, it moves in the waves of bliss.[48]

When the artist creates, he creates in waves of bliss because his creative process involves the creative mechanics of Nature's functioning. Maharishi further elaborates; "art is the expression of life" and such art involves more of the expression of bliss:

> This definition takes art to be Sat (which means eternal, non-changing, ever the same) Chit or consciousness, and Ānanda or bliss. There is bliss involved in the expression of anything, but more of it is involved in the expression of art. The very word "art" indicates such a blending of wholeness into parts, a blending of unboundedness into he boundaries. The expression of these three values—Sat Chit Ānanda or absolute bliss consciousness—is art.[49]

The expression of *Sat Chit Ānanda* is art. An artist, through the process of transporting consciousness onto matter, creates and enlivens bliss. The imagination of the artist, in waves of bliss, is translated into matter.

Creating Art Cultures the Physiology

While having a stress-free nervous system is a prerequisite to creating successful art, the creative process of art itself has a role in refining the nervous system. Maharishi points out that because the artist, in creating a work of art, comprehends the two inner and outer values, with this comprehension comes a corresponding change in the metabolic rate of the artist's physiology. The artist's metabolic rate decreases and breathing is softer; the artist becomes absorbed in this inward experience. For this reason, it is possible for the nervous system to release stress under these circumstances. This process of reducing the metabolic rate is not as profound or marked as that achieved through the practice of the Transcendental Meditation technique. It should be emphasized, therefore, that creative practice alone, as defined above, is not a substitute for meditation. However, it does have the effect of refining the physiology.

Artists are generally considered to be "cultured" people; literally speaking, by comprehending inner and outer values they "culture" their physiology to be less stressed; they have more integrated emotions, understanding, and imagination. As Maharishi points out:

> In creating a piece of art, the awareness of the artist is connecting two levels: a very deep level of feeling in which he imagines what he wants to create and the field of behavior in which he translates his inner feeling into outer performance. This comprehension of two values—inner subtle and outer gross—increases, and with this increase of comprehension, the metabolic rate goes down, the breath becomes finer. As a result, the whole system gets deep rest, and deep rest is very effective for the release of stress. When the artist is fully absorbed in his creation, when he develops the ability to hold onto his still, inner image and translate that image into the outer field of behavior, all aspects of his mind and intellect become very integrated. Through the integration of all aspects of mind, intellect, and ego, the metabolic rate goes down and the breath becomes softer. It's something like Transcendental Meditation, where one is deeply absorbed in the fullness of inner experience.
>
> What Transcendental Meditation brings to the situation, however, is much more complete and full, but a similar situation is available in the creation of a piece of art. That is why artists are, by nature, not stressed people; they enjoy life more, they radiate life more, and others feel as if being an artist is another of the many professions. But the profession of an artist is very different from other professions because this absorption in creation is the joy of the creator, and in that joy, the metabolic rate goes down and cruder emotions don't arise.
>
> In this state, only very fine emotions and great waves of love, beauty, and happiness arise. This is the life of an artist. The life of the artist has a great meaning in terms of release of stress during that kind of creative process which comprehends the gross value of life along with the inner, subtlest emotions. This must be the experience of every artist and more so of the most successful artists.[50]

In this description, Maharishi emphasizes that all aspects of the mind become very integrated in the creation of art—in the translation of the inner image into the outer field of behavior. In the integration of the mind—thinking mind, intellect, finer emotions and ego—the metabolic rate goes down and the breath becomes softer.

In his discussion of the artist and the creative process, Maharishi clearly distinguishes between "refined" emotions—such as love, an appreciation of beauty, and happiness—and "cruder" emotions. The artist is a person who displays finer emotions, because these emotions being more unifying in their character are more fundamental expressions of the field of bliss consciousness. In this respect, the universal human being is able to appreciate more refined emotions, and experience life as waves of bliss. He is able to express those delicate qualities of feeling in the work of art.

Creativity and Suffering

It is often thought that creativity and suffering go hand in hand. But does suffering really enhance creative work? Maharishi emphasizes that it is the increasing experience of happiness in the act of creation, leading to the ultimate goal of bliss, which motivates the artist. Because creativity and happiness go hand in hand, creativity and suffering necessarily oppose one another. Creativity is that underlying force of Natural Law or *Dharma* which creates the different forms and phenomena in the universe; it motivates human life. Maharishi explains that:

> Creativity is that impelling life-force which manifests in different forms, behaviors, and activities. From this definition we find that creativity is the blossoming of life; life as if dances through the waves of creativity—it is the dance of life, it is the laughter of life, it is the music of life. This being the reality of creativity, pain and suffering, if anything, are opposed to it. Creativity is progressive, it is evolutionary, it makes life blossom into greater or higher stages of development; it is the music of life through which life laughs, dances and progresses. Pain, on the other hand, is something that hampers existence. It threatens existence and brings discomfort to the state of existence. Pain and creativity do not seem therefore to have any common ground.[51]

Maharishi goes on to explain that while this is a fundamental principle, history has revealed that many suffering people have been creative. He analyses this phenomenon by indicating that any suffering person wants release from pain:

> It is very simple to see that any suffering man wants to escape from suffering; he wants to be out of suffering and for this he would do anything to come out of suffering. He would therefore start to do anything which would be pleasing to him in any way and to whatever degree.[52]

In painting, or in the composition of poetry, the individual finds solace, and in these moments of relief, he reduces some degree of pain on the level of his awareness. In forgetting pain and becoming absorbed in joy, life moves in a positive direction of creativity:

> In this increasing happiness, creativity blossoms because, as we have seen, life is by nature evolutionary; Creative Intelligence is evolutionary, such that at any moment of greater happiness, that evolutionary force overtakes life and produces something, and the next moment produces a little bit more, and so on. Thus, all works of art, and any work of creative value that anyone ever produced, were

> produced on the steps of increasing joyfulness and, in these acts of creativity, his life danced, amused itself, and evolved.[53]

The creative acts of individuals throughout history, even when committed by an artist who seemed to live a life of great hardship, are expressions of the inner Creative Intelligence of the creator and, as such, are steps in the direction of happiness. Maharishi asserts that suffering, because it is opposed to creativity, cannot contribute anything to the creative process:

> Suffering does not contribute to creativity. If suffering were to contribute to creativity, then more suffering would contribute to more creativity, and still more suffering would contribute to more creativity, and most suffering would contribute to most creativity. But in the state of most suffering, life becomes inert; it's a state of non-existence, inertia. That is zero Creative Intelligence, maybe even minus to the infinite value. Therefore, despite appearances, it's not suffering that should be seen as a means for development of Creative Intelligence.[54]

The experience of suffering is not a platform for the development of creativity; suffering in increasing degrees leads to non-existence or destruction of life, and is, therefore, by definition in opposition to creativity. If creative action increases bliss, what are the mechanics of this process?

Creative action, as the expression of Creative Intelligence, brings increasing happiness at each step of creative expression until finally the artist reaches a stage in his development where bliss—the supreme state of happiness—is permanent. Creativity and happiness are interdependent.

> A painter puts a brush, a writer writes a sentence. The absorption in the joy that he receives from that expression makes his mind more creative; he comprehends another expression, when he writes that, the joy of that next wave of comprehension of Creative Intelligence brings him some added joy, and this new wave of joy absorbs him.
>
> This absorption naturally widens his awareness; he comprehends another expression to enrich the previous expression. In this way, every stroke of Creative Intelligence is attractive, is charming, is joyful, and in this joy, life rejoices in creating another wave, probably higher than the previous. This is how the stream of creativity advances until it reaches the height of advancement in which the individual level of life has reached the universal level of life.[55]

In this state, where universal life is lived by the individual, the artist is able to create true art—art which expresses bliss and the fine levels of feeling now experienced.

Suffering is Opposed to Life

Since the history of life, as is recorded by many cultures, seems to be rife with the problems of war, disease and famine, it is accepted that life is normally a struggle. In this climate, even individuals who devote themselves to the pursuit of creativity have lived with pain and lack of fulfillment. This is why creativity and the life of an artist became synonymous with lack of social integration.[56]

The idea that suffering is natural to life has persisted because there has been no technology to alleviate problems. However, it is not necessary to sacrifice positivity and employ strain and suffering to be creative. Maharishi clearly points out that there is a vast range of positivity within relative degrees of happiness, and that even if one cannot go beyond infinite happiness it is not practical to go beyond zero happiness (suffering or negative happiness) because suffering is opposed to life.

> Relativity does not mean negativity. We can remain within the long, huge, wide range of positivity and be relatively happy, but we don't want to go beyond zero happiness; if we can't go beyond infinite happiness on one side then we definitely don't want to go beyond zero happiness. Suffering is beyond zero happiness, negative happiness.[57]

As Maharishi continues to explain

> Even remaining within the range of happiness life could be lived in many different ways. Even when every man on earth is using his full potential, all men would not be the same.
>
> Differences in taste and understanding remain because it is the differences that make the world, it is the difference that substantiates relative existence. In fact, the whole existence is relative in the manifest field of life. Therefore, one does not have to sacrifice the range of positivity in life and entertain negativity of life for any sense of creativity.[58]

Even when a person lives a completely fulfilled life in bliss consciousness, differences and different qualities of emotion are enjoyed—but nothing overshadows the experience of bliss. Differences, on the basis of unity, constitute the world and the variety of relative existence.

Moreover, in order for difference to flourish and to be expressed in art, it is not necessary to entertain negativity and suffering. There is a vast range of happiness, within the spectrum of relative degrees of positive experience, which can be expressed in art.

Art History is Based on an Incomplete Understanding of Creativity

As Maharishi points out, the history of art, with its accounts of great suffering artists, has been based on an incomplete understanding of the nature and mechanics of creativity:

> All this story of creativity and the statistics drawn from the lives of good writers, good painters, good sculptors, indeed all the geniuses in the world, were defective. Until now, the measuring balance for the increased Creative Intelligence was in a deplorable state, but now it will be on a very laudable level. When life is taken to be a struggle then the utilization of Creative Intelligence is limited to survival. But when life starts to be lived on a natural level of existence where the physical nervous system is natural, then the possibility is for a supernatural state of existence—we would want to call it very natural, the normal state of a human being—when that unbounded awareness is spontaneously lived for the maximum utilization of Creative Intelligence. Until now, we do accept that this has been the understanding of creativity derived from observing how geniuses in the past struggled and suffered in order to create, and that these works may have been enjoyed throughout the ages. But this does not establish a valid principle for the development of Creative Intelligence.[59]

Even though great art has apparently been created on the basis of suffering, according to Maharishi Vedic Science, the idea that suffering contributes to creativity is illogical. When life is a struggle, Creative Intelligence operates at the survival level—resisting any threat to life. However, this consumes energy; it does not allow for the infinite source of creativity to be effortlessly tapped and then spontaneously flow into action. In the case of the normal or natural functioning nervous system (which was thought in the past to be supernatural) the mind and body spontaneously function with least effort, with maximum success, and create bliss in the actor and his or her surroundings. Therefore, creativity thrives on happiness, not its opposite.

Creativity and Freedom

Maharishi adds one further point to the understanding of creativity, happiness and fulfillment. He explains that even an individual performing creative actions is limited when happiness is not present; he or she is further limited if not living the full value of pure consciousness. When we are happy or contented we are more able to apply our creativity because we feel free:

> There is the phenomenon of creation, individuals are constantly creating according to their abilities, but something is missing. Creation, in this sense, is more, we would say, on the outer level of life—it satisfies our environment, it

satisfies our physical, material needs, but it does not seem to bring fulfillment, even though every act of creation is so absorbing during one's activity.[60]

Maharishi continues to describe this experience:

> Every one of us, in our own experience, is aware of this simple phenomenon: when we are happy, no matter for what reason, our mind functions very clearly. The display of Creative Intelligence depends upon this inner feeling, upon whether that level of contentment is present or not. If contentment is there, we are free; if contentment is not there, we are not free. Apply this principle to the work of an architect. You say to him, 'build me a building' and he says 'fine'. If you give him the impression that he doesn't have to worry about the cost, you have automatically opened that awareness deep within him such that his imagination flies in all directions with greatest creativity. He doesn't mind which way he throws the tower, this way or that way, because he is not restricted. If you give him the impression that he can spend only one million dollars on this building, his mind gets restricted. If you give him the impression that only a hundred thousand dollars are available for such a project, more restrictions.
>
> Now if you tell him that you do want to build a building but you are still trying to raise the money, once he knows that there is no bank balance, he would try to think creatively but nothing would dawn in his awareness. Creativity is sealed within the envelope, it doesn't show its face because no building can be erected without money; there is a total restriction on creativity. Just this one, simple piece of information can block the whole mind of the greatest creative artist in the world; the architect's creativity would not come out because nothing can happen without money.[61]

With the experience of pure consciousness, the artist has access to the reservoir of infinite creativity. Like the analogy of architect who has no financial limitations, there are no restrictions to creativity. The artist is free. Freedom is the unbounded experience of pure consciousness—life in fulfillment. Freedom is that state where the individual is no longer bound by the cycle of experience, impression, desire, action and experience, discussed earlier; it is when the individual is no longer tossed about by circumstance but is living higher states of consciousness. In Maharishi Vedic Science, in this state one experiences freedom from boundaries or *Mokṣa.*[62] In this state, creativity is maximum.

The expression of this infinite value of Creative Intelligence depends upon the artist's inner state of consciousness—whether bliss is lively, whether there is the feeling that one is established in the inexhaustible reservoir of Creative Intelligence. Maximum creativity can only be expressed when individual awareness is saturated in bliss consciousness.

> When this bliss consciousness comes to the conscious level of the mind it leaves the conscious mind in fulfillment; this is the ultimate value of fulfillment. There are so many values of fulfillment in the relative, but the ultimate fulfillment we are aiming at is attained through the formula which allows maximum Creative Intelligence to function spontaneously.[63]

Going on to illustrate this principle, Maharishi continues with his analogy of the architect and infinite creativity:

> Just let the architect know that he doesn't have to think of money, immediately beautiful designs flash in his awareness. What we want, therefore, for every man in this progressive, scientific age is to give him the formula whereby in a very natural and simple way he could develop that inner fullness as quickly as possible. What we have seen is that inner fulfillment can be experienced through Transcendental Meditation.[64]

Returning to the discussion of the means through which this goal can be realized, Maharishi emphasizes the practice of his Transcendental Meditation technique. Through this technique the artist's mind can be infused with bliss consciousness, leaving the conscious mind in fulfillment. In that state of fulfillment creativity functions with no boundaries; immediately, beautiful designs flash in the awareness.

A Creator is More than Just a Viewer: System Verses Chance

During the creative process the artist creates in a systematic fashion. She transports the inner picture of her imagination onto the medium. Although spontaneous, this process is not accidental. Because the creative process itself is sequential and orderly and is crucial in the development of the artist's awareness, when art is governed by chance it does not help enliven the value of fine feeling leading to fulfillment. As Maharishi points out, when creativity is governed by chance the artist is really only a viewer—she does not know the mechanics of creation. In art theory, intuition, because it seems unfathomable and is subjective in nature, is associated with rare instances of inspiration and chance. Creativity and intuition cannot be methodically cultured. However, from the perspective of Maharishi Vedic Science, intuition (along with all levels of the mind—ego, intellect, mind, and the senses) can be systematically developed and utilized.

As stated previously, the artist who merely operates without knowing the mechanics of creation does not enliven the deepest value of Creative Intelligence; there is no connection between the universal, absolute source of creation and its relative expression. That fundamental level of creativity which actually inspires imagination and feeling is hidden. Working in this fashion, according to Maharishi Vedic Science, one is not an artist. Operating from a superficial level of the mind, the artist does not know what he is creating. In this instance, Maharishi explains, he is not really a creator:

> It should not be that they, like a modern artist, say, 'I don't know what I'm creating. I take the brush and do something here and there'. That is simply wasting time, because there is no connectedness between consciousness and the process of expression which will exemplify it. Any modern artist who says, 'I don't know what I am creating', just sits in the studio and acts and something comes out. That kind of accidental creation does not contribute to the enlivenment of his heart. In such a case, the gain to the artist is through the appreciation of what he has accidentally produced, so he is just a viewer. Whatever advantage a viewer gets, that's the advantage that the artist gets.[65]

Maharishi goes on to point out that when the artist's awareness remains on the surface level of thinking, his awareness is not involved in the mechanics of creation:

> When the artist's awareness remains on the surface level of thinking, his awareness is not involved in the mechanics through which awareness comes out. Such an artist is not involved in the process of creation; only the hands and eyes are involved, but the inner structuring, the awareness, is untouched by that procedure which structures the steps of manifestation. It is a very beautiful point. The awareness remains untouched. 'Untouched' means that the surface value of awareness touches the creative process but the deeper value of awareness remains completely uninvolved with the steps of manifestation. It remains uninvolved with the mechanics which structure the steps of manifestation.
>
> In this situation, creativity, as such, remains unenlivened. The deep core of creativity remains unenlivened, but the surface value of creation comes into play with the eyes and with the hand, but that level of creativity which inspires imagination and feeling remains out of sight. The wealth of the bank remains aloof, the coins which are available in the market are involved.[66]

When the deepest level of the artist's awareness remains untouched during the creative process, his awareness is not involved with steps which structure meaningful art. The deepest core of creativity is, as if, disconnected. In order to be truly creative, by this definition, (to be an artist and not simply a viewer) the artist must create from the deepest value of awareness, the deepest level of the mind, so that infinite creativity is enlivened.

While artists are commonly held to operate on the level of fine feeling and intuition, Maharishi explains that in any field of activity, whether it is on the level of the intellect, speech, thinking, emotions, or senses and action, the mechanics of creativity are always the same.[67] All levels of the mind should be infused with Creative Intelligence, in the mechanics of the creative process. In this regard,

Maharishi explains that in the teaching of art the student should become acquainted with the mechanics of expression by establishing his awareness on the level of pure consciousness, where complete knowledge is structured. From there consciousness unfolds the manifest work of art in a step-by-step manner. The mechanics which govern individual creative expression should follow the same mechanics by which creation is structured:

> What is most important is to get the student [of art] acquainted with the mechanics of expression and get the agency which structures the mechanics of progress of expression established in the awareness of the student so that any and every phase of his involvement—intellectual, emotional, mental, sensory—breathes in the value of that Creative Intelligence which is responsible for structuring the steps of unfoldment of expression.[68]

In this way, the artist (and the student of art) who is practicing the Transcendental Meditation technique and the TM-Sidhi program can begin to enliven the unmanifest through the steps of manifestation.

It is through the repeated cycle of meditation and artistic activity that the artist develops skill in action. Through the rest of meditation and then dynamic action, focused in a particular channel, the individual can finely hone any skill. In this way, by devoting oneself to one kind of activity, by expressing one's creativity through a specific channel, it is possible to improve and develop great skill. As Maharishi explains "any skill, improves through the application of Creative Intelligence in that field. For this reason, specialization has a very great contribution to make in the unfoldment of Creative Intelligence in increasing degrees."[69] When the artist practices the TM-Sidhi program his skill in action increases as he learns to operate from the field of self-referral consciousness. Developing skill in action, the artist becomes a universal human being, comprehending the detailed mechanics of the creative process, and applying creativity in all aspects of life.

According to the above discussion, in order to represent and embody the creative mechanics of Nature, the artist has to be established in pure consciousness, allowing pure consciousness to flow unimpeded into matter. The artist's pure consciousness, spontaneously expressed in material creation, then follows the dynamics of Nature's creativity—just as the Creator, through infinite Creative Intelligence, creates creation and resides within it.

20

UNIVERSAL ART AND ITS EFFECTS

Art, according to Maharishi Vedic Science, is the expression of the value of consciousness of the artist. Therefore, the art object can be said to be a copy of what is in the artist's consciousness; it is the outer expression of inner vision. When that vision is structured in the infinite value of Creative Intelligence, the art object contains the lively value of the originating life force. Such art is capable of bringing joy to the viewer and promoting the environment because it is generated from the level of infinite correlation. At this level everything is interconnected since it is an unmanifest level beyond space and time, permeating creation. Art "communicates" with everything from this level. A piece of art, then, can have universal significance and be appreciated over time if it embodies this universal value within its boundaries. Art that is universal embodies the absolute and the qualities of Creative Intelligence; it creates a positive feeling or a sense of upliftment in the viewer; it inspires the viewer and thrills the environment.

This view seems to revisit both traditional and modern understandings of art. But modernists had no systematic means through which such a value could be spontaneously embodied within the art object, although they assumed that art (specifically abstract art) could stir absolute emotions. From the perspective of Maharishi Vedic Science, it is possible to create art which has universal value, art which contains the field of all possibilities within the finite expression of performance or object. Universal art is art that can: 1) enliven Natural Law in the environment; 2) represent the culture and period of the artist but communicate to every generation; 3) lead the viewer toward the experience of unboundedness; and 4) allow the viewer to experience joy in the direction of bliss consciousness.

Infinity Within the Finite: A Unique Expression or Copy

Successful art—both universal and individual—is the profound and precise expression of life from the level of pure consciousness, the field of all possibilities, the simplest form of the artist's awareness. As Maharishi points out:

> Universal value is the defining quality of a successful piece of art and is created from the level of pure consciousness which is a field of all possibilities. It has universality, all possibilities, expressed within its individuality. Successful art is the profound and precise expression of life from the level of the simplest form of awareness. From this level, art is capable of displaying all possibilities. Expression from the level of the simplest form of awareness is 'artistic' expression because it has universality imbibed within its individual content.[1]

Successful art, here, is defined specifically as art which has universal value because it is created from the universal field of all possibilities. Therefore, universality can be expressed within its individuality. Successful art is the precise and profound expression of life from the artist's simplest form of awareness.

As Maharishi explains, "art, being expressive is innovative; it involves all the qualities of Creative Intelligence."[2] Like the Creator who creates "no two faces alike" each artistic expression is unique. However, in its creative expression, it could be said that the piece of art represents a "copy" of the structure of consciousness. The structure of consciousness, made up of frequencies or impulses of sound, unfolds in a specific sequential progression into form. Through the creative process, consciousness is manifested in form. In this sense, the artwork is original in that it has its own character; it expresses the originating force of Creative Intelligence. It also is a copy in that it is the outward expression of an inner reality. Art mirrors consciousness. Art is original and copy at the same time.

Maharishi indicates that art helps to enliven the universal character of pure consciousness in the viewer because it is an expression of consciousness; it thereby inspires evolution. Successful art, by this definition, is not just a relative expression of individual creativity, a political statement or intellectual speculation. As Maharishi states, in giving the ever-changing value of the relative the status of the non-changing, eternal value of the absolute, successful art appeals to every heart, whispers a message of love; as a wave or impulse of eternity, it gives life to the futile nature of the lifeless; "art gives more longevity to the ever-changing, futile nature of the lifeless; it gives the lifeless, which is changing and insignificant, the status of longevity":

> This is why it is called an art. It is a small piece within the boundaries of a few inches or a few feet, but the life it radiates speaks of that completeness of life, that unboundedness of Being. It straight away appeals to every heart.
>
> A piece of art that is capable of whispering the songs of life in eternity can clearly whisper a message of love and happiness and 'cheer-up' to every heart, to every mind, to every level of consciousness no matter what—dreaming or sleeping or waking or deep rest or depressed or whatever. A piece of art is just a wave of life, a wave of love, a wave of happiness, a wave of eternity.[3]

Clearly this definition narrows the range of what constitutes art. When the artwork has universal value, it nourishes the viewing public. It cheers up every heart and every mind, every state of consciousness—even if one is dreaming, sleeping, waking, enjoying deep rest, or depressed.

As Maharishi emphasizes, it nourishes the environment and people—no matter what state of consciousness they are experiencing—because it is generated from the level infinite correlation.[4]

Infinite Correlation: Creating an Effect in the Environment

As revealed in Maharishi Vedic Science, the field of pure consciousness is a field of infinite correlation. At this level every point is very well connected with every other point in creation. The artwork created from this level, propagates the same infinite quality; the infinite silence and infinite dynamism of self-referral consciousness is enlivened throughout the field. Such art enlivens the qualities of pure consciousness in everything—all aspects of the environment and surroundings. Referring to pure consciousness as the vacuum state (a term from physics) Maharishi has explained that meditators "use that vacuum state in our consciousness and enjoy the value of infinite correlation in the faint impulse of the heart."[5] The unifying value of infinite correlation registers on the fine level of feeling in human awareness. When the artist creates from this level the art object expresses this quality; "every stroke of art is most effective if it has the backing of faint feelings: the faint fluctuation of feeling, the faint fluctuation of the heart, gets itself beautifully expressed in the way we want, and at the same time it helps the environment."[6] That value of infinite correlation is the quality of consciousness which, when brought to the surface value of life, harmonizes all the differences.

Embodying this infinite correlation value, a work of art can communicate to everything in creation because the essential value of the object and subject are the same; that essential value is Transcendental Consciousness or the "vacuum state" underlying creation:

> The deepest value of all material is the vacuum state, and that state is a field of infinite correlation. The vacuum state, which is the essential value of any object, is our own Self, our own Transcendental Consciousness. They are both the same thing. That is why the melted heart of the artist is able to speak to the soul of the object.[7]

Maharishi continues:

> The more that the artist is able to whisper his breath into the piece of art he creates, the more the art is lively, the longer it will last, and the greater the joy it provides to the whole environment for all times. The ability to whisper from one's own Being is what enlivens every piece of art. This is because that value of infinite correlation, that unmanifest value, permeates every gross expression of creation. Every model that the artist makes, every performance that he performs, every poem that the poet creates, are the fluctuations of that value which is capable of unifying everything with everything else. That is what makes the artist enjoy his creation and what allows him to enjoy everything in creation. Because his inner feeling is so delicate, it is able to capture the depth of any material, any matter. That is why he is an artist, why he is able to give expression to life from within his own consciousness, from the level of infinite

> correlation. The artist is able to communicate with everything from the deepest level of his art, from the deepest level of the object he creates, because everything in the universe has that unmanifest value as its central constituent.[8]

Creating from the level of infinite correlation the artist can unify diverse elements and, through the object he has created, communicate the finest value of his feeling to everything in creation.

The artist is able to communicate with everything because everything in the universe has that unmanifest value as its central constituent. In this context, differences are not dissolved but are enjoyed for their uniqueness in the greater harmonizing panoply of life. Art, created from the level beyond space and time, communicates over time, unifies everything with everything else, and enlivens great joy in the environment and the viewer. This perspective seems to echo some of the ideas held by modernists and Indian theory (even though the two approaches are not commensurate). The difference is that, here, any understanding is founded on a detailed description of the nature and structuring dynamics of consciousness itself. A full explanation of consciousness, of how universal art can be created, and a technique to achieve this goal, are all contained within Maharishi Vedic Science. By presenting the complete disclosure of Nature's creative dynamics, on this basis art and theory can be enlightening.

Successful Art Displays Wholeness

In modern art and theory, artists speak of significant form associated with unified formal values. According to Maharishi Vedic Science, successful art, art which embodies the universal absolute, displays harmony and unity through wholeness. It is made of the same holistic value of self-referral consciousness. In this context, it could be said that the essential, unmanifest structure of the work of art is Veda, the holistic value of Natural Law, pure, self-referral consciousness or intelligence. Maharishi describes how life has two aspects: "a structural value and a value of intelligence. Intelligence makes the structure breathe"[9] and "the material structure and the display of Creative Intelligence through that structure have a union such that neither the structure nor the display of intelligence is visible." Both the structure and display of intelligence are unmanifest or "invisible."

As explained earlier, every grain in creation, every point in creation, contains the totality of Natural Law. Every grain in creation is a wholeness in its own right. The entire mechanics of self-referral consciousness function at every point in creation—as infinity collapses to a point and a point expands to infinity. All the details of this dynamic as described in Part III (the transformations from one to three and three in one, the quantification of consciousness through the unfoldment of sound and gaps in terms of the eight *Prakṛtis*, ten *Maṇḍalas*, the 40 aspects of the Vedic Literature and their divisions), are contained in the structure of the Constitution of the Universe, Ṛk Veda. This eternal structure of pure knowledge can be found in every grain of creation, every cell of the physiology, and in every point in the universe. It is an unmanifest structure, with its own unmanifest dynamic. The orderly, sequential unfoldment of Natural Law can be known in terms of the innumerable points or multiple unities that make up the universe and the grand unified wholeness of Brahman.

Following this line of thinking, it could be said that art that reflects this unity of diversity not only gives us a glimpse of the possibility of a unified self, but actually reflects the ultimate structure of the Self which otherwise is hidden by virtue of *Pragya-Aparadha*. *Pragya-Aparadha*, as mentioned in Chapter 14, is the mistake of the intellect (when the intellect is caught up with the value of diversity at the expense of its own fundamental nature—unity).[10] Successful or 'enlightened' art would enliven *Smṛti*, the value of memory within awareness—memory of the holistic, self-referral nature of consciousness, the value of unity underlying diversity. It can help to reveal the unmanifest mechanics of consciousness going on at the basis of creation by promoting the enlivenment of self-referral awareness, absolute knowledge. While this could be described as the central aim of art—to enliven the wholeness of self-referral consciousness, the Self—Maharishi also points out that "pieces of art speak of the evolution of that generation, of that century, of that nation,"[11] but because art is simultaneously universal and specific, it can tell "the story of life to generations in the eternity of time."[12] Art reveals the spirit of its time but also can speak beyond the confines of its era. As Maharishi notes:

> The value of art is that it has its boundaries, and within those boundaries it is the full expression of life, yet it tells the story of the beyond. It speaks in silence; it speaks of the unboundedness of life, and this is the glory of it. It is true that a piece of art has its value in the vision of the artist or in the vision of the beholder — that is a different story. But so far as the creation of the artist is concerned, spontaneously the piece of art will speak of the fullness of life. Moreover, that speech, that expression, will continue until eternity if the heart of the artist has been at the basis of the evolution of his piece of art. Every stroke of the artist supplies a stroke of love, a tender feeling of love on that hard stone. The hardness of the stone melts into the fine impulses of love, and that the piece radiates. Such a piece of art tells the story of life, and keeps on telling the story of life to generations in the eternity of time.[13]

Successful art displays universal value while also communicating the various 'subtexts' of relative meaning which speak for the age and culture in which the art was created. Both the specific value of art—speaking for its time—and the Transcendental value can be appreciated simultaneously. The work of art has a value for the artist and for the viewer, but if it is really universal, it will have value which endures over time—speaking to generations regardless of different historical periods or social contexts.

Regarding a work of art and its specific characteristics, in terms of style and context, these will be determined by several factors—such as the level of consciousness of the artist, the Laws of Nature that govern the artist's physiology, the geographic and climatic conditions of the environment, and the values etc., which promote his or her culture. The "kind" of artistic expression may be determined by the degree of Natural Law being lived by the artist but will also be influenced by the degree of Natural Law being lived by the collective consciousness of the people, since art speaks "of the evolution of that generation, of that century, of that nation."[14] However, from the perspective of Maharishi Vedic Science, art, music, speech, poetry—all of the arts—become artistic when the Transcendent is promoted through gross expression—the manifest expression of the object, image, word, or sound.

The Transcendent is pure consciousness, the simplest form of everyone's awareness, the source of thought, the foundation of material creation.

The Purpose of Art

As noted in Part I, according to Indian theory, there is no 'art for art's sake'. Any work of art or design must take into account the theme which is appropriate for the patron or spectator. Art is not for its own sake. In this sense, Indian theory departs from modern and postmodern theory and art practice. The purpose of art, as with any "work of the two hands," is directed to an end "over and beyond the fact of expression."[15]

The artist is expected to perform skillful action while working within a set of "grammatical guidelines," which are designed to create a desired outcome. Furthermore, there are different kinds of images with different purposes: *Murti* denotes an image of aesthetic value or beauty; the *Pratima*, or icon, is a presentation of being; a *Yantra*, like an icon, is not an aesthetic object concerned with beauty. In Maharishi Vedic Science, a *Yantra* is an instrument for aiding the development of consciousness (the instruments featured in Maharishi Vedic Observatory mentioned in Part III are *Yantras*). As is clear through the consideration of art in Part I, according to different theories, different activities can be grouped under the heading "art;" different artworks, visual culture or cultural production may take different forms having different relative functions. Not all theories agree on what constitutes art. In Maharishi Vedic Science, that which is defined as art will always serve the underlying purpose of promoting evolution. In Indian theory, as noted in Chapter 2, Pandit stresses the need for perfection of form in all cases of artistic expression. For, without certain formal principles of construction, it is thought that art lacks artistic content. The need for perfect or flawless form relates to the idea of appropriate form and materials to convey aesthetic response and meaning. If the artist does not follow the prescribed rules then the artwork will not achieve its goal—to create aesthetic emotion. This is why, the artist is expected not only to perform skillful action but to work within a set of guidelines when creating art.

As discussed in Part III, Maharishi Sthāpatya Veda also has precise guidelines. However, similar guidelines specifically for the creation of art have not been specifically outlined in Maharishi Vedic Science. Maharishi recommends that the artist's work room and home should be neat and orderly but successful art is not just a matter of working in a tidy studio; it is only possible by allowing the mind to be free of distracting, cloudy thinking. This is why Maharishi emphasizes the need for the practice of a technique—namely the Transcendental Meditation technique and the TM-Sidhi program—to promote clarity of mind. In Maharishi's discussion of art and the creative process, the emphasis is always placed on the development of the artist's consciousness and clear thinking. As discussed previously, orderly, clear thinking means achieving the desired goal without effort. Essentially, development of consciousness is a prerequisite to the spontaneous expression of universal value and the reflection of the orderly principles of Nature in art. However, art education should provide the individual with both theoretical knowledge and practical guidelines.

Maharishi states that "no matter what channel of art one becomes interested in, the teaching of art should provide a man with the theoretical knowledge and practical instructions, practical methods, through which the maximum value of himself is expressed." That maximum value of the artist is bliss consciousness—a "permanent happy mood."[16] This may sound light and airy, but is a profound point since living bliss consciousness means living total freedom and fulfillment. It is the foundation for creating any universal art and enlivening a life-supporting influence throughout the world. With respect to the role of art, as Maharishi indicates, "art is the graphic presentation of the imaginative capacity of the artist to make concrete his abstract imagination."[17] When that abstract imagination comprehends the totality of the infinite value of consciousness it can "move infinity." An awareness that can move infinity or "give concrete shape to infinity—an expression to it, an expressed value to it—will be the greatest achievement of an artist."[18] Then the artist will create a work of art which will "thrill" the atmosphere, thrill the environment.[19]

As discussed in Part III, Maharishi Sthāpatya Veda includes principles with respect to the design and construction of buildings, towns, and cities in accord with Natural Law. These principles, including right placement, right direction and right proportion, take into account the movement of the earth, sun and moon in relation to one another, and are universally applicable.

Art, technically comes under the umbrella of Sthāpatya Veda, since it is involved in the enrichment of the outer environment. It seems that specific guidelines for the creation of universal art, according to Maharishi Sthāpatya Veda, would create desired outcomes; however, the details of this field of knowledge have not yet been formally presented in Maharishi Vedic Science. Nader notes that in Maharishi Sthāpatya Veda, the *Āgamas* are identified as dealing with sculpture and on another level correspond to particular aspects of the physiology. Despite this, there is one key objective of art which has been articulated in Maharishi Vedic Science; art should to lead the viewer/participant toward the experience of unboundedness.

Leading the Viewer Toward Unboundedness

Art is not necessarily limited to any one value because it is capable of expressing all possibilities—by capturing universality within its individual content.[20] Ultimately, whatever the specifics, art should indicate "the direction of unboundedness, immortality, and bliss; if it inspires those values and indicates those qualities of pure consciousness, then it is considered to be successful art."[21] By inspiring the viewer and leading his or her thinking and perception toward pure consciousness, art facilitates the experience of deeper values of consciousness, and expands the awareness in the direction of those qualities of unboundedness, immortality, and bliss. Maharishi emphasizes that art assists the viewer by not only creating a positive emotional response, but by helping the emotions and the physiology of the viewer become more refined—more in the direction of higher states of consciousness. In higher states of consciousness the individual not only enjoys refined emotion but perfect health and life in accord with Natural Law. For example, emotional states have their correlate in the biochemical functioning of the body; higher seratonin levels indicate a greater sense of well-being and happiness. With this understanding, art's purpose can be seen to marry aesthetics and function. Taking the penultimate use-value of anything to be ability to promote evolution, aesthetic value and experience can be redefined and understood to be intimately bound to utility in the broadest sense.

Art can play a social role. As Maharishi notes, "different types of human performance become artistic when they bring fulfillment to both the individual and the society at the same time."[22] Art, therefore, not only inspires the viewer it influences and transforms the environment and collective consciousness. Expanding the definition of art to include the built environment, under the heading of Maharishi Sthāpatya Veda or *Vāstu Śastra*, art can be seen to create an environment which is life-supporting and beneficial on all levels.

Critics like Gablik[23] have already articulated the need for socially-responsible art. Her concern represents a real need for art to have value, appropriateness, and relative meaning in the public arena. In Maharishi Vedic Science, a new holistic and systematic approach to art and theory is emerging—based on complete knowledge of consciousness and its expression as the manifest universe. From this perspective, the artist who is practicing the Transcendental Meditation technique and TM-Sidhi program is a socially responsible human being. As the research on the effect of the collective practice of these technologies shows, such a person eliminates individual and collective stress and nourishes the environment by creating coherence and promoting increasing positive trends in society. In this sense, this artist may begin to create an influence in society through their work but, more importantly, on a daily basis they create a transformative effect through their practice of Maharishi's technologies of consciousness. Their most socially responsible art may be the ongoing performance of creating coherence through the practice of these programs.

In Enlivening Joy Art Promotes Freedom

Art, it seems, can influence not only a viewer/participant but also transform the environment as well. In their discussion of aesthetic response to art, Kuspit and Pandit a seek to clarify the nature of this process. As noted in Chapter 4, Kuspit describes the aesthetic response as one of non-attachment, whereas for Pandit it is a dispassionate feeling, rather than rational understanding, evoked through beauty in art. In Chapter 2, Pandit's view of *Rasa*—or "tasting"—was described as a flavor of emotion generated in response to the work of art. This "tasting" is the experience of bliss. *Rasa* is a unique feeling, unlike everyday feeling, which occurs when everyday feelings are "purified" (as Pandit maintained, in a non-religious, non-moral sense). Common feelings are purified through art and the imaginative faculty of the viewer—by means of aesthetic experience. Aesthetic experience, in turn, results in peace or *Śanta*; this is literally the tasting of one's own consciousness.

According to Maharishi, the word *Rasa* means "juice" or "essence" (as in the "juice of Rām" or "*Rām Ras*," the self-referral value of Rām which unfolds as the story of Rām in the Rāmāyana—the story of bliss).[24] In tasting *Rasa*, one "tastes" pure bliss consciousness. Bliss is the fluctuating value of pure consciousness; through *Rasa* bliss permeates the mind and the physiology. (*Rasa* is also described in Maharishi Āyur-Veda as a subtle aspect of the physiology). In a sense, it could be said that the individual who experiences bliss as a result of interacting with truly universal art enlivens Veda in his physiology. One outcome would may be improved health and well-being—more support of Nature. As mentioned in Part II, the experience of Transcendental Consciousness has been shown to have physiological correlates. Also these has been preliminary research conducted on the effect of reading the Vedic Literature, showing changes in brain wave functioning similar to that created during meditation.

If the work of art could help lead the viewer in direction of the experience of bliss consciousness, then it could be said to help promote the experience of the Self. The experience of the Self, when gained on a permanent basis, is known as freedom from boundaries or *Mokṣa.*[25] *Mokṣa*. is the state of freedom or bliss consciousness. In the state of *Mokṣa*., as noted in Chapter 19, there is no possibility for experience to leave a deep impression in the mind; one is free from the binding influences of the cycle of desire and action. This does not mean that the individual ceases to have desires or ceases to act, but that desires are born of the need of Nature and actions are performed from the level of Natural Law bringing further waves of bliss to the actor. While, according to Maharishi Vedic Science, the Transcendental Meditation and TM-Sidhi program are those technologies which systematically promote development of bliss consciousness, art can indicate a move in the direction of bliss. But even though the goal of art may be to evoke bliss, it is Maharishi's technologies of consciousness that provide the foundation for the systematic development of bliss consciousness, where, tasting *Rasa*, one tastes one's own pure consciousness.

Returning to Indian theory, with regard to the effectiveness of the artwork, the viewer's response is the test.[26] The evidence of *Rasa* in the work of art is revealed through the viewer's experience of *Rasa* in response to art. Taking the definition of *Rasa* outlined in Maharishi Vedic Science, the evidence of *Rasa* in the work of art would be evaluated in terms of the degree to which bliss is enlivened in the viewer. Despite this, as discussed later, according to Maharishi Vedic Science, it is the artist's consciousness and not the viewer's evaluation which determines the success of a work of art. One could say that when the art is successful—i.e. it is created by an artist's with fully developed consciousness—then bliss will be infused in art. Only this art can enliven bliss. The enlightened viewer would appreciate such art as fluctuations of bliss.

In Indian theory, as Pandit maintains, the artist must recreate for the viewer his or her own experience of *Pratibha* or creative energy. Since the role of art is to create an aesthetic response and not intellectual inquiry, art criticism is redundant. In Indian theory, the work of art is expected to stimulate a state of mind which is free from turmoil rather than intellectual discussion. In this sense, a glimpse of freedom, as Pandit defines it, is the purpose of art. Since effective art can produce this result, Indian theorists suggest that art has a moral purpose and helps create a settled state of mind in the viewer; art can transform life from drudgery to fulfillment. Art is, therefore, neither considered to be the individual expression of one human being's experience nor representative of the taste or values of an elite group of society but the expression of a "whole civilization."

While Maharishi explains that the most laudable aim of art is the promotion of evolution, it is clear that art (particularly as defined by modernist and postmodernists) cannot replace systematic technologies for developing consciousness—the Transcendental Meditation and TM-Sidhi techniques. These technologies are designed to develop higher states of consciousness in the individual and create coherence in the environment. Precisely because they are technologies of consciousness, they operate at the level of self-referral consciousness and are therefore most effective and powerful in promoting evolution and *Mokṣa*. However, art can enhance the outer environment, reflect the deeper structure of consciousness, contribute to the enlivenment of universal value in life and refine experience. In this sense, art cultures life toward more refined living—living higher states of consciousness. From this perspective, art can fulfill the aims of Indian theory and, in some instances, the aspirations of modernism. For example, some modern artists define art as that which speaks of a Classical, universal value which can create universal, aesthetic emotion;. Indian aesthetic theory, on the other hand, declares the role of art to be that of spiritual liberation and social advancement. But none of these goals are completely realizable without a systematic technology of consciousness and intellectual understanding of the universal nature and its expression in art. It is only through the development of individual and collective consciousness, through the practice of effective technologies, that artists and art can begin to reflect universal values and principles. Then, art can systematically have an evolutionary effect on the viewer and the environment, help to create universal emotion, promote knowledge, sustain difference on the ground of unity and foster spiritual liberation and social development.

With respect to collective consciousness and the spirit of the time, as discussed in Part IV, art can represent the value of collective consciousness of a culture at a particular time when it reflects the degree of Natural Law being lived by the people. "Pieces of art speak of the evolution of that generation, of that century, of that nation."[27] In this light, for universal art to be created and appreciated, the collective consciousness of the nation must be lively in the full value of Natural Law. This is possible when individuals are living 100 percent Natural Law in daily life—when there is harmony among nations, abundance, prosperity and perfect health in the life of the people. At such a time, art can be predicted to have universal value, capturing infinity within the finite boundaries of the art object, creating a life-supporting effect whether one sees it or not.

21

AESTHETIC VALUE AND AESTHETIC RESPONSE: LEADING THE VIEWER TOWARD BLISS AND A UNIFIED SELF

In a bold statement, Agnes Martin assumes that "true art" is responded to by all people in all cultures in the same way. Although, in Maharishi Vedic Science, successful art is defined as having an evolutionary and uplifting effect on the viewer regardless of cultural background, this does not necessarily imply that art will be responded to by all people in the same way.

Applying Wittgenstein's observations, Postmodernists hold that aesthetic judgment will always be different because no two people are alike; each person has their own specific response. This is the case for aesthetic judgment and any interpretation of art. According to Maharishi Vedic Science, knowledge is different in different states of consciousness. Therefore, a person's response is determined by their state of consciousness. If they are sleepy they will respond differently than if they are alert. Furthermore, in Cosmic Consciousness perception is different than in God Consciousness. As discussed previously, there are seven states of consciousness and each have their own sphere. Different interpretations can also be thought of in terms of the different degrees of Natural Law lived by different people and the various cultural influences determined by the Laws of Nature, geographic and climatic conditions of the land. Ultimately, without an experience of the transcendental value of the object, the full value of art or any object cannot be appreciated. The viewer can only interpret or appreciate art according to: his or her level of consciousness, the culturally-determined values and criteria of judgment, and the influence of the degree of Natural Law lively in society.

As discussed in Part II, even when the individual is established in pure consciousness, experience and knowledge are different in the different states of consciousness. Knowledge in the state of Cosmic Consciousness is different to knowledge in the state of God Consciousness which is different again to knowledge in the state of Brahman Consciousness. While each state of consciousness is different, higher states of consciousness contrast with the relative waking, dreaming and sleeping states; in the relative states there is no experience of absolute, unchanging knowledge.

As we have seen, Maharishi teaches that in higher states of consciousness knowledge is always based upon the absolute structure of unchanging, reliable knowledge—knowledge of the Self. Therefore, in higher states of consciousness, there is a stable reference point for aesthetic judgment—the field of Transcendental Consciousness, the absolute state of knowledge which is beyond relative determinants. A viewer of art who has fully developed consciousness can appreciate the transcendental, universal, absolute value of that expression, regardless of relative, culturally-specific parameters. If the viewer is awake to the infinite value of art he or she will be able to fully appreciate the unbounded nature of it.

Taking an example of the notion of levels of expression and comprehension further, in his description of speech, Maharishi points out that there four levels of expression: 1) a surface value of speech, the speech act itself, called *Vaikhari*, 2) a subtler level of speech—the level of thought—called *Madhyama*, 3) the subtlest value of speech called *Paśyanti*, and; 4) the Transcendental level of speech on the level of pure consciousness called *Para*—the level of bliss.[1] Although four levels of speech can be distinguished, all these can be comprehended, perceived and appreciated simultaneously. But only the speaker, writer and reader who is established on the level of *Para* perceives the entire range of speech and appreciates mechanics of bubbling bliss. If one is functioning only at the *Madhyama* level, the level of thought, the subtler *Paśyanti* level and the *Para* level remain obscured, unavailable.

Applying this same principle to art, the viewer can appreciate the work according to different levels of expression. Ultimately, when the artist and the viewer are both established in pure consciousness, both appreciate the full range and meaning of art. In this sense, Maharishi Vedic Science brings a new insight into the perspectives of modern and postmodern theories; it locates a "vertical" (levels from gross, to subtle, to transcendental) and "horizontal" reading, experience or appreciation of art. In the vertical structure, intuition is a subtle level of the mind.

As discussed in Chapter 1, according to modern theory aesthetic judgment is considered to be intuitive—both in the expression of art and in the process of scientific discovery[2]; qualities such as unity, symmetry, and orderliness determine aesthetic value in art and in science. In Maharishi Vedic Science, the field of pure subjectivity, pure consciousness, is held to be the source of intuition. The impulse of intuitive judgment arises from this deepest level of the mind. When the artist is functioning in accord with Natural Law his or her intuitive judgment is directed or governed from this universal level. Intuition connects the gross outer field and inner transcendental field of life.

With the understanding of Maharishi Vedic Science, various relative meanings can be appreciated along with the universal or absolute level of meaning on the level of Transcendental Consciousness when one is living higher states of consciousness. When the Transcendental value of an artwork is lively, then the viewer's response will be of increasing bliss, feelings of joy, inspiration, or simply "cheer up"—regardless of relative readings. On the level of self-referral consciousness all the relative differences are unified; the relative value and meaning are appreciated on the ground of universality.

The Evaluation of Art

Even though, as Wittgenstein and Bell suggest, different individuals react differently to a work of art, if the work of art really displays pure consciousness it will communicate "to every level of consciousness—no matter what."[3] Such art can radiate the value of pure consciousness whether one is in its presence or not. It mirrors consciousness; it has an orderly, harmonizing effect on the viewer and/or the environment. But what of the consciousness of the viewer?

It is possible for the spectator/participant to evaluate the consciousness of the artist by viewing his or her work. Maharishi indicates that in the perception of an art object a "wise" viewer can evaluate the level of consciousness of the artist who created it. As he explains, "in looking at a piece of art, if one is wise enough, one can see into the structure of the life of the artist and can evaluate the level of consciousness of the artist."[4] The wise viewer can perceive the degree of pure consciousness lively in any art.

This seems to put emphasis on the viewer's evaluation but, in fact, the artist's consciousness still determines the value of the work. As Maharishi indicates, "a stressed artist, full of stress, creates one kind of art. Once he begins to release the stresses he has accumulated, he still creates but there is a difference in the two creations."[5] As Maharishi adds, the two creations "speak of the value of the artist—both states of his awareness—at one point and at another."[6] So, even when one artist creates art, depending on the degree of stress lodged in his nervous system during the creative process, the resultant art will reflect the degree of stress, or, conversely, the degree of pure consciousness, he is living. The less stressed an artist is, the more pure consciousness will be expressed in his creation. With this understanding, the enlightened viewer can appreciate the entire range and structure of the different levels of the work of art.

If the work of art has been created by an enlightened, universal artist, the enlightened viewer will appreciate all the mechanics of creation which have been involved in the creative process. In this context, what is the significance of beauty?

Art, Beauty and Knowledge

Many philosophers and artists have pondered the value of beauty. As discussed in Part I, Agnes Martin describes beauty as the mystery of life and a condition of the mind called perfection. With the insights of Maharishi Vedic Science, beauty can be understood as the embodiment of pure consciousness in form. Beauty, then, would be a universal value—not defined by a relative set of criteria or prescribed, arbitrary preferences governed by the tastes of an elite group. Beauty is the outward expression of pure consciousness in form.

In this sense, a "beautiful" artwork has the ability to radiate pure consciousness, create a life-supporting influence on the environment, and inspire bliss. Beauty would be associated with the experience of bliss. From another perspective, when the individual is living unity consciousness, bliss consciousness is perceived in the object; the Transcendental level of bliss consciousness is appreciated in everything. In this sense, the object can be said to be beautiful because it is seen as the reality of one's own reverberating bliss consciousness. The perception and experience of the object indicates the nature of bliss itself—the source of creation, the self-referral reality of the subject's own consciousness. Beauty, understood in this light, can be lively in art. The work of art which is "beautiful" also has a role in promoting the consciousness of the viewer and uplifting the environment. As with the discussion of relative and absolute knowledge and different states of consciousness mentioned above, beauty will be defined differently according to the state of consciousness of the subject. One could say that only in higher states of consciousness can the Transcendental value of beauty be appreciated; then an unchanging basis for the appreciation of beauty established. The basis of aesthetic emotion is bliss. Beauty helps enliven bliss and mirrors one's own unified, self-referral consciousness as the subtle values of the object. In this sense, beauty would create or reflect a holistic sense of self, indicating the possibility of unifying apparently separate or contradictory elements.

While Martin claims that all positive art is about beauty and any other art is about the lack of happiness, Maharishi goes further by explaining that art as is not just that which creates happiness or the feeling of "cheer up" but it also promotes evolution: Anything else is not art. As noted in Chapter 3, in contrast to Martin's ideas about beauty and the aesthetic value of art, conceptual artist, Joseph Kosuth suggests that "beauty," is merely an arbitrary value of taste that does not form culture or shape consciousness. He defines art as a language game which, unable to express the "unsayable," points to the absence of presence. With the understanding of Maharishi Vedic Science, art—embodying the eternal presence of pure consciousness—is uplifting because it indicates the direction of increasing values of joy, toward the source of happiness, pure bliss consciousness. It promotes evolution, the goal of which is enlightenment—life in freedom and fulfillment. Therefore, beauty and bliss have a role in promoting freedom. Art can capture the unsayable, the indescribable infinite, absolute, within the finite value of an object/expression/performance. It can embody pure knowledge.

As Maharishi emphasizes, the purpose of art is to take the viewer, through the means of one sense, to unboundedness. The value of unboundedness is eventually seen by the viewer as his own Self; in this way, "the unfoldment of the Self in greater degrees is the purpose of art."[7] The Self is the structure of absolute, pure knowledge. In unfolding the Self, art can unfold absolute knowledge—knowledge of the Self as the unified value of Saṁhitā. The field of unboundedness, experienced as the state of pure consciousness or the Self, is a field of all possibilities. Art, if it is an expression of the Self, contains all possibilities. It is all-inclusive in its range. It's success is in expressing "universality imbibed within its individual content."[8]

The Artist's Consciousness, not the Viewer's Assessments, Create Universal Art

With respect to aesthetic judgment, Maharishi emphasizes that "it is the property of the generator," the consciousness of the artist that initially set it forth, and not the "people in this or that generation" that makes a piece of music or a work of art last.[9] The quality of the artist's consciousness, not the criticisms and commentaries of other people, determines the universal value of a work of art. This perspective clearly puts the artist back in center stage—not just any artist, but that artist who is able to create from the resistance-free level of consciousness. As Maharishi indicates, the value of art or a piece of music, for example, is "in that beautiful, pure, resistance-free level of consciousness where impulses initially flowed."[10]

Maharishi also explains that stress and strain in the nervous system of the viewer hampers the appreciation of art. The appreciation of art "has been dim in the present generation due to the domination of stress and strain," but art still wishes to thrive and glorify life on all levels.[11] In this sense, the appreciation of art by the people may wane due to the predominance of stress and strain. It is difficult to appreciate the subtle values of art or beauty when life is overshadowed by suffering and struggle. As Kuspit states, in recent times art no longer speaks of universals and the artist is no longer an exemplary human being because in art "the dregs of the human voice are visible, not its substance."[12] Is it the "stress and strain" of life that has diminished the desire to speak of universals? In a call for change, Kuspit wants art to:

1) speak with a universal voice and not just exist for itself;

2) articulate what seems impossible but is necessary to articulate;

3) spontaneously articulate that which one feels one "naturally" knows but cannot articulate for oneself;

4) speak to people from the inside, from their innermost being, grasp the inner value of life and express it better than one could oneself;

5) articulate people's desire and reality more efficaciously than they could; and

6) give collective and individual desire and reality special human value and respect. He wants art to promote the sense of a possible unified sense of self.[13] Successful art, as defined by Maharishi Vedic Science, can achieve these goals because it speaks from the level of universal, absolute, pure consciousness. It articulates the unbounded nature of that field of all possibilities, which, as discussed earlier, is ultimately the person's own Self—their own unified state of Saṁhitā or inner Being. Successful art, therefore, naturally expresses the inner value of life, from the inside of the universally human; it grasps and expresses the inner value of life, which is often hidden yet so intimate to ourselves. Pure consciousness is the field of infinite correlation which supports individual and collective life; art which is generated from this level gives individual and collective

life the dignity of its own nature—the supreme dignity of the absolute which supports all life. In this way, art can help fulfill man's spiritual needs, even, as Kosuth puts it, "after the end of the age of philosophy and religion."[14]

Lack of Universal Art Results From Lack of Pure Consciousness

The reluctance or inability of artists to express the universally human in art, has been said to stem from materialism[15] and the fragmentary nature of cultural identity where there is no common knowledge or overarching world-view.[16] These observations are revealing; they show a penetrating insight in the state of art, theory and culture. However, the lack of universal value in art, as discussed in Part IV, stems from a deeper problem: the lack of pure consciousness on both individual and collective levels.

On the social level—without the strength of an integrated culture where life is lived in accord with Natural Law—cultural integrity is compromised, nations are plagued by natural disasters, and society is weakened by poor administration in government. Traditions which help structure the evolutionary direction of life are dismantled. Individuals of different political groups or different interests naturally seek to satisfy their needs but often at the expense of others' interests. Some artists have attempted to address these issues in an effort to change consciousness.[17] But, in order to re-establish balance in life, Maharishi emphasizes that it is necessary to begin to function from the level of Natural Law or *Dharma.* Through the collective practice of the Transcendental Meditation technique and TM-Sidhi program the individual and the nation gain the support of Natural Law; the Laws of Nature which govern culture are enlivened. With strengthened cultural integrity art can more effectively serve an evolutionary purpose.

As considered previously, Maharishi teaches that when art is universal, it speaks from the inside—from the level of pure consciousness, the individual's own simplest form of awareness. It speaks from the innermost being of the individual and articulates more completely, in a seemingly spontaneous and effortless way, the deepest reality of life. Art, then, articulates that which, as Kuspit puts it, seems to be "on the tip of the tongue" but seems inexpressible; it articulates that value of life which one knows intrinsically but is not able to articulate. Art which can embody universal value does not "simply address people from the outside," it speaks to one's inner Being and gives significance since it then conveys "special human value" and "social respect." Such art, in voicing the innermost, universal value of human life, is able to speak cross-culturally while being culturally specific. It also can help individuals develop "cognitive mapping"—defining a sense of place in a global system. The enlightened individual not only knows her place within the localized system or arena of her community, her country and nation, but comprehends the significance of her place within the cosmos. Her awareness, established in the infinite, absolute field of pure consciousness, knows the full range of existence from its unmanifest value to its manifest expressions. Such an individual is not "at sea" or without a clear sense of identity and purpose. She is a universal human being who can act as an individual in the world to further universal concerns. Every action is spontaneously supported by Natural Law, nourishing all levels of life.

Artistic Performance Displays the Glory of the Whole Environment

Artistic performance or aesthetic value in art can be said to be both utilitarian and aesthetically significant. It is useful and beautiful. By leading one in the direction of unboundedness, immortality and bliss, aesthetic value in art has a definite practical purpose. In order to achieve this the artist must be able to act "artistically"—he or she must demonstrate artistic performance. Artistic performance is most effective when the artist is totally absorbed in that performance. The full value of the consciousness of the artist must be absorbed in the process of creating art and then it will be enjoyed more fully by the people. As Maharishi points out, "absorption in our own creative display keeps the audience absorbed in it."[18] This means that the mechanics of creation must be lively in the artist's awareness at each point in the unfoldment of the creative process.

When the full value of the heart (which can be understood as the spontaneous expression of bliss from the level of pure consciousness) is expressed in the work of art there is absorption in the creative process. This absorption in the creative display and the consequent full expression of bliss is communicated to all the "hearts viewing" the artist[19] and his creation. It is for this reason that Maharishi states, "the best way to bless the world from our art is to gain effectiveness in operating from within our own unmanifest Self."[20] Ultimately, all performance should be from this level. When all performance is "absolutely artistic" it displays the maximum value or "glory" of the artist while incorporating "the glory of the whole environment."[21] It can be argued that, when all performance is artistic, it has aesthetic value. Maharishi points out that when the artist creates waves of bliss in his own life then the creation of art is more fulfilling to the artist and more appealing to the viewer. But the artist's activity must be fully spontaneous, fully in accord with all the Laws of Nature, because "it is only the laws of nature that connect the deepest experience of life with the outermost experience of life."[22] Aesthetic value can only be imparted to the work of art in a spontaneous manner—when the artist is living in accord with Natural Law. Maharishi explains, to aid the development of life toward bliss, increased positivity, balance, harmony, fulfillment and freedom, spontaneity has to be developed in a purposeful way.

The Laws of Nature facilitate connectedness between the Transcendental field of life and the gross level of activity; the Laws of Nature allow the subsequent spontaneity of action from the field of Natural Law:

> This connectedness, this eternal, infinite connectedness between the transcendental finest and the outermost gross, belongs to the spontaneity of the evolutionary nature of all the laws. Only when we function from the finest level of feeling can we successfully and purposefully perform from that spontaneous level. Purposeful spontaneity develops transcending and coming back to action through the practice of Transcendental Meditation is the basis for the most successful expressions; these types of expressions constitute the glorious field of art.[23]

Spontaneity of performance, as discussed in Part II, is demonstrated in the TM-Sidhi Yogic Flying technique when the individual functions from the self-referral level of consciousness and the body lifts up in the air. This phenomenon creates a positive experience and influence for the practitioner, for the environment and the entire universe. It is all-purposeful activity.

The deepest level of Natural Law is all-purposeful. The level of the Constitution of the Universe structures and administers the entire cosmos. By functioning from this level the artist naturally acts from the switchboard of Nature; then any activity is nourishing, purposeful and harmonizing. Art created from this level is holistic. It is well connected with everything else in the universe because it is created from the level of Transcendental Consciousness "that field of infinite correlation which connects everything with everything else;" this, Maharishi adds, "is the most artistic place in the field of creation."[24]

Aesthetic Disinterestedness and Hyperalertness

In making a distinction between an object which stimulates a psychic or spiritual response and one that creates a sensory or physical response in the viewer, the field of aesthetics attempts to define the effect of art as beyond sensual gratification. In modern theory, the aesthetic attitude is associated with spiritual experience or transcendence. Critics like Kuspit seem to concur with modern theorists like Bell on this issue, suggesting that art has the ability to evoke "aesthetic disinterestedness" through its unified wholeness—a balance of formal forces which create in the viewer a possible unified sense of self.[25]

Kuspit mentions that art can create the feeling of a new sense of self by evoking a "hyperalertness" to the work. This hyperalertness is indifferent to narrative, intellectual meanings or iconographic concerns. It is an experience which goes beyond the relative meaning of the work. However, unlike modernists, Kuspit holds that the new sense of self that is glimpsed, imagined, felt, or speculatively posited, is not a "transcendental illusion" of selfhood but a "real possibility" of achieving a new sense of self. According to Kuspit, a unified self is an unrealistic, unrealizable notion. Kuspit's analysis, varies from that of with Maharishi Vedic Science in several ways. Firstly, aesthetic disinterestedness in response to art, which he compares to the Buddhist definition of non-attachment, does not involve the senses. In Maharishi Vedic Science all the different levels of the mind are engaged in the experience of art, leading the viewer toward pure consciousness. While Transcendental Consciousness is a spontaneous state of "non-attachment" since it is beyond relative experience and the field of the senses, non-attachment is not simply an intellectual phenomenon, as such; it occurs through a refinement in the functioning of the mind and physiology through the practice of the Transcendental Meditation technique, as discussed in Part II.

Furthermore, in higher states of consciousness—Cosmic Consciousness, God Consciousness and Unity Consciousness—the experience of Transcendental Consciousness or the Self is naturally maintained along with activity in the realm of the senses. In Cosmic Consciousness and God Consciousness there is a separation between the Self and activity. However, in Unity Consciousness this separation dissolves into unity and everything is seen in terms of the Self; everything is intimate to oneself. Redefined, aesthetic disinterestedness could involve an experience in any of the higher states of consciousness. The idea of an experience of non-attachment is valid from the perspective of Cosmic Consciousness and God Consciousness, because, as Maharishi points out, the absolute, non-changing Transcendental field of consciousness always remains uninvolved with action; the self has expanded to the Cosmic status of the Self, the unbounded field of Transcendental Consciousness, but action remains in the field of the ever-changing relative—governed by *Prakṛti* and carried out by the three *Guṇas*.[26] In unity or Brahman Consciousness, the object and all phenomena are perceived as fluctuations of the Self, pure, self-referral, bliss consciousness. The separation between subject and object has been unified.

Aesthetic disinterestedness, obviously, relates to experience in response to art. However, it could be redefined as relating to experience in higher states of consciousness when the artist and viewer are enlightened. In enlightenment, the individual enjoys non-attachment to action and its fruits and experiences bliss. In this sense, aesthetic disinterestedness may need to be severally described—taking into account different states of consciousness.

Secondly, Kuspit's "hyperalertness" is not based on the experience of pure consciousness, or the fully awake value of Saṁhitā, which is the experience and reality of the Transcendent. Transcendental Consciousness is the state of total wakefulness, 100 percent wakefulness, which in Cosmic Consciousness permanently underlies dreaming, sleeping and waking states of consciousness. In Maharishi Vedic Science, pure consciousness has the property of being a non-involved silent witness—*Puruṣa,* to its own dynamic creativity, *Prakṛti.* Pure consciousness, thus, remains uninvolved in, and yet awake to, the creative process while generating from within itself the entire creative expression of the universe. Since human awareness is in its basic state pure wakefulness, it is possible for the human mind to experience non-involvement and detachment while being completely wide awake within itself. If hyperalertness were to be understood as a fleeting experience of the state of Transcendental Consciousness this would imply that hyperalertness is a flavor of a transcendental selfhood. But Kuspit emphasizes that transcendental selfhood is not a possibility of human experience. Therefore, hyperalertness as defined by Kuspit is not a glimpse of a permanent, transcendental phenomenon, and should not be confused with the idea of fully awake consciousness as described by Maharishi Vedic Science.

Thirdly, the self, conceived of by virtue of Kuspit's hyperalertness—which he says denotes "a real possibility of achieving a new sense of self" rather than a "transcendental illusion"—is a relative concept of self unlike the Cosmic Self identified in Maharishi Vedic Science. The Self, according to Maharishi Vedic Science, is a permanent Reality which exists whether one knows it or not. The "illusion" lies in identifying oneself with the localized, different values of self (as with the assumption of authorship of action in the endless cycle of impression, desire and action) which constantly change during our common experience. The experience of Transcendental Consciousness is not a 'transcendental illusion' of selfhood; Transcendental Consciousness is the same universal, eternal reality experienced and recorded over time by individuals of different cultures in various scriptures and texts. This transcendental Self can be experienced and verified by any individual in any age through the practice of Maharishi's technologies of consciousness.

As noted in Part IV, when experience of the transcendent is absent from life intellectual conceptions spring up to describe this level. However, intellectual pursuit is not an effective technology for developing experience of the Transcendent. This field of pure subjectivity can only be verified on its own terms. Hence, Maharishi emphasizes the importance of gaining *experience*, along with knowledge, of self-referral consciousness. Self-referral consciousness is expressed as Veda; the Veda, as noted in Part III, exclaims that even its books (the record of the impulses of consciousness) are of little value to the person who has no experience of Transcendental Consciousness. Similarly, intellectual concepts about a Transcendental selfhood are of little value without experience of a Transcendental reality.

As Maharishi teaches, in promoting growth to higher states of consciousness, ideal art can assist in enlivening development toward the full value of the Self—Brahman Consciousness. As discussed previously, in Brahman Consciousness the individual is not only established in the unified value of pure consciousness but the various multiform elements of life are perceived and understood to be an expression of one's own self-referral consciousness. In the progression from one state of consciousness to another—until the final stage of Unity or Brahman Consciousness is reached—the individual realizes an ever new sense of self which becomes progressively more unified. It is first unified in the sense of the individual self becoming the cosmic or infinite value of the Self in Transcendental Consciousness. In the state of Cosmic Consciousness, the Self remains unified but distinct from relative experience. Then, in God Consciousness, one continues to enjoy the infinite status of the Self—Transcendental Consciousness—as a permanent reality. However, now, one also perceives the subtle, celestial values of creation. Finally, in Brahman or Unity

Consciousness, the object of perception and the Self are unified. The object is known to be a fluctuation of one's own self-referral consciousness, the Self. This final stroke of development is the complete unification of Self—object referral consciousness within self-referral consciousness.

From the perspective of Maharishi Vedic Science, one may propose that the work of art which embodies pure consciousness while orchestrating elements in a holistic manner mirrors the functioning of consciousness and stimulates in the viewer the conception and possible experience of such a unified wholeness (which is not out of reach or unrealistic). "Something that has holistic value captures the total appreciation of life. In the Age of Enlightenment, awareness will be holistic, and therefore the task of the artist to express the wholeness of life will be performed in a very spontaneous manner."[27] In this sense, art can help to promote the experience and understanding of the deepest reality, and unfold in the viewer not only a sense or concept of a unified self but an *actual* unified Self, where the entire universe is seen as reverberations of one's own self-referral consciousness.

Ultimately, every discipline and every action can help the individual integrate the experience of pure consciousness with the experience of the relative world. This is why Maharishi speaks of the "art of living". Continued integration of life in this fashion, with the consistent experience of pure consciousness and growth to higher states of consciousness, eventually brings the individual to Brahman Consciousness; the Self (objects of experience are perceived as fluctuations of self-referral consciousness) is unified with the Self (Transcendental Consciousness). In this analysis, it can thus be said that the ultimate purpose of anything in life is to inspire evolution. Any object or behavior can be artistic; it can possess the capacity to promote the experience of a unified Self. Objects can have both varying relative purposes and an underlying universal purpose. This point of view, as will be discussed further in Part VI, is touched upon in Indian aesthetic theory, which identifies all creative acts as art, or *Śilpa*.

As noted, art can articulate the inner value of life which is intimate to us even when it has become hidden from experience. Since everything is infinitely correlated on the level of pure consciousness, art which embodies universal aesthetic value, does not only affect the viewer, it influences the environment. In this sense, the "art vibrations" which McEvilley criticizes in his discussion of modernism and the "music of the spheres" are not completely fanciful ideas. However, it is important to emphasize that not all art (for example, as defined by contemporary criticism) achieves or even aspires to this end. Just because an object or performance is labeled "art" does not mean it has universal value. The criteria for universal value have been outlined above; when these are fulfilled then one can begin to speak of art and aesthetics in a universal sense.

In applying the principles of Maharishi Vedic Science to art and theory, clearly, current ideas about aesthetic disinterestedness and the purpose of aesthetic value can be redefined. Art can promote a new sense of self which is actual and not merely potential, which is fully awake and not merely temporarily hyperalert, which is transcendental rather than illusory.

PART VI

UNCOVERING THE DETAILS OF THE NATURE AND STRUCTURE OF PURE CONSCIOUSNESS IN THE VĀSTUSŪTRA UPANIṢAD

As evidenced in the material covered in Parts II-V, Maharishi has provided unique critical insights into, and arguably the most significant contribution to, the study of the Veda and Vedic Literature—foremost of which is the relationship of the part to the whole and the whole to the Self, the experience of self-referral consciousness. As Maharishi points out, there have been many interpretations of Vedic texts but these analyses do not identify the relationships between the Veda and the Vedic Literature and consciousness or the Self:

> There have been many interpretations of a philosophical nature but none have connected any part (of the Vedic Literature) to the whole (Veda), and none have connected the whole (Veda) to the Self; none have the vision of the whole in every part, and every part in the whole—the entire blueprint of creation in each point of creation; none have identified the Vedic Literature as the structuring dynamics of Veda, the structuring dynamics of creation—the mechanics of transformation through which consciousness evolves into Veda, and Veda evolves into creation, and creation eternally continues in the process of evolution as the ever-expanding universe. [1]

Only a Maharishi, or "great seer", can thoroughly expand any understanding of the Vedic Literature. However, as Maharishi explains, the Transcendental Meditation technique and TM-Sidhi program can allow the individual to develop higher states of consciousness and experience the nature and structure of consciousness itself. These technologies of consciousness can facilitate the verification of the nature of the Veda and the Vedic Literature on the level of the individual's own self-referral consciousness.

Part VI, by examining parallels between the descriptions of consciousness in Maharishi Vedic Science and the sūtras of the Vāstusūtra Upaniṣad, attempts to draw upon Maharishi's insights. The sūtras are considered in the light of the main principles of Maharishi Vedic Science discussed in previous sections: 1) there is an unmanifest field of pure consciousness which generates from within itself the three-in-one structure of pure knowledge—the structure of the Veda—cognized in its detail as the Constitution of the Universe; 2) the Veda is the basis of the subtle and manifest structures of the phenomenal world;[2] 3) one can know the creative dynamics and structure of Veda—pure knowledge—and its infinite organizing power because the human nervous system is able to support the experience of this field of pure consciousness through the practice of the Transcendental Meditation technique and TM-Sidhi program;[3] 4) the artist, by rising to higher states of consciousness through the practice of the technologies of Maharishi Vedic Science, can create as Nature creates and produce art which embodies consciousness; 5) the Vedic Literature as the expression of the mechanics of self-referral consciousness—the sequential unfoldment of impulses of intelligence in the form of sound—is the universal language of Nature; 6) the wholeness of consciousness is contained in each expression of the Vedic Literature while each aspect of the Vedic Literature enlivens and unfolds a specific quality of consciousness; 7) the Veda and the Vedic Literature correspond to specific aspects of the human physiology; and, 8) the recitation and reading of the Vedic Literature enlivens Veda in the physiology.

In the Vedic Literature pure, self-referral consciousness can be located in each part (i.e., in any chapter or sūtra); therefore, it should be possible to clearly identify references to consciousness in the sūtras of the Vāstusūtra Upaniṣad. As discussed earlier, pure, self-referral consciousness is described in different contexts in terms of: the Self; Brahman; infinite silence and infinite dynamism (or *Puruṣa* and *Prakṛti*); infinity and its point; a straight line; a *Maṇḍala* or circle which contains total knowledge; the quantification of wholeness (wholeness moving within itself); the scintillating light of Creative Intelligence; the forms (or syllables) of the Veda and the Vedic Literature; and Laws of Nature. Does the Vāstusūtra Upaniṣad embody, define or describe consciousness in any of these contexts? If it is a part of the Vedic Literature, it seems that it should refer to some of these characteristics and unfold the deeper value of the Self—revealing a vision of the whole in every part.

While Alice Boner's extensive work presents the Vāstusūtra Upaniṣad as conveying a level of meaning beyond simple prescriptions for making sculpture and relief works,[4] in this section, the relationship between selected sūtras and principles of Maharishi Vedic Science is considered. Chapter 22, *Re-Contextualizing the Vāstusūtra Upaniṣad: Uncovering Wholeness* reviews the principle of wholeness and *Vāstu Vidyā*—the science of Vāstu or Sthāpatya Veda—discussing wholeness in terms of the move of consciousness. It also considers the relationship of name and form and the multiple levels of meaning in any expression of the Veda and the Vedic Literature. In addition, the theme of developing artistic sight, mentioned in Part II and V, is considered with reference to an expression preceding the chapters of the Vāstusūtra Upaniṣad.

Following this, Chapter 23, entitled: *The First and Last Sūtras: Containing the Wholeness of the Text in Seed Form*, explores how the wholeness of any text or aspect of the Veda and the Vedic Literature is contained in its first and last expressions. With this understanding, the first and last sūtras of the *Vāstusūtra Upaniṣad* seem to reveal a deep principle of knowledge and may indicate the purpose of the entire text. Then, Chapter 24, *The Artist and the Creative Process: Knowing What Consciousness is and What it is Made Of*, examines particular sūtras that refer to the artist and creative process; these are examined both in terms of Nature's mechanics and the artist's creative endeavor. Chapter 25, *Form or Rūpa: Unmanifest to Manifest*, goes on to consider *Rūpa*; the term *Rūpa* meaning "form" can relate to different levels of expression—manifest to manifest and different effects of form. Finally, Chapter 26, *Point, Line, Grid, Triangle, Square, Circle, and Number as Values of Consciousness*, expands the common notion of geometry by identifying these primary elements as dynamics or aspects of consciousness.

By recontextualizing the Vāstusūtra Upaniṣad according to the principle of wholeness brought out by Maharishi Vedic Science, the following analysis seems to reveal values of consciousness, multiple and profound levels of meaning.

22

RE-CONTEXTUALIZING THE VĀSTUSŪTRA UPANIṢAD: UNCOVERING WHOLENESS

As mentioned in Part II and III of this book, wholeness is self-referral consciousness,[1] Saṁhitā.[2] Wholeness is consciousness moving within itself—Brahman—the relationship of the whole with its parts. Without knowledge of wholeness, or the connection to wholeness, the efficacy and evolutionary purpose of knowledge is lost. One no longer has "true," absolute or eternal knowledge but only partial knowledge which cannot have a completely evolutionary application. Without wholeness (the Saṁhitā level of consciousness) the knower is lost to the parts of knowledge; partial knowledge can never be completely effective because it is not understood or applied from the level of Cosmic Intelligence which computes every detail in the unfoldment of the universe. This is why Maharishi emphasizes the role of his Vedic Science in uncovering wholeness. Even in the study of the Vedic Literature, as with any branch of knowledge, according to Maharishi Vedic Science, it is critical that:

> the WHOLE (of knowledge) is not allowed to be shadowed by the PART (of knowledge), and the PART is always understood with reference to the WHOLE.[3]

Maharishi explains that wholeness, the holistic value of consciousness or Saṁhitā, is complete, unified knowledge and the "part" can be understood as a diversified element of knowledge (governed by Ṛishi, Devatā, and Chhandas values), "knowledge of the WHOLE is the knowledge of consciousness, because consciousness is the most fundamental element in creation;"[4] wholeness is expressed through every aspect of the Vedic Literature.[5] In terms of the physiology, the holistic value of Natural Law has its seat in the Self (*Ātmā*) of everyone, the other aspects of the Vedic Literature, including Sthāpatya Veda, have their seat in the intellect (*Buddhi*). The divisions of each of these values have their seat in the mind (*Manas*) and their subdivisions have their seat in the senses (*Indriyas*).[6] Each division is an elaboration upon the holistic aspect of Natural Law, but contains wholeness within it. Without the experience of pure consciousness, the value of wholeness, the essential meaning and practical value of the Veda and the Vedic Literature are overlooked; they become obscure texts, divorced from everyday life. The essential value of the Vedic texts is found in that quality of wholeness enlivened in the physiology and awareness of listener. In practical terms, without wholeness, without the experience of self-referral consciousness, there is a lack of Natural Law lived in individual and collective life resulting in mistakes and suffering.

In a discussion of Natural Law, Maharishi points out that there are numerous books on the specific areas of Natural Law; the Veda and Vedic Literature have so many divisions and subdivisions. For example, there are several hundred Upaniṣads. While the Vāstusūtra Upaniṣad has not been identified or discussed by Maharishi, in this book, Vāstusūtra Upaniṣad will be seen to be related to Sthāpatya Veda. Maharishi Sthāpatya Veda deals with the enlivenment of wholeness in every part. It is the knowledge of *Vāstu Vidyā,* the science or knowledge of Vāstu.

Sthāpatya Veda: Enlivening Wholeness

As discussed in Part III, Maharishi identifies Sthāpatya Veda as highlighting the establishing quality of intelligence within the self-referral nature of Saṁhitā. The word *Sthāpan*, means "to establish" and Sthāpatya Veda brings out the establishing value of self-referral consciousness or wholeness. Completely established in itself, any isolated value of consciousness is always connected its unified value, the totality of Natural Law. Scientific research illustrates the increase of this quality of consciousness in the individual physiology and environment through the practice of the Transcendental Meditation technique and the TM-Sidhi Program.[7] The *Extended Maharishi Effect* created through the group practice of these technologies of consciousness, for example, promotes:

1) a more effective interaction with the environment and improved resistance to stress,[8]

2) improved right hemisphere functioning—better spatial location,[9]

3) an improved national economy—measured by a monthly index of inflation and unemployment,[10]

4) improved quality of national life,[11]

5) improved quality of provincial life,[12] and

6) improved quality of city life.[13] In all of the above instances, the relationship of part to whole is strengthened. In addition, on the level of consciousness—as noted in Chapter 13, in comprising particular Laws of Nature that promote the quality of Chhandas within Saṁhitā, Maharishi Sthāpatya Veda plays a role in providing a structure to self-referral consciousness. Sthāpatya Veda comprises the sets of Laws of Nature engaged in "promoting the quality of Chhandas within Saṁhitā, providing a structure to [that] eternally silent, self-referral, self-sufficient, fully awake state of consciousness."[14] In the body, Nader notes that the holistic harmony which permeates the different components of the physiology is established through this branch of Vedic knowledge. Described as the knowledge of how everything is established in accord with Natural Law, how the whole is enlivened in every part,[15] Sthāpatya Veda is the outward display of the orderly structure of self-referral consciousness. It is the knowledge of that creativity which holds the universe in one wholeness.

As Maharishi points out, the galaxies just do not run about here and there at random. Order is there in creation; there is system in nature. "That creative intelligence, that knowledge of supreme creativity which holds the ever expanding universe in one wholeness, this is Sthapatya Veda."[16] Maharishi continues to explain that the ultimate purpose of Sthāpatya Veda is to:

> Awaken and enliven consciousness, enliven intelligence, in the structure of inert matter; enliven the energy of Cosmic Intelligence in every material structure; enliven the whole in every part; raise every aspect of life to perfection and render every aspect of living in the evolutionary direction of Cosmic Life.[17]

With respect to the environment, for every material structure to embody Cosmic Intelligence and be integrated with everything else, it must embody the holistic value of consciousness. Sthāpatya Veda puts everything in its proper place so no structure is out of alignment with the whole cosmic structure. It is the science and technology of establishing every individual in harmony with the universe.[18] Then, every created structure can reflect the ordering principles of self-referral consciousness—that consciousness which governs the planets, galaxies and the universe. For this reason, Sthāpatya Veda includes the knowledge of creation of physical structures, architecture and art. It encompasses:

> The most ancient and supreme system of country, town, village, and home planning in accord with Natural Law, taking into account the solar and lunar influences on the earth with reference to the north and south pole and the equator, thereby connecting individual life with cosmic life, individual intelligence with cosmic intelligence, and creating ideal living conditions on earth where everyone will feel: 'I am living in Heaven.' Furthermore, Maharishi Sthāpatya Veda is the only science in the world which has the precise knowledge and time-tested formulas for allocating the rooms in the house according to the path of the sun in the sky. The sun, in its motion from east to west, generates different types of energies in the respective rooms of a building which should correspond to our daily activities so that natural law always supports the cycles of our daily routine and makes life comfortable and activity successful and fulfilling.[19]

It is worth commenting that some scholars suggest that the prescriptions of Vitruvius and Roman architecture utilized guidelines derived from the principles outlined in the *Mānasāra Śilpaśāstra*, the text of Sthāpatya Veda.[20] Consequently, aspects of traditional Western architecture and design may employ similar principles. However, Sthāpatya Veda, as noted above and in earlier chapters, is obviously more than a set of prescriptive rules and regulations. The town, city, house, and work of art, through the principles of Sthāpatya Veda can reflect the deeper structure of consciousness—maintaining balance between the parts and the whole. In awakening the value of self-referral consciousness, the holistic value and energy of Cosmic Intelligence is enlivened in the apparently inert structure of matter; wholeness is enlivened in every isolated element. Discussing Sthāpatya Veda and mathematics in the context of the individual's ability to bring together all the Laws of Nature to spontaneously fulfill a desire—i.e., the manifestation of design in accord with Natural Law—Maharishi points out:

> This is the mathematics of Sthapatya Veda which trains the individual intelligence, awareness, to think and compute or bring together all the laws of nature that will spontaneously fulfill the desire. Every aspect of this undertaking is completely natural and naturally harnesses the creative potential of all the laws of nature. Human brain physiology is that cosmic computer, which could deliver anything through mere desiring. It's a very complete science. It is on the basis of proper calculations that structuring is based. Construction, building, designing—everything is based on mathematics. The mathematics of Sthapatya Veda is accomplishing the infinite dynamism of the universe to run with perfect orderliness. This is the mathematics where steps are not there. It is not based on intellectually counting—intellect is not necessary to ensure the sequence of steps. All the laws of nature spontaneously engage to fulfill the desire. This is the training of Sthapatya Veda, the training of the Vedic architect. He does not have to go through lots of calculations. Spontaneously the thought that comes to him will be a right thought. The steps that he takes will be guided by the laws of nature.[21]

As introduced in Chapter 5, the phenomenon of the expansion of consciousness is the basis of mathematics. Maharishi teaches that Vedic Mathematics is the natural organizing power inherent in the nature of consciousness.[22] It promotes spontaneous evolution of form from name, and the name or sound from the level of pure intelligence or pure consciousness[23] (where name refers to the frequencies of sound at the basis of creation). Vedic Mathematics is at the basis of the influence on physical structures in the field of space, time, direction, causation, etc.[24]

Sthāpatya Veda includes the mathematical formulas of *Vāstu Vidyā*—knowledge of *Vāstu*— utilizing the power of Natural Law, connecting the individual with Cosmic life so that the individual is universal. While *Vāstu* can be understood as the site in a general and specific sense,—i.e., the land, earth, solar system, all the solar systems of the universe— *Vāstu Vidyā* is "the design and structure of a building in harmony with Natural Law, which takes into consideration, for example, the proper orientation of the house with its entrance facing due East."[25] In the context of the site, correct *Vāstu* defines and delineates the site in accordance with Natural Law; the site is calculated or seen in relation to the whole—in relation to the universe. It can be defined by the perimeter which traces the boundary of a place (for example, a dwelling, town, city, state, country, etc.). This is why the mathematical formulas of *Vāstu Vidyā* of Sthāpatya Veda are used in the planning of any particular construction. In neglecting to employ this knowledge, lack of support of Natural Law ensues. As discussed in Chapter

13, by taking care of *Vāstu* through Sthāpatya Veda, the government of any country can gain the support of Natural Law for the people of that country. This principle is demonstrated in the Maharishi Vāstu Effect mentioned in Chapter 13. As with the Meissner Effect of quantum physics which shows that the ability to resist disorder is based on the coherent collective functioning of a system, the ability of a city to resist disorder is also dependent upon the coherence of that city—in terms of its design. The Meissner Effect reveals an example of invincibility in Nature. For example, in a superconductor, the coherent collective functioning of its electrons spontaneously excludes the penetration of a magnetic field. In contrast, in an ordinary electrical conductor the incoherent, disorderly electrons allow penetration by an external magnetic field. Simply put, the first resists outside influence, the second is affected by it. With the Maharishi Vāstu Effect, an analogous principle applies. In a city designed with ideal *Vāstu*—where all roads run North-South, East-West around a central square (the *Brahma-Sthān*)—order, coherence and support of Natural Law is automatically created. In an ordinary city, roads run in all directions. Homes and other buildings have disparate orientations. According to Maharishi Sthapatya Veda this is the cause of chaos and problems in life. The city is unable to disallow any untoward external influence.

Vāstu Vidyā deals with wholeness and the establishment of the parts in relation to the whole, the mathematics of consciousness or Vedic Mathematics (at the basis of the influence on physical structures in the field of space, time, direction, and causation), the relationship of the individual to the cosmos, the relationship of the parts of the body to the whole physiology and all the aspects of site—specific to general, individual to Cosmic.

In addition to the theme of wholeness, Maharishi's understanding of the relationship between name and form, and word and meaning provides a further insight into the nature of the Vedic texts and the issues surrounding Vedic study.

The Relationship of Name and Form in the Vedic Literature

As mentioned previously, there are the four levels of speech—the Transcendental level of pure consciousness or *Para*, the subtle level or *Paśyanti*, the level of the thinking mind or *Madhyama*, and the expressed level of speech or *Vaikari*.[26] The Transcendental level is the source of speech, the source of sound, the source of creation. Name and form are completely unified on this level of pure self-referral consciousness. There is no gap between sound and meaning. In the Veda, the sound is the form and each expression contains all the information of the object to which it refers. As Maharishi points out:

> The name of the object has the content of the form of the object. For example, the seed has all that the tree contains. Everything is there in the seed. The name has all the impulses which are present in the form...now, this is true in the words of the Veda.[27]

Just as a seed contains all the genetic information to structure a tree, the Vedic expression or name contains the structure and tendencies, the Laws of Nature, which give rise to its corresponding form. As Maharishi notes: "the name not only contain those tendencies which structure the form, but it also has all those mechanics which weave those tendencies into one another to produce that particular structure of the form."[28]

While the term, "name," refers to the sounds of the Veda, Maharishi also points out that "name" can refer to the impulse of pure consciousness which, in its more precipitated value, *becomes* form. As Maharishi explains "the form is a more solidified structure of that impulse. Therefore the name is a more delicate expression of the form, and the form is a more precipitated, more manifest value of the name."[29] All the material and non-material expressions of creation have specific frequencies or sounds and "these fundamental frequencies, non-material values, are the sounds of the Vedic Literature." The sounds of the Vedic Literature are actually the "hum of the intellect" which flows and stops in sequence.[30] As Maharishi explains:

> The expression of melody, forming the whole Vedic Literature, gives us the entire process of the basic mechanics of transformation within the self-referral state of consciousness. In its momentum of transformation, the interplay (self-referral dynamism) of Ṛishi, Devatā, Chhandas continues to create sound from sound—from one form of sound to the second more evolved form of sound to the next (third) more evolved form of sound (specific alphabets—vowels and consonants). The evolution of material form commences from the frequencies (vowels and consonants)—speech, through its structured forms, progresses to generate different frequencies and their corresponding material forms.
>
> The infinite diversity and dynamism of creation is just the expression of the eternally silent, self-referral, self-sufficient, unbounded field of consciousness—pure wakefulness, unbounded alertness, pure intelligence, pure existence, all knowingness. Consciousness, functioning within itself in terms of flow and stop, in terms of Saṁhitā of Ṛishi, Devatā, Chhandas, is the 'be-all and end-all' of all life and creation.[31]

In addition, the stages of development of the name or sound from the level of pure consciousness to its expressed value, are equivalent to the stages of development of the corresponding form; the name of an object and the object itself have the same number of steps in their progression. For example, in the case of a rose, the name emerges from the level of pure consciousness and "comes up onto the conscious thinking mind, and from the mind it bursts forth, and then it's a rose."[32] Maharishi explains that

> From the finest level of expression the form develops, which is open to the eyes on the sensory level. When the name "rose" comes on the sensory level of the

> ears and the rose comes on the sensory level of the eyes, both have the same number of steps of progression. Therefore, when we say the name has the same value as the form, we do mean at all levels of expression.[33]

Name and form have the same value at all the levels of their development from their source in pure consciousness to their manifest expression.

In terms of the process of sensory response in the human physiology, this principle reveals that, "it is possible to see the dynamics of the physiology in the sounds of Veda and the Vedic Literature" because the sounds of the Veda correspond to the physiology and the functioning of the senses.[34] The brain's perception of sound, for example, as with all of the senses, takes the same steps of progression as the development of the impulses of consciousness recorded as the Veda. Nader explains how this process occurs through three—multiplied by eight—steps; the three steps correspond to the Ṛishi, Devatā and Chhandas transformations and the eight steps denote the eight stages of transformation within the gap which are governed by the eight *Prakṛtis*—discussed in Part III. Totaling 24 stages of progression, these steps occur in a sequential fashion in the physiological functioning of all the five senses.[35] In fact, all the transformations of one sound to the next, recorded as the Veda and the Vedic Literature, are involved in the functioning of the physiology.

For example, as noted in Chapter 13, the sounds of Sthāpatya Veda constitute the frequencies which structure the spinal cord and nerves which emanate from it. It is possible for the human nervous system, equipped with its sensory apparatus, to cognize the Veda (which is its own structure) because the impulses of the Veda correspond to the form of the human physiology. As mentioned previously, the sound or impulses of consciousness can be heard; the form of the sound, having a specific structure, can be seen, as Maharishi points out:

> Sound has a form, form has a sound; form is physiology, sound is the frequency that structures physiology. Sound and form, being the transformation of consciousness, are appreciated by consciousness as its own expression in terms of *Shruti* (sound) and *Darshana* (form).[36]

The sequential unfoldment of sound is the sequential unfoldment of the form as well; this sequential unfoldment of sound and form is the structure of the Veda heard in one's fully awake, self-referral consciousness as *Śruti* and seen as *Darśana.*[37] As noted earlier, *Śruti* is the Devatā in the form of sound; it is energy and intelligence at the same time, the specific representative of "total creativity," the "scintillating light of Creative Intelligence heard as sound."[38]

Different Levels of Meaning

As explained above, in Maharishi Vedic Science, "name" not only refers to the impulses of consciousness which contains the entire structure of the form but also to the stages of progression of the name (in parallel with the development of the corresponding form) from their unmanifest source to their expression as speech and matter.[39] Due to this relationship, each Vedic word contains numerous levels and layers of meaning; each different value of meaning relates to a step in the range of that word and form's development from the unmanifest to expressed level. This is why Maharishi emphasizes that for the Veda and the Vedic Literature there can be numerous levels of meaning for any expression:

> When we say "carnation," it is just one word, but it can have a meaning at the surface value of the petal. It will have a meaning at any level between the surface and the sap. There could be a thousand levels, and at every level there is "carnation." Such are the expressions of the Veda.[40]

Despite the different levels of meaning, the fundamental level and structure of a word can be cognized by the enlightened seer or Ṛishi. As Maharishi explains, "The words of the hymns are not the words formulated by the seer. He just sees the phenomena in this structure, in this rhythm." "That is why these hymns are said to be cognitions. They are not formulations of the human mind."[41] These are cognitions of the Laws of Nature where the seer sees "the home of all the Laws of Nature, the dwelling place of all creativity, the seed of creation, in his own reverberating consciousness."[42] Seers cognize:

> Their own consciousness taking the shape of a wave, the wave taking the shape of a sound. The wave was seen and the sound was heard. Consciousness reverberated in the vibrant value of sound and form simultaneously.[43]

Without enlightened or fully developed consciousness, in the appreciation of the Vedic Literature only partial values and meaning will be gleaned. Wholeness, the value of consciousness, will be overlooked. Understandably, therefore, any translation of the Vedic Literature would ideally require the attention of a person who possesses an enlightened state of consciousness, a enlightened Ṛishi or knower, so that the deepest, appropriate level of meaning and the complete value of the structure is revealed. One can appreciate, therefore, why the recitation of the Veda and Vedic Literature is considered to be more valuable than translation at this time.

With respect to the discussion of different levels of meaning, in one example Maharishi explains that the Sanskrit word उषस् (*uṣas*), or "dawn," is often poetically referred to as the end of night; but it also means the dawn of Unity or of God Consciousness:

> There is a word उषस् (ushas), which means dawn. Now for a poet dawn is the end of night. This word "dawn" can have a meaning in the dawn of unity, it can have a meaning in the dawn of God Consciousness.[44]

With fully awake consciousness, one can know the deepest level (and all the multiple levels) of meaning of a word. Despite this, as discussed in Part III, the Vedic texts really have their unique value on the level of sound because recitation of these sounds enlivens the intelligence of the physiology.

Recitation of the Vedic Literature Enlivens the Physiology

Maharishi's insights reveal that the oral recitation of the Vedic texts is effective in enlivening and structuring Veda in the physiology. The predicted effect of recitation is growth to higher states of consciousness; preliminary research conducted at Maharishi University of Management examines this principle. With this understanding, Maharishi maintains that intellectual inquiry, alone, into translations of these texts is of limited value. It is the sound value of oral recitation which enlivens Natural Law in the reciter, the listener and the environment. This is why oral tradition is highly valued.

The discovery that the Veda and the Vedic Literature correlate with the different aspects of the physiology has had a significant impact on the understanding of the nature and role of the Veda, the Vedic Literature and Vedic study; as Nader states:

> Veda and the Vedic Literature are the sounds of Natural Law murmuring to itself. It created its own system of maintaining itself on the verbal level. For thousands of years, generation after generation, it has been maintained in the tradition of Vedic families of India. Even though scattered and often misinterpreted, it kept itself reverberating. Its value as explained by Maharishi resides in the mechanics of transformation available in its gaps and sounds. Translating Veda and the Vedic Literature and attempting at intellectually comprehending it therefore is an exercise with very limited scope and significance when compared to the holistic value of Veda which is the total structuring of human life and society.[45]

Obviously, the emphasis in Maharishi Vedic Science is in reciting the Vedic Literature and not simply examining it for intellectual discussion. This is because of the correspondence between the Veda and the physiology. In reading the Veda and the Vedic Literature in Sanskrit, Maharishi points outs, the orderly, evolutionary development of the individual life is promoted:

> Reading the Vedic Literature in sequence is the procedure to spontaneously train the brain physiology and the whole physiology of speech to function in the most orderly way so that every thought, speech, and action is spontaneously promoted

> in the evolutionary direction of Natural Law, and thereby spontaneously enjoys full support of the evolutionary quality of intelligence that upholds order and evolution in the entire universe. The importance of reading the Vedic Literature is very obvious in view of the recent discovery of the Veda and the Vedic Literature in the human physiology.[46]

Clearly, there is a significance to the sequence of the sūtras and the sections of the texts of the Vedic Literature. With the above understanding, in taking the Vāstusūtra Upaniṣad as a "Vedic text" one could read its sūtras (see Appendix), in sequence, simply for the value of sound.

Re-Examining the Vāstusūtra Upaniṣad

As outlined above, from the perspective of Maharishi Vedic Science, different Vedic texts deal with different values of consciousness at different stages of elaboration—from more subtle and abstract to more expressed and concrete. If we take the Vāstusūtra Upaniṣad to be associated with Sthāpatya-Veda, or *Vāstu Vidyā,* it may also support this understanding. In the field of Vedic study, Boner, Śarmā and Bäumer[47] have demonstrated that the Vāstusūtra Upaniṣad is a text on art practice (in particular, stone carving). In her introduction to the text, Boner considers issues such as its origin and historical context. She discusses how the sūtras were translated from five palm leaf inscriptions (of which four are written in Oriya and one in Devanāgarī) and mentions that the manuscripts were found in Orissa between 1973 to 1976. Her translation is based primarily on palm leaf inscriptions (with marginal notes) found by Sombhaṭṭa in 1976. Here, the following chapters (and the complete text provided in the Appendix) cite the translation of the sūtras (and the sūtras themselves) provided by Boner et al.—in the third revised edition published in 1996 (this latest edition includes two additional sūtras and some modification to sūtras as compared to previous editions).

In his introduction to Boner's translation, Bhattacharya refers to Vāstusūtra Upaniṣad as related to the Atharavedic literature. In connection with other Vedic texts, he also discusses issues related to the authenticity and validity of the text. Boner elaborates by noting that:

> The Vāstusūtra Upaniṣad (VSU) attributed to the Paippalāda Kalpa of Atharvaveda presents a challenge to various disciplines: to the indologist, because it is the first text on Śilpa or Vāstu called an Upaniṣad; to the historian, because...its dating and historical position is very difficult to ascertain; to the linguist, because the text contains archaic and popular elements....[48]

Boner goes on to explain that, as with the *Praśna Upaniṣad*, the Vāstusūtra Upaniṣad is attributed to the Ṛishi Pippalāda and, again, like the Praśna Upaniṣad, it is divided into six *prapāṭhakas*, sections or chapters. In both texts, Pippalāda responds to his disciples' questions (in the case of the Praśna Upaniṣad he addresses six disciples; in the Vāstusūtra Upaniṣad, he responds to three). In addition, Chapter One, Sūtra Two of the Vāstusūtra Upaniṣad states:

षट्शिल्पाङ्गप्रयोगेण प्रजनयन्ति रूपाणि ।

Ṣaṭśilpāṅga-prayogeṇa prajanayanti rūpāṇi.
Art forms are produced by means of six disciplines.

(*Vāstusūtra Upaniṣad, 1.2*)

indicating that there are six distinct areas with respect to the creation of art forms.

If we take the Vāstusūtra Upaniṣad to be part of the Vedic Literature as defined by Maharishi Vedic Science, with respect to the issue of "authorship" or "non authorship," it could be stated that the Ṛishi, or seer, Pippalāda *cognized* the details of the Vāstusūtra Upaniṣad—the text itself being, in effect, some aspect of the self-interacting dynamics of consciousness expressed in the form of sound. In this sense, it could be said that the quality of consciousness expressed by the name Pippalāda cognized the details of the text. As discussed in Part III, Maharishi reveals that the six-fold division in other aspects of the Vedic Literature corresponds to the six-fold self-referral feed-back loop of consciousness in terms of Ṛishi, Devatā and Chhandas values in the value of expansion, and Chhandas, Devatā and Ṛishi values in the direction of the source, Saṁhitā. While this book does not assign specific values of consciousness to the chapters, it is worth noting that the text is comprised of six chapters.

The first chapter, *The Six Branches of Art or Śilpa,* is comprised of 10 sūtras. Boner states that *Śilpa* refers to the 64 fine or mechanical arts and can therefore broadly apply to all creative practice;[4)] it can also have the sense of the "the art of variegating" or "artistic work". Chapter One is said to expound the general and foundational principles of art. In Maharishi Vedic Science, as we have seen, artistic performance is defined as performance from the level of pure consciousness, or Natural Law—a theme that will be discussed again later. The second chapter of the Vāstusūtra Upaniṣad, *The Compositional Diagram*, has 27 sūtras (one more than the 26 listed in the earlier editions of the Vāstusūtra Upaniṣad translated by Boner et al.); it deals with composition—making reference to lines, the basic geometric forms of the circle, the triangle, and the square, and the *bindu* (or central point) of the composition or circle. The third chapter, *Carving*, includes 21 sūtras and encompasses the creative process, methods of stone carving. The fourth chapter, *Disposition of Parts of the Image*, has 29 sūtras and deals with proportions and elements of art. The fifth chapter, *The Inner Sense of Form*, consisting of 24 sūtras (previously 23 sūtras), deals with feeling and the effects of art. Finally, the sixth chapter, *Integration of the Composition*, includes 26 sūtras and considers the conceptualization of the composition and how different elements of the image should be orchestrated.

As noted earlier, according to Maharishi Vedic Science, the sequence of expressions in any part of the Vedic Literature is highly significant since it is, in effect, the sequential unfoldment of consciousness in terms of sound. However, in reviewing sūtras of the Vāstusūtra Upaniṣad the following chapters are devoted primarily to particular themes as brought out by specific sūtras. The themes include: 1) the first and last sūtras: 2) the Sthāpaka (sculptor or artist); 3) the creative process in terms of *Brahma* and the artistic practice of envisioning form within consciousness; 4) *Rūpa* or form; and, 5) the significance of point, line, triangle, square, circle, grid and number. Any parallels made between descriptions of consciousness in Maharishi Vedic Science and the sūtras are based on an apparent correspondence, but these relationships have not been specifically identified by Maharishi Vedic Science. Therefore, any observations herein are by no means definitive. In addition, since this section deals with the Vāstusūtra Upaniṣad in the light of Maharishi's description of consciousness, only sūtras (and not the commentary—as provided in Boner's translation) are studied. Furthermore, issues of historical context and authorship with respect to the text and commentary is left to scholars such as Boner et al. and Bhattacharya.[50] The translation provided by Boner is used here. Where terms have been discussed by Maharishi (with respect to consciousness) elsewhere, that translation may be also be considered. For example, the word देव *Deva* meaning "god", is translated in Maharishi Vedic Science as "law of nature."[51] This term law of nature applies to the universal level of meaning with respect to consciousness. This sense of *Deva* is reviewed.

Although all the sūtras are not mentioned, it should not be concluded that they remain outside of the scope of Vedic Science; rather, they remain, at this time, outside the scope of this book.

Developing Artistic Sight

Along with the 137 sūtras of the six chapters of the Vāstusūtra Upaniṣad, a short expression precedes the main text (appearing at the beginning of each palm leaf inscription). This expression is from the verse: भद्रं कर्णेभिः शृणुयाम देवा । *Bhadram Karṇebhiḥ Śriṇuyāma Devā* found in the Ṛk Veda (*1.89.8*) and the *Nrisimhapurvatapaniya Upaniṣad* (*1.1*) which, as discussed in Chapter 19, describes "artistic sight," *Darśana* or cognition.

> Artistic sight is that sight which sees inside the surface expressions of life. So there is the art of seeing in which you see behind the surface expressions, the art of hearing in which you hear behind the words being spoken, and the art of touching in which you feel behind the touch, you feel behind the sight, you sense something there. No matter what you are hearing, you have your target on the divine level in every hearing. This is Vedic hearing. The formula that is sung about it is, *Bhadram karnebhih shrinuyama deva* [Rig Veda, 1.89.8; Nrisimhapurvatapaniya Upanishad, 1.1.]. Bhadram is divine, the finest value of hearing. However, the verse specifies that you hear through the ears, not that you just hear, but that you have divine hearing through the ears. This means that the

> gross is to be experienced in a lively state in terms of the subtle or the subtlest. When the ears have been trained to capture the divine value, when the divine value is there at the subtle level of every word, then you will be hearing the transcendental value of sound and the gross will not be the field of hearing. In such a state of consciousness, the subtle will always be enjoyed, and that will be the art of hearing. No matter what you hear, you will only hear that which nourishes the ears and the mind and the intellect and the ego. This means that you will only hear what is nourishing to life and you will unhear that which should not be heard.[52]

In another context, Maharishi explains that भद्रं कर्णेभिः शृणुयाम देवा भद्रं पश्येमाक्षभिर्यजत्रः । *Bhadraṁ Karṇebhiḥ Śriṇuyāma Devā Bhadraṁ Paśyemā Kṣabir-yajatrā* refers to the principle that all life depends upon the ability to "drink orderliness from the environment" for a "continuing state of creative order."[53] This requires the ability to engage in orderly thinking.

Analogous to the phenomenon of decrease in entropy with temperature decrease and where absolute zero coincides with no activity as described by the Third Law of Thermodynamics, Maharishi explains that through the practice of the Transcendental Meditation technique (a means for "drinking orderliness from the environment"), the brain's capacity for orderly thinking increases:

> The source of creativity is therefore the regime of reduced 'mental temperature.' This natural tendency towards orderliness is the 'natural evolutionary impulse of life.' The physicist Schrödinger found that the orderly, creative (low entropy) aspect of life was closely tied to the order-preserving quality of the quantum-mechanical nature of the DNA molecule, a quality characteristic of the region near absolute zero temperature. He further found that all life depended, for a continuing state of creative order and an avoidance of the disorganization of death, upon the ability to 'drink orderliness from the environment.' We may interpret the process of Transcendental Meditation as a specifically human means of 'drinking orderliness' by a purely mental process. This technique does indeed result in synchronous brain wave pattern of markedly lower entropy. From this point of view, Transcendental Meditation can be seen as something absolutely basic and simple that runs parallel to and communicates with the simplest feature of universal physical laws. The source of creativity tapped by Transcendental Meditation is the same source as for all the Laws of Nature.[54]

This property of orderliness and least entropy created in individual life through the practice of the Transcendental Meditation technique allows the individual to "drink orderliness from the environment" and Maharishi maintains that it is orderly thinking which provides a "productive and useful direction for imagination"[55] and creativity. For creativity to be expressed in practical activity it needs to take "a straight line" from its source in the "pure liveliness in the mind to its goal in achievement through practical activity."[56] In the domain of artistic perception, the development of artistic sight through higher states of consciousness where orderly thinking is at its maximum, is marked by the perception of celestial or subtle values of creation. In this context, the inscription at the beginning of the Vāstusūtra Upaniṣad seems to be referring to the development of refined perception. While this expression precedes other Vedic texts and is not part of the sūtras of the Vāstusūtra Upaniṣad, it is worth noting that Maharishi has commented on its significance in the light of developing artistic sight—a function of enlightened awareness.

23

THE FIRST AND LAST SŪTRAS: CONTAINING THE WHOLENESS OF THE TEXT IN SEED FORM

The first and last expression of Ṛk Veda, and any aspect of the Vedic Literature, according to Maharishi Vedic Science, present a wholeness or compact expression of the entire text.[1] Maharishi discusses the value of this expression of "wholeness on the move" as located in the first and last letter of the Ṛk Veda:

> Because infinity is just a sequentially organized infinite number of points, the relationship between infinity and point presents the wholeness of silence in motion—silent wholeness on the move—infinity of silence on the move—holistic value of silence on the move—holistic value of silence in terms of motion—wholeness of silence in terms of wholeness of motion, wholeness of dynamism—two fullness emerging from one fullness. This is demonstrated by the first letter of Ṛk Veda and by the last letter of Ṛk Veda—from the letter अ ((A)—wholeness of silence) emerges the last letter इ ((I)—wholeness of dynamism).[2]

In this description, Maharishi points out that wholeness expresses itself in the different impulses of Natural Law or sounds of the Veda and the Vedic Literature which form the frequencies which evolve into material creation. The continuous sound of "A", the first letter of Ṛk Veda, embodies the infinity or wholeness of silence. While the first letter embodies the wholeness of silence, the last letter "I", emerging from the first, contains the wholeness of dynamism—the wholeness of silence in terms of motion or dynamism. Infinity, as a series of points representing the wholeness of silence in motion, is wholeness of silence and wholeness of motion or dynamism. As Maharishi elaborates:

> Here is a picture of two values of wholeness—silence and dynamism—in one grand wholeness of Natural Law. One wholeness moving ——> to become another wholeness—wholeness of silence moving between infinity of silence, अ (A), and infinity of dynamism, इ (I).[3]

The two letters both express wholeness but different values of wholeness. Maharishi adds that it is this co-existence of opposites (the values of silence and dynamism) which constitute what we know to be consciousness.[4]

While the first and last expressions of Ṛk Veda contain wholeness, the whole of Ṛk Veda—every word and every gap between the words—are ihe steps of wholeness on the move, the steps of Natural Law moving from infinity to infinity:

> As it is the march of wholeness, every step of progression in the whole length of Ṛk Veda, every word that sequentially follows every other word, every gap between words in every step that the holistic value of Natural Law takes during its move from infinity to infinity, is the step of wholeness expressed in sequence by either a word or gap. The move of Natural Law is demonstrated by the sequentially organized steps of wholeness perpetually maintained by every gap and every syllable, from the beginning to the end of Ṛk Veda. It is this perpetual liveliness of the holistic move of Natural Law—from infinity of silence to infinity of dynamism—that spontaneously maintains the infinite, eternal organizing power at the basis of creation and evolution.[5]

The relationship between the infinity of silence and the infinity of dynamism (silence, and silence in terms of motion, contained within the first and last expressions of the Ṛk Veda) is expressed in the words and gaps of Ṛk Veda. In this way, the expressions of the Veda are significant in terms of their sequence, their expression of wholeness and their governance of the forms and phenomenon which make up the manifest universe.

Just as the first and last letters contain the wholeness of the Veda, the first and last words or verses of any aspect of the Vedic Literature, also contain a compact expression of the wholeness of that text.[6] The first and last chapter of the entire Vedic Literature can also be seen as the starting point and ending point of the circular structure of knowledge; side-by-side they mark the beginning and ending point on the circle.[7] In this sense, the first and last expression of any aspect of the Vedic Literature, according to Maharishi, contain a compact, holistic expression of knowledge[8]—where knowledge is, ultimately, the state of self-referral consciousness. Applying this principle, one can examine the first and last sūtra of the Vāstusūtra Upaniṣad to ascertain whether they may express the wholeness of the entire text and the wholeness of consciousness.

The first sūtra states:

> वास्तोष्पतिर्ज्ञेय इति ।
> *Vāstospatir jñeya iti.*
> (They) should know Vāstoṣpati (the divinity of Vāstu).
> (*Vāstusūtra Upaniṣad, 1.1*)

Vāstospati, the first word of the sūtra and the entire text, is translated as "the divinity of *Vāstu*."[9] However, the words *Pat* and *Pati* can mean "to rule" and "ruler" or "governor." *Vāstospati* in Ṛk Veda (*7.3.21.1-3*) and Atharva-Veda Saṁhitā (*6.73.3*) is described by scholars as the lord or protector of the dwelling.[10]

As we have seen, rulership can only take place from the level of Natural Law—the ultimate administrator of all forms and phenomena. Maharishi describes the "Ruler of the universe" as *Rām*, the embodiment of Natural Law,[11] *Brahma* or "*Purushottam*—the abstract, unmanifest, absolute ruler of the ever-expanding universe" whose nature (*Prakṛti*) is the Veda, the self-interacting dynamics of consciousness.[12] According to Maharishi Vedic Science, *Vāstu* can be understood as the site of the universe. *Vāstospati* can be taken to mean the ruler or governor of *Vāstu*. *Vāstu Vidya* is the power of Natural Law which connects individual life with cosmic life and maintains the universe. *Vāstu Vidya* of Sthāpatya Veda connects the part to the whole. It connects "the reality of the structure and function of the individual with the reality of the structure and function of the whole cosmos."[13]

With respect to consciousness and its dwelling, Creative Intelligence creates its home, the physiology, the universe, and dwells within it. Self-referral consciousness creates creation and resides in (can be found at) every point in creation. The *Ishāvāsyā Upaniṣad* states:

ईशा वास्यमिदं सर्वं यत्किंच जगत्यां जगत् ।
तेन त्यक्तन भुञ्जीथा मा गृधः कस्य स्विद्धनम् ।।

Iśā vāsyam idaṁ sarvaṁ
yat kiṁ-cha jagatyaṁ jagat,
tena tyaktana bhunjīthā
mā gṛdhaḥ kasysa swid dhanam.

(*Ishāvāsyā Upaniṣad, 1*)

Translated by Maharishi, the first line of this expression states: "All this (creation) is the dwelling of the Administrator, the Creator."[14] This verse is further discussed in the context of the one-to-one relationship between the nature and function of the Veda and the Vedic Literature, the structure and function of the human physiology, and the principle that everything everywhere is the expression of Natural Law. The creation, with its forms and phenomenon, is the dwelling place of the Administrator, of Natural Law.

Similarly, as mentioned in the previous chapter, another expression from the Upaniṣads exclaims:

तत्सृट्वा तदेवानुप्राविशत् ।

Tat sṛṣṭva tad evānuprāviśat.
Having created the creation, the Creator entered into it.

(*Taittirīya Upaniṣad*, 2.6)

Vāstu can be understood as the underlying structure within which consciousness dwells; it can be understood as the site of the universe. *Vāstu Vidyā*, Sthāpatya Veda, is involved in giving the value of structure to self-referral consciousness. In knowing *Vāstoṣpati*, one should know the governor of the "dwelling place" of consciousness. The first sūtra of the Vāstusūtra Upaniṣad may be indicate that the one should know the ruler, and inherently the governing principles, which structure form and its orderly functioning. (In addition, if one is considering the role of the artist, in particular, this seems commensurate with the idea of the need for the artist to know what consciousness is and what it is made of).

While knowledge of *Vāstospati* is the theme of the first sūtra, last sūtra of the Vāstusūtra Upaniṣad states:

> प्रज्ञार्थमेतद् वास्तूपाख्यानम् ।
> *Prajñārtham etad vāstūpākhyānam.*
> This exposition of Art (vāstu) is for the purpose of conferring knowledge.
> (*Vāstusūtra Upaniṣad, 6.26)*

On one level, "knowledge" can refer to the knowledge of how to make art (if one takes *Vāstu* to mean art). It can also indicate knowledge of the Self, pure, self-referral consciousness and how it manifests into form.

Prajña means "wisdom".[15] In Maharishi Vedic Science the true nature of wisdom is knowledge of the Self, the structure of pure knowledge, Veda, self-referral consciousness. Knowledge refers to the experience gained in higher states of consciousness when complete knowledge dawns in awareness. It is gained through direct experience[16] and is not merely the development of intellectual acumen. Knowledge is the structure of consciousness; any successful action is based on absolute or complete knowledge. As considered in Part II, Absolute knowledge, knowledge of the infinite, eternal value of the Self, is gained in Transcendental Consciousness; this is the basis of reliable knowledge. This last sūtra may, therefore, refer to the ability of this exposition of *Vāstu* to confer knowledge of the Self or self-referral consciousness. The structure of pure knowledge is Ṛk Veda. "Knowledge" could refer to knowledge of Veda and its expression as *Viśwa*, the universe.

Bhattacharya suggests that the sūtra can be translated literally as "This *Vāstu*-story is for the sake of knowledge."[17] With this meaning, the story of *Vāstu* could be taken to refer to the story of how consciousness expresses itself in the form of the site or as the universe. This "story" is the story of creation—the story of how the structure of pure knowledge unfolds. In this sense, it is the story of knowledge for the sake of knowledge. Maharishi notes that when the artist expresses himself he tells the "whole story of creation."[18] Here, it seems, the story of *Vāstu* could be to confer knowledge or wisdom in a more expanded sense. In referring to the story of *Vāstu*, this sūtra may also contain the idea of *reciting* and *hearing* the expressions of Vāstusūtra Upaniṣad. As Maharishi points out, in practicing the Transcendental Meditation program and then reading the Vedic Literature[19] the individual enlivens the structure of pure knowledge in his or her awareness and physiology because all knowledge is contained in every aspect of the Vedic Literature:

> The Veda and the Vedic Literature is already lively and active as the administrating intelligence within the physiology of everyone. It is also available in the self-referral pure consciousness of everyone, and anyone can enliven this structure of pure knowledge in his own consciousness by opening his awareness to that level of consciousness where it is structured—by reading it or by listening to it—because this whole field of knowledge is available on the level of full awakening of consciousness—because the structure of pure knowledge, the Veda, is available on the self-sufficient, self-referral level of consciousness, and the sound of Veda is the impulse of consciousness (which structures the physiology). Veda is the impulse of consciousness, and by listening to the sound of the Veda (*Shruti*)—by reading it or hearing it—one can enliven it within one's own consciousness and realize the total organizing power of pure knowledge within oneself.[20]

Maharishi continues to explain that, "the theme of imparting complete knowledge through my Vedic Science and Technology is perfect; it maintains complete knowledge at every step of progression of knowledge:"[21]

> Imparting knowledge and gaining knowledge as it naturally evolves in the sequentially progressing structure of the Veda is that perfect theme of education which delivers complete knowledge at every stage of progression of knowledge.[22]

Here, complete knowledge is described as available at every point in the sequential unfoldment of the Veda and the Vedic Literature. Anyone can "enliven the structure of pure knowledge" by opening his or her awareness "to that level of consciousness where it is structured" by reading or listening to the Veda and the Vedic Literature. Knowledge of the Veda is knowledge of the Self. With this knowledge one has access to infinite organizing power.

Pure knowledge, unlike relative knowledge, is holistic—precisely because it contains the organizing power necessary to administer and maintain the creation and evolution of the universe; gaining this level of knowledge the individual can create as Nature creates. At this level one has the support of absolute administration. Absolute administration is perfect. As noted earlier, Maharishi points out that "perfect administration is the phenomenon of knowledge; it is the phenomenon of knowing; it is the phenomenon of knowingness; it is the phenomenon of least action, which is the phenomenon of the self-interacting dynamics of the self-referral state of consciousness."[23] Furthermore, Maharishi explains that while Ṛk Veda is the "reality of the structure and unstructured field of consciousness," the Vedic Literature unfolds the mechanics of the structuring process.[24]

With the understanding of Maharishi Vedic Science, the last sūtra of the Vāstusūtra Upaniṣad, the purpose of "this exposition of *Vāstu*" (the text of the Vāstusūtra Upaniṣad) "is to confer knowledge", can be taken as to refer to knowledge of the Self—self-referral consciousness (and the structure of Veda). *Vāstu* is the value of Natural Law which connects the parts to the whole, individual life with cosmic life. This sūtra may also indicate that by reading the Vāstusūtra Upaniṣad, knowledge of the exposition of *Vāstu*, the wholeness of Natural Law is enlivened in consciousness. As mentioned above, *Vāstoṣpati*, the ruler of *Vāstu*, could be taken to operate on the same principle as the administrator of the universe who, in governing all forms and phenomenon, administers life by virtue of the "phenomenon of knowledge."

In this discussion, its seems that the first and last sūtras may encapsulate the main theme of the text: the administrator of *Vāstu* should be known first; the exposition of *Vāstu* is for knowledge in the broadest sense. The following chapters explore how other sūtras may be understood in the light of principles of Maharishi Vedic Science and how they might possibly elaborate upon this theme.

24

THE ARTIST AND CREATIVE PROCESS: KNOWING WHAT CONSCIOUSNESS IS AND WHAT IT IS MADE OF

As discussed in Part V, Maharishi defines the artist as one who is a genius, able to perform action with minimum expenditure of energy and maximum success. The artist is one who creates as Nature creates. In this sense, an artist is an enlightened individual. This definition of the artist is much broader than established or contemporary definitions; it is not restricted to a specific activity such as painting, sculpture, etc., or generating language games. It refers to enlightenment. The artistic individual maintains a connectedness between the inner value of consciousness and its outer expression in form. This applies in any undertaking. The aim is to fix up the target and achieve the goal with minimum expenditure of energy and maximum life-supporting results. To explore whether the Vāstusūtra Upaniṣad describes such an individual and the mechanics of Nature's functioning, this chapter considers specific sūtras in the light of Maharishi's definition of the artist and his description of the unfoldment of self-referral consciousness.

The Sthāpaka, the Carrier of Tradition, Knows the Line and Circle

Sūtra 6, Chapter One of the Vāstusūtra Upaniṣad states:

स प्रवहणः शिल्पासूत्रध्यायं स्थापकविद्यां चावदत् ।

Sa pravahaṇaḥ śilpā-sūtra-adhyāyaṁ sthāpaka-vidhyāṁ cāvadat.
He, the carrier of the tradition, proclaimed (to them) the teaching of the Śilpasūtra (called) the sthāpakavidyā.

(*Vastusūtra Upanṣad, 1,6*)

Traditions, as discussed in Part IV, are not simply outmoded forms of behavior or rituals; Maharishi explains that, "traditions are those modes of Creative Intelligence which, embedded in the nature of life, have withstood the test of time and therefore serve as a safe ground for currents of creativity to grow and find fulfillment generation after generation."[1] This is why tradition and "cultural values lie at the basis of all progress."[2] Modes of activity or ways righteousness keep life in harmony and are passed down from generation to generation, forming traditions or family *dharmas.*[3] Those traditions which uphold life are the expression of the Laws of Nature upheld by *Dharma*. From this perspective, the custodian of tradition could be defined as one who maintains the ways of righteousness that ensure progression of in an evolutionary direction.

In the Vedic tradition, custodians of complete knowledge preserve Vedic wisdom. This tradition includes the teaching of the technologies to experience pure consciousness and gain pure knowledge; Maharishi points out that "the custodians of Vedic wisdom act as the guardians of the main trunk, from which different branches have sprung from time to time in the form of different religions, faiths, philosophies and cultures in different parts of the world."[4] In this context, the ancient line of teachers is honored[5] since they maintain the teaching in its pure form. Here, tradition is related to preservation of knowledge—and the maintenance of its effectiveness.

The first sūtra in Chapter Six of the Vāstusūtra Upaniṣad (स प्रवहणः शिल्पासूत्रध्यायं स्थापकविद्यां चावदत्। *Sa pravahaṇaḥ śilpā-sūtra-adhyāyaṁ sthāpaka-vidhyāṁ cāvadat*, He, the carrier of the tradition, proclaimed (to them) the teaching of the *Śilpasūtra* (called) the *sthāpakavidyā*) states that the "carrier of tradition" is the one who imparts the knowledge of *Śilpa—Śilpāsūtrādhyāya* (the knowledge of *Śilpa*) called *Sthāpaka Vidyā*. In the light of the earlier discussion, *Sthāpaka Vidyā*. could be related to knowledge of the establishment of the Self. *Sthāpan* means to establish and *Vidyā* means knowledge.[6] The term *Sthāpaka* may refer to one who is established or the establisher; *Śilpāsūtrādhyāya* unfolds knowledge. The sūtra seems to indicate that only the "carrier of the tradition" (i.e., one who enlivens the Laws of Nature which promote life), can impart such knowledge.

With reference to tradition the last sūtra of Chapter Five states:

> एवं दैवभेदान् मार्गभेदा जायन्ते।
>
> *Evaṁ daiva-bhedān mārga-bhedā jāyante.*
>
> Thus from different divinities arise different ways (traditions).
>
> (*Vāstusūtra Upaniṣad*, *5.24*)

As noted above, Laws of Nature, or *Devās*, according to Maharishi Vedic Science, are those governing principles which uphold life. *Devās* are described by Maharishi as "frequencies of Creative Intelligence, the Laws of Nature (mechanics of transformation)—the self-referral performance of Natural Law responsible for the whole manifest universe."[7] The Vedic Literature comprises the different sets of Laws of Nature involved in the structuring dynamics of Ṛk Veda—the Constitution of the Universe, the home of all the Laws of Nature.[8] Maharishi also describes Laws of Nature as *dharmas* which uphold evolution—the evolution of the individual body and society—expressed as specific modes of activity which form traditions.

Bhedah can mean "difference" or "expanding." Here, *Daiva* is translated as "divinities", but can be taken as "Laws of Nature." This sūtra could be referring to the relationship between the Laws of Nature—impulses of consciousness—and the modes of activity in society: "Thus from different Laws of Nature arise different modes of activity (different ways or traditions)."

The next sūtra which mentions Laws of Nature states:

वृत्त्या दैवचिन्तने भेदः सञ्जायते ।

Vṛttyā daiva-cintane bhedaḥ sañjāyate.

According to the (difference of) mental modifications (vṛtti) a difference arises in the conception of divinities.

(*Vāstusūtra Upaniṣad, 6.2*)

The word *daiva* again can be taken as Laws of Nature; as discussed previously, *Vṛtti* is "impulse of consciousness" or "frequency'. *Cint* can mean "to think"[9] and *Saflj* "to be attached";[10] *Safljāyate* can indicate "to be born together", "to arise", or "to unite". The sūtra could convey the sense that according to the *Vṛttis*, or fluctuations of consciousness a difference arises in the conception (or thinking) of the Laws of Nature.

Yet another sūtra makes reference to the *Sthāpaka* as one who knows the circle and line. The fourth sūtra of the Vāstusūtra Upaniṣad states:

वृत्तज्ञानं रेखाज्ञानं च यो जानाति स स्थापकः ।

Vṛtta jñānaṁ rekhā jñānaṁ ca yo jānāti sa sthāpakaḥ.

Who has the knowledge of the circle and line is a sthāpaka.

(*Vāstusūtra Upaniṣad, 1.4*)

Vṛtta can be taken as "turned," "set in motion (as a wheel)," "round," "rounded or circular," or "the turn of a line." The word *Rekhā* can mean "line," "a continuous line," "a row or series." *Jñānam*, or knowledge, as discussed previously, can refer to knowledge of consciousness. This sūtra could also be referring to the *Sthāpaka* as someone who is established in self-referral consciousness (who has knowledge of the science of establishment) and who knows consciousness in terms of line and circle.

The Straight Line: The Transcendental Basis of Creation

As discussed Parts II and III, according to Maharishi Vedic Science, the line and circle describe the fundamental nature and structure of consciousness. The Transcendental basis of creation is the straight line, "an endless unbounded straight line, a straight plane of no boundaries" where "all possibilities are always lively and form the basis of creation."[11] The straight line, in this context, describes the basic nature of consciousness at the Transcendental level. It is a line or plane, a field of no boundaries where all possibilities are latent and form the source of creation. If one knew this level of life, then one would know the basis of creation. Maharishi also mentions the straight line with respect to motion; the straight line represents infinite frequency, the field of silence[12] in which motion is direct and infinitely fast. In this context, on the level of experience, when thinking occurs in the state of silence, dynamism is upheld by silence and thought proceeds in a straight line; it follows the principle of least action.[13] The two values of silence and dynamism describe the phenomenon of progress as a straight dynamism. As Maharishi emphasizes that state of Being is both ways at the same time, "its a "straight line representing silence and dynamism only when the dynamism is of infinite frequency."[14] Here is the "total Constitution of the Universe;" the continuum of infinite silence and of infinite dynamism, by virtue of the infinite frequency of dynamism, is expressed as a straight line. The straight line represents silence and dynamism when dynamism is of an infinite frequency and can, therefore, be said to be "in and out at the same time." Operating from this level, thinking is upheld by silence and progresses in a straight line; one knows the field of Transcendental Consciousness—the state of Being—and how thought functions at that level. With this understanding knowing "line" may refer to knowledge of the Transcendental field, the fundamental value of consciousness within which is structured the Constitution of the Universe.

As noted in Chapters 1 and 5, philosophers described line in relation to point: the point is the indivisible beginning of all magnitudes or an extremity which has no dimension—an extremity of a line. To know the essence of a point, which is simpler than a line, a person is advised to think of the center of the universe and the poles. In Maharishi Vedic Science, "Ṛk Veda is the Constitution of the Universe from that one straight line where infinity collapses onto its own point, 'Ak'."[15] In knowing the line, the Sthāpaka would know the Transcendental level of consciousness and the dynamics of silence and dynamism. वृत्तज्ञानं रेखाज्ञानं च यो जानाति स स्थापकः। *Vṛtta jñānaṁ rekhā jñānaṁ ca yo jānāti sa sthāpakaḥ*—Who has the knowledge of the circle and line is a *Sthāpaka*. *Vṛtta*, meaning "circle", can also denote the turn of a line or series, like the turn of a wheel. If the movement round the circumference of a circle determined by a rotating line (such as the radius of the circle, with its fixed point at the center) is mapped in a single direction, a sine wave is created.

Incidentally, the English word universal, made up "uni" and "versal," has its root in the Latin "ūniuersus" which means turned into one, or combined into a whole— "Ūni" means one or cognate with one, and "uersus" is the past participle of "uertere" meaning "to turn." Representing the self-referral nature of consciousness, the circle would contain the universe—the universe and its observer.

The Circle and the Self-Referral Nature of Consciousness

With respect to the circle, as discussed Part III, Ṛk Veda, the structure of self-referral consciousness, from one point generates *Maṇḍalas* or circles. As Maharishi explains:

> A field without boundaries, an endless unbounded straight line—a straight plane of no boundaries, on that level of life, all possibilities are always lively and form

> the basis of creation. From there the structure of the Veda provides the constitution of all life, the constitution, the law, which governs life everywhere—the eternal law from that level of pure knowledge, Ṛk Veda. Ṛk Veda is that level of eternal law from where the law listens to its own steps of progression and from one point it generates *Maṇḍalas.*[16]

The structure of Ṛk Veda from one point creates *Maṇḍalas* that are "a cyclic performance engaged in eternal steps of progression which construct the steps of evolution in a most orderly way, through the infinite order with which everything in the universe evolves." While the circle or *Maṇḍala* represents the cyclical performance of Natural Law, it is also described by Maharishi as a continuum.

The Circle Represents a Continuum

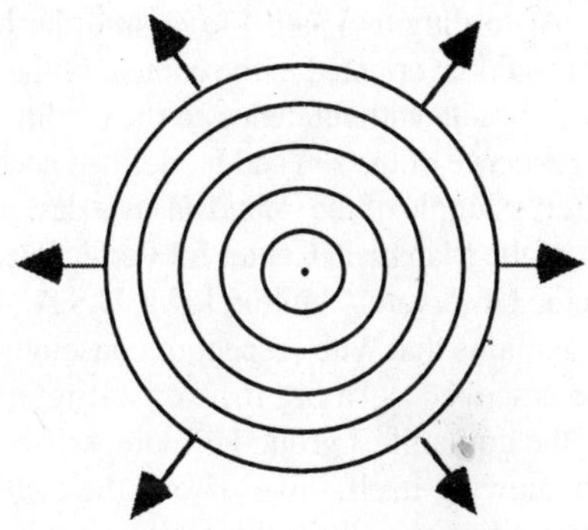

The structure of the Constitution of the Universe can be understood in terms of its self-referral nature expressed in the structure of a circle; small or big, the circle represents a continuum.

The Circle as a Continuum

As discussed in Parts II and III, Maharishi explains that the Constitution of the Universe, Ṛk Veda, the structure of pure knowledge, is expressed as a *Maṇḍala*. Maharishi teaches that:

> Eternal and absolute is the structure of the Constitution of the Universe. This is because the total potential of its infinite organizing power is the field of intelligence which is an eternal continuum. Its self-referral nature is expressed in the structure of a circle (*Maṇḍala* in which Ṛk Veda is structured). A circle can

> be big or small. It can be smaller than the smallest or bigger that the biggest (*Aṇoraṇīyān Mahato-mahīyān*). As long as it is a circle it represents a continuum.[17]

The circle represents a continuum regardless of its size; the structure of the universe, itself, can be understood in terms of the circle.

The circle is the underlying structure of self-referral consciousness. The circle and the many circles of self-referral, the holistic aspect of Ṛk Veda and the different values of the Vedic Literature, are all values of self-referral consciousness. In this way, the circle can be seen to embody more than the concept of a geometric form or mathematical idea.

The Circle and Sthāpatya Veda—Vāstu Vidyā

Maharishi explains that with proper *Vāstu* the individual is well connected with the universe. *Vāstu Vidyā*, the harmonizing power of Natural Law, aligns the parts with the whole. According to *Vāstu Vidyā*, in order to gain the support of Natural Law, the site should be oriented in the context of the earth's relationship to the sun; by determining the site with reference to the cardinal points, a design can take into account the influence of the sun and be defined according with respect to the cycles of Nature (an example of the *Maṇḍala* as a design principle is found in the layout and design of the Maharishi Center for Perfect Health and World Peace and the Maharishi Vedic Observatory built in Iowa, U.S.A.—see page 144).

Maharishi also explains that with respect to consciousness, the self-referral value of *Atmā* can be described as "a big fish" of self-referral "coming up under the water."[18] *Ātmā,* the unmanifest ground of pure, self-referral consciousness, as noted in Part III, in knowing itself, gives rise to the qualities of Ṛishi, Devatā and Chhandas; in their unified state these three values are Saṁhitā, the singularity of self-referral consciousness or Ṛk Veda, the structure of pure knowledge lively within *Ātmā.*[19] *Ātmā* gives rise to Veda; Veda structures and is found within the physiology; it also structures *Viśwa,* the universe. Ultimately, *Viśwa* is found to be *Brahm*—wholeness moving within itself. *Ātmā* is *Brahm.* Maharishi points out that the body, mind, intellect, the Self and the environment are all, ultimately, within consciousness—*Ātmā,* the Self, the ocean of the infinite organizing power of knowledge, the ocean of bliss. In this context, this self-referral move of consciousness can be thought of as the "fish" of self-referral.

The Circular Motion of Self-Referral Consciousness

With respect to the circular motion of self-referral, Maharishi explains that:

> When from any point the all-directional evolution of performance begins, there is a spontaneously created bulging down tendency, which balances the evolution of the point in all directions. This balancing effect is the constant connectedness of

> the source (the point) with the whole process of expansion. This phenomenon of expansion remaining connected to the source presents the form Ṛk.[20]

The circle represents the holistic awareness of self-referral, Transcendental Consciousness. Holistic awareness is equally disposed to all directions; this is why it is referred to as all-directional. In Transcendental Consciousness, the limitations of directions have no validity in this state of wholeness or full alertness. As discussed in Chapter 6, through regular practice of Transcendental Meditation, the process of transcending facilitates the natural ability of comprehending infinity within a point. Every isolated experience remained submerged within an unbounded ocean of bliss.

The Circular Phenomenon of All Directional Awarenesss

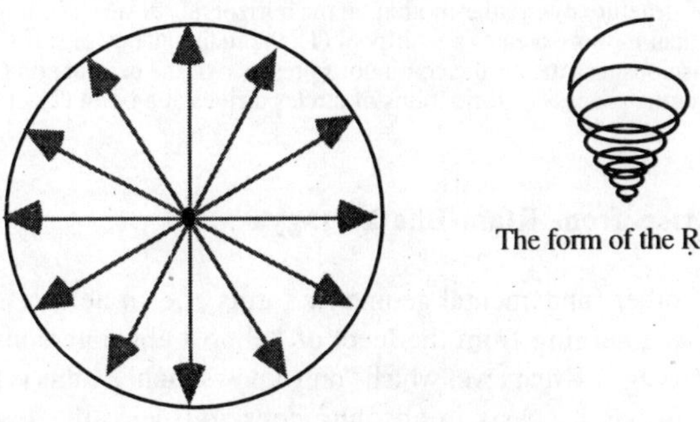

The form of the Ṛk

Holistic awareness, equally disposed to all directions

> The complete picture of knowledge and its organizing power is only available in the state of wholeness or full alertness of Transcendental Consciousness, where the limitations of directions have no meaning.

Maharishi further describes the circular motion or dynamic of consciousness in terms of horizontal and vertical values:

> This structure of circular motion on the horizontal surface, accompanied with vertical motion creating a whirlpool, presents the dynamics of self-referral consciousness. Maintenance of self-referral consciousness means continuous presence of the central point until the dynamic process of formation of circles arrives at a point.[21]

In the process of combined vertical and horizontal motion on the level of self-referral consciousness, the central point is continuously present; simultaneously, the dynamic process of the generation of circles comes to a point.

The Circular Motion of Consciousness

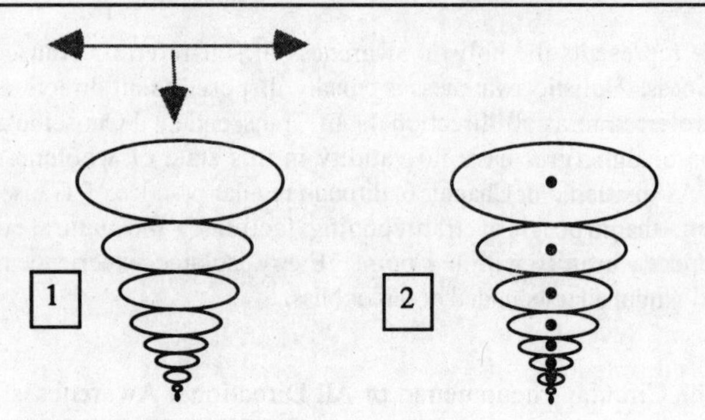

The structure of circular motion on the horizontal surface, accompanied with vertical motion, creates a whirlpool (1). the maintenance of self-referral consciousness means the continuous presence of the central point until the dynamic process of formations of circles arrives at a point (2).

Circles Arise from Ṛtam-Bharā-Pragyā

Along with other fundamental geometric forms, the circle is also described by Maharishi as emerging from the level of "almost absolute consciousness" or *Ṛtam-bharā-pragyā*—that level which "only knows truth";[22] this is the subtle level of life which has its basis in absolute consciousness: the level "where the differences are non-existent but from where all differences arise. It is the source of all differences in creation at a level which in itself is free from all differences, but where there are impulses."[23] From this level of life creation expresses itself.

According to the description of the line and circle outlined in Maharishi Vedic Science, it appears that if the individual (artist or sculptor) or *Sthāpaka* were to know the line and circle, he or she would know the fundamental nature and structure of the universe. Knowing this, any form can be created to embody the structure of life. In this context, the idea of knowing the line and circle would not simply refer to the superficial knowledge of design.

One who knows the circle and line knows the ultimate structure of and dynamics of life at the level of self-referral consciousness, his or her own self-referral awareness. He or she knows the deepest reality of the structure of creation. This understanding seems to extend ideas of the ancient philosophers and mathematicians; as mentioned in Part I, Pythagorean mathematics was thought to reveal the workings of Nature; Euclid laid out five postulates which define the point, line and the circle, from which, he argued, all geometry could be derived.

The Mechanics of Nature's Functioning

According to Maharishi Vedic Science, the creative mechanics of Nature are the creative performance of self-referral consciousness. From within its own singularity, through a process of diversification, pure consciousness creates and dwells within creation. Ideally, the creative process of the artist, as noted in Part V, follows the same progression. In addition, the procedure whereby the artist can successfully create universal art according to Maharishi Vedic Science, involves holding the image within consciousness and transporting that vision onto material form. Several sūtras of the Vāstusūtra Upaniṣad can be viewed in the light of these descriptions.

With respect to Nature's creative mechanics, the details of the Veda and Vedic Literature unfold the structuring mechanics of the Veda, or pure knowledge, giving rise to the universe. Veda emerges from *Ātmā*, the Self, and is expressed as *Viśwa*, the universe. Ultimately, the universe is seen to be nothing other than the impulses of self-referral consciousness, or the Self, in Brahman Consciousness. Maharishi explains that *Brahma*—pure knowledge, the ultimate wholeness, unbounded limitless, infinite, eternal, immortal totality, the Veda lively in human awareness—can be known through levels of cognition. In the process of cognition the intellect is taken from the surface level of the sensory perception to deeper levels of intellectual cognition:

> Cognition is fundamentally the phenomenon of intelligence. Cognition is the path to awaken intelligence to the reality of what one cognizes. Levels of cognition take the intellect from the surface levels of perception to deeper levels of intellectual cognition, until the intellect, transcending the boundaries of the senses, ultimately transcends its own intellectual limitations. What is left is the field of pure existence, pure intelligence—unbounded, limitless, infinite, eternal, immortal totality, the ultimate wholeness, *Brahm*—pure knowledge, the Veda, lively in human awareness—Veda realized on the level of its own intelligence, Saṁhitā of Ṛishi, Devatā, Chhandas, the Ultimate Reality of human consciousness. This is *Brahma Vidyā*, the knowledge of totality, the knowledge of Natural Law.[24]

When the intellect transcends the boundaries of the senses and its own intellectual limitations, what is left is the field of *Brahma*—totality. The creative dynamics of consciousness (from *Ātmā* to Veda, Veda to *Viśwa*, and then *Viśwa* seen aṣ Veda, impulses of self-referral awareness or the Self) are known to be wholeness moving within itself—the totality of consciousness or *Brahma*. The creative mechanics of Nature can, thus, be cognized by individual awareness. *Prajñanam Brahma* is this complete knowledge of Brahman described as "wisdom" by Maharishi.[25]

Brahman and the Creative Process

Brahma corresponds to the infinite organizing power of Natural Law which governs all the Laws of Nature and is "the Ruler of the universe," or the wholeness of Saṁhitā[26]—*Puruṣottama*, the holistic rulership of supreme administration. *Brahma* is the field of pure existence, pure intelligence, the ultimate wholeness, pure knowledge, the Veda, the creator, and the "Absolute."[27] Maharishi also explains that through the "three-step move" of *Brahman*, the "three-step move of Saṁhitā of Ṛishi, Devatā and Chhandas,"[28] the self-referral performance of wholeness, creation emerges.

The Move of Wholeness, or Brahman, in Three Steps

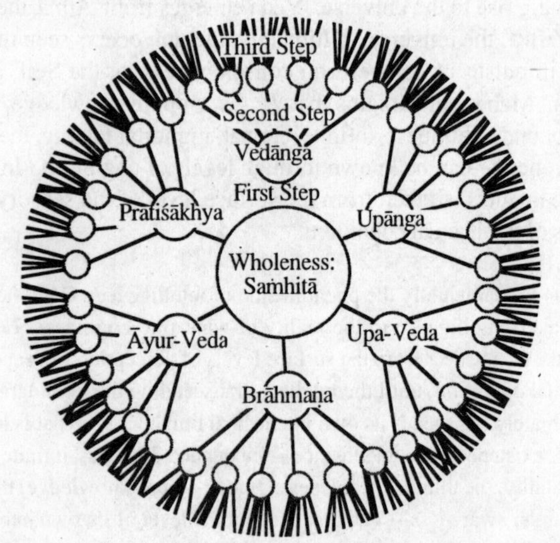

Following the first, basic three-step move of Ṛishi, Devatā and Chhandas within Saṁhitā, the creative mechanics of Nature's functioning unfolds. This symmetrical evolution of Natural Law manifests in the orderly evolution of the ever-expanding universe.

The three-step move of wholeness, involves the entire Veda and Vedic Literature; it reveals the self-interacting dynamics of self-referral consciousness. The move of wholeness is the move of totality, the move of *Brahman*, a move created by virtue of wakefulness or absolute alertness of pure consciousness.

With this understanding, sūtra twelve of the last chapter, of the Vāstusūtra Upaniṣad, can be considered:

ब्रह्म सत्यादौ ।

Brahma satyādau

Brahman and satya (truth) are in the beginning.

(*Vāstusūtra Upaniṣad, 6. 12*)

The sūtra could also be translated as *Satya*, in the beginning, is *Brahman.* From the perspective of Maharishi Vedic Science, *Brahman* is the creator, that value of pure intelligence, pure existence, pure knowledge and its infinite organizing power, which is responsible for the emergence and unfoldment of creation. *Satya* means "truth",[29] or "that which never changes" (*Chit* is intelligence and *Ānanda* is bliss: *Sat Chit Ānanda*—this "unmanifest, non-functioning value of Creative Intelligence is an eternal reality of life, and that is why it is called *Sat*—that which never changes.")[30] Maharishi also translates *Satya* as "absolute alertness":

सत्यमेव जयते ।

Satyam eva jayate.

Wherever there is absolute alertness, there is victory.[31]

(*Mundaka Upaniṣad, 3.1.6*)

The level of absolute alertness is the field pure wakefulness—where consciousness is fully awake to itself. *Satya*, or truth, is that non-changing field of pure intelligence—absolute alertness.

With this understanding of *Satya* and *Brahman*, the sūtra seems to be explaining that *Brahman* is *Satya* or absolute alertness, in the beginning (i.e. at that level where creation is pure potentiality). The beginning can refer to the undifferentiated state of pure consciousness; this is the state of absolute alertness, which, by virtue of its nature to be conscious of itself, differentiates various aspects of its own nature and generates sounds and corresponding forms. These impulses structure the phenomenal world. In this sense, this sūtra may refer to the beginning of the creative process through which, in the three-step move, matter or form arises from the unmanifest.

As discussed in Parts II and III, Maharishi explains that because the field of pure consciousness, the state of absolute alertness, is awake to itself, it discriminates within itself; it creates a duality or division within its undivided nature. This process of diversification gives rise to creation.

Sūtra three of the Vāstusūtra Upaniṣad states:

अतो द्विधा ब्रह्म रूपवन् भवति ।

Ato dvidhā brahma rūpavan bhavati.

Thus, on account of having two aspects Brahman acquires form.

(*Vāstusūtra Upaniṣad, 4. 3*)

It could be said that Brahman—as pure wakefulness or absolute alertness—discriminates within itself, diversifies and acquires form.

Maharishi points out that, "pure wakefulness, being awake in the two values within its structure, exhibits the quality of lively intelligence, the quality of consciousness"[32] and, therefore, knows itself completely. It is the interaction of silence and dynamism within pure wakefulness which presents the mechanics of creation, as Maharishi explains:

> The interchange of silence and dynamism within the nature of pure wakefulness demonstrates the mechanics of creation; it explains how unity is duality and how the process of evolution is sustained within it. Pure wakefulness locates the dynamics of creation within itself and locates the structures of creation within its own unmanifest self-referral state—dynamic silence.[33]

Pure wakefulness is pure silence and infinite dynamism, creating an "eternal interaction" resulting from the collapse of silence into dynamism and dynamism into silence. The two values of silence and dynamism can be said to demonstrate the mechanics of creation. Similarly, Maharishi describes consciousness as the co-existence of two qualities of intelligence: 1) Singularity of self-referral Saṁhitā, 2) Diversity of Ṛishi, Devatā and Chhandas.[34]

Pure consciousness has the silent value of *Puruṣa* and the dynamic value of *Prakṛti*. *Puruṣa* is the "Transcendental Reality which comes into direct experience during Transcendental Meditation,"[35] and is the eternal witness or silent witness of activity. As Maharishi explains, "even though the whole of nature functions under His will, *Purusha* remains a silent witness to its activity."[36] *Puruṣa* is that characteristic within pure consciousness which is "the complete totality of self-sufficiency."[37] Conversely, *Prakṛiti* is the "primal substance out of which the entire creation arises" whose constituents are the three *Guṇas*, *Sattva*, *Rajas* and *Tamas.*"[38] It is that characteristic "which is ready to express the field of all possibilities within itself."[39] While Maharishi refers to *Puruṣa* as the "ruler of the parts of the universe—the individual Creative Intelligence that rules individual values in the universe," he stipulates that the *supreme ruler* or governor of the universe is *Puruṣottama* or *Brahma.*[40]

By virtue of its simultaneously silent and dynamic values absolute alertness creates unmanifest frequencies that give rise to form. As Maharishi notes, sound has a form, form has a sound; form is physiology, sound is the frequency that structures physiology. Sūtra Three, Chapter Four of the Vāstusūtra Upaniṣad seems to be referring to these creative mechanics of Nature's functioning: On account of having two aspects, *Brahma* (the field of almost absolute intelligence which underlies and pervades all activity responsible for the creation and evolution of life) *Rūpavan Bhavati*—acquires form. From the perspective of Maharishi Vedic Science, the sūtra could be said to indicate a foundational principle of Nature's functioning.

In addition, as noted in Part V, Maharishi teaches that the creative mechanics of Nature are the same mechanics through which the enlightened artist creates. In knowing the details of consciousness, in living Brahman Consciousness, the artist can create, embodying the structure and qualities of consciousness in form.

Another sūtra seems to reiterate the above principle; manifest creation emerges from the unmanifest:

> अरूपाद् रूपं तस्य फलम् ।
> *Arūpād rūpaṁ tasya phalam.*
> From the formless arises form, that is the result (of the fourteen stages).
> (*Vāstusūtra Upaniṣad, 5.22*)

Here, the translators Boner et al. make reference to "the fourteen stages" that were mentioned in the preceding sūtra (i.e., sūtra 5, 21 of the text). However, taking *Arūpād rūpaṁ tasya phalam* simply as From the formless arises form, that is the result, it seems to refer to the first principle of Nature's functioning as described in Maharishi Vedic Science. *Rūpa* is "form"; *Arūpa* denotes "the formless". *Phala* is "fruit" or "result".[41] The "formless" can refer to the unmanifest field of pure consciousness, pure intelligence, pure existence or *Ātma*—the unmanifest ground of creation.

This sūtra may indicate that unmanifest, pure consciousness is the basis of form. From that unmanifest field arises the manifest creation—all forms and phenomena. On the level of artistic expression, the same mechanics apply to the creative process in art. For any individual (any artist), in knowing this, he can create as Nature creates.

Envisioning Form and Transporting it onto Matter

An artist, as discussed in Part V, is one who creates as the Creator creates; fully awake in his or her own self-referral value of consciousness, the artist employs the infinite organizing power of Natural Law—creating form which embodies consciousness. As mentioned in Chapter 19, Maharishi outlines the means by which the enlightened artist realizes his or her creation: The artist envisions, and holds, within consciousness, the image he or she wishes to create, transferring the image into form, until the final material "copy" of the original vision is complete. Through this process the artist expands his awareness.[42] But in order to hold that image, to mold consciousness in any shape, it is necessary for the artist to have a stress-free nervous system[43]—cultured through the practice of the Transcendental Meditation technique and TM-Sidhi program.

A similar process of creativity may be indicated by the first sūtra, Chapter Two of the Vāstusūtra Upaniṣad, which states that the image should be envisaged to express a particular meaning.

निदिष्टार्थकप्रतिमा ग्राह्या ।

Nirdiṣṭārthaka-pratimā grāhyā.

An image should be envisaged to express a specified meaning.

(*Vāstusūtra Upaniṣad, 2.1*)

Pratima can signify "to copy"; *Pratimā* is "image," "symbol," or "likeness". *Grāhyā* indicates "to be seized", "held", or "to be perceived or recognized or understood." In the Bhagavad-Gītā, *Grāhya* refers to "gained by"—in the gaining of infinite joy by the intellect which becomes established at that level of pure consciousness.[44]

This sūtra may parallel the description of the enlightened artist's creative process. As noted earlier, Maharishi explains:

> In order to mold in his consciousness any shape, any detailed form, he [the artist] must be able to hold it in his awareness, holding it in his awareness even with his eyes open, with hands moving, and with his sense of discrimination active. He will take red or yellow or this proportion, so many items pulsating in his consciousness, but he is able to hold onto the beautiful shape he wants to create on paper. For this it is necessary that his consciousness is pure and should not have any foreign material in it. For consciousness to be pure, one has to have stress-free nervous system.[45] [emphasis added]

The artist holds the image in consciousness, taking many items pulsating in consciousness and transporting them on paper or material form. Similarly, as noted earlier, in the context of a discussion of creativity and Michelangelo's method of working, Maharishi points out:

> He saw the figure in the marble and what he did was scrape out the figure; he scratched out the undesirable deposits of the marble surrounding the figure. Where was that figure structured? Certainly it existed in the marble, but it was a copy of the structure of the consciousness of the artist. The artist comprehends the outlines of the figure—maybe a long face or a short nose—in his consciousness, and then he wants to depict it on marble, on paper, on clay, or on wood; he carves the wood; he carves the wood, but he carves the wood to match the picture he contains in his awareness.

> To first comprehend in great detail, with great accuracy, and then keep that comprehension alive day after day, week after week, month after month, year after year, until the image has been completely portrayed on the wood or on the marble or on the paper or on the canvas—that is art. The artist enjoys having that figure in his awareness. And he has it permanently fixed in his awareness.[46] [emphasis added]

With the image firmly "fixed" or established in consciousness, the artist simply maintains that image over time on the level of consciousness until it has been transported onto material form. Art is a copy or mirror of that which is in consciousness.

In other instances, Maharishi again refers to this phenomenon:

> Maintaining the intactness of the picture in his awareness and yet allowing it to move, this is the life of an artist. Fixed in immovability and all the time mobile, steadiness and flexibility is the quality of an artist. This ability is an art and this the artist develops with practice. The artist grows in this quality by virtue of his performance, by virtue of his repeated expression in art. Thus, the supreme skill of an artist lies in maintaining the immovability and moveability of consciousness. The artist simultaneously maintains the picture in his awareness while transferring it onto paper; this is art.[47] [emphasis added]

The sense of envisaging, "holding" or "fixing " the image, is important to the creative process. If pure consciousness is to be expressed in art—if wholeness, the value of Saṁhitā awareness, is to be lively in form—then the creative mechanics of Nature's functioning will be lively during action. In this sense, the above sūtra (*Vāstusūtra Upaniṣad, 2, 1*) may refer to the creative process of the individual who is living higher states of consciousness—i.e., at least Cosmic Consciousness.[48]

As Maharishi points out, if the artist loses sight of the goal (the infinite value of life which he seeks to represent in form) his creativity dwindles. This is why the goal should be established in awareness; only when individual awareness in established in pure consciousness and the goal or vision is never lost can the creativity of the individual be at its maximum:

> The goal is infinite value of life, and if that could get established on the level of one's awareness, the goal would never be lost; not only never lost to vision but never lost to life as it is lived from moment to moment. In this state he [the artist] is most creative; in this state of cosmic consciousness, where individual awareness is supported by unbounded pure consciousness.[49]

Maharishi continues to explain that

> The goal is a reality of every moment, and therefore the vision of the goal is never lost and creativity could never dwindle—it is fixed and maximum. That is why we want to create a situation in which the vision of the goal is not lost and we live the state of cosmic consciousness.[50] [emphasis added]

As noted, Maharishi uses the phrase "copy of the structure of the consciousness of the artist" in this discussion. This concept relates to a work of art—defined as such when it is a copy of that which is in consciousness. Considering the sūtra in this light, it seems also that a "specified meaning" can be expressed through this kind of creative process. The work of art is defined as such if it is created in a systematic manner, and not by chance.

25

FORM OR RŪPA: UNMANIFEST TO MANIFEST

In the Vāstusūtra Upaniṣad, the term *Rūpa* occurs in different contexts and is translated as "figure", "image", "nature", "human form", "form", and "symbol." *Rūpa* can also refer to "a known or absolute number, a known quantity as having a specific form." In Maharishi Vedic Science, the word *Rūpa* can refer to: 1) the sounds of the Vedic Literature; 2) the "essence of form" or one of the five *Tanmātrās*; and 3) the material value or forms of creation. *Rūpa* can be understood as the sounds or structure of consciousness in terms of form at various levels of expression. With this understanding, in the sūtras of the Vāstusūtra Upaniṣad, the word *Rūpa* may indicate deeper levels of meaning which relate to consciousness. While are over forty sūtras refer to *Rūpa*, only a few are considered here.

In Maharishi Vedic Science, form can be described as the "more solidified structure" of the impulse of intelligence or "name", where "name" refers to the sounds the Vedic Literature—"the fundamental frequencies", the "non-material values", the "hum of the intellect."[1] In terms of cognition, Maharishi explains that "form" can refer to the *form of the sound*, the structures of sound in terms of spoken and written language,[2] i.e. the letters and words of the Veda and Vedic Literature. It can also refer to the corresponding material forms generated by the progression of these structured forms into different frequencies which appear as matter.[3] In this sense, there are several levels of meaning to the word. With respect to the sounds of the Veda, Maharishi points out that the form or structure of the Veda *is* Saṁhitā of Ṛishi, Devatā and Chhandas; "Saṁhitā of Ṛishi, Devatā and Chhandas is the form (or structure) of the Veda, whose name is Ṛk."[4] The form or structure of the Veda—Saṁhitā of Ṛishi, Devatā and Chhandas—is the Constitution of the Universe, the governor of existence found at every point in creation, the basis of all manifest forms. In the discipline of art, form is considered to be the material expression of artistic conception. In this sense, it is the outward manifestation of the artist's thought. As discussed in Part V, the art form is the expression of inner vision or inner value of form; thought is the "first physical expression of its object" and an expression of Creative Intelligence woven with the "threads of energy and intelligence"[5] and can be thought of as the Veda, *Śruti*—energy and intelligence at the same time.[6] Thought, as an expression of Creative Intelligence—woven with threads of energy and intelligence—is the basis of form.

As described earlier, in this process of the evolution of consciousness, unmanifest sound gives rise to audible frequencies of sound, called *Tanmātrās* or subtle elements—which in turn give rise to material particles.[7] "The basic expression of form is a particle of matter."[8] Discussed in Part III, the word "*Tanmātrā*" means the measure of "That" or Brahman, the totality, where the *Vṛttis* of wakefulness quantify Brahman.[9] The *Tanmātrās* or basic realities or essences of the objects of perception are subtle values corresponding to five *Mahābhūtās* (*Ākaśa, Vāyu, Agni, Jal,* and *Pṛthivi*) out of which the material creation is constituted.[10] As Maharishi explains, each *Tanmātra* is a basic reality, one of which is *Rūpa* —the essence of form which expresses itself in fire (or *Agni*);[11] fire is associated with *Pitta Doṣa* and the sense of sight. Also, it is worth noting that, on the level of cognition, that which is seen—*Darśana*—is the form of the Veda and the Vedic Literature (the different values of Ṛishi, Devatā and Chhandas), "the scintillating light of Creative Intelligence" (heard as *Śruti*).[12]

Furthermore, in the analysis of life and creation, Maharishi explains that Sāṃkhya establishes 25 categories lying at the basis of creation and of the process of cosmic evolution: *Puruṣa, Prakṛti, Mahāt, Ahaṃkāra*—the principle of individuation of *Mahāt*; *Manas*—the cosmic mind, the *Indriyas* (including the five senses of perception (the *Jñanendriya*) and the five organs of action (the *Karmendriya*)), the *Tanmātrās*, and the *Mahābhūtās.*[13] The description of these categories can be verified by direct experience through the practice of the Transcendental Meditation technique, through which the mind travels through the gross and subtle levels of creation to the state of pure consciousness. The *Tanmātrās*, including *Rūpa*, constitute five of these 25 categories at the basis of creation—five of the 25 components of an object.[14] *Rūpa* is also described in Maharishi Vedic Science as one of the special qualities of the *Paramanus* or atoms of three of the nine ultimate substances identified by Vaiśeṣika which form the basis of creation;[15] these nine ultimate substances are earth (*Pṛthivi*), water (*Apas*), fire (*Tejas*), air (*Vāyu*), space (*Ākaśa*), time (*Kala*), direction in space (*Dik*), soul (*Ātman*), mind (*Manas*); the first four are distinguished from one another by the special qualities of their *Paramanus*, or atoms. There are four such special qualities: odor (*Gandha*), taste (*Rasa)*, form (*Rūpa*), touch (*Sparsha*). Earth possesses all four of these qualities; water possess flavor, form and touch; fire possesses form and touch; air possesses touch only.

As discussed in Parts II and III, the essence of form can also be understood in terms of the *Vṛttis* or frequencies of consciousness or intelligence. Thus, it appears that "form" can refer to the vowels and consonants of the Veda and the Vedic Literature, the basis of thought, the essence of form (related to sight), one of the special qualities of the *Paramanus*, and the structure of the physiology and the material world.

The individual can cognize all these different values of form through research in consciousness, by means of the practice of the Transcendental Meditation technique and the TM-Sidhi program.

The Emergence of Form

The most fundamental principle of Maharishi Vedic Science states that manifest form emerges from the unmanifest or Absolute;[16] it seems this principle is expressed in sūtra 22, Chapter Five:

> अरूपाद् रूपं तस्य फलम् ।
> *Arūpād rūpaṁ tasya phalam.*
> From the formless arises form, that is the result.
> (*Vāstusūtra Upaniṣad, 5.22*)

Taking the definition of form as the sounds and letters or words of the Veda, *Rūpa* could refer to the emergence of the Veda from the singularity of pure consciousness or *Ātmā*, which is formless; furthermore, the Veda and Vedic Literature contain those Laws of Nature which give rise to matter. In this sūtra, that which comes first is the formless; this seems to represent the mechanics through which consciousness creates. This principle, as discussed in Part V, is especially important for the artist—since the simplest form of human awareness, the source of thought, is the unmanifest field of pure consciousness—the source of creation.

Perceiving or Cognizing Form

Another sūtra seems to refer to the cognition of form during the process of transcending:

> ध्यानप्रयोगे रूपसाष्ठवं स्पष्टमं भवति ।
> *Dhyāna-prayoge rūpa-sauṣṭhavaṁ spaṣṭaṁ bhavati.*
> The excellence of form becomes clear in the act of meditation (by applying the dhyāna of the divinity).
> (*Vāstusūtra Upaniṣad, 3.14*)

As noted in Part II, Chapter 6, the closest English translation of *Dhyāna* is "to meditate"; according to Maharishi *Dhyāna* refers to the process of transcending—or the sphere of life that lies between the mind and Being or pure consciousness. So *Dhyāna* can be understood as the process of meditation where its realm is marked by the "refining of the mental impulses until the most refined state of mental activity is transcended and the mind gains the state of pure consciousness, absolute existence, or eternal Being."[17] With respect to the practice of meditation, Maharishi further explains that:

> In order to connect the principle of dhyana with practice it may be mentioned that the most valuable practice in the sphere of dhyana is the simple system of Transcendental Meditation. Transcendental Meditation belongs to the sphere of dhyana, but at the same time transcends that sphere and gives rise to the state of Transcendental Consciousness, Samadhi. After this state has been gained the attention returns to the sphere of dhyana, which is a sphere of activity.
>
> This regular passing of the attention from one sphere to the other enables Transcendental Consciousness to be maintained even during activity, first at a very subtle level and later in the gross activity of daily life, so that it may eventually become permanent. In this way the simple system known as Transcendental Meditation, which is a specific type of practice, forms the most effective working tool of these two spheres of life, dhyana and Samadhi.[18]

In this description of mediation and the sphere of *Dhyāna*, Maharishi defines the realm of *Dhyāna* as one of activity, in contrast to the realm or sphere of *Samādhi* or pure consciousness. With respect to sūtra 14, Chapter 3, the word *Sauṣṭhava* is translated as "excellence"; *Spaṣṭa* can be translated as "clearly perceived" or "distinctly visible." With the understanding of form and the cognition of form on the level of self-referral awareness provided by Maharishi Vedic Science, it seems that this sūtra could indicate that form (or possibly the syllables of the Veda) becomes clear, is clearly perceived or discerned, through the process of *Dhyāna* or transcending. It may refer to perception on the self-referral level of the essence of form associated with sight—commensurate with *Darśana*. It may convey different levels of meaning pertaining to perception of the essence of form, perception of the Veda and the Vedic Literature, and the structuring dynamics of consciousness as it assumes form.

Another sūtra of the Vāstusūtra Upaniṣad reads:

> तद्बोधे मानुषा रूपज्ञा भवन्ति ।
>
> *Tadbodhe mānuṣā rūpajñā bhavanti.*
>
> By knowing this, men become knowers of Form.
>
> (*Vāstusūtra Upaniṣad, 4. 23*)

This sūtra directly follows one which deals with fulfillment of desires. Conventionally, "*Tad*" means "this" or "that" and *Bodhā* signifies "knowing", "understanding", "waking", "becoming or being awake", or "consciousness." As Maharishi points out:

> The Vedas reveal the unchanging Unity of life which underlies the evident multiplicity of creation, for Reality is both manifest and unmanifest, and

> That alone is. 'I am That, thou are That and all this is That,' is the Truth; and this is the kernel of the Vedic teaching, which the rishis extol as 'worthy of hearing, contemplating and realizing.'[19]

The three expressions given in the above quote are from the Upaniṣads; along with other expressions they are known as the *Mahāvakyas* or great sayings which refer to the state of Brahman Consciousness when everything is seen as self-referral consciousness. In each instance "this" and "that" are found to be consciousness. Becoming awake to this, men become knowers of form—knowers of the self-referral dynamics of consciousness expressed as Veda and as *Viśwa*, the universe. In knowing the structuring dynamics of one's own consciousness, one knows form.

The Character of Form

Elsewhere in the Vāstusūtra Upaniṣad, Sūtra One, Chapter Three states:

> रूपस्य भावो मुख्यः ।
> *Rūpasya bhāvo mukhyaḥ.*
> The character (bhāva) of the form is essential.
> (*Vāstusūtra Upaniṣad, 3.1*)

Maharishi refers to *Bhāva* as "being", or the quality of existence.[20] The sūtra states that form's character or quality is essential. If taken to refer to the quality of pure existence, then the quality of being or pure existence of the form is essential.

(In art practice, art as form should embodies unboundedness or the various qualities of consciousness). The following sūtra provides another expression from the Vāstusūtra Upaniṣad which makes reference to form:

> यथा प्रकृतिस्तथा रूपलक्षणम् ।
> *Yathā prakṛtistathā rūpa-lakṣaṇam.*
> The features of the images are conform to nature.
> (*Vāstusūtra Upaniṣad, 3.15*)

The term *Lakṣaṇam* is translated as the features—in relation to form. *Lakṣaṇa* also means a characteristic or attribute or can refer to the auspicious quality of the image. The sūtra may be referring to the characteristic of form, which conforms to nature or *Prakṛti.*

As noted in earlier chapters, *Prakṛti* is the creative aspect of intelligence or pure consciousness and means "nature".[21] *Prakṛti* governs creation through the three *guṇas* (*Sattva, Rajas*, and *Tamas*); these are expressed as *Vata, Pitta*, and *Kapha* in material creation.[22]

While the sūtra seems to be referring to the features of an image or artwork, on another level, it could indicate the auspicious qualities or characteristics of the form conform to *Prakṛti*, in terms of the three forces of creation (the three *guṇas*).

On the theme of how forms assumes different values or types, Sūtra Four, Chapter Five states:

> मनसि वृत्तिर्बहुधप्रजायते तदा भिन्नरसाद् रूपं नैकं बवति ।
> *Manasi vṛttir bahudhā prajāyate tadā bhinna rasādrūpaṁ naikaṁ bhavati.*
> Many fluctuations arise in the mind, by their different rasas forms become manifold.
> (*Vāstusūtra Upaniṣad, 5.4*)

Manas can refer to the cosmic mind.[23] *Vṛtti*, discussed previously, is translated by Maharishi as "frequency," "impulse" or "fluctuation of consciousness," or "tendency".[24]

As brought out earlier in the discussion of Atharva Veda, Part III, Chapter 11, on the level of consciousness, the *Vṛttis* of *Ātmā*, are unmanifest sound, the *Tharva* of "A", the reverberating wholeness within the point of speech, vibrating potential, thc self-referral dynamics at the basis of everything.

Atharva Veda brings out this aspect of self-referral consciousness; due to flow in opposite directions, points of non-motion are generated. These points are the juncture where the flow of silence and the flow of dynamism cross; the crossing point is a structure which is lively within itself but is without direction, or is rather all-directional. This point is a pulsating quality.

> This is the vision of ATHARVA—the *Tharva* of अ (A)—reverberating WHOLENESS within क् (K), the point of speech—*Vṛttis* of *Ātmā*, unmanifest sound, emerging from the self-interacting dynamics of WHOLENESS—Transcendental Consciousness—the vibrating potential, the self-referral dynamics at the basis of everything.[25]

Maharishi explains that the self-referral move (*Vṛttis*) of the intelligence of the Unified Field within itself generates the fluctuations of self-referral consciousness, the sounds of the Veda.

Bahudhā can mean "in many ways or parts or forms or directions", or "repeatedly", while *Bhinna* can carry the meaning of "divided into parts". *Tadā* indicates "at that time", or "then", and *Naika* can mean "more than one", "various", "manifold", "numerous", or "many". *Bhavati* has the root of *Bhu* which means "to be" and in various contexts has several meanings: "to arise",[26] "to sustain",[27] "to come into being" or "to come forth"[28] and "to be born."[29] As noted earlier, *Rasa* means "taste";[30] (according to Maharishi

Āyur-Veda, *Rasa* is also the first *Dhatu* or tissue of the physiology) it is a fundamental expression of consciousness on the level of the physiology. As discussed previously, Maharishi teaches that the *Vṛttis* of pure wakefulness are responsible for the creation of the five elements or *Mahābhūtās* which together, in various combinations, constitute the basis of all forms and phenomena, including the human physiology.

Fluctuations of consciousness arise in the mind, by their qualities, forms become manifold or many. It seems that the sūtra could be indicating that the *Vṛttis*, the fluctuations of consciousness, arise in many ways or directions in the (Cosmic) mind; by their different *Rasas* (their different essences) forms become manifold.

Considering the activity of creating art, Maharishi specifically points out that, "every model the artist makes, every performance that he performs, every poem that the poet creates, are the fluctuations of that value which is capable of unifying everything with everything else." Here "that value" refers to the unmanifest basis and the central constituent of the universe.[31] When the artist's mind, as noted in Part V, is established on the Cosmic level, then the functioning of the mind follows the functioning of the Cosmic mind; forms created embody consciousness and its qualities.

Another sūtra, sūtra 24, Chapter Six of the Vāstusūtra Upaniṣad states:

> रूपधाराया वृत्तिरति शेष्ठा ।
>
> *Rūpa-dhārāyā vṛttir iti śreṣṭhā.*
>
> From the sequence of forms comes the condition
> (of the mind), this (procedure) is the best.
>
> (*Vāstusūtra Upaniṣad, 6.24*)

If the word denoting forms were to be taken to be describing consciousness, this sūtra could indicate that from the sequence of forms, (self-referral consciousness—unfolding as Veda) come the *Vṛttis*. Again, the *Vṛttis* are impulses of intelligence which "come to the level of the mind which experiences the five values"[32] of the *Tanmātrās*. The word *Śreṣṭhā* can also mean "most splendid" or "auspicious" and the term *Dhārā* can denote "flowing of water" or "a continuous line or series."

In discussing Atharva Veda—reverberating wholeness, as Maharishi explains, through the flow of silence and the flow of dynamism points of non-flow (or all-directional points) are generated. This phenomenon can be located within Ṛk:

> The phenomenon of flow in two opposite directions in the structure of Ṛk can be seen in terms of neutralizing the flow in each direction and maintaining perpetual silence in the flow. The picture is of a series of points of silence constituting the flow.

> This continuous structure of points of silence within the flowing structures of Ṛk Veda, Sāma Veda, and Yajur-Veda produces such points in the field of self-referral motion in Transcendental Consciousness—points of silence fully awake—points of silence without motion throughout the passage of evolution which is the reality of creation.[33]

This flow of consciousness in terms of silence and dynamism creates the continuous structure of points of silence within the flowing structures of Ṛk, Sāma and Yajur-Veda.

As discussed earlier, the evolution of consciousness unfolds in a sequence of sounds and gaps: the sounds are the forms of the Veda. Consciousness moves and takes a direction; in this move, impulses are generated.

In these sūtras, the characteristic of form or the sequence of forms, it seems, is alluded to. In another instance, in defining specific types of images or forms, the Vāstusūtra Upaniṣad makes reference to the three *Guṇas*:

> गुणानुसृतं रूपत्रयम् ।
>
> *Guṇānusṛtaṁ rūpa-trayam.*
> According to the quality (guṇa) there are three types of images.
> (*Vāstusūtra Upaniṣad, 6.19*)

In Maharishi Vedic Science, the three *Guṇas* of *Sattwa*, *Rajas* and *Tamas* are the three basic forces of Nature born of *Prakṛti*; everything is comprised of these three forces. The sūtra suggests that there are three fundamental forms—*Rūpa-trayam* here translated as three types of images —which may correspond to these three forces of *Sattwa*, *Rajas*, and *Tamas*. The sūtra may be referring to the myriad forms of creation which can be categorized according to the three *Guṇas* while also having the meaning that art forms can embody these three qualities. On a more fundamental level these three qualities are related to Ṛishi, Devatā and Chhandas values of consciousness—a discussion which was covered in Chapter 8. Ultimately, everything in creation can be understood in terms of the three fundamental qualities of consciousness.

Another sūtra exclaims:

> भावस्यारोपणं रूपकर्मणि विधेयम् ।
>
> *Bhāvasyāropaṇaṁ rūpa-karmaṇi vidheyam.*
> In image making the infusion of feeling (bhāva)
> (into the image) is enjoined.
> (*Vāstusūtra Upaniṣad, 5.1*)

As mentioned earlier, *Bhāva* (here translated as feeling) can also refer to being, while *Vidheyam* may indicate "to be established", "bestowed", or "enjoined" and *Karmaṇi* can mean "connected with or being in the action". *Ropa* can refer to the act of "fixing" or "setting up". *Karma* refers to action in general or the action of infinity and its point—the collapse of infinity and its own point or the eternal relationship of infinity and its point.[34] The theme of the creative process itself, in the practice of making art, was examined in detail in Part V, Chapter 19. As elaborated there, Maharishi points out that the successful artist translates inner feeling into the work of art by connecting two levels:

> In creating a piece of art, the awareness of the artist is connecting two levels: a very deep level of feeling in which he imagines what he wants to create and, at the same time, that imagination kept intact, the awareness comes out and translates his inner feeling into outer performance.[35] [emphasis added]

It is "the tender emotions of the artist create form."[36] With this understanding, the sūtra could give the sense of: in form creation or image making, the infusion of fine feeling or pure existence is enjoined. The sūtra may bring out the sense of the creative process as expressing infinity, unboundedness, pure consciousness or Being.

Maharishi explains that

> How much the Self, eternal infinite Being speaks in the strokes of the artist, how much the artist vibrates in the value of infinity, how much the artist vibrates Being in that value of Being—that much will the stroke vibrate into the value of life.[37]

Maharishi further explains, in the context of the creative process and artistic expression, that, "every stroke of the artist supplies a stroke of love, a tender feeling of love, and that the piece radiates. Such a piece of art tells the story of life and keeps on telling the story of life to generations in the eternity of time";[38] art, according to Maharishi, is "a piece of the heart of the artist. It is the expression of life, the expression of love, the expression of happiness."[39]

From this description, it seems that the expression of pure consciousness or Being and the value of feeling into the form is important because that value of Being and the quality of feeling will radiate from the work of art. Love is one of the most refined qualities of feeling; reverence, service, and love are the three aspects of devotion involved in the development to higher states of consciousness.[40] As Maharishi explains, the activity of feeling and emotion is the finest of all the modes of activity, "the activity of the organs of action is the most gross, the activity of the senses of perception is more refined, the mental activity of thought is finer still, and the activity of feeling and emotion is the finest of all."[41] In this context, the practice of the Transcendental

Meditation technique and the TM-Sidhi program are the most effective means through which the individual can develop fine feeling, become established in pure consciousness and express these in art.

Creating A "Meditative" State in the Viewer

In the context of a work of art, form can have a particular effect or purpose to move the awareness in the direction of the Transcendent:

> रूपसौभाग्याद् ध्यानभावो जायते ।
>
> *Rūpa saubhāgyād dhyāna bhāvo jāyate.*
> By a harmonious form a meditative mood is induced.
> (*Vāstusūtra Upaniṣad, 2.23*)

As discussed in Part V, and in the discussion of the first and last sūtras of the Vāstusūtra Upaniṣad, it was noted that according to Maharishi Vedic Science, art should lead the viewer in the direction of the Transcendent or the Self. Maharishi teaches that ideally art unfolds the Self in the viewer:

> A close examination of art reveals that the more attention we give to a work of art the more deeply we are drawn into the work to experience subtler and subtler aspects of its meaning. These subtler aspects spontaneously unfold deeper and deeper levels of awareness through the principle which SCI [the Science of Creative Intelligence] describes as increasing charm. Thus, the ultimate meaning of art, the universal content of art, is a vertical expansion of experience inward from the outer boundary of the art object to the inner boundlessness of the viewer's awareness.[42] [emphasis added]

The experience in the perception and involved attention to a work of art is, ideally, that of increasing charm and a vertical expansion of experience toward boundlessness, the unbounded, Transcendental value of the viewer's awareness. Such works of art, created by an enlightened artist, are formally structured to reflect harmony, as Maharishi points out:

> Works of art are formally structured as ideal domains set apart from everyday life and characterized by harmony and unity. SCI reveals that underlying the diversity and apparent conflict of the parts of life is universal wholeness, oneness. Thus, the function of art is to give a glimpse of the unifying wholeness of life, even in a single isolated part. Art's articulation of the boundless within boundaries simulates the experience of unity consciousness in which the infinite becomes perceptible even on the surface of material existence. Thus, the function of art is to give a glimpse, however brief and artificial, of the goal of life and thereby spur us on to evolution.[43] [emphasis added]

Art should indicate the "direction of unboundedness, immortality and bliss" and inspire "those values" demonstrating those "qualities of pure consciousness."[44] The "flavour of harmony and unity should pervade everything the artist does";[45] Maharishi also explains that works of art consist of objectifying subjectivity:

> Experiencing the work of art, the viewer enjoys a subjective enrichment parallel to the creative experience of the artist. Thus, works of art arise from, express, and lead the viewer back to the unbounded field of creative intelligence.[46]

He continues to point out that:

> The effectiveness of art depends on how much its creator is able to experience and express the qualities of pure creative intelligence. When the artist works at full potential his art enriches the inert world with the values of life, enlivens the senses which refines perception, and stimulates evolution in terms of higher awareness. The more that creative intelligence flows through an artist's work, the more universal and enduring its expression. Similarly, the more creative intelligence the viewer is able to bring to his [awareness] of a work of art, the more pleasurable, enriching, and evolutionary his experience of the work of art will be.[47]

Sūtra 23, Chapter Two, रूपसौभाग्याद् ध्यानभावो जायते । *Rūpasaubhāgyād dhyāna bhāvo jāyate*—By a harmonious form a meditative mood is induced, seems to indicate the purpose of art as described above. In Part V, the nature of the form was described as determining the kind of effect it will have on the viewer. The term *Dhyāna* means transcending; *Saubhāgya* can indicate "good fortune", "happiness", "beauty", "grace", or "loveliness", and is translated here as "harmonious". In Maharishi Vedic Science, "good fortune", as discussed previously, is support of Natural Law and results in harmony.

If the term "form" in this sūtra is also to be taken as the "art form", then it seems this expression could be suggesting that the harmonious art form can create the effect of leading toward the sphere of the intellect, enlivening the quality of Being. "The unfoldment of the Self in greater degrees is the purpose of art"; "it leads the perception of the viewer onto unboundedness."[48]

26

POINT, LINE, GRID, TRIANGLE, SQUARE, CIRCLE AND NUMBER AS VALUES OF CONSCIOUSNESS

Geometry plays an important part in art and design and was traditionally thought to express the divine; however, the point, line, triangle, square and circle are known essentially as mathematical concepts without reference to subjectivity or consciousness. As discussed in previous chapters, in his description of self-referral consciousness, Maharishi considers consciousness in terms of a point or numerous points (where the point is Saṁhitā, the point of infinity or individual values of consciousness) and as line. He mentions that the forms of the triangle, square and circle emerge at the level *Ṛtam bharā prajñā*, which is "fully awake consciousness or all-knowing awareness"[1] and that the chapters and different aspects of the Veda and the Vedic Literature take a circle or *Maṇdala* form. The Vāstusūtra Upaniṣad, by indicating these elements, may refer to the structure and nature of consciousness itself and not simply concepts or design principles.

Point as Saṁhitā or Brahman: The Unmanifest Point of Manifestation

In his description of consciousness, Maharishi refers to point in several instances: 1) infinity collapsing to a point, 2) the point of creation, 3) the value of Saṁhitā. The syllable अक् "Ak," the form of the Veda, describes and embodies the dynamic of the collapse of unbounded field of intelligence (absolute silence) onto its own point; ऋक् "Ṛk," the name of the Veda, is the collapse of absolute dynamism onto a point.[2] The structure of Ṛk, displayed in the sound "Ṛk," is characterized by a whirlpool—the collapse of infinity to a point.[3] In terms of Sanskrit, Maharishi points out that क् "K" is that syllable whose pronunciation stops the flow of speech and it stands for stop or point value. The first syllable of Ṛk Veda, अक् "Ak," represents the stop value of a "A" or wholeness. In either case, for "Ak" and "Ṛk," क् "K" represents the point value. Maharishi points out that infinity is a series of points, "Because infinity is just a sequentially organized infinite number of points, the relationship between infinity and point presents the wholeness of silence in motion."[4] In the phenomenon of flow in two opposite directions within the structure of Ṛk, the picture is of a series of points of silence constituting the flow. This continuous structure of points of silence within the flowing structures of Ṛk, Sāma and Yajur-Veda produces points in the field of self-referral motion in Transcendental Consciousness.[5]

In another context, Maharishi also mentions point in reference to the "point of creation" which he defines as "at the point of manifestation of the unmanifest."[6]

In this instance, the point of creation is described as *Rām*, the embodiment of Natural Law or *Dharma*, the embodiment of absolute order—the "Cosmic Ruler."[7] From the perspective of Maharishi Vedic Science, *Rām* is the embodiment of the totality of self-referral consciousness and, as such, is the administrator of the universe. "Point," thus, is the point where creation emerges. From here all the activity of everyone, all the activity in the universe, can be seen. Maharishi refers to a common Indian proverb to illustrate the idea of *Rām* as the point of creation:

> राम झरोखे बैथके
> सबको मुजरो लेय ।
> जाकी जैसी चाकरी
> ताको तैसो देय ।।
>
> *Rām jharokhe baithake*
> *sabako mujaro leya,*
> *jākī jaisī chākarī*
> *tāko taiso deya.*

> *Rām*, the ruling intelligence—*Rām*, the Cosmic Ruler—ever present at the point of creation (at the point of manifestation of the unmanifest), sees all the activity of everyone and spontaneously bestows due results of everyone's actions.[8]

The mechanics of administration through Natural Law function like a whirlpool as described above; the point at the base of the whirlpool is that level of reality which, Maharishi explains is, "available to everyone in his own Transcendental Consciousness, where consciousness is fully awake in its pure wakefulness;" "where the knower, process of knowing, and known are in their unified state—Saṁhitā."[9] Saṁhitā, as the totality or *Brahma*, is found at every point in creation:

> Each point is Saṁhitā, and each point is Saṁhitā of Ṛishi, Devatā, and Chhandas. Each point has pure wakefulness in three values of knower, knowing, and known, because it is pure wakefulness.[10]

In addition, the underlying unity of infinity is an ocean of points. In the description of wholeness on the move, Maharishi explains that Saṁhitā, the totality of pure wakefulness, creates a move within its own unbounded nature, and when totality moves it is like the stirring of a vast ocean or water in a dish:

> When totality moves it moves to bring together infinity, the two ends of infinity. For example if you take water in a deep dish, fill it and stir it at one end, the moment you start to stir one holistic wave goes through the whole dish. The entire water begins to move. Such is the move of that pure wakefulness which is

> eternally awake within itself. It moves and where does it move? It moves connecting its own point after point, and point after point, and point after point. On that level, the point and point are not separated; points are not separate because pure wakefulness is unified and that unified wholeness we call the infinite correlation level of pure intelligence, where one point is infinitely correlated with every other point.[11]

The totality is *Brahma*, which is wholeness moving within itself, "connecting its own point after point." As discussed earlier, *Brahma* is described as the infinite organizing power of Natural Law, Saṁhitā, the supreme Ruler of the universe; *Rām*, as the embodiment of *Brahma*—the ruling intelligence, "is ever present at the point of creation (at the point of manifestation of the unmanifest)."[12]

With this understanding, three sūtras of the Vāstusūtra Upaniṣad are worth noting. The first states:

> बिन्दुर्ब्रह्मेव ब्रह्मध्रुवम् ।
> *Bindur brahmeva brahma-dhruvam.*
> The bindu is like Brahma, Brahman is immovable.
> (*Vāstusūtra Upaniṣad, 6.11*)

Bindu means point; Indian scholars maintain that:

> It pre-eminently signifies the point which goes to form the body describing itself as —> *nābhi*, the navel or hub in the centre of a triangle or circle. From the *bindu*, the starting point, a triangle or circle makes its appearance. For this reason the point or the *bindu* is considered to be the primary source of everything whether it is a physical form or concept.[13]

Applying the definition of *Brahma*, Brahman and point given in Maharishi Vedic Science, this sūtra could indicate that the *Bindu* is like the unmanifest point of creation; the point of the manifestation of the unmanifest from where the entire creation can be seen. Saṁhitā, or wholeness, is the point, from there creation emerges (as illustrated in Chapter 24 in the figure of the three-step move of Brahman). Another sūtra states:

> नाभौ रूपकर्म प्रारभ्यते ।
> *Nābhau rūpa-karma prārabhyate.*
> The creation of the image starts from the navel.
> (*Vāstusūtra Upaniṣad*, 2.10)

In this translation, *Nābhā* is taken to mean "navel"; however, it can also be translated as "central point. *Rūpa*, as noted earlier, means form and *Karma* is "action".[14] As discussed in Chapter 12, *Karma* can refer to the action of infinity and point on the level of self-referral consciousness as discussed on pages 127 and 173. The sūtra may be indicating that action or the creation of form, begins from the central point. The central point is understood as the value of Saṁhitā available to everyone in their own self-referral consciousness. The creation of form starts from one's own self-referral consciousness.

Sūtra Fourteen, Chapter Two of the Vāstusūtra Upaniṣad also mentions point:

लब्धबिन्दुः रसायाः प्राणः ।

Labdha binduḥ rasāyāḥ prāṇaḥ

The bindu obtained in the centre is the life-breath of the earth.

(*Vāstusūtra Upaniṣad, 2.14*)

Here the point is equated with *Prāṇa*. *Prāṇa* is translated by Maharishi as "life",[15] "life breath",[16] and the "inward breath".[17] With this understanding, the point of creation, the central point, is *Praṇa* or "life".

Sūtra Thirteen of Chapter Six apparently makes reference to the central point with respect to the limbs of the form:

ब्रह्मबिन्द्ववलम्बनेन रूपाङ्गाणि सौभगानि भवन्ति ।

Brahma bindvavalambanena rūpāṅgāṇi saubhagāni bhavanti

When the limbs of the image are depending on the Brahmabindu (central point) they become harmonious.

(*Vāstusūtra Upaniṣad, 6.13*)

Here, the central point is again referred to as the *Brahmabindu*; the term *Bṛahmabindu* seems to denote the point of wholeness, Saṁhitā. When the limbs of the form depend on the *Brahmabindu*, the value of Saṁhitā—the unified state of Ṛishi, Devatā and Chhandas—they become harmonious. In unity, diversified values are netted in harmony. It seems that the limbs (of the image or form) should be expressed, or seen, in relation to the central point, the *Brahmabindu*, the point of creation or emergence.

In Maharishi Vedic Science certain aspects of the Veda, the Vedānga—comprising Śikṣā, Kalp, Vyākaraṇ, Nirukt, Chhand, and Jyotish—are described as the "limbs" or *Aṅgas* of the Veda. The Upa-Veda, encompassing Nyāya, Vaiśeṣik, Sāṁkhya, Yoga, Karma Mīmāṁsā, and Vedānt, are referred to as the subordinate limbs of the Veda. The limbs and subordinate limbs of the Veda reveal the sequential, structuring mechanics of the Ṛk Veda; they can be understood as the parts of the Veda which relate to the whole, Ṛk Veda Saṁhitā (they can also be understood in terms of the three-step move of Brahman illustrated earlier). Without reference to the whole, Ṛk Veda, the practical value and significance of these aspects of the Vedic Literature are misunderstood. In terms of human life, when the totality of self-referral wholeness is lost, the basis of harmony is also lost. This is why the principle of connecting the parts to the whole is central to Maharishi Vedic Science; it is central to the progressive development of human life.

With respect to design, the above principle is upheld in *Vāstu Vidyā;* as discussed in Chapter 13, Maharishi Sthāpatya Veda maintains that for any plan (i.e., in architecture and town and city planning) the total design represents the body of consciousness—the central point of which is called the *Brahma-Sthān.*[18] Wholeness resides at this point; all the parts of the design relate to it. To maintain support of Natural Law, the central area supports the parts of limbs of the design or structure. The design, the house, or the form, has its own physiological structure which embodies the structure of consciousness.

In the above discussion its seems that the point may greater significance than the sense of a dot in a compositional design or the navel of an image. The point could represent the beginning of creation—the point of totality, the level of self-referral consciousness, *Brahman*, or Saṁhitā, from here form emerges and is sustained.

The Straight Line of Consciousness: Various Kinds of Lines and Their Effects

Line is mentioned in more than 20 sūtras of the Vāstusūtra Upaniṣad in the context of geometric forms and the characteristics and effects of different lines. As considered previously, Maharishi also discusses the nature of consciousness in terms of a straight line.[19] Consciousness is "an endless unbounded straight line, a straight plane of no boundaries" on a level where "all possibilities are lively and form the basis of creation".[20] The straight line represents the relationship between silence and dynamism on the level of consciousness:

> Now that state of Being [pure consciousness] is both ways at the same time. Outside lighted, inside lighted, but what do we mean by in and out in that state? In and out is the reality of dynamism and silence. On that level both are the same. Dynamism and silence, dynamism and silence. But if we take it to be in and out, then it is with infinite speed in and out. It's a straight line representing silence and dynamism only when the dynamism is of infinite frequency—when at no time is it in or out; it is in and out at the same time.[21]

In addition to these references to line, Maharishi also mentions that creativity takes a straight line from its source (in the mind) to its goal (in achievement) when there is orderly thinking in the individual. Orderly thinking, means thinking (and resultant actions) in accord with Natural Law—utilizing the infinite orderliness of Nature's functioning. Activity which is promoted from the level of pure liveliness of the mind, or the unmanifest Self—the source of all the Laws of Nature, is "absolutely artistic"[22] and totally spontaneous. It is action performed from the infinite correlation level of the field of Natural Law and "that field of infinite correlation which connects everything with everything else" this is the "most artistic place in the field of creation."[23] As mentioned earlier, the purpose of Maharishi Sthāpatya Veda is to establish life so that everything is connected with everything else.

While some sūtras seem to be simply describing line, others appear to mention line with respect to composition or the effects of certain kinds of line. With regard to the knowledge of line itself, Sūtra Four, Chapter One (discussed at the outset of this chapter and the first sūtra which mentions line) states:

कृत्ताज्ञानं रेखाज्ञानं च यो जानाति स स्थापकः ।

Vṛtta jñānaṁ rekhā jñānaṁ ca yo jānāti sa sthāpakaḥ.
Who has the knowledge of the circle and line is a sthāpaka.
(*Vāstusūtra Upaniṣad, 1.4*)

The *Sthāpaka*, the one who establishes, is defined as one who has the knowledge of the line and circle. As mentioned previously, knowledge of line, *Rekhā jflānam*, as with knowledge of the circle, *Vṛtta jflānam*, could be referring to knowledge of the basic field of consciousness where, as Maharishi states, "all possibilities are lively and form the basis of creation." [24]

Another description of line occurs in the following sūtra which exclaims:

तेजांसि सरलरेखाः ।

Tejāṁsi sarala-rekhāḥ.
Straight lines are as rays of light.
(*Vāstusūtra Upaniṣad, 2.9*)

It is worth noting that not only does Maharishi describe consciousness in terms of a straight line, he also refers to Creative Intelligence as "scintillating light."[25] (In physics, light is described as taking the path of least resistance, a straight line).

An additional sūtra states that knowledge of the line is all comprehensive:

रेखाज्ञानं सर्वमिति ज्ञेयम् ।

Rekhājñānaṁ sarvam iti jñeyam.
The knowledge of the line is to be known as all comprehensive.
(*Vāstusūtra Upaniṣad, 2.27*)

This is the last sūtra in Chapter Two of the Vāstusūtra Upaniṣad, and, therefore, may present a wholeness for that chapter. (In Chapter Two there are a total of 11 sūtras which mention line—more than in any other chapter). *Sarva* is here translated as "all" and is commensurate with सर्वं खल्विदं ब्रह्म । *Sarvaṃ khalvidaṃ Brahma* (*Chāndogya Upaniṣad, 3.14.1*), "All this is That," or "All this is *Brahm*—Totality."[26] *Jfleya* means "to be known". With the understanding from

Maharishi Vedic Science of consciousness as a line, it seems this sūtra may carry the sense that knowledge of the line, *Rekhājflānaṁ*, being knowledge of pure consciousness, the field of all possibilities, is all comprehensive or "everything." Such knowledge would be truly "all comprehensive" and not simply the knowledge of the way to make a mark. Still other sūtras deal with different kinds of lines and their effects.

The Nature and Effect of Lines

The following sūtra states that there are three types of lines:

> तिस्रः रेखाः श्रेष्ठाः ।
>
> *Tisraḥ rekhā śreṣṭhāḥ.*
>
> Three (types of) lines are essential.
>
> (*Vāstusūtra Upaniṣad, 6.5*)

As noted earlier, *Śreṣtha* can be translated as "best "or "most auspicious"; while this sūtra suggests that three lines are essential, or best, the nature of the three lines is not identified. Although there is no obvious connection made in the sūtras, it may be possible that this sūtra, in some way, relates to the sūtra discussed previously, which states that there are three types of form which correspond to the three *guṇas.*

Clearly, in Maharishi Vedic Science, the three-in-one structure of pure knowledge—Saṁhitā of Ṛishi, Devata and Chhandas—is the basis of creation. As discussed Parts II and III, everything in creation is the result of the interaction of these three values and can be understood as expressions of them. It is possible that several sūtras from Chapter Two could indicate that certain lines have particular characteristics which relate to the structure of consciousness although, the nature of any such relationship has not been indicated. However, as one sūtra states:

> उत्थितरेखा अग्निरूपाः पार्श्वगा अब्रूपाः
> तिर्यग्रेखा मारुतरूपा ति ।
>
> *Utthita-rekhā agni-rūpāḥ pārśvagā abarūpāḥ*
> *tiryag-rekhā māruta-rūpā iti.*
>
> Vertical lines have the nature of fire, horizontal lines have the nature of water, diagonal lines have the nature of wind (māruta).
>
> (*Vāstusūtra Upaniṣad, 2.22*)

Given that *Rūpa* can mean form, the sūtra might also read: vertical lines have the form of fire (*Agni*), horizontal lines have the form of water, diagonal lines have the form of wind (*Māruta*). In each case, the directional character of the line seems to correspond to a particular element. As discussed previously, the five elements combine and relate to the three precipitated values of Ṛishi, Devatā and Chhandas— *Vata, Pitta* and *Kapha. Agni* or fire as an element has the quality of *Pitta*; wind has the quality of *Vata* and water the qualities of *Pitta* and *Kapha*. Maharishi Āyur-Veda explains that these qualities affect the physiology and emotions of the individual. With this understanding it is worth considering the following three sūtras which are presented in their sequence:

अग्निरेखायामुत्तुङ्गरूपाणि जायन्ते ।

Agni rekhāyām uttuṅga rūpāṇi jāyante.
On the fire (vertical) lines upright forms are produced.
(*Vāstusūtra Upaniṣad, 2.24*)

अब्रेखायामुत्सुकरूपाणि जायन्ते ।

Abrekhāyām utsuka rūpāni jāyante.
On the water (horizontal) lines forms expressing longing are produced.
(*Vāstusūtra Upaniṣad, 2.25*)

मारुतरेखायां तैजसरूपाणि ।

Māruta rekhāyāṁ taijasa rūpāṇi.
On the diagonal (wind) lines fiery (energetic) forms are produced.
(*Vāstusūtra Upaniṣad, 2.26*)

In the first of these three sūtras, the fire lines or the line of *Agni*, could be referring to the quality of consciousness which is expressed as *Agni* or fire; out of this 'line of *Agni* 'upright forms are born. In the second of the three sūtras, the word *Utsuka* taken as longing can also mean "restless", or "uneasy". This sūtra could also give the sense of forms expressing longing or restlessness, are born in the *Abrekha* (water) lines. Clearly, the different characteristics of the lines mentioned correlate to the various natures of the forms produced.

According to these sūtras, three kinds of lines—vertical, horizontal and diagonal lines—are important for knowledge of *Vāstu*. The Vāstusūtra Upaniṣad includes several sūtras which apparently emphasize the significance of line with respect to the composition:

रेखान्वये सर्वाङ्गाणि न्यासय ।

Rekhānvaye sarvāṅgāṇi nyāsaya.
All limbs have to be set along the lines.
(*Vāstusūtra Upaniṣad, 2.8*)

रेखानुपातेनाङ्गानि निधेयानिति श्रेष्ठकृत्यम् ।

Rekhānupātenāṅgāni nidheyāniti śreṣṭhakṛtyam

Placing the limbs along compositional lines is the best method (action).

(*Vāstusūtra Upaniṣad, 3.12*)

In the above sūtras, the positioning of "limbs" according to compositional lines is important. *Aṅga* or "limb" as noted earlier in the context of the Veda and the Vedic Literature, refers to the parts in relation to the whole. In Maharishi Sthāpatya Veda[27] the layout of the design take the form of a grid; a set of interconnected lines. The lines are determined by direction: east to west, north to south. Diagonal lines constitute the north-east to south-west direction and north-west to south-east direction. Since the layout of the directional lines is important in determining the relationship of the site to the sun and the movement of the constellations and planets, line is very important to *Vāstu*. As discussed in this section, if the straight line refers to more than just a mark but to the actual nature of consciousness itself, the sūtras could be referring to a deeper level of meaning. On an applied level, in terms of composition, the direction of the three kinds of line is significant in establishing the relationship of the site to the universe as a whole.

The Koṣṭhaka or Grid

According to the Vāstusūtra Upaniṣad, lines—in the three variations of vertical, horizontal and diagonal—seem to relate to the grid (which is mentioned in seven sūtras); the grid, as employed in the creation of form, denotes an underlying design principle. As discussed by Hartmann, in Maharishi Sthāpatya Veda the principle of the grid in town and city planning relates to the four cardinal points. It serves the purpose of orientation: wherever one is in the built environment one is never lost.[28] Orientation and movement is always with respect to the movement of the planets, and, specifically, the earth in relation to the sun and moon. The grid in terms of the design of the ideal city or town represents the "structure of the entire universe."[29] This is illustrated by designs for ideal living which have been drawn up and applied all over the world in Maharishi Sthāpatya Veda construction.[30] Each design takes into account the structure of consciousness at both the level of the microcosm and the macrocosm.

The term *Koṣṭhaka* is translated as "grid" and is referred to as "most important":

रूपार्थं कोष्ठका मुख्यः ।

Rūpārthaṁ koṣṭhakā mukhyaḥ

For making images a grid is most important.

(*Vāstusūtra Upaniṣad, 4,4*)

Mukhya, as noted previously, is "principal", "first", or "best"; ***Koṣṭhaka*** is translated above as "grid" but can also mean "receptacle", "vessel", a "surrounding wall", or "surrounded field."

In another sūtra, reference is made to form in relationship to the *Koṣṭhaka*:

> कोष्ठकान्तराले रूपस्यावयवो ध्येयः ।
>
> *Koṣṭhakāntarāle rūpasyāvayavo dhyeyaḥ.*
>
> One should imagine the various parts of the image within the grid.
>
> (*Vāstusūtra Upaniṣad, 4.6*)

The translation of this sūtra states that one should "imagine" the parts of the image within the grid. In this context, the sūtra could be making reference to the act of holding the parts of the form or image (as discussed earlier in the creative process section of this chapter) within a holistic context. It also demonstrates the principle of the part to whole relationship; here the whole is represented by the grid. The grid expresses wholeness, an underlying framework, and the parts of the form the elements which should be imagined within the grid. If the grid can be understood as the framework of consciousness in the design representing the "structure of the entire universe",[31] holding or imagining the parts within the grid, indicates holding or imaging the parts in relation to the whole.

In an account of the creative process, Maharishi explains that:

> The procedure should be to imagine a field, imagine an image, fix up the target and then start creating it. The student should imagine the image they want to create in very concrete terms. What shape, what form, what impression, what they want to put on paper or sand—it doesn't matter what—they must have a clear imagination of it before beginning the process of creation.[32]

He continues to point out that:

> The advantage that the artist gets from creating can be so profound. It will be profound only if he has set up the goal of what he is going to create in his consciousness first. For example, an artist thinks that he wants to create the face of a child—absolutely lovable, full of innocence and expression of life—he just has that image in his mind. Then, on the level of his own imagination, something has been structured and that is the abstract creation he is going to make concrete through his artistic activity. Then there is that blossoming of expression from the faintest unmanifest to the visual expression of the manifest. In this procedure there is some connectedness in the process of expression, in the process of making manifest the unmanifest consciousness within.[33]

Ideally, the artist, Maharishi points out, imagines a field, an image, and then goes about creating it. As discussed in Part V, it is important that the artist starts with the goal within consciousness; only through this process is there a connection between the unmanifest value of unbounded consciousness and the manifest expression of it. In this sense, the value of wholeness, unbounded consciousness, is expressed in the parts.

The term *Dhyeya*, which appears in the above sūtra, can also be taken as "meditation". The possible reference to meditation could indicate a process like "transcending" and "holding"—*Dhyāna* and *Dhāraṇā*—during meditation. This sūtra seems to relate to another sūtra (*Vāstusūtra Upaniṣad, 3.14*) discussed earlier which indicated that the excellence of form becomes clear, or is perceived, through the process of *Dhyāna*—transcending. As discussed in Part V, Maharishi points out:

> When the artist is fully absorbed in his creation, when he develops the ability to hold onto his still, inner image and translate that image into the outer field of behavior, all aspects of his mind and intellect become very integrated. Through the integration of all aspects of mind, intellect, and ego, the metabolic rate goes down and the breath becomes softer. It's something like Transcendental Meditation, where one gets deeply absorbed in the fullness of inner experience. What Transcendental Meditation brings to the situation, however, is much more complete and full, but a similar situation is available in the creation of a piece of art. That is why artist's are, by nature, not stressed people; they enjoy life more, they radiate life more.[34]

He continues:

> The life of the artist has a great meaning in terms of release of stress during that kind of creative process which comprehends the gross value of life along with the inner, subtlest emotions. This must be the experience of every artist and more so of the most successful artists.[35]

By holding the image (and its various details) on the level of consciousness, and creating it in material form on that basis, the artist experiences a more integrated style of psychophysiological functioning. In this process, the metabolic rate goes down. With this understanding, the effect of engaging in the creative process of making art is somewhat akin to Transcendental Meditation where the artist is absorbed in his inner experience. The sūtra, "Imagining the parts of the form within the *Koṣṭhaka*," may be giving an insight into the process of manifesting form from within consciousness; this process, as described by Maharishi, is important in the development of the artist's consciousness.

Of the several remaining sūtras which mention the *Koṣṭhaka*, another states:

कोष्ठके व्यतिक्रान्ते रूपमवद्यं बवति ।

Koṣṭhake vyatikrānte rūpamavadyaṁ bhavati

By transgressing the grid the image becomes imperfect.

(*Vāstusūtra Upaniṣad, 4.8*)

In earlier sūtras, knowledge was equated with line; here the sūtra seems to be indicating that by not conforming to the *Koṣṭhaka* the form becomes imperfect. If one takes perfection or the perfect form to be the expression of Natural Law, in "violating" Natural Law by disconnecting the parts from the whole, perfection cannot be achieved. In this sense, there seems to be deeper significance to the *Koṣṭhaka.* With the above translation, the sūtra seems to be indicating a principle which has its correlate in Sthāpatya Veda which does not advise building on certain lines or critical points of the design which represent important nodes of the design physiology

Vedic Geometry: The Triangle, Circle and Square

The three geometric forms of the triangle, square and circle, as described by Maharishi,[36] emerge from the level of *Ṛtam bharā prajflā.* Starting from this level of consciousness, which is free from differences, is the possibility of all differences. From here all triangles, circles and squares come out.[37] At this level, as Maharishi explains

> Anyone can know anything at anytime, from within himself, without loosing himself (in his *Ṛitam-bharā-pragyā*—fully awake consciousness—*Jyotish-matī-pragyā*).[38]

This value of all-knowing intelligence corresponds to the arithmetic involved in the structuring dynamics of the Veda which is referred, by Maharishi, to as "Vedic Arithmetic."[39] In a further discussion of *Ṛtam bharā prajflā* and Vedic Mathematics, Maharishi teaches that:

> Absolute pure intelligence, Transcendental Consciousness, is endowed with the holistic value of Vedic Mathematics; that is why it has the qualities of *Ṛitam-bharā*—always correct, always precise, always in conformity with absolute order, perfection—the natural quality of pure wakefulness, self-referral consciousness, which is like a 'lamp at the door', which lights inside and outside.
>
> Vedic Mathematics is the mathematics of the absolute, non-changing, eternal, unmanifest ocean of intelligence, which spontaneously designs, with the most systematic, perfect precision, the mechanics of creation emerging from the self-referral nature of pure singularity, self-referral consciousness.[40]

In this sense, the mathematics of the absolute has the qualities of *Ṛtam-bharā*, the correct, precise and orderly nature of pure wakefulness, self-referral consciousness. Vedic Mathematics is the mathematics of the absolute, eternal ocean of intelligence which, as Maharishi points out, spontaneously designs the mechanics of creation emerging from the self-referral nature of pure singularity, self-referral consciousness. With this understanding, knowing this level of *Ṛtam-*

bharā-pragyā, one knows the field of Vedic Mathematics, and the mechanics of creation. This knowledge is, ultimately, the field of the enlightened artist's own awareness.

In defining Vedic Mathematics, Maharishi teaches that not only is Vedic Mathematics expressed in terms of sound (the unfoldment of the Veda) rather than numerical symbols, but that "Vedic Geometry" is the geometry involved in the structuring dynamics of the Veda:

> This field of Vedic Mathematics is expressed in the syllables of speech rather than in numerical symbols: Vedic Algebra is the algebra involved in the structuring dynamics of the Veda; Vedic Analysis is the analysis involved in the structuring dynamics of the Veda; Vedic Arithmetic is the arithmetic involved in the structuring dynamics of the Veda; Vedic Calculus is the calculus involved in the structuring dynamics of the Veda; Vedic Geometry is the geometry involved in the structuring dynamics of the Veda; Vedic Logic is the logic involved in the structuring dynamics of the Veda; Vedic Statistics is the statistics involved in the structuring dynamics of the Veda; Vedic Topology is the topology involved in the structuring dynamics of the Veda; Vedic Trigonometry is the trigonometry involved in the structuring dynamics of the Veda.[41]

Thus, Vedic Mathematics, including the different aspects of mathematics, is the mathematics of consciousness, the unfoldment of syllables of sound in the structuring dynamics of the Veda, self-referral consciousness. In this context, Maharishi teaches that the principle of Vedic Geometry is illustrated by an expression from the Bhagavad-Gītā which he translates as:

> गुणा गुणेषु वर्तन्त...
> *Guṇā guṇeṣu vartanta...*
> The *Guṇas* react with the *Guṇas*.[42]
> (*Bhagavad-Gītā, 3.28*)

According to Maharishi Vedic Science, this theme of the *Guṇas* reacting with the *Guṇas*, corresponds to the field of Vedic Geometry—the geometry involved in the structuring dynamics of the Veda. The structuring dynamics of the Veda involve the three values of Ṛishi, Devatā and Chhandas in the dynamic of the self-referral loop. As discussed in Part III, Maharishi explains that from Ṛishi, Devatā and Chhandas, the three *Guṇas* of *Sattwa, Rajas* and *Tamas* spring. These qualities continue to interact with one another, generating the numerous values of creation.

As noted earlier, one sūtra from the Vāstusūtra Upaniṣad mentioned three types of forms (or images) according to the *Guṇas*: गुणानुसृतं रूपत्रयम् । *Guṇānusṛtam rūpa-trayam*, "According to the quality (*guṇa*) there are three types of images," (*Vāstusūtra Upaniṣad, 6.19*). It seems that the quality of the *guṇa* determines the type of form. There is a relationship between sound, form and the interaction of the *Guṇas* with respect to Vedic Geometry—the geometry involved in the structuring dynamics of the Veda or self-referral consciousness.

In addition, Maharishi teaches that Vedic Trigonometry (where trigonometry is the branch of mathematics dealing with relations of sides and angles of triangles) is defined by another expression from the Bhagavad-Gītā:

> त्रैगुण्यविषया वेदा
>
> *Traiguṇya-viṣayā vedā …*
>
> The Veda's concern is with the three *Guṇas.*[43]
>
> (*Bhagavad-Gītā, 2.45*)

In this way, geometry, and specifically the relations of the mathematical properties of triangles, from the perspective of Maharishi Vedic Science, is the geometry and trigonometry of the structuring dynamics of the Veda, self-referral consciousness, the structure of pure knowledge, the simplest form of human awareness.

Of the sūtras in the Vāstusūtra Upaniṣad which mention the triangle, circle and square, three include the triangle, three discuss the square, and five mention the circle. The sūtras which refer to the triangle follow each other in sequence in the text and seem to describe the characteristics of specific kinds of triangle. However, only the first will be considered here. This sūtra appears to suggest that *Agni* is associated with the triangle:

> त्रिहुताग्निः स्मर्यतेऽपि च लोके ।
>
> *Trihutāgniḥ smaryate'pi ca loke*
>
> Fire in the form of a triangle is known even in the (non-Vedic) world.
>
> (*Vāstusūtra Upaniṣad, 2.15*)

The term *Smaryate* can be translated as "is remembered" and comes from the root *Smṛ*. As discussed in Part III, Maharishi explains that *Smṛti* means memory or awareness—the fully awake value of self-referral consciousness. Thus, "known" may be more fully understood as having the sense of "being awake to" on the level of consciousness.

Loka or "world," refers to the relative field of existence,[44] or "all the people of the world"[45] and "beings."[46] *Agni* can refer to the basic element of fire; it is also the first word of the Veda—the holistic expression of Natural Law—containing the totality of the structuring dynamics of the Veda. Thus, *Agni* can refer to the Veda itself, the self-referral dynamics of consciousness and the interaction of the values of Ṛishi, Devatā and Chhandas. With this understanding, the sūtra may be indicating that *Agni*, as the holistic value of self-referral consciousness (unfolding Vedic Trigonometry i.e. "in the form of a triangle") is lively within consciousness, even in the relative world—the world of the three *guṇas*.

In the context of this discussion, the following section considers the forms of the circle and square. As noted earlier, and as explained in numerous instances by Maharishi, in Maharishi Vedic Science, the circle is a significant form; it is the eternal structure of the Veda; the structure of the Veda unfolds in ten *Maṇḍalas* and, with respect to the Veda and the Vedic Literature, Maharishi points out:

> As every aspect of the Vedic Literature plays the role of the structuring dynamics of the Veda, the structure of the Veda is also moulded in immortality, eternity. For any structure to be immortal, it must be inexhaustible; for any structure to be inexhaustible, it must be self-referral, which means it must refer to its source, it must refer to itself, it must be in a circular form. All aspects of the Vedic Literature, in the process of structuring Veda, function together simultaneously; so the structure of the Veda is structured by those mechanics whose dynamism is always self-referral. That is the reason why the structure of Veda is self-referral, and as such the structure is in a circular form, a *MAṆDALA* form. The obvious conclusion is that the structure of Veda is in the *Maṇḍala* form, and each structure of the Vedic Literature (being the structuring dynamics of Veda) is in a *Maṇḍala* form—we call it a self-referral loop. Being in a circular form, a *Maṇḍala* form, each aspect of the Vedic Literature breathes immortality, eternity.[47]

In this regard, the circular form is the self-referral nature of consciousness, the structure of knowledge. The Vāstusūtra Upaniṣad itself can be thought of as in this circular form; as noted earlier, the first and last sūtras, next to one another, could represent the wholeness of the text.

There are five sūtras in the Vāstusūtra Upaniṣad which refer to the circle. The first of these was discussed at the beginning of this chapter:

> वृत्तज्ञानं रेखाज्ञानं च यो जानाति स स्थापकः ।
> *Vṛtta jñānaṁ rekhā jñānaṁ ca yo jānāti sa sthāpakaḥ.*
> Who has the knowledge of the circle and line is a sthāpaka.
> (*Vāstusūtra Upaniṣad, 1.4*)

The next sūtra which mentions circle or *Vṛtta* states:

> आदौ वृत्तम् वृत्त मिति विश्वम् ।
> *Ādau vṛttam vṛttamiti viśam.*
> In the beginning is a circle. The circle is the All (universe).
> (*Vāstusūtra Upaniṣad, 2.6*)

Ādau means "first";[48] *Vṛtta* meaning "circle", also denotes "meter"; with this understanding it could be said that the sounds of the Veda (expressed in meter) take the eternal form of the *Maṇḍala*. This is the eternal structure of consciousness at the basis of creation from which everything emerges: from *Atmā*, or pure consciousness, to Veda, the structuring dynamics of Saṁhitā of Ṛishi, Devatā and Chhandas taking the form of *Maṇḍalas* or circles, giving rise to *Viśwa*, the universe, all this within *Brahm*, the totality of self-referral consciousness moving within itself. Thus, the circle is "All"; it represents the totality of consciousness—from the emergence of creation within *Ātmā* (the beginning), to the move of self-referral consciousness, the expression of the Veda and the creation of the universe (*Viśwa*). All this is *Brahm.*

In sūtra eleven, Chapter Two of the Vāstusūtra Upaniṣad the circle is also equated with light:

> प्राजापत्यरित्या वृत्तं हि तेजस्तदाऽपां भासे चतुरस्रम् ।
>
> *Prājāpatyarītyā vṛttaṃ hi tejas tadā'pāṃ bhāse caturasram.*
>
> Following the order of Prajāpati the circle represents light (tejas) while the square indicates water.
>
> (*Vāstusūtra Upaniṣad, 2.11*)

This sūtra seems to indicate that there is a relationship between light and the circle. As mentioned earlier, Maharishi refers to consciousness as light—"the scintillating light of Creative Intelligence;"[49] however, he does not mention any specific relationship between the circular structure of the Veda and this aspect of consciousness. In the Vāstusūtra Upaniṣad the square is also referred to in two sūtras, one of which has been mentioned above. The second sūtra which mentions the square, states:

> वगीकरणं मुख्यकृत्यम् ।
>
> *Vargīkaraṇaṁ mukhya-kṛtyam*
>
> Making squares is the principal work.
>
> (*Vāstusūtra Upaniṣad, 4.5*)

As indicated in the *Mānasāra*, the square is determined in the circle by connecting the four points at which the four directions intersect a circle drawn on a specific site. The square has also be referred to as a *Maṇḍala.* In Sthāpatya Veda any design for ideal living, in a town or city for example, is laid out upon a grid format—made up of squares. The orientation of the directional movement of the flow of traffic is always in reference to the cardinal points and the movement of the sun and moon.

While the circle and square are important figures in design, in making reference to these geometric forms, the Vāstusūtra Upaniṣad may also be bringing out another level of meaning which could relate to the description of the almost non-fluctuating value of consciousness from where all triangles, circles and squares emerge. In this sense, the significance of the sūtras extends beyond the description of the creative process of art and architecture, referring to the creative mechanics of consciousness. However, in order to completely comprehend the significance of the above sūtras in this light, it requires further study (and, ultimately, the cognition of the mechanics of self-referral consciousness and its expression on all levels of form). Having considered geometric forms as outlined in the sūtras, the following discussion will examine a few sūtras which mention number.

Consciousness and Number

As noted in Part II, Maharishi explains that, in the quantification of consciousness, any number can be derived from one and two:

> We can keep on deriving any number we want from one and two because three comes out in adding one and two, and once you have three—add one to three make four; add two to three make five; add three to three make six; and then start to add again. Add one to six, seven; add two to six, eight; add three to six, nine; keep on doing it, anything—once you have one and two, and one and three. And where do you have one and two initially? The seer, the intelligence, in its self-referral state, it becomes the observer, and the observer becomes the observed; then there are two. Then we have all the logic to know that one is Ṛishi, Devatā and Chhandas; one is observer, observed, observation. These innumerable values are all the values of intelligence because it is the intelligence which argues within itself—I am one, I am two, I am three, I am the observer, observed, observation, and this and this and this.[50]

More recently, Maharishi explains that any number is the modified state of the number one or Unity and that "Unity is an eternal continuum" which is expressed by the number one circled:

> The number one circled ① expresses the eternal continuum of Unity, which can only be expressed in terms of zero—in terms of a circle. This Unity has two expressions: Saṁhitā, wholeness; 2) Ṛishi, Devatā, Chhandas, the dynamics of wholeness. Unity in its own self-interacting dynamics is expressed by the self-referral loop of a circle. When this self-referral loop is expressed in terms of a number it is expressed as one, circled ①. As any number is the expression of the number one, when the number is zeroed it becomes unmanifest, which means in terms of numbers it becomes the Absolute Number.[51]

In this way, there are two aspects to Unity, wholeness and the dynamics of wholeness. The self-interacting dynamics of wholeness, expressed by the self-referral loop of the circle can be expressed in terms of number as the integer one, contained within a circle. Maharishi continues to explain that:

> By circling any number, the number begins to indicate that it is part and parcel of the Absolute Number—that its boundaries are unmanifest or, in spite of its boundaries, it is a continuum—it plays a part in explaining the eternal order that sustains the evolution of the universe. Its individual status has become Cosmic—as an individual it has been elected to be a ruler—the full potential of its creativity has blossomed.[52]

He also adds that different expressions of the Absolute Number are ①, ②, ③, ④, ⑤, ⑥, ⑦, ⑧, ⑨, and ⑩, circled.

In the context of Maharishi's description of consciousness in terms of its propensity to divide itself and generate numerous values yet remain one wholeness, sūtra seven in Chapter Two of the Vāstusūtra Upaniṣad can be considered.

This sūtra states:

> एकैकस्य संयोगे एकीभवति इति तस्य भावः । वृत्त हि पूर्णम् ।
>
> *Ekaikasya saṁyoge ekībhavati iti tasya bhāvaḥ, vṛtta hi pūrṇam.*
> By the connection of one with one a unity is formed. This is the meaning: The circle verily is the Plenum (fullness, pūrṇam).
> (*Vāstusūtra Upaniṣad*, *2.7*)

Eka is one; *Ekaikasya* can refer to a single state and *Ekībhavati* refers to "becoming one." *Saṁyoga* is "the connection"[53] or "union."[54] In Maharishi Vedic Science, "one" can denote the one ultimate field of singularity or the totality of *Brahma*, Saṁhitā—the three-in-one structure of wholeness, the nature of Unity.[55] The move of wholeness to wholeness (as described in Chapter 23 in the discussion of the first and last letters of Ṛk Veda) represents two fullness emerging from one fullness. This principle is expressed in the verse:

> पूर्णमदः पूर्णमिदं पूर्णात्पूर्णमुदच्यते ।
> पूर्णस्य पूर्णमादाय पूर्णमेवावाशिष्यते ॥
>
> *Pūrṇam adaḥ pūrṇam idaṃ pūrṇāt pūrṇam udachyate,*
> *pūrṇasya pūrṇam ādāya pūrṇam evāvaśiṣyate.*
> (*Shāntipāth*, *Kena Upaniṣad*, *5.1.1*)

This verse states: "That is full; this is full; from fullness, fullness comes out; taking fullness from fullness, what remains is fullness."[56] Maharishi points out that this principle reveals that fullness emerges from fullness. *Pūrṇamadaḥ* represents the fullness of silence contained in the first letter of the Veda, "A"; emerging from this value of fullness is the fullness of dynamism, expressed in *Pūrṇamadaḥ* and contained in the last letter of Ṛk Veda, इ "I".[57] These two values of fullness are contained within the one holistic value of fullness.

In this way, one plus one can be understood as a unity of fullness represented by the circle. There is always only one totality of consciousness, but that fullness is two fullnesses. As also discussed earlier, the totality can be understood as having two aspects, silence and dynamism.

Similarly, another sūtra could also be indicating the nature and mechanics of this infinite, holistic field of consciousness:

अतो द्विध ब्रह्म रूपवन् भवति ।

Ato dvidhā brahma rūpavan bhavati

Thus, on account of having two aspects Brahman acquires form.

(*Vāstusūtra Upaniṣad, 4.3*)

This sūtra, mentioned in Chapter 24, seems to indicate that the totality of Brahman acquires form by virtue of dual aspects (i.e., silence and dynamism, *Puruṣa* and *Prakṛti*, singularity and diversity).

Following on with this discussion, the value of three is also significant; by virtue of its self-referral nature, pure consciousness creates three values in its undivided wholeness—the three-on-one structure of pure knowledge. The term three is mentioned in the following sūtras (previously considered in relation to line and types of form):

तिस्रः रेखा श्रेष्ठाः ।

Tisraḥ rekhā śreṣṭhāḥ.

Three (types of) lines are essential.

(*Vāstusūtra Upaniṣad, 6.5*)

गुणानुसृतं रूपत्रयम् ।

Guṇānusṛtaṃ rūpa-trayam.

According to the quality (guṇa) there are three types of images.

(*Vāstusūtra Upaniṣad, 6.19*)

The three *Guṇas,* the three qualities of *Sattwa*, *Rajas*, and *Tamas* which spring from Ṛishi, Devatā and Chhandas values, correlate to three kinds of image or form and, possibly, three kinds of line. In Maharishi Vedic Science, these three values constitute the forces that govern life in the relative field; the three *Guṇas* spring from the fundamental values of self-referral consciousness that structure everything in creation. As noted above, their interactions are related to Vedic Geometry and Vedic Trigonometry.

It seems that the various aspects of point, line, grid, triangle, square, circle and number mentioned in the Vāstusūtra Upaniṣad can be comprehended in a more expanded sense with respect to consciousness, the mechanics of the unfoldment of Veda and the experience of higher states of consciousness through the practice of the Transcendental Meditation technique and the TM-Sidhi program, by examining sūtras via the unique approach of Maharishi Vedic Science.

In exploring the potential correlation between specific sūtras and fundamental principles of Maharishi Vedic Science, this section has elaborated upon some of the key themes discussed in Parts I through V. Further research, examining in more depth the structure and nature of the text, could yield even deeper insights into this subject.

27

TRANSFORMATIVE FUTURES

At the outset of this book, Thomas McEvilley was quoted—criticizing the traditional Western philosophical point of view adopted by modernism. This viewpoint held that there are universal or absolute values which are inborn in all humans identically in all times and all places. The idea that judgments can be based on perception of these universals, he feels, cannot be supported by anything called "evidence." He emphasizes that quality is subjective and relative rather than objective and universal; therefore, to speak of universal value is to assume that some faculty of judgment lies beyond cultural and historical determinants. As discussed in Parts II to VI, from the perspective of Maharishi Vedic Science, an unmanifest, subjective field of pure consciousness gives rise to all of the "objective" aspects of creation. Furthermore, through subjective technologies, this universal field of pure consciousness can be experienced and enlivened. Although this absolute, universal field gives rise to all subjective and objective values in relative life, and all of their relationships, it lies beyond cultural, historical, and individual determinants. It is beyond time; it remains constant. Precisely because this field of pure consciousness is also the simplest form of human awareness, it is accessible to the individual, regardless of place and in any era.

As we have seen, evidence of this field can be gained through: 1) direct experience, 2) scientific research (which documents the effects of the practice of technologies of consciousness and the enlivenment of this field), and 3) descriptions found in the Veda and Vedic Literature. In this sense, both subjective experience and empirical research endorse the principles unfolded in Maharishi Vedic Science, foremost of which is the principle that there is a universal basis to life. For art and artists this suggests that universal value can be expressed in art and can be appreciated by anyone at any time.

Issues in Twentieth-Century Art and Theory

Other issues related to this debate were also considered. For example, Part I—drawing from modernism, Indian theory and postmodern theory—briefly reviewed some of the key ideas that have occupied artists and theorists over the last fifty years. Indian theory suggests that art can evoke a universal experience—a tasting of ideal beauty—which is an intellectual-ecstatic order of being. Modernists, however, assert that only abstract, avant-garde art can create a universal response; the artist, a hero ever breaking with tradition and propelling history forward, attempts to empty art of all relative reference to reveal an absolute or absolute emotions. Indian theory rejects the notion of avant-gardism, viewing tradition as the tool for creating successful art, art which is expected to have a specific effect on the viewer and society. Certain rules are adhered to; they are like grammar in the language of art. It seems that both modernists and Indian theory support the notion of universal art creating an intuitive aesthetic response, but in fact, the two approaches are at variance with one another. Modernists maintain a distinction between Fine Art and craft or kitsch; Indian theorists suggest that all creative expression is art and that *Śilpa* (or creative practice) indicates "skill" in a general sense. Postmodernism, on the other hand, reveals the limitations of Western philosophy and modern theory, and posits a seemingly more pragmatic yet ironic approach. Art can be understood as a language game within which rules are invented in a constant dynamic. The idea of quality or judgment based on absolute values is invalid, since absolutes are impossible; any attempt to objectively verify a subjective realm or any absolute value is highly problematic. Modernism, with its argument for universal value perceivable by only a few "hyper conscious" individuals (i.e. artists and art critics), is seen as Imperialist.

In modern art, universality was represented through "sameness"; this phenomenon, understandably, came under criticism as "a force for divisiveness and exclusion."[1] Postmodernists, subsequently rejected the idea of a transcendental unity and any special relationship between language or an image and the thing it signifies. Art cannot embody "presence" or the essence of the thing to which it refers (especially so, in the case of abstract art that aimed to indicate the absolute). Conceptual artists assert that art is, in fact, a language game—never able to express an absolute, it can only "point to the unnamable."[2]

Despite the issues raised by postmodernism, many find postmodern art lacking in universal value—abandoning any attempt to evoke a new sense of self or a state of aesthetic disinterestedness (which defines art's role in articulating possibility and the concept of unity). While he laments the lack of universal value, Donald Kuspit clearly states that universality cannot be represented through one formal unity in art because such a formal unity represents an unrealizable unified self. However, there is the possibility of many formal unities positing the illusion of a transcendental unity of form and a unified self. The main thene underlying this debate on universal value hinges on the concept of an absolute.

Subject, Object and their Relationship as Values of Consciousness

In Maharishi Vedic Science the absolute, unmanifest field of existence is common to everyone and everything in the universe. Indeed, in being a field of pure awareness, it is awake to itself, and differentiates three values within its own undivided singularity. The three values of knower or subject (Ṛishi), known or object (Chhandas), and process of knowing or the relationship between subject and object (Devatā), are all shades or values of consciousness discriminated within awareness. These are the basic building blocks of diversity. In their unified state they represent Saṁhitā of Ṛishi, Devatā, and Chhandas—the three-in-one structure of pure knowledge which is the structure of Ṛk Veda. This structure of pure knowledge has inherent within it the infinite organizing power which governs creation. Holding together these two opposite values of singularity and diversity—Saṁhitā and Ṛishi, Devatā, and Chhandas—the phenomenon of infinite organizing power is demonstrated. Here, opposite values do not cancel each other out; their dynamic interaction is the source of difference and the display of creation. Maharishi also explains how this unmanifest field of existence has both the value of silence and dynamism. It is infinite silence but is also silence in motion. Being a field of wholeness, within which everything is contained, it is a field of wholeness as silence and wholeness as dynamism—wholeness moving within itself.

Reliable Knowledge in Higher States of Consciousness

When any individual, through the practice of the Transcendental Meditation technique, experiences his or her own simplest form of awareness, the values of knower, process of knowing and known are unified in Transcendental Consciousness. Maharishi describes this state as absolute knowledge or the state of pure knowledge. It is experienced as pure bliss. Here, the individual self attains the infinite status of the Cosmic Self—unbounded, absolute. The state of pure knowledge is the same infinite field cognized by people throughout the ages and recorded in different traditions. Because it is never changing, it is the only foundation for reliable knowledge. As we have seen, this unchanging, reliable knowledge is gained through direct experience.

The Transcendental Meditation technique and TM-Sidhi program are those technologies which systematically promote this experience and the development of higher states of consciousness. These states of consciousness include Transcendental Consciousness, Cosmic Consciousness, God Consciousness and Unity or Brahman Consciousness; in each state of consciousness knowledge is different. Despite this, in last three states, absolute knowledge is permanently established. This means that the absolute, universal field of pure awareness is a permanent feature of experience. In Brahman Consciousness complete knowledge is gained. Then, everything in creation is known to be nothing other than fluctuations the Self—reverberations of self-referral consciousness. The Self is completely unified in one totality: wholeness moving within itself. When the individual is living higher states of consciousness, he or she can be called a universal human being because all thought, action, and behavior, springs from the universal level of pure consciousness. Furthermore, while it is possible to verify the existence of this field through direct experience by means of Maharishi's technologies of consciousness, physicists[3] also indicate that this field of pure consciousness is the same unified field glimpsed by modern science.

Vedic Language: The Uncreated Commentary of the Veda

The description and understanding of pure consciousness and its expressions does not end here. For example, the understanding of language provided by Maharishi

Vedic Science contrasts with contemporary language theory. The latter suggests that there is no intrinsic relationship between a word and its meaning or a word and the thing to which it refers; there is no intrinsic value to terms in any language. Unlike contemporary language theory, philosophy and deconstruction, Maharishi Vedic Science describes how consciousness, a lively field of all possibilities, presents its own uncreated or unmanifest commentary; this "uncreated commentary" is a record of the sequential unfoldment of consciousness in terms of sounds (syllables) and gaps. The Veda and the Vedic Literature are these sequentially unfolding frequencies of self-referral consciousness. In fact, the 40 aspects of the Veda and Vedic Literature correspond to 40 qualities of intelligence or consciousness and are the structuring dynamics of Ṛk Veda—the structure of pure knowledge itself. Since Nature's creative mechanics are recorded in the language of the Veda, the Vedic language possesses a unique property. The words or sounds are completely correspondent with the form to which they refer. Furthermore, the impulses of consciousness recorded in the Veda and the Vedic Literature are the structuring intelligence of the physiology.

Cycles of Natural Law and Universal Value in Art

On this basis, in examining history according to Maharishi Vedic Science, it is possible to comprehend how a universal value of existence can co-exist with diversified values and how history can be understood as the quantification of pure consciousness in terms of various life-spans—from the innumerable lives of that which has the longest life-span in the relative to the relatively small span of human life. Including specific eras or *Yugas*, history unfolds in a cyclical progression throughout eternity; the longest of these eras, *Sat-Yuga*, is characterized by life in accord with Natural Law where individual and collective life is lived without mistakes and in harmony. In the shortest of these eras, *Kali-Yuga*, the people no longer live 100 percent of Natural Law; perhaps in such a period universal value increasingly becomes invalid since the full experience of pure consciousness is no longer a feature of daily life. When this period reaches its lowest ebb, Natural Law is latent in its pure potentiality and technologies for experiencing pure consciousness are introduced. Life, again, can be lived in its full value—100 percent of Natural Law. It would seem plausible that, during this transition, universal value becomes increasingly expressed in art.

With the rise of Natural Law and universal value in life, differences do not dissolve. Cultures become stronger in themselves. According to Maharishi Vedic Science, the differences between cultures maintain culture. The different mannerisms, habits and customs and artistic expressions of a people maintain and strengthen cultural integrity. As Maharishi explains, while every locality and every physiology has its universal basis in Natural Law, they also have specific Laws of Nature which govern their integrated functioning. The universal holistic value of Natural Law is the source of the specific Laws of Nature that govern life in a particular place—including the climate and geography. The climatic and geographic conditions of a place contribute to culture; therefore, there is an intimate relationship between a place and its people. The local language and accent, the cultural values of a people, support the evolutionary development of the individuals of that group. For this reason, culture is very important; difference in cultures should be respected and maintained. Through the group practice of the Transcendental Meditation technique and TM-Sidhi program invincibility and cultural integrity are strengthened so that the culture is flexible enough to absorb outside influences but stable enough to maintain its own values. It is clear that universality, in Maharishi Vedic Science, does not imply eradication of difference. On the contrary, by enlivening the universal basis of life, differences are strengthened, nourished and expressed.

In addition, there is a unique relationship between the "Language of Nature," the Veda and the Vedic Literature, and the local language or mother tongue. Since the Veda and the Vedic Literature are the frequencies of consciousness which structure the physiology, in reciting or listening to these frequencies, the holistic functioning of the brain physiology is stimulated. Maharishi also maintains, that the mother tongue is the closest linguistic expression to Veda for that particular group. Therefore, it plays a part in maintaining balance and wholeness in the physiology. For this reason, it is important that the mother tongue is spoken. When a foreign language is adopted, the integrity of the host culture risks being eroded—not simply because the new language is foreign, but because there is an intrinsic relationship between the mother tongue and specific Laws of Nature that govern life.

The Artist as Creator Connects Inner and Outer Realms

Given the complete vision of life, language and consciousness provided by Maharishi Vedic Science, new definitions of art and the creative process can be articulated. As discussed in Part V, the creative individual or genius is one who overcomes obstacles, achieves the goal with maximum success and minimum expenditure of energy. Anyone can become a genius—since infinite creativity is an innate property of individual awareness in its most expanded state. In this sense, genius is not restricted to a few individuals: genius is the birthright of everyone.

With respect to the artist, during the phase transition artists should be role models for society; the artist can be a universal human being who, in living higher states of consciousness, brings success to every undertaking. In practicing the Transcendental Meditation technique, the TM-Sidhi program and Yogic Flying, the artist contributes to the transformation of collective consciousness—increasing positive trends in society and enhancing collective life. On the basis of research on the effects of the group practice of these technologies, it could be argued that an artist who is engaged in this practice is involved in the most effective socially responsible performance—the art of promoting harmony in individual and collective life.

With regard to creative practice, ultimately, in order to create universal art—to be a creator and not simply a viewer—the artist must know what consciousness is and what it is made of. Then he or she can create as Nature creates. The procedure for creating art which embodies the absolute, unbounded value of bliss consciousness is to hold the image in consciousness over time and transport that vision onto material form. A work of art created in this manner expresses the originating force of consciousness but is a copy of that which was in consciousness. This process maintains the connectedness between the inner aspect of consciousness and the outer expression in material form. Without this connectedness the artist is not a creator. He or she does not knows the steps of manifestation of consciousness into form.

Art Inspires Bliss and Enlivens Liberation or Mokṣa

Maharishi Vedic Science not only expands opposing propositions of modern and postmodern theory, it also satisfies the aspirations of Indian theory: namely, that art should provide a spiritual role and integrate society. Ideally, art should inspire happiness in the viewer; if it is successful, it will enliven bliss. In this sense, it leads toward the Transcendent—the absolute field of the Self—promoting freedom or *Mokṣa*. The viewer gains more than a state of aesthetic disinterestedness. The awareness and physiology awakens to its own infinite status. This is universal art—art that enlivens unboundedness, immortality and bliss, generating a life-supporting influence in the environment. In aesthetic judgment, if the viewer is wise enough he or she can evaluate the level of consciousness of the artist and also perceive the different subtle values of the art object. However, ultimately, the value of art object, (i.e. whether it is universal or not) is dependent upon the artist and not the viewer. The quality of the consciousness of the creator determines the degree to which it embodies universal value. This is why Maharishi emphasizes that, for any artist, the key to enhanced creativity and successful art is to expand one's own awareness through the practice of his technologies of consciousness.

Art Enhances Life

With respect to aesthetic value and the effects of art, when the art work embodies universal value it has an inspirational effect on the viewer and enlivens the environment—whether one sees it or not. Aesthetic value is, in this instance, seen to be purposeful in that it enhances life and helps to promote evolution by enlivening bliss in the viewer. In this sense, a "beautiful" work of art would be defined as one which has captured universal value in its relative expression. By leading the viewer toward the experience of the Self in greater degrees, the work of art can indicate the unified sense of Self—not simply a transcendental illusion of selfhood but the reality of the Self as the unified state of Saṁhitā or wholeness.

Ideally, then, art unfolds the Self in the viewer. With respect to the experience of a highly successful work of art:

> A close examination of art reveals that the more attention we give to a work of art the more deeply we are drawn into the work to experience subtler and subtler aspects of its meaning. These subtler aspects spontaneously unfold deeper and deeper levels of awareness through the principle which SCI [the Science of Creative Intelligence] describes as increasing charm. Thus, the ultimate meaning of art, the universal content of art, is a vertical expansion of experience inward from the outer boundary of the art object to the inner boundlessness of the viewer's awareness.[4]

This experience can be created through universal works of art which display unity through their formal structure:

> SCI reveals that underlying the diversity and apparent conflict of the parts of life is universal wholeness, oneness. Thus, the function of art is to give a glimpse of the unifying wholeness of life, even in a single isolated part. Art's articulation of the boundless within boundaries simulates the experience of unity consciousness in which the infinite becomes perceptible even on the surface of material existence. Thus, the function of art is to give a glimpse, however brief and artificial, of the goal of life and thereby spur us on to evolution.[5]

This goal is not achieved by focusing on one particular style, but by the artist rising to higher states of consciousness and spontaneously creating from the level of Transcendental Consciousness.

Universal Principles in the Vāstusūtra Upaniṣad

Applying Maharishi's description of consciousness, its creative mechanics, and the nature of the Vedic Literature, the Vāstusūtra Upaniṣad can be said to unfold universal principles of creativity. Sūtras such as "From the formless arises form, that is the result," "The *bindu* is like *Brahma*, *Brahman* is immovable," and "In the beginning is a circle. The circle is All (the Universe)," appear to indicate the process of manifestation of the unmanifest, the value of Saṁhitā, and the generation of *Maṇdalas* or circles from the level of self-referral consciousness. Also, the idea of the *Sthāpaka* as one who knows the line and circle, could refer to the principle of the artist knowing the basic structure and dynamic of consciousness.

Along with the various sūtras examined, the first and last sūtras seem to encapsulate the main theme of the text: "One should know *Vāstoṣpati* (the governor of *Vāstu*) and the purpose of this exposition of *Vāstu* is for conferring knowledge. *Vāstu* encompasses the harmonizing power of Natural Law and knowledge may refer to knowledge of the Self. If this is the purpose of *Vāstu* or the study of *Vāstu* as expressed in the *Vāstusūtra Upaniṣad*, then, applying the understanding of Maharishi Vedic Science, this text could be said to unfold the Self. The purpose of art and the study of the Vedic Literature is to unfold the Self in greater degrees so that individual life is in accord with Cosmic life—lived from the level of self-referral consciousness.

A Technology for Transformative Futures

In this book Maharishi Vedic Science has been presented as more than just philosophy or theory. As a revival, or re-enlivenment of eternal knowledge preserved in the traditions of India, it provides complete knowledge of consciousness and its expressions. While modernism proposed the absolute could be expressed in art, there was no technology to experience such a realm or evidence to substantiate this claim. Postmodernism, apparently less totalizing, dismisses the notion of an absolute. In so doing, it dismisses the very basis of individual and collective life. Neither modernism or postmodernism furnish a means by which universal value in art can be systematically expressed. Maharishi Vedic Science, through complete knowledge and technologies of consciousness, provides a means by which artists can be exemplary human beings. Artists can aspire to create art which enlivens consciousness, radiates life-supporting influence in the environment, embodies universal value and meaning, and stimulates the quality of bliss in the viewer—ultimately promoting the experience of a new sense of Self. Through Maharishi Vedic Science, cultural integrity can be strengthened and differences enriched—bringing a new definition of the role and scope of visual culture.

The recognition of the interconnectedness of inner and outer worlds, the scientific understanding of the role of the subject in creating his universe, the significance of Vedic language theory, and the emergence of new digital media, have all contributed to the re-definition of visual culture. While this book has reviewed important twentieth-century ideas in art and theory, the most significant development at the end of this century is arguably the change in collective consciousness that has permitted the resurfacing of a complete approach to knowledge and the visual arts. Artists working in digital media are creating virtual worlds and exploring the rich yet ephemeral potential of electronic technology. In apparently facilitating the transcendence of space, electronic media seem to mirror the unmanifest workings of consciousness itself.

Steven Holtzman considers the implications of this trend when he writes about the computer as a tool for artists:

> Technology is a tool for investigating the cosmic truths found in structure. The computer—the ultimate tool for manipulating structures—can reveal a new dimension of *Brahman*: a *digital* reflection of *Brahman*. In 1986, Sanskrit provided the key to discovering that Latin, Greek, and Sanskrit all originated from the same source. Sanskrit helped reveal what was not apparent from

> looking only at Latin and Greek. Many explorers have studied the numerical form of structures. The Pythagoreans sought to discover the numerical forms that reflect the harmony of the cosmos. Kandinsky sought to find the numerical representation of visual forms and their corresponding spiritual vibrations. Fractals are effectively numerical expression of visual forms. Music is form and structure and can be expressed numerically. Essentially binary, the digital reflection will be the continuation of the Pythagorean exploration of numbers. Since the times of the Pythagoreans, science and technology and matters of the spirit have been perceived to be at odds. But as we approach the twenty-first century we can return to an integrated view of art, science, and the mystical.... In developing new digital aesthetics, we have the opportunity to integrate technology, science and the mystical to reveal *Brahman*. It is the study of abstract worlds in particular that will help accomplish this goal.[6]

While Holtzman speaks of the unity of science, art and "mysticism", Maharishi Vedic Science effectively "demystifies" the spiritual by providing a systematic means for unfolding this realm in daily life. The twenty-first century will inevitably bring a new approach to knowledge and visual culture—arguably one that will achieve the unification of different disciplines and the creation of transformative futures. However, the most radical technology for the realization of these goals is not the computer but the technologies of consciousness that operate on the level of our simplest form of awareness.[7] With these techniques of consciousness, the full potential and understanding of the nature and structure of the universe can be fathomed by science, applied through technology, and represented in art. The fountainhead of all streams of knowledge can be known; it is, in fact, our own pure awareness. The universal value of life can be appreciated, lived and expressed in terms of fluctuations of our own self-referral awareness or wholeness—in terms of *Brahman*. With this knowledge, in the coming century artists will be uniquely equipped to live, articulate and represent not only new paradigms but, ultimately, this fundamental reality.

NOTES

Introduction

1 Maharishi Mahesh Yogi, *Maharishi Vedic University: Introduction,* Holland, 1994, p. 172.
2 Maharishi Mahesh Yogi, *The Science of Being and the Art of Living,* Washington, D.C., 1966, p. 123; 1994, pp. 58-59 & pp. 260-261.
3 Maharishi Mahesh Yogi, 'Art and the Artist,' [A lecture given at Kössen, West Germany], in M. Cain, *Art and the Science of Creative Intelligence: Interdependence of the Part and Whole,* Fairfield, 1970, pp. v-viii.
4 Maharishi Mahesh Yogi, *Maharishi Vedic University: Introduction,* pp. 67-68.
5 *Ibid.,* pp. 203-214.
6 *Ibid.,* pp. 117-130.
7 *Ibid.,* pp. 326-337.
8 Maharishi Mahesh Yogi, *Maharishi University of Management: Wholeness on the Move,* 1995, pp. 326-337.
9 *Ibid.,* p. 76-124.
10 See: *Modern Science and Vedic Science Journal*, Iowa, 1987-1996, and *Scientific Research on the Transcendental Meditation and TM-Sidhi Programs: Collected Papers,* Volumes 1-6, Holland, 1989-1991.
11 Maharishi Mahesh Yogi, *Maharishi University of Management: Wholeness on the Move,* p. 41.
12 Maharishi Mahesh Yogi, *Maharishi's Absolute Theory of Government: Automation in Administration.* The Netherlands: Maharishi Vedic University Press, 1993, pp. 21-22.
13 Maharishi Mahesh Yogi, *Maharishi University of Management: Wholeness on the Move,* p. 43.

Part I: Art as a Language Game—Lamenting the Loss of Universal Value

1 T. McEvilley, *Art and Otherness: Crisis in Cultural Identity,* New York, 1992, pp. 17-18.
2 I. Kant, 'Critique of Judgment,' in M. Taylor (Ed.), *Deconstruction in Context: Literature and Philosophy,* [pp. 35-66], Chicago, 1985, p. 39.
3 S. Gablik, *Progress in Art,* New York, 1976.
4 I. Kant, *Critique of Judgment,* p. 10.
5 T. McEvilley, *Art and Otherness,* p. 136.
6 S. Gablik, *Progress in Art,* & C. Greenberg, *Art and Culture,* Boston, 1961.
7 C. Greenberg, *Art and Culture.*
8 D. Kuspit, 'The Problem of Art in the Age of Glamor', *Art Criticism,* 6(1), 1990, [pp. 32-42]; F. Jameson, 'Postmodernism, or the Cultural Logic of Late Capitalism', *New Left Review*, 146, 1985, [pp. 53-92]; J-F. Lyotard, *The Postmodern Condition: A Report on Knowledge*, Minneapolis, 1988; C. Harrison & P. Wood, *Art in Theory 1900-1990,* Oxford, 1993.
9 D. Kuspit, Conflicting Logics: Twentieth-century Studies at the Crossroads. *The Art Bulletin*, LXIX, 1987 [pp. 117-132], p. 121.
10 T. Eagleton, *The Illusions of Postmodernism*. Oxford, 1997, pp. vii-viii.

1 Modern Art and Theory

1 T. McEvilley, *Art and Otherness: Crisis in Cultural Identity,* New York, 1992.

2 In the context of this discussion, it is worth noting that the aim of modern movements like Cubism was to present many views simultaneously, defying Plato's definition of painting.
3 Plotinus, in R. Jairazbhoy, *Oriental Influences in Western Art*, Bombay, 1965, p. 2.
4 Lucy Lippard suggests that even since Neolithic times there is recurring evidence of geometric forms (like Platonic solids) and mathematical relationships which were thought to represent the workings of nature.
L. Lippard, *Overlay: Contemporary Art and the Art of Prehistory*, New York, 1983, p. 82.
5 Euclid defined the point as that which has no part while Aristotle defined it as that which is indivisible.
6 G. Engler, 'Aesthetics in Science and Art,' *British Journal of Aesthetics*, 30 (1) [pp. 24-34], 1990, p. 24.
7 N. Ardalan & L. Bahktiar, *The Sense of Unity*, Chicago, 1973. R. Lawlor, Sacred Geometry: Philosophy and Practice, London, 1982.
8 W. Kandinsky, in S. Ross, *Art and its Significance: An Anthology of Aesthetic Theory*, New York, 1994, pp. 550-551.
9 S. Holtzman, *Digital Mantras: The Languages of Abstract and Virtual Worlds*, Cambridge, Massachusetts, 1996.
10 T. McEvilley, *Art and Otherness: Crisis in Cultural Identity*, New York, p. 144.
11 G. Hegel, *Reason in History*, New York, 1953, p. 11.
12 *Ibid.*, p. 15.
13 *Ibid.*, p. 23.
14 *Ibid.*
15 *Ibid.*, p. 24.
16 *Ibid.*, p. 76.
17 Hegel uses the example of the Holy Trinity as a principle of particularization, maintaining that God as one is a dead abstraction of sub-rational understanding because it is incomprehensible on the level of particularity. God as one is the basis of the three aspects of God that form a trinity, but it is only through the particular three aspects of God that we can know Him. Hegel demonstrates a principle of the simultaneity of particularization and universality using the Christian concept of the Holy Trinity.
18 G. Hegel, in S. Ross, *Art and its Significance: An Anthology of Aesthetic Theory*, pp. 146-147.
19 M. Mitias, 'Hegel on the Art Object' in W. Steinkraus and K. Schmitz, *Art and Logic in Hegel's Philosophy*, [pp. 67-76], New Jersey, 1980, p. 70.
20 G. Hegel, in M. Taylor, *Deconstruction in Context, New York*, 1986, pp. 38-39.
21 G. Hegel, in M. Mitias, *Hegel on the Art Object*, p. 74.
22 W. Kandinsky, *The Spiritual in Art*, New York, 1977, pp. 54-55.
23 G. Engler, *Aesthetics in Science and Art*, p. 27.
24 T. McEvilley, *Art and Otherness: Crisis in Cultural Identity*, pp. 149-150.
25 *Ibid.*
26 C. Bell, in Ross, *Art and its Significance: An Anthology of Aesthetic Theory*, p. 189.
27 B. Lake, 'A Study of the Irrefutability of Two Aesthetic Theories,' in W. Elton, *Aesthetics and Language*, Oxford, 1959, p. 109.
28 G. Engler, *Aesthetics in Science and Art*, p. 24.
29 B. Hepworth, *Some Statements by Barbara Hepworth*, Cornwall, 1977, p. 2.
30 *Ibid.*, pp. 4-5.
31 *Ibid.*, pp. 2-3.
32 B. Hepworth, *Sculpture 1937*, p. 374.
33 A. Bonshek & L. Fergusson, 'Agnes Martin on Beauty and Perfection in Art,' *Modern Science and Vedic Science Journal*, 2 (3) [pp. 298-306],1988, p. 299.
34 *Ibid.*
35 *Ibid.*, p. 300.
36 *Ibid.*, pp. 300-301.
37 R. Neher, 'As Stupid as Painter: Jackson Pollock and the Politics of Self,' *Art Criticism*, 10 (2), 1995, pp. 58-60.

38 I. Kant, 'Critique of Judgment,' in M. Taylor, *Deconstruction in Context: Literature and Philosophy* [pp. 35-66], Chicago. 1986, p. 42.
39 *Ibid.*
40 *Ibid.*, p. 43.
41 C. Greenberg, *Art and Culture,* Boston, 1961.
42 *Ibid.*, p. 5.
43 T. McEvilley, 'Heads it's Form, Tails it's not Content,' *Artforum*. XXI (3) [pp. 256-263].1982, p. 256.
44 C. Greenberg, *Art and Culture,* pp. 173-174.
45 B. Newman, 'The Ides of Art, Six Opinions on What is Sublime in Art,' *Tiger's Eye*, 6 (53).1948, p. 53.
46 Kozloff, in R. Neher, *As Stupid as Painter: Jackson Pollack and the Politics of Self,* p. 55.
47 S. Gablik, *Progress in Art,* New York. 1976.
48 T. McEvilley, *Heads it's Form, Tails it's not Content,* p. 263.
49 M. Zakian, "Barnett Newman: Painting and A Sense of Place", *Arts*, [pp. 39-44], 1988, p. 39.
50 T. McEvilley. 'Empyrrhical Thinking (and why Kant can't),' *Artforum*, XXVII (2) [pp. 120-127], 1988, p. 39 & p. 8.

2 Indian Theory: Art and Śanta

1 T. McEvilley, *Art and Otherness: Crisis in Cultural Identity,* New York, 1992, p. 112.
2 S. Pandit, *An Approach to the Indian Theory of Art and Aesthetics*, New Delhi, 1977. A. Coomaraswamy, *Selected Papers: Traditional Art and Symbolism,* Volume 1, New Jersey, 1977.
3 H. Coward, *Derrida and Indian Philosophy*, New York, 1990, pp. 4-5.
4 Coward refers to the Vedas as the first philosophical texts (c. 1500-500 B.C.E.) and therefore he locates the beginning of Indian philosophy around this date. This idea is reviewed in later sections.
5 *Ibid.*, p. 5.
6 In all of the texts reference is made to speech and language in relation to the divine. However, according to Coward, Buddhists reject this connection. The association of the language of philosophical texts with the divine, is discussed by Coward in the context of Derridian deconstruction theory.
Ibid., pp. 22-25.
7 A. Coomaraswamy, *Selected Papers: Traditional Art and Symbolism,* p. 93.
8 *Ibid.*, p. 71.
9 S. Pandit, *An Approach to the Indian Theory of Art and Aesthetics,* p. 32.
10 *Ibid.*, p. 28.
11 I. Kant, *Analytic of the Beautiful,* New York, 1963, pp. 3-19.
12 S. Pandit, *An Approach to the Indian Theory of Art and Aesthetics,* p. 6.
13 *Ibid.*, p. 31.
14 *Ibid.*, pp. 33-34.
15 *Ibid.*, p. 93.
16 A. Coomaraswamy, *Selected Papers: Traditional Art and Symbolism*, p. 93.
17 *Ibid.*, pp. 36-37.
18 S. Pandit, *An Approach to the Indian Theory of Art and Aesthetics*, pp. 39-40.
19 *Ibid.*, p. 51.
20 *Ibid.*, p. 54.
21 A. Coomaraswamy, *Selected Papers: Traditional Art and Symbolism*, p. 82.
22 *Ibid.*
23 This notion of systematization versus chance is addressed in Part V which discusses the creative process and its outcome according to the principles of Maharish Vedic Science.
24 A. Coomaraswamy, *Selected Papers: Traditional Art and Symbolism*, p. 58.
25 S. Pandit, *An Approach to the Indian Theory of Art and Aesthetics*, p. 104.
26 *Ibid.*, p. 106.
27 *Ibid.*, p. 123.

28 *Ibid.*, p. 132.
29 T. McEvilley, *Art and Otherness: Crisis in Cultural Identity*, pp. 114-115 & p. 141.

3 Postmodern Art as a Pluralist Language Game Pointing to the Unnamable

1 F. Fehér & A. Heller, *Reconstructing Aesthetics*, Oxford, 1986, p. 6.
2 T. McEvilley, *Art and Otherness: Crisis in Cultural Identity*, New York, 1992, pp. 9-10.
3 C. Jencks, *What is Postmodernism?*, New York, 1986.
4 F. Jameson, 'Postmodernism or The Cultural Logic of Late-Capitalism,' *New Left Review*, 146, 1985, [pp. 53-92].
5 J. Kosuth, *Art After Philosophy and After*, Cambridge: Massachusetts, 1991, p. 81.
6 T. McEvilley, *Art and Otherness: Crisis in Cultural Identity*, p. 144.
7 *Ibid.*
8 L. Fergusson, *Maharishi Vedic Science and Post-Secondary Art Education.* Dissertation Abstracts International, 52, 9, 1991, pp. 17-18.
9 J. Derrida, 'Différance.' In M. Taylor, *Deconstruction in Context: Literature and Philosophy* [pp. 396-420], Chicago, 1986 p. 419.
10 H. Coward, *Derrida and Indian Philosophy*, New York, 1990, p. 30.
11 This perspective contrasts with the perspective of Vedic language theory brought out in Maharishi Vedic Science (discussed in Part III).
12 K. Green, 'Brain Writing and Derrida,' *Australian Journal of Philosophy*, 71 (3) [pp. 238-255] 1993, p. 241.
13 *Ibid.*, p. 244.
14 *Ibid.*, p. 251.
15 J. Kissick, *Art: Context and Criticism*, Hong Kong, 1991.
16 W. Haney, 'The Self and the Referent in Critical Theory', *The 13th Annual Twentieth Century Literature Conference*, Louisville, 1985.
17 L. Wittgenstein, 'Philosophical Investigations,' In M. Taylor, *Deconstruction in Context: Literature and Philosophy*, [pp. 220-241], Chicago, 1986, p. 229.
18 J-F. Lyotard, *The Postmodern Condition: A Report on Knowledge*, p. 18.
19 T. Kuhn, *The Structure of Scientific Revolutions*, Chicago, 1970, p. 144.
20 R. Rorty, 'Habermas and Lyotard on Postmodernity,' *Praxis International*, 4 (1) [pp. 32-44], 1984, p. 34.
21 S. Best & D. Kellner, *Postmodern Theory: Critical Interrogations*, New York, 1991, p. 171.
22 *Ibid.*, pp. 176-177.
23 J. Wolff , *Aesthetics and the Sociology of Art*, Ann Arbor, Michigan, 1992.
24 T. Eagleton , *Literary Theory*, Oxford, 1983, p. 60.
25 J. Wolff, 'Aesthetic Judgment and Sociological Analysis,' *Aspects: A Journal of Contemporary Art*, 21 [pp. 10-11], 1982/3, p. 10.
26 Maruyama, in E. Sampson, Deconstructing Psychology's Subject,' *The Journal of Mind and Behavior*, 4 (2) [135-164],1983, p. 159.
27 From the perspective of Maharishi Vedic Science (specifically the science of Maharishi Sthāpatya Veda) space is governed by the cycles of Natural Law and the movement of the sun and moon with respect to the earth, as is mentioned in Parts III and VI. There is a local or cultural value to architectural aesthetics but on the foundation of universal principles governed by Natural Law.
28 O. Paz, *Convergences: Essays on Art and Literature*, New York, 1987, p. 26.
29 J. Kosuth, *Art After Philosophy and After*, p. 247.
30 J. Lyotard, In J. Kosuth, *Art After Philosophy and After*, p. xv.
31 J. Kosuth, *Art After Philosophy and After*, p. 247.
32 *Ibid.*, p. 249.
33 *Ibid.*, p. 17.
34 *Ibid.*, p. 16.
35 *Ibid.*
36 T. McEvilley, *Art and Otherness: Crisis in Cultural Identity*, p. 158.

37 R. Krauss, *The Originality of The Avant-Garde and Other Modernist Myths*, Cambridge, 1984 p. 18.
38 *Ibid.*, p. 19.
39 T. McEvilley, '"Grey Geese Descending": The Art of Agnes Martin,' *Artforum*, XXIV (10) [pp. 94-99],1987.
40 R. Krauss, *The Originality of The Avant-Garde and Other Modernist Myths.*
41 H. Belting, *The End of the History of Art*, Chicago, 1987, pp. 46-47.
42 T. McEvilley, *Art and Otherness: Crisis in Cultural Identity*, pp. 136-137.
43 *Ibid.*, p. 137.
44 *Ibid.*, p. 144.
45 *Ibid.*, pp. 144-145.
46 *Ibid.*, p. 145.
47 K. Sangari, in T. McEvilley, *Art and Otherness*, p. 86.
48 I. Hassan, *The Postmodern Turn: Essays in Postmodern Theory and Culture*, Ohio, 1987, p. 230.

4 Universal Value in Art and A New Sense of Self

1 D. Kuspit, 'The Problem of Art in the Age of Glamor,' *Art Criticism*, 1990, & S. Gablik, *The Reenchantment of Art*, New York, 1992.
2 D. Kuspit, *The Problem of Art in the Age of Glamor*, p. 32.
3 *Ibid.*, p. 33.
4 F. Jameson, 'Postmodernism, Or The Cultural Logic of Late Capitalism,' *New Left Review*, 146, [pp. 53-92], 1985, p. 16.
5 D. Kuspit, *The Problem of Art in the Age of Glamor*, p. 34.
6 S. Gablik, *The Reenchantment of Art.*
7 D. Kuspit, *The Problem of Art in the Age of Glamor*, pp. 35-36.
8 *Ibid.*
9 *Ibid.*, p. 36.
10 G. Banks, 'In Defence of Common Knowledge,' *Art Monthly*, 63 [pp. 23-25], 1983, p. 25.
11 M. Beam, 'Global Imaging and Mediated Attention,' in *Consciousness Reframed II: Art and Consciousness in the Post-Biological Era*, Centre for Advanced Inquiry into the Interactive Art, Wales, 1998, p. 4.
12 *Ibid.*
13 J. Bermudez, "Between Reality and Virtuality: Toward a New Consciousness?', in *Consciousness Reframed II: Art and Consciousness in the Post-Biological Era*, p. 6.
14 S. Jones, 'Can There Be Non-Embodied Information?', in *Consciousness Reframed II: Art and Consciousness in the Post-Biological Era*, p 25.
15 D. Kuspit, A Psychoanalytic Reading of Aesthetic Disinterestedness,' *Art Criticism*, 6 (2), [pp. 72-80],1990, p. 75.
16 *Ibid.*, p. 76.
17 *Ibid.*, p. 79.
18 S. Turkle, 'Life on the Screen,' Keynote Address, *The Eighth International Symposium on Electronic Art (ISEA97)*, The School of the Art Institute of Chicago. September 22-27, 1997.

Part II: Accessing and Enlivening A Universal Field of Pure Consciousness

1 Maharishi Mahesh Yogi, Maharishi Mahesh Yogi, *Maharishi Vedic University: Introduction*, Holland, 1994, pp. 2-5.
2 Maharishi Mahesh Yogi, *Life Supported by Natural Law: Lectures by His Holiness Maharishi Mahesh Yogi to the World Assembly on Vedic Science*, July 9-17, 1985, Washington D.C., 1986, p. 34.
3 Maharishi Mahesh Yogi, 'Inaugural Address of His Holiness Maharishi Mahesh Yogi,' in *Maharishi Mahesh Yogi: Maharishi Vedic University Inauguration*, Washington D.C., 1985; *Maharishi's Absolute Theory of Government*, Vlodrop, The Netherlands, 1992; *Maharishi Vedic University: Exhibition*, The Netherlands, 1993;

Maharishi's Absolute Theory of Government: Automation in Administration, Holland, 1993; *Maharishi Vedic University: Introduction,* Vlodrop, 1994; *Maharishi University of Management: Wholeness on the Move,* Holland, 1995; M. Dillbeck, 'The Self-Interacting Dynamics of Consciousness as the Source of the Creative Process in Nature and in Human Life: The Mechanics of Individual Intelligence Arising from the Field of Cosmic Intelligence—the Cosmic Psyche,' *Modern Science and Vedic Science Journal*, 2(3),1988, pp. 245-279; 1989; L. Fergusson, *Maharishi Vedic Science and Postsecondary Art Education,* Dissertation Abstracts International, 52.9, 1991; J. Hagelin,'Restructuring Physics from its Foundation in the Light of Maharishi Vedic Science,' *Modern Science and Vedic Science Journal,* 3(1), 1989, pp. 3-74.

4 Maharishi Mahesh Yogi, *Life Supported by Natural Law: Lectures by His Holiness Maharishi Mahesh Yogi to the World Assembly on Vedic Science July 9-17,* 1985, Washington D.C., 1986, p. 26.

5 S. Dillbeck & M. Dillbeck, 'The Maharishi Technology of the Unified Field in Education: Principles, Practice and Research,' *Modern Science and Vedic Science Journal,* 1(4) 1987, pp. 382-468; D. Meyer-Dinkgräfe, Consciousness and the Actor,' European University Studies: Series 30, *Theatre, Film and Television* : Vol. 67, Peter Lang. 1994; M. Cain, 'Art and the Unified Field,' *Modern Science and Vedic Science Journal,* 2(3), 1988, pp. 280-297; L. Fergusson, *Maharishi Vedic Science and Postsecondary Art Education,*; E. Hartmann, *Maharishi Sthapatya-Veda,*. Presented to the Second International Conference on Maharishi Sthapatya-Veda, Washington D.C., 6-8 July, 1990; W. Haney, 'The Theory of Deconstruction and Maharishi Vedic Science,' *Modern Science and Vedic Science Journal,* 2(4), 1989 pp. 415-441; R. Orme-Johnson, 'A Unified Field Theory of Literature,' *Modern Science and Vedic Science Journal,* 1(3)1987, pp. 322-373; C. Alexander & R. Boyer, 'Seven States of Consciousness: Unfolding the Full Potential of the Cosmic Psyche in Individual Life through Maharishi's Vedic Psychology,' *Modern Science and Vedic Science Journal,* 2(4) 1989, pp. 324-371; J. Hagelin, Restructuring Physics from its Foundation in the Light of Maharishi Vedic Science, *Modern Science and Vedic Science Journal,* 3(1) 1989, pp. 3-74; G. Wells & S. Boothby, 'Absolute Principles of Society in Maharishi's Commentary on the Bhagavad-Gita,' *Modern Science and Vedic Science Journal,* 6(1) 1995, pp. 2-30; W. Sands, *Maharishi's Absolute Theory of Government in the Vālmīki Rāmāyana*, Dissertation Abstracts International, 55(6), 1994.

6 Maharishi Mahesh Yogi, *Life Supported by Natural Law: Lectures by His Holiness Maharishi Mahesh Yogi to the World Assembly on Vedic Science July 9-17*, 1985, Washington D.C., 1986, p. 25.

7 Maharishi Mahesh Yogi, *Maharishi University of Management: Wholeness on the Move,* p. 31.

8 Maharishi Mahesh Yogi, *Thirty Years Around the World: Dawn of the Age of Enlightenment,* The Netherlands, 1986, p. 205.

9 R. Krauss, cited in M. Wood, 'New, Newer, Newest,' *Art of the Western World*. [Film Series] London: British Broadcasting Corporation, 1989.

10 Maharishi Mahesh Yogi, *Thirty Years Around the World: Dawn of the Age of Enlightenment,* pp. 207-208.

11 Maharishi Mahesh Yogi, *Maharishi Mahesh Yogi on the Bhagavad-Gita: A New Translation and Commentary: Chapters 1-6.* Middlesex, 1969, pp. 193-207.

12 Maharishi Mahesh Yogi, *Maharishi's Absolute Theory of Government,* 1992, pp. 27-28.

5 The Universal Self-Referral Source of Creation

1 Maharishi Mahesh Yogi, *Life Supported by Natural Law: Lectures by His Holiness Maharishi Mahesh Yogi to the World Assembly on Vedic Science July 9-17,* 1985," Washington D.C., 1986, pp. 25-22.

2 J. Hagelin, 'Is Consciousness a Unified Field? A Field Theorist's Perspective,' *Modern Science and Vedic Science Journal*, 1(1) 1987, pp. 28-87; 'Restructuring

Physics from its Foundation in the Light of Maharishi Vedic Science,' *Modern Science and Vedic Science Journal,* 3(1), 1989, pp. 3-74.

3 Maharishi Mahesh Yogi, *Maharishi's Absolute Theory of Government: Automation in Administration,* Holland, 1993, p. 27.

4 Maharishi Mahesh Yogi, *Maharishi Vedic University: Introduction,* Holland, 1994, p. 67.

5 *Ibid.,* p. 58 & p. 67.

6 *Ibid.,* p. 58.

7 *Ibid.,* p. 53.

8 J. Hagelin, *Is Consciousness a Unified Field? A Field Theorist's Perspective; Restructuring Physics from its Foundation in the Light of Maharishi Vedic Science;* T. Nader, *Human Physiology: Expression of Veda and the Vedic Literature,* Holland, 1998.

9 Maharishi Mahesh Yogi, *Maharishi Vedic University: Introduction,* p. 54.

10 *Ibid.*

11 *Ibid.*

12 *Ibid.*

13 *Ibid.*

14 *Ibid.,* pp. 54-55.

15 *Ibid.,* p. 55.

16 *Ibid.*

17 *Ibid.,* p. 357.

18 *Ibid.,* pp. 55-56.

19 *Ibid.,* p. 56.

20 Maharishi Mahesh Yogi, 'Inaugural Address of His Holiness Maharishi Mahesh Yogi,' in *Maharishi Mahesh Yogi: Maharishi Vedic University Inauguration,* Washington D.C., 1985, p. 65.

21 *Ibid.*

22 Maharishi Mahesh Yogi, *Maharishi Vedic University: Introduction,* p. 58.

23 Maharishi Mahesh Yogi, *Life Supported by Natural Law: Lectures by His Holiness Maharishi Mahesh Yogi to the World Assembly on Vedic Science July 9-17,* 1985, pp. 25-26.

24 Maharishi Mahesh Yogi, *Thirty Years Around the World: Dawn of the Age of Enlightenment,* The Netherlands, 1986, p. 25.

25 Maharishi Vedic University, *Maharishi Vedic University: Introduction,* Holland, 1994, pp. 58-59.

26 These qualities have also been mathematically derived by physics as characteristics of the Unified Field Maharishi Mahesh Yogi, *Maharishi's Absolute Theory of Government,* Vlodrop, The Netherlands, 1992.

27 A. Bonshek & L. Fergusson, *Signs of Reconciliation: The Recent Work of Michael Kane Taylor,* Fairfield, 1988; M. Cain, 'Art and the Unified Field,' *Modern Science and Vedic Science Journal,* 2(3), 1988, pp. 280-297; L. Fergusson, *Maharishi Vedic Science and Post-Secondary Art Education,* Dissertation Abstracts International, 52, 9. 1991.

28 Maharishi Mahesh Yogi, *Maharishi Vedic University: Introduction,* p. 59.

29 Maharishi Mahesh Yogi, *Maharishi Vedic University: Exhibition,* The Netherlands, 1993, p. 6.

30 Maharishi Mahesh Yogi, *Life Supported by Natural Law,* p. 27.

31 Maharishi Mahesh Yogi, *Maharishi Vedic University: Introduction,* p. 59.

32 Maharishi Mahesh Yogi, *Life Supported by Natural Law,* p.27.

33 Maharishi Mahesh Yogi, 'Inaugural Address of His Holiness Maharishi Mahesh Yogi,' pp. 65-66.

34 *Ibid.,* p. 66.

35 Maharishi Mahesh Yogi, *Maharishi's Absolute Theory of Government,* p. 21.

36 Maharishi Mahesh Yogi, *Maharishi Vedic University: Exhibition,* pp. 12-25.

37 *Ibid.;* pp. 19-20.

38 Maharishi Mahesh Yogi, *Maharishi Vedic University: Introduction,* pp. 59-60.

39 *Ibid.,* p. 163.

40 *Ibid.,* p. 164.

41 *Ibid.*
42 *Ibid.*
43 *Ibid.*, p. 101.
44 Maharishi Mahesh Yogi, in A. Bonshek, *Art—A Mirror of Consciousness: Applying Universal Principles in Art and Theory on the Basis of the Description of Pure Consciousness, the Universal Source of Individual Consciousness, History, Culture, Language and Art, According to Maharishi Vedic Science—with an Analysis of the Vāstusūtra Upaniṣad*, Dissertation Abstracts International, 75, 08A, 1996, p. 102.
45 Maharishi Mahesh Yogi, in J. Muehlman, *Maharishi's Vedic Mathematics at the Elementary Level,* Dissertation Abstracts International, 9431798, 1994, p. 111.
46 Maharishi Mahesh Yogi, *Maharishi Vedic University: Introduction,* p. 65.
47 *Ibid.*, p. 318.
48 Maharishi Mahesh Yogi, *Maharishi Vedic University: Exhibition*, pp. 276-277.
49 Maharishi Mahesh Yogi, in A. Bonshek, *Art—A Mirror of Consciousness*, p. 104.
50 Maharishi Mahesh Yogi, *Maharishi Vedic University: Introduction,* p. 319.
51 Maharishi Mahesh Yogi, in A. Bonshek, *Art—A Mirror of Consciousness*, p. 104.
52 Maharishi Mahesh Yogi, *Maharishi Vedic University: Introduction,* p. 64.
53 *Ibid.*, p. 319.
54 Maharishi Mahesh Yogi, in A. Bonshek, *Art—A Mirror of Consciousness*, p. 104.
55 Maharishi Mahesh Yogi, *Maharishi's Absolute Theory of Government*, pp. 112-119.
56 Maharishi Mahesh Yogi, *Maharishi Vedic University: Introduction*, p. 335.
57 *Ibid.*
58 Maharishi Mahesh Yogi, *Maharishi's Absolute Theory of Government*, p. 109.
59 *Ibid.*, p. 107-108.
60 *Ibid.*, p. 30.
61 *Ibid.*, p. 110.
62 *Ibid.*, p.111.
63 *Ibid.*, p. 160.
64 *Ibid.*
65 *Ibid.*, p. 161.
66 *Ibid.*, pp. 160-162.
67 Maharishi Mahesh Yogi, *Maharishi University of Management: Wholeness on the Move*, Holland, 1995, p.125.
68 Maharishi Mahesh Yogi, in A. Bonshek, *Art—A Mirror of Consciousness*, p. 110.
69 *Ibid.*
70 Maharishi Mahesh Yogi, *Maharishi Vedic University: Introduction*, p. 64.
71 Maharishi Mahesh Yogi, in A. Bonshek, *Art—A Mirror of Consciousness*, p. 110.
72 Maharishi Mahesh Yogi, *Maharishi's Absolute Theory of Government.*
73 Maharishi Mahesh Yogi, in A. Bonshek, *Art—A Mirror of Consciousness*, pp. 110-111.
74 Maharishi Mahesh Yogi, *The Science of Being and the Art of Living*, Washington D.C., 1966 p. 25.
75 *Ibid.*, p. 26.
76 Maharishi Mahesh Yogi, *Life Supported by Natural Law*, p. 75.
77 *Ibid.*
78 Maharishi Mahesh Yogi, 'Art and the Artist.' [Lecture given at Kössen, W. Germany]. In M. Cain, *Art and the Science of Creative Intelligence: Interdependence of Part and Whole*, Fairfield, Iowa, 1970, pp. v-viii.
79 Maharishi Mahesh Yogi, *Art and the Artist.*
80 Maharishi Mahesh Yogi, in A. Bonshek, *Art—A Mirror of Consciousness*, p. 112.
81 Maharishi Mahesh Yogi, *Maharishi Vedic University: Introduction*, p. 285 & p. 288.
82 Maharishi Mahesh Yogi, *Maharishi University of Management: Wholeness on the Move,* p .135.
83 *Ibid.*, pp. 136-137.

6 Developing Higher States of Consciousness through the Practice of the Transcendental Meditation Technique, the TM-Sidhi Program and Yogic Flying

1 Maharishi Mahesh Yogi, *The Science of Being and Art of Living,* Washington, D.C., 1966, p. 50.
2 Maharishi Vedic University, *Maharishi's Master Plan to Create Heaven on Earth,* The Netherlands, 1991, p. 24.
3 *Ibid.,* p. 10.
4 Maharishi Mahesh Yogi, 'Art and the Artist.' [Lecture given at Kössen, W. Germany]. In M. Cain, *Art and the Science of Creative Intelligence: Interdependence of Part and Whole,* Fairfield, Iowa, 1970, pp. v-viii.
5 Maharishi Mahesh Yogi, in A. Bonshek, *Art—A Mirror of Consciousness: Applying Universal Principles in Art and Theory on the Basis of the Description of Pure Consciousness, the Universal Source of Individual Consciousness, History, Culture, Language and Art, According to Maharishi Vedic Science—with an Analysis of the Vāstusūtra Upaniṣad,* Dissertation Abstracts International, 75, 08A, 1996, p. 116.
6 Maharishi Mahesh Yogi, *Maharishi University of Management: Wholeness on the Move,* Holland, 1995, p. 63.
7 Maharishi Mahesh Yogi, *Art and the Artist.* p. vi.
8 Maharishi International University, *Maharishi International University Bulletin*, Los Angeles, 1979-81, p. 43.
9 Maharishi Mahesh Yogi, *Maharishi's Absolute Theory of Government: Automation in Administration*, Holland, 1993, p. 120; *Maharishi University of Management: Wholeness on the Move,* p. 130.
10 Maharishi Mahesh Yogi, *The Science of Being and Art of Living,* p. 123.
11 Maharishi Mahesh Yogi, *Maharishi Vedic University: Introduction,* Holland, 1994, pp. 260-261.
12 Maharishi Mahesh Yogi, *Maharishi Mahesh Yogi on the Bhagavad-Gita: A New Translation and Commentary: Chapters 1-6.* Middlesex, 1969, p. 118.
13 *Ibid.,* p. 144.
14 Maharishi Mahesh Yogi, *Maharishi Vedic University: Introduction,* pp. 260-261.
15 Maharishi Mahesh Yogi, *Maharishi University of Management: Wholeness on the Move,* pp. 31-32.
16 *Ibid.,* p. 32.
17 Maharishi Mahesh Yogi, *Maharishi Mahesh Yogi on the Bhagavad-Gita: A New Translation and Commentary: Chapters 1-6,* p. 314.
18 *Ibid.,* p. 173.
19 *Ibid.,* p. 314.
20 *Ibid.,* p. 313:
21 Maharishi Vedic University, *Maharishi's Master Plan to Create Heaven on Earth*, p. 23.
22 *Ibid.,* pp. 23-24.
23 Maharishi Mahesh Yogi, *Thirty Years Around the World: Dawn of the Age of Enlightenment,* The Netherlands, 1986, pp. 288-289.
24 Maharishi Mahesh Yogi, *Maharishi Mahesh Yogi on the Bhagavad-Gita: A New Translation and Commentary: Chapters 1-6,* p. 314.
25 C. Alexander & R. Boyer, 'Seven States of Consciousness: Unfolding the Full Potential of the Cosmic Psyche in Individual Life through Maharishi's Vedic Psychology,' *Modern Science and Vedic Science Journal,* 2(4), 1989, pp. 343-357.
26 Maharishi Mahesh Yogi, *Maharishi Mahesh Yogi on the Bhagavad-Gita: A New Translation and Commentary: Chapters 1-6,* p. 314.
27 Maharishi Mahesh Yogi, *Maharishi's Absolute Theory of Government: Automation in Administration,* Holland, 1993, p. 17.
28 Maharishi Mahesh Yogi, *Life Supported by Natural Law: Lectures by His Holiness Maharishi Mahesh Yogi to the World Assembly on Vedic Science July 9-17*, 1985, Washington D.C., 1986, p. 115; Maharishi Mahesh Yogi, *Maharishi's Absolute Theory of Government: Automation in Administration,* p. 146.

29 Maharishi Mahesh Yogi, *Maharishi Mahesh Yogi on the Bhagavad-Gita: A New Translation and Commentary: Chapters 1-6,* p. 315.
30 *Ibid.*
31 Maharishi Mahesh Yogi, 'The Artist and the Scientist, Lesson 27,' *The Science of Creative Intelligence: Knowledge and Experience* [Syllabus of Videotaped Course]. Los Angeles, 1972, 23:6
32 *Ibid.*
33 Maharishi Mahesh Yogi, *Maharishi Vedic University: Exhibition,* The Netherlands, 1993, p. 148.
34 Maharishi Mahesh Yogi, *Life Supported by Natural Law,* 1985, p. 34.
35 Maharishi Mahesh Yogi, *The Artist and the Scientist, Lesson 27,* 23:9.
36 Maharishi Mahesh Yogi, *Maharishi Vedic University: Introduction,* p. 44.
37 From the *Bṛihadāraṇyak Upaniṣad,* 1.4.10..
38 Maharishi Mahesh Yogi, *Life Supported by Natural Law*, p. 34; Maharishi Mahesh Yogi, *Maharishi Vedic University: Introduction,* p. 57.
39 Maharishi Mahesh Yogi, Maharishi Mahesh Yogi, *Life Supported by Natural Law,* p. 34.
40 Maharishi Vedic University, *Maharishi's Master Plan to Create Heaven on Earth,* p. 1.
41 *Ibid.*
42 Maharishi Mahesh Yogi, *Maharishi Vedic University: Introduction,* p. 121.
43 Maharishi Mahesh Yogi, *Maharishi's Absolute Theory of Government: Automation in Administration,* p. 200.
44 *Ibid.,* p. 279.
45 *Ibid.,* pp. 277-278.
46 *Ibid.,* p. 278.
47 Maharishi Mahesh Yogi, *Life Supported by Natural Law,* p. 34.
48 Maharishi Mahesh Yogi, *Maharishi Mahesh Yogi on the Bhagavad-Gita: A New Translation and Commentary: Chapters 1-6,* p. 14.
49 Maharishi Mahesh Yogi, *The Science of Being and Art of Living,* pp. 348-349.
50 Maharishi Mahesh Yogi, *Maharishi Mahesh Yogi on the Bhagavad-Gita: A New Translation and Commentary: Chapters 1-6,* p. 316.
51 *Ibid.,* p. 316.
52 *Ibid.,* p. 312.
53 Maharishi Mahesh Yogi, *Life Supported by Natural Law,* p. 27.
54 Maharishi Mahesh Yogi, In S. Dillbeck & M. Dillbeck, 'The Maharishi Technology of the Unified Field in Education: Principles, Practice and Research,' *Modern Science and Vedic Science Journal*, 1987 1(4), p. 391.
55 *Ibid.*
56 Maharishi Mahesh Yogi, *Maharishi Mahesh Yogi on the Bhagavad-Gita: A New Translation and Commentary: Chapters 1-6,* p. 312.
57 Maharishi Vedic University, *Maharishi Vedic University: Introduction*, Vlodrop, 1994, p. 187.
58 *Ibid.,* pp. 17-18.
59 Maharishi Mahesh Yogi, *Life Supported by Natural Law,* p. 42.
60 Maharishi Vedic University, *Maharishi Vedic University: Introduction,* pp. 261-262.
61 Maharishi Mahesh Yogi, *Enlightenment to Every Individual and Invincibility to Every Nation,* Rheinwheiler, W. Germany, 1978, p. 126.
62 Maharishi Mahesh Yogi, *Maharishi University of Management: Wholeness on the Move,* p. 40.
63 Maharishi Mahesh Yogi, *Maharishi Mahesh Yogi on the Bhagavad-Gita: A New Translation and Commentary: Chapters 1-6,* p. 186.
64 P. Gelderloos & W. van den Berg, 'Maharishi's TM-Sidhi Program: Participating in the Infinite Creativity of Nature to Enliven the Totality of the Cosmic Psyche in all Aspects of Life,' *Modern Science and Vedic Science Journal*., 2(4), 1989, pp. 372-412.
65 *Ibid.,* p. 406.
66 Maharishi European Research University, *Global Research Programme*, G 1554, West Germany, 1978, p. 104.

67 Maharishi Mahesh Yogi, *Maharishi Mahesh Yogi: Science, Consciousness and Ageing: Proceedings of the International Conference*, Rheinwheiler, W. Germany, 1980, p. 74.
68 *Ibid.*, p. 75.
69 P. Gelderloos & W. van den Berg, *Maharishi's TM-Sidhi Program: Participating in the Infinite Creativity of Nature to Enliven the Totality of the Cosmic Psyche in all Aspects of Life.*
70 Maharishi Mahesh Yogi, *Maharishi Mahesh Yogi: Science, Consciousness and Ageing: Proceedings of the International Conference*, p. 39.
71 *Ibid.*
72 P. Gelderloos & W. van den Berg, *Maharishi's TM-Sidhi Program: Participating in the Infinite Creativity of Nature to Enliven the Totality of the Cosmic Psyche in all Aspects of Life*, p. 383.
73 Maharishi Mahesh Yogi, *Maharishi Mahesh Yogi: Science, Consciousness and Ageing: Proceedings of the International Conference*, p. 19.
74 *Ibid.*, p. 39.
75 *Ibid.*, p. 19.
76 *Ibid.*
77 Maharishi Mahesh Yogi, *Maharishi University of Management: Wholeness on the Move*, pp. 126-127.
78 *Ibid.*, p. 126.
79 *Ibid.*, pp. 126-127.
80 Maharishi Mahesh Yogi, *Maharishi Vedic University: Introduction*, pp. 350-352.
81 *Ibid.*, pp. 161-350.
82 Maharishi Mahesh Yogi, *Maharishi Vedic University: Introduction*, p. 352.
83 Maharishi Vedic University, *Maharishi's Programme to Create World Peace: Global Inauguration*, The Netherlands, 1987, pp. 18-19.
84 Maharishi Mahesh Yogi, *Life Supported by Natural Law*, p. 29.
85 Maharishi Mahesh Yogi, *Maharishi's Absolute Theory of Government: Automation in Administration*, p. 42.
86 *Ibid.*, p. 42 & p. 118.
87 *Ibid.*, p. 118.
88 *Ibid.*, p. 111.
89 *Ibid.*, pp. 111-112.
90 *Ibid.*, pp. 112-113.
91 *Ibid.*, p. 113.
92 *Ibid.*, p. 116.
93 Maharishi Mahesh Yogi, *Maharishi Mahesh Yogi on the Bhagavad-Gita: A New Translation and Commentary: Chapters 1-6*, p. 355.
94 Maharishi Vedic University, *Maharishi's Programme to Create World Peace: Global Inauguration*, p. 570; Maharishi Mahesh Yogi, *Creating an Ideal Society*, Rheinwheiler, 1977, pp. 76-85.
95 Maharishi Vedic University, *Maharishi's Programme to Create World Peace: Global Inauguration*, p. 25.
96 Maharishi Mahesh Yogi, *Maharishi Vedic University: Exhibition*, p. 212.
97 Maharishi Mahesh Yogi, *Maharishi University of Management; Wholeness on the Move*, p. 213.
98 *Ibid.*, p. 224 & p. 244.
99 Maharishi Mahesh Yogi, *Maharishi Vedic University: Introduction*, p. 224.
100 Maharishi Mahesh Yogi, *Maharishi's Absolute Theory of Government: Automation in Administration*, pp. 200-201.
101 *Ibid.*, p. 100.
102 *Ibid.*

7 Scientific Research on Maharishi's Technologies of Consciousness

1 R. Chalmers, G. Clements, H. Schenkluhn, & M. Weinless, *Scientific Research on Maharishi's Transcendental Meditation and TM-Sidhi Programme: Collected Papers*, Vols. 2-4. The Netherlands, 1989.

2 R. Wallace, 'Physiological Effects of Transcendental Meditation,' *Science,* 167, 1970, pp. 1751-1754; 'A Wakeful Hypometabolic Physiologic State,' *The American Journal of Physiology,* 221, 1971, pp. 795-799.

3 W. van den Berg, & B. Mulder, 'Psychological Research on the Effects of the Transcendental Meditation Technique on a Number of Personality Variables,' *Gedrag: Tijdscrift voor Psychologie* [Behavior: Journal for Psychology], 4, 1976, pp. 206-218; K. Friend, 'Effects of the Transcendental Meditation Program on Work Attitudes and Behavior,' In D. Orme-Johnson & J. Farrow (Eds.), *Scientific Research on the Transcendental Meditation Program: Collected Papers,* Vol. 1 [pp. 630-638]. Rheinweiler, W. Germany, 1977; A. Hjelle, 'Transcendental Meditation and Psychological Health,' *Perceptual and Motor Skills,* 39, 1974, pp. 623-628; S. Nidich, W. Seeman, & M. Seibert, 'Influence of the Transcendental Meditation Program on State Anxiety,' In D. Orme-Johnson & J. Farrow (Eds.), *Scientific Research on the Transcendental Meditation Program: Collected Papers,* Vol. 1 [pp. 434-436]; P. Schilling, 'The Effect of the Regular Practice of the Transcendental Meditation Technique on Behavior and Personality,' In D. Orme-Johnson & J. Farrow (Eds.), *Scientific Research on the Transcendental Meditation Program: Collected Papers,* Vol. 1 [pp. 453-461]; A. Tjoa, 'Increased Intelligence and Reduced Neuroticism through the Transcendental Meditation Program,' *Gedrag: Tijdscrift voor Psychologie* [Behavior: Journal for Psychology], 3, 1975, pp. 167-182.

4 Maharishi Mahesh Yogi, *Creating an Ideal Society.* Rheinweiler, W. Germany, 1977, p. 77.

5 F. Travers, 'Creative Thinking and the Transcendental Meditation Technique,' *The Journal of Creative Behavior,* 13(3) 1979, pp. 169-180.

6 S. Harrison, R. Pagano, & S. Warrenburg, 'Meditation and the Right Hemispheric Functioning-Spatial Localization,' *Proceedings of Biofeedback Research Society, Seventh Annual Meeting,* Colorado Springs, 33, 1976.

7 L. Fergusson, A. Bonshek, & G. Le Masson, 'Vedic Science Based Education and Nonverbal Intelligence: A Preliminary Longitudinal Study in Cambodia,' *Higher Education Research and Development,* 15(1) 1995, pp. 73-82; R. Cranson, D. Orme-Johnson, J. Gackenbach, M. Dillbeck, C. Jones, & C. Alexander, 'Transcendental Meditation and Improved Performance in Intelligence-Related Measures: A Longitudinal Study. *Personality and Individual Differences,* 12 (10), 1991, pp. 1105-1116; A. Tjoa, *Increased Intelligence and Reduced Neuroticism through the Transcendental Meditation Program,* pp. 167-182.

8 D. Miskman, 'The Effect of the Transcendental Meditation Program on the Organization of Thinking and Recall (Secondary Organization),' In D. Orme-Johnson & J. Farrow (Eds.), *Scientific Research on the Transcendental Meditation Program: Collected Papers,* Vol. 1 [pp. 385-392].

9 L. Fergusson, 'Field Independence and Art Achievement in Meditating and Non-Meditating College Students,' *Perceptual and Motor Skills,* 75, 1992, pp. 1171-1175, & 'Field Independence, Transcendental Meditation, and Achievement in College Art: A Re-examination,' *Perceptual and Motor Skills*, 77, 1993, pp. 1104-1106.; K. Pelletier, K. 'Influence of Transcendental Meditation Upon Autokinetic Perception,' *Perceptual and Motor Skills,* 39, 1974, pp. 1031-1034, & 'The Effects of the Transcendental Meditation Program on Perceptual Style: Increased Field-Independence,' In D. Orme-Johnson & J. Farrow (Eds.), *Scientific Research on the Transcendental Meditation Program: Collected Papers,* Vol. 1 [pp. 337-345],.

10 L. Fergusson, *Field Independence and Art Achievement in Meditating and Non-Meditating College Students.*

11 K. Pelletier, *The Effects of the Transcendental Meditation Program on Perceptual Style: Increased Field-Independence.*

12 Maharishi Mahesh Yogi, *Maharishi University of Management: Wholeness on the Move,* Holland, 1995, p. 63 & p. 201.

13 L. Fergusson, *Field Independence and Art Achievement in Meditating and Non-Meditating College Students & Field Independence, Transcendental Meditation, and Achievement in College Art: A Re-examination.*

14 Maharishi Mahesh Yogi, *Maharishi University of Management: Wholeness on the Move,* p. 202.

15 Maharishi Mahesh Yogi, *Maharishi Mahesh Yogi on the Bhagavad-Gita: A New Translation and Commentary: Chapters 1-6.* Middlesex, 1969, p. 428.
16 G. Andrew, & A. Rimol, 'The Transcendental Meditation Technique and its Effects on Sensory-Motor Performance,' In D. Orme-Johnson & J. Farrow (Eds.), *Scientific Research on the Transcendental Meditation Program: Collected Papers,* Vol. 1, [pp. 326-330]; K. Blasdell, 'The effects of the Transcendental Meditation Technique Upon a Complex Perceptual-Motor Task.' In D. Orme-Johnson & J. Farrow (Eds.), *Scientific Research on the Transcendental Meditation Program: Collected Papers*, Vol. 1 [pp. 322-325].
17 Maharishi Mahesh Yogi, *Maharishi University of Management: Wholeness on the Move,* p. 202.
18 L. Fergusson, A. Bonshek, & J-M. Boudigues, 'Personality and Health Characteristics of Cambodian Undergraduates: A Case for Student Development,' *Journal of Instructional Psychology*, 22 (4), 1995, pp. 308-319.
19 L. Fergusson & A. Bonshek, Health and Postsecondary Art Achievement: A Study of Four Universities in Iowa,' *College Student Journal,* 30 (1), 1996, pp. 105-111.
20 D. Orme-Johnson, G. Clements, C. Haynes, & K. Badaoui, 'Higher States of Consciousness: EEG Coherence, Creativity, and Experiences of the Sidhis,' In D. Orme-Johnson & J. Farrow (Eds.), *Scientific Research on the Transcendental Meditation and TM-Sidhi Program: Collected Papers,* Vol. 1 [pp. 705-712].
21 Maharishi Mahesh Yogi, *Maharishi's Absolute Theory of Government: Automation in Administration,* Holland, 1993, p. 119.
22 *Ibid.*
23 Maharishi Mahesh Yogi, *Maharishi Mahesh Yogi on the Bhagavad-Gita: A New Translation and Commentary: Chapters 1-6.* Middlesex, 1969, p. 214.
24 C. Borland, & G. Landrith, 'Improved Quality of City Life Through the Transcendental Meditation Program: Decreased Crime Rate,' In D. Orme-Johnson & J. Farrow (Eds.), *Scientific Research on the Transcendental Meditation Program : Collected Papers,* Vol. 1 [pp. 639-648].
25 S. Gablik, 'Art Beyond the Rectangle: A Call for "Useful" Art,' *New Art Examiner,* 17(4), 1991, pp. 20-24, & *The Reenchantment of Art.* New York, 1992.
26 Maharishi Mahesh Yogi, *Creating an Ideal Society.* pp. 123-124.
27 *Ibid.,* p. 124.
28 D. Orme-Johnson & M. Dillbeck, 'Maharishi's Program to Create World Peace: Theory and Research,' *Modern Science and Vedic Science Journal,* 1(2), 1987, pp. 207-259.
29 Maharishi Mahesh Yogi, *Maharishi Vedic University: Introduction,* Holland, 1994, pp. 286-287.
30 Maharishi European Research University, *Global Research Programme*, G 1554. West Germany, 1978.
31 Maharishi Mahesh Yogi, *Maharishi's Absolute Theory of Government: Automation in Administration,* p. 121.
32 *Ibid.,* p. 304.
33 D. Orme-Johnson, C. Alexander, J. Davies, H. Chandler, & W. Larimore, 'International Peace Project in the Middle East,' *Journal of Conflict Resolution*, 32(4),1988, pp. 776-812; D. Orme-Johnson & M. Dillbeck, *Maharishi's Program to Create World Peace: Theory and Research*.
34 D. Orme-Johnson, M. Dillbeck, J. Bousquet, & C. Alexander, *The World Peace Project of 1978: An Experimental Analysis of Achieving World Peace through the Maharishi Technology of the Unified Field,* Maharishi European University Research Report No. 322.1985; D. Orme-Johnson & M. Dillbeck, *Maharishi's Program to Create World Peace: Theory and Research.*
35 P. Gelderloos, J. Frid, P. Goddard, X. Xue, & S. Löliger, 'Creating World Peace through the Collective Practice of the Maharishi Technology of the Unified Field: Improved U.S.-Soviet Relations,' *Social Science Perspectives Journal,* 2(4), 1988, pp. 80-94.
36 Maharishi Mahesh Yogi, *Maharishi's Absolute Theory of Government: Automation in Administration,* pp. 306-307.

37 Maharishi Mahesh Yogi, *Life Supported by Natural Law: Lectures by His Holiness Maharishi Mahesh Yogi to the World Assembly on Vedic Science July 9-17, 1985,* Washington D.C., 1986, pp. 80-82.
38 Institute of Science, Technology and Public Policy, *Results of the National Demonstration Project to Reduce Violent Crime and Improve Governmental Effectiveness in Washington D.C. June 7 to July 30, 1993.* Institute of Science, Technology and Public Policy Technical Report, September, 1994, ITR-94:1.

Part III: The Veda and the Vedic Literature: The Complete Disclosure of Nature's Creative Mechanics

1 Maharishi Mahesh Yogi, Maharishi University of Management: *Wholeness on the Move,* Holland, 1995, pp. 25-29.
2 Maharishi Mahesh Yogi, *Inauguration of Maharishi Vedic University,* Washington D.C., 1985, p. 78.
3 *Ibid.*
4 Maharishi Mahesh Yogi, *Maharishi Vedic University: Introduction,* Holland, 1994, p. 317.
5 *Ibid.,* p. 149.
6 Maharishi Mahesh Yogi, *Maharishi University of Management: Wholeness on the Move,* p. 20.
7 Maharishi Mahesh Yogi, *Maharishi's Absolute Theory of Government: Automation in Administration,* 1993, p. 209.
8 *Ibid.,* p. 207.
9 *Ibid.,* p. 210.

8 Self-Referral Conciousness as the Structure of Ṛk Veda: The Holistic Value of Natural Law at the Basis of Creation

1 Maharishi Mahesh Yogi, *Maharishi's Absolute Theory of Government: Automation in Administration,* Holland, 1993, p. 224.
2 *Ibid.,* p. 225.
3 *Ibid.,* pp. 18-19.
4 *Ibid.,* p. 20.
5 *Ibid.,* p. 99.
6 *Ibid.,* pp. 19-20.
7 *Ibid.,* p. 59.
8 *Ibid.,* pp. 5-7.
9 *Ibid.,* p. 8.
10 *Ibid.,* p. 175.
11 *Ibid.,* p. 94.
12 *Ibid.,* p. 4 & p. 94.
13 Maharishi Mahesh Yogi, *Maharishi Mahesh Yogi on the Bhagavad-Gita: A New Translation and Commentary: Chapters 1-6,* Middlesex, 1969, p. 26.
14 *Ibid.*
15 *Ibid.,* p. 64.
16 *Ibid.*
17 T. Nader, *Human Physiology: Expression of Veda and the Vedic Literature,* Vlodrop, The Netherlands, 1993.
18 Maharishi Mahesh Yogi, *Maharishi's Absolute Theory of Government: Automation in Administration,* p. 8.
19 *Ibid.,* p. 33.
20 *Ibid.,* p. 16.
21 Maharishi Mahesh Yogi, in A. Bonshek, *Art—A Mirror of Consciousness: Applying Universal Principles in Art and Theory on the Basis of the Description of Pure Consciousness, the Universal Source of Individual Consciousness, History, Culture, Language and Art, According to Maharishi Vedic Science—with an Analysis of the Vāstusūtra Upaniṣad,* Dissertation Abstracts International, 75, 08A, 1996, p. 169.

22 Maharishi Mahesh Yogi, *Maharishi Vedic University: Introduction*, Holland, 1994, p. 357.
23 *Ibid.*, p. 158.
24 *Ibid.*, p. 55.
25 Maharishi Mahesh Yogi, in A. Bonshek, *Art—A Mirror of Consciousness*, p. 170.
26 Maharishi Mahesh Yogi, *Maharishi Mahesh Yogi on the Bhagavad-Gita: A New Translation and Commentary: Chapters 1-6*, p. 483.
27 Maharishi Mahesh Yogi, *Maharishi's Absolute Theory of Government: Automation in Administration*, p. 33.
28 T. Nader, *Human Physiology: Expression of Veda and the Vedic Literature*, p. 95.
29 Maharishi Mahesh Yogi, *Maharishi Vedic University: Introduction*, p. 117 & p. 356.
30 Maharishi Mahesh Yogi, in A. Bonshek, *Art—A Mirror of Consciousness*, p. 170.
31 Maharishi Mahesh Yogi, *Maharishi University of Management: Wholeness on the Move*, Holland, 1995, p. 43.
32 Maharishi Mahesh Yogi, *Maharishi Vedic University: Introduction*, p. 165.
33 H. Coward, *Derrida and Indian Philosophy*, New York, 1990, p. 61.
34 Maharishi Mahesh Yogi, *Maharishi Vedic University: Introduction*, p. 253 & p. 356.
35 Maharishi Mahesh Yogi, in A. Bonshek, *Art—A Mirror of Consciousness*, p. 171.
36 *Ibid.*
37 *Ibid.*
38 *Ibid.*
39 *Ibid.*
40 Maharishi Mahesh Yogi, *Maharishi Mahesh Yogi on the Bhagavad-Gita: A New Translation and Commentary: Chapters 1-6*, p, 128.
41 *Ibid.*, p. 128.
42 T. Nader, *Human Physiology: Expression of Veda and the Vedic Literature*, p. 122.
43 J. Hagelin, 'Is Consciousness a Unified Field? A Field Theorist's Perspective,' *Modern Science and Vedic Science Journal*, 1(1) 1987, pp. 28-87.
44 T. Nader, *Human Physiology: Expression of Veda and the Vedic Literature.*
45 J. Hagelin, *Is Consciousness a Unified Field? A Field Theorist's Perspective*, pp. 75-77.
46 *Ibid.*, pp. 75-76.
47 Maharishi Mahesh Yogi, *Maharishi Vedic University: Introduction*, p. 66.
48 *Ibid.*, p. 65.
49 Maharishi Mahesh Yogi, *Maharishi's Absolute Theory of Government: Automation in Administration*, p. 174.
50 Maharishi Mahesh Yogi, *Maharishi's Absolute Theory of Government: Automation in Administration*; Nader, *Human Physiology: Expression of Veda and the Vedic Literature*, pp. 14-15 & pp. 52-53.
51 Maharishi Mahesh Yogi, *Maharishi's Absolute Theory of Government: Automation in Administration*, p. 182.
52 *Ibid.*, pp. 175-176.
53 *Ibid.*, p. 177.
54 Maharishi Mahesh Yogi, *Maharishi Vedic University: Introduction*, p. 139.
55 Maharishi Mahesh Yogi, *Maharishi's Absolute Theory of Government: Automation in Administration*, pp. 174-175.
56 Maharishi Mahesh Yogi, *Maharishi Vedic University: Introduction*, p. 336.
57 *Ibid.*
58 Maharishi Mahesh Yogi, *Maharishi's Absolute Theory of Government: Automation in Administration*, p. 188 & pp. 202-203.
59 Maharishi Mahesh Yogi, *Maharishi Vedic University: Introduction*, pp. 195-196.
60 *Ibid.*, p. 317.
61 *Ibid.*, p. 66.
62 Maharishi Mahesh Yogi, *Maharishi Vedic University: Introduction*, p. 212.
63 *Ibid.*, pp. 339-340.
64 *Ibid.*
65 T. Nader, *Human Physiology: Expression of Veda and the Vedic Literature*, p. 22.
66 Maharishi Mahesh Yogi, *Maharishi Vedic University: Introduction*, pp. 340-341.
67 *Ibid.*, pp. 308-309.

68 Maharishi Mahesh Yogi, *Maharishi's Absolute Theory of Government: Automation in Administration*, p. 295.
69 *Ibid.*
70 *Ibid.*, p. 296.
71 *Ibid.*, p. 165.
72 *Ibid.*, p. 166.
73 *Ibid.*, p. 167.
74 *Ibid.*, pp. 282-283.
75 *Ibid.*, p. 286.
76 *Ibid.*
77 *Ibid.*, p. 283.
78 *Ibid.*
79 *Ibid.*
80 T. Nader, *Human Physiology: Expression of Veda and the Vedic Literature*, p. 12.
81 Maharishi Mahesh Yogi, *Maharishi Vedic University: Exhibition,* The Netherlands, 1993, pp. 164-165.
82 See diagram: T. Nader, *Human Physiology: Expression of Veda and the Vedic Literature*, pp. 52-53.
83 *Ibid.*, pp. 12-15.
84 *Ibid.*, p. 15.
85 *Ibid.*, pp. 52-53.
86 Maharishi Mahesh Yogi Vedic Vishwavidyalaya, *Constitution of India Fulfilled through Maharishi's Transcendental Meditation,* Age of Enlightenment Publications, India. 1996, pp. 24-25.
87 *Ibid.*, p. 25.
88 *Ibid.*, p. 89.
89 T. Nader, *Human Physiology: Expression of Veda and the Vedic Literature*, pp. 52-53.
90 Maharishi Mahesh Yogi, *Maharishi's Absolute Theory of Government: Automation in Administration,* pp. 179-180.
91 *Ibid.*, p. 180.

10 The Forty Aspects of the Veda and the Vedic Literature and their Qualities of Intelligence: Impulses of Consciousness and the Structuring Mechanics of Ṛk Veda

1 Maharishi Mahesh Yogi, *Maharishi's Absolute Theory of Government: Automation in Administration*, Holland, 1993, p. 206.
2 *Ibid.*, p. 207.
3 Maharishi Mahesh Yogi, *Constitution of India Fulfilled through Maharishi's Transcendental Meditation*, India, 1997, p. 30.
4 Maharishi Mahesh Yogi, *Maharishi's Absolute Theory of Government: Automation in Administration*, pp. 94-95.
5 The Vāstusūtra Upaniṣad is discussed in Part VI as one of the textbooks of the Vedic Literature.
6 Maharishi Mahesh Yogi, *Maharishi University of Management: Wholeness on the Move,* Holland, 1995, p. 39.
7 Maharishi Mahesh Yogi, *Constitution of India Fulfilled through Maharishi's Transcendental Meditation*, 1997, p. 82.
8 Maharishi Mahesh Yogi, *Celebrating Perfection in Education,* India, 1997, p. 146.
9 Maharishi Mahesh Yogi, *Inaugurating Maharishi Vedic University*, India, 1996, p. 100.
10 Maharishi Mahesh Yogi, *Celebrating Perfection in Education,* p. 146.
11 *Ibid.*, pp. 35-37 & p. 47.
Maharishi Mahesh Yogi, *Maharishi's Absolute Theory of Government: Automation in Administration*, pp. 246-261.
12 T. Nader, *Human Physiology: Expression of Veda and Vedic Literature*, Vlodrop, The Netherlands, 1993, p. 33.
13 *Ibid.*

14 *Ibid.*
15 Maharishi Mahesh Yogi, *Celebrating Perfection in Education,* p. 146.
16 Maharishi Mahesh Yogi, *Maharishi Vedic University: Introduction, Holland,* 1994, p. 129.
17 *Ibid.,* p. 143.
18 *Ibid.,* p. 74.
19 Maharishi Mahesh Yogi, *Maharishi University of Management: Wholeness on the Move,* p. 32.

11 The Absolute Values of Each of the Four Vedas: Ṛk, Sāma, Yajur and Atharva Veda

1 Maharishi Mahesh Yogi, *Constitution of India Fulfilled through Maharishi's Transcendental Meditation.* Maharishi Mahesh Yogi Vedic Vishwavidyalaya, India, 1997, p. 82.
2 *Ibid.,* p. 83.
3 *Ibid.,* pp. 20-21.
4 Maharishi Mahesh Yogi, *Inaugurating Maharishi Vedic University,* Age of Enlightenment Publications, India, 1996, p. 59.
5 T. Nader, *Human Physiology: Expression of Veda and Vedic Literature,* Vlodrop, The Netherlands, 1993, pp. 33-53.
6` Maharishi Mahesh Yogi, *Constitution of India Fulfilled through Maharishi's Transcendental Meditation,* p. 82.
7 *Ibid.*
8 *Ibid.*
9 *Ibid.*
10 *Ibid.*
11 *Ibid.*, p. 86.
12 *Ibid.*
13 *Ibid.*
14 *Ibid.*
15 *Ibid.* p. 87.
16 Maharishi Mahesh Yogi, I*naugurating Maharishi Vedic University,* p. 60.
17 Maharishi Mahesh Yogi, *Constitution of India Fulfilled through Maharishi's Transcendental Meditation*, p. 87.
18 Maharishi Mahesh Yogi, *Inaugurating Maharishi Vedic University,* p. 61.
19 Maharishi Mahesh Yogi, *Constitution of India Fulfilled through Maharishi's Transcendental Meditation,* p. 88.
20 *Ibid.*
21 *Ibid.*
22 *Ibid.*
23 *Ibid.*
24 *Ibid.*
25 *Ibid.*
26 Maharishi Mahesh Yogi, *Inaugurating Maharishi Vedic University,* p. 62.
27 Maharishi Mahesh Yogi, *Constitution of India Fulfilled through Maharishi's Transcendental Meditation,* p. 89.
28 *Ibid.*

12 The Vedāṅga and the Darśana: The Expansion and Submergence of Self-Referral Consciousness and the Phenomenon of Cognition

1 Maharishi Vedic University, *Maharishi Vedic University Inauguration*, Washington D.C., 1985, p. 116.
2 Maharishi Mahesh Yogi, *Maharishi Vedic University: Introduction,* 1994, pp. 86-87.
3 Maharishi Mahesh Yogi, *Maharishi's Absolute Theory of Government: Automation in Administration,* 1993, p. 230-231; *Maharishi Vedic University: Introduction*, Holland, 1994, pp. 87-88.
4 *Ibid.,* pp. 231-232; *Ibid.,* pp. 89-90.

5 Maharishi Mahesh Yogi, *Celebrating Perfection in Education,* India, 1997, p. 30.
6 Maharishi Mahesh Yogi, *Maharishi Vedic Astrology and Maharishi Yagya Programs,* Maharishi Vedic Foundation, New Hampshire, 1997, p.1.
7 Maharishi Mahesh Yogi, *Celebrating Perfection in Administration*, India, 1998, pp. 248-251.
8 Maharishi Mahesh Yogi, *Constitution of India Fulfilled through Maharishi's Transcendental Meditation*, India, 1997, p. 30.
9 Maharishi Vedic University, *Maharishi Vedic University Inauguration,* p. 116.
10 Maharishi Mahesh Yogi, *Maharishi University of Management: Wholeness on the Move,* Holland, 1995, p. 95.
11 *Ibid.*, pp. 95-100; T. Nader, *Human Physiology: Expression of Veda and Vedic Literature,* Vlopdrop, The Netherlands, 1993, pp. 59-85.
12 *Ibid.*
13 Maharishi Mahesh Yogi, *Maharishi Mahesh Yogi on the Bhagavad-Gita: A New Translation and Commentary: Chapters 1-6,* Middlesex, 1969, pp. 472-494; Maharishi Vedic University, *Maharishi Vedic University Inauguration,* p. 116.
14 H. Coward, *Derrida and Indian Philosophy,* Albany, NY., 1990, pp. 4-5.
15 Maharishi Mahesh Yogi, *Maharishi University of Management: Wholeness on the Move,* p. 317.
16 *Ibid.* p. 314.
17 Maharishi Mahesh Yogi, *Maharishi Vedic University: Introduction,* pp. 314-315.
18 Maharishi Mahesh Yogi, in A. Bonshek, *Art—A Mirror of Consciousness: Applying Universal Principles in Art and Theory on the Basis of the Description of Pure Consciousness, the Universal Source of Individual Consciousness, History, Culture, Language and Art, According to Maharishi Vedic Science—with an Analysis of the Vāstusūtra Upaniṣad,* Dissertation Abstracts International, 75, 08A, 1996, p. 217.
19 Maharishi Mahesh Yogi, *Maharishi's Absolute Theory of Defence: Sovereignty in Invincibility*, India, 1996, p. 343.
20 *Ibid.*, pp. 340-341.
21 *Ibid.*, pp. 343-344.
22 *Ibid.*, p. 342.
23 *Ibid.*, pp. 343-344.
24 *Ibid.*, p. 345.
25 *Ibid.*
26 T. Nader, *Human Physiology: Expression of Veda and Vedic Literature,* p. 92
27 Maharishi Mahesh Yogi, *Maharishi Mahesh Yogi: A Commentary on the Bhagavad-Gita: Chapters 1-6,* pp. 477-480.
28 Maharishi Mahesh Yogi, *Maharishi Vedic University: Introduction,* p. 314.
29 Maharishi Vedic University, *Maharishi Vedic University Inauguration,* p. 117.
30 Maharishi Mahesh Yogi, *Maharishi's Absolute Theory of Government: Automation in Administration,* p. 235.
31 Maharishi Mahesh Yogi, *Maharishi Mahesh Yogi on the Bhagavad-Gita: A New Translation and Commentary: Chapters 1-6,* p. 116.
32 *Ibid.*, p. 483-487.
33 *Ibid.*, p. 486.
34 *Ibid.*
35 *Ibid.*
36 T. Nader, *Human Physiology: Expression of Veda and Vedic Literature,* pp. 97-100.
37 Maharishi Mahesh Yogi, *Maharishi's Absolute Theory of Government: Automation in Administration,* p. 463.
38 *Ibid.*, pp. 276-277.
39 *Ibid.*, p. 274.
40 *Ibid.*, pp. 275-276.
41 *Ibid.*, p. 458.
42 *Ibid.*
43 Maharishi Mahesh Yogi, *Maharishi Mahesh Yogi on the Bhagavad-Gita: A New Translation and Commentary: Chapters 1-6,* pp. 472-494.
44 Maharishi Mahesh Yogi, *Maharishi's Absolute Theory of Government: Automation in Administration,* p. 236.

45 *Ibid.*, pp. 274-275.
46 *Ibid.*, p. 461.
47 *Ibid.*, p. 458.

13 Upa-Veda: The Subordinate Veda or Third Cluster of Natural Law

1 Maharishi Mahesh Yogi, *Maharishi's Absolute Theory of Government: Automation in Administration*, India, 1995, pp. 427-428.
2 *Ibid.*, p. 427.
3 Maharishi Mahesh Yogi, I*naugurating Maharishi Vedic University*, India, 1996, p. 81.
4 *Ibid.*, p. 82.
5 Maharishi Mahesh Yogi, *Celebrating Perfection in Administration: Creating Invincible India*, India, 1998, p. 243.
6 *Ibid.*
7 *Ibid.*, pp. 150-151.
8 *Ibid.*, p. 152.
9 *Ibid.*, pp. 153-154.
10 *Ibid.*, p. 154.
11 Maharishi Mahesh Yogi, *Maharishi Vedic University Introduction*, Holland, 1994, p. 85.
12 Maharishi Mahesh Yogi, *Maharishi's Absolute Theory of Government: Automation in Administration*, Holland, 1993, p. 227.
13 T. Nader, *Human Physiology: Expression of Veda and Vedic Literature*, Vlodrop, 1993, p. 30.
14 Maharishi Mahesh Yogi, *Maharishi University of Management: Wholeness on the Move*, 1995, p. 92.
15 *Ibid.*, p. 92.
16 T. Nader, *Human Physiology: Expression of Veda and Vedic Literature*, p. 43.
17 *Ibid.*, p. 33.
18 A. Coomaraswamy, *Selected Papers: Traditional Art and Symbolism*, Volume One, Princeton, 1977, pp. 376-404.
19 Maharishi Mahesh Yogi, *Celebrating Perfection in Administration*, p. 165.
20 Maharishi Mahesh Yogi, *Buidling for the Health and Happiness of Everyone*, The Netherlands, 1998, p. 7.
21 Maharishi Vedic University Press, 1991, p. 37.
22 Maharishi Vedic University, *Celebrating Perfection in Administration*, India, 1998, pp. 165-166.
23 *Ibid.*, p. 166.
24 *Ibid.*, p. 167.
25 *Ibid.*
26 see: *Progress in Neurobiology*, 13, 1979, pp. 419-439; *Journal of Neuroscience*, 15 (9), 1995, pp. 6260-6270; "Processing the Head Direction Cell Signal: A Review and Commentary", *Brain Research Bulletin*, 40 (5-6), 1996, pp. 477-484.
27 Maharishi Vedic University, *Building for the Health and Happiness of Everyone*, p. 13.
28 Maharishi Mahesh Yogi, *Celebrating Perfection in Administration*, p. 179.
29 Maharishi Mahesh Yogi, *Celebrating Perfection in Education*, India, 1997, p. 32.

14 Ayur-Veda, Brāhmaṇa and Prātiśākhya: The Final Three Clusters of Natural Law

1 Maharishi Mahesh Yogi, *Maharishi's Absolute Theory of Government: Automation in Administration*, India, 1995, pp. 205-234.
2 Maharishi Mahesh Yogi, *Celebrating Perfection in Education*, India, 1997, p. 32 & p. 41.
3 *Ibid.*, p. 41.
4 *Ibid.*
5 *Ibid.*

6 *Ibid.*
7 *Ibid.*, p. 43.
8 *Ibid.*, p. 33.
9 *Ibid.*, p. 42-43.
10 *Ibid.*, p. 45.
11 *Ibid.*, p. 44.
12 Maharishi Mahesh Yogi, *Maharishi's Absolute Theory of Government: Automation in Administration*, pp. 201-480.
13 Maharishi Mahesh Yogi, *Celebrating Perfection in Education*, p. 33.
14 *Ibid.*
15 *Ibid.*
16 *Ibid.*, p. 34.
17 *Ibid.*
18 Maharishi Mahesh Yogi, *Inaugurating Maharishi Vedic University*, p. 143.
19 Maharishi Mahesh Yogi, *Celebrating Perfection in Education*, p. 34.
20 T. Nader, *Human Physiology: Expression of Veda and Vedic Literature*, Vlodrop, 1993, p. 132.
21 *Ibid.*
22 *Ibid.*
23 Maharishi Mahesh Yogi, *Maharishi Mahesh Yogi on the Bhagavad-Gita: A New Translation and Commentary: Chapters 1-6*, Middlesex: GB, 1969, pp. 250-251.
24 Maharishi Mahesh Yogi, *Maharishi Vedic University: Introduction*, Holland, 1994, p. 46, p. 57, p. 201 & p. 314.
25 *Ibid.*, p. 99.
26 *Ibid.*, p. 165.
27 Maharishi Mahesh Yogi, *Maharishi's Absolute Theory of Government: Automation in Administration*, India, 1993, pp. 240-290.
28 *Ibid.*, p. 290.
29 *Ibid.*, p. 256.
30 *Ibid.*, p. 290.
31 V. Bedekar, 'The Legend of the Churning of the Ocean in the Epics and the Purāṇas: A Comparative Study.' *Puranam*, IX, 7-61, 1967, p. 8.
32 Maharishi Mahesh Yogi, *Maharishi's Absolute Theory of Government: Automation in Administration*, 1993, p. 10.
33 *Ibid.*, p. 291.
34 *Ibid.*
35 *Ibid.*, pp. 291-292.
36 T. Nader, *Human Physiology: Expression of Veda and Vedic Literature*, p. 131.
37 Maharishi Mahesh Yogi, *Celebrating Perfection in Education*, p. 41.
38 Maharishi Mahesh Yogi, *Maharishi Vedic University: Introduction*, p. 95.
39 Maharishi Mahesh Yogi in W. Sands, *Maharishi's Absolute Theory of Government in the Vālmīki Rāmāyaṇa*. Dissertation Abstracts International, 55, 6, 1994, p. 113.
40 Maharishi Vedic University, *Inaugurating Maharishi Vedic University*, Washington, D.C., 1985, p. 117 & p. 242.
41 W. Sands, *Maharishi's Absolute Theory of Government in the Vālmīki Rāmāyaṇa*. Dissertation Abstracts International, 55, 6, 1994, p. 113.
42 *Ibid.*
43 Maharishi Mahesh Yogi, *Maharishi's Absolute Theory of Government: Automation in Administration*, 1993, p. 239.
44 P. Richman, (Ed.), *Many Rāmāyaṇas: The Diversity of a Narrative Tradition in South Asia*, California, 1991; Asian Civilizations Museum, *Ramayan: A Living Tradition*, Singapore, 1997.
45 Maharishi Mahesh Yogi, in W. Sands, *Maharishi's Absolute Theory of Government in the Vālmīki Rāmāyaṇa*, p. 113.
46 W. Sands, *Maharishi's Absolute Theory of Government in the Vālmīki Rāmāyaṇa*.
47 Maharishi Mahesh Yogi, *Maharishi's Absolute Theory of Government: Automation in Administration*, 1993, p. 46.
48 *Ibid.*, p. 51.
49 *Ibid.*

50 *Ibid.*, pp. 280-281.
51 *Ibid.*, pp. 284-285.
52 *Ibid.*, pp. 285-286.
53 Maharishi Vedic University, *Inaugurating Maharishi Vedic University*, Washington, D.C., p. 117.
54 Maharishi Mahesh Yogi, *Maharishi Mahesh Yogi: Science, Consciousness and Aging: Proceedings of the International Conference*, Rheinwheiler, West Germany, 1980, p. 16.
55 *Ibid.*, p. 17.
56 K. Green, 'Brain Writing and Derrida,' *Australian Journal of Philosophy*, 71 (3), 1993, pp. 238-255.
57 Maharishi Vedic University, *Inaugurating Maharishi Vedic University*, Washington, D.C., pp. 117-118.
58 Maharishi Mahesh Yogi, *Maharishi Mahesh Yogi on the Bhagavad-Gita: A New Translation and Commentary: Chapters 1-6*, p. 164.
59 *Ibid.*, p. 164.
60 Maharishi Mahesh Yogi, *Maharishi Mahesh Yogi: Science, Consciousness and Aging: Proceedings of the International Conference*, p.17.
61 *Ibid.*, p.16.
62 Maharishi Mahesh Yogi, *Maharishi Mahesh Yogi on the Bhagavad-Gita: A New Translation and Commentary: Chapters 1-6*, p. 350.
63 *Ibid.*, p. 164.
64 T. Nader, *Human Physiology: Expression of Veda and Vedic Literature*, p. 5.
65 *Ibid.*, p. 134.
66 Maharishi Mahesh Yogi, *Maharishi's Absolute Theory of Government: Automation in Administration*, 1993, pp. 247-248.
67 *Ibid.*, p. 257.
68 *Ibid.*, p. 258 & p. 268.
69 *Ibid.*, pp. 241-243.
70 *Ibid.*, pp. 260-261.
71 *Ibid.*, pp. 261-262.
72 *Ibid.*, p. 259.
73 *Ibid.*, p. 243.
74 Maharishi Mahesh Yogi, *Maharishi's Absolute Theory of Government*, The Netherlands, 1994, pp. 205-234.
75 Maharishi Mahesh Yogi, *Maharishi University of Management: Wholeness on the Move*, India, 1995, pp. 41-43.
76 Maharishi Mahesh Yogi, *Maharishi Vedic University: Introduction*, Holland, 1994, pp. 326-333.

Part IV Natural Law: The Universal Foundation of History, Traditions, Culture and Language

1 Maharishi Mahesh Yogi, *Maharishi Mahesh Yogi on the Bhagavad-Gītā: A New Translation and Commentary: Chapters 1-6*, Middlesex, GB, 1969, pp. 254-255.
2 *Ibid.*, p. 64 & 68.
3 *Ibid.*, p. 69 & 232.
4 Maharishi Mahesh Yogi, *Maharishi University of Management: Wholeness on the Move*, Holland, 1995, p. 72.
5 Maharishi Mahesh Yogi, *Enlightenment to Every Individual and Invincibility to Every Nation*, Rheinwheiler, West Germany, 1978, pp. 136-138; Maharishi Mahesh Yogi, *Maharishi University of Management: Wholeness on the Move*, p. 72.
6 Maharishi Mahesh Yogi, *Enlightenment to Every Individual and Invincibility to Every Nation*, pp. 138-139.
7 Maharishi Mahesh Yogi, *Maharishi Vedic University: Introduction*, Holland, 1994, p. 361; *Maharishi University of Management: Wholeness on the Move*, p. 73.

15 The Purpose and Dynamic of History: The Rise and Fall of Natural Law in the Cyclical Unfoldment of Consciousness

1 Maharishi Mahesh Yogi, *Maharishi Mahesh Yogi on the Bhagavad-Gita: A New Translation and Commentary: Chapters 1-6,* Middlesex, 1969, p. 252.
2 *Ibid.*, p. 254.
3 *Ibid.*
4 *Ibid.*
5 *Ibid.*
6 *Ibid.*
7 P. Novick, in R. Martin, 'Progress in Historical Studies', *History and Theory,* 37 (1), 14-39, 1998, p. 15.
8 *Ibid.*, pp. 254-255.
9 Maharishi Mahesh Yogi, *Maharishi's Absolute Theory of Government: Automation in Administration*, Holland, 1993, p. 277.
10 *Ibid.*, p. 278.
11 Maharishi Mahesh Yogi, *Maharishi Mahesh Yogi on the Bhagavad-Gita: A New Translation and Commentary: Chapters 1-6,* p. 254.
12 *Ibid.*, p. 252.
13 Maharishi Mahesh Yogi, *Maharishi Vedic University: Introduction*, Holland, 1994, pp. 216-218.
14 *Ibid.*, pp. 216-217 & p. 352.
15 *Ibid.*, p. 218.
16 Maharishi European Research University, *Enlightenment to Every Individual: Invincibility to Every Nation*, West Germany, 1978, pp. 470-603; Maharishi Vedic University, *Maharishi's Master Plan to Create Heaven on Earth,* The Netherlands, 1991, pp. 4-10.
17 Maharishi Mahesh Yogi, *Maharishi Vedic University: Introduction*, p. 222.
18 *Ibid.*, pp. 222-223.
19 *Ibid.*, p. 220.
20 Maharishi Mahesh Yogi, *Maharishi's Absolute Theory of Government*, The Netherlands, 1992, p. 144.
21 Maharishi Mahesh Yogi, *Maharishi Vedic University: Introduction*, pp. 215-216.
22 *Ibid.*
23 *Ibid.*, p. 223.
24 *Ibid.*, pp. 219-220.
25 Maharishi Vedic Foundation, *Maharishi Yagya Performances Around the Year to Create Heaven on Earth in Everyone's Life: Auspicious Days for the Months of April 2000 to June 2000,* New Hampshire, 2000, p. 2.
26 Maharishi Mahesh Yogi, *Maharishi Vedic University: Introduction*, p. 251.
27 J. Legge, *The Texts of Taoism*, New York, 1959, p. 37.
28 Maharishi Mahesh Yogi, "Natural Law and the Evolutionary Perspective of Religious Codes", *World Government News,* 11,1979, p. 35.
29 Maharishi European Research University, *World Government News,* 11, 1979, p. 35.
30 *Ibid.*
31 Maharishi Mahesh Yogi, *Natural Law and the Evolutionary Perspective of Religious Codes,* p. 35.
32 Maharishi European Research University, *World Government News*, p. 35.
33 *Ibid.*
34 Maharishi Mahesh Yogi, *Enlightenment to Every Individual: Invincibility to Every Nation,* West Germany, 1978, p. 136.
35 Maharishi Mahesh Yogi, *Maharishi Vedic University: Introduction,* pp. 221-222.
36 Maharishi Mahesh Yogi, *Maharishi's Absolute Theory of Government: Automation in Administration*, pp. 29-35.
37 *Ibid.*
38 Maharishi Mahesh Yogi, *Maharishi Vedic University: Introduction*, p. 223.
39 *Ibid.*
40 Maharishi Mahesh Yogi, in A. Bonshek, *Art—A Mirror of Consciousness: Applying Universal Principles in Art and Theory on the Basis of the Description of Pure*

Consciousness, the Universal Source of Individual Consciousness, History, Culture, Language and Art, According to Maharishi's Vedic Science—with an Analysis of the Vāstusūtra Upaniṣad, Dissertation Abstracts International, 75, 08A, 1996, p. 259.

41 Maharishi Mahesh Yogi, "A Message from His Holiness Maharishi Mahesh Yogi," *Creative Intelligence,* 1, 1973, pp. 2-5.

42 Maharishi Mahesh Yogi, *Maharishi Vedic University: Introduction,* p. 248.

43 H. Belting, *The End of the History of Art,* Chicago, 1987; V. Burgin, *The End of Art Theory,* London, 1986.

16 Traditions: Different Modes of Activity Governed by Dharmas

1 Maharishi Mahesh Yogi, *Maharishi University of Management: Wholeness on the Move,* Holland, 1995, pp. 29-32; T. Nader, *Human Physiology: Expression of Veda and the Vedic Literature,* The Netherlands, 1993.

2 Maharishi Mahesh Yogi, *Maharishi Mahesh Yogi on the Bhagavad-Gita: A New Translation and Commentary: Chapters 1-6,* Middlesex, 1969, p. 64.

3 *Ibid.,* p. 68.

4 *Ibid.,* p. 64.

5 *Ibid.,* pp. 68-69.

6 Maharishi Mahesh Yogi, *The Science of Being and Art of Living,* Washington, D.C., 1966, p. 229.

7 Maharishi Mahesh Yogi, *Maharishi Mahesh Yogi on the Bhagavad-Gita: A New Translation and Commentary: Chapters 1-6,* p. 65.

8 *Ibid.,* pp. 64-65.

9 Maharishi Mahesh Yogi, *World Government News,* 1978-9, p. 29.

10 Maharishi Mahesh Yogi, *Maharishi Mahesh Yogi on the Bhagavad-Gita: A New Translation and Commentary: Chapters 1-6,* pp. 66-67.

11 *Ibid.,* pp. 68-69.

12 *Ibid.,* p. 69.

13 *Ibid.*

14 *Ibid.*

15 Maharishi Mahesh Yogi, 'The Artist and the Scientist: Lesson 27', *The Science of Creative Intelligence: Knowledge and Experience.* [Syllabus of Videotaped Course], Los Angeles, 1972.

16 *Ibid.,* p. 27:3-4.

17 *Ibid.,* p. 27:3.

18 *Ibid.,* p. 27:4.

19 *Ibid.*

20 *Ibid.*

21 *Ibid.*

22 *Ibid.*

23 *Ibid.,* p. 27:5.

24 Maharishi Mahesh Yogi, *Maharishi Mahesh Yogi on the Bhagavad-Gita: A New Translation and Commentary: Chapters 1-6,* pp. 76-86.

25 Maharishi Mahesh Yogi, *The Artist and the Scientist: Lesson 27,* p. 27:12.

26 *Ibid.*

27 Maharishi Mahesh Yogi, *Maharishi Mahesh Yogi on the Bhagavad-Gita: A New Translation and Commentary: Chapters 1-6,* p. 232.

28 *Ibid.*

29 *Ibid.*

30 *Ibid.,* p. 233.

31 *Ibid.,* p. 63.

32 *Ibid.*

33 Maharishi Mahesh Yogi, *The Science of Being and Art of Living,* pp. 221-222.

34 Maharishi Mahesh Yogi, *Maharishi Mahesh Yogi on the Bhagavad-Gita: A New Translation and Commentary: Chapters 1-6,* p. 63.

35 *Ibid.*

36 *Ibid.*

37 *Ibid.*

38 Maharishi Mahesh Yogi, *Enlightenment to Every Individual and Invincibility to Every Nation,* West Germany, 1978, p. 143.
39 Maharishi Mahesh Yogi, *Maharishi Mahesh Yogi on the Bhagavad-Gita: A New Translation and Commentary: Chapters 1-6*, pp. 231-234.
40 *Ibid.*, pp. 233-234.
41 Maharishi Vedic University, *Celebrating Perfection in Administration: Creating Invincible India,* India, 1998, pp.338-339.
42 *Ibid.*
43 *Ibid.*
44 *Ibid.* pp. 334-336.
45 *Ibid.*
46 *Ibid.* p. 337.
47 *Ibid.* p. 339.

17 Culture as the Expression of Specific Laws of Nature —Governing Geography, Climate, Mannerisms, Language and Accents of Different Peoples

1 Maharishi Mahesh Yogi, *Maharishi University of Management: Wholeness on the Move,* Holland, 1995, p. 72.
2 Maharishi Mahesh Yogi, *Enlightenment to Every Individual and Invincibility to Every Nation*, West Germany, 1978, p. 136.
3 Maharishi Mahesh Yogi, *Maharishi Mahesh Yogi on the Bhagavad-Gita: A New Translation and Commentary: Chapters 1-6*, Middlesex, 1969, p. 273.
4 *Ibid.*, p. 196.
5 Maharishi Mahesh Yogi, *Enlightenment to Every Individual and Invincibility to Every Nation*, pp. 91-92.
6 Maharishi Mahesh Yogi, *Maharishi Vedic University: Introduction*, Holland, 1994, p. 148.
7 Maharishi Mahesh Yogi, *Enlightenment to Every Individual and Invincibility to Every Nation*, p. 136.
8 *Ibid.*, pp. 317-318.
9 *Ibid.*, p. 318.
10 *Ibid.*, pp. 318-319.
11 Maharishi Mahesh Yogi, *Maharishi University of Management: Wholeness on the Move*, Holland, p. 70.
12 Maharishi Mahesh Yogi, *Enlightenment to Every Individual and Invincibility to Every Nation*, p. 319
13 *Ibid.*
14 *Ibid.*, p. 138.
15 *Ibid.*, p. 139.
16 *Ibid.*
17 *Ibid.*, p. 141.
18 Maharishi Mahesh Yogi, *Maharishi University of Management: Wholeness on the Move*, p. 71.
19 *Ibid.*, p. 72.
20 Maharishi Mahesh Yogi, *Enlightenment to Every Individual and Invincibility to Every Nation*, p. 142.
21 *Ibid.*, p. 142.
22 *Ibid.*, p. 143.
23 *Ibid.*, p. 135.
24 Maharishi Mahesh Yogi, *Maharishi Vedic University: Introduction*, p. 225.
25 *Ibid.*, pp. 227-228.
26 *Ibid.*, p. 228
27 *Ibid.*, pp. 226-227.
28 Maharishi Mahesh Yogi, 'Art and the Artist.' [A lecture given at Kōssen, West Germany]. In M. Cain, *Art and the Science of Creative Intelligence: Interdependence of Part and Whole,* Fairfield, IA, .pp. v-viii.
29 Maharishi Mahesh Yogi, *Maharishi Vedic University: Introduction*, p. 361.

30 *Ibid.*
31 Maharishi Mahesh Yogi, *Maharishi University of Management: Wholeness on the Move*, p. 73.
32 Maharishi Mahesh Yogi, *Maharishi Vedic University: Introduction*, p. 361.
33 Maharishi Mahesh Yogi, *Enlightenment to Every Individual and Invincibility to Every Nation*, 319.
34 *Ibid.*
35 Maharishi Mahesh Yogi, *Maharishi's Absolute Theory of Government: Automation in Administration*, Holland, p. 95.

Part V: The Artist as a Universal Human Being Creating Universal Value in Art and Aesthetics

1 Maharishi Mahesh Yogi, 'Art and the Artist', [A lecture given in Kōssen, W. Germany]. In M. Cain, *Art and the Science of Creative Intelligence; Interdependence of Part and Whole*, v-viii, 1970, pp. v-viii; *Maharishi University of Management: Wholeness on the Move*, Holland, 1995, pp. 129-133; Maharishi Mahesh Yogi, in L. Fergusson, *Maharishi's Vedic Science and Post-Secondary Art Education*, Dissertation Abstracts International, 52,9.1991, p. 195 & p. 197.
2 Maharishi Mahesh Yogi, in L. Fergusson, *Maharishi's Vedic Science and Post-Secondary Art Education*, p. 169, p. 178, p. 182, p. 192, & p. 200.

18 The Role of the Artist: Spontaneously Functioning from the Level of Natural Law

1 The Science of Creative Intelligence is the discipline which connects the main conclusions of modern science to the main principles of Maharishi Vedic Science and also includes Maharishi's technologies of consciousness.
2 Maharishi Mahesh Yogi, in L. Fergusson, *Maharishi's Vedic Science and Post-Secondary Art Education*, Dissertation Abstracts International, 52,9, 1991, p. 170, p. 177, & p. 194.
3 *Ibid.*, p. 188.
4 *Ibid.*
5 *Ibid.*, p. 182.
6 *Ibid.*, p. 171.
7 *Ibid.*, p. 195.
8 *Ibid.*
9 *Ibid.*, p. 171.
10 *Ibid.*, p. 177.
11 Maharishi Mahesh Yogi, in A. Bonshek, *Art—A Mirror of Consciousness: Applying Universal Principles in Art and Theory on the Basis of the Description of Pure Consciousness, the Universal Source of Individual Consciousness, History, Culture, Language and Art, According to Maharishi's Vedic Science—with an Analysis of the Vāstusūtra Upaniṣad,* Dissertation Abstracts International, 75, 08A, 1996, p. 304-305.
12 *Ibid.*, p. 305.
13 *Ibid.*
14 Maharishi Mahesh Yogi, in L. Fergusson, *Maharishi's Vedic Science and Post-Secondary Art Education*, p. 164 & p. 175.
15 *Ibid.*, p. 164.
16 *Ibid.*
17 *Ibid.*
18 Maharishi Mahesh Yogi, in A. Bonshek, *Art—A Mirror of Consciousness*, p. 306.
19 *Ibid.*
20 *Ibid.*, p. 307.
21 *Ibid.*
22 Maharishi Mahesh Yogi, in L. Fergusson, *Maharishi's Vedic Science and Post-Secondary Art Education*, p. 168.
23 *Ibid.* p. 170.
24 Maharishi Mahesh Yogi, in A. Bonshek, *Art—A Mirror of Consciousness*, p. 308.

25 *Ibid.*
26 Maharishi Mahesh Yogi, in L. Fergusson, *Maharishi's Vedic Science and Post-Secondary Art Education,* p. 180.
27 *Ibid.*
28 *Ibid.*
29 Maharishi Mahesh Yogi, 'The Artist and the Scientist, Lesson 27', *In The Science of Creative Intelligence: Knowledge and Experience* [Syllabus of Videotaped Course]. 1972, p. 13.
30 *Ibid.,* pp. 13-14.
31 Maharishi Mahesh Yogi, in L. Fergusson, *Maharishi's Vedic Science and Post-Secondary Art Education,* p. 194.

19 The Creative Process: Operating From the Level of Nature's Creative Mechanics

1 Maharishi Mahesh Yogi, in L. Fergusson, *Maharishi's Vedic Science and Post-Secondary Art Education,* Dissertation Abstracts International, 52,9, 1991, p. 166.
2 Maharishi Mahesh Yogi, 'Art and the Artist', [A lecture given at Kōssen, W. Germany]. In M. Cain, *Art and the Science of Creative Intelligence; Interdependence of Part and Whole,* [pp. v-viii], 1970, p. v.
3 *Ibid.*
4 Maharishi Mahesh Yogi, *Maharishi Vedic University: Introduction*, Holland, 1994, p. 173.
5 *Ibid.*, p. 212.
6 Maharishi Mahesh Yogi, *Maharishi's Absolute Theory of Government: Automation in Administration,* Holland, 1993, p. 23.
7 Maharishi Mahesh Yogi, *Art and the Artist,* p. v.
8 *Ibid.*
9 Maharishi Mahesh Yogi, *Maharishi Mahesh Yogi on the Bhagavad-Gita: A New Translation and Commentary: Chapters 1-6,* Middlesex, GB, 1969, p. 284.
10 *Ibid.*
11 *Ibid.,* pp. 283-284.
12 Maharishi Mahesh Yogi, *The Science of Being and the Art of Living,* Washington D.C., 1966, p. 120.
13 Maharishi Mahesh Yogi, *Maharishi Mahesh Yogi on the Bhagavad-Gita: A New Translation and Commentary: Chapters 1-6,* p. 284.
14 Maharishi Mahesh Yogi, *The Science of Being and the Art of Living,* p. 118.
15 *Ibid.,* p. 120
16 Maharishi Mahesh Yogi, *Maharishi Mahesh Yogi on the Bhagavad-Gita: A New Translation and Commentary: Chapters 1-6,* p. 285.
17 Maharishi Mahesh Yogi, *The Science of Being and the Art of Living,* p. 120.
18 N. King, 'Psychology of Retrieval: Personal and Fictional Archives', *Artlink,* 19 (1), 49-51, 1999, p. 49.
19 D. Kuspit, 'A Psychoanalytic Reading of Aesthetic Disinterestedness', *Art Criticism*, 6 (2), 1990, pp. 72-80.
20 C. Alexander & R. Boyer, 'Seven States of Consciousness:: Unfolding the Full Potential of the Cosmic Psyche in Individual Life Through Maharishi's Vedic Psychology', *Modern Science and Vedic Science Journal,* 2 (4), 1989, pp. 324-371.
21 D. Kuspit, *A Psychoanalytic Reading of Aesthetic Disinterestedness,* pp. 72-80.
22 Maharishi Mahesh Yogi, *The Science of Being and the Art of Living,* p. 264.
23 *Ibid.,* p. 264.
24 *Ibid.,* p. 265.
25 *Ibid.*
26 Maharishi Mahesh Yogi, 'A Message from His Holiness Maharishi Mahesh Yogi', *Creative Intelligence,* 1, 2-5, 1973, p. 2.
27 *Ibid.*
28 *Ibid.,* p. 4.
29 *Ibid.,* p. 3.
30 *Ibid.,* p. 2.

31 *Ibid.*, p. 3.
32 Maharishi Mahesh Yogi, *Maharishi Vedic University: Introduction*, p. 356.
33 *Ibid.*, p. 357.
34 Maharishi Mahesh Yogi, *A Message from His Holiness Maharishi Mahesh Yogi*, pp. 3-4.
35 *Ibid.*, p. 3.
36 *Ibid.*
37 Maharishi Mahesh Yogi, *Maharishi's Absolute Theory of Government: Automation in Administration,* pp. 294-295.
38 T. Nader, *Human Physiology: Expression of Veda and Vedic Literature*, Vlodrop, The Netherlands, 1993, p. 22.
39 Maharishi Mahesh Yogi, in A. Bonshek, *Art—A Mirror of Consciousness: Applying Universal Principles in Art and Theory on the Basis of the Description of Pure Consciousness, the Universal Source of Individual Consciousness, History, Culture, Language and Art, According to Maharishi's Vedic Science—with an Analysis of the Vāstusūtra Upaniṣad,* Dissertation Abstracts International, 75, 08A, 1996, p. 328.
40 Maharishi Mahesh Yogi, in L. Fergusson, *Maharishi's Vedic Science and Post-Secondary Art Education*, p. 169.
41 Maharishi Mahesh Yogi, in A. Bonshek, *Art—A Mirror of Consciousness*, p. 328.
42 Maharishi Mahesh Yogi, in L. Fergusson, *Maharishi's Vedic Science and Post-Secondary Art Education*, p. 171.
43 Maharishi Mahesh Yogi, *A Message from His Holiness Maharishi Mahesh Yogi,* p. 4.
44 Maharishi Mahesh Yogi, in L. Fergusson, *Maharishi's Vedic Science and Post-Secondary Art Education,* pp. 174-175.
45 Maharishi Mahesh Yogi, in A. Bonshek, *Art—A Mirror of Consciousness*, p. 333.
46 A. Coomaraswamy, *Selected Papers: Traditional Art and Symbolism*, 1, Princeton, 1977; S. Pandit, *An Approach to the Indian Theory of Art and Aesthetics,* New Delhi, 1977, p. 71.
47 Maharishi Mahesh Yogi, in A. Bonshek, *Art—A Mirror of Consciousness,* p. 334.
48 *Ibid.*, p. 331.
49 Maharishi Mahesh Yogi, in L. Fergusson, *Maharishi's Vedic Science and Post-Secondary Art Education*, p. 178.
50 *Ibid.*, pp. 193-194.
51 *Ibid.*, p. 179.
52 Maharishi Mahesh Yogi, in A. Bonshek, *Art—A Mirror of Consciousness*, p. 337.
53 *Ibid.*
54 *Ibid.*
55 *Ibid.*, pp. 337-338.
56 R. Neher, "As Stupid as a Painter: Jackson Pollock and the Politics of Self,' *Art Criticism*, 10 (2) 55-67, 1995, p. 60.
57 Maharishi Mahesh Yogi, in A. Bonshek, *Art—A Mirror of Consciousness*, p. 338.
58 *Ibid.*
59 *Ibid.*, p. 339.
60 *Ibid.*, p. 340.
61 *Ibid.*
62 Maharishi Mahesh Yogi, *Maharishi University of Management: Wholeness on the Move*, Holland, 1995, p. 202.
63 Maharishi Mahesh Yogi, in A. Bonshek, *Art—A Mirror of Consciousness*, p. 341.
64 *Ibid.*
65 *Ibid.*, p. 342.
66 *Ibid.*, pp. 342-343.
67 *Ibid.*, p.343.
68 *Ibid.*
69 *Ibid.*, p. 344.

20 Universal Art and its Effects

1 Maharishi Mahesh Yogi, in A. Bonshek, *Art—A Mirror of Consciousness: Applying Universal Principles in Art and Theory on the Basis of the Description of Pure Consciousness, the Universal Source of Individual Consciousness, History, Culture, Language and Art, According to Maharishi's Vedic Science—with an Analysis of the Vāstusūtra Upaniṣad,* Dissertation Abstracts International, 75, 08A, 1996, p. 347.
2 *Ibid.*
3 Maharishi Mahesh Yogi, 'Art and the Artist', [A lecture given at Kōssen, W. Germany]. In M. Cain, *Art and the Science of Creative Intelligence; Interdependence of Part and Whole,* v-viii, 1970, pp. vi-vii.
4 Maharishi Mahesh Yogi, in A. Bonshek, *Art—A Mirror of Consciousness,* p. 348.
5 *Ibid.,* p. 349.
6 *Ibid.*
7 *Ibid.*
8 *Ibid.*
9 *Ibid.,* p. 350.
10 see Part III, Chapter 14.
11 Mahariṣhi Mahesh Yogi, *Art and the Artist,* p. v.
12 *Ibid.,* p. vi.
13 *Ibid.,* p. vi-vii.
14 *Ibid.*, p. v.
15 A. Coomaraswamy, *Selected Papers: Traditional Art and Symbolism,* 1, Princeton, 1977, p. 71.
16 Maharishi Mahesh Yogi, in A. Bonshek, *Art—A Mirror of Consciousness,* p. 352.
17 *Ibid.,* p. 353.
18 *Ibid.*
19 *Ibid.*
20 *Ibid.*
21 *Ibid.*
22 *Ibid.*
23 S. Gablik, 'Art Beyond the Rectangle: A Call for "Useful" Art', *New Art Examiner,* 17 (4), 1991, pp. 20-24; *The Reenchantment of Art,* New York, 1992.
24 Maharishi Mahesh Yogi, in W. Sands, *Maharishi's Absolute Theory of Government in the Vālmīki Rāmāyana*. Dissertation Abstracts International, 55,6, 1994, p. 113.
25 Maharishi Mahesh Yogi, *Maharishi University of Management: Wholeness on the Move,* Holland, 1995, p. 202.
26 S. Pandit, *An Approach to the Indian Theory of Art and Aesthetics*, New Delhi, 1977.
27 Maharishi Mahesh Yogi, *Art and the Artist,* p. v.

21 Aesthetic Value and Aesthetic Response: Leading the Viewer Toward Bliss and a Unified Self

1 Maharishi Mahesh Yogi, in R. Orme-Johnson, 'A Unified Field Theory of Literature', *Modern Science and Vedic Science Journal*, 1 (3), 322-373, 1987, pp. 343-346.
2 G. Engler, 'Aesthetics in Science and Art', *British Journal of Aesthetics,* 30 (1), 24-34, 1990.
3 Maharishi Mahesh Yogi, 'Art and the Artist', [A lecture given at Kōssen, W. Germany]. In M. Cain, *Art and the Science of Creative Intelligence; Interdependence of Part and Whole,* v-viii, 1970, pp. vii-viii.
4 Maharishi Mahesh Yogi, in A. Bonshek, *Art—A Mirror of Consciousness: Applying Universal Principles in Art and Theory on the Basis of the Description of Pure Consciousness, the Universal Source of Individual Consciousness, History, Culture, Language and Art, According to Maharishi's Vedic Science—with an Analysis of the Vāstusūtra Upaniṣad,* Dissertation Abstracts International, 75, 08A, 1996, p. 360.
5 Maharishi Mahesh Yogi, in L. Fergusson, *Maharishi's Vedic Science and Post-Secondary Art Education,* Dissertation Abstracts International, 52,9., 1991, p. 183.
6 Maharishi Mahesh Yogi, in A. Bonshek, *Art—A Mirror of Consciousness,* p. 360.

7 *Ibid.*, p. 362.
8 *Ibid.*
9 *Ibid.*
10 *Ibid.*
11 *Ibid.*
12 D. Kuspit, 'The Problem of Art in the Age of Glamor', *Art Criticism*, 6(1), [pp. 32 - 42], 1990.
13 D. Kuspit, 'A Psychoanalytic Reading of Aesthetic Disinterestedness', *Art Criticism*, 6 (2), [pp. 72-80], 1990.
14 J, Kosuth, *Art After Philosophy and After*, Cambridge, MA, 1991.
15 D. Kuspit, *The Problem of Art in the Age of Glamor*, S. Pandit, *An Approach to the Indian Theory of Art and Aesthetics*, New Delhi, 1977.
16 G. Banks, 'In Defence of Common Knowledge', *Art Monthly*, 63, 23-25, 1983.
17 S. Gablik, *The Reenchantment of Art*, New York, 1992.
18 Maharishi Mahesh Yogi, in L. Fergusson, *Maharishi's Vedic Science and Post-Secondary Art Education*, p. 193.
19 *Ibid.*
20 Maharishi Mahesh Yogi, in A. Bonshek, *Art—A Mirror of Consciousness*, p. 366.
21 *Ibid.*
22 Maharishi Mahesh Yogi, in L. Fergusson, *Maharishi's Vedic Science and Post-Secondary Art Education*, p. 169.
23 *Ibid.*
24 Maharishi Mahesh Yogi, in A. Bonshek, *Art—A Mirror of Consciousness*, p. 367.
25 D. Kuspit, *A Psychoanalytic Reading of Aesthetic Disinterestedness.*
26 Maharishi Mahesh Yogi, *Maharishi Mahesh Yogi on the Bhagavad-Gita: A New Translation and Commentary: Chapters 1-6*, Middlesex, GB, 1969, pp. 270-285.
27 Maharishi Mahesh Yogi, in L. Fergusson, *Maharishi's Vedic Science and Post-Secondary Art Education*, p. 181.

Part VI: Uncovering the Details of the Nature and Structure of Pure Consciousness in the Vāstusūtra Upaniṣad

1 Maharishi Mahesh Yogi, *Maharishi Vedic University: Introduction*, Holland, 1994, pp. 252-253.
2 *Ibid.*, pp. 129-130 & pp. 204-214.
3 *Ibid.*, p. 209.
4 A. Boner, S. Śarma, & B. Bāumer, *Vāstusūtra Upaniṣad: The Essence of Form in Sacred Art*, Delhi, 1982.

22 Re-Contextualizing The Vāstusūtra Upaniṣad: Uncovering Wholeness

1 Maharishi Mahesh Yogi, *Maharishi University of Management: Wholeness on the Move*, Holland, 1995, p. 52.
2 *Ibid.*, p.191.
3 Maharishi Mahesh Yogi, *Maharishi Vedic University: Introduction*, Holland, 1994, p. 23.
4 *Ibid.*, p. 7.
5 Maharishi Mahesh Yogi, *Maharishi University of Management: Wholeness on the Move*, pp. 57-59.
6 *Ibid.*, p. 32.
7 T. Nader, *Human Physiology: Expression of the Veda and the Vedic Literature*, Vlodrop, 1993, p.155-156.
8 D. Orme-Johnson & J, Farrow, (Eds.), *Scientific Research on Maharishi's Transcendental Meditation and TM-Sidhi Programme: Collected Papers*, Volume 1, Rheinwheiler, West Germany, 1977, pp. 25-28; R. Chalmers, G. Clements, H. Schenkluhn, & M. Weinless, (Eds.), *Scientific Research on Maharishi's Transcendental Meditation and TM-Sidhi Programme: Collected Papers*, Volume 3-5, The Netherlands, 1989, Volume 2, p. 123; & Volume 5, p. 370,
9 *Ibid.*, Volume 2, p. 135.

10 *Ibid.*, Volume 5, pp. 403-406.
11 *Ibid.*, Volume 4, pp. 332-333; Volume 5, p. 401, p. 407, p. 408.
12 *Ibid.*, Volume 4, p. 321; Volume 5, p. 401.
13 *Ibid.*, Volume 4, p. 333.
14 Maharishi Mahesh Yogi, *Maharishi Vedic University: Introduction*, p. 85
15 Maharishi Mahesh Yogi, *Maharishi's Absolute Theory of Government: Automation in Administration*, The Netherlands, 1993, p. 179.
16 Maharishi Mahesh Yogi, in J. Muehlman, *Maharishi's Vedic Mathematics at the Elementary Level*, Dissertation Abstracts International, 9431798, 1994, p. 135.
17 Maharishi Mahesh Yogi, *Maharishi Vedic University: Exhibition*, Vlodrop, The Netherlands, 1993, p. 179.
18 T. Nader, *Human Physiology: Expression of the Veda and the Vedic Literature*, p. 57.
19 Maharishi Vedic University, *Maharishi's Master Plan to Create Heaven on Earth*, Vlodrop, The Netherlands, 1991, p. 37.
20 E. Hartmann, 'Maharishi Sthapatya-Veda', Presented to the *Second International Symposium on Maharishi Sthapatya-Veda*, Washington D.C., (6-8 July), 1990.
21 Maharishi Mahesh Yogi, in J. Muehlman, *Maharishi's Vedic Mathematics at the Elementary Level*, p. 136.
22 Maharishi Mahesh Yogi, *Maharishi's Absolute Theory of Defence*, India, 1996, p. 390.
23 *Ibid.*, p. 391.
24 Maharishi Mahesh Yogi, *Maharishi Forum of Natural Law for Doctors*, India, 1996, p. 391.
25 Maharishi Vedic University, *Building for the Health and Happiness of Everyone*, 1998, The Netherlands, p. 9.
26 R. Orme-Johnson, 'A Unified Field Theory of Literature,' *Modern Science and Vedic Science Journal*, 1 (3), 1987, pp. 322-373.
27 Maharishi Mahesh Yogi, in W. Sands, *Maharishi's Absolute Theory of Government in the Vālmīki Rāmāyana*, Dissertation Abstracts International, 55, 6, 1994, p. 98.
28 *Ibid.*, p. 99.
29 *Ibid.*, p. 100.
30 Maharishi Mahesh Yogi, *Maharishi Vedic University: Introduction*, p. 66.
31 *Ibid.*, p. 66-67.
32 Maharishi Mahesh Yogi, in W. Sands, *Maharishi's Absolute Theory of Government in the Vālmīki Rāmāyana*, p. 99.
33 *Ibid.*
34 T. Nader, *Human Physiology: Expression of the Veda and the Vedic Literature*, p. 23 & pp. 98-115.
35 *Ibid.*, pp. 34-37.
36 Maharishi Mahesh Yogi, *Maharishi Vedic University: Introduction*, pp. 316-317.
37 *Ibid.*, pp. 356-357.
38 *Ibid.*
39 W. Sands, *Maharishi's Absolute Theory of Government in the Vālmīki Rāmāyana*.
40 Maharishi Mahesh Yogi, in W. Sands, *Maharishi's Absolute Theory of Government in the Vālmīki Rāmāyana*, p. 101.
41 *Ibid.*, p. 102.
42 *Ibid.*, p. 103.
43 *Ibid.*
44 *Ibid.* p. 101.
45 T. Nader, *Human Physiology: Expression of the Veda and the Vedic Literature*, p. 145.
46 Maharishi Mahesh Yogi, *Maharishi Vedic University: Introduction*, pp.182-184.
47 A. Boner, S. Śarma, & B. Bāumer, *Vāstiusūtra Upaniṣad: The Essence of Form in Sacred Art.*, Delhi, 1996.
48 *Ibid.*, p. 1.
49 *Ibid.*, p. 2.
50 A. Boner, S. Śarma, & B. Bāumer, *Vāstiusūtra Upaniṣad: The Essence of Form in Sacred Art.*

51 Maharishi Mahesh Yogi, *Maharishi Vedic University: Introduction*, p. 8.
52 Maharishi Mahesh Yogi, in L. Fergusson, *Maharishi's Vedic Science and Post-Secondary Art Education*, Dissertation Abstracts International, 52, 9, 1991, p. 171.
53 Maharishi Mahesh Yogi, *Maharishi University of Management: Wholeness on the Move*, p. 172.
54 *Ibid.*, p. 173.
55 *Ibid.*
56 *Ibid.*

23 The First and Last Sūtras: Containing the Wholeness of the Text in Seed Form

1 Maharishi Mahesh Yogi, in A. Bonshek, *Art—A Mirror of Consciousness: Applying Universal Principles in Art and Theory on the Basis of the Description of Pure Consciousness, the Universal Source of Individual Consciousness, History, Culture, Language and Art, According to Maharishi's Vedic Science—with an Analysis of the Vāstusūtra Upaniṣad*, Dissertation Abstracts International, 75, 08A, 1996, p. 384.
2 Maharishi Mahesh Yogi, Maharishi University of Management: *Wholeness on the Move*, pp. 43-45.
3 *Ibid.*, p. 45.
4 *Ibid.*, pp. 48-49.
5 *Ibid.*, p. 47.
6 Maharishi Mahesh Yogi, in A. Bonshek, *Art—A Mirror of Consciousness*, p. 385.
7 Maharishi Mahesh Yogi, *Maharishi's Absolute Theory of Government: Automation in Administration*, p. 255.
8 Maharishi Mahesh Yogi, in A. Bonshek, *Art—A Mirror of Consciousness*, p. 397.
9 A. Boner, S. Śarma, & B. Bāumer, *Vāstusūtra Upaniṣad: The Essence of Form in Sacred Art*, Delhi, 1996.
10 H. Wilson, (Trans.) *Ṛg Veda-Saṁhitā* [Vol. 4], Iawahaṛ Nagar: Delhi, 1977, p. 338.
11 Maharishi Mahesh Yogi, *Maharishi's Absolute Theory of Government: Automation in Administration*, The Netherlands, 1993, p. 91.
12 *Ibid.*, p. 46.
13 Maharishi Ved Vigyān Vishwa Vidyā Peetham, *Maharishi's Absolute Theory of Government: Automation in Administration*, [2nd Editioṇ] India, 1993, p. 229.
14 Maharishi Mahesh Yogi, *Maharishi's Absolute Theory of Government: Automation in Administration*, India, 1993, p. 85.
15 Maharishi Mahesh Yogi, *Maharishi Mahesh Yogi on the Bhagavad-Gita: A New Translation and Commentary: Chapters 1-6*, Middlesex, 1969, p. 355.
16 *Ibid.*, p. 355.
17 D. Bhattacharya, 'The Position of the Vāstusutraūpaniṣad in the Atharvavedic Literature,' in A. Boner, S. Śarma, & B. Bāumer, *Vāstusūtra Upaniṣad: The Essence of Form in Sacred Art*, p. 32.
18 Maharishi Mahesh Yogi, 'Art and the Artist,' [A Lecture given at Kōssen, West Germany]. In M. Cain, *Art and the Science of Creative Intelligence: interdependence of Part and Whole*, [pp. v-viii], Fairfield: IA, 1970.
19 Maharishi Mahesh Yogi, *Maharishi Vedic University: Introduction*, p. 117.
20 *Ibid.*, pp. 122-123.
21 *Ibid.*, p. 125.
22 *Ibid.*, p. 127.
23 Maharishi Mahesh Yogi, *Maharishi's Absolute Theory of Government: Automation in Administration*, 1st Edition, p. 5.
24 Maharishi Mahesh Yogi, *Maharishi Vedic University: Introduction*, p. 143.

24 The Artist and the Creative Process: Knowing What Consciousness is and What it is Made of

1 Maharishi Mahesh Yogi, *The Science of Creative Intelligence for Secondary Education: First Year Core Course*, Rheinwheiler, West Germany, 1975, p. 244.
2 *Ibid.*, p. 249.

3 Maharishi Mahesh Yogi, *Maharishi Mahesh Yogi on the Bhagavad-Gita: A New Translation and Commentary: Chapters 1-6,* Middlesex, 1969, p. 64.
4 *Ibid.*, p. 256.
5 *Ibid.*
6 Maharishi Mahesh Yogi, *Maharishi Vedic University: Introduction,* Holland, 1994, p. 315.
7 *Ibid.*, p. 174.
8 *Ibid.*, p. 82-98.
9 *Ibid.*, p. 432.
10 *Ibid.*, p. 221.
11 Maharishi Mahesh Yogi, in A. Bonshek, *Art—A Mirror of Consciousness: Applying Universal Principles in Art and Theory on the Basis of the Description of Pure Consciousness, the Universal Source of Individual Consciousness, History, Culture, Language and Art, According to Maharishi's Vedic Science—with an Analysis of the Vāstusūtra Upaniṣad,* Dissertation Abstracts International, 75, 08A, 1996, p. 405.
12 Maharishi Mahesh Yogi, *Maharishi University of Management: Wholeness on the Move,* [1st Edition], India, 1995, p. 125.
13 Maharishi Mahesh Yogi, *Maharishi University of Management: Wholeness on the Move,* [2nd Edition] India, 1995.
14 Maharishi Mahesh Yogi, in A. Bonshek, *Art—A Mirror of Consciousness,* p. 405.
15 *Ibid.*, p. 406.
16 *Ibid.*, p. 407.
17 Maharishi Mahesh Yogi, *Maharishi Forum of Natural Law and National Law for Doctors,* India, 1996, p. 199.
18 Maharishi Mahesh Yogi, in A. Bonshek, *Art—A Mirror of Consciousness,* p. 411.
19 *Ibid.*
20 Maharishi Ved Vigyān Vishwa Vidyā Peetham, *Maharishi's Absolute Theory of Government: Automation in Administration*, Holland, 1995, pp. 449-450.
21 *Ibid.*, p. 450.
22 Maharishi Mahesh Yogi, in A. Bonshek, *Art—A Mirror of Consciousness,* p. 412.
23 *Ibid.*, p. 413.
24 Maharishi Mahesh Yogi, *Maharishi Vedic University: Introduction,* p. 314-315.
25 Maharishi Mahesh Yogi, *Maharishi Mahesh Yogi on the Bhagavad-Gita: A New Translation and Commentary: Chapters 1-6,* p. 355.
26 *Maharishi's Absolute Theory of Government: Automation in Administration,* Holland, 1993, pp. 91-92.
27 *Maharishi's Absolute Theory of Government: Automation in Administration,* Holland, 1992, p. 12.
28 Maharishi Mahesh Yogi, *Maharishi University of Management: Wholeness on the Move,* [2nd Edition], p. 191.
29 Maharishi Mahesh Yogi, in A. Bonshek, *Art—A Mirror of Consciousness,* p. 416.
30 *Ibid.*
31 *Maharishi's Absolute Theory of Government: Automation in Administration,* 1993, p. 199.
32 *Ibid.*, p. 160.
33 *Ibid.*, pp. 160-162.
34 Maharishi Mahesh Yogi, *Maharishi Vedic University: Introduction,* pp. 59-60.
35 Maharishi Mahesh Yogi, *Maharishi Mahesh Yogi on the Bhagavad-Gita: A New Translation and Commentary: Chapters 1-6,* p. 481.
36 *Ibid.*
37 Maharishi Mahesh Yogi, 'The Structure of Pure Knowledge', *Maharishi Mahesh Yogi: Science, Consciousness and Aging: Proceedings of the International Conference,* [pp. 73-80], Rheinwheiler, West Germany, 1980, p. 80.
38 Maharishi Mahesh Yogi, *Maharishi Mahesh Yogi on the Bhagavad-Gita: A New Translation and Commentary: Chapters 1-6,* p. 481.
39 Maharishi Mahesh Yogi, *The Structure of Pure Knowledge,* p. 80.
40 *Maharishi's Absolute Theory of Government: Automation in Administration*, 1993, p. 44.

41 Maharishi Mahesh Yogi, *Maharishi Mahesh Yogi on the Bhagavad-Gita: A New Translation and Commentary: Chapters 1-6*, p. 133.
42 Maharishi Mahesh Yogi, in A. Bonshek, *Art—A Mirror of Consciousness*, p. 419.
43 *Ibid.*
44 Maharishi Mahesh Yogi, *Maharishi Mahesh Yogi on the Bhagavad-Gita: A New Translation and Commentary: Chapters 1-6*, p. 424.
45 Maharishi Mahesh Yogi, in L. Fergusson, *Maharishi's Vedic Science and Post-Secondary Art Education*, Dissertation Abstracts International, 52,9, 1991, p. 174.
46 *Ibid.*
47 *Ibid.*, p. 175.
48 Maharishi Mahesh Yogi, in A. Bonshek, *Art—A Mirror of Consciousness*, p. 421.
49 *Ibid.*
50 *Ibid.*

25 Form or Rūpa: Unmanifest to Manifest

1 Maharishi Mahesh Yogi, *Maharishi Vedic University: Introduction, Holland*, 1994, p. 66-67.
2 *Ibid.*, pp. 316-317.
3 *Ibid.*, pp. 66-67.
4 *Ibid.*, p. 310.
5 Maharishi Mahesh Yogi, 'A Message from His Holiness Maharishi Mahesh Yogi', *Creative Intelligence*, 1 [2-5], 1973, p. 3.
6 Maharishi Mahesh Yogi, *Maharishi University of Management: Wholeness on the Move*, Holland, 1995, p. 356.
7 Maharishi Mahesh Yogi, *Maharishi's Absolute Theory of Government: Automation in Administration*, Holland, 1993, p. 16.
8 *Ibid.*, pp. 312-313.
9 Maharishi Mahesh Yogi, in A. Bonshek, *Art—A Mirror of Consciousness: Applying Universal Principles in Art and Theory on the Basis of the Description of Pure Consciousness, the Universal Source of Individual Consciousness, History, Culture, Language and Art, According to Maharishi's Vedic Science—with an Analysis of the Vāstusūtra Upaniṣad*, Dissertation Abstracts International, 75, 08A, 1996, p.170.
10 Maharishi Mahesh Yogi, *Maharishi Mahesh Yogi on the Bhagavad-Gita: A New Translation and Commentary: Chapters 1-6*, Middlesex, 1969, p. 482.
11 *Ibid.*, p. 483.
12 Maharishi Mahesh Yogi, *Maharishi University of Management: Wholeness on the Move*, p. 357.
13 *Ibid.*, pp. 480-483.
14 Maharishi Mahesh Yogi, *Maharishi Mahesh Yogi on the Bhagavad-Gita: A New Translation and Commentary: Chapters 1-6*, p. 483.
15 *Ibid.*, p. 478.
16 *Ibid.*, p. 10.
17 *Ibid.*, p. 485.
18 *Ibid.*
19 *Ibid.*, p. 9.
20 *Ibid.*, p. 95.
21 Maharishi Mahesh Yogi, *Maharishi's Absolute Theory of Government: Automation in Administration*, p. 108.
22 Maharishi Mahesh Yogi, in A. Bonshek, *Art—A Mirror of Consciousness*, pp. 172-173.
23 Maharishi Mahesh Yogi, *Maharishi Mahesh Yogi on the Bhagavad-Gita: A New Translation and Commentary: Chapters 1-6*, p. 482.
24 Maharishi Mahesh Yogi, *Maharishi Vedic University: Introduction*, p. 55.
25 Maharishi Mahesh Yogi, *Constitution of India Fulfilled through Maharishi's Transcendental Meditation*. Maharishi Mahesh Yogi Vedic Vishwavidyalaya, India, 1997, p. 82.
26 Maharishi Mahesh Yogi, *Maharishi Mahesh Yogi on the Bhagavad-Gita: A New Translation and Commentary: Chapters 1-6*, p. 91 & p. 99.

27 *Ibid.*, p. 197.
28 *Ibid.*, p. 204.
29 *Ibid.*, p. 461.
30 *Ibid.*, p. 160.
31 Maharishi Mahesh Yogi, in A. Bonshek, *Art—A Mirror of Consciousness*, p 349.
32 *Ibid.*, p. 430.
33 Maharishi Mahesh Yogi, *Constitution of India Fulfilled through Maharishi's Transcendental Meditation*, p. 88.
34 Maharishi Mahesh Yogi, *Maharishi's Absolute Theory of Government: Automation in Administration*, pp. 275-276.
35 *Ibid.*, p. 432.
36 *Ibid.*
37 Maharishi Mahesh Yogi, 'Art and the Artist', [A lecture given at Kōssen, W. Germany]. In M. Cain, *Art and the Science of Creative Intelligence; Interdependence of Part and Whole*, [pp. v-viii], 1970, p. vi.
38 *Ibid.*, p. vii.
39 *Ibid.*
40 Maharishi Mahesh Yogi, *Maharishi Mahesh Yogi on the Bhagavad-Gita: A New Translation and Commentary: Chapters 1-6*, p. 315.
41 *Ibid.*, p. 315.
42 Maharishi Mahesh Yogi, in L. Fergusson, *Maharishi's Vedic Science and Post-Secondary Art Education*, Dissertation Abstracts International, 52,9, 1991, p. 191.
43 *Ibid.*
44 *Ibid.*
45 Maharishi Mahesh Yogi, in A. Bonshek, *Art—A Mirror of Consciousness*, p. 434.
46 Maharishi Mahesh Yogi, in L. Fergusson, *Maharishi's Vedic Science and Post-Secondary Art Education*, p. 191.
47 *Ibid.*
48 *Ibid.*

26 Point, Line, Grid, Triangle and Number as Values of Consciousness

1 Maharishi Yogi, *Maharishi Forum of Natural Law and National Law for Doctors*, India, 1996, p. 136.
2 Maharishi Mahesh Yogi, *Maharishi's Absolute Theory of Government: Automation in Administration*, Holland, 1993, pp. 188-203.
3 Maharishi Mahesh Yogi, *Maharishi University of Management: Introduction*, Holland, 1994, pp. 309-339.
4 Maharishi Mahesh Yogi, *Maharishi University of Management: Wholeness on the Move*, Holland, 1995, p. 45.
5 Maharishi Mahesh Yogi, *Constitution of India Fulfilled through Maharishi's Transcendental Meditation*, Maharishi Mahesh Yogi Vedic Vishwavidyalaya, India, 1997, p. 82.
6 Maharishi Mahesh Yogi, *Maharishi's Absolute Theory of Government: Automation in Administration*, p. 9.
7 *Ibid.*
8 *Ibid.*
9 Maharishi Mahesh Yogi, *Maharishi University of Management: Wholeness on the Move*, p. 80.
10 Maharishi Mahesh Yogi, in A. Bonshek, *Art—A Mirror of Consciousness: Applying Universal Principles in Art and Theory on the Basis of the Description of Pure Consciousness, the Universal Source of Individual Consciousness, History, Culture, Language and Art, According to Maharishi's Vedic Science—with an Analysis of the Vāstusūtra Upaniṣad*, Dissertation Abstracts International, 75, 08A, 1996, p. 437.
11 *Ibid.*
12 Maharishi Mahesh Yogi, *Maharishi's Absolute Theory of Government: Automation in Administration*, p. 9.
13 K. Vatsyayan, [Ed.] *Kalātattvakośa: A Lexicon of Fundamental Concepts of the Indian Arts.* Volume II, Delhi, India, 1992, p. 3.

14 Maharishi Mahesh Yogi, *Maharishi Mahesh Yogi on the Bhagavad-Gita: A New Translation and Commentary: Chapters 1-6,* Middlesex, 1969, pp. 116-117 & pp. 133-145.
15 *Ibid.,* p. 57.
16 *Ibid.,* p. 295.
17 *Ibid.,* p. 297.
18 E. Hartmann, Maharishi Sthapatya Veda, Presented to the *Second International Symposium on Maharishi Sthapatya-Veda,* Washington, D.C., [6-8 July], 1990.
19 Maharishi Mahesh Yogi, in A. Bonshek, *Art—A Mirror of Consciousness*, p. 440; Maharishi Mahesh Yogi, *Maharishi University of Management: Wholeness on the Move,* p. 173.
20 Maharishi Mahesh Yogi, in A. Bonshek, *Art—A Mirror of Consciousness,* p. 441.
21 *Ibid.*
22 *Ibid.*
23 *Ibid.*
24 *Ibid.,* p. 442.
25 Maharishi Mahesh Yogi, *Maharishi University of Management: Wholeness on the Move,* p. 357.
26 Maharishi Mahesh Yogi, *Maharishi's Absolute Theory of Government: Automation in Administration,* p. 266.
27 Maharishi Vedic University, *Maharishi's Master Plan to Create Heaven on Earth,* Vlodrop, The Netherlands, 1991, pp. 36, i-iv.
28 E. Hartmann, Maharishi Sthapatya Veda, Presented to the *Second International Symposium on Maharishi Sthapatya-Veda.*
29 Maharishi Vedic University, *Maharishi's Master Plan to Create Heaven on Earth,* p. 36, iii.
30 *Ibid.,* pp. 36, i-iv.
31 *Ibid.,* p. 36, iii.
32 Maharishi Mahesh Yogi, in L. Fergusson, *Maharishi's Vedic Science and Post-Secondary Art Education,* Dissertation Abstracts International, 52,9, 1991, p. 200.
33 *Ibid.*
34 *Ibid.,* p. 194.
35 *Ibid.*
36 Maharishi Mahesh Yogi, in A. Bonshek, *Art—A Mirror of Consciousness,* p. 450.
37 *Ibid.,* p. 194.
38 Maharishi Mahesh Yogi, *Maharishi Forum of Natural Law and National Law for Doctors,* p. 376.
39 *Ibid.,* p. 386.
40 *Ibid.,* pp. 368-639.
41 *Ibid.,* pp. 386-387.
42 *Ibid.,* p. 386.
43 *Ibid.,* p. 387.
44 Maharishi Mahesh Yogi, *Maharishi Mahesh Yogi on the Bhagavad-Gita: A New Translation and Commentary: Chapters 1-6,* p. 183.
45 *Ibid.,* p. 214.
46 *Ibid.,* p. 351.
47 Maharishi Mahesh Yogi, *Maharishi Vedic University: Introduction,* p. 75-76.
48 Maharishi Mahesh Yogi, *Maharishi Mahesh Yogi on the Bhagavad-Gita: A New Translation and Commentary: Chapters 1-6,* p. 241.
49 Maharishi Mahesh Yogi, *Maharishi University of Management: Wholeness on the Move,* p. 357.
50 Maharishi Mahesh Yogi, in A. Bonshek, *Art—A Mirror of Consciousness,* p. 456.
51 Maharishi Mahesh Yogi, *Maharishi's Absolute Theory of Defence,* India, 1996, pp. 613-614.
52 *Ibid.,* p. 614.
53 Maharishi Mahesh Yogi, *Maharishi Mahesh Yogi on the Bhagavad-Gita: A New Translation and Commentary: Chapters 1-6,* p. 350.
54 *Ibid.,* p. 426.

55 Maharishi Mahesh Yogi, *Maharishi University of Management: Wholeness on the Move*, p. 53.
56 *Ibid.*, p. 185.
57 *Ibid.*, p. 184.

27 Transformative Futures

1 T. McEvilley, *Art and Otherness: Crisis in Cultural Identity*, New York, 1992, p. 10.
2 J. Kosuth, *Art After Philosophy and After*, Cambridge: MA, 1991, p. 17.
3 J. Hagelin, 'Is Consciousness a Unified Filed? A Field Theorist's Perspective.' *Modern Science and Vedic Science Journal*, 1 (1), 1987, pp. 28-87.
4 Maharishi Mahesh Yogi, in L. Fergusson, *Maharishi's Vedic Science and Post-Secondary Art Education*. Dissertation Abstracts International, 52, 9, 1991, p. 191.
5 *Ibid.*
6 S. Holzman, *Digital Mantras*, Cambridge, MA., 1996, p. 291.
7 A. Bonshek & G. Leete, 'Future Present: Reaesthetizing Life through a New Technology of Consciousness', *Reframing Consciousness*, Exeter, UK, 1999, pp. 285-290; A. Bonshek & G. Leete, *The Shock of Refinement*, International Symposium for the Electronic Arts (ISEA'98), England, 1998.

APPENDIX

वास्तुसूत्र उपनिषद्

Vāstusūtra Upaniṣad

प्रथमप्रपाठकस्य सूत्राणि

Prathamaprapāṭhakasya sūtrāṇi

1.1 वास्तोष्पतिर्ज्ञेय इति ।

Vāstoṣpatir jñeya iti.

(They) should know Vāstoṣpati (the divinity of Vāstu).

1.2 षट् शिल्पाङ्गप्रयोगेण प्रजनयन्ति रूपाणि ।

Ṣaṭśilpāṅga-prayogeṇa prajanayanti rūpāṇi.

Art forms are produced by means of six disciplines.

1.3 यूप इदं ज्योतिः ।

Yūpa idaṁ jyotiḥ.

The Yūpa (sacrificial post) is this light.

1.4 वृत्तज्ञानं रेखाज्ञानं च यो जानाति स स्थापकः ।

Vṛtta jñānaṁ rekhā jñānaṁ ca yo jānāti sa sthāpakaḥ.

Who has the knowledge of circle and line is a sthāpaka.

1.5 शिल्पात् प्रतिमा जायन्ते ।

Śilpāt pratimā jāyante.

By Śilpa images are produced.

1.6 स प्रवहणः शिल्पसूत्राध्यायं स्थापकविद्यां
चावदत् ।

Sa pravahaṇaḥ śilpa-sūtra-adhyāyaṁ
sthāpaka-vidhyāṁ cāvadat.
He, the carrier of the tradition, proclaimed (to them) the teaching of the Śilpasūtra (called) the sthāpakavidyā.

1.7 शरिरमूर्तिरहिते मन आवेश्य विशेषेण
विकल्पिदोषयुक्तं भवति इति ।

Śarira-mūrtirahite mana āveśya viśeṣeṇa
vikalpi-doṣa-yuktaṁ bhavati iti.
When worship is done without bodily images, the mind becomes particularly vitiated by indiscriminate imagination.

1.8 वास्तु षडङ्गमिति श्रेष्ठम् ।

Vāstu-ṣaḍ-aṅgam iti śreṣṭham.
Six disciplines of Art are essential.

1.9 षड्धा शैलं ज्ञेयम् ।

Śaḍdhā śailaṁ jñeyam.
Six kinds of stone are to be known.

1.10 शैलादङ्गरागज्ञानं प्रसरति ।

Śailād-aṅga rāgajñānaṁ prasarati.
By the type of stone the colour (rāga) of the image is known.

द्वितीयप्रपाठकस्य सूत्राणि

Dvitīyaprapāṭhakasya sūtrāṇi

2.1 निर्दिष्टार्थकप्रतिमा ग्राह्या ।

Nirdiṣṭārthaka-pratimā grāhyā.

An image should be envisaged to express a specified meaning.

2.2 पतनं प्रथमा क्रिया ।

Pātanaṁ prathamā kriyā.

Setting the stone is the first action.

2.3 मर्दनं द्वितीया क्रिया ।

Mardanaṁ dvitīyā kriyā.

Polishing it is the second action.

2.4 विलमिति मर्म ज्ञेयम् ।

Vilam iti marma-jñeyam.

This hole is consdered as the central point (marman = core).

2.5 न कृत्यरूपार्थं रेखाकरणं कर्त्तव्यम् ।

Na kṛtya rūpārthaṃ rekhākaraṇaṁ karttavyam.

For kṛtya-images (clay figures) a line-diagram need not be made.

2.6 आदौ वृत्तम् वृत्त मिति विश्वम् ।

Ādau vṛttam vṛttam iti viśvam.

In the beginning is a circle. The circle is the All (universe).

2.7 एकैकस्य संयोगे एकीभवति इति तस्य भावः ।
वृत्त हि पूर्णम् ।

Ekaikasya saṁyoge ekī-bhavati iti tasya bhāvaḥ, vṛtta hi purṇam.

By the connection of one with one a unity is formed. This is the meaning: The circle verily is the Plenum (fullness, pūrṇam).

2.8 रेखान्वये सर्वाङ्गाणि न्यासय ।

Rekhānvaye sarvāṅgāṇi nyāsaya.
All limbs have to be set along the lines.

2.9 तेजांसि सरलरेखाः ।

Tejāṁsi sarala-rekhāḥ
Straight lines are as rays of light.

2.10 नाभौ रूपकर्म प्रारभ्यते ।

Nābhau rūpa-karma prārabhyate.
The creation of the image starts from the navel.

2.11 प्राजापत्यरीत्या वृत्तं हि तेजस्तदाऽपांभासे
चतुरस्रम् ।

Prājāpatyarītyā vṛttaṁ hi tejas tadā'pāṁ bhāse caturasram.
Following the order of Prajāpati the circle represents light (tejas) while the square indicates water.

2.12 कर्णाद्वयं मरुद्भावेन आचरन्ति ।

Karṇa-dvayaṁ marud bhāvena ācaranti.
Two diagonals are drawn in the nature of wind.

2.13 धरेव कर्णिकक्षेत्रमाकर्षयन्ति स्थापकाः ।

Dhareva karṇikakṣetramākarṣayanti sthāpakāḥ.
The sthāpakas trace the karṇikakṣetra (rhombus) as the earth.

2.14 लब्धबिन्दुः रसायाः प्राणः ।

Labdha binduḥ rasāyāḥ prāṇaḥ.
The bindu obtained in the centre is the life-breath of the earth.

2.15 त्रिहुताग्निः स्मर्यतेऽपि च लोके ।

Trihutāgniḥ smaryate'pi ca loke.
Fire in the form of a triangle is known even in the (non-Vedic) world.

2.16 निम्नगास्त्रिहुता आप इति ।

Nimnagāstrihutā āpa iti.
The inverted triangle is water.

2.17 स षट्कोणको हि आकर्षणीविद्याविशेषः ।

Sa ṣaṭkoṇako hi ākarṣṇīvidyā viśeṣaḥ.
The hexagram is the special science of attraction.

2.18 यथा रूपे तथा यूपेऽनुच्छेदान्ता ग्राह्याः ।

Yathā rūpe tathā yūpe 'nucchedāntā grāhyāḥ.
As for images thus for Yūpas cutting along the line-divisions should be done.

2.19 खनित्रप्रकारो ध्येयः ।

Khanitraprakāro dhyeyaḥ.
Observe the method of (using) the chisels.

2.20 सूत्रायने रेखाः सुभगा भवन्ति ।

Sūtrāyane rekhāḥ subhagā bhavanti.
Lines following the Sūtra become harmonious.

2.21 खिलपञ्जरज्ञानं श्रेष्ठम् ।

Khilapañjarajñānaṁ śreṣṭham.
The knowledge of the compositional diagram (khilapañjara) is the best.

2.22 उत्थितरेखा अग्निरूपाः पार्श्वगा अबरूपाः तिर्यग्रेखा मरुद्रूपा इति ।

Utthita-rekhā agni-rūpāḥ pārśvagā abarūpāḥ tiryag-rekhā marud-rūpā iti
Vertical lines have the nature of fire, horizontal lines have the nature of water, diagonal lines have the nature of wind (māruta).

2.23 रूपसौभगद् ध्यानभावो जायते ।

Rūpa saubhagād dhyāna bhāvo jāyate.
By a harmonious form a meditative mood is induced.

2.24 अग्निरेखायामुत्तुङ्गरूपाणि जायन्ते ।

Agni rekhāyām uttuṅga rūpāṇi jāyante.
On the fire (vertical) lines upright forms are produced.

2.25 अब्रेखायामुत्सुकरूपाणि जायन्ते ।

Abrekhāyām utsuka rūpāṇi jāyante.
On the water (horizontal) lines forms expressing longing are produced.

2.26 मारुतरेखायां तैजसरूपाणि ।

Māruta-rekhāyāṁ taijasa rūpāṇi.
On the diagonal (wind) lines fiery (energetic) forms are produced.

2.27 रेखाज्ञानं सर्वमिति ज्ञेयम् ।

Rekhājñānaṃ sarvam iti jñeyam.
The knowledge of the line is to be known as all comprehensive.

तृतीयप्रपाठकस्य सूत्राणि

Tṛtīyaprapāṭhakasya sūtrāṇi

3.1 रूपस्य भावो मुख्यः ।

Rūpasya bhāvo mukhyaḥ.
The character (bhāva) of the form is essential.

3.2 भावानुसारतो रेखाविधानमिति ज्ञेयम् ।

Bhāvānusārato rekhā-vidhānam iti jñeyam.
The lay-out of the lines has to be established according to the character (of the image).

3.3 तेषां बहुधा कृत्यं श्रेयः ।

Teṣāṃ bahudhā kṛtyaṁ śreyaḥ.
For these (artists) many work-processes are important.

3.4 न्यासार्थं कालबोधो ध्येय इति ।

Nyāsārthaṁ kālābodho dhyeya iti.
One should observe the proper time for setting the stone (nyāsa).

3.5 तद्भेदनेऽभिमन्त्रेयन्ते खनित्राणि ।

Tadbhedane bhimantreyante khanitrāṇi.
For carving the chisels must be consecrated with a mantra.

3.6 खनित्रपञ्चकं श्रेष्ठम् ।

Khanitra-pañcakaṁ śreṣṭham.
Five types of chisels are the best.

3.7 रूपप्रकर्षार्थं रूपाङ्गं स्निग्धमिति ।

Rūpa prakarṣārthaṁ rūpāṇgaṁ snigdhamiti.
The limbs of the images should be smooth to bring out a clear form.

3.8 शिल्पकाराः प्रलेपयन्ति द्रावकरसम् ।

Śilpākārāḥ pralepayanti drāvakarasam.
The śilpakāras apply a softening mixture.

3.9 एषा हेतिविद्या श्रेष्ठा ।

Eṣā hetividyā śreṣṭhā.
This is the best method of (using) the instruments.

3.10 रक्षार्थं पर्णमणिः परिधेयः ।

Rakṣārthaṁ parṇamaṇiḥ paridheyaḥ.
For protection parṇamaṇi should be worn (in an amulet).

3.11 भेदनादङ्गसौभगं प्रभवति ।

Bhedanādaṅgasaubhagaṁ prabhavati.
Perfection of limbs is achieved by carving.

3.12 रेखानुपातेनाङ्गानि निधेयानीति श्रेष्ठाकृत्यम् ।

Rekhānupātenāṅgāni nidheyānīti śreṣṭhākṛtyam.
Placing the limbs along compositional lines is the best method (action).

3.13 गाथानुप्रासे लक्षणं व्यक्तं भवति ।

Gāthānuprāse lakṣaṇaṁ vyaktaṁ bhavati.
In the sacred songs the features (of the gods) are revealed.

3.14 धयानप्रयोगे रूपसौष्ठवं स्पष्टं भवति ।

Dhyāna-prayoge rūpa-sauṣṭhavaṁ spaṣṭaṁ bhavati.
The excellence of form becomes clear in the act of meditation (by applying the dhyāna of the divinity).

3.15 यथा प्रकृतिस्तथा रूपलक्षणम् ।

Yathā prakṛti-stathā rūpa lakṣaṇam.
The features of the images conform to nature.

3.16 अङ्गानि अर्धाकले सुषमं ध्येयानि ।

Aṅgāni ardhākale suṣamaṁ dhyeyāni.
Figures in half relief are beautiful (suitable) for meditation.

3.17 हर्सावधि उभयदिशि चोर्ध्वे वर्धयेत् ।

Harsāvadhi ubhayadiśi cordhve vardhayet.
Figures in half relief should not extend beyond the border-line on both sides and above.

3.18 रक्षाविधानेन विघ्नघातयः ।

Rakṣāvidhānena vighna-ghātayaḥ.
Obstacles are removed by the protective covering.

3.19 रेखाक्रमेण भेदनं चतुर्धा ज्ञेयम् ।

Rekhā-krameṇa bhedanaṁ caturdhā jñeyam.
There are four known ways of carving (the limbs) along the lines.

3.20 नेम्योत्तरे रूपाङ्गं न वर्धयेत् ।

Nemyottare rūpāṅgaṁ na vardhayet.
No limb of the image should exceed the circle.

3.21 खनित्रचालनविधिर्ध्येयविशेषः ।

Khanitracālanavidhir-dhyeya viśeṣaḥ.
The method of handling the chisels should be studied particularly.

चतुर्थप्रपाठकस्य सूत्राणि

Caturthaprapāṭhakasya sūtrāṇi

4.1 प्रतीतात् प्रतीकः ।

Pratītāt pratīkaḥ.

From the realization comes the symbol.

4.2 रूपादङ्गानि सञ्जायन्ते ।

Rūpādaṅgani sañjāyante.

From the form (of the symbol) arise the limbs (of images).

4.3 अतो द्विधा ब्रह्म रूपवान् भवति ।

Ato dvidhā brahma rūpavan bhavati.

Thus, on account of having two aspects Brahman acquires form.

4.4 रूपार्थं कोष्ठका मुख्याः ।

Rūpārthaṁ koṣṭhakā mukhyāḥ.

For making images a grid is most important.

4.5 वर्गीकरणं मुख्यकृत्यम् ।

Vargīkaraṇaṁ mukhya-kṛtyam.

Making squares is the principal work.

4.6 कोष्ठकान्तराले रूपस्यावयवो ध्येयः ।

Koṣṭhakāntarāle rūpasyāvayavo dhyeyaḥ.

One should imagine the various parts of the image within the grid.

4.7 परिमिताङ्गहाराद् भावलक्षणानि जायन्ते ।

Parimitāṅgahārād bhāvālakṣaṇāni jāyante.

The features of the character (bhāva) arise from the measured gestures of the body (or limbs).

4.8 कोष्ठके व्यतिक्रान्ते रूपमवद्यं भवति ।

Koṣṭhake vyatikrānte rūpamavadyaṁ bhavati.
By transgressing the grid the image becomes imperfect.

4.9 शुल्वं यज्ञस्य साधनं शिल्पं रूपस्य साधनम् ।

Śulvaṁ yajñasya sādhanaṁ śilpaṁ rūpasya sādhanam.
Śulva is the discipline for sacrifice, Śilpa is the discipline for form-creation (image-making).

4.10 शिल्पकाराणां रूपशैले रूपशालादि ध्येयम् ।

Śilpakārāṇāṃ rūpaśaile rūpaśālādi dhyeyam.
The śilpakaras make image-halls in the cave-temples and such things.

4.11 यूपाद्रूपं रूपाद् यूप इति स्वभावः ।

Yūpād rūpaṁ rūpād yūpa iti svabhāvaḥ.
From the Yūpa comes the (human) form, from the (human) form comes the Yūpa, that is their (common) fundamental nature.

4.12 यूपस्य मानं ध्येयम् ।

Yūpasya mānaṁ dhyeyam.
Study the measurement of the Yūpa.

4.13 षड्भागस्य प्रयोगो ध्येयः ।

Ṣaḍbhāgasya prayogo dhyeyaḥ.
The function of six parts should be understood.

4.14 पुरुषस्य रूपेऽङ्गचत्वारोऽष्टाङ्गक्रमेणोपजायनो ।

Puruṣasya rūpe'ṅga-catvāro'ṣṭāṅga-krameṇopa-jāyano.
The four parts (of the pillar) become eight parts in the form (image) of the Puruṣa, in their respective order.

4.15 पालाशदण्डरज्जुसंयोगे रेखामानय ।

Pālāśa-daṇḍaraj jusaṃyoge rekhāmānaya.
Draw the lines with a measuring rod of pālāśa wood and a rope.

4.16 निम्नादूर्ध्वावधि सदा रेखादीनाचर ।

Nimnādūrdhvāvadhi sadārekhādīnācara.
Lines and other (forms) are always to be traced from below upwards.

4.17 पुरुषस्तम्भ इव स्तम्भो वै यज्ञस्य रूपम् ।

Puruṣa-stambha iva stambho vai yajñasya rūpam.
The Puruṣa is like the pillar (of the universe), the pillar is the very symbol of sacrifice.

4.18 यथा स्तम्भस्य दशाङ्गं तथा पुरुषस्य दशयज्ञ
-प्रज्ञाश्च ।

Yathā stambhasya daśāṅgaṁ tathā puruṣasya daśa-yajña-prajñāś ca.
As there are ten parts in the pillar, thus the Pusruṣa is understood as consisting of ten sacrifices.

4.19 स्थापकाचार्या स्तम्भाद्रूपं बोधयन्ति ।

Sthāpakācāryā stambhād rūpaṁ bodhayanti.
The masters of art understand the (human) image as derived from the pillar.

4.20 स्तम्भः कामचारिणास्त्रिधामानयन्ति ।

Stambhaḥ kāma-cāriṇastridhāmānayanti.
Those who have desires set up pillars of three types.

4.21 दैवयज्ञार्थं यूपः ।

Daiva-yajñārthaṁ yūpaḥ.
A Yūpa is set up for sacrifices to the gods.

4.22 तदा पितृमेधार्थं वृषस्तम्भं मिथुनस्तम्भं कामचारा
होमे रोपयन्ति ।

Tadā pitṛ-medhārthaṁ vṛṣa-stambhaṁ mithunastambhaṁ kāmacārā home ropayanti.
Those who want to fulfill desires set up bull-pillars (vṛṣa-stambha) for ancestor-worship and mithuna-stambhas in homa-ceremonies.

4.23 तद्बोधे मानुषा रूपज्ञा भवन्ति ।

Tadbodhe mānuṣā rūpajñā bhavanti.
By knowing this, men become knowers of Form.

4.24 पुरुषस्य रूपाकले कोष्ठकस्याधो भावरूपं
प्रसरति ।

Puruṣasya rūpākale koṣṭhakasyādho bhāvarūpaṁ prasarati.
In the complete figure of the Puruṣa (human body) the form expressing its character (bhāvarūpa) arises from the lower compartments of the grid.

4.25 दशाङ्गयूपे रूपे इति तस्य भावः समानः ।

Daśāṅga-yūpe rūpe iti tasya bhāvaḥ samānaḥ.
The significance of the ten sections is the same in both the Yūpa and the human form (image).

4.26 ब्रह्मकीलाधारः ब्रह्मकीलेन सह क्षेत्रं विभाजय ।

Brahma-kīlādhāraḥ brahma-kīlena saha kṣetraṁ vibhājaya
The middle line (brahmakīla) is the support, and the field (panel) should be divided by this middle line.

4.27 अङ्गादङ्गं सञ्जायते ।

Aṅgād aṅgaṁ sañjāyate.
From one limb arises the other limb.

4.28 रेखासंयोगे तत्क्षेत्रेऽङ्गानि सौभगानि भवन्ति ।

Rekhāsaṁyoge tat kṣetre'ṅgāni saubhagāni bhavanti.
When the limbs in that panel adhere to the lines they become well-proportioned (harmonious).

4.29 क्षेत्रनेमिं रोधयेदिति ।

Kṣetra-nemiṁ rodhayed iti.
One should establish the circle of the panel.

पञ्चमप्रपाठकस्य सूत्राणि

Pañcamaprapaṭhakasya sūtrāṇi

5.1 भावस्यारोपणं रूपकर्मणि विधेयम् ।

Bhāvasyāropaṇaṁ rūpa-karmaṇi vidheyam.

In image-making the infusion of feeling (bhāva) (into the image) is enjoined.

5.2 कर्म भावस्य प्रदायकम् ।

Karma bhāvasya pradāyakam.

Action bestows the mood (bhāva).

5.3 भावस्याऽधारो रसः ।

Bhāvasyā'dhāro rasaḥ.

The support of the emotional attitude (bhāva) (of the image) is rasa.

5.4 मनसि वृत्तिर्बहुधा प्रजायते । तदा भिन्नरसाद्रूपं नैकं भवति ।

Manasi vṛttir bahudhā prajāyate, tadā bhinna-rasādrūpaṁ naikaṁ bhavati.

Many fluctuations arise in the mind, by their different rasas forms become manifold.

5.5 नवधा रसः ।

Navadhā rasaḥ.

There are nine rasas.

5.6 प्रथमरसः शृङ्गारः ।

Prathama-rasaḥ śṛṅgāraḥ.

The first rasa is love (śṛingāra).

5.7 शृङ्गाररूपार्थमब्रेखा ग्राह्याः ।

Śṛṅgāra rūpārtham-abrekhā grāhyāḥ.

For love-images horizontal lines should be used.

5.8 स हासो द्वितीयरसः ।

Sa hāso dvitīya-rasaḥ.
Laughter (hāsa) is the second rasa.

5.9 मुखलक्षणाद् रसं जानन्ति सर्वे ईक्षणेन ।

Mukha-lakṣaṇād rasaṁ jānanti sarve īkṣaṇena.
By seeing the features of the face all people can know the rasa.

5.10 स तृतयिः करुणारस भाव इति ।

Sa tṛtiyaḥ karuṇa-rasa-bhāva iti.
Compassion (karuṇa) is the third rasa or sentiment.

5.11 रौद्रः चतुर्थो रसः ।

Raudraḥ caturtho rasaḥ
The furious sentiment (raudra) is the fourth rasa.

5.12 तिर्यगरेखायां रूपाङ्गभावः प्रकटो भवति ।

Tiryag rekhāyām rūpāṅgabhāvaḥ prakaṭo bhavati
This sentiment becomes evident in the oblique lines in the image.

5.13 स वीरभावः पञ्चमः ।

Sa vīra-bhāvaḥ pañcamaḥ.
The heroic sentiment (*vīrabhāva*) is the fifth (*rasa*).

5.14 वैरभावे उत्कटे भयङ्करो भवति । स वैलक्षणः षष्ठरसः ।

Vaira-bhāve ut̃kaṭe bhayaṅkaro bhavati, sa vailakṣaṇaḥ ṣaṣṭha-rasaḥ.
When the heroic sentiment becomes excessive it becomes terrifying (bhayaṅkara), this is the sixth rasa which is different (from vīra).

5.15 कुरुपाः क्षिप्ताङ्गाः मारुतरेखायामिति स सप्तमः ।

Kurupāḥ kṣiptāṅgaḥ māruta-rekhāyām iti sa saptamaḥ.
The deformed figures with their limbs in disarray are placed on diagonal lines, this is the seventh sentiment (bībhatsā, disgust).

5.16 शान्तभावः सोऽष्टमो रसः ।

Śānta-bhāvaḥ so'ṣṭamo rasaḥ.

The sentiment of peace is the eighth rasa.

5.17 भावानुगतरूपाणि चतुर्धा मुख्यानि ।

Bhāvānugata-rūpāṇi caturdhā mukhyāni.

In conformity with the sentiment images are of four main types.

5.18 लोके भावबोधस्य हेतुर्मनः ।

Loke bhāva-bodhasya hetur manaḥ.

In this world mind is the cause of experiencing sentiments.

5.19 मनुष्याणां वृत्तिर्मुख्येति ।

Manusyāṇāṁ vṛttir mukhyeti.

Of humans it is the mental modification (vṛtti) which is important.

5.20 सङ्कल्पाद् विकल्पः ।

Saṅkalpād vikalpaḥ.

The intention to worship (saṅkalpa) is the cause for the imagination (vikalpa), (of the particular form of God in which he is worshipped).

5.21 एष भुवनकोषो देहानुभूत्याः क्रमः ।

Eṣa bhuvanakoṣo dehānubhūtyāḥ kramaḥ.

This arrangement of the (fourteen) worlds (stages) constitutes the order of bodily realization.

5.22 अरूपाद्रूपं तस्य फलम् ।

Arūpād rūpaṁ tasya phalam.

From the formless arises form, that is the result (of the fourteen stages).

5.23 दिशानुसृतेर्दिशापालानुपासन्ते ।

Diśānusṛterdiśāpālānupāsante.

According to space-directions the guardians of the quarters are worshipped.

5.24 एवं दैवभेदान्मार्गभेदा जायन्ते ।

Evaṁ daiva-bhedān mārga-bhedā jāyante.
Thus from different divinities arise different ways (traditions).

षष्ठः प्रपाठकस्य सूत्राणि

Ṣaṣṭhaḥ prapāṭhakasya sūtrāṇi

6.1 न्यासधारणा श्रेष्ठा ।

Nyāsa-dhāraṇā śreṣṭhā.
The conception of the composition (nyāsadhāraṇā).
is most essential.

6.2 वृत्तया दैवचिन्तने भेदः सञ्जायते ।

Vṛttyā daiva-cintane bhedaḥ sañjāyate.
According to the (difference of) mental modifications (vṛtti) a difference arises in the conception of divinities.

6.3 लक्षणप्रकाशार्थं शिल्पविद्या ।

Lakṣaṇa-prakāśārthaṃ śilpa vidyā.
The science of Śilpa is to make manifest the (divine) features.

6.4 न्यासोऽलङ्कारमुद्रायुध-
बाध्रकक्षवाहनोपदेवारिस्तुवकक्रमेण
रूपनवाङ्गमिति ध्येयम् ।

Nyāso'laṅkāramudrāyudha-bādhrakakṣavāhanopadevāristuvaka-krameṇa rūpānavaṅgam iti dhyeyam.
One should remember the nine different elements constituting images in their order: composition, ornamentation, gestures, weapons, postures, vehicles, secondary divinities, enemies and devotees.

6.5 तिस्रः रेखाः श्रेष्ठाः ।

Tisraḥ rekhā śreṣṭhāḥ.
Three (types of) lines are essential.

6.6 रूपक्षेत्रे कोष्ठकालिर्मुख्या ।

Rūpa-kṣetre koṣṭhakālir mukhyā.
The sequence of lines of the grid on the image panel is most important.

6.7 षोडशकोष्ठकमध्ये रूपाणि प्रभवन्ति तद्रूपार्थ श्रेष्ठम् ।

Ṣoḍaśakoṣṭha-kamadhye rūpāṇi prabhavanti tad rūpārthaṃ śreṣṭham.
The forms appear within the grid of sixteen compartments, this is the best for making images.

6.8 विलमिति मर्म ब्रह्मेव निधेयम् ।

Vilam iti marma brahmeva nidheyam.
The hole is the centre (*marma*), (it is to be) contemplated as *Brahman.*

6.9 षोडशकोष्ठकप्रमाणविभागस्तु ब्राह्मदैवजैवोपदैवयाजकक्रमेण पञ्चधा ध्येयः ।

Ṣoḍaśakoṣṭhaka-pramāṇa vibhāgastu brahma-daiva-jaivopadaiva-yājaka-kramena pañcadhā dhyeyaḥ.
The compartments in the measure of the sixteenfold grid are known to be of five types: the field of Brahman, of the gods (daiva), of living beings (jaiva), of secondary divinities (upadaiva) and of worshippers.

6.10 रूपाङ्गं चतुर्धेति विशेषः ।

Rūpāṅgaṁ caturdheti viśeṣaḥ.
There are four parts in the figure, this is the particularity.

6.11 बिन्दुर्ब्रह्मेव ब्रह्मध्रुवम् ।

Bindur brahmeva brahma-dhruvam.
The bindu is like Brahma, Brahman is immovable.

6.12 ब्रह्म सत्यादौ ।

Brahma satyādau.
Brahman and satya (truth) are in the beginning.

6.13 ब्रह्मबिन्द्ववलम्बनेन रूपाङ्गाणि सौभगानि भवन्ति ।

Brahma-bindvavalambanena rūpāṅgāṇi saubhagāni bhavanti.
When the limbs of the image are depending on the brahmabindu (central point) they become harmonious.

6.14 अलङ्करणं दैवभूषणमिति ।

Alaṅkaraṇaṁ daiva bhuṣaṇam iti.
Ornamentation means the decoration of divine images.

6.15 प्रतिमुचः रतिः प्रसरति ।

Pratimucaḥ ratiḥ prasarati.
From the ornamentation (of the image) arises delight.

6.16 करमुद्रा रूपस्य भावं ज्ञापयति ।

Karamudrā rūpasya bhāvaṁ jñāpayati.
Hand gestures manifest the emotional attitude of the image.

6.17 बाध्रं बलं ज्ञापयति रूपे ।

Bādhraṁ balaṁ jñāpayati rūpe.
The bādhra (weapons) communicate the power of the figure.

6.18 आसनंषट्धं मुख्यम् ।

Āsanaṁ ṣaḍdhaṁ mukhyam.
Six are the principal types of postures (āsana).

6.19 गुणानुसृतं रूपत्रयम् ।

Guṇānusṛtaṁ rūpa-trayam.
According to the quality (guṇa) there are three types of images.

6.20 वाहनं रूपस्य प्रकृतिज्ञापकविशेषः ।

Vāhanaṁ rūpasya prakṛti-jñāpaka-viśeṣaḥ.
The vehicle is a special means for revealing the nature of the figure.

6.21 उपदैवतं प्रतिरूपमिति ।

Upadaivataṁ pratirūpam iti.

Attendent divinities are secondary figures.

6.22 उपदैवताद्रूपज्ञानं प्रसरति ।

Upadaiva tād rūpa jñānaṁ prasarati.

The (aspects of the) main image are known by the attendent divinities.

6.23 अरिसन्धा ध्येया ।

Arisandhā dhyeyā.

The connection (of the main figure) with adversaries should be remembered.

6.24 रूपधाराया वृत्तिरिति श्रेष्ठा ।

Rūpa-dhārāyā vṛttir iti śreṣṭhā.

From the sequence of forms comes the condition (of the mind), this (procedure) is the best.

6.25 स्तोतॄणां रूपे सुभगविशेषः ।

Stotṝṇāṁ rūpe subhaga-viśeṣaḥ.

Through the (representation of the) singers of praises images become particularly beautiful.

6. 26 प्रज्ञार्थमेतद् वास्तूपाख्यानम् ।

Prajñārtham etad vāstūpākhyānam.

This exposition of Art (vāstu) is for the purpose of conferring knowledge.

BIBLIOGRAPHY

Alexander, C.N., Nader, T., & Davies, J. (1989). The Maharishi Technology of the Unified Field and Reduction of Armed Conflict: A Comparative Longitudinal Study of Lebanese Villages. In R.A. Chalmers, G. Clements, H. Schenkluhn, & M. Weinless (Eds.), *Scientific Research on the Transcendental Meditation and TM-Sidhi Programme: Collected Papers, Vol. 4*, [pp. 2623-2634]. Vlodrop, The Netherlands: Maharishi Vedic University Press.

Alexander, C. N. & Boyer, R. W. (1989). Seven States of Consciousness: Unfolding the Full Potential of the Cosmic Psyche in Individual Life Through Maharishi's Vedic Psychology. *Modern Science and Vedic Science*, 2(4), 324-371.

Alexander, C. N., Cranson, R.W., Boyer, R.W., & Orme-Johnson, D.W. (1987). Transcendental Consciousness: A Fourth State of Consciousness Beyond Sleep, Dreaming, and Waking. In J. Gackenbach (Ed.), *Sleep and Dreams: A Sourcebook*, [pp. 282-315]. New York: Garland.

Ardalan, N., & Bakhtiar, L. (1973). *The Sense of Unity*. Chicago: University of Chicago Press.

Ascott, R. (Ed.) (1999). *Reframing Consciousness*, Exeter, UK: Intellect Books.

Banks, G. (1983). In Defence of Common Knowledge. *Art Monthly*, 63, 23-25.

Bedekar, V. (1967). The Legend of the Churning of the Ocean in the Epics and the Purānas: A Comparative Study. *Puranam* IX, 7-61.

Belting, H. (1987). *The End of the History of Art*. Chicago: University of Chicago Press.

Berleant, A. (1988). Aesthetic Perception in Environmental Design. In J. Nasar (Ed.) *Environmental Aesthetics: Theory, Research, and Applications*, [pp. 84-97]. Cambridge: Cambridge University Press.

Berg, W.P. van den, & Mulder, B. (1976). Psychological Research on the Effects of the Transcendental Meditation Technique on a Number of Personality Variables. *Gedrag: Tijdscrift voor Psychologie*, [Behavior: Journal for Psychology], 4, 206-218.

Best, S., & Kellner, D. (1991). *Postmodern Theory: Critical Interrogations*. New York: Guilford Press.

Bhattacharya, D. (1982). The Position of the Vāstusutraūpaniṣad in the Atharvavedic Literature. In A. Boner, S.R. Śarma, & B. Bäumer [pp. 30-36], *Vāstusūtra Upaniṣad: The Essence of Form in Sacred Art*. Delhi: Motilal Banarsidass.

Blasdell, K. (1977). The Effects of the Transcendental Meditation Technique upon a Complex Perceptual-Motor Task. In D.W. Orme-Johnson & J.T. Farrow (Eds.), *Scientific Research on the Transcendental Meditation Program: Collected Papers*, Vol. 1, [pp. 322-325]. Rheinweiler, W. Germany: Maharishi European Research University Press.

Boner, A., Śarma, S. R., & Bäumer, B. (1982). *Vāstusūtra Upaniṣad: The Essence of Form in Sacred Art*. Delhi: Motilal Banarsidass.

Bonshek, A. J. (1986). Feminist Romantic Painting—A Re-Constellation, in H. Robinson (Ed.) *Visibly Female: Feminism and Art Today* [pp. 118-129]. Camden Press, London: Camden Press.

——— (1995) The Use of Aesthetics: Food for Thought. *Artlink*, 15 (1), 16-19.

Bonshek, A. J., & Fergusson, L. C. (1988). Agnes Martin on Beauty and Perfection in Art. *Modern Science and Vedic Science*, 2 (3), 298-306.

——— (1989) *Allegories of Consciousness: Perfection in Printmaking Since the Renaissance*, Exhibition Catalogue. Iowa: Des Moines Art Center.

Bonshek, A. & Leete, G. (1999). 'Future Present: Reaestheticizing Life through a New Technology of Consciousness,' *Reframing Consciousness*, Exeter, UK: Intellect Books, pp. 285-290.

Borges, J. L (1962). *Labyrinths*. New York: New Directions.

Borland, C., & Landrith, G. (1977) Improved Quality of City Life through the Transcendental Meditation Program: Decreased crime rate. In D.W. Orme-Johnson & J.T. Farrow (Eds.), *Scientific Research on the Transcendental Meditation Program: Collected Papers*, Vol.1 [pp. 639-648]. Rheinwheiler, W. Germany: Maharishi European Research University Press.

Burgin, V. (1986). The Absence of Presence: Conceptualism and Postmodernism. In V. Burgin (Ed.), *The End of Art Theory* [pp. 29-50]. London: Macmillan.

Cain, M. (1988). Art and the Unified Field. *Modern Science and Vedic Science*, 2(3), 280-297.

Chandler, K. (1987). Modern Science and Vedic Science: An Introduction. *Modern Science and Vedic Science*, 1(1), 5-26.

Coomaraswamy, A. (1977). *Selected Papers: Traditional Art and Symbolism*, Vol. 1. Princeton, NJ: Princeton University Press.

Coward, H. (1990). *Derrida and Indian Philosophy*. Albany, NY: State University of New York Press.

Cranson, R.W., Orme-Johnson, D.W., Gackenbach, J., Dillbeck, M.C., Jones, C.H. & Alexander, C.N. (1991). Transcendental Meditation and Improved Performance in Intelligence-Related Measures: A Longitudinal Study. *Personality and Individual Differences*, 12 (10), 1105-1116.

Dehejia, V. (1997) *Indian Art*, London: Phaidon.

Derrida, J. (1981). *Positions*. Chicago: University of Chicago Press.

——— (1986). Différance. In M. Taylor (Ed.), *Deconstruction in Context: Literature and Philosophy* [pp. 396-420]. Chicago: University of Chicago Press.

——— (1987). Structure, Sign and Play in the Discourse of the Human Sciences. In A. Blass (Trans.), *Writing and Difference* [pp. 278-293]. Chicago: University of Chicago Press.

Dillbeck, S., & Dillbeck, M. C. (1987). The Maharishi Technology of the Unified Field in Education: Principles, Practice and Research. *Modern Science and Vedic Science*, 1(4), 382-468.

Dillbeck, M. C. (1988). The Self-Interacting Dynamics of Consciousness as the Source of the Creative Process in Nature and in Human Life: The Mechanics of Individual Intelligence Arising from the Field of Cosmic Intelligence—the Cosmic Psyche. *Modern Science and Vedic Science*, 2(3), 245-279.

——— (1989) Experience of the Ved, Realization of the Cosmic Psyche by Direct Perception: Opening Individual Awareness to the Self-interacting Dynamics of Consciousness. *Modern Science and Vedic Science*, 3(2), 116-152.

Dillbeck, M.C., Orme-Johnson, D.W., & Wallace, R. (1981). Frontal EEG coherence, H-reflex Recovery, Concept Learning, and the TM-Sidhi Program. *International Journal of Neuroscience*, 15, 151-157.

Eagleton, T. (1983). *Literary Theory*. Oxford: Basil Blackwell.

——— (1997). *Illusions of Postmodernism*, Oxford: Basil Blackwell.

Engler, G. (1990). Aesthetics in Science and in Art. *British Journal of Aesthetics*, 30 (1), 24-34.

Fehér, F., & Heller, A. (1986). *Reconstructing Aesthetics.* Oxford: Basil Blackwell.

Fergusson, L. C.(1991). Maharishi's Vedic Science and Post-Secondary Art Education. *Dissertation Abstracts International,* 52, 9.

——— (1992). Field Independence and Art Achievement in Meditating and Non-meditating College Students. *Perceptual and Motor Skills,* 75, 1171-1175.

——— (1993). Field Independence, Transcendental Meditation, and Achievement in College Art: A Re-examination. *Perceptual and Motor Skills,* 77, 1104-1106.

Fergusson, L.C., Bonshek, A.J., Norman, M.C. & Norman C.W. (1990). *The Socio-Environmental Impact of Sthapatya-Veda.* In Conference Proceedings: The First Annual National Social Science Conference, Washington, D.C.

Fergusson, L.C., Bonshek, A.J. & Boudigues, M. (1994). Transcendental Meditation and Five Factors Relevant to Higher Education in Cambodia. *College Student Journal,* 28 (1), 103-107.

Fergusson, L.C., Bonshek, A.J. & Boudigues, J-M. (1995). Personality and Health Characteristics of Cambodian Undergraduates: A Case for Student Development. *Journal of Instructional Psychology,* 22 (4), 308-319.

Foster, H. (1984). *(Post)modern Polemics.* New German Critique, 30, 67-78.

Fuller, P. (1983). *Aesthetics After Modernism.* London: Writers and Readers.

Gablik, S. (1976). *Progress in Art.* New York: Rizzoli.

——— (1984). *Has Modernism Failed?* London: Thames and Hudson.

——— (1991). Art Beyond the Rectangle: A Call for "Useful" Art. *New Art Examiner,* 17(4), 20-24.

——— (1992). *The Reenchantment of Art.* New York: Thames and Hudson.

Gelderloos, P., Frid, J.F., Goddard, P.H., Xue, X., & Löliger, S. (1988). Creating World Peace through the Collective Practice of the Maharishi Technology of the Unified Field: Improved U.S.-Soviet Relations. *Social Science Perspectives Journal,* 2(4), 80-94.

Gelderloos, P., & van den Berg, W.P. (1989). Maharishi's TM-Sidhi Program: Participating in the Infinite Creativity of Nature to Enliven the Totality of the Cosmic Psyche in all Aspects of Life. *Modern Science and Vedic Science,* 2(4), 372-412.

Gómez-Peña, G. (1998).*The New World Border,* San Francisco: City Lights.

Green, M. (1986). Superstrings. *Scientific American,* 255(3), 48-53.

Green, K. (1993). Brain Writing and Derrida. *Australasian Journal of Philosophy,* 71(3), 238-255.

Greenberg, C. (1961) *Art and Culture.* Boston, MA: Beacon.

Hagelin, J. (1987). Is Consciousness the Unified Field? A Field Theorists Perspective. *Modern Science and Vedic Science, 1(1),* 28-87.

——— (1989). Restructuring Physics from its Foundation in the Light of Maharishi's Vedic Science. *Modern Science and Vedic Science,* 3(1), 3-74.

Haney, W. (1989). The Theory of Deconstruction and Maharishi's Vedic Science. *Modern Science and Vedic Science Journal,* 2(4), 415-441.

Harrison, C., & Wood, P. (Eds.) (1992). *Art in Theory 1900-1990.* Oxford: Blackwell.

Hartmann, E. (6-8 July, 1990). *Maharishi Sthapatya-Veda.* Presented to the Second International Symposium on Maharishi Sthapatya-Veda. Washington D.C..

Hassan, I. (1987). *The Postmodern Turn: Essays in Postmodern Theory and Culture.* Ohio: Ohio State University Press.

Hegel, G. W. (1975). *Lectures on the Philosophy of World History.* New York: Cambridge University Press.

Heim, M. (1998). *Virtual Realism.* Oxford: Oxford University Press.

——— (1975). *The Philosophy of Fine Art.* New York: Hacker Art Books.

Hepworth, B., (1992). 'Sculpture 1937'. In C. Harrison & P. Wood (Eds.), *Art in Theory 1900-1990* [pp. 374-376]. Oxford: Basil Blackwell.

——— (1977). *Some Statements by Barbara Hepworth.* Hayle, Cornwall: Rowe.

Hofstadter, A., & Kuhns, R. (Eds.) (1964). *Philosophies of Art and Beauty: Readings in Aesthetics from Plato to Heidegger.* New York: Random House.

Holtzman, S. (1996). *Digital Mantras.* Massachusetts: MIT Press.

Institute of Science, Technology and Public Policy. (September, 1994). *Results of the National Demonstration Project to Reduce Violent Crime and Improve Governmental Effectiveness in Washington D.C. June 7 to July 30, 1993.* Institute of Science, Technology and Public Policy Technical Report, ITR-94:1.

Jairazbhoy, R.A. (1965). *Oriental Influences in Western Art.* Bombay: Asia Publishing House.

Jameson, F. (1985). Postmodernism, or the Cultural Logic of Late Capitalism. *New Left Review*, 146, 53-92.

Jencks, C. (1986). *What is Post-modernism?* New York: St. Martin's Press.

Kant, I. (1986). Critique of Judgment. In M. Taylor (Ed.), *Deconstruction in Context: Literature and Philosophy* [pp. 35-66]. Chicago: University of Chicago Press.

——— (1963). *Analytic of the Beautiful.* New York: Bobbs-Merrill.

Kemal, S. (1986). *Kant and Fine Art.* (Trans. Cerf, W.) Oxford: Clarendon Press.

Kesterson, J., & Clinch, N.F. (1989). Metabolic Rate, Respiratory Exchange Ratio and Apneas During Meditation. *American Journal of Physiology, 256 Regulatory, Integrative and Comparative Physiology*, 25, R632-R638.

Kissick, J. (1993). *Art: Context and Criticism.* Hong Kong: Brown and Benchmark.

Kosuth, J. (1991). *Art After Philosophy and After.* Cambridge, MA: Massachusetts Institute of Technology Press.

Kramrisch, S. (1986). *The Hindu Temple* (Vol.1). Delhi: Motilal Barnarsidass.

——— (1986). *The Hindu Temple* (Vol.2). Delhi: Motilal Barnarsidass.

Krauss, R.E. (1987). *The Originality of the Avant-garde and Other Modernist Myths.* Cambridge, MA: MIT Press.

Krishnan, G.P. (1997). *Ramayana: A Living Tradition.* Singapore: National Heritage Board.

Kumar Acharya, P. (1980). (trans.) *Architecture of Manasara,* Vol. IV. New Delhi: Oriental Books Reprint Corporation.

Kumar Acharya, P. (1980). *Architecture of Manasara,* Vol. V. New Delhi: Oriental Books Reprint Corporation.

Kuspit, D. (1987). Conflicting Logics: Twentieth-Century Studies at the Crossroads. *The Art Bulletin*, LXIX, 117-132.

——— (1990). The Problem of Art in the Age of Glamor. *Art Criticism*, 6(1), 32-42.

——— (1990). A Psychoanalytic Understanding of Aesthetic Disinterestedness. *Art Criticism*, 6(2), 72-80.

Lake, B. (1959). A Study of the Irrefutability of Two Aesthetic Theories. In W. Elton (Ed.), *Aesthetics and Language.* Oxford: Basil Blackwell.

Legge, J. (trans.) (1959). *The Texts of Taoism.* New York: Julian Press.

Levine, P., Hebert, J., Haynes, C., & Strobel, U. (1975). EEG coherence during the Transcendental Meditation technique. In D.W. Orme-Johnson & J.T. Farrow (Eds.), *Scientific Research on the Transcendental Meditation Program: Collected Papers*, Vol. 1 [pp. 187-207]. Rheinweiler, W. Germany: Maharishi European Research University Press.

Lippard, L. (1983). *Overlay: Contemporary Art and the Art of Prehistory.* New York: Pantheon.

Lawlor, R. (1982). *Sacred Geometry: Philosophy and Practice.* London: Thames and Hudson.

Los Angeles County Museum of Art. (1986). *The Spiritual in Art: Abstract Painting 1890-1985.* New York: Abbeville Press.

Lyotard, J-F. (1988). *The Postmodern Condition: A Report on Knowledge.* Minneapolis: University of Minnesota Press.

——— (1991) In Joseph Kosuth, *Art after Philosophy and After.* Foreword, [pp. xv-xviii], (Ed). G. Guercio. Cambridge, MA: MIT Press.

Maharishi European Research University. (1978). *Enlightenment to Every Individual: Invincibility to Every Nation.* West Germany: Maharishi European Research University Press.

Maharishi European Research University. (1979). *World Government News,* 11. West Germany: Maharishi European Research University Press.

Maharishi International University. (1979). Maharishi International University Bulletin, 1979-81. Los Angeles: Maharishi International University Press.

Maharishi Mahesh Yogi. (1966). *The Science of Being and the Art of Living.* Washington, D.C.: Age of Enlightenment Press.

——— (1969). *Maharishi Mahesh Yogi on the Bhagavad-Gita: A New Translation and Commentary: Chapters 1-6.* Middlesex, GB: Penguin.

——— (1970). *Art and the Artist.* [A lecture given at Kössen, W. Germany]. In M. Cain, Art and the Science of Creative Intelligence: Interdependence of part and whole [pp. v-viii]. Fairfield, IA: Maharishi International University Press.

——— (1972). The Artist and the Scientist, Lesson 27. In *The Science of Creative Intelligence: Knowledge and Experience* [Syllabus of Videotaped course]. Los Angeles: Maharishi International University Press.

——— (1973). A Message From His Holiness Maharishi Mahesh Yogi. *Creative Intelligence,* 1, 2-5.

——— (1973). Creativity and World Problems. *Creative Intelligence,* 3, 2.

——— (1974). Creative Intelligence and Art. *Creative Intelligence,* 4, 2.

——— (1975) *Science of Creative Intelligence for Secondary Education: First-year Core Course.* Rheinweiler, W. Germany: Maharishi International University Press.

——— (1977). *Creating an Ideal Society.* Rheinweiler, W. Germany: Maharishi European Research University Press.

——— (1977). Inaugural Address. In *Maharishi Mahesh Yogi, First World Assembly of Law, Justice and Rehabilitation* [pp. 21-27]. Rheinweiler, W. Germany: Maharishi European Research University Press.

——— (1977). *Enlightenment and the Siddhis: A New Breakthrough in Human Potential.* Rheinweiler, W. Germany: Maharishi European Research University Press.

——— (1978). The Global Maharishi Effect: New Principles of Life Taking Over in the Dawning Age of Enlightenment. *World Government News,* 8, 4-5.

——— (1979). Natural Law and the Evolutionary Perspective of Religious Codes. *World Government News.* 11, 34-36.

——— (1980). *Maharishi Mahesh Yogi: Science, Consciousness and Aging: Proceedings of the International Conference.* Rheinweiler, West Germany: Maharishi European Research University Press.

——— (1985). Inaugural address of His Holiness Maharishi Mahesh Yogi. In *Maharishi Mahesh Yogi: Maharishi Vedic University Inauguration.* Washington, D.C.: Age of Enlightenment Press.

——— (1986). *Thirty Years Around the World: Dawn of the Age of Enlightenment.* The Netherlands: Maharishi Vedic University Press.
——— (1986). *Life Supported by Natural Law: Lectures by His Holiness Maharishi Mahesh Yogi to the World Assembly on Vedic Science July 9-17, 1985.* Washington, D.C.: Age of Enlightenment Press.
——— (1990). Maharishi Offers to Every Government Alliance with Nature's Government. January 6, *Economist*, 314, 19.
——— (1993). *Maharishi Vedic University: Exhibition.* The Netherlands: Maharishi Vedic University Press.
——— (1993). *Maharishi's Absolute Theory of Government: Automation in Administration.* Holland: Maharishi Vedic University Press.
——— (1994). *Maharishi Vedic University: Introduction.* Holland: Maharishi Vedic University Press.
——— (1995). *Maharishi University of Management: Wholeness on the Move.* Holland: Maharishi Vedic University Press.
——— (1996). *Maharishi Forum of Natural Law and National Law for Doctors.* India: Age of Enlightenment Publications.
——— (1996). *Maharishi's Absolute Theory of Defence.* India: Age of Enlightenment Publications.
——— (1996). *Inaugurating Maharishi Vedic University.* India: Maharishi Mahesh Yogi Vedic Vishwavidyalaya.
——— (1997). *Constitution of India Fulfilled through Maharishi's Transcendental Meditation.* India: Maharishi Mahesh Yogi Vedic Vishwavidyalaya.
——— (1997). *Celebrating Perfection in Education.* India: Maharishi Mahesh Vedic University Press.
——— (1998). *Celebrating Perfection in Administration.* India: Age of Enlightenment Publications.
Maharishi University of Management. (1996). *Maharishi University of Management World*, 5 (1). Fairfield, Iowa: Maharishi University of Management Press.
Maharishi Vedic University. (1987). *Maharishi's Programme to Create World Peace: Global Inauguration.* Vlodrop, The Netherlands: Maharishi Vedic University Press.
——— (1991). *Maharishi's Master Plan to Create Heaven on Earth.* Vlodrop, The Netherlands: Maharishi Vedic University Press.
——— (1998). *Building for the Health and Happiness of Everyone.* The Netherlands: Maharishi Vedic University Press.
McEvilley, T. (1982). Heads it's Form, Tails it's Not Content. *Artforum*, XXI, 3, 256-263.
——— (1984). On the Manner of Addressing Clouds. *Artforum*, XXII, 10, 61-70.
——— (1984). Doctor, Lawyer, Indian Chief: "'Primitivism' in Twentieth-Century Art at the MOMA in 984" *Artforum*, XXIII, 3, 54-60.
——— (1988). Empyrrhical Thinking (and Why Kant can't). *Artforum*, XXVII, 2, 120-127.
——— (1989). Postmodernism: Yes, No, Maybe. *The Journal of Art*, 1(6), 8-9.
——— (1992). *Art and Otherness: Crisis in Cultural Identity.* New York: McPherson Press.
Mitias, M.H. (1980). Hegel on the Art Object. In W. Steinkraus & K. Schmitz. (Eds.), *Art and Logic in Hegel's Philosophy* New Jersey: Humanities Press.
Müller, F.M. (Ed.) (1882). *The Śatapatha Brāhmana.* Delhi: Motilal Banarsidass.
Nader, T. (1995). *Human Physiology: Expression of Veda and the Vedic Literature.* Vlodrop, The Netherlands: Maharishi Vedic University Press.

Neher, R. (1995). As Stupid as a Painter: Jackson Pollock and the Politics of Self. *Art Criticism.* 10 (2), 55-67.
Newman, B. (1948). The Ides of Art, Six Opinions on What is Sublime in Art. *Tiger's Eye*, 6, 53.
Norris, C. (1982). *Deconstruction: Theory and Practice.* New York: Methuen.
Orme-Johnson, D.W., & Dillbeck, M. C. (1987). Maharishi's Program to Create World Peace: Theory and Research. *Modern Science and Vedic Science*, 1(2), 207-259.
Orme-Johnson, D.W., Alexander, C.N., Davies, J., Chandler, H., & Larimore, W. (1988). International Peace Project in the Middle East. *Journal of Conflict Resolution*, 32(4), 776-812.
Orme-Johnson, D.W., Clements, G., Haynes, C.T., & Badaoui, K. (1977). Higher States of Consciousness: EEG coherence, Creativity, and Experiences of the Sidhis. In D.W. Orme-Johnson & J.T. Farrow (Eds.), *Scientific Research on the Transcendental Meditation and TM-Sidhi program: Collected Papers*, Vol. 1 [pp. 705-712]. Vlodrop, The Netherlands: Maharishi Vedic University Press.
Orme-Johnson, R. (1987). A Unified Field Theory of Literature. *Modern Science and Vedic Science*, 1 (3), 322-373.
Pandit, S. (1977). *An Approach to the Indian Theory of Art and Aesthetics.* New Delhi: Sterling.
Paz, O. (1987). *Convergences: Essays on Art and Literature.* New York: Harcourt, Brace and Jovanovich.
Pelletier, K. (1974). Influence of Transcendental Meditation upon Autokinetic Perception. *Perceptual and Motor Skills*, 39, 1031-1034.
——— (1977). The Effects of the Transcendental Meditation Program on Perceptual Style: Increased Field-Independence. In D.W. Orme-Johnson & J.T. Farrow (Eds.), *Scientific Research on the Transcendental Meditation program: Collected Papers*, Vol. 1 [pp. 337-345]. Rheinweiler, W. Germany: Maharishi European Research University Press.
Raj Bahadur Srisa Chandra Vasu (Trans.) (1984). *Śiva Saṃhitā*. India: Sat Guru Publications.
Richman, P. (1991). (Ed.) *Many Rāmāyaṇas.* Los Angeles: University of California Press.
Rorty, R. (1984). Habermas and Lyotard on Postmodernity. *Praxis International*, 4 (1), 32-44.
Ross, S. (1994) *Art and its Significance: An Anthology of Aesthetic Theory.* Albany, NY: State University of New York Press.
Said, E.W. (1979). *Orientalism.* New York: Random House.
Sampson, E. (1983). Deconstructing Psychology's Subject. *The Journal of Mind and Behavior*, 4 (2), 135-164.
Sands, W. (1994). *Maharishi's Absolute Theory of Government in the Vālmiki Rāmāyana.* Dissertation Abstracts International, 55, 6.
Schillinger, J. (1976). *The Mathematical Basis of the Arts.* New York, NY: Da Capo Press.
Schumacher, P. J. (1990). Art for Existence's Sake: A Heideggerian Revision. *Journal of Aesthetic Education*, 24(2), 83-89.
Smith, B. (1988). *The Death of the Artist as Hero: Essays in History and Culture.* Melbourne: Oxford University Press.
Travers, F. (1979). Creative Thinking and the Transcendental Meditation Technique. *The Journal of Creative Behavior*, 13(3), 169-180.
Tuchman, M. (1986). Hidden Meanings in Abstract Art. In Los Angeles County Museum of Art, *The Spiritual in Art: Abstract Painting 1890-1985* [pp. 17-60]. New York: Abbeville Press.
Wallace, R. (1970). Physiological Effects of Transcendental Meditation. *Science*, 167, 1751-1754.
——— (1971). A Wakeful Hypometabolic Physiologic State. *The American Journal of Physiology*, 221, 795-799.

——— (1986). *The Maharishi Technology of the Unified Field: The Neurophysiology of Enlightenment.* Fairfield, IA: Maharishi International University Press.

Wallace, R.K., Dillbeck, M., Jacobe, E., & Harrington, B. (1982). The effects of the Transcendental Meditation and TM-Sidhi Program on the Aging Process. *International Journal of Neuroscience,* 16, 53-58.

Weisberg, R. W. (1986). *Creativity, Genius and Other Myths.* San Francisco, CA: W.H. Freeman.

Wells, G.A., & Boothby, S.Y. (1995). Absolute Principles of Society in Maharishi's Commentary on the Bhagavad-Gita. *Modern Science and Vedic Science Journal,* 6 (1), 2-30.

Wilber, K. (1983). *Eye to Eye: The Quest for a New Paradigm.* New York: Doubleday.

Wilson, H. H.(1977). (Trans.) Ṛg-Veda-Saṁhitā [Vol. 4]. Iawahar Nagar, Delhi: Nag.

Wittgenstein, L. (1986). Philosophical Investigations. In M. Taylor (Ed.), *Deconstruction in Context* [pp. 220-241]. Chicago: University of Chicago Press.

Wolff, J. (1982/83). Aesthetic Judgment and Sociological Analysis. *Aspects: A Journal of Contemporary Art,* 21, 10-11.

——— (1992). *Aesthetics and the Sociology of Art.* Ann Arbor: University of Michigan Press.

Wood, M. (1989). New, Newer, Newest. In *Art of the Western World.* [Film series] London: British Broadcasting Corporation.

Zakian, M. (March, 1988). Barnett Newman: Painting and a Sense of Place. *Arts,* 39-44.

INDEX

B

D

E

J

M

U

V

W

N

O

P

Q

R